NATIONAL GEOGRAPHIC
FIELD GUIDE TO THE
BIRDS
OF NORTH AMERICA

FIFTH EDITION

NATIONAL GEOGRAPHIC
FIELD GUIDE TO THE
BIRDS
OF NORTH AMERICA

FIFTH EDITION

EDITED BY JON L. DUNN AND JONATHAN ALDERFER

NATIONAL
GEOGRAPHIC
WASHINGTON, D.C.

Contents

Introduction

Accidental:
Mugimaki Flycatcher

Resident in southern Texas:
White-collared Seedeater

Nonbreeding
offshore visitor:
Buller's Shearwater

It has been more than 20 years since the first edition of this field guide was published in 1983. The second edition appeared in 1987. Twelve years after that (1999), the guide had a major revision with the publication of the third edition. Relatively minor changes (a few new plates and many revised maps) were reflected in the fourth edition (2002).

The present edition, the fifth, includes new plates and figures, updated maps, quick-reference information on the cover flaps, and a revised text reflecting our current knowledge of both identification and distribution. In this edition, we include 14 pages of accidentals, species that have been recorded on only one or a few occasions in North America. These 71 species are generally illustrated in the plumage in which they were recorded. As of this date (spring 2006), we cover every species of bird recorded in North America, although some new species could occur at any moment, which would make the work "out of date." We have also added short sections on Greenland and Bermuda (see pages 480, 481), both of which are part of the American Ornithologists' Union's area of coverage and might, at some future date, became part of the American Birding Association's area too. These organizations are referred to hereafter as the AOU and the ABA, respectively.

In many ways, the various editions of the field guide are works in progress, for we continue to learn more about our avifauna. Birding is a worldwide activity, and we have benefited greatly from the contributions of others, notably the Europeans, for increasing our overall knowledge.

In each edition of this guide, museum specimens have been an essential tool in preparing detailed and accurate illustrations. There is simply no substitute for having a series of carefully cataloged, archived specimens for reference, especially for studying a species' geographical variation. Many institutions have loaned specimens to the artists (see acknowledgments, page 502) through the five editions of this guide, and we are grateful to them.

Species Selection

This guide includes all species that have occurred in North America, which is defined here as the land extending northward from the northern border of Mexico, plus adjacent islands and seas within about two hundred miles of the coast.

For those accidental visitors that are seen in North America only when they wander off course, our standard generally requires that in order to be included in the main text, they have been seen at least three times in the past two decades or five times in the last 100 years. The more accidental species with even fewer records are included in an end section along with the specific details of their occurrence. This section also includes the four species that are known to have gone extinct during the 19th and 20th centuries. In a few cases we have chosen to include those accidentals in the main section (e.g., Parkinson's Petrel, Cape Verde Shearwater, and Asian Brown Flycatcher) because we felt a direct comparison with similar species would be useful. Exotic species from other continents that have been introduced into North America as game, park, or cage birds are seen in the wild frequently, and the list is seemingly endless. We have chosen to show those that have at least some degree of establishment (e.g., Red Bishop). The criterion for acceptance and inclusion differs between the AOU and the ABA. The ABA Checklist Committee is in the process of redefining its policies for treating these "exotics," but in general it requires a significant population that has been present for at least 15 years. Some exotics (e.g., European Starling) have spread continent-wide and are a nuisance, while others have maintained more stable populations or even have declined. One such species, the Crested Myna, after thriving for nearly a century, has been extirpated, perhaps as a result of competition with European Starlings.

For issues of taxonomy and nomenclature—English and scientific names—we strictly adhere to the Committee on Classification and Nomenclature of the American Ornithologists' Union, as determined in the 7th edition of the AOU Check-list (1997) and its six subsequent supplements, published annually in the July issue of the AOU's journal, *The Auk*. Completed and ongoing molecular and traditional studies will refine, and continue to refine, our knowledge of speciation (what is and what is not a species) and higher level systematics (relationships of families to one another and their linear sequence). We follow either the ABA Checklist Committee or the above-mentioned AOU committee on deciding which species to include. Apart from the list of exotics, the differences are few (see page 480).

Typically, when a new species is reported from the North American area, it is first reviewed by the respective state or provincial committee. (Nearly all states and provinces now have established committees.) Then it is reviewed by the ABA Checklist Committee. If ABA accepts the species, the AOU committee then reviews it and, if in agreement with the ABA, determines its linear placement within the Check-list. Occasionally, state or provisional committees have accepted records that are subsequently not accepted by both the ABA and the AOU. For instance, the Texas committee has accepted records of White-chinned Petrel, Dark-billed Cukoo, and Black Catbird; the North Carolina committee has accepted a record of a Swinhoe's Storm-Petrel; the British Columbia committee has accepted a record of Blue Rock-Thrush; and the California committee has accepted two records of Swallow-tailed Gull. Usually, but not always, these debates concern the origin of the record (identification accepted), often without much evidence pointing one way or the other. Both of the AOU and ABA committees, as well as some state and provincial committees, require verifiable diagnostic evidence (photographic or audio) before adding a new species to a checklist.

Accidental:
Asian Brown
Flycatcher

Introduced:
Orange
Bishop

Extirpated:
Crested Myna

Families

Scientists organize animal species into family groups that share certain structural or molecular characteristics. Among the birds,

Sapsuckers: Red-breasted *daggetti,* Williamson's, Yellow-bellied

Downy Woodpecker

some families encompass more than a hundred members; others have only one. Characteristics within a family are often helpful in identifying birds in the field. Take the members of the Picidae family (page 282), for example. Strong, sharp bills, strong claws, and short legs are among the features that make them easily recognized as woodpeckers. Their family resemblance narrows down the list of possible identifications to a manageable number.

Brief family descriptions can be found at the beginning of each group in this field guide for information applicable to all members of the family. Additionally, a description of a smaller group within a family is provided, such as that given for the sapsuckers (three shown here), which share some unique traits.

Scientific Names

Each species has a two-part scientific name, derived from Greek or Latin, which is given in italics. The first part, always capitalized, indicates the genus, a group of closely related species more narrowly defined than that of the family. For example, nine members of the family Picidae are placed in the genus *Picoides.* Together with the second part of the name (often referred to as the specific epithet), not capitalized, this identifies the species. *Picoides pubescens* is the name of one specific kind of woodpecker, commonly known as the Downy Woodpecker. *Picoides dorsalis,* or *P. dorsalis,* is the American Three-toed Woodpecker. In scientific nomenclature, no two species share the same two-part scientific name, or binomial.

family	Woodpeckers	Picidae
genus	Sapsuckers	***Sphyrapicus***
species	Red-breasted Sapsucker	*Sphyrapicus **ruber***
subspecies or **race**	Red-breasted Sapsucker (southern subspecies)	*Sphyrapicus ruber **daggetti***
nominate race	Red-breasted Sapsucker (northern subspecies)	*Sphyrapicus ruber **ruber***

Subspecies

Since about the latter half of the 19th century, species have been further divided into subspecies (*race* is a synonym), when populations from different geographical regions show recognizable differences. Each subspecies bears a third scientific name, or trinomial. Out of three subspecies (all found in North America) of American Three-toed Woodpecker, *Picoides dorsalis bacatus* (often abbreviated as *P. d. bacatus* or simply *bacatus*) identifies the dark-backed subspecies of Three-toed Woodpecker that inhabits the boreal forest of eastern North America. The Rockies subspecies is the paler-backed race, *dorsalis;* a third and intermediate subspecies, *fasciatus,* is found from Alaska to Oregon.

If the third part of a scientific name is the same as the second, the subspecies in question is the *nominate* subspecies, the type of the species that was originally described. The subspecies *dorsalis* was named and described in 1858, earlier then *fasciatus* (1870) or *bacatus* (1900). Birders might be surprised to learn that the nominate race of the widespread Red-tailed Hawk, *jamaicensis*, is found only on the island of Jamaica, although one might deduce that from the name. It was described to science in 1788.

Scientific names are used in this book for learning and clarity. We have illustrated or described the extremes of variations that look distinctly different from other races of the same species. For example, of the roughly 25 races of Horned Lark in North America, we show the most typical or widespread, the extremes within the species, and an Asian vagrant (*flava*) that occurs casually in Alaska in fall (page 328). For polytypic species where our figures are mainly or entirely of only one subspecies, we italicize that subspecies name under the English name; the other figures will also be of that subspecies, unless indicated otherwise.

American Three-toed Woodpeckers: *bacatus, dorsalis, fasciatus*

As with species, taxonomists frequently differ as to what constitutes a valid subspecies. One widely used definition is that 75 percent of the individuals from one region differ from all of the individuals from another described subspecies. Some taxonomists would prefer a 90 percent or even 95 percent criterion. Slight differences in size or a very slight and gradual change in coloration, with no sharp breaks, are usually considered clinal differences; and while the differences are important to our understanding the variation within a species as a whole, usually the differing groups are not recognized with separate subspecies names. If the species is considered monotypic (e.g., Cerulean Warbler), with no recognized subspecies, then only the scientific binomial is used (e.g., *Dendroica caerulea*). We have relied on the 5th edition of the AOU Check-list (1957), the last edition in which the AOU treated subspecies. (The next edition of the Check-list will again treat subspecies.) For more recent treatments we have also followed *The Howard and Moore Complete Checklist of the Birds of the World*, 3rd edition (2003).

Monotypic: Cerulean Warbler

Since for the most part the artists have used museum specimens for their figures, we have labeled those figures with an italicized subspecies name, if that information is known.

How to Identify Birds

Field marks, a bird's physical aspects, are the clues by which birds are identified. Field marks include plumage, or the bird's overall feathering, as well as the shape of the body and its individual parts and any actual markings such as bars, bands, spots, or rings. A field mark can be as obvious as the Northern Cardinal's color or the Killdeer's double breast bands (page 158), or as subtle as the difference in head markings between a Clay-colored and a winter-plumaged Chipping Sparrow or the difference in the head shapes of Greater and Lesser Scaup, a much more reliable field mark than head color. Some field marks are plainly visible only in good light, or from a certain angle, or when the bird is in flight.

Lesser Scaup, Greater Scaup

Lark Sparrow

supercilium
postocular stripe
ear coverts
(auricular)
moustachial stripe
submoustachial stripe

median crown stripe
lateral crown stripe
supraloral area
lores
malar stripe

The most important thing to do when birding is just to look at the actual bird—there's plenty of time later to consult the field guide. In this guide, the most distinctive features for each species in each plumage are usually listed first in the text account, and boldface terms (e.g., **adult female** or **first-winter male**) in the accounts correspond to the illustrated figures.

Keep in mind that not every bird seen can be identified, even by experts. Remember this the next time you look at a badly worn and bleached immature gull on the beach in July!

Parts of a Bird

Because size, shape, and the configuration of birds' various parts vary from family to family and from species to species, you should become acquainted with all the terms used to describe those parts and their locations—bird topography. For easy reference in the field, the front inside cover has additional bird topography drawings.

Shape

Most birds have a shape that is characteristic of their species or family. Even at great range and in poor light, the short-tailed, pointed-billed, rather chunky body shape of the perched European Starling is distinctive. Shape can change, though, depending on environmental conditions. In cold weather many species fluff their feathers and hunker down. This makes them look bigger, and often shorter, and alters their characteristic posture.

Head

A careful look at a bird's head can nearly always provide a correct identification of a species. The boldly marked head of an adult Lark Sparrow offers a nearly complete course in common head markings. Sparrows are a confusing group, and it is the often subtle differences in head markings that can help sort them out. At the top of the head there is often a pale or white *median crown stripe* bordered by dark *lateral crown stripes*. A line running from base of the bill up and over the eye is known as the *eyebrow,* or *supercilium.* Sometimes the area between bill and eye, the *lores,* has its own marking. The front part of the eyebrow, or *supraloral area,* may be of a different color—another useful marking. The eye color itself may be diagnostic in some species. Bird pupils are always black, but the *iris* can be colored, as it is in many subadult and adult gulls. A ring of naked flesh, the *orbital ring,* may surround the eye, as may a feathered one, usually called an *eye ring.* The Least Flycatcher has an unbroken, feathered, white eye ring. In some species the ring is interrupted, forming *eye crescents* instead. The dark stripe extending

eye line

Chipping Sparrow

eye crescent

Northern Parula

orbital ring

cere

Common Black-Hawk

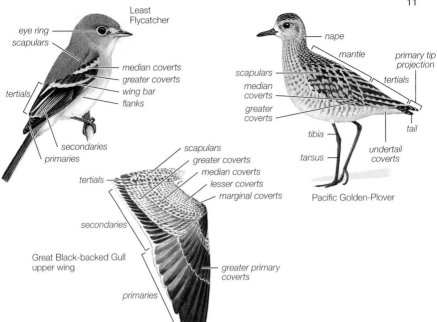

Least Flycatcher

eye ring
scapulars
median coverts
greater coverts
wing bar
flanks
tertials
secondaries
primaries

scapulars
greater coverts
median coverts
lesser coverts
marginal coverts

tertials
secondaries

Great Black-backed Gull
upper wing

greater primary
coverts

primaries

nape
mantle
primary tip
projection
scapulars
tertials
median
coverts
greater
coverts
tibia
tarsus
undertail
coverts
tail

Pacific Golden-Plover

back from the Lark Sparrow's eye is known as a *postocular stripe*. If it extended through the eye itself, as in the Chipping Sparrow, it would be known as an *eye line,* or a *transocular line*. A distinctive brown patch, bordered in black on the Lark Sparrow, marks the *ear coverts,* or *auricular*. Its lower border is a *moustachial stripe*. Below that is a white *submoustachial stripe,* bordered with yet another dark line, the *malar stripe*.

The shape of the bill must not be overlooked. Bills are specialized according to diet and method of feeding. The Lark Sparrow's short, stout bill indicates a seedeater. The Tennessee Warbler's is a fine-pointed insect probe, as is the case with many warblers, but it is also used for sipping nectar. The *gonys,* the junction of the two sides of the lower mandible, forms a prominent ridge in some species, and its shape can be important in identification. For instance on the Western Gull it is more acute, giving the bill a bulbous tip, while on the California Gull the angle is much broader and the bill looks almost straight. The top of the bill is known as the *culmen*. In raptors, such as the Common Black-Hawk, the patch of bare skin covering the base of the upper mandible is called the *cere*. Some species, such as pelicans or cormorants, have a fold of loose skin called a *gular pouch* hanging from the throat.

gonys

California Gull, Western Gull

trailing
edge
rump
scapulars
humerals

Short-tailed
Albatross

leading
edge

Wings

Wings can be most critically observed in the folded position, and while this position provides useful clues, not all of the wing is visible. A bird's wing is composed basically of groups of strong *flight feathers,* covered on the upper and lower side by shorter, protective feathers called *coverts*. Each feather's shaft divides its

wing lining
speculum

uppertail   American
coverts   Black Duck

carpal bar

Common Tern, first summer

axillaries

Black-bellied Plover

Myiarchus Flycatcher
tails from below:
Brown-crested, Ash-throated

inner web from its *outer web*. The *primaries* comprise the outer 9 or 10 tapering flight feathers; some non-passerines have up to 12. They are followed by the *secondaries*. The three innermost flight feathers are the *tertials*.

Joining the wing and body are rows of short, protective feathers, called the *scapulars*. A series of wing coverts are found on the wing above the secondaries. From *leading edge* to *trailing edge* they are the *marginal, lesser, median,* and *greater* wing coverts. The lesser and marginal coverts have multiple rows of feathers; the others have a single row each. On long-winged species such as albatrosses, another set of feathers, the *humerals,* is well developed. The overall plumage of the back, extending to the scapulars and upperwing coverts, is called the *mantle,* a term used almost exclusively for gulls.

In some species the white tips of the greater and median coverts above the secondaries form *wing bars,* often an important diagnostic feature. In some ducks, such as the American Black Duck, the secondaries themselves are uniquely colored, forming a pronounced bar known as a *speculum.* When a bird (e.g, the immature Common Tern) shows a contrasting bar on the forward part of the upper wing, it is referred to as a *carpal bar.*

The spread underwing displays the undersides of the flight feathers and the underwing coverts, and it offers features that prove useful in identifying birds in flight. The coverts of the *wing linings* often contrast with the rest of the underwing, as may the *axillaries,* the bird's "armpit."

A feature to notice in the folded bird wing is how far the primaries extend past the longest tertial. This length—known as the *primary tip projection*—can help distinguish between similar species such as the American and Pacific Golden-Plovers. On such shorebirds, note the prominence of the scapulars, and that the secondaries are completely hidden.

Tail

Lastly, tail shape and pattern can be very important aids to identification. Most bird species have 12 tail feathers, called *rectrices.* A good part of the time we see only the folded tail. From above, usually only the one or two central tail feathers show; from below, only the outermost tail feather on each side is visible. Similar-looking species, such as MacGillivray's and Connecticut Warblers (page 390), may be distinguished from each other from below by the length of tail projecting past the undertail coverts. In order to view the undertail properly, get in front of the bird and look at the tail from below. Subtle differences in undertail pattern, for instance, help distinguish the members of the perplexing flycatcher genus *Myiarchus.*

But sometimes it takes more than the outer tail feathers to discern the pattern of a tail. Then it is best to see the bird in flight, as in the case of the four longspurs (pages 428, 430). In flight, too, tail shape shows well. Thus, we can distinguish the fan-shaped tail of the American Crow from the wedge-shaped tail of the Common Raven (page 326). The distinctive forked tail of the

Barn Swallow (page 332) gets its shape from short central tail feathers and long outer ones.

Molt

Regular renewal of plumage, called *molt,* is essential to a bird's well-being and ability to fly. Yet molt produces variations of plumage within a species and between ages that create additional obstacles to identification. It is not enough for us to know what a bird's plumage looks like in only one season or sex or at one age. Most species undergo a complete molt in late summer or early fall, replacing all their feathers.

Adult male Scarlet Tanagers change their entire body plumage color from summer to fall. Adult Acadian Flycatchers are brightest in spring, becoming worn and faded by late summer. Fresh fall plumage after molt can be brighter than the colors of August. This plumage is usually held through the fall and through most of the winter (and is usually labeled winter plumage).

In some songbirds, such as the House Sparrow, the more patterned plumage of spring appears with the gradual wearing away of dull tips on the feathers of the winter plumage, with very little actual molting involved.

Scarlet Tanagers:
fall adult ♂, breeding adult ♂

Often the molt occurs before the birds migrate, and thus we see the birds in this fresh plumage even if they spend the winter outside North America. In late winter or early spring, many birds undergo a partial molt—usually involving the head, body, and some wing coverts—to the plumage we see in spring and summer. Some species suspend the molt during migration and complete it upon arrival at the wintering or breeding grounds. This applies to many shorebird species. On the whole, fall and winter plumage may vary considerably from spring and summer plumage.

Some species molt over a considerably longer period than others. Birds of prey must rely on their wing feathers for successful hunting and thus molt very gradually so that only a few feathers are missing at any one time.

Acadian Flycatchers:
spring adult, worn summer adult

Plumage Variation

In many species, the male and female look quite different, and young birds are unlike either parent. And some species—usually, but not always, of the same genus—occasionally breed with other species, producing *hybrid* offspring that often look intermediate. Different subspecies also interbreed, resulting in *intergrade* individuals or populations.

Some species have two or more *color morphs*—variations, in plumage color occurring regionally or within the same population. The Red-tailed Hawk (page 132) comes in multiple morphs, which include *dark, light,* and *rufous* (rust colored). Common terms, such as *rufous* and *buffy,* alternate with rarer usages, such as *hepatic* (reddish brown), in describing the nuances of shading in a bird's plumage.

House Sparrows:
fall ♂, breeding ♂

Where adult males and females of a species are similar, we show only one. When male (♂) and female (♀) look different, we usually show both. If spring and fall, or *breeding* and *nonbreeding*, plumages differ only slightly, or if only one of these plumages is usually seen in North America, we tend to show only one figure. Juvenile and immature birds are illustrated when they hold a different-looking plumage after they are old enough to be seen away from their more easily recognizable parents.

Painted Redstart:
adult, top, and juvenile

Plumage Sequence

After hatching, not all birds go through the same sequence of plumages. Some young birds, such as the Painted Redstart (page 398), hold this juvenal plumage for a few weeks and then move right into adult or adultlike plumage. Others, such as the Herring Gull (page 206) and the Bald Eagle (page 124), take years to acquire their adult look.

Some nestlings are active immediately after hatching (termed *precocial*) and wear a fluffy *down*, while others are hatched naked, remain in the nest and are completely helpless (termed *altricial*). The first coat of true feathers, acquired before the bird leaves the nest, is called the *juvenal* plumage, and birds holding it are referred to as *juveniles*. True hawks and loons, as well as many other waterbirds, hold juvenal plumage well into the winter. In many species, juvenal plumage is replaced in late summer or early fall by a *first-fall* or *first-winter* plumage that more closely resembles the adult. First-fall and any subsequent plumages that do not resemble the adult are termed *immature* plumages. These may continue in a series that includes *first-spring* (when the bird is almost a year old), *first-summer*, and so on, until *adult* plumage is attained. When birds, such as the Bald Eagle, take several years to reach adult plumage, we have labeled the interim plumages as *subadult* or with the specific year or season shown. This terminology is often used with gulls.

American Golden-Plover:
April male, top, and
breeding male

Some species wear colorful plumage in the breeding season and molt to different colors for fall and winter. In other species, *breeding* plumage looks much like *winter* plumage. Some changes are evident only during the brief period of courtship. In herons, for example, the colors of bill, lores, legs, and feet may change. When these colors are at their height, the birds are said to be in *high breeding* plumage.

After breeding, most ducks molt into an *eclipse* plumage in which males acquire a femalelike plumage and females show little change, although some become paler and duller. Eclipse plumage is usually held for several weeks. In eclipse, all the flight feathers are lost simultaneously in some species, rendering them unable to fly until new feathers grow in.

Measurements

Knowing the size of a bird is another key. When identifying a kinglet, for example, it helps to know that the bird in question is tiny (only about four inches long). Relative size is also important.

In mixed flocks, Greater and Lesser Yellowlegs (page 162) are easily distinguished from each other by size alone.

The measurements in this book come from a large number of published works. Technical books give a variety of precise measurements, such as the *wing chord* (the measurement of a folded wing). Body length and wingspread measurements are by their nature more imprecise and may vary slightly from one source to another. For birders in the field, however, we felt that these were the most helpful aids. Thus, average length (L) from tip of bill to tip of tail for each species is given, with figures rounded off. Where size varies greatly within a species, either because of sex or geographical variation among subspecies, a range of smallest to largest is provided. And for large birds, often seen in flight, we give the wingspan (WS), measured from wing tip to wing tip.

Voice

A bird's songs and calls reveal not only its presence, but also, in many cases, its identity. Some species—particularly nocturnal or secretive birds such as owls, nightjars, and rails—are more often heard than seen. A few species are most reliably identified by voice even when they are seen well. Willow and Alder Flycatchers, for example, are nearly identical in appearance, but they have different songs as well as call notes: Willow gives a liquid *wit* call, while Alder delivers a loud *pip.*

When birds assemble or travel in flocks, they often keep in touch with a *contact* or *flight call* that may be markedly different from their other calls. Flight calls are especially important for identifying individuals (or flocks) overhead. Flying Blackpoll Warblers and other warblers, for example, announce their identity with buzzy *zeet* notes.

Birds sensing danger give an *alarm call,* which may be the same as or a variant of their basic call, though delivered in a more urgent tone. Dowitchers execute a series of call notes that increases in rapidity according to the birds' degree of alarm. Bushtits give an excited twittering when raptors are about.

While bird species have a number of vocalizations that are used for different purposes, some are multipurpose. The primary song is sung mainly by males on or near the breeding grounds, although some species sing year-round; and its purpose is to announce territorial claims to attract females. Females of some species, such as the Northern Cardinal, sometimes sing also. Many of our songbirds (where song is learned) sing two or more different types of songs (e.g., Black-throated Green Warbler), and these are often used for different purposes.

Learning songs and calls makes birding a more rewarding experience. Distinctive songs and calls are described in our text. Transcription into words, such as *cheerily cheer-up cheerio* for the American Robin's song, helps to express tone and pattern but is very subjective. You may find it best to transcribe sounds into your own words as you hear them; one birder's *chip* is another's *tsip* or *chik* or even *peek.*

Willow Flycatcher (left) song: a sneezy *fitz-bew*
Alder Flycatcher (right) song: a falling, wheezy *weeb-ew*

Behavior

Behavioral traits also provide many clues to species identity. Look, for example, at a bird's flight. Is it direct or undulating? Does the bird beat its wings rapidly or slowly? Turkey Vultures soar with their wings held slightly raised in a shallow V, known as a *dihedral,* while Black Vultures soar on level wings.

Short-billed Dowitcher

Observe feeding. Does the bird forage on the ground or in the treetops? Among shorebirds, the two species of Yellowlegs and the Solitary Sandpiper peck at the water to get food, while the dowitchers drill the mud like the needle in a sewing machine.

Look for personality clues. Is the bird usually visible and approachable, or is it shy and difficult to locate? How does the bird move? Mourning and MacGillivray's Warblers hop; Connecticut Warblers walk deliberately. Black-and-white Warblers climb up and down and around tree trunks; the superficially similar Blackpoll Warbler does not. How does the bird use its tail? Among the hard-to-identify flycatchers of the genus *Empidonax,* nearly all species flick their tails up—except for the Gray Flycatcher, which drops its tail down.

Abundance and Habitat

Abundance must be considered in relation to habitat. Habitat information included in the text will help you find a particular species within its range. Under the heading **Range** in our species accounts, we include supplemental information about habitat, abundance (such as casual or accidental), and seasonal status that cannot be shown in a single map. Some species are highly local, found only in a very specialized habitat. Bank Swallows, for example, are common in summer only near the steep sandy or gravelly banks they require for nesting. Common Loons are fairly common to common on large bodies of water; but away from large lakes, as in parts of the Southwest, they are very rare.

Abundant:
European Starling

Common:
Indigo Bunting

Seasons of the year, of course, also affect numbers. In spring, the Semipalmated Sandpiper is abundant on its northern breeding grounds; during migration it is common in the Midwest and on the East Coast but rare in the West; in the winter a few are still found, in North America, in southernmost Florida only.

The following categories of abundance are used in this guide:

Abundant means a species is present in great numbers in an area. The European Starling is abundant in varied habitats throughout most of North America.

Common means that a species is very likely to be seen in a given area, but in fewer numbers than an abundant one. The Indigo Bunting is common over much of eastern North America.

Fairly common is rather numerous, but there are fewer still than those designated as common.

Uncommon species can have a large range and still be seen infrequently. The Northern Goshawk, for example, is uncommon over much of its resident range.

Rare are species that occur in very low numbers, but annually in North America. These include visitors and rare breeding residents. For instance the Ruff, an Old World visitor, is rare over much of North America.

Very rare species are annual in North America, but only one or a few will occur in a season.

Casual is used for species that do not occur annually in North America, but over decades there is a pattern of their occurrence, as with the Redwing in Newfoundland.

Accidental refers to species that have been seen only once or a few times in an area that is far out of their normal range. In fact, it may be decades, or even centuries, before another one is seen there again. The Eurasian Hoopoe has been recorded only once in North America (from coastal southwestern Alaska in fall).

Rare: Ruff

Other references may use different abundance terms, or they may give the same terms a slightly different meaning, but it is worth noting that both the AOU and ABA committees have adopted the same general definitions for the terms *rare, casual,* and *accidental.*

Some other terms that are used herein include the following: *Vagrant* is a bird that is found well off its usual migration route.

Irruptive species, such as the Snowy Owl or the Bohemian Waxwing, are erratic in their movements over much of their winter range. One year they may be numerous in a given region and the next year, or even the next decade, totally absent.

Casual: Redwing

Range Maps

Maps are provided for all species with two general exceptions. One is for certain introduced exotic species with very limited ranges that instead are described in the text. The other is those species that do not breed in North America and are of only rare, casual, or accidental occurrence.

On each map, range boundaries are drawn where the species ceases to be regularly seen. Keep in mind that nearly every species will be rare at the edges of its range. The sample map (next page) explains the colors and symbols used on our maps; the map on the inside back cover gives an overview of North America.

Accidental:
Eurasian Hoopoe

Birds are not, however, bound by maps. Their ranges continually expand and contract. The Shiny Cowbird, for instance, was not even included in the first two editions of this field guide. Now it is found regularly in small numbers in south Florida and has been recorded as an accidental as far north as New Brunswick and Nova Scotia. Irruptive species move southward in some years in large or small numbers and for great or small distances. These irregular movements are generally but not specifically predictable; certainly they cannot be precisely mapped. In some species, birds leave the nesting grounds in late summer and then move northward. These post-breeding wanderers, principally young birds, will subsequently migrate southward by winter. Range maps of pelagic species, which spend most of their time over the open sea, are somewhat conjectural.

Range information is based on actual sightings and therefore depends on the number of knowledgeable and active birders in each area. There is much to learn about bird distribution in every

Recent arrival:
Shiny Cowbird

Range Map Symbols

Breeding range, generally in spring and summer *(or summer range of some nonbreeding seabirds)*

Year-round range

Winter range *(if no winter or year-round range is shown, winters outside North America)*

Principal direction of migration

Extent of irregular breeding range, or of post-breeding dispersal in summer and fall

Extent of irregular year-round range

Extent of irregular or irruptive range in some winters

Species migrates chiefly east of this line

 Selected breeding colonies

Irruptive: Snowy Owl

part of North America. Participation by birders is necessary to the monitoring of expanding and contracting ranges. Breeding-bird surveys and atlas projects undertaken by federal and state governments and by birding clubs make a vital contribution to the general fund of information about each species. The Cornell Laboratory of Ornithology has created eBird (www.ebird.org), a way in which birders can send in their observations of species and, after screening for accuracy, a better overall understanding is reached about abundance and distribution.

How to Be a Better Birder

The time you spend at home with your field guide will be repaid when you go out birding. But much is also learned only from experience. When you have seen the Northern Harrier many times, for instance, its distinctive flight pattern signals its identity for you long before you can see its facial disk or white rump. Experienced birders know how to move quietly and to stand patiently still. They know that a sudden riot of scolding songbirds may mean that an owl is roosting nearby or that a flock of familiar Bonaparte's Gulls should be studied closely to determine whether a Little or Black-headed Gull might also be present.

Beyond learning field marks and birding strategies, it is essential to learn the distribution patterns of your area. Most states and provinces have their own detailed distribution books that provide these details, and there are many other publications detailing bird distribution for other specific places. *North American Birds*, a journal published quarterly by the ABA, chronicles—region by region—the significant observations and trends for North and Middle America.

If you know a species is unusual, you are much more likely to look at it carefully and document it better. Mistakes are made when birds aren't critically examined. As Louis Pasteur said, "Chance favors the prepared mind." If you find something that you believe is unusual, be sure to document it well (with notes taken in the field and photos too), and call other birders as soon as possible to share in your find.

The bird life of our continent has, on the whole, declined with the advance of human populations, and the resultant destruction of habitat, over-hunting, and other hazards. In just over the last 160 years, we have lost the Labrador Duck, the Great Auk, the Passenger Pigeon, and the Carolina Parakeet. Since the publication of the last edition of this guide, it now appears virtually certain that the Eskimo Curlew and the Bachman's Warbler have gone extinct, the last certain record of the curlew being from Barbados in 1963 and of the warbler from near Charleston, South Carolina, in 1962. We can only hope that additional comprehensive searches now under way better document remnant individuals or small populations of Ivory-billed Woodpeckers. We have also lost various subspecies, such as the "Heath Hen," the eastern seaboard nominate race of the Greater Prairie-Chicken, in the 1930s. More recently, the "Dusky Seaside Sparrow" (*A. m. nigrescens*) from Atlantic coastal north Florida, has become extinct, the last one dying in captivity in 1987.

In the accounts of birds presently on the U.S. federal list of threatened or endangered species—such as the Red-cockaded Woodpecker species and the *extimus* subspecies of Willow Flycatcher (endangered), or the Florida Scrub-Jay (threatened)—we have placed the symbols **E** (endangered) or **T** (threatened). Canada also has its own list of threatened species, as do many states and provinces. Extinct species are indicated with the symbol **EX**.

With birding's increasing popularity, birders are becoming powerful advocates for the protection and stewardship of our natural resources. Observing and studying birds can be an enriching, pleasurable experience with far-reaching rewards.

THE EDITORS

Extinct species:
Carolina Parakeet

Endangered species:
Red-cockaded Woodpecker

Extinct subspecies:
Dusky Seaside Sparrow
nigrescens

Ducks, Geese, Swans (Family Anatidae)

Worldwide family. Web-footed, gregarious birds, ranging from small ducks to large swans. Largely aquatic, but geese, swans, and some "puddle ducks" also graze on land. *Species: 158 World, 62 N.A.*

Greater White-fronted Goose   *Anser albifrons*

L 28" (71 cm) Named for the distinctive white band at base of bill. Medium-size, grayish brown goose, with irregular black barring on underparts; orange feet and legs. Bill pink or orangish with whitish tip. In flight, note grayish blue wash on wing coverts and white, U-shaped rump band. Most **immatures** acquire white front above bill and white bill tip during first winter; acquire black belly markings by second fall; distinguished from similar Bean Goose by bill color; from Pink-footed Goose by bill and leg color; compare also with immature blue-morph Snow Goose (next page). Color and size vary in **adults:** Small, pale, Arctic tundra birds have heavy barring; taiga-breeding (central Alaska) race, *elgasi*, is larger, with bigger bill, darker neck, and less barring on belly; Greenland's intermediate-size tundra subspecies, *flavirostris,* rare in the Northeast, is darkest, with the heaviest barring and an orange bill. **Range:** Large populations are found on eastern Great Plains (fewer east to Mississippi Valley) and Pacific states. Rare on western Great Plains and in eastern North America. **Call** is a high-pitched, laughing *kah-lah-aluck*. Rare winter visitor outside mapped range in all western states and north into southern Canada.

Bean Goose   *Anser fabalis   L 31" (79 cm)*

Range: Eurasian species; rare spring migrant on western and central Aleutians, casual on islands in Bering Sea; a few scattered records elsewhere in North America. Similar to plain-bellied, immature Greater White-fronted Goose. Best distinguished by different bill color—black with orange-yellow band above the tip in Russian Far East races; lacks white front, though some show a narrow white ring at base of bill. In flight, Bean Goose shows browner primary coverts and greater secondary coverts than Greater White-fronted. Of the two East Asian races shown here, *middendorffii* of the taiga, largest of all Bean Goose races, is rarer; bill is long and of moderate depth; bill of tundra race *serrirostris* is shorter with an extremely thick base. **Call** is a low, reedy *ung-unk,* suggestive of barnyard geese.

Pink-footed Goose   *Anser brachyrhynchus   L 26" (66 cm)*

Range: East Coast vagrant from breeding grounds in eastern Greenland. A scattering of records between eastern Pennsylvania and Newfoundland; most sightings thought to be wild birds. Distinguished from plain-bellied immature Greater White-fronted Goose by pink legs and variable dark base and tip to stubbier pinkish bill; neck shorter than Greater White-fronted. Juvenile is browner, looks more scaly than barred; legs duller. In flight, shows an extensive area of bluish gray on mantle and all wing coverts; darker head and neck contrast with grayish body; tail base is grayer and paler than Greater White-fronted and Bean Goose.

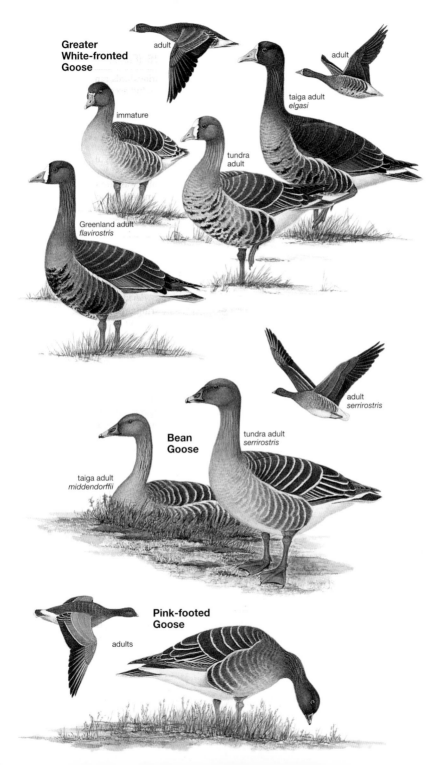

Greater White-fronted Goose

adult

immature

tundra adult

Greenland adult *flavirostris*

taiga adult *elgasi*

adult

Bean Goose

taiga adult *middendorffii*

tundra adult *serrirostris*

adult *serrirostris*

Pink-footed Goose

adults

Snow Goose *Chen caerulescens*
L 26-33" (66-84 cm) Two color morphs. Adults distinguished from smaller Ross's Goose by larger, pinkish bill with black "grinning patch." Flies with slower wingbeat than Ross's; rusty stains often visible on face in summer. **White-morph juvenile** is grayish above, with dark bill. **Blue-morph adult** has mostly white head and neck, brown back, variable amount of white on underparts. Juvenile has dark head and neck, overall slaty body coloring; distinguished from Greater White-fronted Goose (preceding page) by dark legs and bill and lack of white on face. Intermediates between white and blue morphs have mainly white underparts and whitish wing coverts. **Range:** Abundant. Occasionally hybridizes with Ross's Goose. A larger subspecies, the "Greater Snow Goose" (not shown), breeds around Baffin Bay, winters only along mid-Atlantic coast; blue morph almost unknown. Smaller race, the "Lesser Snow Goose" (morphs shown here), is rare in winter throughout interior U.S. and in southern Canada outside mapped range. Blue morph is abundant in central North America; rare west of the Great Plains; uncommon in East.

Ross's Goose *Chen rossii L 23" (58 cm)*
Stubby, triangular bill, mostly deep pinkish red. Neck shorter, head rounder than Snow Goose, white head generally lacks rusty stains; **calls** higher pitched. Ross's has two color morphs. **White-morph juvenile** may have very pale gray wash on head, back, and flanks, but far less than juvenile white-morph Snow Goose. Extremely rare **blue morph** is darker than blue-morph Snow Goose; face and belly are white. **Range:** Seen during migration in grasslands and grainfields in eastern Great Plains and Mississippi Valley; rare but regular farther east to western Vermont. Rare winter visitor to mid-Atlantic states; rare visitor also to much of West outside mapped range. Usually seen with Snow Geese.

Emperor Goose *Chen canagica L 26" (66 cm)*
Fairly stocky, small goose with short, thick neck. Head and back of neck white; chin and throat black; face often stained rusty in summer. Bill pinkish; lower mandible is sometimes black. Black-and-white edging to silvery gray plumage creates a scaled effect below; upperparts appear barred. **Juvenile** has dark head and bill. During first fall, acquires white flecking on head; resembles adult by first winter. **Range:** Emperor Goose breeds in tidewater marsh and tundra; winters on seashores, reefs. Casual south on Pacific coast to central California and inland to Sacramento Valley.

Barnacle Goose *Branta leucopsis L 27" (69 cm)*
Part of world population breeds in northeastern Greenland; accidental vagrant in Maritime Provinces. Note distinctive head pattern and stubby bill. Bluish gray upperparts, barred with black, and white, U-shaped rump band. Silver-gray wing linings show in flight. **Range:** More of a land goose than the Brant, feeding in fields near the ocean. Fairly common in captivity. Numerous sightings from eastern North America are of uncertain origin; perhaps most are escapes, especially away from Atlantic seaboard.

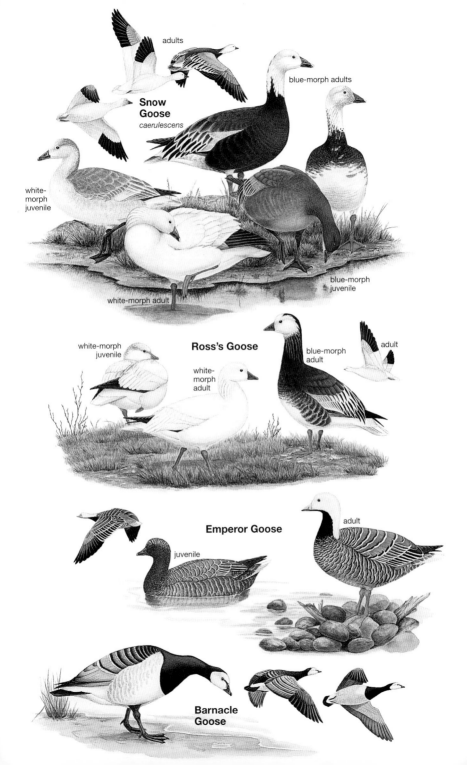

adults

Snow Goose
caerulescens

blue-morph adults

white-morph juvenile

white-morph adult

blue-morph juvenile

Ross's Goose

white-morph juvenile

white-morph adult

blue-morph adult

adult

Emperor Goose

juvenile

adult

Barnacle Goose

Cackling Goose *Branta hutchinsii* L 23-33" (58-84 cm)
Formerly considered part of the Canada Goose complex, this species is smaller with a rounder head and a stubbier bill. Its shorter neck is most obvious in flight. Four subspecies vary from smallest and darkest *minima*, breeding in southwest Alaska, to largest *taverneri*, breeding in western and northern Alaska; both winter in the Pacific states. Aleutian breeding *leucopareia*, with a prominent white neck ring (sometimes present on other subspecies), winters in California's Central Valley. Intermediately sized and palest *hutchinsii*, breeding in Canada's Arctic archipelago and wintering from southern Great Plains to western Gulf Coast region, is generally otherwise rare to casual in eastern North America. Size of *parvipes* Canada and *taverneri* Cackling overlap; *taverneri* averages darker with stubbier bill, but identification criterion is still not adequately worked out. **Calls** are much higher pitched than Canada Goose.

Canada Goose *Branta canadensis* L 30-43" (76-109 cm)
Our most common and familiar goose. Black head and neck marked with distinctive white "chin strap," stretching from ear to ear. In flight, shows large dark wings; white undertail coverts; white, U-shaped rump band; and long neck. The approximately seven named subspecies vary in overall color, generally darker in West; ranges from pale *canadensis* of eastern seaboard to dark *occidentalis*, which breeds on eastern Gulf of Alaska coast. Size decreases northward: The smallest subspecies, *parvipes* (**"Lesser Canada Goose"**) breeds from central Alaska to north-central Canada and winters in central portions of U.S. with some in the Pacific states. **Call** is a deep, musical *honk-a-lonk*. **Range:** Flocks usually migrate in V-formations, stopping to feed in wetlands, grasslands, or agricultural areas. Breeding programs have now produced expanding populations that are resident south of mapped range and along Pacific and Atlantic coasts; explosive increase has prompted control measures in East.

Brant *Branta bernicla* L 25" (64 cm)
A small, dark, stocky sea goose. Note whitish patch on side of neck. White uppertail coverts almost conceal black tail. White undertail coverts conspicuous in flight. Wings comparatively long and pointed, wingbeat rather rapid. **Immature** birds show bold white edging to wing coverts and secondaries, and fainter neck patches than **adults.** Juveniles usually lack neck patches entirely. In more easterly subspecies *hrota*, **"American Brant,"** pale belly contrasts with black chest, and neck patches do not meet in front. Western *nigricans*, **"Black Brant,"** has dark belly, and neck patches meet in front. **Call** is a low, rolling, slightly upslurred *raunk-raunk*. **Range:** Primarily a sea goose; flocks fly low in ragged formation and feed on aquatic plants of shallow bays and estuaries. Locally common. Western *nigricans* is regular at Salton Sea in spring and sometimes summers. Brant is rare inland, but some *hrota* are sighted during migrations through the Great Lakes region, particularly in fall. Both races are casual during migration and winter on opposite coasts. Eastern *hrota* also casual south of mapped range.

"Aleutian" *leucopareia*

hutchinsii

"Taverner's" *taverneri*

"Cackling" *minima*

Cackling Goose

"Richardson's" *hutchinsii*

"Lesser" *parvipes*

Canada Goose

"Dusky" *occidentalis*

"Atlantic" *canadensis*

adult

adults

adult

Brant

"American Brant" *hrota*

immature

"Black Brant" adult *nigricans*

Swans

Large, long-necked birds; North American species are white overall as adults; browner immatures are difficult to identify.

Tundra Swan *Cygnus columbianus L 52" (132 cm)*
In **adult,** black facial skin tapers to a point in front of eye and cuts straight across forehead; most birds have a yellow spot of variable size in front of eye. Head is rounded, bill slightly concave. In Eurasian race, **"Bewick's Swan,"** seen very rarely in the Pacific states, facial skin and base of bill are yellow, but usually only above the nostril; compare with Whooper Swan. **Juvenile** Tundras molt earlier than immature Trumpeter and Whooper Swans; appear much whiter by late winter. Immature "Bewick's" has whitish bill patch. Tundra's **call** is a noisy, high-pitched whooping or yodeling. **Range:** Nests on tundra or sheltered marshes; winters in flocks on shallow ponds, lakes, estuaries. Rare to uncommon in winter over parts of interior U.S.; casual south to the Gulf Coast and north to the Maritimes.

Whooper Swan *Cygnus cygnus L 60" (152 cm)*
Range: Eurasian species closely related to Trumpeter Swan. Regular winter visitor to outer and central Aleutians; has bred on Attu Island. Casual elsewhere in northwestern North America (south to northern California). Records from eastern North America are all treated as escapes. Large yellow patch on lores and bill usually extends in a point to the nostrils; compare with "Bewick's Swan." Forehead slopes evenly to the straight bill. Common **call** is a buglelike double note. **Juvenile** retains dusky plumage through first winter; by first fall, bill attains whitish patches in same shape as adult's bill patch.

Trumpeter Swan *Cygnus buccinator L 60" (152 cm)*
Adult's black facial skin tapers to broad point at the eye, dips down in a V on forehead. Forehead slopes evenly to straight bill. **Juveniles** retain gray-brown plumage through first spring. Common **call** is a single or double *honk* like an old car horn. **Range:** Locally fairly common in its breeding areas. Reintroduced into parts of former range and introduced elsewhere. Rare in winter south to California and in western interior south of mapped range.

Mute Swan *Cygnus olor L 60" (152 cm)*
Prominent black knob at base of orange bill. **Juvenile** may be white or brownish; bill gray with black base. Darker juvenile begins to molt to white plumage by midwinter; bill becomes pinkish. Mute Swan often holds its long neck in an S-shaped curve, with bill pointed down. Often swims with wings arched over back. Gives a variety of hisses and snorts, but generally silent. **Range:** An Old World species, introduced in the U.S. Seen in parks. East Coast populations are increasing. Mute Swan is now established on the southeastern portion of Vancouver Island, British Columbia, and in parts of the Midwest. It is being systematically removed from the Great Lakes and other areas.

juvenile

adult

"Bewick's Swan"
adult
bewickii

**Tundra
Swan**
columbianus

Whooper Swan

**Trumpeter
Swan**

adult   juvenile

juvenile

adult

Mute Swan

adult   juvenile

Whistling-Ducks

Named for their whistling calls, these gooselike ducks have long legs and long necks. Wingbeats are slower than ducks, faster than geese.

Fulvous Whistling-Duck *Dendrocygna bicolor*
L 20" (51 cm) Rich tawny color overall; back darker, edged with tawny. Dark stripe along hindneck is continuous in female, usually broken in male. Bill and legs dark. Whitish rump band conspicuous in flight. **Call,** a squealing *pe-chee.* Forages in rice fields, marshes, shallow waters; often dives to feed. More active at night than day. **Range:** Irregular summer wanderer north to dashed line on map; casual farther north. Nearly extirpated in the West.

Black-bellied Whistling-Duck
Dendrocygna autumnalis L 21" (53 cm) Gray face with white eye ring, red bill. Legs red or pink; belly, rump, and tail black. White wing patch shows as broad white stripe in flight. **Juvenile** is paler, with gray bill. **Call** is a high-pitched, four-note whistle. Inhabits wetlands; nests in trees, nest boxes. **Range:** Casual west to southeastern California; recent sightings in the East, north to Canada, may include wild birds.

Perching Ducks

These surface-feeding, woodland ducks are equipped with sharp claws for perching in trees. They nest in tree cavities or nest boxes.

Wood Duck *Aix sponsa L 18½" (47 cm)*
Male's glossy, colorful plumage and sleek crest are distinctive. Head pattern and bill colors are retained in drab eclipse plumage. **Female** identified by short crest and large, white, teardrop-shaped eye patch; compare with female Mandarin Duck (page 50). **Juvenile** resembles female but is spotted below. In all plumages, flight profile (page 52) is distinctive: large head with bill angled downward; long, squared-off tail. Male gives soft, upslurred whistle when swimming; female's squealing flight **call** is a rising *oo-eek.* **Range:** Fairly common in open woodlands near water. Rare during winter throughout most of breeding range.

Muscovy Duck *Cairina moschata L 26-33" (66-84 cm)*
Range: Tropical species; tame escaped birds found in parks across North America (now established in Florida). A nest box program in northeastern Mexico helped spread of wild Muscovies to Rio Grande area, where they are now present near Falcon Dam, Texas. Large, blackish duck with green and purple gloss above with white patches on upper- and underwing. **Male** has blackish to dark reddish knob at base of bill, bare facial skin (usually brighter red in **domestic male,** whose color varies; can be all-white). Female is smaller, duller; lacks knob and bare facial skin. **Juvenile** even duller; slowly acquires wing patches in first winter. Wild Muscovies are shy, usually silent; seen mostly in slow, gooselike flight at dawn and dusk.

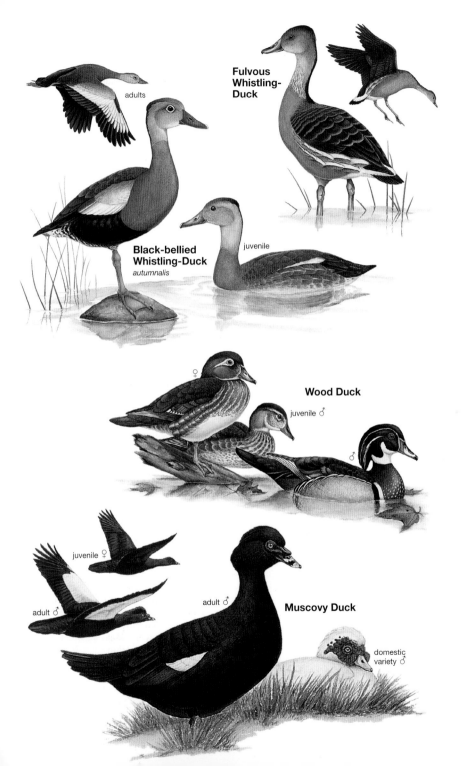

Fulvous Whistling-Duck

adults

Black-bellied Whistling-Duck
autumnalis

juvenile

Wood Duck

♀

juvenile ♂

♂

juvenile ♀

adult ♂

adult ♂

Muscovy Duck

domestic variety ♂

Dabbling Ducks

Surface-feeding members of the genus *Anas:* the familiar "puddle ducks" of freshwater shallows and, chiefly in winter, salt marshes. Dabblers feed by tipping, tail up, to reach aquatic plants, seeds, and snails. They require no running start to take off but spring directly into flight. Most species show a distinguishing swatch of bright color, the speculum, on the secondaries. Many are known to hybridize.

Mallard *Anas platyrhynchos* L 23" (58 cm)
Male readily identified by metallic green head and neck, yellow bill, narrow white collar, chestnut breast. Black central tail feathers curl up. Both sexes have white tail, white underwings, bright blue speculum with both sides bordered in white (see also page 53). **Female**'s mottled plumage resembles other *Anas* species; look for orange bill marked with black. **Juvenile** and **eclipse male** resemble female but bill is dull olive. Abundant and widespread. Mallards in central Mexico, formerly considered a separate species, "Mexican Duck," are darker, lack distinctive male plumage; **intergrades** occur in southwestern U.S.

Mottled Duck *Anas fulvigula* L 22" (56 cm)
Both sexes closely resemble American Black Duck but body is slightly paler, throat and face are buffy and unstreaked; speculum bluish. Differs from female Mallard by darker plumage and absence of white in tail or black on bill. Western Gulf Coast race, *maculosa,* is darker than nominate Florida race. **Range:** Mottled Duck has been introduced to coastal South Carolina. Common year-round in coastal marshes. Very rare north to Kentucky and Kansas. Begins pairing in Jan. or Feb., earlier than the migratory American Black Ducks and Mallards. Some authorities consider the Mottled Duck to be a subspecies of the Mallard.

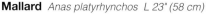

American Black Duck *Anas rubripes* L 23" (58 cm)
Blackish brown, paler on face and foreneck. In flight (page 52), white wing linings contrast more sharply with otherwise dark plumage than in similar female Mallard. Violet speculum is bordered in black, may show a thin white trailing edge. **Male**'s bill is yellow; **female**'s dull green, may be flecked with black. **Range:** Nesting pairs favor woodland lakes and streams, freshwater or tidal marshes. Small introduced populations from western British Columbia and Washington appear to be extirpated. In many parts of range, especially deforested areas, Mallards are replacing American Black Ducks; the two species **hybridize** frequently.

Spot-billed Duck *Anas poecilorhyncha* L 22" (56 cm)
Range: Asian species, casual vagrant to Aleutians and Kodiak Island. Pale tertials and sharply defined yellow tip of black bill, visible at a great distance, set this species apart from similar American Black Duck and female Mallard. The subspecies, *zonorhyncha,* which has reached North America, lacks the red spots at base of bill for which this duck is named.

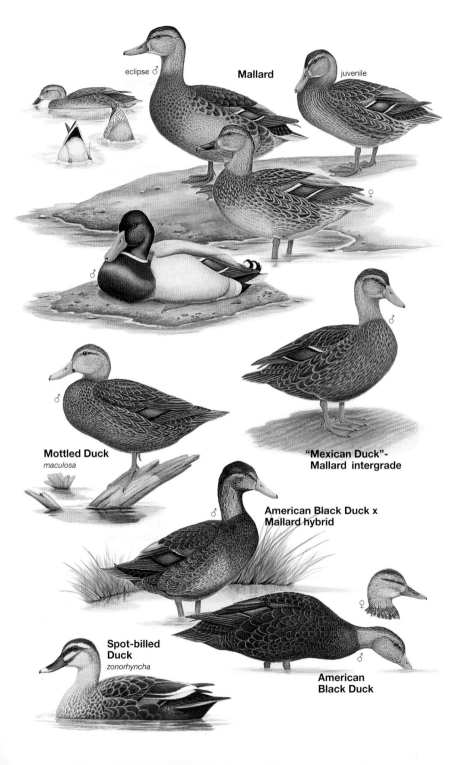

eclipse ♂

Mallard

juvenile

♀

♂

Mottled Duck
maculosa

♂

♂

**"Mexican Duck"-
Mallard intergrade**

♂

**American Black Duck x
Mallard hybrid**

♀

♂

**Spot-billed
Duck**
zonorhyncha

**American
Black Duck**

Gadwall *Anas strepera L 20" (51 cm)*
Male is mostly gray, with white belly, black tail coverts, pale chestnut on wings. **Female**'s mottled brown plumage resembles female Mallard (preceding page), but belly is white, forehead steeper, upper mandible gray with orange sides. Both sexes have white inner secondaries that may show as small patch on swimming bird and identify the species in flight (page 53).

Falcated Duck *Anas falcata L 19" (48 cm)*
Range: East Asian species, rare visitor to the western Aleutians; casual to Pribilofs and from West Coast region. Named for **male**'s long, falcated (sickle-shaped) tertials that overhang tail. Both sexes are chunky, with large head. **Female**'s all-dark bill distinguishes her from female wigeons (next page) and Gadwall; note slight bump on back of head. In flight (page 53), both sexes show a broad, dark speculum bordered in white.

Green-winged Teal *Anas crecca L 14½" (37 cm)*
Our smallest dabbler. **Male**'s chestnut head has dark green ear patch outlined in white. **Female** distinguished from other female teals (see also page 37) by smaller bill and by largely white undertail coverts that contrast with mottled flanks. A fast-flying, agile duck. In flight (page 52), shows green speculum bordered in buff on leading edge, white on trailing edge. In the subspecies seen in most of North America, *carolinensis*, male has vertical white bar on side. Eurasian race, *crecca*, is fairly common on the Aleutians and Pribilofs; rare to very rare elsewhere on West and East Coasts; was formerly considered a separate species, the Common Teal. It lacks the vertical bar, but has white stripe on scapulars.

Baikal Teal *Anas formosa L 17" (43 cm)*
Range: Asian species. After several decades of decline, Asian populations appear to have rebounded recently with a corresponding increase of records from western Alaska, and two others on West Coast (Washington and California). Records away from Pacific region may be of escapes. **Adult male**'s intricately patterned head is distinctive. Long, dropping dark scapulars are edged in rufous and white. Gray sides are set off front and rear by vertical white bars. **Female** similar to smaller female Green-winged Teal, but tail appears a bit longer; note distinct face pattern with a well-defined white spot at base of bill and white throat that angles up to rear of eye. Distinct eyebrow is bordered by darker crown. "Female" birds with **bridle** marking may be immature males. In flight (page 52), Baikal Teal's underwing is like Green-winged, but has more extensive and darker leading edge. Green speculum has an indistinct cinnamon-buff inner border.

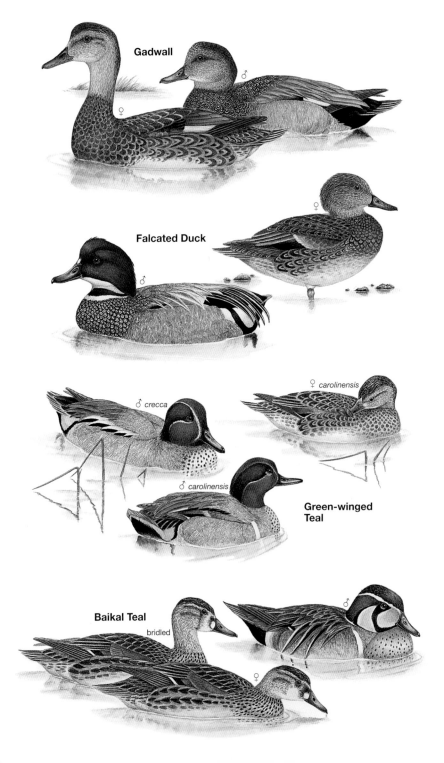

Gadwall

♀

♂

Falcated Duck

♀

♂

♂ crecca

♀ carolinensis

♂ carolinensis

Green-winged
Teal

Baikal Teal

bridled

♀

♂

American Wigeon   *Anas americana*   L 19" (48 cm)

Male's white forehead and cap are conspicuous in mixed flocks foraging in fields, marshes, and shallow waters; in flight (page 52), identified by mainly white wing linings and, in **adult males,** by large white patches on upperwing. Wing patches are grayish on **adult female** and immatures. Female lacks white on head, closely resembles gray-morph female Eurasian Wigeon; distinguishing field marks in flight are female American's white wing linings and contrast between gray throat and brown breast; Eurasian female's throat and breast are of uniform color. **Range:** Common. A recently established breeder on the East Coast. Fairly common during winter north to Lake Erie, rare on northern Great Lakes; rare to the Aleutians.

Eurasian Wigeon   *Anas penelope*   L 20" (51 cm)

Dark rufous head and gray back and sides make males conspicuous in flocks of American Wigeons; dusky wing linings are distinctive in all plumages (page 52). Hybridizes regularly with American Wigeon. **Adult male** has reddish brown head and neck with creamy crown; large white patches on upperwings. Many fall males retain some brown eclipse feathers but show distinctive reddish head. **Immature male** begins to acquire adult head and breast color but retains some brown juvenal plumage, particularly on forewing, similar to American Wigeon. **Gray-morph female** more closely resembles female American. **Rufous morph** has a more reddish head. **Range:** Eurasian Wigeon is a rare but regular winter visitor along both coasts, more common in the West; rare in interior of North America. Regular migrant and winter visitor on western and central Aleutians and Bering Sea islands.

Northern Pintail   *Anas acuta*   ♂ L 26" (66 cm)   ♀ L 20" (51 cm)

Male's chocolate brown head tops long, slender white neck, the white extending in a thin line onto head. Black central tail feathers extend far beyond rest of long, wedge-shaped tail. **Female** is mottled brown, paler on head and neck; bill uniformly grayish. In both sexes, flight profile (page 52) shows long neck; slender body; long, pointed wings; dark speculum bordered in white on trailing edge. In flight, female's mottled brown wing linings contrast with white belly; long, wedge-shaped tail lacks male's extended feathers. **Range:** A common, widespread duck, found in marshes and open areas with ponds, lakes; in winter often feeds in grainfields. Much more common in West than in East. Rare in winter north to southern Alaska and Great Lakes region.

White-cheeked Pintail   *Anas bahamensis*   L 17" (43 cm)

Range: Casual vagrant from the West Indies to southern Florida. White cheeks and throat contrast with dark forehead and cap; blue bill has a red spot near base. Long, pointed tail is buffy; tawny or reddish underparts are heavily spotted. Female is paler than **male;** tail slightly shorter. In flight, both sexes show green speculum broadly bordered on each side with buff. Sightings even from Florida are of uncertain origin; those away from Florida are most likely birds escaped from captivity.

**American
Wigeon**

adult ♂

eclipse
adult ♂

♀

rufous-morph ♀

gray-morph ♀

adult ♂

**Eurasian
Wigeon**

immature ♂

♂

♀

Northern Pintail

♂

**White-cheeked
Pintail**
bahamensis

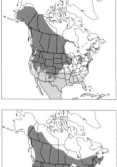

Northern Shoveler   *Anas clypeata*   L 19" (48 cm)

Large, spatulate bill, longer than head, identifies both sexes. **Male** distinguished by green head, white breast, brown sides; in early **fall** has a white crescent on each side of face, like Blue-winged Teal. **Female**'s grayish bill is tinged with orange on cutting edges and lower mandible. In flight (page 53), both sexes show blue forewing patch. **Range:** Common to abundant in the West; increasing in the East. Found in marshes, ponds, and bays.

Blue-winged Teal   *Anas discors*   L 15½" (39 cm)

Violet-gray head with white crescent on each side identifies **male**. **Female** distinguished from smaller female Green-winged Teal (page 32) by larger bill, more heavily spotted undertail coverts, yellowish legs. Compare also with female Cinnamon Teal; note Blue-winged's grayer plumage, smaller bill, and bolder facial markings, including whiter lore and more prominent, broken eye ring. Male in eclipse plumage resembles female. In flight (page 53), wing patterns of both sexes match those of Cinnamon. **Range:** Blue-winged Teal is fairly common in marshes and on ponds and lakes in open country. Uncommon on the West Coast.

Cinnamon Teal   *Anas cyanoptera*   L 16" (41 cm)

Cinnamon head, neck, and underparts identify **male. Female** closely resembles female Blue-winged Teal but plumage is a richer brown; lore spot, eye line, and broken eye ring less distinct; bill longer and more spatulate. Compare also with Green-winged Teal (page 32). Young birds and males in eclipse plumage resemble female. Males more than a couple of months old have red-orange eyes; Blue-winged's eyes are dark. Wing pattern (page 53) is almost identical to Blue-winged. **Range:** Common in marshes, ponds, and lakes. Regular from eastern Great Plains south to eastern Texas. Casual to eastern Midwest and farther east. Some sightings may be escaped birds. Cinnamon Teal is known to interbreed with Blue-winged Teal.

Garganey   *Anas querquedula*   L 15½" (39 cm)

Range: Old World species. Regular migrant on western Aleutians; very rare on Pribilofs and in Pacific states; casual elsewhere in North America. Prominent whitish edge to tertials is an important field mark in swimming birds; head shape is less rounded than in Blue-winged and Cinnamon Teal. **Male**'s bold white eyebrows separate dark crown, red-brown face; in flight (page 53), shows gray-blue forewing and green speculum bordered fore and aft with white. Wing pattern is retained when male acquires femalelike supplemental plumage, held into winter. **Female** has strong facial pattern: dark crown, pale eyebrow, dark eye line, white lore spot bordered by a second dark line; note also dark bill and legs, dark undertail coverts. Larger and paler overall than female Green-winged Teal (page 32). Female in flight shows gray-brown forewing, dark green speculum bordered in white. Note pale gray inner webs of primaries, visible in flight from above.

Northern Shoveler

fall ♂

♀

♂

Blue-winged Teal

♂

Cinnamon Teal

♂

♀

Garganey

♀

♂

fall ♂

Pochards

Diving ducks of the genus *Aythya* have legs set far back and far apart, which makes walking awkward. Heavy bodies require a running start on water for takeoff. Various species hybridize. Always carefully check potential vagrants to make sure they are not hybrids.

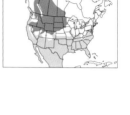

Canvasback *Aythya valisineria* L 21" (53 cm)
Forehead slopes to long, black bill. **Male**'s head and neck are chestnut, back and sides whitish. **Female** and eclipse male have pale brown head and neck, pale brownish gray back and sides. In flight (page 54), whitish belly contrasts with dark breast, dark undertail coverts. Wings lack contrasting pale stripe of smaller Common Pochard and Redhead. **Range:** Locally common in marshes, lakes; feeds in large flocks; has decreased significantly but decline has stabilized. Migrating flocks fly in irregular V-formations or in lines.

Common Pochard *Aythya ferina* L 18" (46 cm)
Range: Eurasian species, rare migrant to Pribilofs and to western and central Aleutians; accidental to south coastal Alaska and southern California. Resembles Canvasback in plumage and head shape. Bill similar to Redhead's but dark at base and tip, gray in center. Gray on upperparts immediately distinguishes **female** from female Redhead and Ring-necked Duck (next page). In flight (page 54), wings show gray stripe along trailing edge.

Redhead *Aythya americana* L 19" (48 cm)
Rounded head and shorter, tricolored bill separate this species from Canvasback. Bill is mostly pale blue (male) or slate (female), with narrow white ring bordering black tip. **Male**'s back and sides are smoky gray. **Female** and eclipse male are tawny brown, with slightly darker crown, pale patch bordering black bill tip; compare female scaup (next page). Redheads in flight (page 54) show gray stripe on trailing edge of wings. **Range:** Locally common in marshes, ponds, and lakes; is declining in the East.

Canvasback

Common Pochard

Redhead

Ring-necked Duck *Aythya collaris L 17" (43 cm)*
Peaked head; bold white ring near tip of bill. **Male** has second
white ring at base of bill; white crescent separates black breast
from gray sides. Cinnamon collar is often hard to see in the field.
Female has dark crown, white eye ring; may have a pale line
extending back from eye; face is mainly gray. In flight (page 54),
all plumages show a gray stripe on secondaries. **Range:** Fairly
common in freshwater marshes and on woodland ponds, lakes;
during winter, found also in southern coastal marshes. Range is
variable; may breed south or winter north of mapped range.

Tufted Duck *Aythya fuligula L 17" (43 cm)*
Range: Old World species; regular visitor to western Alaska. Rare
winter visitor along East Coast as far south as Maryland, and on
West Coast to southern California; casual elsewhere in West; very
rare in Great Lakes region. Found on ponds, rivers, bays, often
with Ring-necked Ducks and especially scaup. Head is rounded;
crest distinct in **male,** smaller in **female** and immatures; may be
absent in eclipse male. Gleaming white sides further distinguish
male from male Ring-necked Duck. **First-winter male** has gray
sides but lacks the white crescent conspicuous in male Ring-
necked. Female is blackish brown above; lacks white eye ring and
white bill ring of female Ring-necked. Bills of both male and
female Tufted have a wide black tip. Some females also have a small
white area at base of bill. In flight (page 54), all plumages show a
broad white stripe on secondaries and extending onto primaries.

Greater Scaup *Aythya marila L 18" (46 cm)*
Larger size and smoothly rounded head help distinguish this
species from Lesser Scaup. In close view, note Greater Scaup's
slightly larger bill with wider black tip. **Male** averages paler on
back and flanks; in good light, head may show a green gloss. In
both species, **female** has bold white patch at base of bill. Some
female Greater Scaup, especially in spring and summer, have a
paler head with a distinct whitish ear patch. In flight (page 54),
Greater Scaup typically shows a bold white stripe on secondaries
and well out onto primaries, unlike Lesser Scaup. **Range:** Locally
common; found on large, open lakes and bays. Migrates and
winters in small or large flocks, often with Lesser Scaup. Rare to
uncommon winter visitor throughout the Gulf Coast states.

Lesser Scaup *Aythya affinis L 16½" (42 cm)*
Smaller size and peaked crown help distinguish from Greater
Scaup. In close view, note Lesser Scaup's slightly smaller bill with
smaller black tip. In good light, **male**'s head may show a purple
gloss, sometimes mixed with green. **Female** is brown overall, with
bold white patch at base of bill. In some females, especially in
spring and summer, head is paler, with whitish ear patch less distinct than in female Greater Scaup. In flight (page 54), Lesser
Scaup shows bold white stripe on secondaries only. **Range:** Common; breeds in marshes, small lakes, and ponds. In winter, found
in large flocks on sheltered bays, inlets, and lakes.

Ring-necked Duck

adult ♂

♀

Tufted Duck

1st winter ♂

♀

adult ♂

♀

Greater Scaup

nearctica

1st winter ♂

♀

♀

adult ♂

Lesser Scaup

adult ♂

♀

Eiders

These large, bulky diving sea ducks have dense down feathers that help insulate them from the cold northern waters. Females pluck their own down to line nests.

Common Eider *Somateria mollissima* L 24" (61 cm)
Female distinguished from female King Eider by larger size, sloping forehead, and evenly barred sides and scapulars. Feathering extends along sides of bill to or beyond nostril, with minimal feathering on top of bill. Females range in overall color from rust to gray. Eastern *dresseri* is reddish brown. Western *v-nigrum* is duller brown. **Male**'s head pattern is distinctive. Most western and a few eastern males show a thin black V on throat; *v-nigrum* male has orange-yellow bill. **Eclipse** and **first-winter males** are dark; first-winter has white on breast; full adult plumage is attained by fourth winter. In flight (page 54), adult male shows solid white back and wing coverts. **Range:** Locally abundant on shallow bays, rocky shores; casual on Great Lakes. Rare in winter to North Carolina; casual on East Coast to Florida; accidental on West Coast.

King Eider *Somateria spectabilis* L 22" (56 cm)
Female distinguished from female Common Eider by smaller size, more rounded head, and crescent or V-shaped markings on sides and scapulars. Feathering extends only slightly along sides of bill but extensively down the top, making bill look stubby. **Male**'s head pattern is distinctive. In flight (page 55), shows partly black back, black wings with white patches. **First-winter male** has brown head, pinkish or buffy bill, buffy eye line; lacks white wing patches; full adult plumage attained by third winter. **Range:** Common on tundra and coastal waters in northern part of range; generally very rare on Great Lakes except on Lake Ontario, where rare and increasing. Rare in winter on East Coast to Virginia; casual to Florida and on West Coast.

Spectacled Eider *Somateria fischeri* **T** L 21" (53 cm)
Male has green head with white, black-bordered eye patches and orange bill. In flight (page 55), black breast separates adult male from other eiders, smaller size from Common Eider. Drab **female** has fainter spectacle pattern; bill is gray-blue; feathering extends far down upper mandible. **Range:** Uncommon and declining; found on coastal tundra near lakes and ponds. Flocks winter in openings in ice pack on Bering Sea. Casual on Aleutians.

Steller's Eider *Polysticta stelleri* **T** L 17" (43 cm)
Greenish head tufts, black eye patch, chin, and collar identify **male. Female** is dark cinnamon brown with pale eye ring, unfeathered dark bill. In flight (page 55), adults, immature males, and some immature females show blue speculum bordered fore and aft in white. **Range:** Found along rocky coasts; nests on inland grassy areas or tundra. Winters casually south to northern California coast. Numbers reduced over last two decades.

Common Eider

eclipse adult ♂
v-nigrum

♀ *v-nigrum*

♀ *dresseri*

adult ♂
dresseri

1st winter ♂
dresseri

adult ♂
v-nigrum

King Eider

1st winter ♂

adult ♂

♀

Spectacled Eider

adult ♂

♀

Common Eiders in flight

Steller's Eider

1st winter ♂

adult ♂

♀

Sea Ducks

Stocky, short-necked diving ducks, most species breed in the far north and migrate in large, compact flocks to and from their coastal wintering grounds.

Black Scoter *Melanitta nigra L 19" (48 cm)*

Male is black, with orange-yellow knob at base of dark bill. **Female**'s dark crown and nape contrast with pale face and throat; feathering does not extend onto bill. In both, forehead is rounded. In flight (page 55), adult male's blackish wing linings contrast with paler flight feathers. Juveniles resemble females but are whitish on belly; **first-winter male** has some yellow at base of bill by winter. **Range:** Nests on tundra. Small numbers seen in fall on Great Lakes (common on Lake Ontario, where some winter); rare elsewhere in eastern interior; casual in western interior.

White-winged Scoter *Melanitta fusca L 21" (53 cm)*

White secondaries, conspicuous in flight (page 54), may show as a small white patch on swimming bird. Forehead slightly rounded. Feathering extends almost to nostrils on top and sides of bill. **Female** and juveniles lack contrasting dark crown and paler face of other scoters; white facial patches are distinct on juveniles, often indistinct on adult female. Juveniles and immatures are whitish below. **Adult male** has black knob at base of colorful bill; crescent-shaped white patch below white eye, brownish flanks. Black-flanked adult male Asian *stejnegeri*, casual to western Alaska, has more obvious nasal hook and different bill color pattern. **Range:** Fairly common on inland lakes in breeding season, coastal areas in winter. Uncommon inland migrant. Large numbers winter on Lake Ontario since introduction of zebra mussels. Rarest scoter in the South.

Surf Scoter *Melanitta perspicillata L 20" (51 cm)*

Male's black plumage sets off colorful bill, white eye, white patch on forehead and nape; forehead is sloping, not rounded. **Female** is brown, with dark crown; usually has two white patches on each side of face; feathering extends down top of bill only. Adult female and **first-winter male** may have whitish nape patch. All juveniles have whitish belly, usually white face patches. In flight (page 54), more uniform color of underwings helps distinguish Surf from Black Scoter; also orangish, not dark, legs and feet. **Range:** Common; nests on tundra and in wooded areas near water. Rare inland migrant. A few winter on Great Lakes; most in coastal waters.

Harlequin Duck *Histrionicus histrionicus L 16½" (42 cm)*

Small duck, with rounded head, stubby bill. **Male**'s colorful plumage appears dark at a distance. **Female** has three white spots on each side of head. Juvenile resembles adult female. Flight is rapid, low. Compare female in flight (page 55) with female Bufflehead. Male's **call** is a high-pitched nasal squeaking. **Range:** Locally common on rocky coasts; moves inland along swift streams for nesting. Rare on Great Lakes in migration and winter.

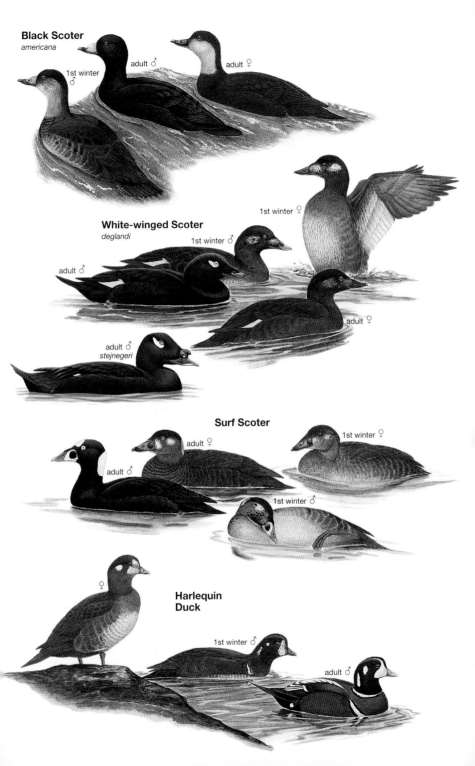

Black Scoter
americana

1st winter ♂

adult ♂

adult ♀

White-winged Scoter
deglandi

1st winter ♀

adult ♂

1st winter ♂

adult ♀

adult ♂
stejnegeri

Surf Scoter

adult ♂

adult ♀

1st winter ♀

1st winter ♂

♀

Harlequin Duck

1st winter ♂

adult ♂

Long-tailed Duck *Clangula hyemalis*

♂ L 22" (56 cm) ♀ 16" (41 cm) Formerly Oldsquaw. **Male**'s long tail is conspicuous in flight, may be submerged in swimming bird. Male in winter and spring is largely white; breast and back dark brown, scapulars pearl gray; stubby bill shows pink band. By late spring, male becomes mostly dark, with pale facial patch, bi-colored scapulars; in later, supplemental molt, acquires paler crown and shorter, buff-edged scapulars. Molt into full eclipse plumage continues until early fall. **Female** lacks long tail; bill is dark; plumage whiter in winter, darker in summer. First-fall birds (see page 55) are even darker. Long-taileds are identifiable at some distance by their swift, careening flight and loud, yodeling, three-part **calls,** heard all year. Both sexes show uniformly dark underwings. **Range:** Away from Great Lakes, rare in the interior and south to Gulf Coast.

Barrow's Goldeneye *Bucephala islandica* L 18" (46 cm)

Male has white crescent on each side of face; white patches on scapulars show on swimming bird as a row of spots; dark color of back extends forward in a bar partially separating white breast from white sides. **Female** and male in eclipse plumage closely resemble the Common Goldeneye. Puffy, oval-shaped head, steep forehead, and stubby, triangular bill help identify Barrow's. Adult female's head is slightly darker than female Common; bill mostly yellow, except in young females, which may have only a yellow band near tip of bill. In all plumages, white wing patches visible in flight (page 55) differ subtly between the two species. **Hybrids** between the two goldeneye species are regularly noted. **Range:** Both summer on open lakes and small ponds; winter in sheltered coastal areas, inland lakes, and rivers. Overall, Barrow's is much less common; rare to casual outside mapped winter range.

Common Goldeneye *Bucephala clangula* L 18½" (47 cm)

Male has round white spot on each side of face; scapulars are mostly white. **Female** and eclipse male closely resemble Barrow's Goldeneye. Head of Common is more triangular; forehead more sloped; bill longer. Female's head is slightly paler than female Barrow's; bill generally all-dark or with yellow near tip only; rarely completely dull yellow. In all plumages, there are subtle differences between the two species in white wing patches visible in flight (page 55).

Bufflehead *Bucephala albeola* L 13½" (34 cm)

A small duck with a large, puffy head, steep forehead, short bill. **Male** is glossy black above, white below, with large white patch on head. **Female** is duller, with small, elongated white patch on each side of head. **First-winter male** and male in eclipse resemble female. In flight (page 55), males show white patch across entire wing; female has white patch only on inner secondaries. **Range:** Generally common, Buffleheads nest in woodlands near small lakes and ponds. During migration and winter, found also on sheltered bays, rivers, and lakes.

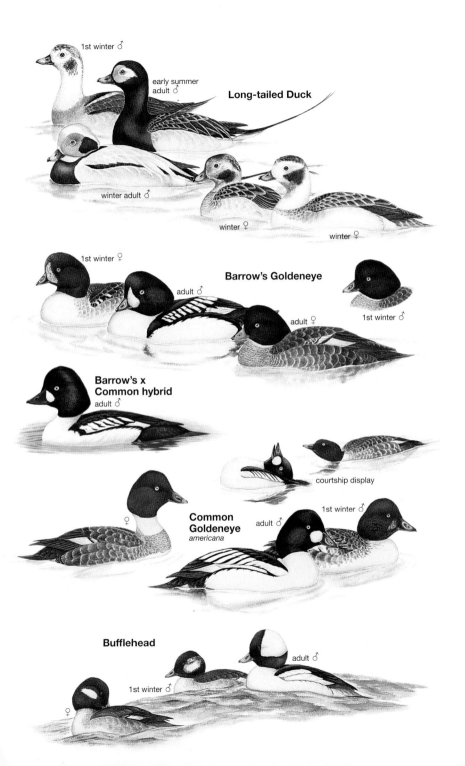

1st winter ♂

early summer
adult ♂

Long-tailed Duck

winter adult ♂

winter ♀

winter ♀

1st winter ♀

Barrow's Goldeneye

adult ♂

adult ♀

1st winter ♂

**Barrow's x
Common hybrid**
adult ♂

courtship display

♀

**Common
Goldeneye**
americana

adult ♂

1st winter ♂

Bufflehead

adult ♂

1st winter ♂

♀

Mergansers

Long, thin, serrated bills help these divers catch fish, crustaceans, and aquatic insects. Mergansers in flight show pointed wings.

Common Merganser *Mergus merganser L 25" (64 cm)*
Large duck with long, slim neck and thick-based, hooked, red bill. White breast and sides, often tinged with pink, and lack of crest distinguish **male** from Red-breasted Merganser. **Female**'s bright chestnut, crested head and neck contrast sharply with white chin, white breast. Adult male in flight (page 54) shows white patch on upper surface of entire inner wing, partially crossed by a single black bar. Eclipse male resembles female but retains wing pattern. Female's white inner secondaries and greater coverts are partially crossed by a black bar. Old World "**Goosander**" (nominate *merganser*), recorded from western Aleutians, lacks dark bar on wing. Note different bill shape. As in all species on this page, young male resembles adult female. **Range:** Common Mergansers nest in woodlands near lakes and rivers; in winter, sometimes also found on brackish water. Casual to Gulf Coast.

Red-breasted Merganser *Mergus serrator L 23" (58 cm)*
Shaggy double crest, white collar, and streaked breast distinguish **male** from male Common Merganser. **Female**'s head and neck are paler than female Common; chin and foreneck whitish. Adult male in flight (page 54) shows white patch on upper surface of inner wing, partly crossed by two black bars. Eclipse male resembles female but retains male wing pattern. Female's white inner secondaries and greater coverts are crossed by a single black bar. Smaller size and thinner bill help distinguish Red-breasted Merganser in mixed flocks. **Range:** Nests in woodlands near fresh water or in sheltered coastal areas; prefers brackish or salt water in winter. Abundant migrant on Great Lakes, where moderate numbers winter; elsewhere, fairly common to common migrant in interior.

Hooded Merganser *Lophodytes cucullatus L 18" (46 cm)*
Puffy, rounded crest; thin bill. **Male**'s bill is dark; white head patches are fan shaped and conspicuous when crest is raised. Compare with male Bufflehead (preceding page). **Female** brownish overall; upper mandible dark, lower yellowish. Rapid wingbeats in flight (page 55); both sexes show black-and-white inner secondaries. Crest is flattened in flight, male's head patch shows only as a white line. **Range:** Uncommon in West; common over much of East. In breeding season, found on woodland ponds, rivers, and backwaters. Winters chiefly on fresh water.

Smew *Mergellus albellus L 16" (41 cm)*
Range: Eurasian species, rare visitor to Aleutians; casual on Pribilofs; accidental in Pacific states and in East. Bill is dark and relatively short. In **female,** white throat and lower face contrast sharply with reddish head and nape. **Adult male** is white with black markings; black-and-white wings are conspicuous in flight (page 55).

Common Merganser
americanus

♀

1st spring ♂

adult ♂

"Goosander"
adult ♂
merganser

**Red-breasted
Merganser**

adult ♂

1st winter ♂

♀

**Hooded
Merganser**

1st spring ♂

adult ♂

♀

Smew

♀

1st spring ♂

adult ♂

Stiff-tailed Ducks

Long, stiff tail feathers serve as a rudder for these diving ducks. In both species, male's bill is blue in breeding season.

Ruddy Duck *Oxyura jamaicensis L 15" (38 cm)*
Chunky, with large head, broad bill, long tail, often cocked up. **Male**'s white cheeks are conspicuous both in **breeding** plumage and in dull **winter** plumage. In **female,** single dark line crosses cheek. Young resemble female through first winter. **Range:** Common; nests in dense vegetation of freshwater wetlands. During migration and winter, found on lakes, bays, and salt marshes.

Masked Duck *Nomonyx dominicus L 13½" (34 cm)*
Range: Tropical species, rare and irregular visitor to southern and southeastern Texas; casual in Louisiana and Florida. Accidental in East, north to Wisconsin and New England. Shy; found on densely vegetated ponds. **Male**'s black face on reddish brown head is distinctive. In **female, winter male,** and **juvenile,** two dark stripes cross face and barred back. White wing patches show in flight (page 53).

Exotic Waterfowl

Many waterfowl species are brought into North America from other continents for zoos and private collections. Escapes are frequent. The species shown here are among those seen most frequently.

Ruddy Shelduck *Tadorna ferruginea L 26" (66 cm)*
Afro-Eurasian species often kept in captivity. A record of a flock of six on 23 July 2000 from Southampton Island, Nunavut, Canada, may have been vagrants from Old World.

Common Shelduck *Tadorna tadorna L 25" (64 cm)*
Eurasian species. Female smaller, lacks knob on bill.

Egyptian Goose *Alopochen aegyptiacus L 27" (68 cm)*
African species. Widespread escape. Note white wing patches.

Swan Goose *Anser cygnoides L 45" (114 cm)*
Asian species, domesticated type often called Chinese Goose. Wild race is slim, has long, swanlike bill lacking knob at base.

Mandarin Duck *Aix galericulata L 16" (41 cm)*
Asian species. Compare female to female Wood Duck (page 28).

Bar-headed Goose *Anser indicus L 30" (76 cm)*
Asian species. Fairly common in zoos and private collections.

Graylag Goose *Anser anser L 34" (86 cm)*
Eurasian species, progenitor of most domestic geese. A recent record of a wild bird off Newfoundland (page 466). Compare carefully to Greater White-fronted Goose (page 20).

Ruddy Duck

breeding ♂

winter ♂

winter ♀

breeding ♀

Masked Duck

breeding ♂

winter ♀

winter ♂

breeding ♀

juvenile

Egyptian Goose

adults

Common Shelduck

adult ♂

Ruddy Shelduck

adult ♂

Swan Goose
domestic type

Mandarin Duck

♀

♂

adult

Bar-headed Goose

Graylag Goose

wild type

domestic type

Ducks in Flight

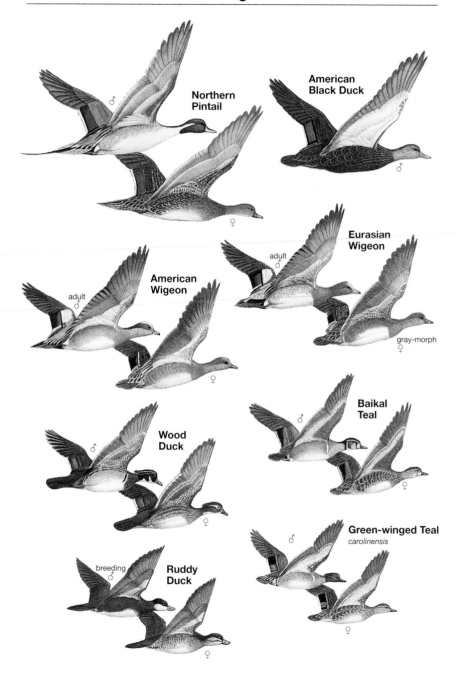

Northern Pintail
♂
♀

American Black Duck
♂

Eurasian Wigeon
adult ♂
gray-morph ♀

American Wigeon
adult ♂
♀

Wood Duck
♂
♀

Baikal Teal
♂
♀

Green-winged Teal
carolinensis
♂
♀

Ruddy Duck
breeding ♂
♀

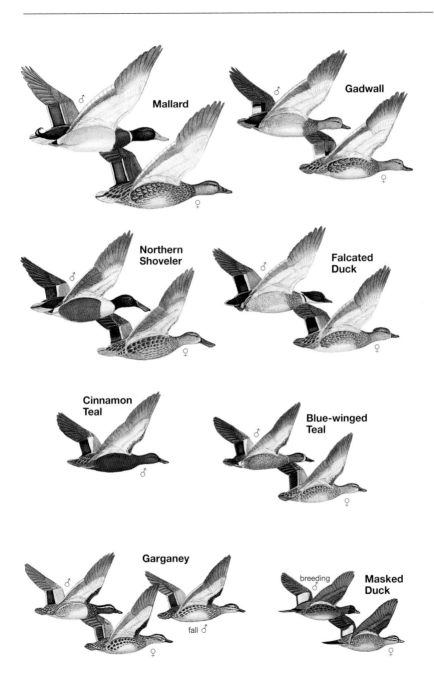

Mallard

Gadwall

Northern Shoveler

Falcated Duck

Cinnamon Teal

Blue-winged Teal

Garganey

fall ♂

Masked Duck

breeding ♂

Ducks in Flight

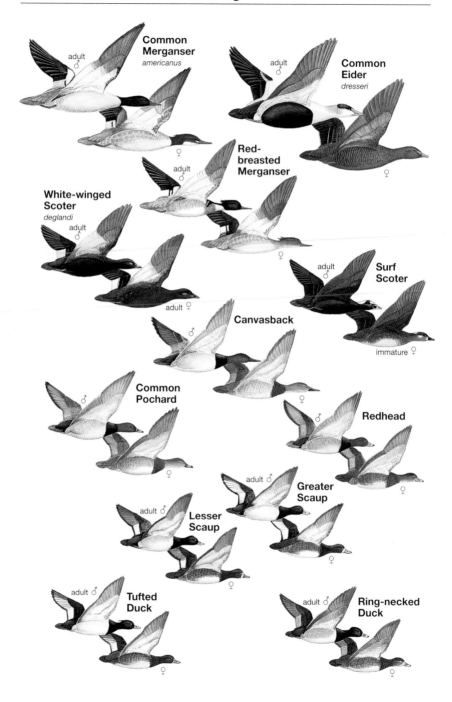

Common Merganser
americanus
adult ♂
♀

Common Eider
dresseri
adult ♂
♀

Red-breasted Merganser
adult ♂
♀

White-winged Scoter
deglandi
adult ♂
adult ♀

Surf Scoter
adult ♂
immature ♀

Canvasback
♂
♀

Common Pochard
♂
♀

Redhead
♂
♀

Greater Scaup
adult ♂
♀

Lesser Scaup
adult ♂
♀

Tufted Duck
adult ♂
♀

Ring-necked Duck
adult ♂
♀

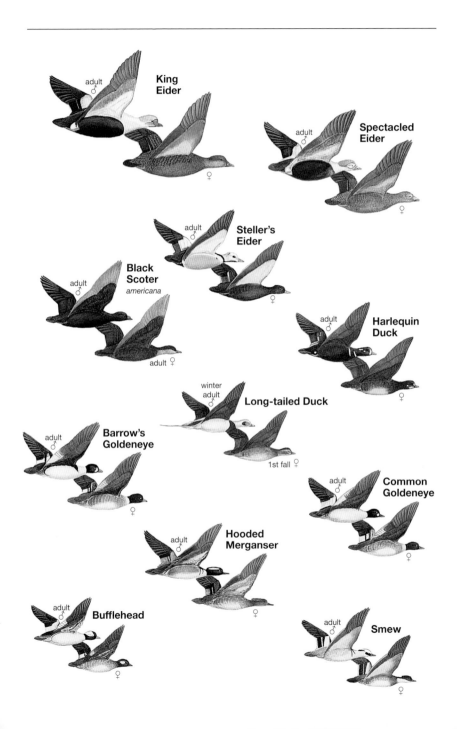

King
Eider

adult ♂

Spectacled
Eider

adult ♂

♀

♀

Steller's
Eider

adult ♂

Black
Scoter
americana

adult ♂

♀

Harlequin
Duck

adult ♂

adult ♀

♀

Long-tailed Duck

winter
adult ♂

Barrow's
Goldeneye

adult ♂

1st fall ♀

Common
Goldeneye

adult ♂

♀

♀

Hooded
Merganser

adult ♂

Bufflehead

adult ♂

♀

Smew

adult ♂

♀

Curassows, Guans (Family Cracidae)

These tropical-forest birds have short, rounded wings and long tails. Generally secretive but highly vocal. One species of this family is found in the United States. *Species: 50 World, 1 N.A.*

Plain Chachalaca *Ortalis vetula* L 22" (56 cm)
Gray to brownish olive above, with small head, slight crest; long and rounded, lustrous, dark green tail tipped with white. Patch of bare skin on throat, usually grayish, is pinkish red in **breeding male.** Male's **call** is a deep, ringing *cha-cha-lac,* often given in a loud chorus with other birds; female's voice is higher pitched. **Range:** Inhabits tall chaparral thickets along the Rio Grande; feeds in trees, chiefly on leaves and buds; often best seen at feeding stations, which many habituate. Introduced to Georgia's Sapelo Island.

Partridges, Grouse, Turkeys, Old World Quail (Family Phasianidae)

Ground dwellers with feathered nostrils, short, strong bills, and short, rounded wings. Flight is brief but strong. Males perform elaborate courting displays. In some species, birds gather at the same strutting grounds, known as leks, every year. *Species: 180 World, 17 N.A.*

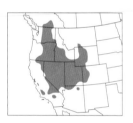

Chukar *Alectoris chukar* L 14" (36 cm)
Old World species, introduced in North America as a game bird in the 1930s. Gray-brown above; flanks boldly barred black and white; buffy face and throat outlined in black; breast gray; belly buff; outer tail feathers chestnut (best seen in flight just prior to landing). Bill and legs are red. Sexes are similar, but males are slightly larger and have small leg spurs. **Juvenile** is smaller and mottled; lacks bold black markings of **adults. Calls** include a series of loud, rapid *chuck chuck chuck* notes and a shrill *whitoo* alarm note. **Range:** Chukars have become established in rocky, arid, mountainous areas of the West. Game farm Chukars or hybrids with Rock Partridge (*A. graeca*) are released for hunting in the East. In fall and winter, Chukars feed in coveys of 5 to 40 birds.

Gray Partridge *Perdix perdix* L 12½" (32 cm)
Grayish brown bird with rusty face and throat, paler in **female. Male** has dark chestnut patch on belly; patch is smaller or absent in females. Flanks are barred with reddish brown; outer tail feathers rusty. **Calls** include a hoarse *kee-uck,* likened to a rusty gate. **Range:** Widely introduced from Europe in early 1900s. Has declined over parts of North American range. Inhabits open farmlands, grassy fields. In fall, forms coveys of 12 to 15 birds.

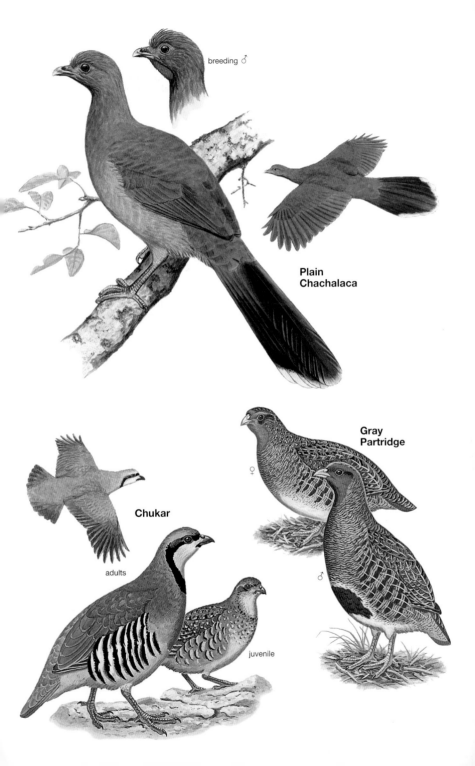

breeding ♂

Plain Chachalaca

Gray Partridge

♀

Chukar

adults

juvenile

♂

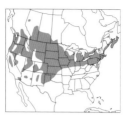

Ring-necked Pheasant *Phasianus colchicus*
♂ *L 33" (84 cm)* ♀ *L 21" (53 cm)* Introduced from Asia, this large, flashy bird has a long, pointed tail and short, rounded wings. **Male** is iridescent bronze overall, mottled with brown, black, and green; head varies from dark, glossy green to purplish, with fleshy red eye patches and iridescent ear tufts. Often shows a broad white neck ring. **Female** is buffy overall, much smaller and duller than male. Distinguished from female Sharp-tailed Grouse (page 64) by larger size, longer tail, lack of barring below, and white in tail. Male's territorial **call** is a loud, penetrating *kok-cack.* Both sexes give hoarse, croaking alarm notes. When flushed, rise almost vertically with a loud whirring of wings. **Range:** Locally common; declining in parts of the East. Found in open country, farmlands, brushy areas, and woodland edges. A group of subspecies with white wing coverts (not shown) has become established in parts of the West. The Japanese subspecies **"Green Pheasant,"** *versicolor,* introduced in tidewater Virginia and southern Delaware, is apparently gone.

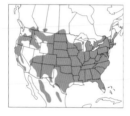

Wild Turkey *Meleagris gallopavo*
♂ *L 46" (117 cm)* ♀ *L 37" (94 cm)* Largest game bird in North America; slightly smaller, more slender than the domesticated bird. **Male** has dark, iridescent body, flight feathers barred with white, red wattles, blackish breast tuft, spurred legs; bare-skinned head is blue and pink. Tail, uppertail coverts, and lower rump feathers are tipped with chestnut on eastern birds, buffy white on western birds. **Female** and immature are smaller and duller than male, often lack breast tuft. Of the races seen in North America, *silvestris* predominates in the East, *merriami* in the West. Birds from Kansas to Mexico (*intermedia*) are intermediate. Birds from Peninsular Florida (*osceola*) are like *silvestris,* but smaller. Birds of the open forest and forest openings, Wild Turkeys forage mostly on the ground for seeds, nuts, acorns, and insects. At night they roost in trees. In spring a male's gobbling **call** may be heard a mile away. **Range:** Restocked in much of its former range and introduced in other areas.

Himalayan Snowcock *Tetraogallus himalayensis*
L 28" (71 cm) **Range:** Large Asian bird, successfully established (introduced 1963) only at high elevations in the Ruby Mountains of northeastern Nevada. Gray-brown overall, with tan streaking above. Whitish face and throat, outlined with chestnut stripes; undertail coverts white. Note white in wing in flight. **Male** almost identical to female, except female slightly smaller, lacks spurs, forehead buff and area around eye grayer. Inhabits mountainous terrain; flies downhill in the morning, then walks back up, feeding. **Calls** include various clucks and cackles while feeding; one advertising call suggestive of Long-billed Curlew (male's call rises, female's descends).

Ring-necked Pheasant

♂

♀

"Green Pheasant"

♂

♀

eastern *silvestris*

♂

♀

Wild Turkey

Himalayan Snowcock

♂

western *merriami*

♂

Ruffed Grouse *Bonasa umbellus* L 17" (43 cm)

Small crest; black ruff on sides of neck, usually inconspicuous; banded tail with wide dark band near tip, incomplete in **female.** The two color **morphs, red** and **gray,** are most apparent by tail color. Red morphs predominate in the humid Pacific Northwest and Appalachian region; gray morphs in the North and West outside the Pacific Northwest. Ten subspecies. In spring, the **male** displays by raising ruff and crest, fanning tail, and beating wings to make a hollow, accelerating, drumming noise. **Range:** Uncommon to fairly common in deciduous and mixed woodlands.

Spruce Grouse *Falcipennis canadensis* L 16" (41 cm)

Male has dark throat and breast, edged with white; red eye combs. Over most of range, both sexes have black tail with chestnut tip. Birds of the northern Rockies and Cascades, **"Franklin's Grouse,"** *franklinii,* have white spots on uppertail coverts; **male**'s tail is all-dark. In all subspecies, **females** have two color **morphs, red** and **gray;** resemble female Sooty and Dusky Grouse but are smaller and have black barring and white spots below. Juveniles resemble red-morph female. Spruce Grouse inhabit open coniferous forests with dense undergrowth. Frequents roadsides, especially in fall. Female's high-pitched **call** is thought to be territorial. In courtship display, male spreads his tail, erects the red eye combs, and rapidly beats wings. In territorial flight display, male flutters upward on shallow wingstrokes; "Franklin's Grouse" ends this performance by beating wings together, making a clapping sound.

Sooty Grouse *Dendragapus fuliginosus* L 20" (51 cm)

Formerly (with Dusky Grouse) known as Blue Grouse. Larger than Spruce Grouse. **Male**'s sooty gray plumage sets off yellow-orange eye comb. On neck, white-based feathers cover an inflatable bare yellow sac. Female is mottled brown above, with plain gray belly. On both sexes, the 18 tail feathers are round and tipped with a gray terminal band. Chicks are yellowish. Male display **call** is series of loud low hoots audible at considerable distance, usually delivered from perch in tree; neck sacs are inflated to amplify sound. **Range:** Inhabits coniferous forest but will forage at meadow edges. Believed extirpated from mountains of southern California.

Dusky Grouse *Dendragapus obscurus* L 20" (51 cm)

All plumages similar to Sooty Grouse, but paler overall; closed tail squarer (less graduated), the 20 tail feathers are more square tipped. Northern subspecies (*richardsonii* and *pallidus*) lack or virtually lack the gray terminal band. **Male** neck sac is purplish and smoother, with broader white-feathered border than in Sooty. Male's display, usually from ground, often involves low fluttering or making short circular flights, then strutting with tail fanned, body tipped forward, head drawn in, wings dragging. Male's display **call,** usually given from ground, is softer and lower pitched than Sooty and audible only at close range. Chicks are grayish. **Range:** Often prefers more open forest than Sooty; sometimes found in sagebrush. Range almost entirely separate from Sooty; hybrids recorded from interior of British Columbia.

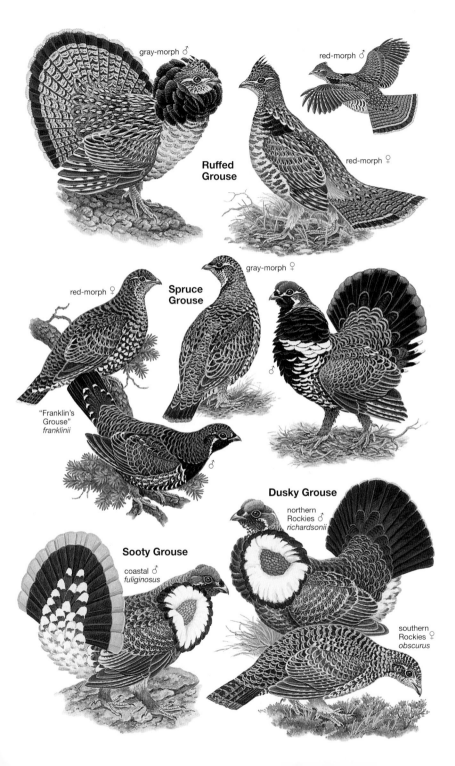

gray-morph ♂

red-morph ♂

Ruffed Grouse

red-morph ♀

red-morph ♀

Spruce Grouse

gray-morph ♀

"Franklin's Grouse" *franklinii*

♂

♂

Dusky Grouse

northern Rockies ♂ *richardsonii*

Sooty Grouse

coastal ♂ *fuliginosus*

southern Rockies ♀ *obscurus*

White-tailed Ptarmigan *Lagopus leucura* L 12½" (32 cm)

As with all ptarmigans, legs and feet are feathered and plumage is molted three times a year, matching seasonal changes in habitat. Distinguished from other ptarmigans in all seasons by white tail. **Winter** bird is white except for small dark bill and eyes and red eye combs. In **summer,** body is mottled blackish or brown with white belly, wings, and tail. Spring and **fall molts** give a patchy appearance. **Calls** include a henlike clucking and soft, low hoots. **Range:** Locally common on rocky alpine slopes, high meadows. Small numbers have been successfully introduced in the central Sierra Nevada, Wallowa, and Uinta Mountains and on Pike's Peak. Reintroduced into northern New Mexico. Moves to lower elevations during severe weather.

Rock Ptarmigan *Lagopus muta* L 14" (36 cm)

Mottled **summer** plumage is black, dark brown, or grayish brown; **male** generally lacks the reddish tones of male Willow Ptarmigan. There are many recognized subspecies, with color variations according to geography. In **winter** plumage, **male** has a black line from bill through eye, lacking in male Willow. Acquires breeding plumage later in spring than does Willow. In both sexes, bill and overall size are slightly smaller than in Willow. **Females** are otherwise difficult to distinguish from Willows. Plumage is patchy white during spring and fall molts. Both species retain white wings and black tail year-round. **Calls** include low growls and croaks and noisy cackles. **Range:** The Rock Ptarmigan is common on high, rocky slopes and tundra. In breeding season, generally prefers higher and more barren habitat than does Willow Ptarmigan. Accidental in northern Minnesota and Queen Charlotte Islands, British Columbia, in spring.

Willow Ptarmigan *Lagopus lagopus* L 15" (38 cm)

Largest ptarmigan. Mottled **summer** plumage of **male** is generally redder than in Rock Ptarmigan. White **winter** plumage lacks the black eye line of male Rock Ptarmigan; bill and overall size are slightly larger in Willow Ptarmigan. **Female** is otherwise difficult to distinguish from Rock Ptarmigan. Both species retain white wings and black tail year-round. Plumage is patchy white during **spring** and fall **molts. Calls** include low growls and croaks, noisy cackles. In courtship and territorial displays, male utters a raucous *go-back go-back go-backa go-backa go-backa.* Ptarmigans' red eye combs can be concealed or raised during courtship and aggression. **Range:** Willow Ptarmigan is common on tundra, especially in thickets of willow and alder. In breeding season, generally prefers wetter, brushier habitat than Rock Ptarmigan. Casual in spring and winter to northern tier of U.S. states.

White-tailed Ptarmigan

winter

summer ♀

molting fall ♂

summer ♂

Rock Ptarmigan

winter ♀

winter ♂

summer ♀

summer ♂

fall ♂

Willow Ptarmigan

summer ♀

molting spring ♂

winter

summer ♂

summer ♂

Greater Prairie-Chicken *Tympanuchus cupido*
L 17" (43 cm) Heavily barred with dark brown, cinnamon, and pale buff above and below. Short, rounded tail is all-dark in **male,** barred in **female.** Male has fleshy yellow-orange eye combs. Both sexes have elongated dark neck feathers, longer in males and erected during courtship to display inflated golden neck sacs. Courting males make a deep *oo-loo-woo* sound known as "booming," like blowing over top of an empty bottle. **Range:** Uncommon, local, and declining. Found in areas of natural tallgrass prairie interspersed with cropland. A smaller, darker race, endangered "Attwater's Prairie-Chicken," *attwateri* (**E**) of southeastern Texas, is nearly extinct. The "Heath Hen" (nominate *cupido*), formerly resident along the Atlantic seaboard from Massachusetts to Virginia, is now extinct—last record on Martha's Vineyard in 1932.

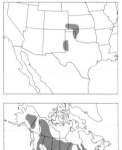

Lesser Prairie-Chicken *Tympanuchus pallidicinctus*
L 16" (41 cm) Resembles Greater Prairie-Chicken, but slightly smaller, paler, less heavily barred below. Male's courtship notes are higher pitched than Greater. Courting male displays dull orange-red neck sacs and erects dark neck tufts. **Range:** Uncommon, local, and declining; found in sagebrush and shortgrass prairie country, especially where shinnery oak grows.

Sharp-tailed Grouse *Tympanuchus phasianellus*
L 17" (43 cm) Similar to prairie-chickens, but underparts are scaled and spotted; tail is mostly white and pointed; yellowish eye combs are less prominent. Compare with female Ring-necked Pheasant (page 58). Birds are darkest in Alaska and northern Canada (standing figure), palest in the Plains (flying figure). **Male**'s purplish neck sacs are inflated during courtship display. His courting notes include cackling and a single, low *coo-oo* **call** accompanied by the rattling of wing quills. **Range:** Inhabits grasslands, sagebrush, woodland edges, and river canyons. Fairly common over range; rare in western U.S. Where ranges overlap, can hybridize with Greater Prairie-Chicken and Dusky Grouse.

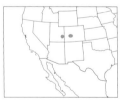

Gunnison Sage-Grouse *Centrocercus minimus*
♂ L 22" (56 cm) ♀ L 18" (46 cm) Distinguished from Greater Sage-Grouse by smaller size and more strongly white-banded tail. Longer, denser filoplumes are erected to form a distinct, recurved crest on **displaying male. Range:** Small, declining population in south-central Colorado and southeastern Utah is geographically isolated from Greater Sage-Grouse.

Greater Sage-Grouse *Centrocercus urophasianus*
♂ L 28" (71 cm) ♀ L 22" (56 cm) Blackish belly, long pointed tail feathers, and large size are distinctive. **Male** is larger than **female** and has yellow eye combs, black throat and bib, and large white ruff on breast. In flight, dark belly, absence of white outer tail feathers, and larger size distinguish it from Sharp-tailed Grouse. **Displaying male** fans tail and rapidly inflates and deflates air sacs, emitting a loud, bubbling popping. **Range:** Fairly common but local; found in sagebrush areas of foothills and plains.

Greater Prairie-Chicken

displaying ♂

♀

Lesser Prairie-Chicken

displaying ♂

♀

Sharp-tailed Grouse

displaying ♂

♀

Gunnison Sage-Grouse

displaying ♂

Greater Sage-Grouse

displaying ♂

♂

♀

♀

displaying males on lek

New World Quail (Family Odontophoridae)

Scientific evidence has recently placed the New World Quail in their own family. All have chunky bodies and crests or head plumes. In North America, most live in the West. *Species: 32 World, 6 N.A.*

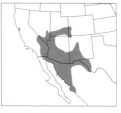

Gambel's Quail *Callipepla gambelii* L 11" (28 cm)

Grayish above, with prominent teardrop-shaped plume or double plume. Chestnut sides and crown, and lack of scaling on underparts, distinguish Gambel's from California Quail. **Male** has dark forehead, black throat, black patch on belly. Smaller **juvenile** is tan and gray with pale mottling and streaking. Shows less scaling and streaking than darker California juvenile; nape and throat are grayer. **Calls** include varied grunts and cackles and a plaintive *qua-el;* loud, querulous *chi-ca-go-go* call is similar to California Quail but higher pitched and usually has four notes. **Range:** Common in desert scrublands and thickets, usually near permanent water source. Gregarious; in fall and winter, forms large coveys. Sometimes **hybridizes** with Scaled Quail (next page) and California Quail where ranges overlap. Introduced populations exist in Idaho and on California's San Clemente Island.

California Quail *Callipepla californica* L 10" (25 cm)

Gray and brown above, with prominent teardrop-shaped plume or double plume. Scaled underparts and brown sides and crown separate California from Gambel's Quail. Body color varies from grayish, seen over most of range, to brown in coastal mountains of California; extremes are shown here in **females. Male** has pale forehead, black throat, and chestnut patch on belly. **Juvenile** is smaller; resembles Gambel's juvenile, but is darker, with traces of scaling on underparts. **Calls** include varied grunts and cackles; loud, emphatic *chi-ca-go* call is similar to Gambel's Quail but lower pitched and usually has three notes rather than four. **Range:** Common in open woodlands, brushy foothills, stream valleys, suburbs, usually near permanent water source. Gregarious; in fall and winter, assembles in large coveys. Populations in northeastern portion of range and Utah are probably introduced.

Mountain Quail *Oreortyx pictus* L 11" (28 cm)

Gray and brown above, with two long, thin head plumes that often appear to be one plume. Gray breast; chestnut sides boldly barred with white; chestnut throat outlined in white. **Male** and **female** are alike; female has shorter head plumes. Amount of brown and gray in upperparts varies in different races; birds of humid coastal Northwest are browner than three gray interior subspecies. Smaller **juvenile** has grayer underparts and longer head plumes than Gambel's or California Quail juveniles. Male's mating **call,** a loud, clear, descending *quee-ark;* both sexes give whistled notes. **Range:** Uncommon to fairly common, but declining in parts of range; in chaparral, brushy ravines, mountain slopes, at altitudes up to 10,000 feet. Nonmigratory but descends to lower altitudes in winter. Gregarious, forming small coveys in fall and winter. Secretive; best seen in late summer in family groups along roadsides.

Gambel's Quail

juvenile

Scaled x Gambel's hybrid

♂

♀ *californica*

coastal ♀ *brunescens*

California Quail

coastal juvenile *brunescens*

♂ *californica*

Mountain Quail

coastal ♂ *palmeri*

interior ♀

juvenile

Northern Bobwhite *Colinus virginianus L 9¾" (25 cm)*
Mottled, reddish brown quail with short gray tail. Flanks are striped with reddish brown. Throat and eye stripe are white in **male,** buffy in **female. Juvenile** is smaller and duller. Male's **call** is a rising, whistled *bob-white,* heard chiefly in late spring and summer; whistled *hoy* call is heard year-round. **Range:** Uncommon to common in brushlands and open woodlands, the bobwhite feeds and roosts in coveys except during nesting season. The population in the Northwest is introduced. At northern edge of range, numbers have greatly declined over the last couple of decades. **"Masked Bobwhite,"** *ridgwayi* (**E**), which was formerly found from southeastern Arizona to central Sonora, Mexico, was eliminated from the U.S. part of its range by the early 1900s. Reintroduced in 1970 from Mexico (Sonora) to Altar Valley in southeastern Arizona, it remains endangered. Male has black throat and cinnamon underparts.

Montezuma Quail *Cyrtonyx montezumae L 8¾" (22 cm)*
Plump, short-tailed, round-winged quail. **Male** has distinctive facial pattern and rounded pale brown crest on back of head. Back and wings mottled black, brown, and tan; breast dark chestnut; sides and flanks dark gray with white spots. **Female** is mottled pinkish brown below with less distinct head markings. **Juvenile** is smaller, paler, with dark spotting on underparts. **Call** given by male in breeding season is a loud, quavering, descending whistle. **Range:** Uncommon, secretive, and local in grassy undergrowth of open juniper-oak or pine-oak woodlands on semiarid mountain slopes. Recently rediscovered in Chisos Mountains of southwest Texas.

Scaled Quail *Callipepla squamata L 10" (25 cm)*
Grayish quail with conspicuous white-tipped crest. Bluish gray breast and mantle feathers have dark edges, creating a shingled or scaly effect. Female's crest is buffy and smaller. **Males** in southernmost Texas (*castanogastris*) tend to show a dark chestnut patch on belly, unlike the common subspecies, *pallida,* found over much of the U.S. range. **Juvenile** resembles adult but is more mottled above, with less conspicuous scaling. During breeding season, both sexes give a location **call** when separated, a low, nasal *chip-churr,* accented on the second syllable. **Range:** Fairly common; found on barren mesas and plateaus, semidesert scrublands, and grasslands with mixed scrub; often frequents roadsides. In fall, forms large coveys.

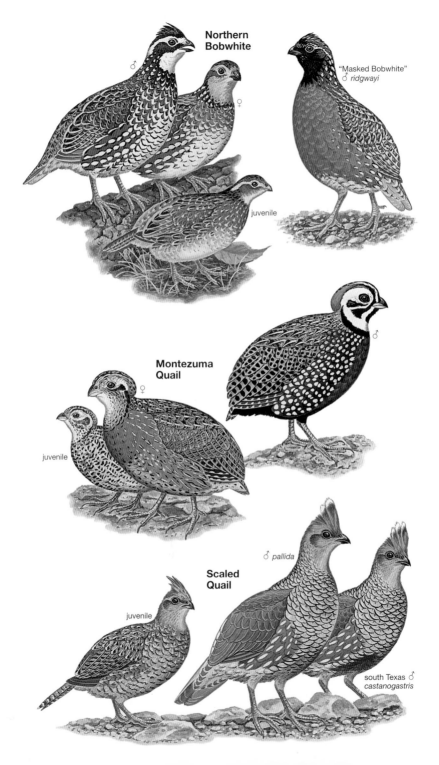

Northern Bobwhite

♂

♀

juvenile

"Masked Bobwhite"
♂ *ridgwayi*

Montezuma Quail

♀

juvenile

♂

Scaled Quail

juvenile

♂ *pallida*

south Texas ♂
castanogastris

Loons (Family Gaviidae)

In all species, juvenal-like plumage is held through the first summer.
Species: 5 World, 5 N.A.

Red-throated Loon *Gavia stellata L 25" (64 cm)*
Thin bill often appears slightly upturned; tends to hold head tilted up. **Breeding adult** has gray head with brick red throat patch that appears dark in flight; dark brown upperparts with no contrasting white patches on scapulars as in all other loons in breeding plumage. **Winter adult** has sharply defined white on face and extensive white spotting on back. **Juvenile**'s head is grayish brown; throat may have dull red markings. In all plumages, white on flanks extends upward a bit on sides of rump, which may cause confusion with Arctic Loon. In flight, shows smaller head and feet than Common and Yellow-billed Loon (next page); wingbeat is quicker; often flies with drooping neck, unlike other loons. Flight **call,** heard on breeding range, is a rapid, gooselike *kak-kak-kak.* **Range:** Migrates coastally; also overland in the East, where most numerous on northern and eastern Great Lakes. Always casual inland in western North America, and in the eastern interior during winter.

Pacific Loon *Gavia pacifica L 26" (66 cm)*
In all plumages, has dark flanks, with no white extending upward on sides of rump. Bill is slim and straight; head smoothly rounded and held level. **Breeding adult**'s head and nape are pale gray; white stripes on sides of neck show only moderate contrast; throat's iridescent purple patch, sometimes washed with green, usually appears black unless seen clearly on swimming bird. **Juvenile**'s crown and nape are slightly paler than back, unlike Common Loon (next page); in juveniles and **winter adults,** dark cap extends to eye. Winter adults and most juveniles have a thin, brown "chin strap," though it may be faint in juveniles. In flight, resembles Common, but head and feet are smaller. **Range:** A coastal and offshore migrant; unlike other loons, often migrates in small to moderate-size flocks. Rare inland throughout the West; very rare in Midwest; casual on East Coast.

Arctic Loon *Gavia arctica L 28" (73 cm)*
Range: Old World species. To date, only the larger Siberian race, *viridigularis,* has been recorded in North America. Breeds in northwestern Alaska. Seen in migration in coastal western Alaska, especially at St. Lawrence Island. Casual elsewhere on West Coast. Larger than Pacific Loon, with less-rounded head; best distinguished in all plumages from Pacific by more extensive white on flanks, coming up over sides of rump. Visibility of white area depends on how buoyantly the bird is swimming. When diving, often only a small white rump patch is evident. At rest, Arctic Loon shows much more white; note Pacific can also show some white. Nape in **breeding adult** is darker, and black-and-white stripes are bolder, than in Pacific; white stripes on face connect more to sides of neck; greenish on throat very hard to see.

winter adult

1st spring

Red-throated Loon

breeding adult

juvenile

winter adult

Red-throated

breeding adults for comparison

Pacific

Arctic

breeding adult

winter adult

Pacific Loon

winter adult

juveniles

winter adult

breeding adults

Arctic Loon
viridigularis

juvenile

winter adult

winter adult

Common Loon   *Gavia immer*   L 32" (81 cm)

Large, thick-billed loon with slightly curved culmen. Bill is black in **breeding** plumage, blue-gray in **winter adults** and **juveniles,** but the culmen remains dark. In winter plumage, crown and nape are darker than back; dark on nape extends around sides of neck, but note the white indentation above this. In winter adults the white extends up and around the eye; the face pattern is more blended in juveniles. Forehead is steep, crown is peaked at front. Holds head level. Juvenile Common and Yellow-billed Loons have whitish scalloping on their scapulars, distinguishing them from the plainer-backed winter adults. Full juvenal plumage is kept through most of the winter, with a partial molt in spring. Most winter adults retain at least a few spotted coverts, often visible on swimming birds. In flight, large head and feet help distinguish Common from Arctic, Pacific, and Red-throated Loons (preceding page). Loud yodeling **calls** delivered on water and in flight are heard all year, but most often on breeding grounds. **Range:** Fairly common; nests on large lakes. Migrates overland as well as coastally. Under most conditions, Common and Yellow-billed fly quite high above the water when migrating, while the other loon species fly lower. Note their slower wingbeats and the paddle-shaped feet that are usually visible beyond the tail. Winters mainly in coastal waters or on large, ice-free inland bodies of water.

Yellow-billed Loon   *Gavia adamsii*   L 34" (86 cm)

Breeding adult has straw-yellow bill, usually longer than in Common Loon; culmen is straight, giving bill a slightly uptilted look; head often tilted back, which enhances this effect. Crown is peaked at front and rear, giving a subtle double-bump effect. Bill is duskier at the base in **winter adults** and **juveniles,** but always shows strong yellow cast toward the tip. Note also pale face and distinct dark mark behind eye; eye is smaller, back and crown are paler and browner than in Common. **Calls** are similar to Common. **Range:** Yellow-billed Loon breeds on tundra lakes and rivers. Migrates coastally; rare south of Canada on West Coast, where it is recorded annually south to northern California, casually to southern California. Very rare inland in West; casual east to Great Lakes region and south to Texas and Georgia.

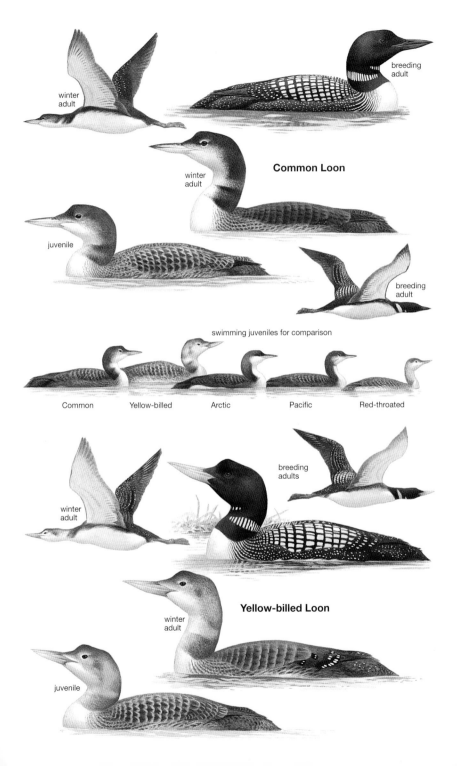

winter adult

breeding adult

Common Loon

winter adult

juvenile

breeding adult

swimming juveniles for comparison

Common   Yellow-billed   Arctic   Pacific   Red-throated

winter adult

breeding adults

Yellow-billed Loon

winter adult

juvenile

Grebes (Family Podicipedidae)

A worldwide family of aquatic diving birds. Lobed toes make them strong swimmers. Grebes are infrequently seen on land or in flight. *Species: 22 World, 7 N.A.*

Least Grebe *Tachybaptus dominicus* L 9¾" (25 cm)
A small, short-necked grebe with golden yellow eyes, a slim, dark bill, and purplish gray face and foreneck. **Breeding adult** has blackish crown, hindneck, throat, and back. **Winter** birds have white throat, paler bill, less black on crown. In flight, shows large white wing patch. **Range:** Rather uncommon and local; may hide in vegetation near shores of ponds, sloughs, ditches. May nest at any season on any quiet, inland water. Casual straggler to southern Arizona, southeast California, south Florida, and upper Texas coast.

Pied-billed Grebe *Podilymbus podiceps* L 13½" (34 cm)
Breeding adult is brown overall, with black ring around stout, whitish bill; black chin and throat; pale belly. **Winter** birds lose bill ring; chin is white, throat tinged with pale rufous. **Juveniles** resemble winter adult but throat is much redder, eye ring absent, head and neck streaked with brown and white. First-winter birds lack streaking; throat is duller. A short-necked, big-headed, stocky grebe. In flight, shows almost no white on wing. **Range:** Nests around marshy ponds and sloughs; sometimes hides from intruders by sinking until only its head shows. Common but not gregarious. Winters on fresh or salt water. Casual to Alaska.

Horned Grebe *Podiceps auritus* L 13½" (34 cm)
Breeding adult has chestnut foreneck, golden "horns." In **winter** plumage, white cheeks and throat contrast with dark crown and nape; some are dusky on lower foreneck. Black on nape narrows to a thin stripe. All birds show a pale spot in front of eye. In flight (next page), white secondaries show as patch on trailing edge of wing. Bill is short and straight, thicker than Eared Grebe's; neck is thicker too, crown flatter. Smaller size and shorter, dark bill most readily separate winter Horned from Red-necked Grebe (next page). **Range:** Breeds on lakes and ponds. Winters mostly on salt water but also on ice-free lakes of eastern North America; a few winter inland in West. Casual in Newfoundland.

Eared Grebe *Podiceps nigricollis* L 12½" (32 cm)
Breeding adult has blackish neck, golden "ears" fanning out behind eye. In **winter** plumage, throat is variably dusky; cheek dark; whitish on chin extends up as a crescent behind eye; compare with Horned Grebe. Note also Eared Grebe's longer, thinner bill; thinner neck; more peaked crown. Lacks pale spot in front of eye. Generally rides higher in the water than Horned Grebe, exposing fluffy white undertail coverts. In flight, white secondaries show as white patch on trailing edge of wing. **Range:** Usually nests in large colonies on freshwater lakes. Rare in eastern North America.

juvenile

Least Grebe
brachypterus

winter

breeding
adult

breeding
adult

juvenile

winter

downy young

Pied-billed Grebe
podiceps

Horned Grebe
cornutus

adult in
spring molt

darker
winter

breeding adult,
with "horns" raised

breeding
adult

winter

Horned   Eared

winter

Eared Grebe
californicus

1st fall

paler
winter

breeding
adult

downy
young

winter

Red-necked Grebe *Podiceps grisegena L 20" (51 cm)*

Large grebe with heavy, tapered, yellowish bill almost as long as the head. **Breeding adult**'s whitish throat and cheeks contrast with reddish foreneck. In **winter** plumage, throat is dusky, white of chin extends onto rear of face in a crescent. **First-winter** bird has rounder head, paler eye; lacks strong facial crescent. **Juvenile** has striped head. In flight, Red-necked Grebe shows a white leading and trailing edge on inner wing; thick neck is often held slouched down. **Calls,** usually heard only on breeding grounds, include a *crick-crick* note and drawn out braying calls. Generally solitary. **Range:** Breeds on shallow lakes; winters mostly along coasts. Rare in interior south of northern tier of states; occasionally, moderate numbers winter in mid-Atlantic region, especially in years when Great Lakes freeze. Casual south to Southwest and Gulf Coast states.

Clark's Grebe *Aechmophorus clarkii L 25" (64 cm)*

Resembles Western Grebe but bill is orange; back and flanks are paler; black cap does not extend to eye in **breeding** plumage; **downy young** are paler. In **winter adult,** lore region acquires more dark color, pattern looks more like Western; best distinction then is bill color. In flight, Clark Grebe's white wing stripe is more extensive than on Western. **Call** is a single, two-syllabled, upslurred *kree-eek* note. **Range:** Limits of range in both species are not well known; Clark's occupies same general area and habitat as Western but is much less common in northern and eastern part of range. Accidental to eastern North America. Formerly considered one species with Western.

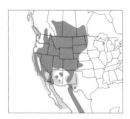

Western Grebe *Aechmophorus occidentalis L 25" (64 cm)*

Large grebe, strikingly black and white, with a long, thin neck and long bill. Resembles Clark's Grebe but bill is yellow-green; black cap extends to include eyes; back and flanks are darker; **downy young** are darker. In **winter adult,** lore region acquires more whitish color, and pattern can closely resemble winter Clark's. In flight, Western Grebe's white wing stripe is less extensive than Clark's. **Call** is a loud, two-note *crick-kreek*. **Range:** Gregarious; nests in reeds along broad, freshwater lakes. Winters on seacoasts and sheltered bays and large inland bodies of water. Occupies same general range and habitat as Clark's but greatly predominates in northern and eastern part of range. Casual during migration and winter to eastern North America. Formerly considered one species with Clark's; hybrids are regularly noted.

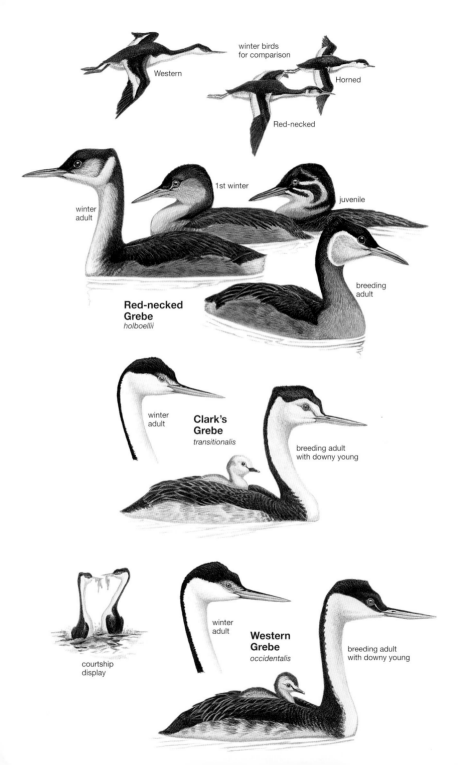

Western

winter birds
for comparison

Horned

Red-necked

winter
adult

1st winter

juvenile

breeding
adult

**Red-necked
Grebe**
holboellii

winter
adult

**Clark's
Grebe**
transitionalis

breeding adult
with downy young

courtship
display

winter
adult

**Western
Grebe**
occidentalis

breeding adult
with downy young

Albatrosses (Family Diomedeidae)

Gliding on extremely long narrow wings, these largest of seabirds spend most of their lives at sea, alighting on the water when becalmed or when feeding on squid, fish, and refuse. Pelagic; most species nest in colonies on oceanic islands; pairs mate for life. A number of species, especially those in Southern Hemisphere, are threatened by long-line fishing. *Species: 13 World, 8 N.A.*

Short-tailed Albatross *Phoebastria albatrus* **E**

L 36" (91 cm) WS 85-91" (215-230 cm) **Range:** Common until end of 19th century, then decimated and was on verge of extinction by 1930s. Very small numbers of breeders reappeared on Torishima Island, beginning in 1951. Now protected and population slowly recovering—global population believed to number about 2,000. Presently breeds on Torishima (most) and Minami-kojima Islands off southern Japan. Still very rare to rare, but sightings are increasing in North Pacific off North America from Aleutians to central California. The great majority of these sightings are of juveniles and subadults. Large size, but best field mark is the long and massive pink (initially dark on very young juveniles) bill with pale bluish tip. Dark humerals and pale feet distinctive in post juvenal plumages. **Adult** is mostly white, with golden wash on head. **Juvenile** is blackish brown, except for traces of white below and behind eye and on chin. Older juvenile has more white around bill; compare with Black-footed Albatross. **Subadult** shows white forehead and face, dark cap; acquires white patches on scapulars and inner secondary coverts; with age becomes progressively white, but retains dark hindneck. Full adult plumage takes more than a decade to acquire, but can breed in subadult plumages.

Laysan Albatross *Phoebastria immutabilis*

L 32" (81 cm) WS 77-80" (195-203 cm) Back, upperwing blackish brown, except for white flash in primaries; underwings with black margins and variable internal markings. Note blurry dark mark surrounding eye; pinkish bill. Adults and juveniles similar. Occasionally hybridizes with Black-footed Albatross. Most numerous spring through summer off Alaska; rare to uncommon off West Coast from late fall through spring; casual inland in winter and spring; most records from southeastern California in spring. Breeds mainly on Hawaiian Islands; small colonies recently established in the Revillagigedo Archipelago and Isla Guadalupe, Mexico.

Black-footed Albatross *Phoebastria nigripes*

L 32" (81 cm) WS 80" (203 cm) Mostly dark in all plumages. White area around bill is more extensive on **old** birds; reduced or absent on immatures. Most birds of all ages have dark undertail coverts. Some **adults** have white undertail coverts, and white may extend onto belly; these birds can be confused with subadult Short-tailed Albatross, but lack white upperwing patches and have thinner, shorter, darker bills. **Range:** Seen year-round off West Coast; most common in spring and summer. Breeds mainly on Hawaiian Islands; overall population declining.

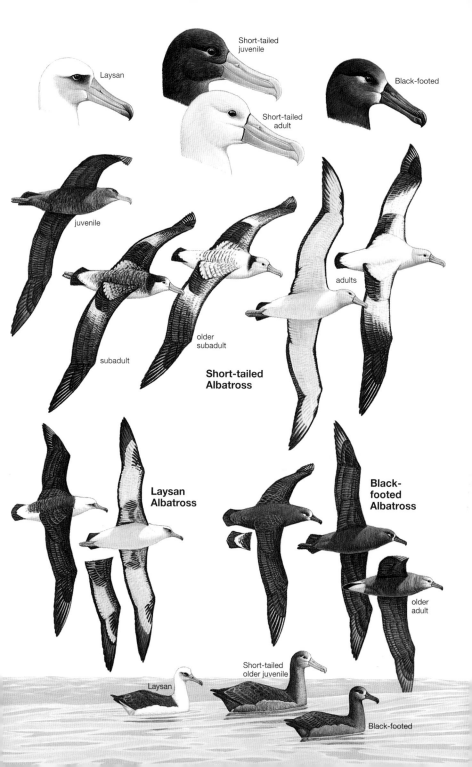

Laysan

Short-tailed
juvenile

Short-tailed
adult

Black-footed

juvenile

subadult

older
subadult

**Short-tailed
Albatross**

adults

**Laysan
Albatross**

**Black-
footed
Albatross**

older
adult

Laysan

Short-tailed
older juvenile

Black-footed

Shy Albatross *Thalassarche cauta*
L 35-39" (90-99 cm) WS 87-101" (220-256 cm) **Range:** Casual
off Pacific coast from Washington to northern California; once off
Kasatochi Island, Aleutians. Only specimen (nominate *cauta*) was
off Washington in 1951; nine other records since 1996. Taxonomic
opinions differ, but presently divided into four subspecies breeding in the following locations: *cauta* breeds on islands off Tasma-
nia; nearly identical *steadi* breeds on Auckland, Antipodes, and
Chatham Islands, New Zealand; *salvini* breeds on Snares and
Bounty Islands off New Zealand, and on Iles Crozet in southwest
Indian Ocean; and unrecorded *eremita* group (dark gray head)
breeds on Chatham Island. Remaining nine North American
records are divided between those of *cauta/steadi* and those
believed to be of *salvini* (including the Aleutians record). **Adults**
of *cauta/steadi* are white-headed, unlike all ages of *salvini*, which
have a grayish washed head; younger *cauta/steadi* head also grayish. Distinctive in all ages is underwing pattern: primaries more
extensively dark in *salvini* (and *eremita*); larger than Laysan, which
has smaller, thinner, mostly pinkish bill. Note Shy's paler back,
longer and grayer tail, more extensive white on the rump, and more
languid flight style; all ages show extensively white underwings and
characteristic dark "thumb mark" at beginning of leading edge.
Yellow-tipped bill in *cauta* adults (*steadi* very similar); grayer and
darker-tipped bill in all younger birds. Bill is dusky with a dull yellow ridge and dark lower tip in adult *salvini*.

Yellow-nosed Albatross *Thalassarche chlororhynchos*
L 32" (81 cm) WS 80" (203 cm) **Range:** Casual off Atlantic and
Gulf coasts; a few inland sightings in East. Most of nominate subspecies breed on Tristan de Cunha and Gough Islands in south
Atlantic, the probable source of North American records. The
other subspecies, *bassi*, breeding on south Indian Ocean islands,
has purer white head and reduced dark smudge in front of eye.
Confused with Black-browed, but Yellow-nosed is smaller and
slimmer, with longer neck. **Adult**'s bill appears black; at close range,
yellow ridge on top and reddish tip are visible. Note light grayish
wash on head and blackish triangular patch in front of eye of nominate race. Underwing extensively white with a narrow dark border; some **juveniles** show more dark on leading edge, which can
cause confusion with adult Black-browed. Otherwise juvenile
resembles adult, except for all-dark bill and reduced eye patch.

Black-browed Albatross *Thalassarche melanophris*
L 35" (89 cm) WS 88" (224 cm) **Range:** A circumpolar Southern
Hemisphere species. Casual in North Atlantic, most recorded in
northeast portion. One certain record of immature photographed
off Virginia Beach on 6 Feb. 1999; about 20 other reports (some
possibly correct). From similar Yellow-nosed, note larger size with
thicker neck and chunkier body. **Adult** has broad dark leading edge
to underwing and heavier orange bill with redder tip; black eyebrow. **Juveniles** have darker bills and gray shading about head and
neck forming collar; underwing mainly dark. **Subadults** have more
yellowish bill with dark tip and some white in underwings.

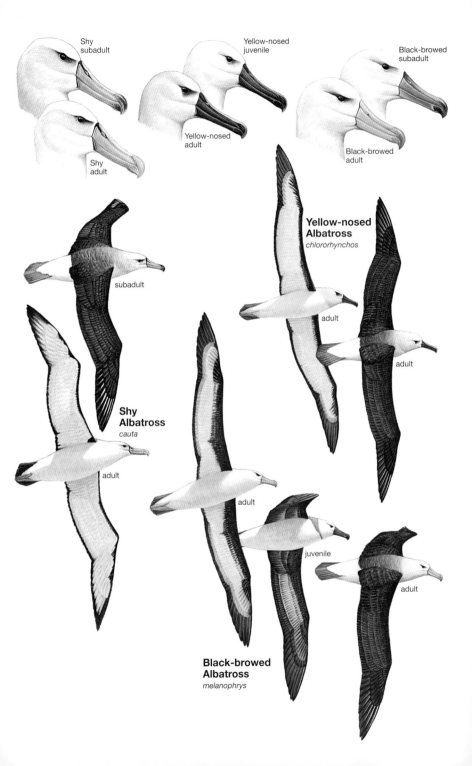

Shy subadult

Shy adult

Yellow-nosed juvenile

Yellow-nosed adult

Black-browed subadult

Black-browed adult

subadult

Yellow-nosed Albatross
chlororhynchos

adult

adult

Shy Albatross
cauta

adult

adult

juvenile

adult

Black-browed Albatross
melanophrys

Shearwaters, Petrels (Family Procellariidae)

Pelagic seabirds rarely seen from shore; bills have nostril tubes. Fly with rapid wingbeats, stiff-winged glides. *Species: 75 World, 28 N.A.*

Northern Fulmar *Fulmarus glacialis*
L 19" (48 cm) WS 42" (107 cm) **Light morphs** predominate over much of North Atlantic. In Pacific light morphs predominate in Bering Sea; **dark morphs** farther south. Pacific subspecies (*rodgersii*) has a more slender bill; shows greater variation in color morphs (darker dark morphs and paler lights), and darker tail contrasts with rump. **Intermediates** of all shades are frequent. Distinguished from gulls by short, thick bill with nostril tubes, and shearwater-like flight; from shearwaters by thick, yellow bill, stockier shape, and rounder wings. **Range:** Common and increasing. Within winter range, numbers fluctuate annually; some summer.

Parkinson's Petrel *Procellaria parkinsoni*
L 18" (46 cm) WS 45" (115 cm) **Range:** Breeds on islands off New Zealand; ranges north in austral winter to east-central Pacific, north to southern Mexico. One certain record (1 Oct. 2005, about 18 miles off Point Reyes, California). Almost wholly blackish petrel; rather thick yellowish bill, with black lines and tip; feet and legs dark. Compare to similarly colored Flesh-footed Shearwater (page 90), note bill shape and color. Westland Petrel (*P. westlandica*) from South Pacific is similar but is even larger and thicker billed; unrecorded north of Equator.

Gadfly Petrels

Fast-flying petrels with arcing, acrobatic flight in high winds. Unlike shearwaters, they typically hold their wings slightly forward from the shoulder and bent sharply back at the "wrist."

Great-winged Petrel *Pterodroma macroptera*
L 16" (41 cm) WS 38" (97 cm) **Range:** Southern oceans species; two records (late summer, Oct.) off central California of presumed *gouldi* subspecies with whiter face. Similar to Murphy's, but browner (less gray); more uniform underwing; white more evenly distributed around bill; and dark legs and feet.

Murphy's Petrel *Pterodroma ultima*
L 16" (41 cm) WS 38" (97 cm) **Range:** Breeds on remote central South Pacific islands. Fairly common spring visitor far off California coast; recorded at least north to Washington. Dark brownish gray color with faint dark M pattern on back, wedge-shaped tail, and white underwing flash; white most conspicuous below bill; legs and feet pink. The similar but larger Solander's Petrel (*P. solandri*), reported off California and Washington (no accepted records), has heavier bill with equal or more white above bill than below; prominent dark primary covert tips. Compare to dark morph Northern Fulmar.

Northern Fulmar

intermediate

dark morph

light morph

Parkinson's Petrel

Murphy's Petrel

Great-winged Petrel
gouldi

Hawaiian Petrel *Pterodroma sandwichensis* **E**

L 17" (43 cm) WS 39" (98 cm) Recently split from Galapagos Petrel (*P. phaeopygia*), which together were formerly known as Dark-rumped Petrel. The two are not known to be separable with certainty in the field. **Range:** Casual, recorded off California and Oregon from May to Oct., over 20 records, but no specimens. Hawaiian is heavier than Galapagos Petrel, with shorter wings and shorter, deeper bill. Galapagos often has a freckled rather than pure white forehead. Both species have mostly black crown that extends down sides of neck forming a partial collar. Both uniformly dark above, but may show a slight M pattern and white on the upper tail coverts. Note underwing pattern. The endangered Hawaiian Petrel nests only on Hawaiian Islands.

Mottled Petrel *Pterodroma inexpectata*

L 14" (36 cm) WS 32" (81 cm) White throat, breast, and vent contrast with rest of mostly gray underparts. Shows prominent black bar on otherwise white underwings; dark M across upperwings. **Range:** Breeds on islands off New Zealand. Probably regular well off southern Alaska and Aleutians in summer; rare and irregular well off the West Coast, chiefly in late fall. Accidental in western New York (Livingston County, early Apr. 1880).

Cook's Petrel *Pterodroma cookii*

L 10¾" (27 cm) WS 26" (66 cm) **Range:** Breeds on islands off New Zealand. Found well off California coast from spring through late fall, where it is the most numerous *Pterodroma* petrel. Casual off Aleutians and on the Salton Sea in summer. This and Stejneger's considered part of the *Cookilaria* petrel subgenus. They are smaller sized and more acrobatic than the larger *Pterodroma* petrels. All show a dark M across the dorsal surface. Cook's is small, with long wings and rather short tail. Crown and back uniformly gray; blackish eye patch. Note mainly white underwings and distinct dark M across upperwings. White on outer tail feathers and dark tip to central tail feathers can be hard to see. Two other *Cookilaria* petrels are very similar; the thicker-billed Masatierra or De Filippi's Petrel (*P. defilippiana*) from off west coast of South America and smaller Pycroft's Petrel (*P. pycrofti*) from New Zealand have not been recorded in North Pacific.

Stejneger's Petrel *Pterodroma longirostris*

L 11" (28 cm) WS 23" (58 cm) **Range:** Breeds on Juan Fernandez Islands off Chile. Casual well off the California coast, chiefly in fall. Resembles Cook's Petrel but distinct, dark half hood contrasts with grayish back and extensive white forehead; tail is longer and more uniformly colored, with less white in outer tail feathers. Accidental coastal Texas (Port Aransas, 15 Sept. 1995, tideline corpse).

Hawaiian
Petrel

Mottled
Petrel

Cook's
Petrel

Stejneger's
Petrel

Black-capped Petrel　*Pterodroma hasitata*

L 16" (41 cm) WS 37" (94 cm)　Distinct dark cap; white collar; broad white band on uppertail coverts and base of tail. White wing lining, with variable dark diagonal bar on leading edge. Wing and bill shape, white forehead, broader band on tail, and languid, arching flight distinguish this species from Greater Shearwater (page 88). Some birds have less white at base of tail and duskier collar. **Range:** Breeds on Hispaniola and Cuba. Common in Gulf Stream off North Carolina from late May to mid-Oct.; uncommon in winter; casual north to Nova Scotia and in Gulf of Mexico. Recorded inland in the East after hurricanes.

Fea's Petrel　*Pterodroma feae*

L 14" (36 cm) WS 37" (94 cm)　**Range:** Breeds in the Madeira and Cape Verde Islands off West Africa. Rare visitor off North Carolina in late May and early June, casual into the fall; accidental to Nova Scotia. Sightings (supported by excellent photos but no specimens) here believed to be Fea's, not Zino's Petrel (*P. madeira*, a highly endangered species breeding only on Madeira), based on larger bill size and likelihood. Fea's is brownish gray above with dark M pattern, pale uppertail coverts and tail. White below; partial breast band; mostly dark underwings.

Bermuda Petrel　*Pterodroma cahow*　**E**

L 15" (38 cm) WS 35" (89 cm)　Endangered species. Believed extinct, but rediscovered in 1951; population increasing, now estimated at about 200. **Range:** Nests only on islets off Bermuda; since mid-1990s, about 20 well-documented records, in late spring (mostly) and summer off Outer Banks, North Carolina. Note that larger Black-capped Petrel has heavier bill and disproportionately shorter wings. Bermuda Petrel's whitish rump, sometimes lacking, is restricted to base of uppertail coverts. Without Black-capped's white collar, dark on head is more like cowl than cap; Bermuda more buoyant in flight, with darker underwings than Black-capped.

Herald Petrel　*Pterodroma arminjoniana*

L 15½" (39 cm) WS 37½" (95 cm)　**Range:** Tropical Southern Hemisphere species. South Atlantic birds of the nominate race nest on islands off Brazil; mid-Atlantic region sightings likely from these populations. Rare visitor late May to late Sept. in Gulf Stream off North Carolina. Accidental inland after hurricanes. Long-winged, slender-bodied species with languid wingbeats. Occurs in three morphs; **dark morph,** predominant in U.S., has pale-based flight feathers and greater primary coverts on underwing. Compare to chunkier Sooty Shearwater with its shorter tail, thinner bill, paler underwings, and faster wingbeats. **Light morph** has brownish gray head and chest, variably whitish throat, white belly, pale underwings. **Intermediate morphs** are variably mottled below.

typical

Black-capped Petrel

darker variant

Black-capped Petrel

Greater Shearwater

Fea's Petrel

darker rump

Bermuda Petrel

dark morph

Herald Petrel

dark morph

light morph

intermediate morph

Herald Petrel

Sooty Shearwater

Cory's Shearwater *Calonectris diomedea*
L 18" (46 cm) WS 46" (117 cm) Grayish brown upperparts merge into white underparts without sharp contrast; bill is yellowish. Flight is more languid than most other shearwaters. **Range:** Nominate *diomedea* breeds in the Mediterranean; slightly larger *borealis* breeds on the Azores, Canary, and Salvage Islands. Underside of primaries darker in *borealis*. Both occur (*borealis* much more common) off East Coast, mainly late spring through fall. Uncommon in Gulf of Mexico.

Cape Verde Shearwater *Calonectris edwardsii*
L 15½" (39 cm) WS 39½" (101 cm) **Range:** Breeds Cape Verde archipelago, ranges to West African coast. Accidental off Hatteras Inlet, North Carolina (15 Aug. 2004). Much smaller, slightly longer tailed than Cory's with darker gray upperparts and more contrasting face; much slimmer bill is olive-gray, not yellowish.

Greater Shearwater *Puffinus gravis*
L 18" (46 cm) WS 44" (112 cm) Dark brown cap contrasts with grayish brown upperparts and white cheeks. Rump usually shows a narrow, white, U-shaped band. Bill is dark; underparts white with indistinct dusky patch on belly. Many Greater Shearwaters have a white nape. Similar to Black-capped Petrel (page 86), but lacks white forehead and wide black bar on underwing; also has shorter, less wedge-shaped tail with less extensive white at base. **Range:** Breeds in South Atlantic. Fairly common off the East Coast during migration, chiefly in spring. Summers in large numbers from the Gulf of Maine north. Casual off West Coast.

Manx Shearwater *Puffinus puffinus*
L 13½" (34 cm) WS 33" (84 cm) Blackish above, white below with white wing linings. Pure white undertail coverts extend to end of short tail. White wraps around dark ear coverts. **Range:** Most breed on islands around United Kingdom; one small colony in Newfoundland. Winters off eastern South America. Fairly common off the northern Atlantic coast in summer. Rare in winter from Maryland south. Rare in summer and fall off West Coast to Alaska.

Audubon's Shearwater *Puffinus lherminieri*
L 12" (31 cm) WS 27" (69 cm) Dark brown above, white below, with long tail, dark undertail coverts (a few with pale ones). **Range:** Breeds on Caribbean islands. Common off the southern Atlantic coast, chiefly from May through Oct. Rare in winter.

Little Shearwater *Puffinus assimilis*
L 11" (28 cm) WS 25" (64 cm) **Range:** Casual, two fall specimens from Nova Scotia and South Carolina (*baroli*, breeds Azores); sight records from off North Carolina and Nova Scotia; photo record from Monterey County, California (29 Oct. 2003) likely Southern Hemisphere subspecies. Similar to larger Audubon's Shearwater, but has shorter tail, whiter underwings, and grayer two-toned upperwing; white undertail coverts; face whiter. Flies with rapid, stiff, shallow wingbeats.

Cory's Shearwater *borealis*

diomedea

Cory's

Greater

Cape Verde Shearwater

Black-capped Petrel

Greater Shearwater

Manx Shearwater

Audubon's Shearwater *lherminieri*

Little Shearwater *baroli*

Wedge-tailed Shearwater *Puffinus pacificus*
L 18" (46 cm) WS 40" (101 cm) **Range:** Polymorphic species from warm waters of Pacific and Indian Oceans. Casual in summer and fall to waters off central California; accidental on Salton Sea. Long tail held in a point; wedge shape visible only when fanned. Slender, grayish bill has darker tip. Head and upperparts of **light morph** grayish brown; mostly white with mottled brown below. Most sightings are of wholly brown **dark morph,** which has paler base to flight feathers. Languid flight with prolonged soaring on bowed wings angled forward to "wrist," then swept back.

Flesh-footed Shearwater *Puffinus carneipes*
L 17" (43 cm) WS 41" (104 cm) Dark above and below except for pale flight feathers, distinctive pale pink base of bill. Compare especially with Sooty Shearwater, which has whitish wing linings, all-dark bill, less languid flight. **Range:** Breeds on islands off Australia and New Zealand. Winters (our summer) in North Pacific; rare off West Coast.

Bulwer's Petrel *Bulweria bulwerii*
L 10" (26 cm) WS 26" (66 cm) **Range:** Bird of tropical and subtropical oceans; accidental summer visitor off Monterey, California, and Outer Banks, North Carolina. Sooty brown overall with pale diagonal bar across secondary coverts. Long tail usually held in a point; wedge shape visible only when fanned. Flight is buoyant and erratic, long wings slightly bowed and held forward. Flies within a few feet of the water; flight, when it is windy, is more like gadfly petrels.

Short-tailed Shearwater *Puffinus tenuirostris*
L 17" (43 cm) WS 39" (99 cm) Plumage variable. Usually dark overall, but often with pale wing linings like Sooty Shearwater; white is more evenly distributed, when present, forming a panel. Has shorter bill than Sooty, slightly steeper forehead, more rounded crown. Some birds, unlike Sooty, have pale throat and dark-capped appearance. **Range:** Breeds off Australia. Winters (our summer) in North Pacific to Alaska. Seen along West Coast from British Columbia to California during southward migration in fall and winter.

Sooty Shearwater *Puffinus griseus*
L 18" (46 cm) WS 40" (101 cm) Whitish underwing coverts contrast with overall dark plumage. Flies with fast wingbeats and, except when it is windy, short glides. Almost identical to Short-tailed Shearwater. White on underwings usually most prominent on primary coverts. **Range:** Breeds in Southern Hemisphere. Fairly common off East Coast in spring, and in summer off New England and Canada. Abundant off West Coast, often seen from shore. Very rare in Gulf of Mexico.

Wedge-tailed Shearwater

dark morph

dark morph

light morph

Flesh-footed Shearwater

Bulwer's Petrel

Short-tailed Shearwater

Sooty Shearwater

Short-tailed

Sooty

Buller's Shearwater *Puffinus bulleri*
L 16" (41 cm) WS 40" (102 cm) Gleaming white below, including wing linings. Gray above, with a darker cap and a long, dark, wedge-shaped tail. Dark bar across leading edge of upperwing extends across back, forming a distinct M. Flight is graceful, buoyant, with long periods of gliding. **Range:** Breeds on islands off New Zealand. Irregular off West Coast during southward migration. Most common from Washington to central California; rarer north and south along West Coast. Accidental off New Jersey.

Streaked Shearwater *Calonectris leucomelas*
L 19" (48 cm) WS 48" (122 cm) **Range:** Asian species, casual off California (most records from Monterey Bay) in the fall, accidental inland in California's upper Central Valley. Head is variable, largely white to rather heavily streaked; often looks white at a distance. Pale fringes give upperparts a scaly look. White uppertail coverts form a pale "horseshoe," but can be absent. Bill color varies from pale gray to pale pink. Note the white axillaries and dark underwing primary coverts. Languid, soaring flight is typical of *Calonectris* shearwaters (see also Cory's, page 88).

Pink-footed Shearwater *Puffinus creatopus*
L 19" (48 cm) WS 43" (109 cm) Uniformly blackish brown above; white wing linings and underparts are variably mottled (sight records of much darker birds than illustrated); pink bill and feet distinctive at close range. Flies with slower wingbeats and more soaring than Sooty Shearwater (page 90). Spring birds of this and other Southern Hemisphere species may be in heavy **molt,** often resulting in whitish wing bars and odd wing shape. **Range:** Breeds on islands off Chile; winters (our summer) in the northern Pacific. Common from spring through fall; rare throughout the rest of the year.

Black-vented Shearwater *Puffinus opisthomelas*
L 14" (36 cm) WS 34" (86 cm) Dark brown above, white below, with dark undertail coverts. Variable dusky mottling on sides of breast, often extending across entire breast. **Range:** Seen off California from Aug. to May; often visible from shore. Nests chiefly on islands off Mexico's Baja peninsula. Strictly casual north of central California to southwestern British Columbia. Formerly considered a subspecies of the Atlantic species Manx Shearwater, which is rare in fall off central California. Manx is much darker above and much cleaner white below, including pure white undertail coverts; it has the pale wrapping around the dark ear coverts; and its flight is more buoyant.

Buller's Shearwater

Streaked Shearwater

worn

variant with white uppertail coverts

dark

light

Black-vented Shearwater

typical

typical

in molt

light

dark

Pink-footed Shearwater

dark

Manx Shearwater for comparison

Storm-Petrels (Family Hydrobatidae)

These small seabirds hover close to the water, pattering or hopping across the waves to pluck up small fish and plankton. Some species follow ships. Identification is often difficult. Flight behavior helps to distinguish the various species, but can vary deceptively depending on weather. *Species: 21 World, 12 N.A.*

European Storm-Petrel *Hydrobates pelagicus*
L 5½-6½" (14-17 cm) WS 15" (38 cm) **Range:** Nests on islands in northeastern Atlantic and Mediterranean. Specimen record from Sable Island, Nova Scotia (Aug. 1970), and multiple recent records in late spring off Outer Banks. Small, dark storm-petrel with white underwing bar; feet do not project beyond tail.

Wilson's Storm-Petrel *Oceanites oceanicus*
L 7¼" (18 cm) WS 16" (41 cm) Flies with shallow, fluttery wing-beats. Wings short and rounded; long legs; in flight, feet trail behind tip of squarish or rounded tail. Often hovers to feed, pattering its yellow-webbed feet on the water. Bold white, U-shaped rump band extends onto undertail coverts; visible even on sitting bird. Smaller than Leach's and Band-rumped Storm-Petrels. **Range:** Common off Atlantic coast; rare off eastern Gulf Coast and California (fall).

Band-rumped Storm-Petrel *Oceanodroma castro*
L 9" (23 cm) WS 17" (43 cm) **Range:** Breeds on tropical islands. Fairly common from late May to late Aug. in Gulf Stream, especially off North Carolina; rare or casual farther north to waters off Massachusetts; uncommon well off Gulf Coast. Rather shallow wingstrokes are followed by stiff-winged glides, like the flight of a shearwater but unlike the erratic flight of Leach's Storm-Petrel or the fluttery flight of Wilson's. White rump patch narrower and less extensive on undertail coverts than on Wilson's. Tail squarish or very slightly notched; no foot projection in flight. Larger, longer winged than Wilson's; darker than Leach's, with fainter carpal bar.

Leach's Storm-Petrel *Oceanodroma leucorhoa*
L 8" (20 cm) WS 18" (46 cm) Distinctive erratic flight, with deep strokes of long, pointed wings. In close view, note dusky line dividing white rump band on most birds. No white is visible on flanks of sitting bird. Brown overall, with pale wing stripes and forked tail. Amount of white on rump varies; a few birds seen off southern California have dark rumps. **Range:** Fairly common well off Pacific coast; uncommon south of breeding range along Atlantic coast. Very rare in Gulf of Mexico; casual on Salton Sea.

White-faced Storm-Petrel *Pelagodroma marina*
L 7½" (19 cm) WS 17" (43 cm) **Range:** Very rare off the Atlantic coast from North Carolina to Massachusetts in late summer. Flies with stiff, shallow wingbeats and short glides. Habitually angles to water at 45 degrees, then bounces off the surface with long legs in a pogo-stick fashion. Distinctive white underparts, wing linings, and face. Dark eye stripe, crown, and upperparts; paler rump.

European Storm-Petrel

Wilson's Storm-Petrel

Band-rumped Storm-Petrel

Leach's Storm-Petrel
leucorhoa

White-faced Storm-Petrel

Wilson's

Band-rumped

Leach's
West Coast

northern

intermediate

southern

Wedge-rumped
kelsalli

Black Storm-Petrel *Oceanodroma melania*

L 9" (23 cm) WS 19" (48 cm) Deep, languid wingstrokes, graceful flight. Largest of the all-dark storm-petrels. Blackish brown
overall with pale bar on upper surface of wing. Tail forked and
fairly long. Slow, deep wingbeats and larger size distinguish Black
Storm-Petrel from dark-rumped individuals of Leach's Storm-
Petrel (preceding page). **Range:** Breeds from May to Dec. off Baja
California and in Gulf of California; small colony in vicinity of
Santa Barbara Island. Fairly common off southern California
coast from late spring; by late summer north to Monterey Bay.
Casual in interior of southern California and in southwest Ari-
zona after tropical storms.

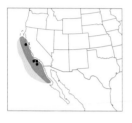

Ashy Storm-Petrel *Oceanodroma homochroa*

L 8" (20 cm) WS 17" (43 cm) Fluttery wingbeats, but flight fairly
direct; not as swallowlike as Wilson's Storm-Petrel (preceding
page). Gray-brown overall; pale mottling on underwing coverts
may be visible at close range. Viewed from the side, Ashy appears
to have long tail, unless in molt. Distinguished from Black Storm-
Petrel by rapid, shallow wingbeats and overall paler, grayer
appearance. **Range:** Fairly common most of the year; rare in winter. Breeds on islands off central and southern California.

Least Storm-Petrel *Oceanodroma microsoma*

L 5¾" (15 cm) WS 15" (38 cm) Our smallest storm-petrel. Swift,
indirect flight, low over the water, with deep wingbeats like the
much larger Black Storm-Petrel. Blackish brown overall. Short
tailed; appears almost tailless in flight; often confused with molting Ashies. **Range:** Irregular; rare to common off the coast of
southern California in late summer and fall; in peak years, small
numbers occur to central California; after tropical storms, may
be seen in southeast California and southwest Arizona.

Fork-tailed Storm-Petrel *Oceanodroma furcata*

L 8½" (22 cm) WS 18" (46 cm) Wingbeats shallow, rapid, often
followed by glides. Looks fairly long tailed in flight. Occasionally makes shallow dives for food. Distinctively bluish gray above,
pearl gray below. Note also dark gray forehead and eye patch,
dark wing linings. Nominate *furcata* from coastal northeast Asia
and Aleutians is larger and paler than *plumbea* from off south-
coastal to northern California. **Range:** Found regularly south to
central California; rare off southern California coast.

Wedge-rumped Storm-Petrel *Oceanodroma tethys*

L 6½" (17 cm) WS 13¼" (34 cm) **Range:** Breeds on the Galápagos Islands (nominate *tethys*) and on islets off Peru (much
smaller *kelsalli*). Casual off the California coast from Aug. to Jan.;
single specimen (Jan.) is of *kelsalli*. Distinctive bold white triangular patch of uppertail coverts gives the appearance of a
white tail with dark corners. Compare with the rounded rump
band and white flanks of Wilson's Storm-Petrel (preceding
page). Wedge-rumped is almost as small as Least Storm-Petrel,
with similar deep wingbeats.

Ashy
Storm-Petrel

Black
Storm-Petrel

Fork-tailed
Storm-Petrel

Least Storm-Petrel

Wedge-rumped
Storm-Petrel
kelsalli

Frigatebirds (Family Fregatidae)

These large, dark seabirds have the longest wingspan, in proportion to weight, of all birds. *Species: 5 World, 3 N.A.*

Magnificent Frigatebird *Fregata magnificens*
L 40" (102 cm) WS 90" (229 cm) Long, forked tail; long, narrow wings. **Male** is glossy black; orange throat pouch becomes bright red when inflated in courtship display. **Female** is blackish brown, with white at center of underparts. **Juveniles** show varying amount of white on head and underparts; require four to six years to reach adult plumage. Frigatebirds skim the sea, snatching up food from surface; also harass other birds in flight, forcing them to disgorge food. **Range:** Generally seen along coast, but also casual inland, especially after storms. Breeds on Dry Tortugas off Florida. Very rare at Salton Sea and north along California coast, casual farther north; rare on East Coast north to North Carolina, casual farther north.

Tropicbirds (Family Phaethontidae)

Long central tail feathers identify adults. They are usually seen far out at sea. *Species: 3 World, 3 N.A.*

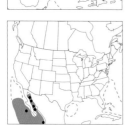

White-tailed Tropicbird *Phaethon lepturus*
L 30" (76 cm) WS 37" (94 cm) **Range:** Tropical species, rare but regular in Gulf Stream off North Carolina in summer; casual on Dry Tortugas, Florida, and elsewhere off East Coast. Smaller than Red-billed Tropicbird; distinctive black stripe on upperwing coverts; primaries show less black than in Red-billed. Bill orange in Atlantic subspecies (*catesbyi*) **adults. Juvenile** lacks tail streamers; upperparts are boldly barred, bill more yellowish.

Red-billed Tropicbird *Phaethon aethereus*
L 40" (102 cm) WS 44" (112 cm) **Range:** Tropical species, rare well off southern California coast; very rare in Gulf of Mexico and off Atlantic coast to North Carolina; casual to Massachusetts. Flies with rapid, stiff, shallow wingbeats, unlike other tropicbirds, whose flight is more ternlike. **Adult** has red bill, black primaries, barring on back and wings, white tail streamers. **Juvenile** has black collar; lacks streamers; tail is tipped with black; barring on upperparts is finer than in other young tropicbirds. Also bill is yellowish, but soon becomes orange-red.

Red-tailed Tropicbird *Phaethon rubricauda*
L 37" (94 cm) WS 44" (112 cm) **Range:** Species from tropical and subtropical Pacific and Indian Oceans. Very rare, usually well off California coast. Broadest-winged tropicbird; flies with languid wingbeats. Flight feathers mostly white. **Adult** has red bill; red tail streamers, narrower than in other tropicbirds. **Juvenile**'s all-white tail lacks streamers; upperparts barred; bill black, gradually changing to yellow and then red. Note also lack of black collar on nape.

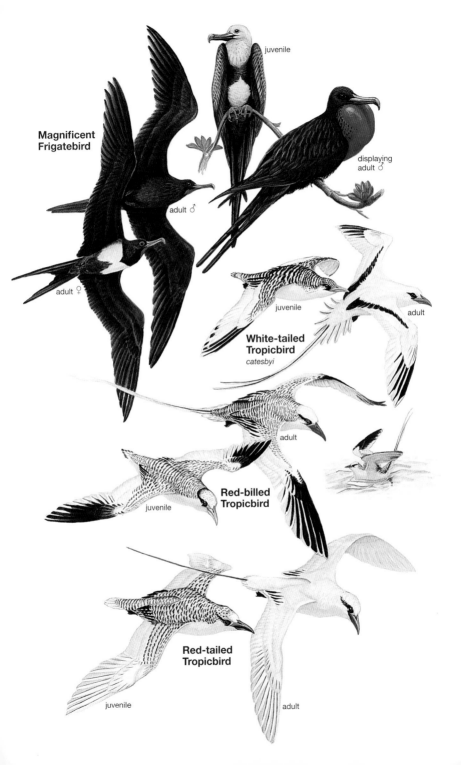

Magnificent Frigatebird

juvenile

displaying adult ♂

adult ♂

adult ♀

White-tailed Tropicbird
catesbyi

juvenile

adult

Red-billed Tropicbird

adult

juvenile

Red-tailed Tropicbird

juvenile

adult

Boobies, Gannets (Family Sulidae)

High-diving seabirds that plunge into water. Gregarious, nesting in colonies on small islands. The rest of the year, gannets roost at sea, boobies primarily on land. *Species: 10 World, 6 N.A.*

Red-footed Booby *Sula sula*
L 28" (71 cm) WS 60" (152 cm) Smallest booby, with rounded head. **Range:** Tropical species; casual on Florida's Dry Tortugas and California coast. All **adults** show bright coral red feet, and blue and pink at base of bill. Four principal morphs occur: **brown morph, white-tailed brown morph, white morph,** and **black-tailed white morph;** note that white morphs have black primaries, secondaries, and underwing median primary coverts. All **juveniles** and **subadults** are brownish overall with darker chest band, with mainly dark underwings and flesh pink legs and feet.

Brown Booby *Sula leucogaster*

L 30" (76 cm) WS 57" (145 cm) **Adults** of nominate race and female *brewsteri* from western Mexico have dark brown heads and necks with sharply contrasting white bellies and underwing coverts; **adult male** *brewsteri* has white on head and neck. Adult female's bill, facial skin, legs, and feet are bright yellow; male's soft parts washed with grayish green, throat bluish. **Juveniles** are dark brown, with little or no contrast between breast and belly; underwing muted. **Subadults** show white on belly and sharp line of contrast with darker neck. **Range:** A few found on Dry Tortugas and vicinity; rare north off both Florida coasts. Very rare through Gulf of Mexico; casual up Atlantic coast to Nova Scotia, and in California and the Southwest (*brewsteri*).

Blue-footed Booby *Sula nebouxii*

L 32" (81 cm) WS 62" (158 cm) Feet bright blue in adults, darker in young; long, attenuated bill is dark bluish gray. **Adults** have streaked heads, whitish patches on upper back and rump. **Juvenile** has darker head and neck; compare with immature Masked Booby; note pale dorsal patches, all-dark underwing primary coverts. **Range:** Breeds on islands in Gulf of California. Rare and irregular to inland California and southwest Arizona in late summer and fall (most to Salton Sea). Casual to California coast; accidental to Washington and Texas. Absent in U.S. most years.

Masked Booby *Sula dactylatra*

L 32" (81 cm) WS 62" (158 cm) Proportionately, the shortest tailed booby. **Adult** distinguished from Northern Gannet (next page) by yellow bill and extensive black facial skin; black tail; and solid black trailing edge to wing. On **juvenile,** note more white on underwing, with contrasting dark median primary coverts and pale collar. **Subadult** has paler head and broader collar; note yellow on bill. **Range:** Breeds on Dry Tortugas, Florida; uncommon in Gulf of Mexico in summer. Rare in Gulf Stream north to Outer Banks, North Carolina. Casual to coastal California, where it must be separated from Nazca Booby (page 467).

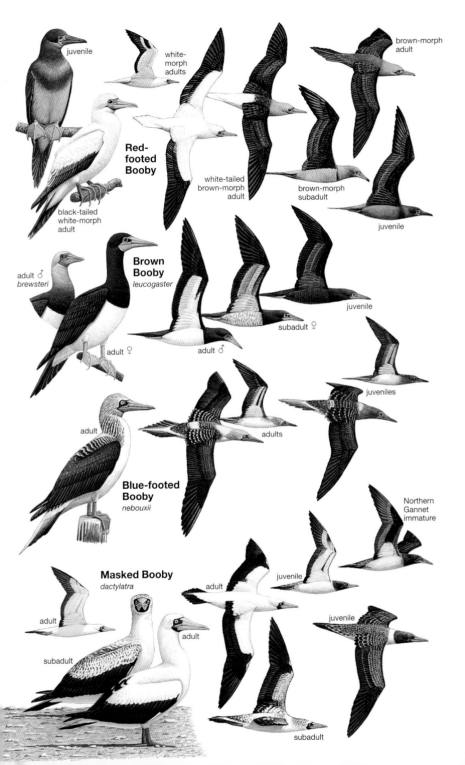

Red-footed Booby

juvenile

white-morph adults

brown-morph adult

black-tailed white-morph adult

white-tailed brown-morph adult

brown-morph subadult

juvenile

Brown Booby
leucogaster

adult ♂
brewsteri

adult ♀

adult ♂

subadult ♀

juvenile

juveniles

adult

adults

Blue-footed Booby
nebouxii

Northern Gannet immature

Masked Booby
dactylatra

adult

adult

subadult

adult

adult

juvenile

juvenile

subadult

Northern Gannet *Morus bassanus*

L 37" (94 cm) WS 72" (183 cm) Large, white seabird with long, black-tipped wings, pointed white tail. **Juvenile** is dark gray above, with pale speckling; grayish below. **First-year** birds are whiter below; distinguished from juvenile and immature Masked Booby (preceding page) by more uniformly dark underwings and, at close range, by different feathering pattern around the bill. Full **adult** plumage is acquired in three to four years. **Range:** Common; breeds in large colonies on rocky cliffs; winters at sea. Often seen from shore during migration and winter. Casual in Great Lakes region in late fall.

Pelicans (Family Pelecanidae)

These large, heavy waterbirds have massive bills and huge throat pouches used as dip nets to catch fish. In flight, pelicans hold their heads drawn back. *Species: 7 World, 2 N.A.*

American White Pelican *Pelecanus erythrorhynchos*

L 62" (158 cm) WS 108" (274 cm) White, with black primaries and outer secondaries. **Breeding adult** has pale yellow crest; bill is bright orange, usually with a fibrous plate on upper mandible. Plate is shed after eggs are laid; crown and nape become grayish. Juvenile is white with brownish wash on head, neck, and lesser coverts; soft parts more dully colored. White Pelicans do not dive for food but dip their bills into the water while swimming. Usually found in flocks. **Range: Nonbreeding** birds are seen in summer throughout area enclosed by dashed line on map. In fall, vagrants may appear almost anywhere, increasingly in Northeast.

Brown Pelican *Pelecanus occidentalis* **E**

L 48" (122 cm) WS 84" (213 cm) **Nonbreeding adult** has white head and neck, often washed with yellow; grayish brown body; blackish belly. In **breeding** bird, hindneck is dark chestnut; yellow patch appears at base of foreneck. On eastern race, *carolinensis* (shown here), gular pouch is grayish; breeding *californicus* from the West Coast has a bright red gular pouch. Molt during incubation and **chick feeding** produces speckled head and foreneck. Adult eye color is light except during chick feeding, when it darkens. Juvenile is grayish brown above, tipped with pale buff; underparts whitish. **Immatures** are browner; acquire adult plumage by third year. Dives from the air after prey, capturing fish in its pouch. **Range:** Very rare, but widely recorded from interior U.S. and southern Ontario, inland except at Salton Sea, where may be common. Wanderers are seen mainly in spring and summer, to limit of dashed line on map, rarely to British Columbia and casually to Nova Scotia.

Northern Gannet

adult

adult

juvenile

2nd year

1st year

American White Pelican

nonbreeding adult

immature

chick-feeding adult

breeding adult

nonbreeding adult

Brown Pelican
carolinensis

subadult

nonbreeding adult

chick-feeding adult

immature

breeding adult

Darters (Family Anhingidae)

Long, slim neck helps to distinguish anhingas from cormorants. Anhingas often swim submerged to the neck. Sharply pointed bill is used to spear fish. *Species: 2 World, 1 N.A.*

Anhinga *Anhinga anhinga L 35" (89 cm) WS 45" (114 cm)*
Black above, with green gloss; silvery white spots and streaks on wings and upper back. During breeding season, **male** acquires pale, wispy plumes on upper neck; bill and bare facial skin become brightly colored. **Female** has buffy neck and breast. Immatures resemble adult female but are browner overall. Anhingas prefer freshwater habitats; often seen perched on branches or stumps with wings spread. In flight, profile looks headless. Flies with slow, regular wingbeats and circles like raptor on thermals. **Range:** Casual wanderer north of breeding range.

Cormorants (Family Phalacrocoracidae)

Dark birds with set-back legs; long, hooked bill; and colorful bare facial skin and throat pouch. Dive from the surface for fish. May briefly soar; may swim partially submerged. *Species: 36 World, 6 N.A.*

Neotropic Cormorant *Phalacrocorax brasilianus*
L 26" (66 cm) WS 40" (102 cm) Small, long-tailed cormorant with white-bordered, yellow-brown or dull yellow throat pouch that tapers to a sharp point behind bill. In **breeding** plumage, **adult** acquires short white plumes on sides of neck. Distinguished from Double-crested Cormorant (next page) by smaller size, longer tail, and smaller, angled throat pouch that does not extend around eye. Neotropic **juveniles** are overall browner than adults, particularly on underparts. **Range:** Fairly common; found at marshy ponds or shallow inlets near perching stumps and snags. Regular to Arizona; casual to southeast California, Colorado, and the western Midwest; accidental mid-Atlantic region. Formerly called Olivaceous Cormorant.

Great Cormorant *Phalacrocorax carbo*
L 36" (91 cm) WS 63" (160 cm) Large, short-tailed cormorant with small, lemon yellow throat pouch broadly bordered with white feathering. **Breeding adult** shows white flank patches and wispy white plumes on head. Smaller Double-crested Cormorant (next page) has orange throat pouch; lacks flank patches; note also Great Cormorant's larger, blockier head and heavier bill. **First-year** birds are brown above; white belly contrasts with streaked brown neck, breast, and flanks. **Second-year** immatures resemble nonbreeding adults more closely but have a brown tinge above; compare with young Double-crested, which has a slimmer bill, deep orange facial skin, and, often, a darker belly. **Range:** Winters in small numbers regularly south to South Carolina, very rarely as far south as Florida. Casual on Lake Ontario.

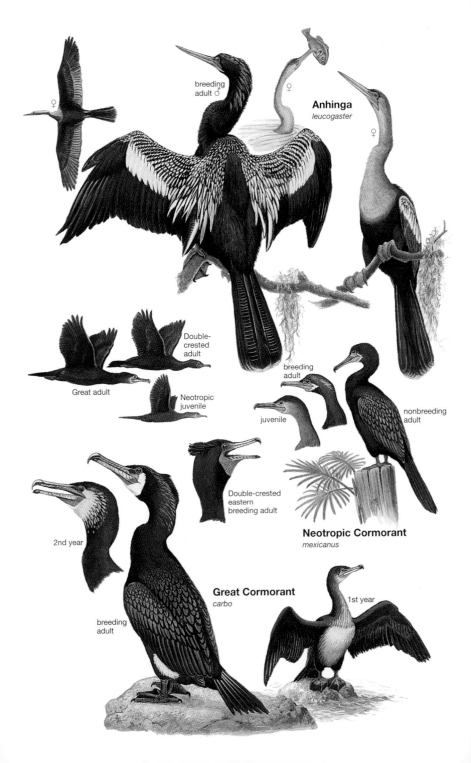

breeding
adult ♂

♀

Anhinga
leucogaster

♀

♀

Double-
crested
adult

Great adult

Neotropic
juvenile

breeding
adult

juvenile

nonbreeding
adult

Double-crested
eastern
breeding adult

Neotropic Cormorant
mexicanus

2nd year

Great Cormorant
carbo

1st year

breeding
adult

Pelagic Cormorant *Phalacrocorax pelagicus*

L 26" (66 cm) WS 39" (99 cm) **Adults** are dark and glossy over-all; bill dark. Smaller and slenderer than other western cormorants. **Breeding adult** has tufts on crown and nape; fine white plumes on sides of neck; white patches on flanks. Distinguished from Red-faced Cormorant by darker and less extensive red facial skin and lack of yellow in bill. **Juvenile** is uniformly dark brown; closely resembles young Red-faced, but note dark bill and smaller size. Pelagic Cormorant is distinguished in flight from Brandt's by smaller head, slimmer neck, smaller overall size, and dispropor-tionately longer tail. Its bill is thinner and different in color than the Red-Faced Cormorant's. Less gregarious than other species; breeds in smaller colonies. Despite name, rare out over open ocean.

Red-faced Cormorant *Phalacrocorax urile*

L 31" (79 cm) WS 46" (117 cm) Heavier and paler bill distin-guishes all ages from Pelagic Cormorant. In **adult,** dull brown wings contrast with glossy upperparts; more uniform in Pelagic. Extensive yellow on bill with bluish at base. Facial skin is red and becomes enlarged and brighter in the **breeding** season. **Juvenile** is uniformly dark brown, with pale yellowish gray bill. More gre-garious than Pelagics, Red-faced Cormorants nest in colonies on the ledges of steep coastal cliffs and on rocky sea islands, along-side gulls, murres, and auklets.

Brandt's Cormorant *Phalacrocorax penicillatus*

L 35" (89 cm) WS 48" (122 cm) A band of pale buffy feathers bordering the throat pouch identifies all ages. Throat pouch becomes bright blue in **breeding** plumage; head, neck, and scapu-lars acquire fine, white plumes. **Juvenile** is dark brown above, slightly paler below. In all ages, appears more uniformly dark above than Double-crested Cormorant; wings and tail are shorter. Head and bill are larger than in Pelagic Cormorant. **Range:** Com-mon and gregarious; often fishes in large flocks; flies in long lines between feeding and roosting grounds. Much more likely to be seen over open ocean than Pelagic Cormorant. A tiny breeding colony may still exist on Seal Rocks near Prince William Sound, Alaska; very rare in southeast Alaska.

Double-crested Cormorant *Phalacrocorax auritus*

L 32" (81 cm) WS 52" (132 cm) Large, rounded throat pouch is yellow-orange year-round. **Breeding adult** has a tuft curving back on either side of its head from behind eyes. Tufts are largely white in western birds, black and less conspicuous in eastern birds (see figure preceding page). **Juvenile** is brown above, variably pale below, but usually palest on upper breast and neck. Immatures sometimes have pouch edged with white, which can cause con-fusion with Neotropic Cormorant (preceding page). Among West Coast cormorants, Double-crested's kinked neck is distinctive in flight; its wings are also longer and more pointed than Brandt's and Pelagic. **Range:** Common and widespread; found along coasts, inland lakes, and rivers. Breeding populations in the inte-rior have greatly increased in the last three decades.

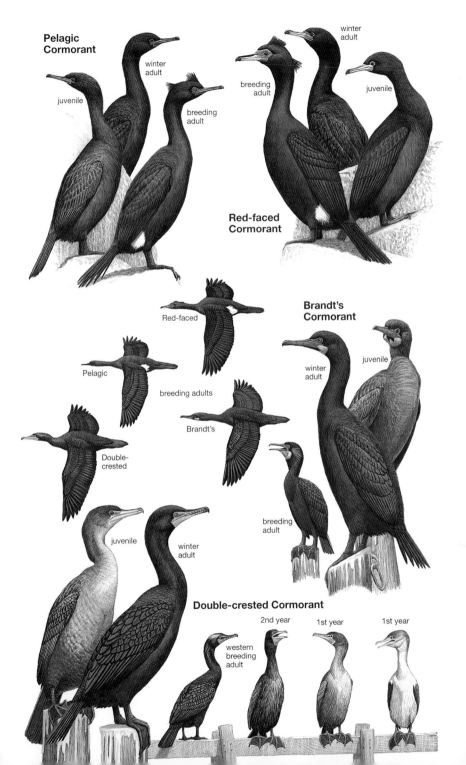

Pelagic Cormorant

juvenile

winter adult

breeding adult

Red-faced Cormorant

breeding adult

winter adult

juvenile

Red-faced

Pelagic

breeding adults

Brandt's

Double-crested

Brandt's Cormorant

winter adult

juvenile

breeding adult

juvenile

winter adult

Double-crested Cormorant

western breeding adult

2nd year

1st year

1st year

Herons, Bitterns, Allies
(Family Ardeidae)

Wading birds; most have long legs, neck, and bill for stalking food in shallow water. Graceful crests and plumes adorn some species in breeding season. *Species: 65 World, 18 N.A.*

American Bittern *Botaurus lentiginosus*
L 28" (71 cm) WS 42" (107 cm) Mottled brown upperparts and brownish neck streaks. Contrasting dark flight feathers are conspicuous in flight; note also that wings are longer, narrower, and more pointed, not rounded as in night-herons. **Juvenile** lacks neck patches. Distinctive spring and early summer **song,** *oonk-a-lunk,* is most often heard at dusk in dense marsh reeds. When alarmed, freezes with bill pointing up, or flushes with rapid wing-beats. **Range:** Fairly common; casual breeder south of range.

Least Bittern *Ixobrychus exilis* L 13" (33 cm) WS 17" (43 cm)
Buffy inner wing patches identify this small, rather secretive heron as it flushes briefly from dense marsh cover. When alarmed, it may freeze with bill pointing up. In **male** back and crown are black; in **female** they are browner. **Juvenile** resembles female but has more prominent streaking on back and breast. Rare dark morph, **"Cory's Least Bittern"** not documented since mid-20th century, is chestnut where typical plumage is pale. Least Bittern's **calls** include a series of harsh *kek* notes; **song,** a softer series of *ku* notes, is heard only on the breeding ground. Fairly common. May breed sporadically beyond mapped range in West.

Yellow-crowned Night-Heron *Nyctanassa violacea*
L 24" (61 cm) WS 42" (107 cm) **Adult** has buffy white crown, black face with white cheeks; acquires head plumes in breeding season. **Juvenile** told from young Black-crowned Night-Heron by grayer upperparts with less conspicuous white spotting; longer neck; stouter, mostly dark bill; and larger eyes. In flight, its legs extend well beyond its tail and it shows darker flight feathers and trailing edge on wings. Full adult plumage is acquired in third year. **Calls** include a short *woc,* higher and less harsh than in Black-crowned. **Range:** Uncommon to fairly common; roosts in trees in wet woods and swamps. Casual in California and north to dashed line on map; casual also in Newfoundland.

Black-crowned Night-Heron *Nycticorax nycticorax*
L 25" (64 cm) WS 44" (112 cm) Stocky heron with short neck and legs. **Adult** has black crown and back; white hindneck plumes are longest in breeding season. **Juvenile** distinguished from young Yellow-crowned Night-Heron by browner upperparts with bolder white spotting; thicker neck; paler, less contrasting face with smaller eyes; and longer, thinner bill with mostly pale lower mandible. In flight, legs barely extend beyond tail. Full adult plumage is not acquired until third year. **Calls** include a low, harsh *woc,* more guttural than in Yellow-crowned. Mainly nocturnal feeder. Typically roosts in trees. Fairly common to common.

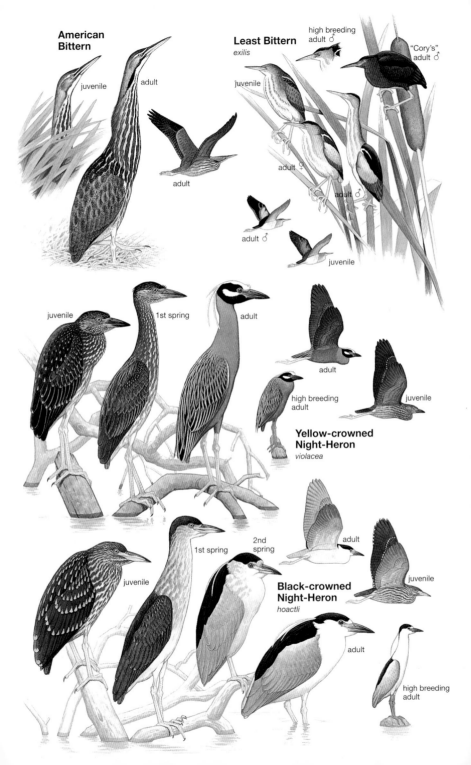

American Bittern

juvenile

adult

adult

Least Bittern
exilis

high breeding
adult ♂

"Cory's"
adult ♂

juvenile

adult ♀

adult ♂

adult ♂

juvenile

juvenile

1st spring

adult

adult

high breeding
adult

juvenile

**Yellow-crowned
Night-Heron**
violacea

juvenile

1st spring

2nd
spring

adult

juvenile

**Black-crowned
Night-Heron**
hoactli

adult

high breeding
adult

Green Heron *Butorides virescens*

L 18" (46 cm) WS 26" (66 cm) Small, chunky heron with short legs. Back and sides of **adult**'s neck are deep chestnut; green on upperparts is mixed with blue-gray; center of throat and neck white. Greenish black crown feathers, sometimes raised to form shaggy crest. Legs are usually dull yellow but in male turn bright orange in high breeding plumage. **Juvenile** is browner above; white throat and underparts heavily streaked with brown. Common **call** is a loud, sharp *kyowk*. When alarmed, raises crest and flicks tail. **Range:** Usually solitary; found in a variety of habitats, but prefers streams, ponds, and marshes with woodland cover; often perches in trees. Generally common; a few winter north of resident limit.

Tricolored Heron *Egretta tricolor*

L 26" (66 cm) WS 36" (91 cm) White belly and foreneck contrast with mainly dark blue upperparts; bill long and slender. **Juvenile** has chestnut hindneck and wing coverts. **Range:** Common inhabitant of salt marshes and mangrove swamps of the East and Gulf Coasts. Rare inland, but has bred in North Dakota and Kansas. Rare but regular on southern California coast, chiefly in winter; casual in the Southwest.

Little Blue Heron *Egretta caerulea*

L 24" (61 cm) WS 40" (102 cm) Slate blue overall. During most of the year, plumage, head, and neck are dark purple; legs and feet dull green. In high **breeding** plumage, head and neck become reddish purple, legs and feet black. **Juvenile** is easily confused with immature Snowy Egret (next page); note Little Blue Heron's dull yellow legs and feet; two-toned bill with thicker, gray base and dark tip; mostly grayish lores; and, often, narrow, dusky primary tips. During first spring, juvenile's white plumage begins gradual **molt** to adult plumage. Little Blue Herons are slow, methodical feeders in freshwater ponds, lakes, and marshes and coastal saltwater wetlands. **Range:** Common; disperses north in spring and during post-breeding dispersal. Casual north on the West Coast to southern British Columbia, and on the East Coast to Newfoundland.

Reddish Egret *Egretta rufescens*

L 30" (76 cm) WS 46" (117 cm) While feeding, this heron lurches, dashing about with wings spread in a canopy. **Dark-morph breeding adult** has shaggy plumes on rufous head, neck. Bill is pink with black tip; legs cobalt blue. Nonbreeding plumage varies, but in general duller, with shorter plumes, darker bill. **Dark-morph juvenile** is gray; some pale cinnamon on head, neck, inner wing; bill is dark. **White-morph adult** resembles immature Little Blue Heron or Snowy Egret (next page); note larger size, longer bill, dark legs and feet. A few dark-morph birds have much white on wings and resemble molting immature Little Blue Heron. **Range:** Inhabits shallow, open salt pans. Wanders along Gulf Coast in post-breeding dispersal; casual inland to Midwest, Southwest, up the Atlantic coast to New England; rare to coastal southern California.

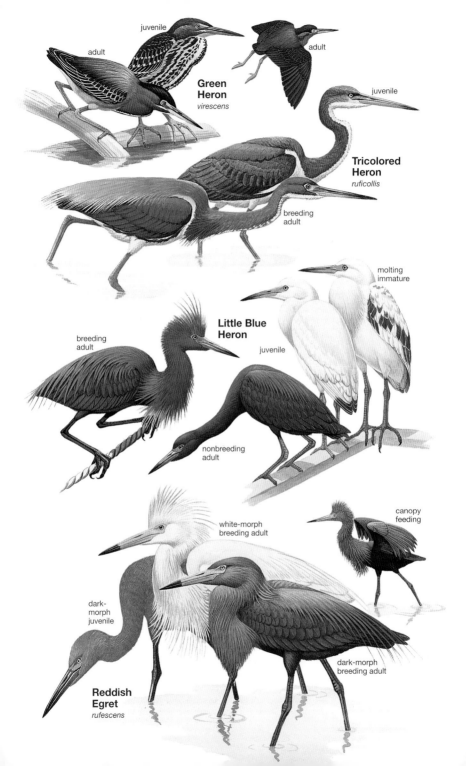

juvenile

adult

Green Heron
virescens

adult

juvenile

Tricolored Heron
ruficollis

breeding adult

Little Blue Heron

breeding adult

juvenile

molting immature

nonbreeding adult

canopy feeding

white-morph breeding adult

dark-morph juvenile

dark-morph breeding adult

Reddish Egret
rufescens

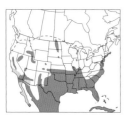

Cattle Egret *Bubulcus ibis L 20" (51 cm) WS 36" (91 cm)*
Small, stocky white heron with large, rounded head; note throat feathering extends far out on bill. **Breeding adult** is adorned with orange-buff plumes on crown, back, and foreneck. At height of breeding season, bill is red-orange, lores purplish, legs dusky red. **Nonbreeding adult** has short yellow bill, yellowish legs. Juvenile's bill is black; begins to turn yellow in late summer; resembles nonbreeding adult. Often seen among livestock in fields, feeding on insects. In flight, resembles Snowy Egret but is smaller; bill and legs shorter; wingbeats faster. **Range:** An Old World species, Cattle Egret came to South America from Africa, spread to Florida in the early 1950s, reached California by the mid-1960s. In spring, summer, and especially fall, wanders well north of breeding range.

Little Egret *Egretta garzetta L 24" (60 cm) WS 36" (91 cm)*
Range: Old World species. Casual spring and summer visitor to East Coast, from Newfoundland to mid-Atlantic states. Closely resembles Snowy Egret, but often appears larger, with longer neck; longer, thicker bill and legs, the latter always entirely black; mostly grayish lores; and more extensive throat feathering out on lower mandible. Little Egret's crown is flatter; feet are yellow, like Snowy, but average slightly duller. In **breeding** plumage, lore color is variable, but can be yellow. Note the two or three long, tapering plumes on back, rather than Snowy's many curved plumes. Often feeds less frenetically than Snowy, with long neck bent over in a posture like Little Blue Heron.

Snowy Egret *Egretta thula L 24" (61 cm) WS 41" (104 cm)*
White heron with slender black bill, yellow eyes, black legs, and bright golden yellow feet. Graceful plumes on head, neck, and back (where they curve upward) are striking in **breeding adult**. In **high breeding** plumage, lores turn red, feet orange. Nonbreeding plumage is similar but plumes shorter; also note yellow on backs of legs. Compare to Little Egret. **Juvenile** resembles nonbreeding adult, but lacks plumes and shows some bluish gray at base of lower mandible. Can be confused with immature Little Blue Heron (preceding page); note young Snowy Egret's slimmer, mostly black bill; yellow lores; predominantly dark legs; and white wing tips. Snowy Egrets are active feeders. **Range:** Common in various wetland habitats. Disperses north of mapped range in spring and after breeding season.

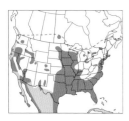

Great Egret *Ardea alba L 39" (99 cm) WS 51" (130 cm)*
Large white heron with heavy yellow bill, blackish legs and feet. In **breeding** plumage, long plumes trail from back, extending beyond tail. In immature and **nonbreeding adult,** bill and leg colors are duller, plumes absent. Distinguished from most other white herons by large size; from white morph of the larger Great Blue Heron by black legs and feet. **Range:** Common in wetlands. Partial to open habitats for feeding; stalks prey slowly, methodically. Occasionally breeds far north of usual range. Post-breeding wanderers reach far north of mapped breeding range.

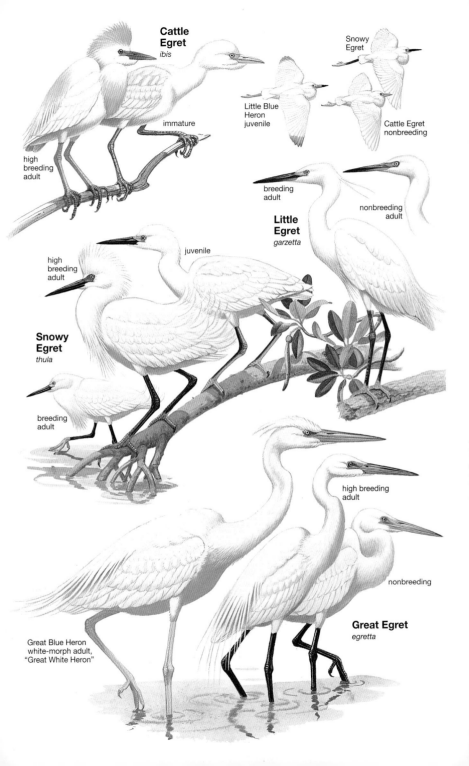

Cattle Egret
ibis

immature

high breeding adult

Snowy Egret

Little Blue Heron juvenile

Cattle Egret nonbreeding

breeding adult

nonbreeding adult

Little Egret
garzetta

juvenile

high breeding adult

Snowy Egret
thula

breeding adult

high breeding adult

nonbreeding

Great Egret
egretta

Great Blue Heron white-morph adult, "Great White Heron"

Great Blue Heron   Ardea herodias
L 46" (117 cm) WS 72" (183 cm) Large, gray-blue heron; black stripe extends above eye; white foreneck is streaked with black. **Breeding adult** has yellowish bill and ornate plumes on head, neck, and back. Nonbreeding adult lacks plumes; bill is yellower. **Juvenile** has black crown, no plumes. All-white morph found in southern Florida formerly considered a separate species, **"Great White Heron"** (preceding page). **"Wurdemann's Heron"** morph, found chiefly in Florida Keys, has all-white head. **Range:** Common. A few winter far north into breeding range.

Storks (Family Ciconiidae)

Large, long-legged birds that fly with slow beats of their long, broad wings, soaring and circling like hawks. *Species: 19 World, 2 N.A.*

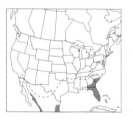

Wood Stork   Mycteria americana   E
L 40" (102 cm) WS 61" (155 cm) Black flight feathers and tail contrast with white body. **Adult** has bald, blackish gray head; thick, dusky, downcurved bill. **Juvenile**'s head is feathered largely with grayish brown; bill is yellow. **Range:** Wood Storks inhabit wet meadows, swamps, ponds, and coastal shallows. A few wander north in late summer; accidental north to Maine and British Columbia.

Jabiru   Jabiru mycteria   L 52" (132 cm) WS 90" (229 cm)
Range: Huge stork of Central and South America, casual straggler in south Texas; recorded once in Oklahoma. Distinguished from Wood Stork by larger size; large bill, slightly upturned; and all-white wings and tail. Red throat pouch brightens and inflates during breeding season. **Juvenile** is patchy brown-gray; head is blackish brown. Usually seen with flocks of Wood Storks.

Flamingos (Family Phoenicopteridae)

Large waders with big, bent bills, used to strain food from the waters of shallow lakes and lagoons. *Species: 5 World, 1 N.A.*

Greater Flamingo   Phoenicopterus ruber
L 46" (117 cm) WS 60" (152 cm) **Range:** Birds seen in New World are of the nominate race, treated by some as separate species, which breeds as close to Florida as southern Bahamas, Cuba, and the Yucatan Peninsula. Note pink legs, black flight feathers, tricolored bill. **Immature** is grayer, with pink wash below; paler bill. South Florida (rare) and south Texas (casual) sightings include wild birds; others, especially away from these regions, more likely escapes. In addition, escapes include a widespread Old World subspecies (*roseus*), with pink-and-white plumage; the Chilean Flamingo (*P. chilensis*), with grayish legs with pink joints; and the Lesser Flamingo (*Phoeniconaias minor*), with dark red bill and blotchy red wing coverts and axillaries.

Great Blue Heron
herodias

breeding
adult

adult

"Wurdemann's
Heron"
breeding adult

juvenile

adult

juvenile

adult

Wood Stork

**Greater
Flamingo**
ruber

juvenile

Jabiru

adult

immature

breeding
adult

Ibises, Spoonbills (Family Threskiornithidae)

Gregarious, heronlike birds, these long-legged waders feed with long, specialized bills: slender and curved downward in ibises, wide and spatulate in spoonbills. *Species: 32 World, 5 N.A.*

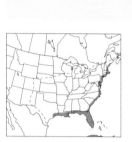

Glossy Ibis *Plegadis falcinellus*

L 23" (58 cm) WS 36" (91 cm) **Breeding adult**'s chestnut plumage is glossed with green or purple; looks all-dark at a distance. Distinguished from White-faced Ibis by brown eye, gray-green legs with red joints, and lack of distinct white border to bare facial skin. Blue edge to gray facial skin does not extend behind eye or under chin. **Winter adult** closely resembles winter White-faced; look for gray facial skin partially bordered by blue line. **Juvenile** closely resembles juvenile White-faced Ibis, but note gray facial skin and at least trace of blue line on most birds. Adult breeding plumage is acquired in second spring. **Range:** Glossy Ibises inhabit freshwater and saltwater marshes. Fairly common but local. Expanding north along the East Coast. Rare but annual in Texas. Rare inland wanderer, chiefly in spring; casual west to California.

White-faced Ibis *Plegadis chihi*

L 23" (58 cm) WS 36" (91 cm) **Breeding adult** distinguished from Glossy Ibis, with which it sometimes hybridizes, by bronzer tones in chestnut plumage, reddish bill, red eye, all-red legs, and white feathered border around red facial skin; border extends behind eye and under chin. **Winter adult** plumage is like Glossy, but lacks pale blue line from eye to bill; facial skin is pale pink. **Juvenile** closely resembles juvenile Glossy until winter, when facial skin turns pinkish; look for lack of blue line (or a hint of white border) and reddish tinge to eye. **Range:** Breeds in freshwater marshes. Very rare in Midwest; casual on East Coast north to New England.

White Ibis *Eudocimus albus* L 25" (64 cm) WS 38" (97 cm)

Adult's white plumage and pink facial skin are distinctive. In **breeding adult,** facial skin, bill, and legs turn scarlet. Dark tips of primaries most easily seen in flight. Immatures have white underparts and wing linings, pinkish bill; gradually molt into adult plumage by second fall. **Range:** Locally common to abundant in coastal salt marshes, swamps, mangroves. Expanding north, now breeds to Virginia. Casual north to New Jersey, Midwest, Southwest. Closely related **Scarlet Ibis** (*E. ruber*), a South American species introduced or escaped in Florida, hybridizes with White Ibis; offspring are various shades of pink or scarlet.

Roseate Spoonbill *Platalea ajaja*

L 32" (81 cm) WS 50" (127 cm) **Adult** has pink body with red highlights; long, spatulate bill; unfeathered greenish head. The head may become buffy during courtship. **Juvenile** has white feathering on head; body is mostly pale pink. Spoonbills feed in shallow waters, swinging their bills from side to side. **Range:** Fairly common locally along the Gulf Coast; casual north to mid-Atlantic, Midwest, and Southwest regions.

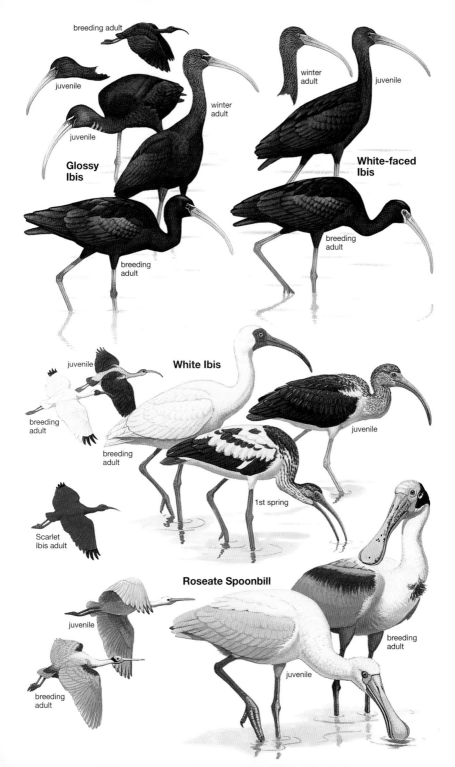

Glossy Ibis

breeding adult

juvenile

juvenile

winter adult

White-faced Ibis

winter adult

juvenile

breeding adult

White Ibis

juvenile

breeding adult

breeding adult

juvenile

1st spring

Scarlet Ibis adult

Roseate Spoonbill

juvenile

breeding adult

breeding adult

juvenile

New World Vultures (Family Cathartidae)

Small, unfeathered head and hooked bill aid in consuming carrion.
Species: 7 World, 3 N.A.

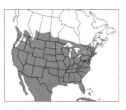

Turkey Vulture *Cathartes aura*
L 27" (69 cm) WS 69" (175 cm) In flight, rocks side to side with little flapping and wings held upward in a shallow V; dark wing linings contrast with silvery flight feathers. Rather long tailed. **Adult** has red head, white bill, brown legs; **juvenile**'s head and bill are dark, legs are paler. Feeds chiefly on carrion and refuse. **Range:** Common in mapped range.

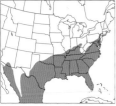

Black Vulture *Coragyps atratus*
L 25" (64 cm) WS 57" (145 cm) In flight, shows large white patches at base of primaries. Tail is shorter than Turkey Vulture; wings shorter and broader; legs white; feet usually extend to edge of tail or beyond. Flight includes rapid flapping and short glides, usually with wings flat. Gregarious and aggressive, but less efficient at spotting carrion than Turkey Vulture. **Range:** Common in open country and near human settlements, often scavenge in garbage dumps. Range expanding in the Northeast; casual north to Ontario, Maritimes, and northern California; accidental to New Mexico.

California Condor *Gymnogyps californianus* **E**
L 47" (119 cm) WS 108" (274 cm) **Range:** Last wild birds captured in Apr. 1987. Before that, found in arid foothills and mountains of southern and central California. Decline to near extinction caused largely by lead poisoning and illegal shooting. Recently reintroduced in California and introduced in northern Arizona. Huge size distinctive. **Adult** has white wing linings, orange head; **juvenile**'s wing linings mottled, head dusky. Soars on flat wings, without flapping, in search of large carrion. Population in wild now about 100; 100 more in captivity.

Hawks, Kites, Eagles, Allies
(Family Accipitridae)

Worldwide family of diurnal birds of prey, with hooked bills and strong talons. *Species: 233 World, 28 N.A.*

Osprey *Pandion haliaetus*
L 22-25" (56-64 cm) WS 58-72" (147-183 cm) Dark brown above, white below, with white head, prominent dark eye stripe. Females average darker streaking on neck; **juvenile** plumage is fringed with pale buff above. In flight, long, narrow wings are bent back at "wrist," dark carpal patches conspicuous; wings slightly arched in soaring. Nests near fresh or salt water; eats mostly fish. Hovering over water, dives down, then plunges feetfirst to snatch prey. Bulky nests are built in trees, on sheds, poles, docks, and special platforms. **Call** is a series of loud, whistled *kyew* notes. **Range:** Conservation programs successful and now fairly common.

Turkey Vulture

adults

adult

juvenile

adult

Black Vulture

adult

juvenile

adult

adult

California Condor

Osprey
carolinensis

adult

adult

juvenile

adult

Mississippi Kite *Ictinia mississippiensis*
L 14½" (37 cm) WS 35" (89 cm) Long, pointed wings with first primary distinctly shorter; long, flared tail. Dark gray above, paler below, with pale gray head, averaging paler on **male. Female** with white shaft on outer tail feather and often whitish in vent region. White secondaries show in flight as white wing patch. Black tail readily distinguishes Mississippi from White-tailed Kite. Compare also with male Northern Harrier (next page); note Mississippi never hovers. **Juvenile** is heavily streaked and spotted, with pale bands on tail, but pattern and overall darkness highly variable on underparts, underwings, and tail. **First-summer** bird (page 142) more like adult but retains juvenal flight feathers. At all ages, may be confused with Peregrine Falcon (page 142); compare wing and tail shapes. Mississippi Kites capture and eat their prey, mainly insects, on the wing. Gregarious; often hunt in groups, nest in loose colonies. **Range:** Found in woodlands, swamps, rangelands. Regular straggler (chiefly immatures in spring) to mid-Atlantic states. Casual north to Great Lakes region and California. Winters in South America.

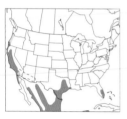

White-tailed Kite *Elanus leucurus*
L 16" (41 cm) WS 42" (107 cm) Long, pointed wings; long tail. White underparts and mostly white tail distinguish **adults** from similar Mississippi Kite. Compare also with male Northern Harrier (next page). **Juvenile**'s underparts and head are lightly streaked with rufous, which rapidly fades. In all ages, black shoulders show in flight as black leading edge of inner wings from above, small black patches from below. Hovers while hunting, unlike any other North American kite. Eats mainly rodents, insects. **Range:** Populations fluctuate. Fairly common in grasslands, farmlands, even highway median strips. Casual well north of mapped range to British Columbia, Wyoming, and New York. Often forms winter roosts of more than a hundred birds.

Swallow-tailed Kite *Elanoides forficatus*
L 23" (58 cm) WS 48" (122 cm) Seen in flight, deeply forked tail and sharply defined pattern of black and white are like no other large bird except the young Magnificent Frigatebird (page 98). Perched, Swallow-tailed Kite's coloring more closely resembles White-tailed and Mississippi Kites; again, note long, forked tail. Juvenile is similar to **adult,** but tail is shorter, flight feathers and tail narrowly tipped with white. Agile and graceful, Swallow-tailed snatches flying insects; also drops down upon snakes, lizards, young birds; does not hover. Often eats prey in flight; also drinks in flight, skimming the water like a swallow. Found in open woods, bottomlands, and wetlands. Nests in the tops of tall trees. Somewhat social; several may hunt in the same territory. **Range:** Casual in spring and summer as far north as Ontario and Nova Scotia; accidental as far west as Arizona. Most winter in South America.

Mississippi Kite

juvenile

adult ♂

adult ♀

adult ♂

Swallow-tailed Kite

adults

adults

juvenile

adult

White-tailed Kite
majusculus

Snail Kite *Rostrhamus sociabilis* **E**

L 17" (43 cm) WS 46" (117 cm) This kite's wings are paddle shaped, bill thin and deeply hooked. **Male** is gray-black above and below, with white uppertail and undertail coverts; square, white tail with broad, dark band and paler terminal band; legs orange-red; eyes and facial skin reddish. **Female** is dark brown, with distinctive head pattern. **Juvenile** has dark brown eyes, duller facial skin and legs, streaked crown and underparts. Hunting flight is slow, with considerable flapping of wings, and head held down as the kite searches for apple snails, its chief and perhaps only food. **Range:** A tropical species. Endangered; uncommon and local resident in southern Florida.

Hook-billed Kite *Chondrohierax uncinatus*

L 18" (46 cm) WS 36" (91 cm) **Range:** Tropical species, uncommon over most of its range. Rare resident in lower Rio Grande Valley from Santa Ana to Falcon Dam. Found in dense woodlands, from which it thermals upward in late morning. Plumage varies considerably, but look for large, heavy bill with long hook, white eyes, banded tail, and heavily barred underparts, including underwings. **Males** are generally gray overall. **Females** are brown, with a rufous collar and rufous, barred underparts. **Juveniles** have brown eyes, white collar, and whitish underparts with variable dark brown barring. In the **black morph,** rarely seen in the U.S., **adult** is all-black except for a single white or grayish tail band and whitish tail tip; **juveniles** are mostly brownish black, with two or more grayish tail bands. Hook-billed Kite flies with deep, languid wingbeats, its "wrists" slightly cocked upward and "hands" angled down. Wings are paddle shaped, slightly tapered in at the base. It eats insects and small amphibians, but prefers snails of various kinds. A pile of broken snail shells beneath a tree may indicate a favorite perch or a nest site above.

Northern Harrier *Circus cyaneus*

L 16-20" (41-51 cm) WS 38-48" (97-122 cm) White uppertail coverts and owl-like facial disk distinctive in all ages and both sexes. Body slim; wings long and narrow with somewhat rounded tips; tail long. **Adult male** is grayish above; mostly white below with variable chestnut spotting; has black wing tips and black tips to secondaries. **Female** is brown above, whitish below with heavy brown streaking on breast and flanks, lighter streaking and spotting on belly. **Juveniles** resemble adult female but are cinnamon below, fading to creamy buff by spring; streaked only on the breast; wing linings are cinnamon, distinctly darker on inner half. Harriers generally perch low and fly close to the ground, wings upraised, as they search for birds, mice, frogs, and other prey. Seldom soar high except during migration and in exuberant, acrobatic courtship display. **Range:** Fairly common in wetlands and open fields. Adult males migrate later in fall and earlier in spring than females and immatures. In winter, harriers form communal ground roosts, sometimes with Short-eared Owls.

Snail Kite
plumbeus

adult ♂

adult ♀

adult ♂

juvenile

black-morph
adult

black-morph
juvenile

juvenile

adult ♂

adult ♀

**Hook-billed
Kite**
uncinatus

juvenile

**Northern
Harrier**
hudsonicus

adult ♂

adult ♂

juvenile

adult ♂

juveniles

adult ♀

adult ♂

Golden Eagle *Aquila chrysaetos*

L 30-40" (76-102 cm) WS 80-88" (203-224 cm) Brown, with variable yellow to tawny brown wash over back of head and neck; bill mostly horn colored; tail faintly banded. Tawny greater upperwing coverts form a bar. **Juveniles,** seen in flight from below, show well-defined white patches at base of primaries, white tail with distinct dark terminal band. Compare with juvenile Bald Eagle's larger head, shorter tail, blotchier tail and underwing pattern. **Adult** plumage is acquired in four years. Golden Eagle often soars with wings slightly uplifted. **Range:** Inhabits mountainous or hilly terrain, hunting over open country for small mammals, snakes, birds, and carrion. Also found in valleys and western plains, especially in migration and winter. Nests on cliffs or in trees. Uncommon to rare in the East; uncommon to fairly common in the West.

White-tailed Eagle *Haliaeetus albicilla*

L 26-35" (66-89 cm) WS 72-94" (183-239 cm) **Range:** Flies over northern Eurasia and Greenland in diminishing numbers. Very rare visitor to outer Aleutians, especially Attu Island, where it has nested. Note short, wedge-shaped white tail. Plumage mottled; head may be very pale and appear white at a distance; undertail coverts are dark, unlike subadult and adult Bald Eagles. **Juvenile's** tail has variable dark mottling and tip and is less wedge shaped, underwing darker, than Bald Eagle.

Steller's Sea-Eagle *Haliaeetus pelagicus*

L 33-41" (84-104 cm) WS 87-96" (221-244 cm) **Range:** Nests in northeastern Asia; casual in Alaska; recorded on Aleutians, Pribilofs, Kodiak Island, near Juneau in southeast Alaska. In flight, white shoulders show as white leading edge of wings; trailing edge of wing more curved than in White-tailed or Bald Eagles. Immense yellow-orange bill; long, white, wedge-shaped tail; white thighs. **Juvenile** lacks white shoulders; end of tail is dark.

Bald Eagle *Haliaeetus leucocephalus* **T**

L 31-37" (79-94 cm) WS 70-90" (178-229 cm) **Adults** readily identified by white head and tail, large yellow bill. **Juveniles** are mostly dark, may be confused with juvenile Golden Eagle; compare blotchy white on underwing coverts, axillaries, and tail with Golden Eagle's more sharply defined pattern; note also Bald Eagle's disproportionately larger head, shorter tail. Neck is shorter and tail longer than White-tailed Eagle; Steller's Sea-Eagle has longer, wedge-shaped tail. Flat-winged soar distinguishes young Bald Eagle from Turkey Vulture (page 118). Bald Eagles require four or five years to reach full adult plumage. Seen most often on seacoasts or near rivers and lakes. Feed mainly on fish in breeding season, regularly on carrion, and on roadkill in winter, particularly in the Southwest. Nest in tall trees or on cliffs. **Range:** Most abundant in Alaska; common in winter along Mississippi and Missouri Rivers, fairly common in the Northwest. Banning of pesticides and intense recovery programs have increased populations that had been seriously diminished in the East.

juvenile

Golden Eagle
canadensis

adult

adult

White-tailed Eagle

juvenile

adult

Steller's Sea-Eagle

adult

juvenile

juvenile

2nd year

3rd year

juvenile

Bald Eagle

adults

Accipiters

Comparatively long tails and short, rounded wings give these wood-land hawks great agility. Flight is several quick wingbeats and a glide. The three species in North America are confusingly similar.

Sharp-shinned Hawk *Accipiter striatus*

L 10-14" (25-36 cm) WS 20-28" (51-71 cm) Distinguished from Cooper's Hawk by shorter, squared tail, often appearing notched when folded, thinner legs, and by smaller head and neck. **Adult** lacks Cooper's strong contrast between crown and back. **Juveniles** are whitish below, some streaked with brown (like Cooper's), others spotted with reddish brown. Note also the pale eyebrows, narrow white tip on tail, entirely white undertail coverts, less tawny head than other accipiters. In flight (see also page 143), again compare smaller head and proportionately shorter tail than Cooper's; wingbeats quick and choppy, slower on Cooper's. **Range:** Sharp-shinned Hawk is fairly common over much of its range; found in mixed woodlands. Preys chiefly on small birds. Migrates singly or in loose groups.

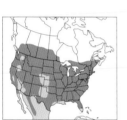

Cooper's Hawk *Accipiter cooperii*

L 14-20" (36-51 cm) WS 29-37" (74-94 cm) Distinguished from Sharp-shinned Hawk by longer, rounded tail, larger head, and, in **adult,** stronger contrast between back and crown. **Juvenile** has whitish or buffy underparts with fine streaks on breast, streaking reduced or absent on belly; tawny rufous color on head is much richer, white tip on tail is broader, than in Sharp-shinned; undertail coverts entirely white. Note that some juveniles may have a pale eyebrow like Sharp-shinned. In flight (see also page 143), again compare larger head and longer tail. Preys largely on songbirds, some small mammals. Often perches on telephone poles, unlike Sharp-shinned. **Range:** Inhabits broken woodlands or streamside groves, especially deciduous. Usually migrates singly. Rare, mainly in fall, in the Maritimes.

Northern Goshawk *Accipiter gentilis*

L 21-26" (53-66 cm) WS 40-46" (102-117 cm) Conspicuous eyebrow, flaring behind eye, separates **adult**'s dark crown from blue-gray back. Underparts are white with dense gray barring; appear gray at a distance; has wedge-shaped tail with fluffy undertail coverts. Note disproportionately shorter tail, longer wings, than Cooper's Hawk. **Juvenile** is brown above, buffy below, with thick, blackish brown streaks, heaviest on flanks; tail has wavy dark bands bordered with white and a thin white tip; undertail coverts usually have dark streaks. In flight (see also page 143), note tawny bar on upperwing on greater secondary coverts. Juvenile also can be confused with Gyrfalcon (page 140) and Red-shouldered Hawk (page 130). **Range:** The Northern Goshawk inhabits deep, conifer-dominated, mixed woodlands; preys on birds and mammals as large as hares. Uncommon; winters irregularly south of mapped range in the East. Southward irruptions occur in some winters.

Sharp-shinned Hawk
velox

adult ♂

juvenile ♀

juvenile

Cooper's Hawk

juvenile ♀

adult ♂

juvenile

Northern Goshawk
atricapillus

juvenile ♀

juvenile

adult ♂

Buteos

High-soaring hawks, amongst easiest of birds of prey to spot.

Common Black-Hawk *Buteogallus anthracinus*
L 21" (53 cm) WS 50" (127 cm) Wings broad and rounded; tail short, broad. **Adult** blackish overall; tail has broad white band. Legs and cere orange-yellow. Distinguished from Zone-tailed Hawk by broader wings; broader, less banded tail; larger bill; more orange-yellow in lore region. **Juvenile** has strong face pattern; heavily streaked underparts; many-banded tail; buffy wing panel visible from above and below. **Call** is a series of loud whistles. **Range:** Found along waterways. Rare, local, and declining; very rare in southwestern Utah and southern Texas; casual in California.

Harris's Hawk *Parabuteo unicinctus*
L 21" (53 cm) WS 46" (117 cm) Chocolate brown overall, with chestnut shoulder patches, leggings, and wing linings; white at base and tip of long tail; rounded wingtips. **Juvenile** is heavily streaked below; chestnut shoulder patches are less distinct. Inhabits semiarid woodland, and brushland. Gregarious; sometimes hunts in small, cooperative groups. **Range:** May straggle north and west of mapped range, but many may be escapes.

Zone-tailed Hawk *Buteo albonotatus*
L 20" (51 cm) WS 51" (130 cm) Grayish black overall, with barred flight feathers. Legs and cere yellow. Slimmer winged than Common Black-Hawk; longer tail, variably banded according to sex and age. Flies like Turkey Vulture; compare Zone-tailed's banded tail; smaller bill; yellow cere; larger, feathered head. **Juvenile** has grayish tail, some white flecking on breast. **Call,** a squealing whistle. **Range:** Uncommon; found in mesa and mountain country, often near watercourses; drops from low glide on small birds, rodents, lizards, and fish. Rare in southern California and southern Texas.

Short-tailed Hawk *Buteo brachyurus*
L 15½" (39 cm) WS 35" (89 cm) Small hawk with two color morphs. Secondaries seen from below are darker than primaries. **Light morph** has dark helmet and underwing resembling Swainson's Hawk (page 132), wings and tail are shorter, broader; lacks chest band. **Adults** have wide, dark subterminal tail band; of equal width on juveniles. Faint streaks on sides of light morph; spotted with white on wing linings and underparts on dark-morph juveniles. Most often seen in flight. **Range:** Found in mixed woodland-grassland. Casual to south Texas and mountains of southeast Arizona (has bred) in spring and summer; accidental Michigan.

Roadside Hawk *Buteo magnirostris*
L 14" (36 cm) WS 30" (75 cm) **Range:** Tropical species, casual in winter in lower Rio Grande Valley, Texas. A small, slim, long-legged raptor with banded tail. **Adult** with brown bib, barred belly. **Juvenile** with some streaking on chest. Flies with stiff, rapid wingbeats; wingtips rounded with rufous patch on inner primaries.

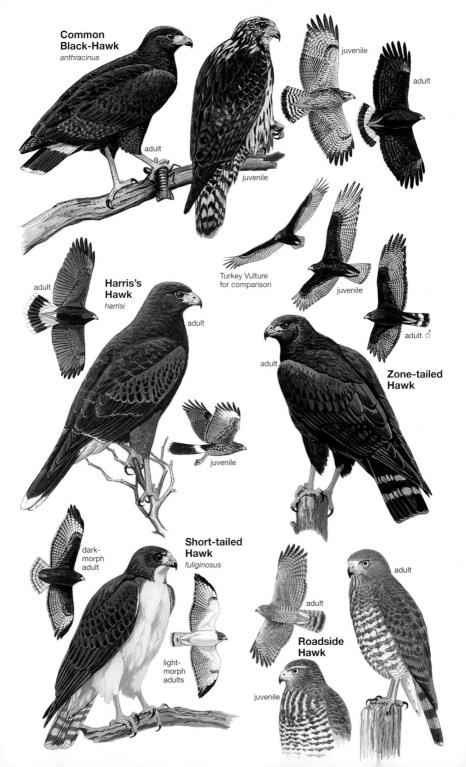

Common Black-Hawk
anthracinus

adult

juvenile

juvenile

adult

Harris's Hawk
harrisi

adult

adult

Turkey Vulture for comparison

juvenile

adult ♂

juvenile

Zone-tailed Hawk

adult

dark-morph adult

Short-tailed Hawk
fuliginosus

light-morph adults

adult

Roadside Hawk

juvenile

Broad-winged Hawk *Buteo platypterus*

L 16" (41 cm) WS 34" (86 cm) Pointed wing tips; white under-wings have dark borders; tail has broad black and white bands, with last white band broader than the others. Wings broad but more pointed than in Red-shouldered Hawk; wing linings buffy or white; tail shorter, broader. Wingbeats are slower than in *elegans* race of Red-shouldered. **Juveniles** typically have black moustachial streak; dark-bordered underwings, indistinct bands on tail; very similar to juvenile eastern Red-shouldered but paler below; may have a pale area at base of primaries but lack the distinct pale crescent. Rare **dark morph** breeds in western and central Canada. Broad-winged is a woodland species. **Call,** heard on breeding and winter grounds, is a thin, shrill, slightly descending whistle: *pee-teee.* **Range:** Often migrates in very large flocks. Rare migrant in the West. Most winter in South America; a few winter in southern Florida and very rarely in coastal California.

Gray Hawk *Buteo nitidus*

L 17" (43 cm) WS 35" (89 cm) Gray upperparts, gray-barred underparts and wing linings, and rounded wing tips distinguish Gray from Broad-winged Hawk (see also page 143). Flight is accipiter-like: several rapid, shallow wingbeats and a glide. **Juvenile** resembles juvenile Broad-winged, but has much longer tail projection, stronger face pattern with outlined white cheek, and white, U-shaped rump band; dark trailing edge on wings is smaller or absent. Gray Hawk inhabits deciduous growth along streams with nearby open land. **Calls** include a loud, descending whistle. **Range:** Tropical species; local nester in southeastern Arizona. Rare in lower Rio Grande Valley year-round. Rare in summer upriver to Big Bend and in southwest New Mexico.

Red-shouldered Hawk *Buteo lineatus*

L 15-19" (38-48 cm) WS 37-42" (94-107 cm) Relatively long tailed and long legged. In flight, shows pale crescent at base of primaries. **Adult** has reddish shoulders and wing linings and extensive pale spotting above. Widespread eastern nominate race *lineatus* shows dark streaks on reddish chest. Southeastern *alleni* (not shown) is smaller, with grayish cast to head and back; usually lacks breast streaking. South Florida *extimus* is the smallest and palest race. California *elegans* and central Texas *texanus* (not shown) are decidedly more rufous below; *elegans* is often solidly rufous across the chest and has broader white tail bands. **Juveniles** show extensive variations; *lineatus* shows more finely streaked breast and more closely resembles juvenile Broad-winged Hawk; other eastern races show more coarsely marked underparts; *elegans* is quite dark and has more adultlike features, including some rufous on shoulders and wing linings. Flight of all ages of *elegans* is accipiter-like, with several quick wingbeats and a glide, while *lineatus* flies with slower wingbeats, more like Broad-winged. **Call** is an evenly spaced series of clear, high *kee-ah* or *kah* notes. **Range:** Found in moist, mixed woodlands; often seen near water.

juveniles

juveniles

juveniles

adult

dark-morph
adult

adult

**Broad-winged
Hawk**
platypterus

**Gray
Hawk**
plagiata

juvenile

adult

juvenile

adult

juvenile

adult
lineatus

juvenile
lineatus

California
adult
elegans

juvenile
elegans

juvenile
lineatus

**Red-shouldered
Hawk**

Florida
adult
extimus

Eastern
adult
lineatus

juvenile
lineatus

juvenile
elegans

Red-tailed Hawk *Buteo jamaicensis*

L 22" (56 cm) WS 50" (127 cm) Our most common buteo; wings broad and fairly rounded; plumage extremely variable. Looks heavy billed, unlike Rough-legged (next page) and Swainson's Hawks. Variable pale mottling on scapulars contrasts with dark mantle, often forming a broad-sided V on perched birds. Most **adults,** especially in the East, show a belly band of dark streaks on whitish underparts; dark bar on leading edge of underwing, contrasting with paler wing linings (see also page 144). Note reddish uppertail; paler red undertail. Great Plains race *krideri,* known as **"Krider's Red-tailed,"** has paler upperparts and whitish tail with pale reddish wash; in flight, shows pale rectangular patches at base of primaries on upperwing. Many southwestern birds of the *fuertesi* race (not shown) lack belly band and have entirely light underparts. Widespread dark and **rufous morphs** of western race, *calurus,* have dark wing linings and underparts, obscuring the bar on leading edge and belly band; tail is dark reddish above. In *harlani,* **"Harlan's Hawk,"** formerly considered a separate species, dark morph has dusky white tail, diffuse blackish terminal band; shows some white streaking on its dark breast; may lack scapular mottling; rare *harlani* light morph has typical tail pattern, but plumage resembles *krideri.* "Harlan's Hawk" breeds in Alaska and east to northwestern Canada; winters primarily in central U.S. **Juveniles** of all morphs except *harlani* have gray-brown tails with many blackish bands; otherwise heavily streaked and spotted with brown below. Distinctive **call,** a harsh, descending *keeeeer.* Habitat variable: woods with nearby open land; also plains, prairie groves, and desert. Preys on rodents.

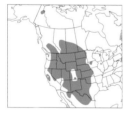

Swainson's Hawk *Buteo swainsoni*

L 21" (53 cm) WS 52" (132 cm) Distinguished from most other buteos by long, narrow, pointed wings; plumage is extremely variable. Lacks Red-tailed Hawk's pale mottling on scapulars; bill is smaller. All but darkest birds show contrast between paler wing linings and dark flight feathers; most show pale uppertail coverts. In **light morph,** whitish or buffy white wing linings contrast with darkly barred brown flight feathers (see also page 144); dark bib; underparts otherwise whitish to pale buff. **Dark-morph** bird is dark brown with white undertail coverts; shows less sharp contrast between wing linings and flight feathers; darkest birds show none. Compare with first-year White-tailed Hawk (next page). **Intermediate** colorations between light and dark morphs include a rufous morph. Intermediate and **light-morph juveniles** have dark moustachial stripe and conspicuous whitish eyebrows that meet on the forehead; variable streaking below, very heavy on dark morphs. Show less contrast between wing linings and flight feathers than adult birds (page 144). Swainson's soars over open plains and prairie with uptilted wings in teetering, vulturelike flight. **Range:** Very rare spring and fall migrant in eastern North America. Gregarious; usually migrates in large flocks, often with Broadwinged Hawks (preceding page). Winters chiefly in South America; rarely in southern Florida and Central Valley of California.

Red-tailed Hawk

eastern adult *borealis*

eastern juvenile *borealis*

"Harlan's Hawk" adult *harlani*

"Krider's Red-tailed" adult *krideri*

rufous-morph adult *calurus*

eastern adult *borealis*

light-morph juvenile

Swainson's Hawk

dark-morph adult

light-morph adult

light-morph adult

intermediate-morph adult

Rough-legged Hawk   *Buteo lagopus*

L 21" (53 cm) WS 53" (135 cm) Long, white tail with dark band or bands helps to identify this hawk in all plumages; bill small. Thin legs are feathered to the toes, the feathering barred in adults, unbarred in juveniles. **Adult male** has multibanded tail with a broad blackish subterminal band. **Adult female**'s tail is brown toward tip with a thin, black subterminal band. **Juveniles** have a single broad, brown tail band. Wings are long, fairly narrow. Seen in flight from above, white at base of tail is conspicuous; note also the small white patches at base of primaries on upper-wings. In the common light morph, pale head contrasts with darker back and dark belly band, especially in females and imma-tures. Adult male has darker breast markings that may create a bib effect; belly is paler. Observe the square, black carpal patches at the "wrists" of the wings. **Dark morph** is less common. A bird of the open country also seen in marshes in winter, Rough-legged often hovers while hunting. During breeding season gives a soft, plaintive courting whistle. Alarm **call** is a loud screech or squeal.

Ferruginous Hawk   *Buteo regalis*

L 23" (58 cm) WS 56" (142 cm) This hawk has a pale head; extended "gape line" going back under eye; tail is a mixture of pale rust, white, and gray. Wings are long, broad, and pointed; note large, white, crescent-shaped patches on upperwing surface. Seen from below, flight feathers lack barring. **Adults** show rusty color on back and shoulders; rusty leggings form a conspicuous V against whitish underparts spotted with rufous. **Dark morph** is rare; varies from dark rufous to dark brown, with dark undertail coverts. Absence of dark tail bands separates it from dark-morph Rough-legged Hawk. **Juvenile** Ferruginous Hawk almost or entirely lacks rusty leggings and is less rufous above; resembles "Krider's" type of Red-tailed Hawk (preceding page), but wings longer and more pointed. Ferruginous gives harsh alarm **calls,** *kree-a* or *kaah,* chiefly in breeding season. Inhabits dry, open country. Often hovers when hunting or soars in a dihedral. Often sits on ground. **Range:** Casual east to Wisconsin, Illinois, Arkansas, Louisiana, Florida in migra-tion, winter. Very rare migrant to Minnesota; casual in summer.

White-tailed Hawk   *Buteo albicaudatus*

L 20" (51 cm) WS 51" (130 cm) Legs longest of any North Amer-ican buteo. Wings fairly long and pointed; at rest, **adult**'s wing tips project well beyond end of short tail; tail is white with sin-gle black band and other finer bands. Rusty shoulders are highly visible against dark gray upperparts. Underparts and wing lin-ings vary from white on most to lightly barred. Females are darker above, more barred below. **Juveniles** brown above, variable below from mostly blackish to paler; most show a white patch on breast; tail is pale gray; undertail and uppertail coverts whitish, the latter forming a pale U at tail base. Compare with dark morphs of Swainson's (preceding page) and Ferruginous Hawks. Identifiable second-year plumage is intermediate. **Range:** Rare to fairly common in open coastal grasslands and semiarid brush country. Casual to southwest Louisiana.

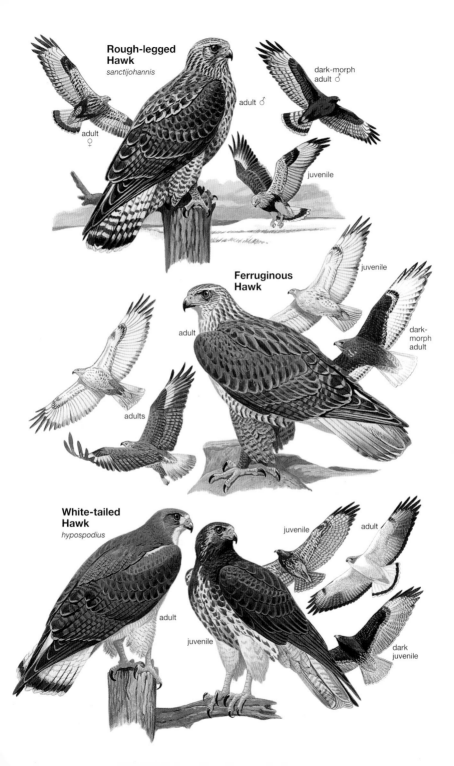

Rough-legged Hawk
sanctijohannis

adult ♀

adult ♂

dark-morph
adult ♂

juvenile

**Ferruginous
Hawk**

juvenile

adult

dark-
morph
adult

adults

**White-tailed
Hawk**
hypospodius

juvenile

adult

adult

juvenile

dark
juvenile

Caracaras, Falcons (Family Falconidae)

These powerful hunters are distinguished from hawks by their long wings, which are bent back at the "wrist" and, except in the Crested Caracara, narrow and pointed. Females are larger than the males. Birds of the genus *Falco* use their notched bills to kill prey by severing its spinal column at the neck. *Species: 64 World, 11 N.A.*

Eurasian Hobby *Falco subbuteo*

L 12¼" (31 cm) WS 30¼" (77 cm) **Range:** Old World species. Casual in late spring and summer in Bering Sea region and on western Aleutians. Record of a bird on a ship off Newfoundland and an Oct. record from Seattle. Small, short-tailed falcon with long, slender wings; in folded wing, wing tips extend well past tip of tail. Graceful and powerful flier. White cheeks; thin, pale eyebrow; thin, dark moustachial stripe; heavily streaked below. **Adult** has rufous-red undertail coverts; is dark gray above. **Juveniles** are blackish brown above with buffy feather fringes; lack rufous below. By following spring some look like adults, others intermediate in appearance. Compare all ages carefully to Merlin and Peregrine Falcon (next two pages).

Aplomado Falcon *Falco femoralis* **E**

L 15-16½" (38-42 cm) WS 40-48" (102-122 cm) **Range:** Once found in open grasslands and deserts from southern Texas to southeastern Arizona. Disappeared by the early 20th century; birds seen in New Mexico and west Texas from 1990s probably from a small extant population in northern Chihuahua, Mexico; recent nesting records southern New Mexico. A reintroduction project is now under way in south coastal Texas and is starting in New Mexico. In flight, often hovers; long, pointed wings and long, banded tail resemble young Mississippi Kite (page 120); underwings are dark, with pale trailing edge. Note slate gray crown, boldly marked head. Pale eyebrows join at back of head. Dark patches on sides sometimes extend across breast. **Juvenile** is cinnamon below with a streaked breast, and browner above.

Crested Caracara *Caracara cheriway* **T**

L 23" (58 cm) WS 50" (127 cm) Large head, long neck, and long legs. Blackish brown overall, with white throat and neck and red-orange to yellow bare facial skin; underparts barred with black. **Juvenile** is browner; upperparts are edged and spotted with buff; underparts streaked with buff, unlike **adult** barring; second-year plumage closer to adult. In flight, shows whitish patches near ends of rounded wings. Flapping, ravenlike flight; soars with flat wings. **Calls** include a low rattle and a single *wuck* note. Inhabits open brushlands; often seen on the ground in company with vultures. Feeds chiefly on carrion; also hunts insects and small animals. **Range:** Fairly common in Texas part of range. Rare in Louisiana and southern Arizona. Casual to southern New Mexico. Records from well outside known range are of debatable origin.

Eurasian Hobby
subbuteo

adult

juvenile

adult

juvenile

adult ♀

juvenile

juvenile ♀

adult ♂

Aplomado Falcon
septentrionalis

Crested Caracara

adult

juvenile

adults

American Kestrel *Falco sparverius*
L 10½" (27 cm) WS 23" (58 cm) Smallest and most common of our falcons. Identified by russet back and tail, double black stripes on white face. Seen in flight from below, **adults** show pale underwings, and **males** a distinctive row of white, circular spots on trailing edge of wings. Male also has blue-gray wing coverts; compare with Merlin and much larger Peregrine Falcon (next page). **Juvenile male** is like adult male, but breast heavily streaked, back completely barred; by first fall looks more like adult, but some dark markings remain. **Call** is a shrill *killy killy killy.* Found in open country and in cities, American Kestrel feeds on insects, reptiles, and small mammals, hovering over prey before plunging. Also eats small birds, chiefly in winter. Often perches on telephone wires; frequently bobs its tail.

Eurasian Kestrel *Falco tinnunculus*
L 13½" (34 cm) WS 29" (74 cm) **Range:** Casual on western Aleutians and in Bering Sea region; accidental in fall, winter, and spring on the East Coast from New Brunswick and Nova Scotia to New Jersey and Florida; and on the West Coast to Washington. Resembles American Kestrel, but note larger size and single, not double, dark facial stripe. In flight, distinguished by wedge-shaped tail and two-toned upperwing, with back and inner wing paler. Hovers as it hunts. **Adult male** has russet wings, gray tail; **female** duller, often with gray rump. **Juvenile** similar to adult female, but dark barring heavier on upperparts and tail.

Merlin *Falco columbarius L 12" (31 cm) WS 25" (64 cm)*
Adult male is gray-blue above; **female** and juveniles usually dark brown. Merlins lack the strong facial markings and russet upperparts of kestrels, and have broader wings than American Kestrel. Plumage varies geographically from the very dark race, *suckleyi,* of the Pacific Northwest to the pale *richardsonii* that breeds on northern Great Plains from southern Canada to northern U.S. A few *suckleyi* winter to southern California; this race has dark cheeks and narrow, incomplete tail bands. All *richardsonii* have pale cheeks; male is paler blue-gray above; female and juvenile are pale brown, the latter with wide, pale tail bands. Winter to southern Great Plains, a few to the Great Basin and Pacific states. The widespread nominate race, *columbarius,* which breeds in the taiga region, is intermediate in plumage; western *columbarius* average slightly paler than eastern. In flight, strongly barred tail distinguishes Merlin from the much larger Peregrine and Prairie Falcons (next page). Underparts and underwings darker than in kestrels, particularly in *suckleyi* and *columbarius,* and head larger. Nests in open woods or wooded prairies; otherwise found in a variety of habitats. Powerful flyer; does not hover. Catches birds in flight by a sudden burst of speed rather than by diving. Also eats large insects and small rodents. **Range:** Fairly common to common on East Coast during fall migration. Many individuals in the Prairie Provinces do not migrate but winter in or near cities. Generally uncommon throughout U.S. in winter.

adult ♀

adult ♂

American Kestrel

adult ♂

adult ♀

juvenile

Eurasian Kestrel

adult ♀

adult ♂

adult ♂

adult ♂

Merlin
columbarius

♀

adult ♂

♀ *suckleyi*

adult ♂
suckleyi

♀ *richardsonii*

adult ♂

adult ♂ *richardsonii*

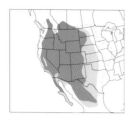

Prairie Falcon *Falco mexicanus*

L 15½-19½" (39-50 cm) WS 35-43" (89-109 cm) Pale brown above; creamy white and heavily spotted below. Brown crown, dark moustachial, and broad pale area below and behind eye; facial markings narrower and plumage paler overall than Peregrine Falcon. Compare also with female and juvenile male Merlin (preceding page), especially subspecies *richardsonii*. In flight (see also next page), all ages show distinctive dark axillaries and dark bar on wing lining, broader on **females.** Juvenile is streaked below (not spotted) and darker above; bluish cere. Preys chiefly on birds and small mammals. **Range:** Inhabits dry, open country, prairies. Uncommon to fairly common. Rare migrant and winter visitor in western Midwest. Casual elsewhere in Midwest and Southeast. Small numbers winter throughout breeding range.

Peregrine Falcon *Falco peregrinus*

L 16-20" (41-51 cm) WS 36-44" (91-112 cm) Crown and nape black; black wedge extends below eye, forming a distinctive helmet, absent in Prairie Falcon and smaller Merlin (preceding page). Tail is shorter than in Prairie; wing tips almost reach the end; also lacks dark bar and axillaries on underwings. Plumage varies from pale in subspecies *tundrius* of the North to very dark in *pealei,* found from Queen Charlotte Islands to the Aleutians. In *pealei,* the largest race, adult has heavy spotting on whitish breast, underparts very dark. Intermediate *anatum* race has thickest moustachial stripe; **adult** shows rufous wash below; **juvenile** is dark brownish above, and underparts are heavily streaked. Juvenile *tundrius* has a pale eyebrow and larger pale area on side of face; underparts more finely streaked. **Range:** Peregrines inhabit open wetlands near cliffs; prey chiefly on birds. Now established also in cities; nest on bridges, tall buildings. Use of pesticides helped eliminate eastern *anatum* breeding populations; now reintroduced in parts of their former range, Peregrines are seen year-round. Most East Coast sightings in the fall are of *tundrius* birds. Uncommon to rare in winter in U.S.

Gyrfalcon *Falco rusticolus*

L 20-25" (51-64 cm) WS 50-64" (127-163 cm) Heavily built; wings broader based than in other falcons. **Adult** has yellow-orange eye ring, cere, and legs (bluish gray in juveniles). Tail broad and tapered; may be barred or unbarred; in perched bird, tail extends far beyond wing tips, unlike other falcons. Compare also with Northern Goshawk (page 126). Plumages vary from **white morph** to **gray morph,** to very **dark morph,** with paler gray morphs intermediate between typical gray and white. Facial markings range from none on white morph to all-dark cheeks on dark morph. Juveniles of white and gray morphs are much browner above; **juveniles** of gray and dark morphs show darker wing linings and paler flight feathers. Gyrfalcon inhabits open tundra near rocky outcrops and cliffs. Flies with slow, powerful wingbeats. Preys chiefly on birds. **Range:** Uncommon; winters irregularly south to dashed line on map. Casual to central California, southern Great Plains, southern Great Lakes, and mid-Atlantic regions.

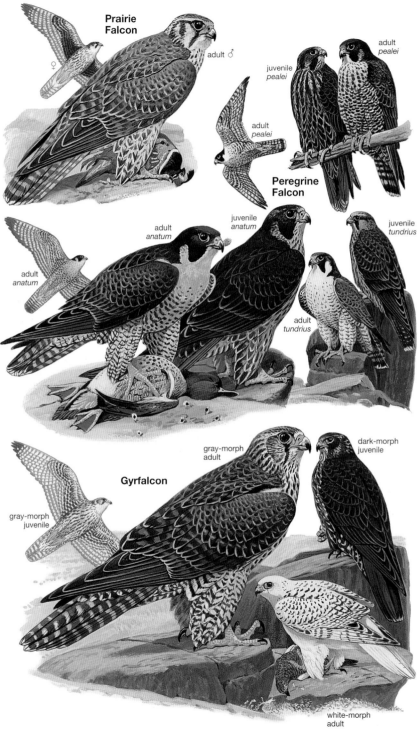

Prairie Falcon

adult ♂

♀

juvenile *pealei*

adult *pealei*

adult *pealei*

Peregrine Falcon

adult *anatum*

juvenile *anatum*

adult *anatum*

adult *tundrius*

juvenile *tundrius*

Gyrfalcon

gray-morph adult

dark-morph juvenile

gray-morph juvenile

white-morph adult

Female Hawks in Flight

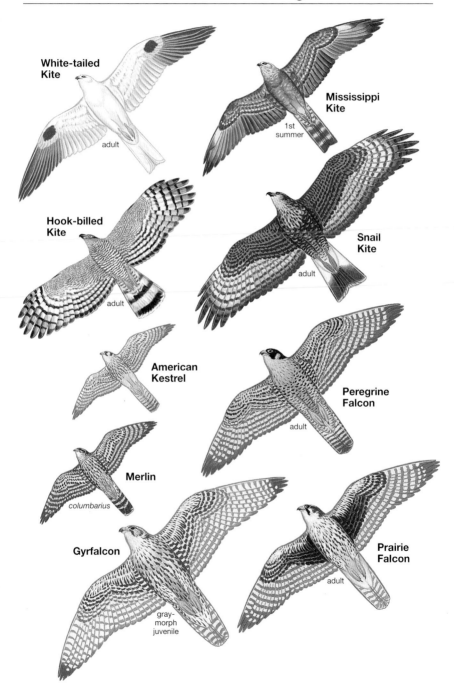

White-tailed Kite — adult

Mississippi Kite — 1st summer

Hook-billed Kite — adult

Snail Kite — adult

American Kestrel

Peregrine Falcon — adult

Merlin — columbarius

Gyrfalcon — gray-morph juvenile

Prairie Falcon — adult

Sharp-shinned
Hawk

adult

Cooper's
Hawk

adult

Northern
Goshawk

adult

Northern
Harrier

adult

Gray
Hawk

adult

Broad-winged
Hawk

adult

Broad-winged
Hawk

dark-
morph
adult

Red-shouldered
Hawk

adult
lineatus

Female Hawks in Flight

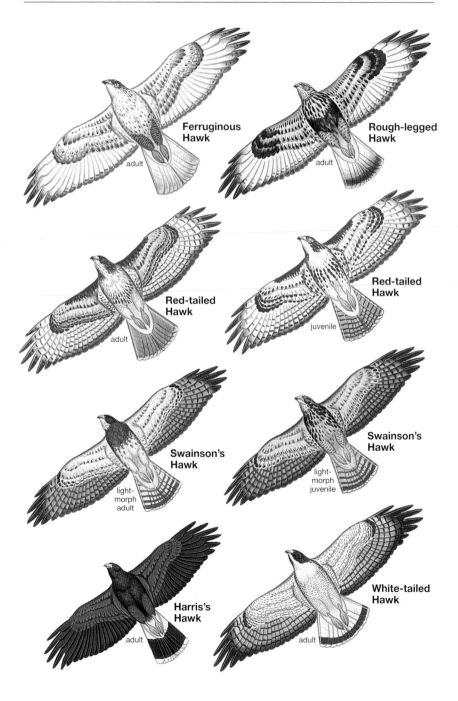

Ferruginous Hawk adult

Rough-legged Hawk adult

Red-tailed Hawk adult

Red-tailed Hawk juvenile

Swainson's Hawk light-morph adult

Swainson's Hawk light-morph juvenile

Harris's Hawk adult

White-tailed Hawk adult

Crested Caracara
adult

Osprey
adult

Zone-tailed Hawk
juvenile

Bald Eagle
2nd year

Common Black-Hawk
adult

Golden Eagle
adult

Black Vulture
adult

Turkey Vulture
adult

Limpkins (Family Aramidae)

Large, long-necked wading bird, named for its unusual limping gait.
Species: 1 World, 1 N.A.

Limpkin *Aramus guarauna* L 26" (66 cm)
Chocolate brown overall, densely streaked with white above.
Long bill, slightly downcurved. Long legs and large, webless feet
are dull grayish green. Juvenile is paler than **adult. Call,** heard
chiefly at night, is a wailing *krr-oww.* **Range:** Generally uncommon in swamps and wetlands, where it wades or swims in search
of snails, frogs, and insects. Rare to fairly common in Florida;
casual in southern Georgia; accidental north to Maryland.

Rails, Gallinules, Coots (Family Rallidae)

These marsh birds have short tails and short, rounded wings. Most
species are local and secretive. Some, especially the rails, are identified chiefly by call and habitat. *Species: 141 World, 14 N.A.*

King Rail *Rallus elegans* L 15" (38 cm)
Large freshwater rail with long, slightly downcurved bill. Much
larger than similar Virginia Rail (next page). Adult distinguished
from Clapper Rail by tawny edges on black-centered back feathers, tawny wing coverts. Head slate, with brown or grayish cheeks,
buffy eyebrow; underparts cinnamon; flanks strongly barred
black-and-white. **Juvenile** is darker above, paler below. King Rail
favors freshwater and brackish swamps and marshes but hard to
see. As with Clapper Rail, most often heard at dusk and dawn.
Usually distinctive **call** is a series of fewer than ten *kek kek kek*
notes, fairly evenly spaced. **Range:** Fairly common to common
in freshwater habitat near Gulf Coast; generally rather rare and
local well inland in East. Rare in west Texas, where it may breed.
Casual west to Colorado. Some birds winter in coastal marshes
with Clapper Rails. Hybridizes with Clapper Rail in narrow zone
of overlap; some calls of the two are identical.

Clapper Rail *Rallus longirostris* L 14½" (37 cm)
Much larger than Virginia Rail (next page). Plumage variable but
always has grayish edges on brown-centered back feathers, olive
wing coverts. East Coast subspecies such as *crepitans* are much
duller than King Rail: buffy below; cheeks gray; flanks less
strongly barred than in King. Gulf Coast races such as *scottii* are
brighter cinnamon below. West Coast races such as *levipes* (**E**)
and inland *yumanensis* (**E**) are brighter below than East Coast
birds; cheeks brownish gray. Clapper's **call** is a series of ten or
more dry *kek kek kek* notes, like King but accelerating and then
slowing. **Range:** Common in coastal salt marshes except on West
Coast, where populations have declined since introduction of the
red fox; also found along lower Colorado River and at Salton Sea.
In East, casual north to Maritimes.

Limpkin
pictus

adult

King Rail
elegans

adult

juvenile

crepitans

yumanensis

Clapper Rail

scottii

"Light-footed"
levipes

Virginia Rail *Rallus limicola L 9½" (24 cm)*
Similar to King Rail (preceding page) but smaller; cheeks grayer; wings richer chestnut; legs and bill often redder. **Juvenile** is blackish brown above, mottled black or gray below. **Song** a series of *kid kid kidick kidick* phrases, heard chiefly in breeding season; common **call,** heard year-round, is a descending series of *oink* notes. **Range:** Common but a bit secretive; found in freshwater and brackish marshes and wetlands; also in coastal salt marshes.

Sora *Porzana carolina L 8¾" (22 cm)*
Short, thick bill, yellow or greenish yellow. **Breeding adult** is coarsely streaked above. Face and center of throat and breast are black. In **winter** plumage, black throat is somewhat obscured by gray edgings. **Juvenile** lacks black on face and throat; underparts are paler. Compare with Yellow Rail; juvenile Sora is not as black above; upperparts streaked, not barred, with white. **Calls** heard year-round are a descending whinny and a sharp, high-pitched *keek;* a whistled *ker-wheer* is heard on breeding grounds. **Range:** Common in freshwater and brackish marshes, rice fields, grainfields; found in saltwater marshes during migration and winter.

Yellow Rail *Coturnicops noveboracensis L 7¼" (18 cm)*
A small, dark rail, deep tawny yellow above with wide dark stripes crossed by white bars. In flight, shows a large white patch on trailing edges of wings. Bill is short and thick; color varies from yellowish to greenish gray. **Juvenile** is darker than adult. Distinctive **call,** heard chiefly in breeding season, a four- or five-note *tick-tick, tick-tick-tick* in alternate twos or twos and threes, sounds like tapping two pebbles together. **Range:** Uncommon and local; secretive. Breeds in grassy marshes, boggy swales, damp fields; not found in deepwater marshes or swamps. Rare in the West. Winters in fresh, brackish, or salt marshes, rice fields, dry fields.

Black Rail *Laterallus jamaicensis L 6" (15 cm)*
Very small, extremely secretive. Blackish above, with white speckling; chestnut nape. Bill short and black. Underparts grayish black, with narrow white barring on flanks. Newly hatched juveniles of other rails resemble Black Rail. Unlike other rails, most vocal in the middle of the night. Distinctive **call,** heard chiefly in breeding season, is a repeated *kik-kee-do* or *kik-kee-derr;* sometimes four notes: *kik-kik-kee-do.* **Range:** Uncommon and local; inhabits marshes, swamps, wet meadows. Very irregular inland; range speculative; declining in some coastal areas.

Corn Crake *Crex crex L 10½" (27 cm)*
Range: European species, formerly a very rare vagrant in fall along the East Coast; recently only three fall records: Saint-Pierre, Nova Scotia, and Avalon Peninsula, Newfoundland. Western European populations have seriously declined over last decades. Found in damp, grassy fields, croplands, not in marshes. Dull buffy yellow overall, with short, thick, brownish bill; distinctive large chestnut wing patch.

juvenile

Virginia Rail
limicola

Sora

winter
♀

juvenile   breeding adult ♂

juvenile

Yellow Rail
noveboracensis

**Black
Rail**
jamaicensis

**Corn
Crake**

Purple Gallinule *Porphyrio martinica* L 13" (33 cm)

Bright purplish blue head, neck, and underparts, with pale blue forehead shield, red-and-yellow bill. Legs and feet bright yellow. **Juvenile** is buffy brown overall, with brownish olive back, greenish wings; bill mostly dark olive, legs and feet dull olive. Molts into winter plumage after fall migration but may retain traces of juvenal plumage into first spring. In all ages, all-white undertail coverts are conspicuous. **Range:** Fairly common in overgrown swamps, lagoons, and marshes. Highly migratory; winters from southern Florida to Argentina. Wanderers are seen in all seasons far north of mapped range; frequently breeds north of area shown.

Purple Swamphen *Porphyrio porphyrio*

L 18-20" (45-50 cm) **Range:** Widespread species from southern Europe to island groups in tropical South Pacific. Various subspecies groups are recognized, some of which perhaps deserve recognition as separate species. Introduced into south Florida in 1996 and has slowly spread. Resembles a huge Purple Gallinule with reddish bill and frontal shield, iris and legs. Florida birds appear to belong to the *poliocephalus* group subspecies (three included) from southern Asia with grayish blue neck, or possibly closely allied *viridis* (mainland Southeast Asia), but some bluer-headed swamphens likely represent other subspecies.

Common Moorhen *Gallinula chloropus* L 14" (36 cm)

Black head and neck, with red forehead shield, red bill with yellow tip. Back brownish olive; underparts slate; white along flanks is diagnostic. Outer undertail coverts white, inner ones black. Legs and feet yellow. **Juvenile** is paler, browner; throat whitish; bill and legs dusky. **Winter adult** has brownish facial shield and usually a brownish bill with dusky yellow tip. **Range:** Common in freshwater marshes, ponds, and placid rivers; now uncommon to rare and declining from much of interior range.

American Coot *Fulica americana* L 15½" (39 cm)

Overall blackish, darker on head and neck; outer undertail coverts white. Whitish bill has dark subterminal band; note reddish brown forehead shield. Leg color ranges from greenish gray in **juvenile** birds to yellow or orangish in adults. Toes are lobed, unlike gallinules. Juvenile is quite pale; by first winter more like adult, but still paler, with whitish feather tips, especially below. In flight, white trailing edge on most of wing is distinctive. A few **variant** American Coots have extensively white facial shields like Caribbean Coot, *F. caribaea*, of the West Indies. Regarded by some as a subspecies of American, Caribbean has not yet been verified in Florida. **Range:** American Coot is common to abundant. Nests in freshwater marshes, wetlands, or near lakes and ponds; winters in both fresh and salt water, usually in large flocks. Often dives to feed.

Eurasian Coot *Fulica atra* L 15¾" (40 cm)

Range: Accidental straggler to Newfoundland, Labrador, Quebec, and the Pribilofs. Slightly larger and darker than American Coot; undertail coverts all-black. Forehead shield and bill entirely white.

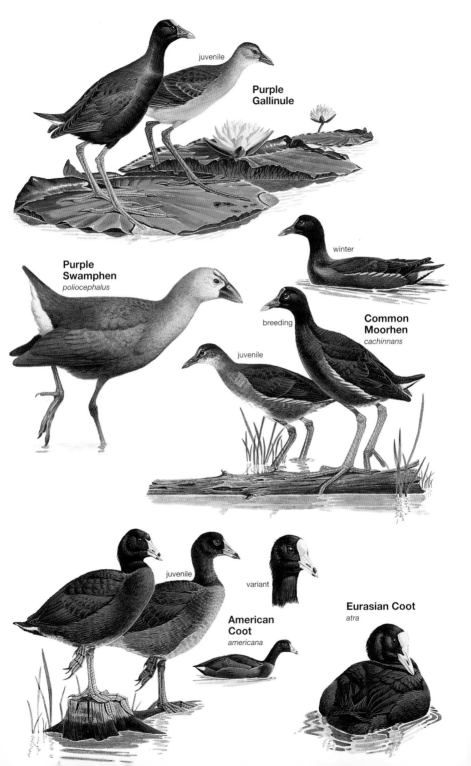

juvenile

Purple Gallinule

winter

Purple Swamphen
poliocephalus

breeding

Common Moorhen
cachinnans

juvenile

juvenile

variant

American Coot
americana

Eurasian Coot
atra

Cranes (Family Gruidae)

Tall birds with long necks and legs. Tertials droop over the rump in a "bustle" that distinguishes cranes from herons. Cranes fly with their necks fully extended and circle in thermals like raptors. Courtship includes a frenzied, leaping dance. *Species: 15 World, 3 N.A.*

Sandhill Crane *Grus canadensis*

L 34-48" (86-122 cm) WS 73-90" (185-229 cm) Races vary in size: northern nominate race smallest; more southerly *tabida* largest. Resident Florida race, *pratensis,* and endangered Gulf Coast race, *pulla* (**E**), are intermediate. **Adult** is gray, with dull red skin on crown and lores; whitish chin, cheek, and upper throat; and slaty primaries. **Juvenile** lacks red patch; head and neck vary from pale to tawny; gray body is irregularly mottled with brownish red; full adult plumage reached after two and a half years. Great Blue Heron (page 114), sometimes confused with Sandhill Crane, lacks bustle. Preening with muddy bills, cranes may stain feathers of upper back, lower neck, and breast with ferrous solution in mud. Common **call** is a trumpeting, rattling *gar-oo-oo,* audible for more than a mile. **Range:** Locally common; breeds on tundra and in marshes and grasslands. In winter, regularly feeds in dry fields, returning to water at night. Resident near parts of the Gulf Coast, in Florida, and in Cuba; other North American subspecies migratory. Rare during fall and winter on East Coast from Massachusetts south. Migrating flocks fly at great heights, sometimes too high to be seen from the ground.

Common Crane *Grus grus*

L 44-51" (112-130 cm) WS 79-91" (202-231 cm) **Range:** Eurasian species, casual vagrant on the Great Plains, accidental farther east; almost always with migrating flocks of Sandhill Cranes. Some records involve a mixed Common-Sandhill pair with accompanying hybrid young. **Adult** distinguished from Sandhill Crane by blackish head and neck marked by broad white stripe. **Juvenile** like juvenile Sandhill; may show trace of white head stripe by spring. In flight, in all ages, black primaries and secondaries show as a broad black trailing edge on gray wings.

Whooping Crane *Grus americana* **E**

L 52" (132 cm) WS 87" (221 cm) **Range:** Sparse wild population breeds in freshwater marshes of Wood Buffalo National Park, Canada, and winters in Aransas National Wildlife Refuge on Gulf Coast of Texas. A small population has been introduced in Florida. **Adult** is white overall, with red facial skin; black primaries show in flight. **Juvenile** bird is whitish, with pale reddish brown head and neck and scattered reddish brown feathers over the rest of its body; begins to acquire adult plumage after first summer. A few abnormally colored Sandhill Cranes of *tabida* race ("Greater Sandhill Crane") have been taken for Whooping Cranes; check wingtip pattern. **Call** is a shrill, trumpeting *ker-loo ker-lee-loo.* Endangered: Wild population is now about 150, including introductions. Intensive management and protection seem to be slowly succeeding.

juvenile

adult

Sandhill Crane
rowani

stained
adult

adult

juvenile

adult

Common Crane
lilfordi

adult

adult

adult

juvenile

Whooping Crane

Lapwings, Plovers (Family Charadriidae)

These compact birds run and stop abruptly when foraging. Shape and behavior identify plovers in general. *Species: 66 World, 17 N.A.*

Black-bellied Plover *Pluvialis squatarola L 11½" (29 cm)*
Black-and-white **breeding male** has frosty crown and nape, white belly region; **female** averages less black. **Winter** and **juvenile** birds distinguished from Pacific and American Golden-Plovers by larger size, larger bill, and grayer plumage (including crown); underparts streaked rather than softly barred, but note that juvenile can be speckled with gold above. In flight, shows black axillaries and white uppertail coverts, barred white tail, and bold white wing stripe. **Call** is a drawn-out, three-note whistle, the second note lower-pitched. **Range:** Nests on Arctic tundra. Common migrant in Great Lakes region. Uncommon to rare elsewhere in interior.

American Golden-Plover *Pluvialis dominica*
L 10¼" (26 cm) Smaller, with a smaller bill than Black-bellied Plover; wing stripe is indistinct, and underwings are smoky gray with no black in axillaries; no contrasting white rump. Note the four evenly spaced primary tips. **Breeding male** shows broad white patches on sides of neck; underparts otherwise black. **Female** has less black. Flight **call** is a shrill *ku-wheep.* **Range:** Mar. arrivals are in winter plumage; breeding plumage slowly acquired on migration north. Rare fall migrant in West (apparently all **juveniles**). Winters in South America.

Pacific Golden-Plover *Pluvialis fulva L 9¾" (25 cm)*
Similar to American, but shorter primary tip projection with three, not four, staggered primary tips, the outer two close together; bill appears thicker, legs longer. **Breeding male** has less extensive white on sides of neck than American; white continues down sides and flanks; undertail coverts whiter; slightly larger gold markings above. Female has less black below. **Juveniles** and **winter** birds typically appear brighter than American. **Call,** a loud, rich *chu-wheet.* In Alaska, Americans favor less vegetated slopes; Pacifics, the coast and river valleys. **Range:** Breeds from northern Russia to western Alaska. Winters from southern Asia to Pacific islands; a few on West Coast and in central California. Some adults migrate earlier in fall than other golden-plovers.

European Golden-Plover *Pluvialis apricaria*
L 11" (28 cm) **Range:** Breeds from Greenland and Iceland to northwestern Russia. Winters from Europe to North Africa. Irregular spring migrant to Newfoundland and Labrador; casually to eastern Quebec and Nova Scotia. Similar to Pacific Golden-Plover; note larger size, plumper body shape, white underwings; also small bill and bolder wing bar. On **breeding males,** white nearly meets on front of breast; sides, flanks, and undertail coverts are more purely white than on Pacific; note dense pattern of smaller gold spots on upperparts, unlike coarser pattern of larger spots on other golden-plovers. **Call** is a mournful, drawn-out whistle.

juveniles in flight

European   Pacific   American   Black-bellied

bright
juvenile

winter   breeding ♀

juvenile

**Black-bellied
Plover**

breeding ♂

bright
juvenile   juvenile   April ♂   breeding ♀

breeding ♂

**American
Golden-Plover**

juveniles   winter   breeding ♂

breeding
♀

breeding ♂

**Pacific
Golden-Plover**

juveniles   breeding ♂   breeding ♀

**European
Golden-Plover**
altifrons

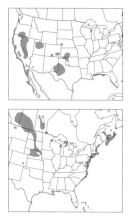

Snowy Plover *Charadrius alexandrinus* L 6¼" (16 cm)
Pale above, very pale in Gulf Coast birds; thin dark bill; dark or grayish legs; partial breast band; dark ear patch. **Females** and **juveniles** resemble Piping Plover; note Snowy Plover's thinner bill, darker legs. **Calls** include a low *krut* and a soft, whistled *ku-wheet*. **Range:** Inhabits barren sandy beaches and flats. Uncommon and declining on Gulf Coast. Western *nivosus* is threatened (**T**).

Piping Plover *Charadrius melodus* **E** L 7¼" (18 cm)
Very pale above; orange legs; white rump conspicuous in flight (page 196). In **breeding** plumage, shows dark narrow breast band usually complete in *circumcinctus*, sometimes incomplete, especially in **females** and paler-faced East Coast birds, *melodus*. In **winter,** bill is all-dark. Distinguished from Snowy Plover by thicker bill, paler back; legs are brighter than in Semipalmated Plover. Distinctive **call,** a clear *peep-lo.* **Range:** Found on sandy beaches, lakeshores, and dunes. Endangered: generally uncommon; rare and declining breeder in the Midwest; rare migrant in interior. In winter, *melodus* winters mainly on south Atlantic coast and northern Bahamas; *circumcinctus* on Gulf Coast. Casual in winter to coastal southern California.

Wilson's Plover *Charadrius wilsonia* L 7¾" (20 cm)
Long, very heavy, black bill; broad neck band is black in **breeding male,** brown in **female** and winter male; legs grayish pink. **Juvenile** resembles adult female but note scaly-looking upperparts. Breeding male may have cinnamon-buff ear patch. **Call** is a sharp, whistled *whit.* **Range:** Fairly common but declining on barrier islands, sandy beaches, mud flats. Recorded casually to California and the Maritimes and inland to Great Lakes region.

Semipalmated Plover *Charadrius semipalmatus*
L 7¼" (18 cm) Dark back distinguishes this species from Piping and Snowy Plovers; bill much smaller than in Wilson's Plover (flight figures page 196). At very close range, Semipalmated shows partial webbing between toes. **Breeding male** often lacks white above eye; shows orangish eye ring. **Juvenile** has darker legs than adults'. Distinctive **call** is a whistled, upslurred *chu-weet;* **song** a series of same. **Range:** Common on beaches, lakeshores, and tidal flats; seen throughout the continent in migration.

Common Ringed Plover *Charadrius hiaticula*
L 7½" (19 cm) Almost identical to Semipalmated Plover; best distinguished by **call,** a soft, fluted *pooee;* **song,** delivered in display flight, is a series of these notes. Breast band averages slightly broader in center than in Semipalmated. White eyebrow is more distinct; eye ring is partial or lacking altogether; webbing between toes less extensive. Bill is slightly longer, of more even thickness, and shows more orange at base; black on face meets bill where mandibles join. **Range:** Regular but rare spring migrant on western Alaska islands; occasionally breeds on St. Lawrence Island. Casual on East Coast south to Massachusetts.

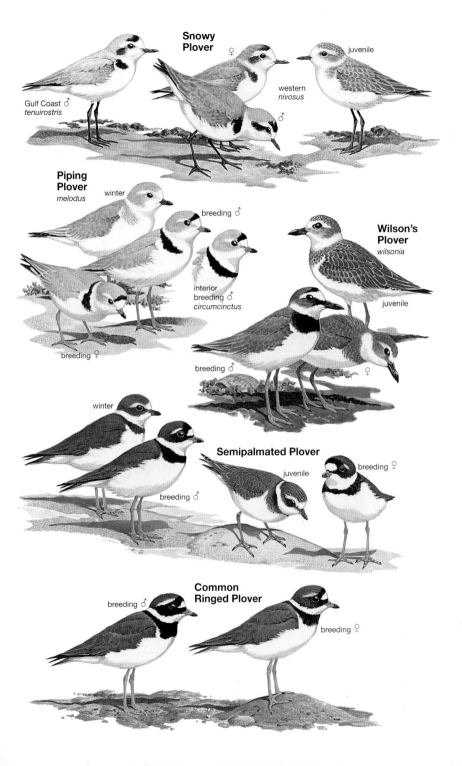

Snowy Plover ♀

western *nivosus*

juvenile

Gulf Coast ♂
tenuirostris

♂

Piping Plover
melodus

winter

breeding ♂

interior
breeding ♂
circumcinctus

breeding ♀

Wilson's Plover
wilsonia

juvenile

breeding ♂

♀

winter

breeding ♂

Semipalmated Plover

juvenile

breeding ♀

Common Ringed Plover

breeding ♂

breeding ♀

Lesser Sand-Plover *Charadrius mongolus L 7½" (19 cm)*
Range: Asian species, rare migrant on Aleutians and on islands off western Alaska; casual along West Coast. Casual in summer in western and northwestern Alaska, where it has bred. Accidental in eastern North America. Bright rusty red breast; black-and-white facial pattern. **Females** are duller. **Juvenile** has broad buffy wash across breast; edged with buff above. In **winter** birds, underparts are white except for broad grayish patches on sides of breast.

Little Ringed Plover *Charadrius dubius L 6" (15 cm)*
Range: Old World species. Casual spring vagrant to western Aleutians. A small, slim plover with conspicuous yellow eye ring; legs rather dull color. In flight (page 196), note lack of wing bar. In **breeding** adult, white line separates brown forecrown from rear of head. On winter birds and **juveniles,** brown replaces black on head and breast, and eye ring is slightly duller; juvenile often shows yellow-buff tint to pale areas on head and throat. Rather solitary. **Call** is a descending *pee-oo* that carries a long way.

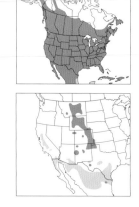

Killdeer *Charadrius vociferus L 10½" (27 cm)*
Double breast bands distinctive, as is Killdeer's loud, piercing **call,** *kill-dee* or *dee-dee-dee*. Bright reddish orange rump is visible in flight (page 196). Downy young have only one breast band. **Range:** Common in grassy fields and on shores. Nests on open ground, usually on gravel. May form loose flocks and linger into early winter in summer range. Vagrant north of breeding range.

Mountain Plover *Charadrius montanus L 9" (23 cm)*
In **breeding** plumage, unbanded white underparts separate this plover from all other brown-backed plovers. Buffy tinge on breast is more extensive in **winter** plumage; compare with winter American Golden-Plover (page 154). In flight, Mountain Plover shows white underwings; American Golden-Plover's are grayish. **Calls** heard on breeding grounds include low, drawn-out whistles and harsh notes. In migration and winter, gives a harsh *krrr* note. **Range:** Inhabits plains; local and declining in many areas. Gregarious in winter; usually found on grassy or bare dirt fields.

Northern Lapwing *Vanellus vanellus L 12½" (32 cm)*
Range: Eurasian species, casual primarily in late fall in northeast states and provinces; accidental elsewhere in East; recorded south to Florida. Most sightings of birds in **winter** plumage: dark, iridescent above, white below, with black breast; wispy but prominent crest. Wings broad and rounded, with white tips, white wing linings. Flight **call** is a whistled *pee-wit.*

Eurasian Dotterel *Charadrius morinellus L 8¼" (21 cm)*
Range: Eurasian species, very approachable; uncommon, sporadic breeder in northwestern Alaska; casual along West Coast in fall. Whitish band on lower breast is somewhat obscured in young and **winter** birds. Bold white eyebrow extends around entire head. Unlike other plovers, **females** are brighter than males. **Juvenile** is darker above, buffy below.

breeding ♀

Little Ringed Plover
curonicus

juvenile

breeding ♂

Lesser Sand-Plover
stegmanni

breeding ♂

winter

juvenile

winter

Killdeer

Mountain Plover

winter

breeding

breeding ♂

winter

juvenile

Eurasian Dotterel

winter

breeding ♀

Northern Lapwing

winter

winter

winter

juvenile

Jacanas (Family Jacanidae)

Extremely long toes and claws allow these tropical birds to walk on lily pads and other floating plants. *Species: 8 World, 1 N.A.*

Northern Jacana *Jacana spinosa L 9½" (24 cm)*
Range: Mexican and Central American species, casual visitor to ponds and marshes in southern Texas, where it has probably bred. Accidental to west Texas and southern Arizona. Often raises its wings, revealing yellow flight feathers.

Oystercatchers (Family Haematopodidae)

These chunky shorebirds have laterally flattened, heavy bills that can reach into mollusks and pry the shells open; they also probe sand for worms and crabs. *Species: 11 World, 3 N.A.*

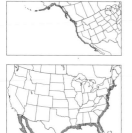

Black Oystercatcher *Haematopus bachmani*
L 17½" (45 cm) Large red-orange bill, all-dark body, pinkish legs. On immatures, outer half of bill is dusky during first year. **Range:** Resident on rocky shores and islands along the Pacific coast.

American Oystercatcher *Haematopus palliatus*
L 18½" (47 cm) Large red-orange bill. Black head and dark brown back; white wing and tail patches, white underparts. **Juvenile** appears scaly above; dark tip on bill is kept through first year. Birds feed in small, noisy flocks on coastal beaches and mudflats. **Range:** Expanding northward in the East; recently established as a breeder on Cape Sable Island, Nova Scotia. Casual in southern California, where has hybridized with Black Oystercatcher.

Stilts, Avocets (Family Recurvirostridae)

Sleek and graceful waders with long, slender bills and spindly legs. Two species inhabit North America. *Species: 7 World, 3 N.A.*

American Avocet *Recurvirostra americana L 18" (46 cm)*
Black-and-white above, white below; head and neck rusty in breeding plumage, gray in winter. **Juveniles** have cinnamon wash on head and neck. Avocets feed by sweeping their bills from side to side through the water. **Male**'s bill is longer, straighter than **female**'s. Common **call** is a loud *wheet*. **Range:** Fairly common on shallow ponds, marshes, and lakeshores.

Black-necked Stilt *Himantopus mexicanus L 14" (36 cm)*
Male's glossy black back and bill contrast sharply with white under-parts, long red or pink legs. Female is browner on back. **Juvenile** is brown above, with buffy edgings. Common **call** is a loud *kek kek kek*. **Range:** Breeds and winters in a wide variety of wet habitats; breeding range is spreading north. Casual north to Great Lakes.

Northern Jacana
gymnostoma

immature

adult

Black Oystercatcher
adult

adults

juvenile

American Oystercatcher
palliatus

breeding ♀

juvenile ♂

breeding ♀

winter ♂

American Avocet

juvenile

Black-necked Stilt

♂

Sandpipers, Phalaropes, Allies
(Family Scolopacidae)

The majority of these shorebirds have three distinct plumages. Most begin molting to winter plumage as they near or reach their winter grounds. *Species: 92 World, 65 N.A.*

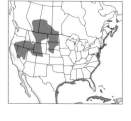

Willet *Tringa semipalmata* L 15" (38 cm)

Large, plump, and grayish overall with grayish legs. In flight, note black-and-white wing pattern. Two subspecies: eastern *semipalmata* is smaller, darker, browner, and thicker billed than western *inornata* in all plumages. **Breeding** *semipalmata* is more heavily barred below with more pinkish-based bill than *inornata*. **Juvenile** *semipalmata* has more contrasting scapulars than *inornata*. Separating winter birds to subspecies best done by structural features and range. Winter-plumaged *semipalmata* typically not seen in North America, except for early Mar. arrivals on Gulf Coast. Territorial call is *pill-will-willet*, distinctly faster and higher-pitched in nominate race. Other raucous calls are given year-round, all averaging higher-pitched in the nominate race. **Range:** Nominate *semipalmata* nests in coastal Atlantic and Gulf salt marshes; *inornata* in interior marshes. In fall *semipalmata* is an early migrant, most departing by early Aug., and winters entirely outside North America (mainly South America).

Lesser Yellowlegs *Tringa flavipes* L 10½" (27 cm)

Legs yellow to rarely orange. Smaller than Greater Yellowlegs; all-dark bill is shorter, thinner, and straighter. In **breeding** plumage, not nearly as heavily as marked as Greater Yellowlegs, especially on sides and flanks. **Juvenile** and **winter** birds are overall darker than Greater; juvenile Lessers are washed with grayish brown across the neck and lack the streaks that are present in Greater. A more sedate feeder than Greater, leisurely picks at prey from a more vertical position. **Call** is one to three *tew* notes, a little higher than Greater Yellowlegs, the individual notes being more clipped and all on one pitch. **Range:** Common in the East (often abundant on Great Plains and Midwest); uncommon in far West, especially in spring (more numerous in fall). Nests on tundra or in woodland. On nesting grounds, like Greater, often perches in trees and yelps at intruders. Most winter in South America, a few in U.S.

Greater Yellowlegs *Tringa melanoleuca* L 14" (36 cm)

Legs yellow to orange. Larger than Lesser Yellowlegs; bill longer, stouter, often slightly upturned, and, in all plumages except breeding, two toned. In **breeding** plumage, throat and breast are heavily streaked; sides and belly are spotted and barred with black; bill is all black. In **juvenile** birds the neck is distinctly streaked. Behavior is more active than Lesser Yellowlegs, often racing about with extended neck while pursuing prey (often very small fish). **Call** is a loud, slightly descending series of three or more *tew* notes. **Range:** Fairly common; nests on muskeg, winters in wetland habitats. Compared to Lesser Yellowlegs, Greater is overall a later fall migrant and is much more capable of wintering at interior locations.

Willet

early March in molt

western

eastern

breeding

eastern *semipalmata*

juvenile

winter

worn breeding

western *inornata*

winter

breeding

juvenile

Lesser Yellowlegs

breeding

winter

juvenile

winter

winter

breeding

winter

juvenile

Greater Yellowlegs

Common Greenshank *Tringa nebularia L 13½" (34 cm)*
Range: Common Eurasian species that annually visits western
Alaska in spring: rare to Aleutian and Pribilof Islands; casual to
St. Lawrence Island; casual in western Alaska in fall. Accidental to
northeast Canada and coastal northwest California. In plumage
and structure resembles Greater Yellowlegs, but less heavily
streaked; legs are greenish. In flight, white wedge extends up the
middle of back. Typical flight **call** is a loud *tew-tew-tew*, very
much like Greater Yellowlegs, but the notes are all on one pitch.

Marsh Sandpiper *Tringa stagnatilis L 8½" (21 cm)*
Range: Old World species. Common in Asia. Casual in central
and western Aleutians (three fall records). One wintered recently
on Oahu. A small and slender *Tringa* with a long needle-like bill
and disproportionately long, greenish legs; distinct supercilium
in all plumages. Plumages overall suggestive of Common Greenshank. In **breeding** neck and sides are streaked and spotted with
brown and mottled with black above. **Juvenile** is faintly streaked
on sides of breast, brownish above with pale buff edges. **Winter**
adult pale gray and uniform above and with long needle bill suggests a winter-plumaged Wilson's Phalarope; Marsh has much
longer legs. In flight, white wedge extends up back; note long leg
projection past tail. **Call** is a *tew* note, like call of Lesser Yellowlegs; often delivered in a series.

Common Redshank *Tringa totanus L 11" (28 cm)*
Range: Eurasian species; breeds as close to North America as Iceland; numerous records for Greenland. Casual to Newfoundland
in spring, once in winter. Bright orange legs, stout bill with reddish orange base, overall brownish plumage with distinct eye ring.
Juvenile and **breeding** birds are extensively streaked below; winter birds (not illustrated) are diffusely mottled below. In flight,
shows white dorsal wedge up back and distinctive broad white
trailing edge to secondaries and inner primaries. **Calls** include
a musical *tew* or more mournful *tew-hieu*. Alarm note is a series
of *twek* notes.

Spotted Redshank *Tringa erythropus L 12½" (32 cm)*
Range: Eurasian species, rare spring and fall visitor to Aleutian
and Pribilof Islands; casual on both coasts during migration and
winter; accidental elsewhere. Long bill with red-based lower
mandible, droops at tip. **Breeding adult** is black overall with
white spots above; legs dark red to blackish. Many underparts
variably marked with white. **Juvenile** is brownish gray and is
heavily barred and spotted below. **Winter** birds are pale gray
above, spotted with white on coverts and tertials. Some fall North
American sightings involve young birds in transitional plumage.
Both plumages show brighter orange legs. In flight, shows white
wedge on back and white wing linings. Distinctive **call,** a loud
rising *chu-weet* closely resembles the call of Semipalmated Plover.

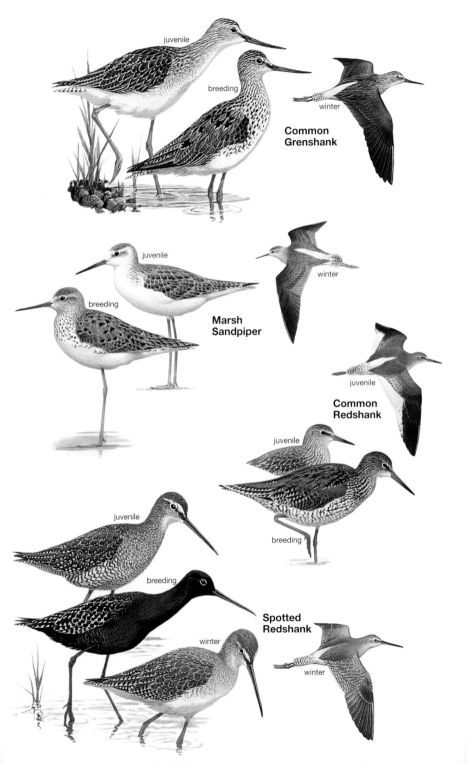

juvenile

breeding

winter

Common Grenshank

juvenile

breeding

winter

Marsh Sandpiper

juvenile

Common Redshank

juvenile

breeding

juvenile

breeding

winter

Spotted Redshank

winter

Wood Sandpiper *Tringa glareola L 8" (20 cm)*

Range: Eurasian species, fairly common spring migrant and occasional breeder on the outer Aleutians; uncommon on the Pribilofs; rare on St. Lawrence Island. Casual to British Columbia and northeast North America. Dark upperparts are heavily spotted with buff; prominent whitish eyebrow. In flight (page 195), distinguished from Green Sandpiper by paler wing linings, smaller white rump patch, and more densely barred tail. Bill is straight like Green, but shorter. Common **call** is a loud, sharp whistling of three or more notes, similar to the call of Long-billed Dowitcher.

Green Sandpiper *Tringa ochropus L 8¾" (22 cm)*

Range: Eurasian species, casual in spring on outer Aleutians, Pribilofs, and St. Lawrence Island. Resembles Solitary Sandpiper in plumage, behavior, and calls. Structure also similar, but a little plumper, straighter billed. Note white rump and uppertail coverts, with less extensively barred tail; lacks solidly dark central tail feathers of Solitary; upperparts and wing linings are darker. Similar Wood Sandpiper has more spotting above, more barring on tail, and paler wing linings. **Call** is like Solitary, but louder.

Solitary Sandpiper *Tringa solitaria L 8½" (22 cm)*

Dark brown above, heavily spotted with buffy white. White below; lower throat, breast, and sides streaked with blackish brown. Bolder white eye ring and shorter, olive legs distinguish Solitary Sandpiper from Lesser Yellowlegs (page 162). In flight (page 195), shows dark central tail feathers, white outer feathers barred with black. Underwing is dark. Two subspecies: nominate *solitaria* (illustrated) from East is spotted with white in breeding plumage; spots more cinnamon-buff in western *cinnamomea*. **Calls** include a shrill *peet-weet,* higher-pitched than calls of Spotted Sandpiper. Often keeps wings raised briefly after alighting; on the ground, often bobs its tail. Generally seen singly or in small flocks. Fairly common at shallow backwaters, pools, small estuaries, even rain puddles.

Terek Sandpiper *Xenus cinereus L 9" (23 cm)*

Range: Eurasian species, rare migrant on outer Aleutians; casual on Pribilofs, St. Lawrence Island, and in Anchorage area. Accidental in fall to coastal British Columbia, California, and Massachusetts. Note long, upturned bill and short orange-yellow legs. In **breeding adult,** dark-centered scapulars form two dark lines on back. In flight, shows distinctive wing pattern: dark leading edge, grayer median coverts, dark greater coverts, and white-tipped secondaries. Flight **call** is a series of shrill whistled notes on one pitch, usually in threes.

Wood Sandpiper

juvenile

breeding

breeding

Solitary Sandpiper breeding

juvenile

Green Sandpiper breeding

breeding

Green Sandpiper

breeding

juvenile

Solitary Sandpiper
solitaria

breeding

breeding

juvenile

Terek Sandpiper

Wandering Tattler   *Tringa incana   L 11" (28 cm)*

Uniformly dark gray above; white eyebrow flecked with gray; bill dark, legs dull yellow. In **breeding** plumage, underparts are heavily barred. **Juvenile** and **winter** birds have only a dark gray wash over breast, sides, and flanks; juvenile has pale spots above. Closely resembles Gray-tailed Tattler; best distinguished by voice. Wandering Tattler's **call** is a rapid series of clear, hollow whistles, all on one pitch. Often teeters and bobs as it feeds. **Range:** Breeds chiefly on gravelly stream banks. Winters on rocky coasts. Generally seen singly or in small groups. Casual inland during migration. Accidental to eastern North America.

Gray-tailed Tattler   *Tringa brevipes   L 10" (25 cm)*

Range: Asian species, regular spring and fall migrant on outer Aleutians, Pribilofs, and St. Lawrence Island; casual visitor to northern Alaska. Accidental in fall to Washington and California. Closely resembles Wandering Tattler; upperparts are slightly paler; barring on underparts finer and less extensive; whitish eyebrows are more distinct and meet on forehead. Diagnostic shorter nasal groove hard to see in field. **Juvenile** has less extensive gray on underparts; white flanks and belly; more pale spotting above. Best distinction is voice. Gray-tailed Tattler's common **call** is a loud, ascending *too-weet,* similar to call of Common Ringed Plover.

Common Sandpiper   *Actitis hypoleucos   L 8" (20 cm)*

Range: Eurasian species, rare but regular migrant, usually in spring, on the outer Aleutians, Pribilofs, and St. Lawrence Island; casual to Seward Peninsula. **Breeding adult** is brown above with dark barring and streaking; white below; upper breast finely streaked. **Juvenile** and winter birds resemble Spotted Sandpiper. Note Common Sandpiper's longer tail; in juvenile, barring on edge of tertials extends along the entire feather. In flight, shows longer white wing stripe and longer white trailing edge; wingbeats not as shallow and rapid. **Call** in flight is a shrill, piping *twee-wee-wee.*

Spotted Sandpiper   *Actitis macularius   L 7½" (19 cm)*

Striking in **breeding** plumage, with barred upperparts, spotted underparts. **Juvenile** and **winter** birds lack spotting below, resemble Common Sandpiper. Note Spotted Sandpiper's shorter tail; in flight, shows shorter white wing stripe, shorter white trailing edge. In juvenile and first-winter birds, barred wing coverts contrast with back; tertials have a black bar on tip; and barring, if any, on edge of tertials extends no farther than halfway along each feather. **Calls** include a shrill *peet-weet* and, in flight, a series of *weet* notes, lower-pitched than the calls of Solitary Sandpiper. Both Spotted and Common Sandpipers fly with stiff, rapid, fluttering wingbeats. On the ground, both nod and teeter constantly. **Range:** Spotted is common and widespread, found at sheltered streams, ponds, lakes, or marshes. Generally seen singly; may form small flocks in migration. Most winter in Central and South America. Rare in winter to southern edge of breeding range.

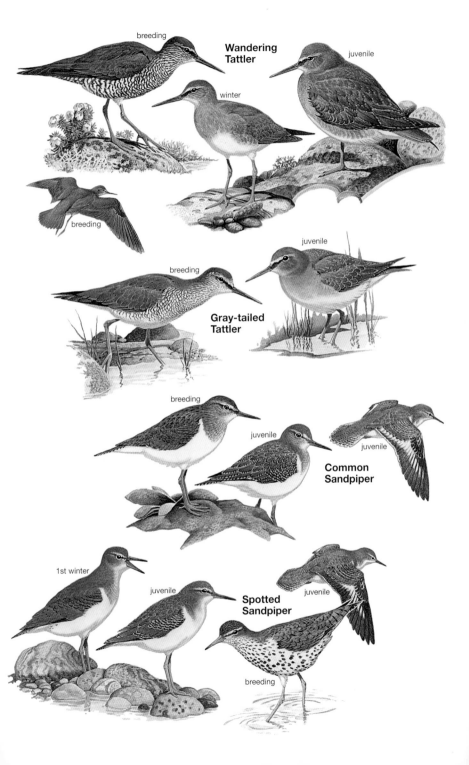

Wandering Tattler

breeding

winter

juvenile

breeding

Gray-tailed Tattler

breeding

juvenile

Common Sandpiper

breeding

juvenile

juvenile

Spotted Sandpiper

1st winter

juvenile

juvenile

breeding

Little Curlew *Numenius minutus L 12" (30 cm)*

Range: Breeds in Russian Far East; winters mainly northern Australia. Casual fall vagrant to coastal central California (four fall records involving both adult and juvenile birds) and one well-documented record in late spring for Gambell, St. Lawrence Island, Alaska. Also, an accepted spring record of a flyover in western Washington. Like a diminutive Whimbrel, with shorter and only slight curved bill; note mostly pale lores. **Calls** include a musical *quee-dlee* and a loud *tchew-tchew-tchew.*

Eskimo Curlew *Numenius borealis* **E** *L 14" (36 cm)*

Range: Formerly bred on Arctic tundra. Only known nesting area was Anderson River region, Northwest Territories (nests found 1862-1866), but breeding range may have extended west to Alaska and perhaps Russian Far East. Wintered mainly on the Pampas of Argentina. Migrated up through Great Plains in spring; to northeast Arctic Canada and then over the Atlantic to South America in fall. Formerly common, now probably extinct, the last certain record was of an adult female shot by a "sportsman" on Barbados on 4 Sept. 1963 (specimen eventually secured). Other more recent sightings not adequately documented. Main cause of likely extinction was unregulated market hunting, especially prevalent on central Great Plains in the two decades following the Civil War. Rare by 1900, thought possibly extinct by 1940; but a few persisted, as up to two were well photographed in Mar. and Apr. from 1959 to 1962 at Galveston Island, Texas, the last verified North American records. Resembles a small Whimbrel, but upperparts darker, bill less curved; wing linings pale cinnamon. Closer in size to Little Curlew but slightly larger (though shorter legged), longer winged, with wingtips extending beyond tail tip at rest, overall more cinnamon coloration (pale buffy in Little Curlew), and more heavily barred breast and flanks with bold Y-shaped marks on the flanks (slight brown barring on Little). The lores are dark, like Whimbrel, not like Little Curlew. **Calls** are poorly known; one call reportedly a rippling *tr-tr-tr* and a soft whistle.

Whimbrel *Numenius phaeopus L 17½" (45 cm)*

Bold, dark-striped crown; dark eye line extending through lores; long downcurved bill. **Call,** a series of hollow whistles on one pitch. Fairly common; nests on open tundra; most winter south of U.S. Generally rare in interior, except Great Lakes and California. In flight, North American *hudsonicus* shows dark rump and underwings; European *phaeopus,* casual vagrant to east (mainly Atlantic coast), white rump and underwings; Asian *variegatus,* rare migrant on islands in western Alaska, casual elsewhere in Pacific region, has whitish, variably streaked rump and underwings. Some argue that based on distinct plumage and genetic differences, the Palearctic subspecies should be split from North American Whimbrels; however, all subspecies give similar vocalizations. In North America, the western (*rufiventris,* if recognized) breeding population (migrating through Pacific states) is a little darker brown and larger than eastern birds.

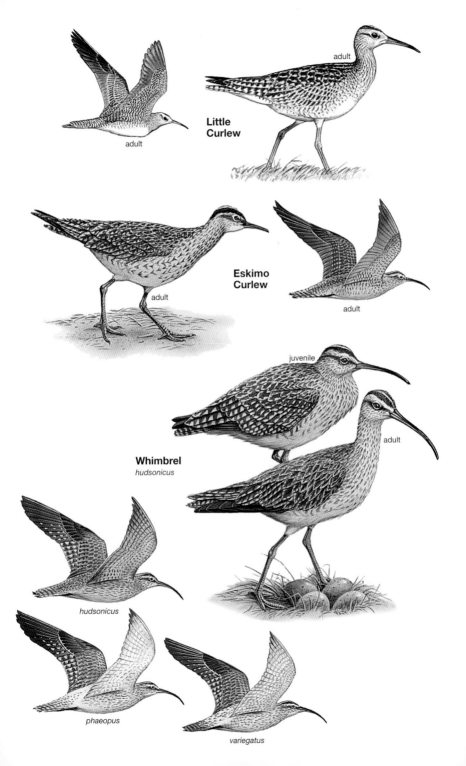

Little Curlew

adult

adult

Eskimo Curlew

adult

adult

juvenile

adult

Whimbrel
hudsonicus

hudsonicus

phaeopus

variegatus

Bristle-thighed Curlew *Numenius tahitiensis*

L 18" (46 cm) Bright buff rump and tail (paler when worn) and extensive pattern of large buff spots on upperparts distinguish this species from slightly smaller Whimbrel. The bill is also slightly more strongly decurved near tip. The stiff feathers on the sides and flanks are very hard to see in the field. Main **call,** a loud whistled *chu-a-whit,* and all other vocalizations are completely different from Whimbrel. **Range:** Winters South Pacific islands. Migration chiefly over water to western Alaskan breeding grounds. Rare spring migrant on Middleton Island and on Pribilof Islands. Casual on St. Lawrence Island and on the Aleutians. Casual to West Coast in spring, after storms, as in May 1998 when over a dozen were found from coastal Washington to northern California.

Long-billed Curlew *Numenius americanus* L 23" (58 cm)

Cinnamon-brown above, buff below, with very long, strongly downcurved bill. Lacks dark head stripes of Whimbrel. Males and juveniles have shorter bills. Cinnamon-buff wing linings and flight feathers, visible in flight, distinctive in all plumages. At rest closely resembles the smaller Marbled Godwit, if bill is hidden; note paler legs. Two weakly differentiated subspecies; more southerly breeding *americanus* is larger and longer billed than more northerly *parvus,* but differences are clinal. Still, bill length extremes are significant and shorter-billed juveniles look much more Whimbrel-like in structure. **Call,** a loud musical, ascending *cur-lee.* **Range:** Fairly common; nests in wet and dry uplands; in migration and winter found on wetlands and agricultural fields. Rare on Gulf Coast east of Texas and on Atlantic coast from Virginia south. Casual farther north on Atlantic coast, and in Midwest.

Eurasian Curlew *Numenius arquata* L 22" (56 cm)

Range: A widespread Eurasian species. Casual on East Coast in fall and winter. The seven records are from Newfoundland to Long Island, New York, except for one at Middle Cheyne Lake, Nunavut. A large curlew that is heavily streaked below. The long bill is long and strongly decurved. Distinguished from Long-billed Curlew by paler overall coloration and by white rump and wing linings, readily visible in flight; from Eurasian races of Whimbrel by larger size, longer bill, and lack of dark stripes on head. Overall very similar to Far Eastern Curlew at rest, but paler, especially from lower belly to undertail; easily told in flight by white rump and wing linings.

Far Eastern Curlew *Numenius madagascariensis*

L 25" (64 cm) **Range:** Despite scientific name, found nowhere near Madagascar! Breeds in Russian Far East, winters in the Sunda Isles, New Guinea, Australia, New Zealand; a few on mainland Southeast Asia. Casual in spring and early summer on Aleutians and Pribilofs; accidental (Sept. 1984) from coastal British Columbia. A large curlew with a very long, decurved bill. Closely resembles Eurasian Curlew, but overall browner, especially from lower belly to undertail coverts. In flight, underwings are heavily barred with dark; rump is the same color as remainder of upperparts.

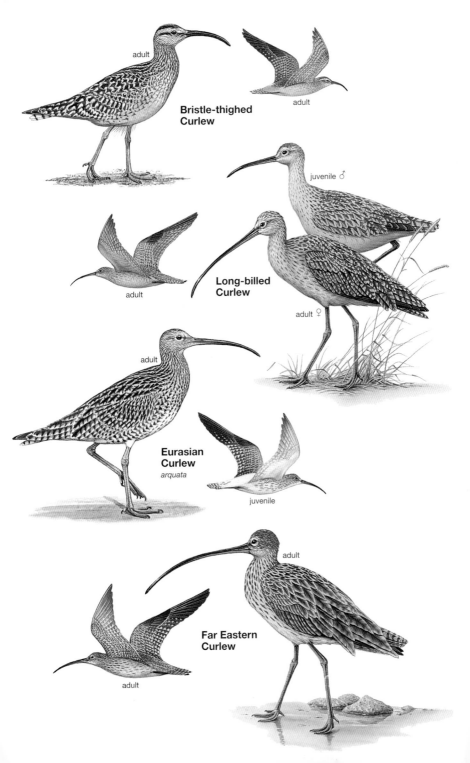

adult

Bristle-thighed Curlew

adult

juvenile ♂

adult

Long-billed Curlew

adult ♀

adult

Eurasian Curlew
arquata

juvenile

adult

Far Eastern Curlew

adult

Black-tailed Godwit *Limosa limosa* L 16½" (42 cm)
Range: Eurasian species, rare but regular spring migrant on western Aleutians; casual to Pribilofs; casual along Atlantic coast; accidental to eastern Ontario and Louisiana. Long, bicolored bill is straight or only slightly upcurved. Tail is mostly black, upper-tail coverts white. In **breeding** plumage, shows chestnut head and neck and heavily barred sides and flanks. East Coast records are of *islandica*, which in the breeding male is of a deeper and more extensive reddish color below. **Winter** birds are gray above, whitish below. In all plumages, white wing linings and broad wing stripe are conspicuous in flight (page 194).

Hudsonian Godwit *Limosa haemastica* L 15½" (39 cm)
Long, bicolored bill, slightly upcurved. Tail is black, uppertail coverts white. **Breeding male** is dark chestnut below, finely barred. **Female** is larger and much duller. **Juvenile**'s buff feather edges give upperparts a scaly look. Winter adult resembles Black-tailed Godwit; dark wing linings and narrower white wing stripe are distinctive in flight (page 194). **Range:** Breeding range not fully known. Migrates through central and eastern Great Plains in spring, much farther east in fall. Casual to Pacific states.

Bar-tailed Godwit *Limosa lapponica* L 16" (41 cm)
Long, bicolored bill, slightly upcurved. **Breeding male** is reddish brown below; lacks heavy barring of Black-tailed Godwit. **Female** is larger and much paler than male. In **winter** plumage, Bar-tailed resembles Marbled Godwit but lacks cinnamon tones. Note also shorter bill and shorter legs. Black-and-white barred tail distinctive but hard to see at rest. **Juvenile** resembles winter adult but is buffier overall. Two subspecies of this Eurasian godwit occur in North America. Alaska-breeding *baueri* (shown opposite) appears casually in migration along Pacific coast and also recorded from Massachusetts; rump is heavily mottled, wing linings brown with white barring. European *lapponica*, very rare migrant along Atlantic coast, has a whiter rump, white wing linings, and brown-barred axillaries. (Both races are shown in flight on page 194.)

Marbled Godwit *Limosa fedoa* L 18" (46 cm)
Long, bicolored bill, slightly upcurved. Tawny brown; mottled with black above, barred below. Barring is much less extensive on **winter** birds and **juveniles.** The wing coverts are also less patterned on juveniles. Legs are longer than in Bar-tailed Godwit. In flight (page 194), cinnamon wing linings and cinnamon on primaries and secondaries are distinctive. Nests in grassy meadows, near lakes and ponds. **Range:** Common on West Coast in winter, fairly common on Texas Gulf Coast and in Florida; rare but regular in the East.

Black-tailed Godwit
melanuroides

juvenile

juvenile

winter

breeding ♂
islandica

breeding ♂

breeding ♀

juvenile

juvenile

Hudsonian Godwit

molting fall
adult ♂

breeding ♀

breeding ♂

juvenile

winter

breeding ♀

Bar-tailed Godwit
baueri

breeding ♂

Marbled Godwit
fedoa

juvenile Hudsonian,
Bar-tailed, and Marbled
(left to right)

breeding ♂

winter ♀

Ruddy Turnstone *Arenaria interpres L 9½" (24 cm)*
Striking black-and-white head and bib, black-and-chestnut back, and orange legs mark this stout bird in **breeding** plumage. Female is duller than **male.** Bib pattern and orange leg color are retained in **winter** plumage. **Juvenile** resembles winter adult but back has a scaly appearance. Distinctive **call** is a low-pitched, guttural rattle. Turnstones use their slender bills to flip aside shells and pebbles in search of food. In flight, complex pattern on back and wings identifies both Ruddy and Black Turnstones. **Range:** Nests on coastal tundra. Rare inland migrant except in Great Lakes region, where much more numerous.

Black Turnstone *Arenaria melanocephala L 9¼" (24 cm)*
Black upperparts. In **breeding** plumage head is marked by white eyebrow and lore spot; white spotting visible on sides of neck and breast. Legs dark reddish brown in all plumages. Juvenile and **winter adult** are slate gray, lack lore spot and mottling. **Calls** include a guttural rattle, higher than call of Ruddy Turnstone. **Range:** Breeds in coastal Alaska. Winters on rocky coasts.

Surfbird *Aphriza virgata L 10" (25 cm)*
Base of short, stout bill is yellow; legs yellowish green. **Breeding adult**'s head and underparts are heavily streaked and spotted with dusky black; upperparts edged with white and chestnut; scapulars mostly rufous. **Winter adult** has a solid dark gray head and breast. **Juvenile**'s head and breast are flecked with white; back appears scaly. In flight, all plumages show a conspicuous black band at end of white tail and rump. **Range:** Nests on mountain tundra; winters along rocky beaches and reefs. Casual in spring on Texas coast, also at Salton Sea.

Rock Sandpiper *Calidris ptilocnemis L 9" (23 cm)*
Black patch on lower breast in **breeding** plumage; compare with belly patch of Dunlin (next page). Crown and back are black, edged with chestnut. In flight (page 197), shows white wing stripe and all-dark tail. Nominate *ptilocnemis* breeding on Pribilofs is larger, has paler chestnut above, less black below, bolder white wing stripe. Long, slender bill is slightly downcurved, base greenish yellow. Legs greenish yellow. **Winter** bird separated from Purple Sandpiper by range, duller bill base and legs; from Surfbird by longer bill, smaller size, more patterned upperparts and breast. **Range:** Nests on tundra; most winter on rocky shores, often with Black Turnstones and Surfbirds. Migrates late in fall.

Purple Sandpiper *Calidris maritima L 9" (23 cm)*
Breeding adult has tawny buff crown, streaked with black; back is edged with white and tawny buff; breast and flanks spotted with blackish brown. Long, slender bill is slightly downcurved, base orange-yellow. Legs orange-yellow. In flight (page 197) and in **winter,** adult resembles Rock Sandpiper. **Range:** Migrates late in fall. Rare fall migrant on Great Lakes. Casual elsewhere inland in the East and in winter on the Gulf Coast. Winters on rocky shores, jetties, often with Ruddy Turnstones and Sanderlings.

juvenile

winter

Ruddy Turnstone

breeding ♂

breeding ♂

Black Turnstone

winter

winter

breeding

winter

winter

juvenile

breeding

winter

Surfbird

Rock Sandpiper
tschuktschorum

juvenile

Pribilofs breeding
ptilocnemis

breeding

Purple Sandpiper

juvenile

breeding

winter

Great Knot *Calidris tenuirostris L 11" (28 cm)*

Range: Asian species, casual in spring to western Alaska. Larger than Red Knot, with longer bill. Compare to Surfbird and Rock Sandpiper (preceding page). In **breeding** plumage, shows black breast and black flank pattern. **Juvenile** has buffy wash and distinct spotting below; dark back feathers edged with rust. Resembles Red Knot in flight but primary coverts darker, wing bar fainter.

Red Knot *Calidris canutus L 10½" (27 cm)*

Chunky and short legged. **Breeding adult** is dappled brown, black, and chestnut above, with buffy chestnut face and breast. In **winter,** back is pale gray; underparts white. Distinguished from dowitchers (page 188) by shorter bill, paler crown, and, in flight (page 195), by whitish rump finely barred with gray. **Juveniles** similar to winter adults but have distinct spotting below, scaly-looking upperparts. **Range:** Feeds along sandy beaches and mudflats. Eastern populations declining; rare migrant in the interior.

Sanderling *Calidris alba L 8" (20 cm)*

Palest sandpiper of **winter;** pale gray above, white below. Bill, legs black. Bold white wing stripe shows in flight (page 197). In **breeding** plumage (acquired late Apr.), head, mantle, and breast are rusty. Feeds on sandy beaches, running to snatch mollusks and crustaceans exposed by retreating waves. **Juveniles** blackish above, with pale edges near tips of feathers. **Call,** a *kip*, often in a series.

Dunlin *Calidris alpina L 8½" (22 cm)*

Medium sized; long bill, curved at tip; in flight (page 197) shows dark center to rump. **Breeding** plumage with reddish upperparts, black belly. Subspecies differ in size, structure, and breeding plumage: more ventrally streaked in *hudsonia,* found in eastern North America; *pacifica* in western Alaska and Pacific region; similar *arcticola* (breeds northern Alaska) and *sakhalina* (migrant western Alaska) winter in Asia. Three races from Greenland and western Palearctic (*arctica, schinzii,* and *alpina*) are smaller, shorter billed, and darker above in breeding plumage; *arctica* and *alpina* accidental on East Coast. Compare to Rock Sandpiper (preceding page). In **winter** plumage, upperparts and chest brownish gray. **Juveniles** rusty above, spotted below. **Call,** a harsh, reedy *kree.* **Range:** Rare on Great Plains. In North America, adults and juveniles stay north and molt into winter plumage, then migrate south.

Curlew Sandpiper *Calidris ferruginea L 8½" (22 cm)*

Range: Eurasian species, rare on East Coast, casual elsewhere. Long, downcurved bill has whitish area at base. In **breeding** plumage, rich chestnut underparts, mottled chestnut back distinctive. Female slightly paler than male. Many sightings are of birds in patchy spring plumage or molting to winter plumage, showing grayer upperparts and partly white underparts. **Juvenile** appears scaly above; shows rich buff wash across breast; young birds seen in southern Canada and U.S. are in full juvenal plumage; compare with winter Dunlins. White rump is conspicuous in flight (page 195). **Call** is a soft, rippling *chirrup.* Has bred in northern Alaska.

Great Knot

juvenile

breeding

juvenile

Red Knot

winter

breeding

Sanderling

winter

breeding

juvenile

breeding
sakhalina

breeding
pacifica

breeding
schinzii

Dunlin
hudsonia

juvenile

breeding

winter

Curlew Sandpiper

juvenile

breeding ♂

winter

Peeps

These are seven species of small *Calidris* sandpipers that are difficult to identify. Collectively known as stints, by Old World English speakers, they can be roughly divided into four Old World and three New World species. Sometimes the larger Baird's and White-rumped Sandpipers are also included. Keys to identification include learning overall structure and feather topography, behavior, and the distribution patterns of each. It is essential to thoroughly learn our three common species before attempting to identify one of the Eurasian ones.

Semipalmated Sandpiper   *Calidris pusilla*   L 6¼" (16 cm)
Black legs; tubular-looking, straight bill, of variable length. Easily confused with Western Sandpiper. In **breeding** birds, note that Semipalmated usually lacks spotting on flanks and shows only a tinge of rust on crown, ear patch, and scapulars. **Juveniles** are distinguished by stronger supercilium contrasting with darker crown and ear coverts and by more uniform upperparts. Some are brighter above than illustrated. **Winter** plumage (in North America seen most often on Gulf Coast in late Mar.) of these two species is very similar (see also page 197), but rounder-headed Semipalmated is plumper; note bill shape; face shows slightly more contrast; center of breast never shows the faint streaks visible on some winter Westerns. Semipalmateds tend to pick at the water surface, often just at the water's edge. **Call** is a short *churk*. **Range:** Abundant. A common migrant in eastern half of continent; generally a rare migrant in the West, south of British Columbia; very rare in winter in south Florida; no valid winter records elsewhere.

Western Sandpiper   *Calidris mauri*   L 6½" (17 cm)
Black legs; tapered bill, of variable length (longer in females); distal portion usually slightly drooped. Easily confused with Semipalmated Sandpiper, but blockier-headed Western has more attenuated body. In **breeding** plumage, Western has arrow-shaped spots along sides, rufous at base of scapulars, and a bright rufous wash on crown and ear patch. **Juvenile** is distinguished from juvenile Semipalmated by less prominent supercilium, paler crown and face, and brighter rufous edges on back and inner scapulars. **Winter** plumage is very similar. Note structure (especially bill shape). In North America, especially away from south Florida, any winter-plumaged individual in fall or winter is likely to be this species. Found in similar situations to Semipalmated Sandpipers, but often feeds a little farther out in the water away from the shore's edge. **Call** is a raspy *jeet*.

Least Sandpiper   *Calidris minutilla*   L 6" (15 cm)
Note small size and short, thin bill, slightly downcurved. Always darker above than Western and Semipalmated Sandpipers. Legs are yellowish, but can appear dark in poor light or when smeared with mud. In **winter** plumage, has prominent brown breast band. **Juvenile** has strong buffy wash across breast. Feeds in a variety of wet habitats, but forages less in the water, often preferring to feed back from the shore's edge. **Call** is a high plaintive *kree*.

breeding

Semipalmated Sandpiper

juvenile

winter

winter

juvenile

Western Sandpiper

breeding

winter

Least Sandpiper

breeding

juvenile

Rare Stints

These are the four Old World species of peeps that have been found in North America. Of these, Red-necked Stint is the most regular. Of the remaining three, both Temminck's and Long-toed Stints are almost unknown in North America away from Alaska. With any potential find of a rare stint it is essential to get documentation, preferably photographs. Even in migration, shorebirds hold feeding territories, and if flocks are disturbed, they soon return and sort themselves out. If the potential rarity can't be refound, chances are it was a commoner species.

Red-necked Stint *Calidris ruficollis L 6¼" (16 cm)*
Rufous on throat and upper breast may be pale and indistinct; look for necklace of dark streaks on white lower breast. **Juvenile** distinguished from Little Stint by plainer wing coverts and tertials, more uniform crown pattern, and plainer breast sides. **Range:** Asian species, regular migrant on western Alaska coast and islands. Breeding documented on Seward Peninsula coast; breeding range on map is conjectural. Casual migrant on both coasts; accidental in interior.

Little Stint *Calidris minuta L 6" (15 cm)*
Range: Eurasian species, very rare on western Alaska islands in spring and fall; casual on East and West Coasts, and accidental elsewhere. **Breeding** birds are brightly fringed with rufous above; throat and underparts white (more suffused with color in later summer adults), with bright buff wash and bold spotting on sides of breast. Redder above than Western and Semipalmated Sandpipers (preceding page); compare also with Red-necked Stint. **Juvenile** best distinguished from juvenile Red-necked by extensively black-centered wing coverts and tertials, usually edged with rufous; also note split supercilium and streaking on sides of chest.

Long-toed Stint *Calidris subminuta L 6" (15 cm)*
Asian species, casual in spring on St. Lawrence Island and the Pribilofs; can be fairly common on the outer Aleutians. Accidental in fall from coastal Oregon and California. Distinguished in all plumages from Least Sandpiper by dark forehead, which pinches off prominent white supercilium before it meets the bill (dark forms J shape on its side); also shows a split supercilium. Median coverts are white edged; note also greenish base of lower mandible; yellowish legs. Gives a lower-pitched **call** than Least Sandpiper.

Temminck's Stint *Calidris temminckii L 6¼" (16 cm)*
Range: Eurasian species; rare spring and fall migrant on Pribilofs, Aleutians, and St. Lawrence Island. Accidental northern Alaska and coastal Pacific Northwest. White outer tail feathers distinctive in all plumages. **Breeding adult** resembles the larger Baird's Sandpiper in plumage and shape (preceding page), but legs are yellow or greenish yellow; note Baird's dark legs and distinct primary tip projection past tertials. In Temminck's Stint **juvenile,** feathers of upperparts have a dark subterminal edge, buffy fringe. **Call** is a very distinctive, repeated, rapid dry rattle.

juvenile

breeding

**Red-necked
Stint**

Little Stint

juvenile

breeding

juvenile

**Long-toed
Stint**

breeding

**Temminck's
Stint**

juvenile

breeding

White-rumped Sandpiper   *Calidris fuscicollis*

L 7½" (19 cm) Long primary tip projection beyond tertials and tail on standing bird. Similar to Baird's Sandpiper structurally, but grayer overall and usually has an entirely white rump. In **breeding** plumage, streaking extends to flanks. **Juvenile** (see also page 197) shows rusty edges on crown and back. In winter, head and neck are dark gray, giving a hooded look. **Call** note, a very high-pitched insect-like *jeet*. **Range:** Fairly common; common spring and rare fall migrant through Great Plains. Casual spring (mainly) and fall (all records are adults) in West. Spring migration late, extends to late June; juveniles don't migrate south until the end of Sept. Winters in southern South America; no valid midwinter records for North America. Feeds on mudflats.

Baird's Sandpiper   *Calidris bairdii*   L 7½" (19 cm)

Long primary tip projection beyond tertials and tail on standing bird gives the bird a horizontal profile. Buff-brown above and across breast. Pale fringing on **juvenile**'s back gives a scaly appearance (see also page 197). Distinguished from White-rumped Sandpiper by more buffy brown color and uniform plumage; in flight by dark rump. Distinguished from Least Sandpiper by much larger size, longer and straighter bill, and primary projection. **Call** is a low raspy *kreep*, similar to call of Pectoral Sandpiper, but less rich. **Range:** Fairly common to common; found on upper beaches and inland on lakeshores, wet fields, even beaches. Migration is through Great Plains. Uncommon (usually juveniles) to both coasts in fall. Winters in South America; accidental in North America in midwinter.

Spoon-billed Sandpiper   *Eurynorhynchus pygmeus*

L 6" (15 cm) **Range:** Globally threatened species. Recent estimated population on breeding grounds of between 600 and 1,000 individuals represents a greater than 50 percent reduction in the last 15 years. Breeds on coast of Russian Far East; winters coastal Southeast Asia; casual migrant (about six records) to western and northern Alaska. One record of a fall migrant, a breeding-plumaged adult, from Vancouver region, British Columbia (30 July to 3 Aug. 1978). Spoon-shaped bill is diagnostic and gives bill a longer look, but spoon is sometimes hard to see with clarity at a distance; beware of other small *Calidris* with mud on bill tip. In **breeding** plumage is easily mistaken for Red-necked Stint, apart from bill. **Juvenile** has darker cheek and more contrasting supercilium than Red-necked Stint. On winter grounds in Southeast Asia, feeds farther out into the water than Red-necked Stints; probes like Western Sandpiper but often with a side-to-side motion.

Broad-billed Sandpiper   *Limicola falcinellus*

L 7" (18 cm) **Range:** Eurasian species, casual fall migrant on western and central Aleutians. Accidental in fall from coastal New York. All sightings so far of juveniles. Plump body with short legs and long, broad-based bill with distinctive drooped tip give it a distinctive profile. Note also the distinctive split supercilium. **Call** is a dry and high-pitched buzzy trill; also shorter calls.

White-rumped Sandpiper

juvenile

breeding

fall-molting adult

Baird's Sandpiper

breeding

juvenile

Spoon-billed Sandpiper

juvenile

breeding

Broad-billed Sandpiper

breeding

juvenile

Pectoral Sandpiper *Calidris melanotos* L 8¾" (22 cm)

Prominent streaking on breast, darker in **male,** contrasts sharply with clear white belly. Male is larger than **female. Juvenile** has buffy wash on streaked breast. Compare especially with juvenile Sharp-tailed Sandpiper (see also page 197). **Call** is a rich, low *churk.* **Range:** Often feeds in wet meadows, marshes, pond edges. Common in Midwest; fairly common on East Coast; scarcer from Great Plains to West Coast, where mainly juveniles are seen in fall.

Sharp-tailed Sandpiper *Calidris acuminata*

L 8½" (22 cm) **Range:** Breeds in Russian Far East; casual spring and fairly common fall migrant in western Alaska; rare fall migrant along entire Pacific coast. Casual in fall across rest of continent. Most sightings are **juveniles,** distinguished from juvenile Pectoral Sandpiper by white eyebrow that broadens behind the eye; bright buffy breast lightly streaked on upper breast and sides; streaked undertail coverts; and brighter rufous cap and edging on upperparts (see also page 197). **Adult** in **breeding** plumage is similar to juvenile, but more spotted below with dark chevrons on flanks; also distinct white eye ring. **Call** is a mellow, two-note whistle.

Upland Sandpiper *Bartramia longicauda* L 12" (31 cm)

Small head, with large, dark, prominent eyes; long, thin neck, long tail, long wings. Legs yellow. Prefers fields, where often only its head and neck are visible above the grass. Also perches on posts on breeding grounds. In flight (page 195), blackish primaries contrast with mottled brown upperparts. **Calls,** a rolling *pulip pulip,* and a call like a wolf whistle, heard in flight on breeding grounds. **Range:** Fairly common except in eastern range, where declining. Casual on West Coast and in the Southwest in migration.

Buff-breasted Sandpiper *Tryngites subruficollis*

L 8¼" (21 cm) Dark eye stands out prominently on buffy face; underparts paler buff; legs orange-yellow. In flight, shows flashy white wing linings. **Juveniles** are paler below, with scaly white fringing to feathers above. **Range:** Prefers plowed fields, turf farms, and wet rice fields. Migrates through the interior of the continent. In fall, rare on the West Coast, uncommon in the East; most sightings west or east of eastern Great Plains are of juveniles (see also page 195).

Ruff *Philomachus pugnax* ♂L 12" (31 cm) ♀L 10" (25 cm)

Range: Old World species. Rare migrant in western Alaska and along West and East Coasts and in Great Lakes region. Casual elsewhere. Very rare in winter in California; has bred in Alaska. **Breeding males** acquire dramatic ruffs in colors that range from black to rufous to white. **Female** lacks ruff, is smaller, and has a variable amount of black below. Both sexes have a plump body, small head, and white underwings. Leg color may be yellow, orange, or red. **Juvenile** is buffy below, has prominently fringed feathers above. In flight (page 197), the U-shaped white band on rump is distinctive in all plumages. Ruff and Buff-breasted Sandpiper are both silent away from breeding grounds.

Pectoral Sandpiper

breeding ♂

breeding ♀

juvenile

juvenile Sharp-tailed (center) with juvenile Pectorals

breeding adult

Sharp-tailed Sandpiper

juvenile

Upland Sandpiper

adult

juvenile

displaying adult

juvenile

Buff-breasted Sandpiper

breeding adult

breeding males

♀

summer molting ♂

Ruff

juvenile ♀

summer molting ♀

winter ♂

Dowitchers

Medium-size, chunky, dark shorebirds, dowitchers have long, straight bills and distinct pale eyebrows. Feeding in mud or shallow water, they probe with a rapid jabbing motion. Dowitchers in flight show a white wedge from barred tail to middle of back. Separating the two species is easiest with juveniles, more difficult with breeding adults, and very difficult in winter except by distinctive calls. Both species give the same song, a rapid *di di da doo,* year-round.

Short-billed Dowitcher *Limnodromus griseus*

L 11" (28 cm) In flight, tail usually looks paler than in Long-billed Dowitcher. **Breeding** plumage varies among the three subspecies: *griseus* (which breeds in northeast Canada), *hendersoni* (central and western Canada), and *caurinus* (Alaska). Unlike Long-billed, most Short-billed show some white on the belly, especially *griseus,* which also has a heavily spotted breast and may have densely barred flanks; *caurinus* is variable but similar to *griseus.* In *hendersoni,* which may be mostly reddish below, foreneck is much less heavily spotted than in Long-billed; sides have less or no barring; upperparts are brighter. In all subspecies, **juvenile** is brighter above, buffier and more spotted below than juvenile Long-billed; tertials and visible greater wing coverts have broad reddish-buff edges and internal bars, loops, or stripes. **Winter** birds are brownish gray above, white below, with gray breast; at close range note fine dark speckling on and below the breast on many birds. **Call** is a mellow *tu tu tu,* repeated in a rapid series as an alarm call. **Range:** Common in migration along the Atlantic coast (*griseus*); from the eastern plains to Atlantic coast from New Jersey south (*hendersoni*); and along the Pacific coast (*caurinus*); a few *griseus* are seen on eastern Great Lakes in late spring. Fall migration begins earlier than Long-billed, usually in late June or early July for adults; early Aug. for juveniles. Migrant juveniles are seen through early Oct.

Long-billed Dowitcher *Limnodromus scolopaceus*

L 11½" (29 cm) **Male**'s bill is no longer than on Short-billed Dowitcher, **female**'s is. In flight, tail usually looks darker than in Short-billed. **Breeding adult** is entirely reddish below; foreneck heavily spotted; sides usually barred. Bold white scapular tips in spring help separate this species from Short-billed. **Juvenile** is darker above, grayer below than Short-billed; tertials and greater wing coverts are plain, with thin gray edges and rufous tips; some birds show two pale spots near the tips. In **winter** birds, breast is unspotted and more extensively dark than on most Short-billed. **Call** is a sharp, high-pitched *keek,* given singly or in a rapid series. Adult Long-billeds go to favored locations in late summer to molt; Short-billeds molt when they reach winter grounds. **Range:** Common in migration in western half of continent; less common in the East in fall, rare in spring. Fall migration begins later than Short-billed, in mid-July (West) or late July (East). Juveniles migrate later than adults; rare before Sept. Dowitchers seen inland after mid-Oct. are almost certainly Long-billed.

Short-billed Dowitcher

breeding *caurinus*

worn breeding *griseus*

breeding *griseus*

breeding *hendersoni*

molting juvenile

juvenile

winter

griseus

winter *hendersoni*

juvenile tertials

Long-billed Dowitcher

molting juvenile

juvenile

winter

winter

juvenile tertials

worn breeding ♀

fresh breeding ♂

Stilt Sandpiper *Calidris himantopus* L 8½" (22 cm)

Breeding adult has pale eyebrow, chestnut on head, slender, slightly downcurved bill, and heavily barred underparts. **Winter adult** is grayer above, whiter below; **juvenile** has more sharply patterned upperparts; the two resemble Curlew Sandpiper (page 178), but note straighter bill, yellow-green legs, and, in flight (page 195), lack of prominent wing stripe, paler tail; early juvenile has a buffy wash on breast. Feeds like dowitchers, with which it often associates, but note smaller size and disproportionately longer legs. **Call** is a low, hoarse *querp*. **Range:** Common to East in fall.

Wilson's Snipe *Gallinago delicata* L 10¼" (26 cm)

Stocky, with very long bill; boldly striped head; barred flanks. Usually seen when flushed, as it gives a harsh two-syllable *ski-ape* **call** in rapid, twisting flight. Where breeding, males deliver loud *wheet* notes from perches. In swooping display flight, vibrating outer tail feathers make quavering hoots, like song of Boreal Owl.

Common Snipe *Gallinago gallinago* L 10½" (27 cm)

Range: Eurasian species, regular migrant to the western Aleutians where it has bred and been found casually in winter; rarer to the central Aleutians, Pribilofs; casual to St. Lawrence Island. Paler, buffier color overall than Wilson's Snipe; broader white trailing edge to secondaries, fainter flank markings; paler white-striped underwings. Flight-display notes of the male are lower-pitched.

Pin-tailed Snipe *Gallinago stenura* L 10" (26 cm).

Range: Breeds in Siberia and Russian Far East; winters chiefly in Southeast Asia. Two certain records from western Aleutians. Chunkier, shorter billed, and shorter tailed than Common Snipe. On ground, note barred secondary coverts and even-width pale edges on inner and outer webs of scapulars for a scalloped look. In flight, note buffy secondary covert panel, uniformly dark underwings, no pale edge to secondaries, distinct foot projection past tail. Larger Swinhoe's Snipe (*G. megala*) from Asia (unrecorded in North America) perhaps not separable in field. In hand, razor-thin outer tail feathers are diagnostic. **Call** is high, ducklike *squak*.

American Woodcock *Scolopax minor* L 11" (28 cm)

Chunky, with long bill, barred crown, large eyes set high in head. Rounded wings. Nocturnal, secretive. Flies up abruptly; wings make a twittering sound. Males give an elaborate flight display; visible at dusk and dawn. **Call,** heard mainly in spring, a nasal *peent*. **Range:** Common; nests in moist woodlands. In mild winters, a few are found farther north. Casual to Colorado, New Mexico.

Jack Snipe *Lymnocryptes minimus* L 7" (18 cm)

Range: Small, chunky Eurasian species. Three late fall records for California and Labrador; one, possibly two, spring records for Pribilofs. Secretive, reluctant to flush. Flight is low, short, fluttery, on rounded wings. Bobs while feeding. Pale base to short bill, pale split eyebrow stripes with no median crown stripe, broad buffy back stripes, streaked flanks, pale underparts.

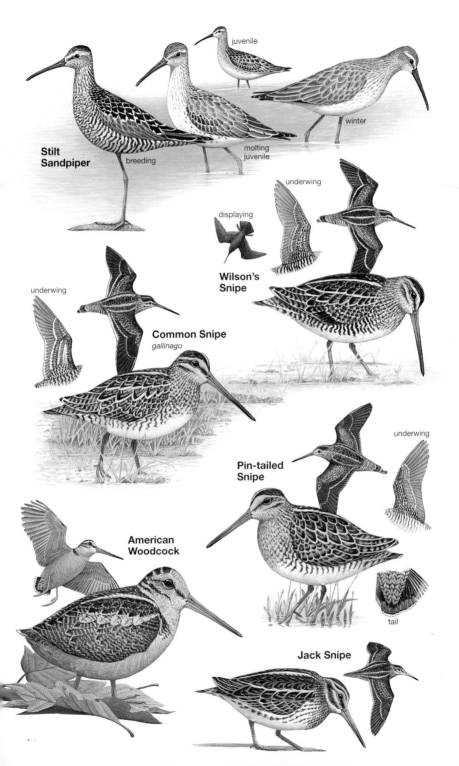

Stilt Sandpiper

juvenile

molting juvenile

breeding

winter

underwing

displaying

Wilson's Snipe

underwing

Common Snipe
gallinago

underwing

Pin-tailed Snipe

American Woodcock

tail

Jack Snipe

Phalaropes

These elegant shorebirds have partially lobed feet and dense, soft plumage. Feeding on the water, phalaropes often spin like tops, stirring up larvae, crustaceans, and insects. Females, larger and more brightly colored than the males, do the courting; males incubate the eggs and care for the chicks. In fall, adults and juveniles (particularly Wilson's and Red Phalaropes) rapidly molt to winter plumage; many are seen in transitional plumage farther south.

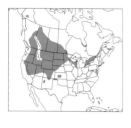

Wilson's Phalarope   *Phalaropus tricolor*   *L 9¼" (24 cm)*

Long, thin bill; bold blackish stripe on face and neck. In **winter** plumage, upperparts are gray, underparts white; note also lack of distinct dark ear patch; legs yellowish. Briefly held **juvenal** plumage resembles winter adult but back is browner with buffy edge to feathers, breast buffy. In flight, white uppertail coverts, whitish tail, and absence of white wing stripe distinguish juvenile and winter birds from other phalaropes. **Calls** include a hoarse *wurk* and other low, croaking notes. **Range:** Wilson's is chiefly an inland phalarope, nesting on grassy borders of shallow lakes, marshes, and reservoirs. Feeds as often on land as on water. Common to abundant in western North America; uncommon to rare in the East; rare in southern California in winter.

Red-necked Phalarope   *Phalaropus lobatus*

L 7¾" (20 cm)   Chestnut on front and sides of neck distinctive in **breeding female,** less prominent in **male.** Both have dark back with bright buff stripes along sides; bill shorter than in Wilson's Phalarope, thinner than in Red Phalarope. **Winter** birds are blue-gray above with whitish stripes; underparts and front of crown white; dark patch extends back from eye. In flight, show white wing stripe, whitish stripes on back, dark central tail coverts. Fresh **juvenile** resembles winter adult but is blacker above, with bright buff stripes. **Call,** a high, sharp *kit,* often given in a series. **Range:** Breeds on Arctic and subarctic tundra; winters chiefly at sea in Southern Hemisphere. Common inland in West and off West Coast during migration; rare in Midwest and East; uncommon off East Coast; more numerous off Maine and Maritimes.

Red Phalarope   *Phalaropus fulicarius*   *L 8½" (22 cm)*

Bill shorter and much thicker than in other phalaropes; yellow with black tip in breeding adult, usually all-dark in juvenile and winter adult. **Female** in breeding plumage has black crown, white face, chestnut red underparts. **Male** is duller. **Juvenile** resembles male but is much paler below; juveniles seen in southern Canada and the U.S. are **molting** to winter plumage; more closely resemble Red-necked Phalaropes. **Winter** bird is pale gray above. In flight, shows a bolder white wing stripe than Red-necked and dark central tail coverts. **Call** is a sharp *keip,* is higher-pitched than Red-necked's. **Range:** Breeds on Arctic shores; winters at sea. Irregularly common off West Coast during fall migration; rare to very rare inland, chiefly seen in fall. Generally uncommon off East Coast in spring and fall.

juvenile

winter

molting
juvenile

winter

**Wilson's
Phalarope**

breeding ♀

breeding ♂

juvenile

breeding adults with juvenile

winter

Red-necked Phalarope

breeding ♀

molting
juvenile

breeding ♂

winter

juvenile

molting
fall adults

winter

molting juvenile

**Red
Phalarope**

breeding
♀

winter

breeding
♂

Shorebirds in Flight

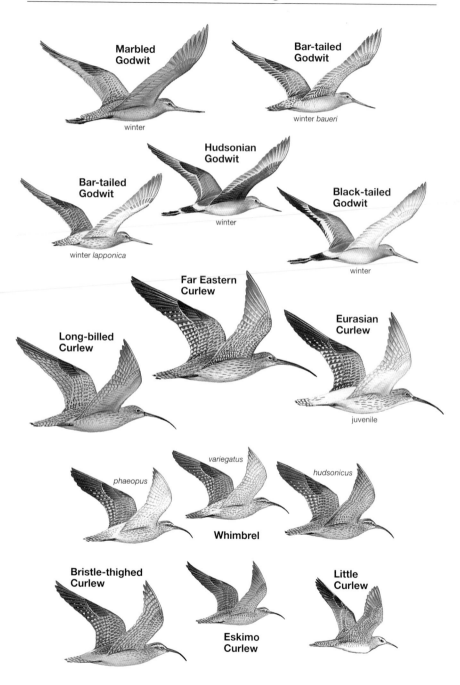

Marbled Godwit
winter

Bar-tailed Godwit
winter *baueri*

Bar-tailed Godwit
winter *lapponica*

Hudsonian Godwit
winter

Black-tailed Godwit
winter

Long-billed Curlew

Far Eastern Curlew

Eurasian Curlew
juvenile

phaeopus

variegatus

hudsonicus

Whimbrel

Bristle-thighed Curlew

Eskimo Curlew

Little Curlew

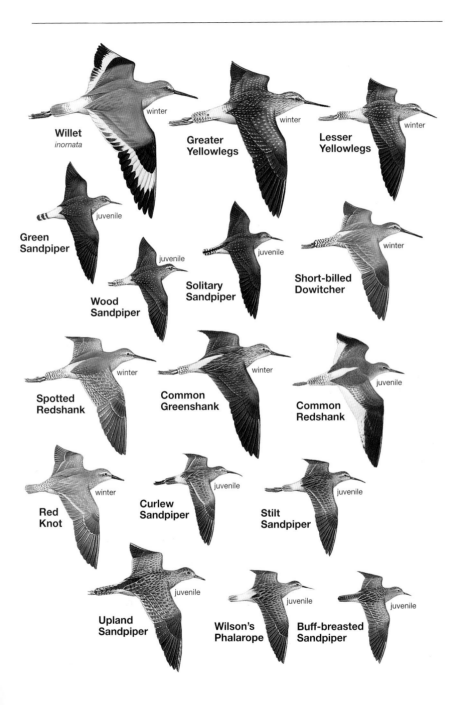

Willet
inornata   winter

**Greater
Yellowlegs**   winter

**Lesser
Yellowlegs**   winter

juvenile

**Green
Sandpiper**

juvenile

**Wood
Sandpiper**

juvenile

**Solitary
Sandpiper**

**Short-billed
Dowitcher**   winter

**Spotted
Redshank**   winter

**Common
Greenshank**   winter

**Common
Redshank**   juvenile

**Red
Knot**   winter

**Curlew
Sandpiper**   juvenile

**Stilt
Sandpiper**   juvenile

**Upland
Sandpiper**   juvenile

**Wilson's
Phalarope**   juvenile

**Buff-breasted
Sandpiper**   juvenile

Shorebirds in Flight

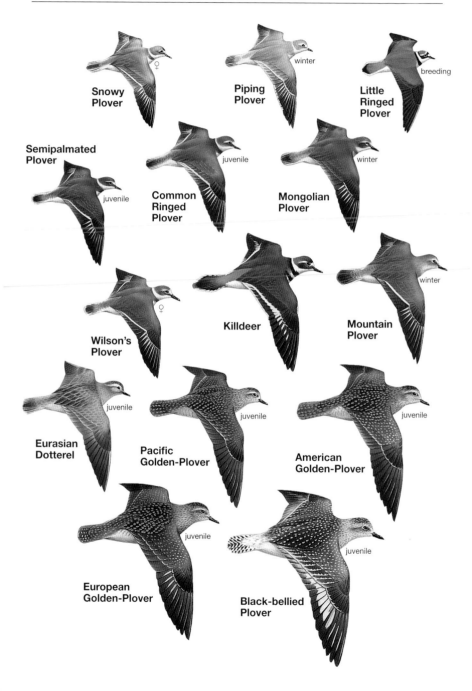

Snowy Plover ♀

Piping Plover winter

Little Ringed Plover breeding

Semipalmated Plover juvenile

Common Ringed Plover juvenile

Mongolian Plover winter

Wilson's Plover ♀

Killdeer

Mountain Plover winter

Eurasian Dotterel juvenile

Pacific Golden-Plover juvenile

American Golden-Plover juvenile

European Golden-Plover juvenile

Black-bellied Plover juvenile

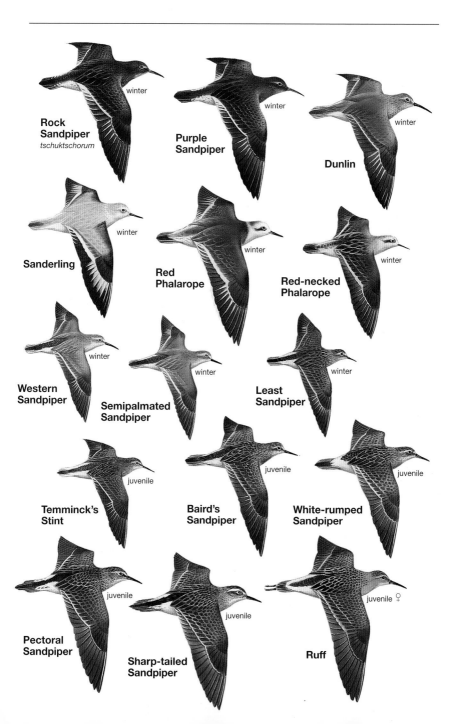

Rock Sandpiper *tschuktschorum* · winter

Purple Sandpiper · winter

Dunlin · winter

Sanderling · winter

Red Phalarope · winter

Red-necked Phalarope · winter

Western Sandpiper · winter

Semipalmated Sandpiper · winter

Least Sandpiper · winter

Temminck's Stint · juvenile

Baird's Sandpiper · juvenile

White-rumped Sandpiper · juvenile

Pectoral Sandpiper · juvenile

Sharp-tailed Sandpiper · juvenile

Ruff · juvenile ♀

Gulls, Terns, Skimmers (Family Laridae)

A large, diverse family with strong wings and powerful flight. Some species are largely pelagic; others frequent coastal waters or inland lakes and wetlands. Gulls take from about two to four years to reach adult plumage; immatures are often variable and hard to identify. In general, male gulls are larger than females. *Species: 97 World, 49 N.A.*

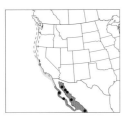

Heermann's Gull *Larus heermanni*
L 19" (48 cm) WS 51" (130 cm) Four-year gull. **Adult** distinctive with white head, streaked gray-brown in winter; red bill; dark gray body; black tail with white terminal band; white trailing edge on wings. **Second-winter** bird is browner, with two-toned bill and buff tail band. **First-winter** bird has dark brown body, lacks contrasting tail tip and trailing edge on wing. Wings are fairly long, flight buoyant. **Range:** Common post-breeding visitor along the West Coast; rare at Salton Sea. Casual elsewhere inland in California and the Southwest; accidental to west Texas, Great Lakes, southeast Alaska, Florida, and Virginia.

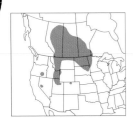

Franklin's Gull *Larus pipixcan*
L 14½" (37 cm) WS 36" (91 cm) Three-year gull. **Breeding adult** has black hood, white underparts variably tinged with pink, slate gray wings with white bar and black-and-white tips on primaries. Distinguished from Laughing Gull by white bar and large white tips on primaries, pale gray central tail feathers, and broader white eye crescents. All **winter** birds have a dark half-hood, more extensive than in any winter Laughing Gull. Second-summer Franklin's has partial or no bar on primaries. **First-summer** bird is like winter adult but lacks white primary bar; bill and legs black. **First-winter** bird resembles first-winter Laughing; note white outer tail feathers, half-hood, broader eye crescents, white underparts, and, in flight (page 216), pale inner primaries. Juvenile is like first-winter bird but back is brown. At all ages, distinguished from Laughing Gull by smaller size, smaller bill with less prominent hook, rounder forehead, less extensive dark on underside of primaries; shorter legs and wings give a stocky look when standing. **Range:** Rare migrant along both coasts; very rare in winter along Gulf Coast and in southern California.

Laughing Gull *Larus atricilla*
L 16½" (42 cm) WS 40" (102 cm) Three-year gull. **Breeding adult** has black hood, white underparts, slate gray wings with black outer primaries. In **winter**, shows gray wash on nape; compare with the half-hood of Franklin's Gull. Second-summer bird has partial hood, some spotting on tip of tail. **Second-winter** bird (see also page 216) is similar to second-summer but has gray wash on sides of breast, lacks hood. **First-winter** bird has extensively gray sides, complete tail band, gray wash on nape, slate gray back, dark brown wings; compare with first-winter Franklin's Gull. **Juvenile** is like first-winter bird but brown on head and body. **Range:** Common along Gulf and Atlantic coasts; rare inland except at Salton Sea where it is fairly common, chiefly as a post-breeding visitor.

Heermann's Gull

breeding adult

winter adult

2nd winter

1st winter

breeding adult

Franklin's Gull

breeding adult

winter adult

1st winter

breeding adult

1st summer

Laughing Gull

breeding adult

2nd winter

breeding adult

winter adult

1st winter

juvenile

Bonaparte's Gull *Larus philadelphia*

L 13½" (34 cm) WS 33" (84 cm) Two-year gull. **Breeding adult** has slate black hood, black bill, gray mantle with black wing tips that are pale on underside; white underparts, orange-red legs. In flight, shows white wedge on wing. **Winter** bird lacks hood. **First-winter** bird has a dark brown carpal bar on leading edge of wing, dark band on secondaries, black tail band; compare with juvenile Black-legged Kittiwake (pages 214, 216). First-summer bird may show partial hood; wings and tail are like first-winter. Flight is buoyant, wingbeats rapid. **Range:** Uncommon inland migrant in West; common to abundant on Great Lakes.

Black-headed Gull *Larus ridibundus*

L 16" (41 cm) WS 40" (102 cm) Two-year gull. **Breeding adult** has dark brown hood; maroon-red bill and legs; mantle slightly paler gray than Bonaparte's Gull; black wing tips; white underparts. **Winter adult** lacks hood; bill brighter red. **First-winter** birds have orange-red bill, pale legs, dark tail band, dark brown carpal bar (page 216). Distinguished from Bonaparte's by larger size and bill color. **First-summer** bird's hood varies from minimal, like first-winter's, to nearly complete; wings and tail like first-winter. In all plumages, shows dark underside of primaries in flight, darker on adults; compare with Bonaparte's. **Range:** Colonizer from Europe. Fairly common in winter in Newfoundland, where a few breed; rare off western Alaska, Maritimes, and coastal New England; casual elsewhere in North America.

Little Gull *Larus minutus L 11" (28 cm) WS 24" (61 cm)*

Two- to three-year gull. **Breeding adult** has black hood, black bill, pale gray mantle, white wing tips, white underparts, red legs. **Winter adult** has dusky cap, dark spot behind eye. Wings uniformly pale gray above, dark gray to black below, with white trailing edge. Some second-winter birds are like adult but underwing pattern is incomplete; show some dusky slate in primaries (page 216). **First-winter** is like Bonaparte's but primaries blackish above, lack white wedge; wings show strong blackish W; crown shows more black. In all plumages, note short, rounded wings, fluttery wingbeat. **Range:** Western Palearctic species, has bred irregularly from Great Lakes to Hudson Bay. Generally rare on Great Lakes in migration and in winter on East Coast; very rare to casual elsewhere in North America.

Ross's Gull *Rhodostethia rosea*

L 13½" (34 cm) WS 33" (84 cm) **Range:** Arctic species of the Russian Far East, has bred in northern Canada and Greenland in last two decades. Common fall migrant along northern coast of Alaska; presumably winters at sea. Casual south to northern U.S. Two-year gull. Variably pink below; upperwing pale gray; underwing pale to dark gray. Black collar in summer, partial or absent in winter. **First-winter** bird has black at tip of tail, dark spot behind eye; acquires black collar by first summer; in flight (page 216), shows W pattern like Little Gull. In all plumages, note long, pointed wings; long, wedge-shaped tail; and broad, white trailing edge to wings.

breeding
adult

**Bonaparte's
Gull**

winter
adult

1st winter

winter
adult

breeding
adult

1st summer

winter
adult

1st
winter

winter
adult

**Black-headed
Gull**

winter
adult

breeding
adult

**Little
Gull**

1st winter

breeding
adult

winter
adult

**Ross's
Gull**

winter
adult

1st winter

breeding
adult

Ring-billed Gull   *Larus delawarensis*

L 17½" (45 cm) WS 48" (122 cm) Three-year gull. **Adult** has pale gray mantle; yellow bill with black subterminal ring; pale eyes; yellowish legs; head streaked with brown in **winter**. **Second-winter** birds are like winter adult but bill has broader band, black on primaries is more extensive, tail usually has some blackish terminal spots. **First-winter** bird has gray back, brown wings with dark blackish-brown primaries, brown-streaked head and nape; underparts white with brown spots and scalloping on breast and throat; tail has medium-wide but variable brown band and extensive mottling above band; uppertail and undertail coverts are lightly barred; secondary coverts medium gray; wing linings mostly white, with some barring (page 216). Distinguished from first-winter Mew Gull (*brachyrhynchus*) by white underparts spotted on breast and throat, tail pattern, darker primaries, heavier bill, and paler back. **Juvenal** plumage may be largely kept into early winter; resembles first-winter but back is brown, spotting below more extensive, bill has more black. **Range:** Abundant and widespread; winters uncommonly outside mapped range.

Mew Gull   *Larus canus*   L 16" (41 cm) WS 43" (109 cm)

Three-year gull. North American race *brachyrhynchus* is the smallest of three subspecies found here; has least black on wing tips; in flight, shows much more white on primaries than Ring-billed Gull. European nominate race, *canus* ("Common Gull"), and East Asian *kamtschatschensis* (the largest race) have more extensive black on wing tips. All **adults** have white head, washed with brown in **winter;** dark gray mantle; thin yellow bill; most have large, dark eyes. **Second-winter** bird is like adult but has two-toned bill; has less white on primaries; variably spotted tail band. **First-winter** *brachyrhynchus* is heavily washed with brown below, almost solid brown on belly; spotted with white on breast. The head and nape are washed with soft brown; mantle dark gray; primaries light brown with pale edges. Tail is almost entirely brown, with heavily barred tail coverts; wing linings evenly pale brown (page 216). **Juvenile** is like first-winter, but brown on the back and head, darker below. Second-winter and adult *kamtschatschensis* have pale eyes; first-winter birds are more like *brachyrhynchus*, but note dark tail band rather than all-dark tail, and paler tail coverts. In flight, first-winter's underwing coverts show intermediate coloration between *brachyrhynchus* (dark) and *canus* (pale). European *canus* resembles Ring-billed Gull in first winter; but note *canus*'s mostly white tail with dark subterminal band, unbarred white tail coverts, darker gray back, white wing linings mottled with brown. Mew Gulls average smaller than Ring-billed Gulls, especially *brachyrhynchus,* with rounder heads, larger eyes, thinner bills. **Range:** Asian race, rare on the Aleutians and islands in the Bering Sea. American race, rare inland in winter in Pacific states, casual east to Great Lakes region. European race, casual on East Coast in winter, annual in Newfoundland.

Ring-billed Gull

winter adult

breeding adult

2nd winter

breeding adult

juvenile

1st winter tail

1st winter

1st winter tail

winter adult

2nd winter

breeding adults

juvenile

Mew Gull
brachyrhynchus

1st winter

kamtschatschensis

winter adult

1st winter

winter adult

canus

1st winter

adult *kamtschatschensis*

adult *canus*

California Gull *Larus californicus*

L 21" (53 cm) WS 54" (137 cm) Four-year gull. **Adult** has darker gray mantle than Herring Gull (next page), paler than Lesser Black-backed Gull (page 212); white head, heavily streaked with brown in winter; dark eyes; yellow bill with black and red spots; black spot often smaller in breeding season; gray-green or greenish-yellow legs. In flight, shows dusky trailing edge on underwing. Third-winter plumage is like adult but bill is more extensively smudged with black; wings show some brown; tail has some brown spotting. **Second-winter** has gray back, brown wings, grayish legs, two-toned bill; compare to first-winter Ring-billed Gull (preceding page). **First-winter** is brown overall with veiled gray on scapulars; usually palest on throat, breast, and upper belly; legs pinkish; bill two-toned, the colors sharply defined. In flight (page 217), first-winter birds show double dark bar on inner half of wing, caused by darker secondaries and greater secondary covert bases. Distinctly smaller than Western Gull (page 210), with thinner bill. Compare first-winter birds to first- and second-winter Herring and Lesser Black-backed. **Juveniles** are variably pale below, lack pale bill base. **Range:** Casual on East Coast and Gulf Coast in winter.

Black-tailed Gull *Larus crassirostris*

L 18½" (47 cm) WS 47¼" (120 cm) **Range:** East Asian species, casual in coastal Alaska and eastern North America; accidental in California. Three-year or four-year gull, about size of Ring-billed Gull (page 202); bill and wings long; legs short. Distinctive white eye crescents except on **breeding adult** and third-winter bird. Adult has black ring near red tip of bill; yellow iris; red orbital ring. Mantle dark slate gray; tail has broad subterminal band. Head of **winter adult** heavily streaked. **First-winter** bird has white on face, otherwise heavily washed with brown.

Belcher's Gull *Larus belcheri*

L 20" (51 cm) WS 49" (124 cm) **Range:** Resident on west coast of South America; accidental to California and Florida. Medium-size, three-year gull. Plumages and bill color similar to Black-tailed Gull, but Belcher's has dark eyes, longer legs, and thicker bill. **Winter adults** and **second-winter** birds have dark hood, red only on tip of bill. Adult has yellow orbital ring. **First-winter**'s head and breast are smoky brown; belly white; mottled above.

Kelp Gull *Larus dominicanus*

L 23" (58 cm), WS 53" (135 cm) **Range:** Widespread Southern Hemisphere species; casual to Gulf Coast. A few Kelps nested on Chandeleur Islands off southeast Louisiana for about a decade starting in early 1990s. This resulted in pure Kelp pairings, and mixed pairings with Herring Gull that produced **hybrids.** Accidental elsewhere. Three-year gull; size, structure, and bill shape suggest Western Gull (page 210). **Adult** Kelp has black back and dull greenish legs; head streaking in winter indistinct. Eye color variable. Note restricted white in outer primaries, unlike Great Black-backed (page 212). Change to adult plumage rapid; mantle blackish by **second summer.**

California Gull

breeding adult

winter adult

2nd winter

breeding adult

1st winter

pale juvenile

dark juvenile

Black-tailed Gull

breeding adult

winter adult

1st winter

2nd winter

breeding adult

Belcher's Gull

breeding adult

winter adult

2nd winter

1st winter

breeding adult

Kelp Gull

molting juvenile

Kelp x Herring hybrid winter adult

winter adult

2nd summer

breeding adult

Herring Gull *Larus argentatus*

L 25" (64 cm) WS 58" (147 cm) Highly variable four-year gull. **Adult** has pale gray mantle; white head streaked with brown in winter; legs and feet pink; bill yellow with red spot. **Third-winter** plumage is like winter adult but with black smudge on bill, some brown on body and wing coverts. **Second-winter** bird has pale gray back; brown wings; pale eyes; two-toned bill. **First-winter** birds are brown overall, with dark brownish black primaries and tail band, dark eyes, dark bill, with variable pink at base; some may have bill like first-winter California Gull (preceding page); but usually distinguished by darker bill, paler face and throat, and, in flight (page 217), by pale panel at base of primaries and single dark bar on secondaries. Distinguished from first-winter Western Gull (page 210) by smaller bill, paler and more mottled body plumage, and, in flight, by paler wings with pale panel, and lack of contrast between back and rump. Distinguished from first-winter Lesser Black-backed Gull (page 212) by browner, less-contrasting body plumage, usually darker belly, and, in flight, by pale primary and outer secondary coverts and less-contrasting rump pattern. Widespread North American race is *smithsonianus;* Bering Sea region *vegae* has darker mantle in adult plumage and similar wing-tip pattern to Slaty-backed Gull (page 212); usually has dark eyes; head heavily streaked in winter. First-year birds are paler and more checkered; tail base is white. West European race, *argenteus*, noted casually from Newfoundland, is similar in adult plumage to *smithsonianus*, but first-winter bird is paler. **Range:** Herring Gull is generally local in the West; common in some regions, uncommon to rare in most. Common in eastern North America.

Yellow-legged Gull *Larus cachinnans*

L 24" (61 cm) WS 57" (144 cm) **Range:** Palearctic species. Casual winter visitor to northeastern coast from Newfoundland to mid-Atlantic, possibly south Texas. Size similar to Herring Gull, but Yellow-legged has squarer head, peaked at rear of crown; bill stouter and shorter. Adult mantle darker gray than *smithonianus* Herring. From above, wing tip darker than Herring; from below more gray, less black, on outermost primaries. Red gonys spot often extends onto upper mandible; orbital ring is redder than on Herring. Yellow legs distinctive, but some *smithsonianus* Herrings may show some yellow during winter. In Yellow-legged, fainter winter head streaking is restricted to nape and crown, making white head stand out; by midwinter most **adults** are white headed. **First-winter** birds are much paler on head and underparts than first-winter Herring; blocky head and extensive white on uppertail coverts and base of tail suggests same-age Great Black-backed Gull (page 212). Compare also to first-winter Lesser Black-backed. Molt to first-winter occurs earlier than in Herring; by fall, young Yellow-legged often appear worn. Recent evidence indicates that nominate *cachinnans* from Black Sea eastward is probably a distinct species from *michahellis* of Black and Mediterranean Seas and slightly darker-mantled *atlantis* of eastern Atlantic islands. Current North American records believed to be either *michahellis* or *atlantis*.

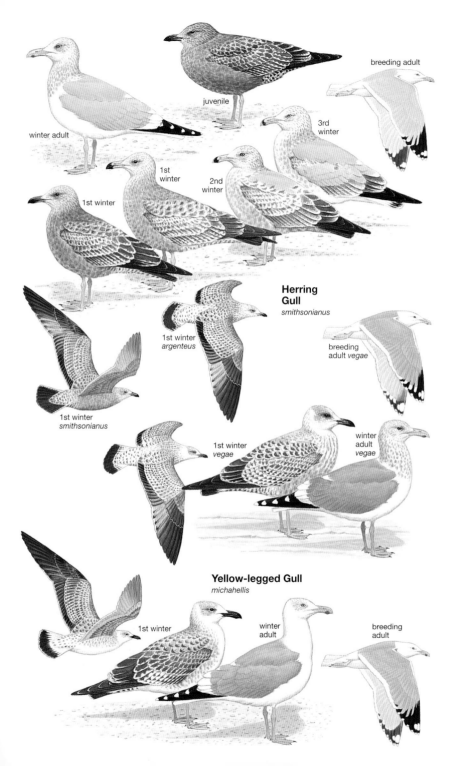

breeding adult

winter adult

juvenile

3rd winter

1st winter

2nd winter

1st winter

1st winter

Herring Gull
smithsonianus

1st winter *argenteus*

breeding adult *vegae*

1st winter *smithsonianus*

1st winter *vegae*

winter adult *vegae*

Yellow-legged Gull
michahellis

1st winter

winter adult

breeding adult

Glaucous Gull *Larus hyperboreus*

L 27" (69 cm) WS 60" (152 cm) Heavy-bodied, four-year gull. All have translucent tips to white primaries. **Adult** has very pale gray mantle, yellow eye. Head is streaked with brown in winter. Late **second-winter** bird has pale gray back and pale eye. **First-winter** birds may be buffy or almost all-white; bill is bicolored. Distinguished from Iceland Gull by size; heavier, longer bill; flatter crown; slightly paler mantle of adults; disproportionately shorter wings, barely extending beyond tail. At all ages, distinguished from Glaucous-winged Gull (pages 210, 217) by more buffy white color, contrasting pale primaries; in first-winter birds by sharply two-toned bill. **Range:** Rare in winter south to Gulf states and southern California. Northern Alaskan birds are slightly smaller, and adults have slightly darker mantles, than birds from eastern Canada and Bering Sea. Occasionally hybridizes with Herring Gull.

Iceland Gull *Larus glaucoides*

L 22" (56 cm) WS 54" (137 cm) Highly variable four-year gull. **Adults** have white heads, suffused with brown in winter; most have yellow eyes, a few brown. Late **second-winter** birds have pale eyes, gray back, two-toned bill. **First-winter** birds are buffy to mostly white; chiefly dark bill is short; eyes dark; wing tips white or irregularly washed with brown. Canadian-breeding adult *kumlieni* have wing tips variably marked with gray; a few are pure white. Greenland breeding *glaucoides* is slightly smaller and paler overall in all plumages; adults are slightly paler mantled and have pure white wing tips; most migrate southeast to Iceland, a few to Europe; rare or casual to northeast North America. First-winter birds distinguished from Thayer's by paler primaries, checkered tertials, usually paler body plumage and on some by checkered tail (see also page 217); from Glaucous by usually darker bill and structural features (smaller size, rounder head, and longer wings that extend beyond tail at rest). **Range:** Casual south to Gulf Coast states; uncommon to rare on Great Lakes; casual to Pacific region.

Thayer's Gull *Larus thayeri*

L 23" (58 cm) WS 55" (140 cm) Variable four-year gull. In most **adults,** eye is dark brown, mantle slightly darker than Iceland Gull or Herring Gull (preceding page); bill yellow with dark red spot; legs darker pink than Herring. Primaries pale gray below, with thin, dark trailing edge; show some black or slaty gray from above. Many have paler eyes. **Second-winter** has gray mantle, contrasting gray-brown tail band, dark eye. **First-winter** variable but primaries always entirely pale below, darker than mantle above. Distinguished from Herring Gull by smaller size, paler checkered markings in plumage (see also page 217), and paler primaries with whitish edges; from Iceland Gull by generally darker plumage, primaries darker than mantle, and usually by unspeckled tail. Compare to larger-sized and bigger-billed Glaucous-winged Gull (next page), in which the immatures are less mottled and the wing tips are uniform with the mantle. **Range:** Rare winter visitor to Great Lakes region and through the interior, but identification difficult. Casual on East Coast. Considered by some a race of Iceland Gull.

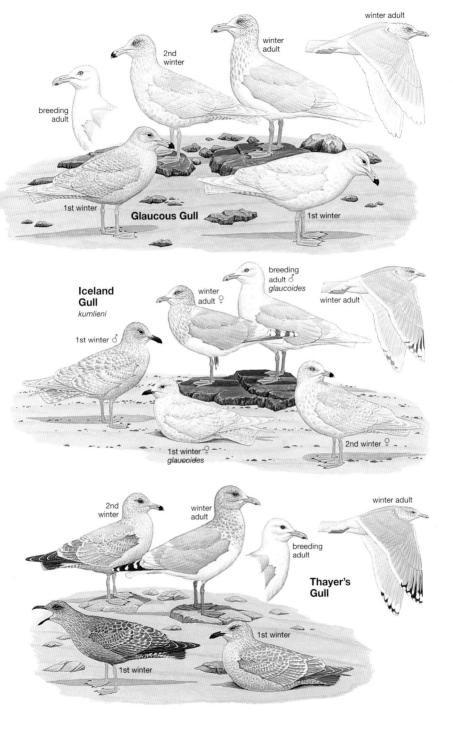

winter adult

2nd
winter

winter
adult

breeding
adult

1st winter

Glaucous Gull

1st winter

**Iceland
Gull**
kumlieni

breeding
adult ♂
glaucoides

winter
adult ♀

winter adult

1st winter ♂

1st winter ♀
glaucoides

2nd winter ♀

2nd
winter

winter
adult

breeding
adult

winter adult

**Thayer's
Gull**

1st winter

1st winter

Yellow-footed Gull *Larus livens*

L 27" (69 cm) WS 60" (152 cm) **Range:** Breeds in the Gulf of California. Fairly common post-breeding visitor in summer to Salton Sea; a few usually linger into winter; rarest in spring. Casual to coastal southern California. Three-year gull. **Adult** is like Western Gull but has yellow legs and feet; note also thicker yellow bill with red spot; dark slate gray wings; yellow eyes. **Second-winter** bird is like adult but tail looks entirely black, bill two-toned. In first-winter plumage (seen in flight page 217), head and body are mostly white, back and wings brown, eyes dark, bill mostly dark, legs pinkish. **Juvenile** resembles first-winter Western but white belly contrasts sharply with streaked breast; upperparts are more boldly patterned; rump whiter. Yellow-footed Gull's **calls** are lower-pitched than Western.

Western Gull *Larus occidentalis*

L 25" (64 cm) WS 58" (147 cm) Four-year gull. **Adults** north of Monterey, California, have paler backs and darker eyes than southern birds. All adults have white head, dark gray back, pink legs, very large bill. In **winter,** head is moderately streaked with brown in northern birds, faintly streaked in southern. **Third-winter** plumage resembles second-winter Yellow-footed Gull but tail is mostly white. **Second-winter** bird has a dark gray back, yellow eyes, two-toned bill, dark brown wings. **First-winter** bird is one of the darkest young gulls; bill is black; in flight (page 217), distinguished from young Herring Gull by contrast of dark back with paler rump. Note also the often sootier underparts and head, heavier bill. **Juvenile** is like first-winter but darker. Western Gulls hybridize extensively with Glaucous-winged Gulls in the Northwest; **hybrids** are seen all along the West Coast in winter; two ages are shown here. These are easily confused with Thayer's Gull (page 208); note large bill, pattern of wing tips. **Range:** Western Gulls are very rare to casual well inland; definite records as far east as Illinois and Texas. Casual to southeastern Alaska.

Glaucous-winged Gull *Larus glaucescens*

L 26" (66 cm) WS 58" (147 cm) Four-year gull. **Adult** has white head, moderately streaked with brown in winter. Body is white, mantle pale gray; primaries are the same color as rest of wing above, paler below. Eyes dark; large bill yellow with red spot; legs pink. Third-winter bird is like adult but has some buff on body, bill is smudged black; some have a partial tail band. **Second-winter**'s back is gray, rest of body and wings are pale buff to white with little mottling; tail evenly gray; bill mostly dark. **First-winter** bird (shown in flight on page 217) is uniformly pale gray-brown to whitish with subtle mottling; primaries are the same color as the mantle; note young Glaucous Gull (pages 208, 217) has sharply two-toned bill, pale primaries; and young Thayer's Gull (previous page) is smaller, with smaller bill, more speckled body plumage, and darker primaries. Glaucous-winged Gull hybridizes with Western Gull; and with Herring Gull (page 206) in south-central Alaska. Hybrids are extremely variable. **Range:** Rare well inland in Pacific states; casual east to Great Lakes region.

Yellow-footed Gull

2nd winter

adult

juvenile

adult

1st summer

Western Gull

southern 3rd winter *wymani*

southern winter adult *wymani*

northern breeding adult *occidentalis*

southern breeding adult *wymani*

juvenile *occidentalis*

southern 2nd winter *wymani*

1st winter *occidentalis*

1st winter

breeding adult

Glaucous-winged x Western hybrid

breeding adult

2nd winter

Glaucous-winged Gull

breeding adult

1st winter

Slaty-backed Gull *Larus schistisagus*

L 25" (64 cm) WS 58" (147 cm) **Range:** Coastal species of northeast Asia. Rare in coastal Alaska, most frequent in the Bering Sea. Very rare in winter south through Pacific states; casual elsewhere in North America. Four-year gull. **Adult** has dark slate gray back and wings, blackish outer primaries separated from mantle by a staggered row of whitish spots. Underside of primaries gray. Note broad white trailing edge to wings. Legs bright pink; pale eyes. Head heavily mottled in winter. **Second-summer** bird has dark back, very pale wings. First-year birds show almost entirely dark tail and wing pattern like Thayer's Gull (page 208); also compare with *vegae* race of Herring Gull (page 206); *vegae* adult has slightly paler upperparts, lacks broad white trailing edge; underside of primaries darker than Slaty-backed.

Lesser Black-backed Gull *Larus fuscus*

L 21" (53 cm) WS 54" (137 cm) **Range:** Western Palearctic species; generally rare to locally uncommon in eastern North America. Casual to West Coast and Alaska. A four-year gull. **Adult** has white head, heavily streaked with brown in winter; white underparts; yellow legs. Third-winter bird has dark smudge on bill; some brown in wings. **Second-winter** bird resembles second-winter Herring Gull (page 206) but note dark gray back, much darker underwings. **First-winter** bird similar to first-winter Herring Gull but head and belly are paler, upperparts more contrastingly dark and light; bill is always entirely black. Identified in flight (page 217) by darker primary and secondary coverts, more extensively dark primaries and white outer tail feathers; paler rump contrasts with back. Much smaller than Great Black-backed Gull. Smaller on average than Herring Gull, with smaller bill, but there is substantial range of overlap; also note longer wings, usually extending well beyond tail at rest. Most birds seen here are of northern European race *graellsii*. A few darker mantled adults in eastern North America likely of Baltic race *intermedius*.

Great Black-backed Gull *Larus marinus*

L 30" (76 cm) WS 65" (165 cm) Four-year gull. Huge size and large bill are distinctive. **Adult**'s white head is virtually unstreaked in winter; black upperparts; white underparts; variably pale eyes; pink legs. In flight, note extensive white on outer primary that merges with white spot on second primary to form solid white area. **Third-winter** bird is like adult but shows some dark on bill, some brown in wings, sometimes dark in tail. **Second-summer** bird has pale eye, black back; wings and tail are like first-winter. Second-winter is like first-winter, but base of bill is paler, secondary coverts more evenly brown. **First-winter** bird resembles Herring Gull (page 206) but head and body are much paler, back and wings have the checkered look of young Lesser Black-backed Gull; in flight (page 217), shows almost white rump, checkered tail band. **Range:** Breeding range expanding southward on the Atlantic coast. Fairly common on eastern Great Lakes, rarer on western; casual inland throughout the East. Very rare on Gulf Coast; casual west to Great Plains; accidental to Alaska and Washington.

Slaty-backed Gull

winter adult

breeding adult

2nd summer

1st summer

Lesser Black-backed Gull *graellsii*

winter adult *intermedius*

breeding adult

winter adult

winter adult

2nd winter

1st winter

Great Black-backed Gull

breeding adult

3rd winter

winter adult

2nd summer

1st winter

Black-legged Kittiwake *Rissa tridactyla*

L 17" (43 cm) WS 36" (91 cm) Pelagic three-year gull. **Adult** has white head, nape smudged with gray in **winter;** dark eye; yellow bill; white body with gray mantle. Inner primaries are pale, wing tips inky black; legs black. Second-year bird is like adult but with more black on outermost primary. **Juvenile** has dark half collar, retained into early winter; black bill; black spot behind eye; dark tail band; and, in flight (page 216), dark W across the wings. Distinguished from young Sabine's Gull by half collar, dark carpal bar. A very few young birds have pinkish legs. **Call** is a series of *kittiwake*'s. **Range:** Nests in large cliff colonies; winters at sea. Seen uncommonly from shore on the West Coast, commonly in some years when a few may summer; rarely on the East Coast.

Red-legged Kittiwake *Rissa brevirostris*

L 15" (38 cm) WS 33" (84 cm) Pelagic two-year gull. **Adult** distinguished from Black-legged Kittiwake by coral red legs; shorter, thicker bill; darker mantle; wings are not paler on flight feathers as in Black-legged; broader white trailing edge on wings; dusky underside of primaries. In first-year, wing pattern resembles Sabine's Gull (page 216), but Red-legged Kittiwake is the only gull to have an all-white tail in first winter. Similar to young Black-legged but lacks W pattern on wings. **Call** is higher-pitched and squeakier than Black-legged. **Range:** Breeds in cliff colonies, usually close to Black-legged Kittiwake. Very rare away from breeding grounds, even in winter. Casual on and off West Coast.

Sabine's Gull *Xema sabini* *L 13½" (34 cm) WS 33" (84 cm)*

Two-year gull with striking black-gray-and-white wing pattern in all ages. **Breeding adult** has dark gray hood with thin black ring at bottom; black bill with yellow tip; forked tail. First-summer bird is like adult but hood not complete; faint dusky nape. In **juvenal** plumage (see also page 216), wing pattern is like adult; crown and nape are soft gray-brown; bill black; tail has dark band. **Range:** Sabine's Gull winters at sea mainly in the Southern Hemisphere. Most adults migrate out of North America before acquiring white head and dark nape of winter plumage. Juveniles depart before acquiring more adultlike plumage. Common migrant off West Coast, rarely seen from shore. Rare in fall, casual in spring, in western interior. Very rare in fall east to Great Lakes region. Casual on and off East Coast and in the South.

Ivory Gull *Pagophila eburnea* *L 17" (43 cm) WS 37" (94 cm)*

Two-year arctic gull, ghostly pale. **Adults** in all plumages are strikingly white with a yellow-tipped bill, black eyes, black legs. **First-winter** birds show a variable amount of speckling on the body, heaviest and often patchy on the face; have tail band, and spots on tips of primaries. A short-necked, stocky gull with long wings. **Range:** Winters primarily in Arctic seas. Uncommon in northern and western Alaska. Casual along the Atlantic coast to New York, and inland to the northern tier of states. Accidental to southern California and southern Tennessee. Global warming imperils species.

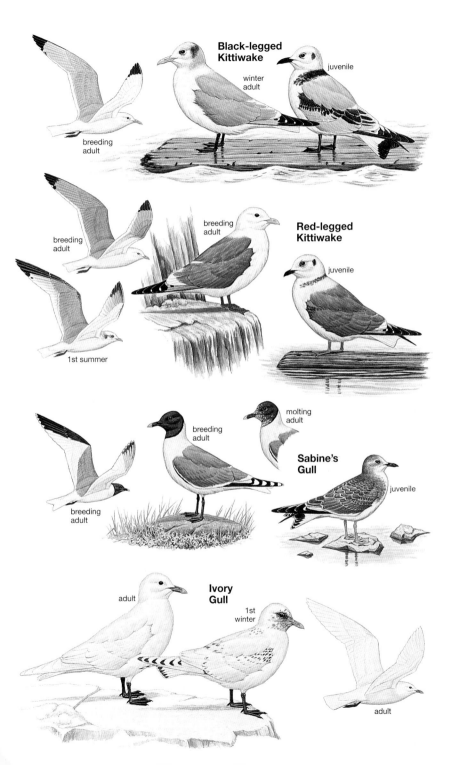

Black-legged Kittiwake

breeding adult

winter adult

juvenile

Red-legged Kittiwake

breeding adult

breeding adult

1st summer

juvenile

breeding adult

molting adult

breeding adult

Sabine's Gull

juvenile

adult

Ivory Gull

1st winter

adult

Immature Gulls in Flight

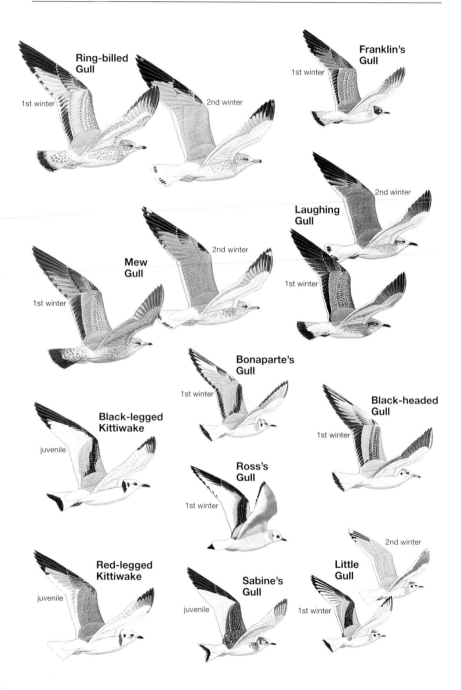

Ring-billed Gull — 1st winter, 2nd winter

Franklin's Gull — 1st winter

Laughing Gull — 2nd winter, 1st winter

Mew Gull — 1st winter, 2nd winter

Bonaparte's Gull — 1st winter

Black-headed Gull — 1st winter

Black-legged Kittiwake — juvenile

Ross's Gull — 1st winter

Red-legged Kittiwake — juvenile

Sabine's Gull — juvenile

Little Gull — 2nd winter, 1st winter

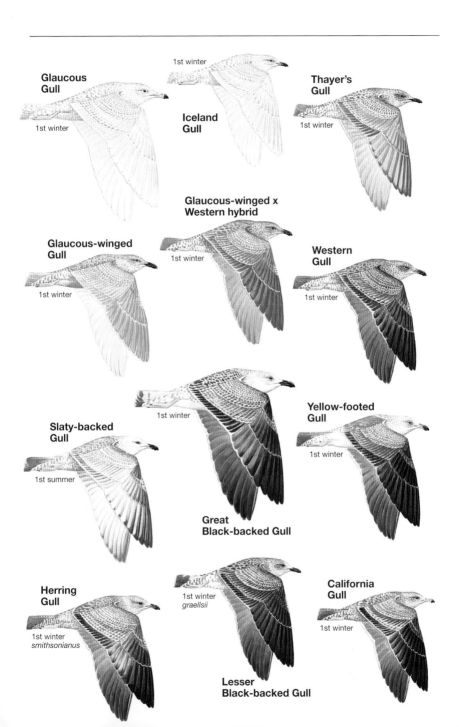

Glaucous
Gull

1st winter

1st winter
Iceland
Gull

Thayer's
Gull

1st winter

Glaucous-winged x
Western hybrid

Glaucous-winged
Gull

1st winter

1st winter

Western
Gull

1st winter

Slaty-backed
Gull

1st summer

1st winter

Yellow-footed
Gull

1st winter

Great
Black-backed Gull

Herring
Gull

1st winter
smithsonianus

1st winter
graellsii

California
Gull

1st winter

Lesser
Black-backed Gull

Terns

Distinguished from gulls by long, pointed wings and bill and by feeding technique. Most terns plunge-dive into the water after prey. Most species have a forked tail.

Sandwich Tern *Thalasseus sandvicensis*
L 15" (38 cm) WS 34" (86 cm) Slender, black bill, tipped with yellow. **Breeding adult** is pale gray above with black crown, short black crest. In flight, shows some dark in outer primaries. White tail is deeply forked, comparatively short. Adult in **winter** plumage, seen as early as July, has a white forehead, streaked crown, grayer tail. **Juvenile**'s tail less deeply forked; bill often lacks yellow tip; in a few it is entirely yellow. By late summer, juvenile loses dark V-shaped markings and spots on back and scapulars. **Calls** include abrupt *gwit gwit* and *skee-rick* notes, like calls of Elegant Tern. **Range:** Nests on coastal beaches and islands. Casual spring and summer visitor to coastal southern California.

Elegant Tern *Thalasseus elegans*
L 17" (43 cm) WS 34" (86 cm) Bill longer, thinner than in larger Royal Tern; reddish orange in adults, yellow in some juveniles. In flight, shows mostly pale underside of primaries; compare to Caspian Tern. **Breeding adult** is pale gray above with black crown and nape, black crest; white below, often with pinkish tinge. **Winter adult** and **juvenile** have white forehead; black over top of crown extends forward around eye; compare with Royal. Juveniles variably mottled above, may have orange legs; some have less black on crown, like juvenile Royal. Sharp *kee-rick* **call** very similar to Sandwich Tern. **Range:** Post-breeding dispersal to northern Washington; casual to British Columbia; very rare spring and summer at Salton Sea; accidental in Southwest, Gulf and Atlantic coasts.

Royal Tern *Thalasseus maxima*
L 20" (51 cm) WS 41" (104 cm) Orange-red bill, thinner than Caspian. In flight, shows mostly pale underside of primaries; tail more deeply forked than Caspian. **Adult** shows white crown most of year; black cap acquired briefly early in **breeding** season. In **winter adult** and **juvenile,** black on nape does not usually extend to encompass eye; compare Elegant Tern. **Calls** include a bleating *kee-rer* and ploverlike whistled *tourreee.* **Range:** Nests in dense colonies. Fairly common in winter on southern California coast, where a few breed; uncommon to rare north of breeding range along Atlantic coast in late summer; casual in North American interior.

Caspian Tern *Hydroprogne caspia*
L 21" (53 cm) WS 50" (127 cm) Large, stocky; bill orange to coral red, much thicker than in Royal Tern. In flight, shows dark underside of primaries; tail less deeply forked than Royal. **Adult** acquires black cap in **breeding** season; in **winter adult** and **juvenile,** crown streaked; never shows fully white forehead of Royal. Adult's **calls** include a harsh *kowk* and *ca-arr;* immature's a distinctive, whistled *whee-you.* **Range:** Small colonies nest on coasts, in wetlands.

Sandwich Tern

juvenile

winter adult

breeding adult

juvenile

Elegant Tern

winter adult

juvenile

breeding adult

winter adult

juvenile

Royal Tern

breeding adult

juvenile

Caspian Tern

winter adult

breeding adult

juvenile

Roseate Tern *Sterna dougallii* **E**

L 15½" (39 cm) WS 29" (74 cm) **Breeding adult** is white below with slight, variable pinkish cast visible in good light; pale gray above with black cap and nape. Much paler overall than Common and Arctic Terns (next page). Lacks dark trailing edge on underside of outer wing. Bill mostly black; during summer more red appears at base. Wings shorter than in Common and Arctic; flies with rapid wingbeats suggestive of Least Tern (page 224). Deeply forked all-white tail extends well beyond wings in standing bird. Legs and feet bright red-orange. **Juvenile**'s brownish cap extends over forehead; mantle looks coarsely scaled, lower back barred with black; bill and legs black. **First-summer** bird has white forehead; lacks dark secondaries of immature Common. Full adult plumage is attained by second spring. **Call** is a soft *chi-weep;* alarm signal a drawn-out *zra-ap,* like ripping cloth. **Range:** Uncommon and highly maritime, Roseate Terns usually come ashore only to nest. Rare on mid-Atlantic coast in late spring.

Forster's Tern *Sterna forsteri*

L 14½" (37 cm) WS 31" (79 cm) **Breeding adult** is snow white below, pale gray above, with black cap and nape; mostly orange bill, orange legs and feet. Wingbeat much slower than in Roseate Tern. Legs and bill longer than in Common and Arctic Terns (next page). Long, deeply forked gray tail has white outer edges. In flight, shows pale upperwing area formed by silvery primaries; white rump contrasts with gray back, gray tail. **Winter** plumage resembles Common and Arctic but is acquired by mid- to late Aug., much earlier than those species, which molt chiefly after migration out of U.S. Note also lack of dark shoulder bars; most have dark eye patches not joined at nape as in Common, but many have dark streaks on nape. **Juvenile** and **first-winter** bird have shorter tails than adults and more dark color in wings. Juvenile has ginger brown cap and dark eye patch; shoulder bar is faint or absent. **Calls** include a hoarse *kyarr,* lower and shorter than in Common. **Range:** Forster's Terns nest in widely scattered colonies in marshes.

Gull-billed Tern *Gelochelidon nilotica*

L 14" (36 cm) WS 34" (86 cm) **Breeding adult** is white below, pale gray above, with black crown and nape, stout black bill, black legs and feet. Stockier and paler than Common Tern (next page); wings broader; tail shorter and only moderately forked. **Juveniles** and **winter** birds appear largely white headed apart from some fine streaking. Juvenile has pale edgings on upperparts, bill is brownish. Adult **call** is a raspy, sharp *kay-wack;* call of juvenile is a faint, high-pitched *peep peep.* **Range:** Fairly common but local; nests in salt marshes and on beaches; often seen hunting for insects over fields and marshes in direct powerful flight. Does not hover or dive in water. Casual in interior of North America, New England, and Atlantic Canada, except at Salton Sea, where it nests. Breeds also in California in coastal San Diego County.

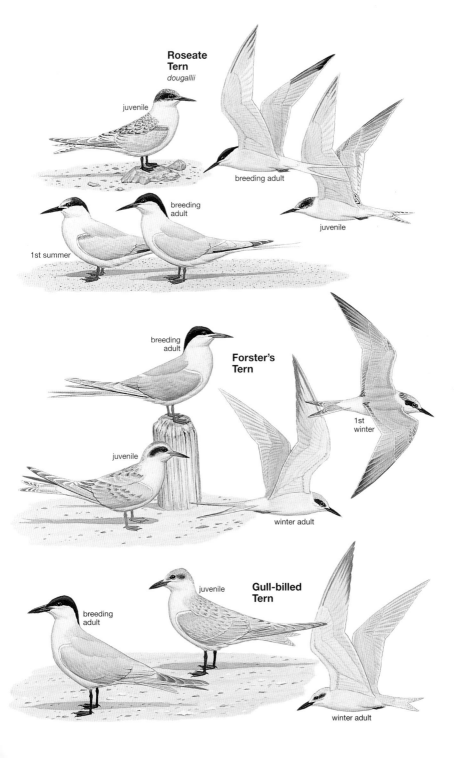

Roseate Tern
dougallii

juvenile

breeding adult

juvenile

1st summer

breeding adult

breeding adult

Forster's Tern

juvenile

1st winter

winter adult

breeding adult

juvenile

Gull-billed Tern

winter adult

Common Tern *Sterna hirundo*

L 14½" (37 cm) WS 30" (76 cm) Medium gray above, with black cap and nape; paler below. Bill red, usually tipped with black. Slightly stockier than the Arctic Tern, with flatter crown, longer neck and bill. In flight, usually displays a dark wedge, variably shaped, near tip of upperwing; in late summer all outer primaries can appear dark. Note also that head projects farther than in Arctic. Common Tern's shorter tail gives it a chunkier look. Early **juvenile** shows some brown above, white below, with mostly dark bill. Juvenile's forehead is white, crown and nape blackish, secondaries dark gray; compare with juvenile Forster's Tern (preceding page). All immature and winter plumages have a dark shoulder bar. Full **adult breeding** plumage is acquired by third spring. Some **calls** are similar to Arctic Tern; distinctive in Common, a low, piercing, drawn-out *kee-ar-r-r-r*. **Range:** Common Terns nest in large colonies. Common throughout breeding range. Uncommon and declining migrant on Pacific coast from Washington south; uncommon in fall in western interior. An East Asian subspecies, *longipennis,* seen regularly on the islands of western Alaska, is darker overall; bill and legs black.

Arctic Tern *Sterna paradisaea*

L 15½" (39 cm) WS 31" (79 cm) Medium gray above, with black cap and nape; paler below. Bill deep red. Slightly slimmer than Common Tern, with rounder head, shorter neck and bill. In flight, upperwing appears uniformly gray, lacking dark wedge of Common; underwing shows very narrow black line on trailing edge of primaries; all flight feathers appear translucent. Note also that tail is longer and head does not project as far as in Common. **Juvenile** largely lacks brownish wash of early juvenile Common; shoulder bar less distinct; secondaries whitish and a portion of coverts whitish too, creating an effect like Sabine's Gull (page 214). Forehead is white, crown and nape blackish; compare juvenile Forster's Tern (preceding page). Full adult breeding plumage is acquired by third spring. **Calls** include a raspy *tr-tee-ar,* higher than Common Tern's call. **Range:** Arctic Terns migrate well offshore; casual inland during migration, especially in late spring.

Aleutian Tern *Onychoprion aleutica*

L 13½" (34 cm) WS 29" (74 cm) Dark gray above and below, with white forehead, black cap, black bill, black legs. In flight, distinguished from Common and Arctic Terns by shorter tail, white forehead, and dark, white-edged bar on secondaries, most visible from below. **Juvenile** is buff and brown above; legs and lower mandible reddish. **Call** is a squeaky *twee-ee-ee,* unlike any other tern. **Range:** Aleutian Terns nest in loose colonies, sometimes with Arctic Terns. Casual in spring off British Columbia. Migration routes uncertain; has been seen in fall and winter off Hong Kong, the Philippines, and Sumatra. Main winter grounds still unknown, probably southwest Pacific and Indian Oceans.

Common Tern
hirundo

1st summer

breeding
adult

juvenile

2nd
summer

breeding adult
longipennis

1st fall

breeding adult

Arctic Tern

juvenile

1st summer

breeding adult

breeding
adult

juvenile

Aleutian Tern

juvenile

breeding
adult

Least Tern *Sternula antillarum* **E**
L 9" (23 cm) WS 20" (51 cm) Smallest North American tern.
Breeding adult is gray above, with black cap and nape, white forehead, orange-yellow bill with dark tip; underparts are white; legs orange-yellow. By late summer, bill base is more greenish. In flight, black wedge on outer primaries is conspicuous; note also the short, deeply forked tail. **Juvenile** shows brownish, U-shaped markings; crown is dusky; wings show dark shoulder bar. By first fall, upperparts are gray, crown whiter, but dark shoulder bar is retained. **First-summer** birds are more like adults but have dark bill and legs, shoulder bar, black line through eye, dusky primaries. Flight is rapid and buoyant. **Calls** include high-pitched *kip* notes and a harsh *chir-ee-eep*. **Range:** Nests in colonies on beaches and sandbars; also on rooftops. Fairly common but local on East and Gulf Coasts; declining inland and on the California coast. Winters from Central America south.

Black Tern *Chlidonias niger*
L 9¾" (25 cm) WS 24" (61 cm) **Breeding adult** is mostly black, with dark gray back, wings, and tail; white undertail coverts. In flight, shows uniformly pale gray underwing and fairly short tail, slightly forked. Bill is black in all plumages. **Juvenile** and winter birds are white below, with dark gray mantle and tail; dark ear patch extends from dark crown; flying birds show dark bar on side of breast. Some juveniles show a contrastingly paler rump. Shoulder bar on upper wing is much darker than in juvenile White-winged Tern. First-summer birds can be like winter adults or may have some dark feathers on head and underparts; second-summer birds are like breeding adults, but show some whitish on head; full breeding plumage is acquired by third spring. **Molting fall adults** appear patchy black-and-white as they acquire winter plumage in late summer; these birds are easily confused with the White-winged Tern. **Calls** include a metallic *kik* and a slurred *k-seek*. **Range:** Black Terns nest on lakeshores and in marshes; declining over part of range inland and on East Coast; rare migrant on West Coast.

White-winged Tern *Chlidonias leucopterus*
L 9½" (24 cm) WS 23" (58 cm) **Range:** Eurasian species, very rare vagrant to East Coast; casual to Great Lakes region; accidental in West, where recorded in western Aleutians, south coastal Alaska, coastal California. Bill and tail shorter than in Black Tern; tail less deeply notched. In **breeding** plumage, bill usually black, but sometimes red; white tail, whitish upperwing coverts, and black wing linings are distinctive; upperwing shows black outer primaries. **Molting** birds are patchy black-and-white, but whitish tail and rump are distinctive; black wing linings often last until late summer. **Winter adult** has white wing linings; lacks dark breast bar of Black Tern; crown, speckled rather than solid black, not usually connected to dark ear patch. First-summer bird resembles winter adult; second-summer usually like breeding adult; adult plumage reached by third spring. **Juvenile**'s head pattern resembles Black, but browner back shows greater contrast with grayish wing coverts and whitish rump than juvenile Black.

Least Tern *antillarum*

breeding adult

juvenile

breeding adult

1st summer

Black Tern *surinamensis*

breeding adult

molting fall adult

juvenile

breeding adult

juvenile

White-winged Tern

winter adult

juvenile

breeding adult

molting adult

Bridled Tern *Onychoprion anaethetus*

L 15" (38 cm) WS 30" (76 cm) **Range:** Nests in the West Indies and locally off Florida Keys. Regular in summer well offshore in the Gulf of Mexico, and in the Gulf Stream to North Carolina; rarely to New Jersey; after tropical storms, casual to New England. Note white collar between brownish gray upperparts and black cap on **breeding adult.** Similar to Sooty Tern, but slimmer; wings more pointed; underwings and tail edges more extensively white; tail grayer. Bridled's white forehead patch extends behind the eye, while Sooty's stops at the eye. **Juvenile** has pale mottling above.

Sooty Tern *Onychoprion fuscata*

L 16" (41 cm) WS 32" (81 cm) **Range:** Large breeding colony on Dry Tortugas, Florida; also nests on islands off Texas and Louisiana. Regular in summer to North Carolina. Casual in southern coastal California. Tropical storms can carry birds inland to Great Lakes and north to Maritime Provinces. Blackish above, white below; white forehead. Lacks white collar of Bridled Tern. Tail is deeply forked, edged with white. **Juvenile** is sooty brown overall, with whitish stippling on back; pale lower belly and undertail coverts; pale wing linings. Typical **call** is a high, nasal *wacky-wack.*

Black Noddy *Anous minutus* *L 13½" (34 cm) WS 30" (76 cm)*

Range: Tropical species, rare and now irregular visitor among Brown Noddies on Dry Tortugas (mostly immatures). Casual on Texas Gulf Coast. Black Noddy is smaller, with shorter legs; bill is thinner and disproportionately longer; overall color is slightly blacker. In **immatures,** white area on head is very sharply defined.

Brown Noddy *Anous stolidus*

L 15½" (39 cm) WS 32" (81 cm) **Range:** Nests in a colony on Dry Tortugas, Florida. Casual to Texas coast and off Outer Banks, North Carolina. Overall dark gray-brown with whitish gray cap, blending at back; **immature** shows only a whitish line on forehead. Unlike other terns, noddies have long, wedge-shaped tail with only a small notch at tip. Usually silent; a crowlike *karrk* **call** is heard mostly around the breeding colonies.

Large-billed Tern *Phaetusa simplex*

L 14½" (37 cm) WS 36" (92 cm) **Range:** A South American freshwater species. Accidental; recorded in late spring and summer from Illinois, Ohio, and New Jersey; additionally from Cuba and Bermuda. Mantle and short tail dark gray; white below with white forehead and black cap; legs and stout bill yellow. In flight, shows striking Sabine's Gull-like pattern (page 214).

Black Skimmer *Rynchops niger*

L 18" (46 cm) WS 44" (112 cm) No other bird has a lower mandible longer than the upper. A long-winged coastal bird, it furrows the shallows with its red, black-tipped bill. Black above and white below; red legs and bill shape are distinctive. Female is distinctly smaller than the male. **Juvenile** is mottled dingy brown above. **Winter adults** show a white collar. **Range:** Casual inland.

Bridled Tern
melanoptera

breeding
adult

juvenile

Sooty Tern
fuscata

juvenile

breeding adult

Black Noddy
americanus

adult

immature

Brown Noddy
stolidus

adults

immature

Large-billed Tern

breeding
adult

juvenile

winter adults

Black Skimmer
niger

breeding
adult

Skuas, Jaegers (Family Stercorariidae)

Formerly placed with the Gulls, Terns, and Skimmers, recent molecular evidence indicates that they are most closely related to Alcidae and belong in their own family. Predatory and piratic seabirds, skuas are broader winged than jaegers. *Species: 7 World, 5 N.A.*

Great Skua *Stercorarius skua*
L 22" (56 cm) WS 54" (137 cm) Large, heavy, and barrel-chested; wings broader and more rounded than jaegers (next page); tail shorter and broader. Shows a distinctly hunchbacked appearance in flight and a conspicuous white bar at base of primaries; bill is heavier than in jaegers. Great Skua is distinguished from South Polar Skua by overall reddish or ginger brown color and heavy streaking on back, wing coverts, and much of underparts; sometimes shows dark brown cap. **Juvenile** and immature show less streaking, especially on underparts. A small number of juvenile dark morphs have much less rufous streaking; resemble juvenile South Polar Skuas. Strong, powerful fliers, skuas pursue gulls and other seabirds and rob them of their prey. **Range:** Uncommon; breeds in Iceland and northern Europe; winters in North Atlantic. Seen well offshore from Nov. to Apr.; rare in summer off Canadian coast.

South Polar Skua *Stercorarius maccormicki*
L 21" (53 cm) WS 52" (132 cm) Large, heavy, and barrel-chested; wings broader and more rounded than jaegers (next page); tail shorter and broader. Like Great Skua, shows a distinctly hunchbacked appearance in flight, a bold white bar at base of primaries, and a heavier bill than in jaegers. In all ages, South Polar Skua shows a uniform mantle coloring and lacks the reddish tones and streaking seen on upperparts of Great Skua. In **light-morph** birds, contrastingly pale gray nape is distinctive; light morph also shows grayish head and underparts. **Dark morph** is uniformly blackish brown across mantle, with golden hackles on nape; distinguished from subadult Pomarine Jaeger by larger size, broader and more rounded wings, more distinct white wing bar. **Juveniles** and immatures of both color morphs are darker than light-morph adults, ranging from dark brown to dark gray. In the field, birds under two years of age are generally indistinguishable from juveniles; birds over two years old are generally indistinguishable from full adults. **Range:** South Polar Skua winters (our summer) in the North Atlantic and North Pacific, usually from May to early Nov. Most numerous in spring and fall off the West Coast, in spring off the East Coast; casual off the south coast of Alaska; accidental in North Dakota; a record from Tennessee after Hurricane Katrina likely this species. Very rarely seen from shore. Difficulty of identification makes range information somewhat speculative for both skua species. Several records (photos) of birds off mid-Atlantic coast could pertain to Brown Skua (*S. antarcticus*), of Southern Hemisphere, or possibly hybrids between that species and South Polar Skua.

Great Skua

typical adult

dark adult

juvenile

pale adult

dark-morph adult

intermediate-morph adult

juvenile

South Polar Skua

light-morph adults

juvenile

Jaegers

Arctic breeders. Wings are longer, slimmer, and more powerful than skuas. Adult plumage and long central tail feathers take three or four years to develop. Complex and variable plumages make identification extremely difficult. Most molts occur after the fall migration.

Pomarine Jaeger *Stercorarius pomarinus*
L 21" (53 cm) WS 48" (122 cm) Body bulkier, bicolored bill longer and thicker, wingbeats slower than Parasitic Jaeger. Most birds show a distinctive second pale underwing patch at base of primaries (fainter or lacking in Parasitic). **Adult**'s tail streamers, twisted at ends, form dark blobs when seen from side; length is variable, averages longer in male. Note extensive helmet on sides of head. Compare **dark-morph adults** and subadults with South Polar Skuas (preceding page). Some grayish brown **juveniles** are dark, some pale, but none shows the foxy red tones of most juvenile Parasitics; underwing is paler than body; pale, barred uppertail covert forms a contrasting patch above. **Range:** Seen less often from shore than Parasitic. Common off West Coast in spring migration and especially late in fall; often migrates in flocks. Uncommon in winter; casual inland away from Great Lakes.

Parasitic Jaeger *Stercorarius parasiticus*
L 19" (48 cm) WS 42" (107 cm) Smaller size, more slender body, faster wingbeats than Pomarine Jaeger; also smaller head, thinner bill, pointed tail streamers. **Adult** lacks helmeted effect of Pomarine; is paler near bill, as juveniles sometimes are also. **Juvenile** is highly variable; shows rufous tips on primaries; distinctive rusty tones particularly evident on **light morphs;** tail coverts have fainter, wavier bars than Pomarine. **Range:** Fairly common; the jaeger species most often seen from shore in migration. Casual fall migrant inland; more regular on Great Lakes and Salton Sea.

Long-tailed Jaeger *Stercorarius longicaudus*
L 22" (56 cm) WS 40" (102 cm) Most lightly built jaeger, with round chest, flat belly, narrow wings, and disproportionately long tail in all ages; bill rather short and thick. Flight is more graceful, ternlike. Note distinctive contrast between grayish mantle and darker flight feathers; usually has only two to three white primary shafts; no pale underwing patch except on **juvenile. Adult** has well-defined black cap, no breast band as in most jaegers, and usually very long, pointed central tail streamers. Juvenile's central tail feathers have round, often white-edged tips; bill is half dark, half gray; is grayer overall than Parasitic except for dark morph; fringing above whitish, never rusty. **Light-morph juveniles** show distinctive white belly and strong, even, black barring on upper- and undertail coverts; palest birds may have very pale gray heads. **Dark-morph juveniles** often lack barring on uppertail coverts. **Range:** Common in dry, upland-tundra breeding area; migrating birds uncommon to fairly common well off West Coast (fall); rare closer to shore and off East Coast (mainly in fall); rare inland (mainly in fall), and casual off Gulf Coast.

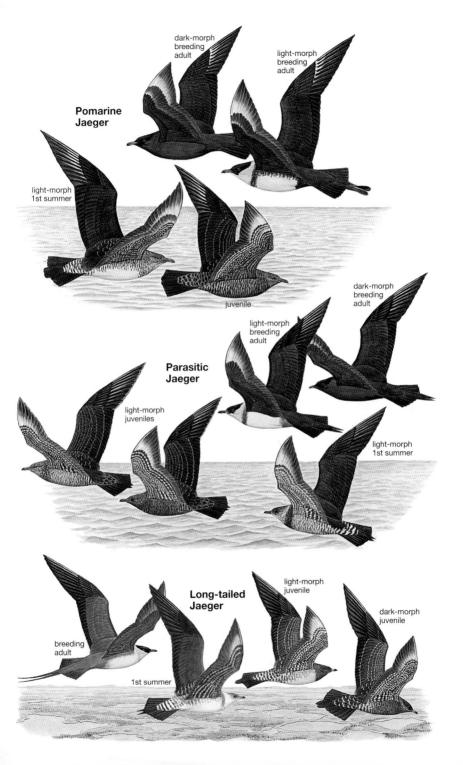

Pomarine Jaeger

dark-morph breeding adult

light-morph breeding adult

light-morph 1st summer

juvenile

Parasitic Jaeger

light-morph breeding adult

dark-morph breeding adult

light-morph juveniles

light-morph 1st summer

Long-tailed Jaeger

light-morph juvenile

dark-morph juvenile

breeding adult

1st summer

Auks, Murres, Puffins (Family Alcidae)

These black-and-white "penguins of the north" have set-back legs
that give them an upright stance on land. In flight, wingbeats are
rapid and shallow. *Species: 24 World, 22 N.A.*

Dovekie *Alle alle* L 8¼" (21 cm)

Small and plump with short neck, stubby bill. **Breeding adult** is
black above, white below; black upper breast contrasts sharply
with white underparts; dark wing linings. Usually swims tilted
forward in the water. In **winter** plumage, throat, chin, and lower
face are white, with white curving around behind eye. **Range:**
Abundant on breeding grounds. Winters irregularly in North
Atlantic south to off coast of North Carolina; rarely to Florida,
but occasionally in large numbers; casual inland.

Common Murre *Uria aalge* L 17½" (45 cm)

Large, with a long, slender, pointed bill. Upperparts dark sooty
gray, head brownish; underparts white. Some Atlantic birds have
a **"bridle,"** a white eye ring and spur. In **winter** plumage, a dark
stripe extends from eye across white cheek. **Juvenile** has shorter
bill; distinguished from Thick-billed Murre by white facial stripe,
paler upperparts, mottled flanks, and thinner bill. **Range:**
Numerous off East and West Coasts. Nests in dense colonies on
rocky cliffs. Chick accompanies adult at sea and can be mistaken
for Xantus's Murrelets (page 236).

Thick-billed Murre *Uria lomvia* L 18" (46 cm)

Stocky, with a thick, fairly short bill, arched at tip to form a blunt
hook. Upperparts and throat of **adult** are darker than Common
Murre; white of underparts usually rises to a sharp point on the
foreneck. Most birds show a distinct white line on cutting edge of
upper mandible; in Pacific birds, bill is slightly longer and thinner
than in Atlantic birds. In immature and **winter adult,** face and neck
are more extensively dark than in Common. First-summer bird is
browner above than adult; otherwise similar to winter bird. **Range:**
Nests in colonies on rocky cliffs. Common on breeding grounds.
On East Coast, much more regular in winter south of Canada than
Common; casual to mid-Atlantic states; recorded to Florida. Casual
on West Coast south of breeding range, where most records are
from the Monterey area in California.

Razorbill *Alca torda* L 17" (43 cm)

A chunky bird, with a big head and thick neck; black above, white
below. Rather long, pointed tail; heavy head; and massive, arching bill distinguish Razorbill from murres. Swimming birds often
hold tail cocked up. A white band crosses the bill; in **breeding**
plumage, a white line runs from bill to eye. **Immature** lacks white
band; bill is smaller but still distinctively shaped. **Range:** Nests
on rocky cliffs and among boulders. Winters in large numbers
on the Grand Banks off Newfoundland. A few winter well offshore as far south as North Carolina, casually to Florida; irregular along the coast south of Long Island.

Dovekie

breeding adult

winter

breeding adult

winter

bridled breeding adult

breeding adult

breeding adult

Common Murre

winter

juvenile

Thick-billed Murre

Pacific winter *arra*

Atlantic breeding adults *lomvia*

immature

breeding adult

Razorbill

winter adult

breeding adult

Black Guillemot   Cepphus grylle L 13" (33 cm)

Breeding adult black overall, with large white patch on upper-wing. **Winter adult** white; upperparts heavily mottled with black except on nape; wing patch less distinct. **Juvenile** is sooty above; sides and wing patches mottled. First-summer birds are patchily black-and-white; wing patches mottled. In all plumages, white axillaries and wing linings distinguish Black from Pigeon Guillemot. In East Coast race *arcticus*, juveniles and winter birds are darker than in high Arctic race, *mandtii*. **Range:** Fairly common in the East; usually seen close to shore in breeding season.

Pigeon Guillemot   Cepphus columba L 13½" (34 cm)

Breeding and **winter adults'** plumage similar to smaller Black Guillemot, but note black bar on white upperwing patch; bar may be obscured in swimming bird. **Juvenile** is dusky above; crown and nape darker; wing patch marked with black edgings; breast and sides mottled gray. Compare with juvenile Marbled Murrelet. First-winter Pigeon Guillemot resembles winter adult but is darker. In all plumages, dusky axillaries and wing linings distinguish Pigeon from Black Guillemot. **Range:** Fairly common; seen near shore in breeding season. Winter range not well-known.

Long-billed Murrelet   Brachyramphus perdix

L 11½" (29 cm) **Range:** Found in coastal northeast Asia. Casual throughout North America; most records are in fall of winter-plumaged birds. In **winter,** lacks conspicuous white collar of similar Marbled Murrelet; shows small pale oval patches on sides of nape; in **breeding** plumage upperparts are less rufous, throat paler. Formerly considered a race of Marbled.

Marbled Murrelet   Brachyramphus marmoratus **T**

L 10" (25 cm) Bill longer than in Kittlitz's Murrelet. Tail all-dark, but white on overlapping uppertail coverts. **Breeding adult** dark above, heavily mottled below. In **winter** plumage, white on scapulars distinguishes Marbled from other murrelets except Long-billed and Kittlitz's with shorter bill and breast band; white on face of Marbled is variable but less than Kittlitz's. **Juvenile** is like winter adult but mottled below; by first winter, underparts are mostly white. Highly vocal; **call** is a series of loud, high *kree* notes. **Range:** Nests inland, usually in trees. Fairly common in breeding range; rare in southern California. All murrelets have more pointed wings and faster flight than auklets.

Kittlitz's Murrelet   Brachyramphus brevirostris

L 9½" (24 cm) Bill shorter than in Marbled Murrelet. Outer tail feathers white. **Breeding adult**'s buffy grayish brown upperparts are heavily patterned; throat, breast, and flanks mottled; belly white. In **winter,** note extensive white on face, making eye conspicuous; nearly complete breast band; and white edges on secondaries. **Juvenile** distinguished from Marbled by shorter bill, paler face, white outer tail feathers. **Range:** Fairly common but local. Accidental to British Columbia and southern California.

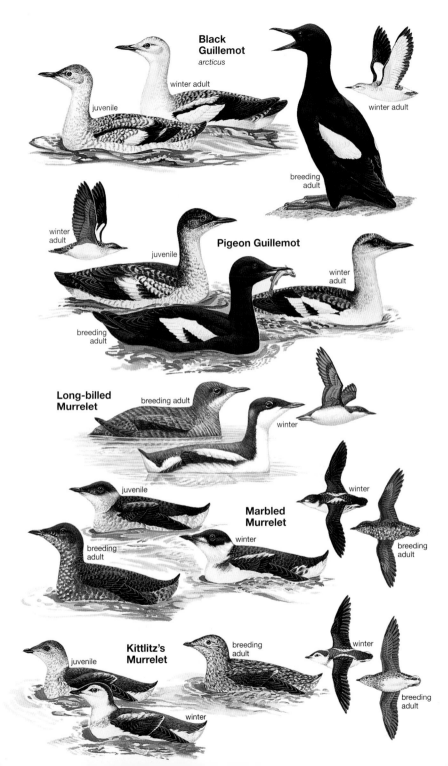

Black Guillemot
arcticus

juvenile

winter adult

winter adult

breeding adult

winter adult

juvenile

Pigeon Guillemot

winter adult

breeding adult

Long-billed Murrelet

breeding adult

winter

juvenile

Marbled Murrelet

winter

breeding adult

winter

breeding adult

winter

juvenile

Kittlitz's Murrelet

breeding adult

winter

winter

breeding adult

Xantus's Murrelet *Synthliboramphus hypoleucus*

L 9¾" (25 cm) Slate black above, white below. The more southerly breeding race, nominate *hypoleucus,* has much more white in face than southern California-breeding *scrippsi.* Both races distinguished from Craveri's Murrelet by lack of partial dark collar; slightly shorter, stouter bill; lack of black under the bill; and white wing linings, visible when birds rise to flap wings before taking off. Usually seen a few miles offshore; nests in colonies on rocky islands, ledges, and sometimes in dense vegetation. **Call,** a piping whistle or series of whistles, is heard year-round. **Range:** Uncommon to fairly common; both subspecies move north after breeding as far as Washington; *scrippsi* casually to southern British Columbia; *hypoleucus* is generally rare in North American waters.

Craveri's Murrelet *Synthliboramphus craveri*

L 8½" (22 cm) Slate black above, white below. Distinguished from Xantus's Murrelet by variably dusky gray wing linings; dark partial collar extending onto breast; slightly slimmer, longer bill; and black color of face extending under the bill. In good light, upperparts have a brownish tinge. Usually seen a few or many miles offshore. **Call,** very different from *scrippsi* Xantus's, is a cicada-like rattle, rising to a reedy trilling when agitated. **Range:** Breeds on rocky islands off Baja California. Regular late-summer and fall post-breeding visitor to coast of southern and central California. Rarely seen from shore.

Ancient Murrelet *Synthliboramphus antiquus*

L 10" (25 cm) Black crown and nape contrast with gray back. White streaks on head and nape of **breeding adult** give it an "ancient" look. Note also black chin and throat, yellowish bill. **Winter adult**'s bib is smaller and flecked with white, streaks on head less distinct. **Immature** lacks head streaks; throat is mostly white; distinguished from winter Marbled Murrelet (preceding page) by heavier, paler bill and by sharp contrast between head and back. In flight, the Ancient Murrelet holds its head higher than other murrelets; dark stripe on body at base of wing contrasts with white underparts, white wing linings. Call is a short, emphatic *chirrup.* **Range:** Uncommon to common; breeds primarily on the Aleutians and other Alaska islands; winters to central California, rarely to southern California. Casual inland throughout North America.

Cassin's Auklet *Ptychoramphus aleuticus* *L 9" (23 cm)*

Small, plump, dark gray bird; wings more rounded than in murrelets; bill short and stout, with pale spot at base of lower mandible; pale eyes. Upperparts are dark gray, shading to paler gray below, with whitish belly. Prominent white crescent above eye. Juvenile is paler overall; throat whitish; has darker eye and black bill. **Call,** heard only on the breeding grounds, is a weak croaking. **Range:** Common; nests in colonies on islands and on isolated coastal cliffs and headlands. Highly pelagic; usually seen farther from shore than murrelets.

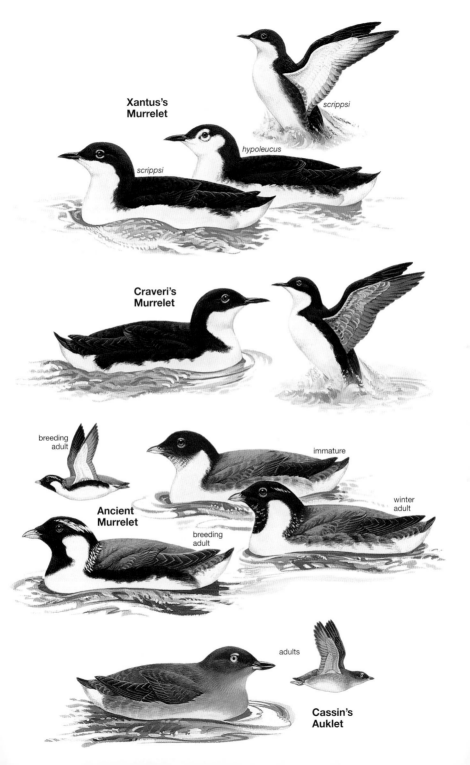

Xantus's Murrelet

scrippsi

hypoleucus

scrippsi

Craveri's Murrelet

breeding adult

immature

Ancient Murrelet

breeding adult

winter adult

adults

Cassin's Auklet

Least Auklet *Aethia pusilla* L 6¼" (16 cm)

Small and chubby, with short neck; dark above, with variably white-tipped scapulars, secondaries and greater coverts; forehead and lores streaked with white bristly feathers. Stubby, knobbed bill is dark red, with pale tip. In **breeding** plumage, acquired by Jan., a streak of white plumes extends back from behind eye; underparts are variable: heavily mottled with gray to nearly all-white. In **winter** plumage, underparts are entirely white. **Juvenile** resembles winter adult. **Range:** Abundant and gregarious, Least Auklets are found in immense flocks. Nest on boulder-strewn beaches and islands. Often seen far from shore. Accidental in Northwest Territories, Canada, and coastal California. Winters throughout Aleutians.

Parakeet Auklet *Aethia psittacula* L 10" (25 cm)

In **breeding** plumage, acquired by late Jan., broad upturned bill is orange-red; white plume extends back from behind the eye; dark slate upperparts and throat contrast sharply with white underparts; sides are mottled gray. In **winter** plumage, bill becomes duskier; underparts, including throat, are entirely white. Compare especially with larger Rhinoceros Auklet (next page). **Juvenile** resembles winter adult. Silent except on breeding grounds, when **call** is a musical trill, rising in pitch. **Range:** Fairly common on breeding grounds; nests in scattered pairs on rocky shores and sea cliffs. Found in pairs or small flocks in winter, well out to sea. Winters irregularly as far south as California. Like other auklets, wings are rounded and wingbeats are fluttery in comparison to those of murrelets.

Whiskered Auklet *Aethia pygmaea* L 7¾" (20 cm)

Overall color like Crested Auklet, but note Whiskered is paler on belly and undertail coverts. Three white plumes splay from each side of face; thin crest curls forward. In **breeding** plumage, bill is deep red with white tip. In **winter,** bill is dusky, plumes and crest less conspicuous. **Juvenile** is paler below; bill smaller; lacks crest; less striking head pattern. First-summer bird may lack crest and show reduced plumes. Often seen feeding in riptides. **Range:** Fairly common but local; nests in Aleutians from Baby Islands off Unalaska Island west to Buldir; and on islands off Russian Far East.

Crested Auklet *Aethia cristatella* L 9" (23 cm)

Sooty black overall; prominent quail-like crest curves forward from forehead; narrow white plume trails from behind yellow eye. **Breeding adult**'s bill is enlarged by bright orange plates. In **winter,** bill is smaller and browner; crest and plume reduced. **Juvenile** has short crest, faint plume; bill smaller. Compare with smaller Whiskered Auklet. **First-summer** bird has more evident plume back from eye, but bill is still small. Common and gregarious; often seen in large flocks that may include Parakeet and Least Auklets. In flight, note more pointed wing tips. **Range:** Nests in crevices of sea cliffs and rocky shores. Accidental south to Baja California.

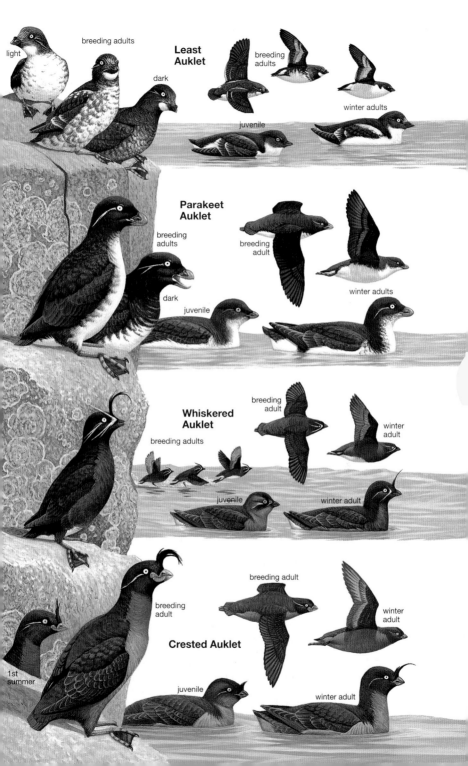

Least Auklet

light

breeding adults

dark

breeding adults

winter adults

juvenile

Parakeet Auklet

breeding adults

breeding adult

dark

juvenile

winter adults

Whiskered Auklet

breeding adult

breeding adults

winter adult

juvenile

winter adult

winter adult

Crested Auklet

breeding adult

breeding adult

1st summer

juvenile

winter adult

winter adult

Rhinoceros Auklet *Cerorhinca monocerata L 15" (38 cm)*
Large, heavy-billed auklet with large head and short, thick neck.
Blackish brown above; paler on sides, neck, and throat. In flight,
whitish on belly blends into dark breast; compare with extensively white underparts of similar Parakeet Auklet (preceding
page). In **breeding** plumage, acquired by Feb., Rhinoceros Auklet has distinct white plumes and a pale yellow "horn" at base of
orange bill. **Winter adult** lacks horn; plumes are less distinct,
bill paler. Juvenile and **immature** lack horn and plumes; bill is
dusky, eyes darker. Compare with much smaller Cassin's Auklet (page 236). **Range:** Rhinoceros Auklets are common along
most of the West Coast in fall and winter; often seen in large
numbers close inshore.

Atlantic Puffin *Fratercula arctica L 12½" (32 cm)*
The only East Coast puffin. **Breeding adult** identified by massive, brightly colored bill; pale face and underparts contrast with
dark upperparts. **Winter adult** has smaller, duller bill, dusky face.
In **juvenile** and first-winter birds, face is even duskier, bill much
paler and smaller. Full adult bill takes about five years to develop.
In flight, distinguished from murres and Razorbill (page 232) by
red-orange legs, rounded wings, grayish wing linings, absence of
white trailing edge on wing. **Range:** Locally common in breeding season; winters at sea, rarely south to North Carolina.

Horned Puffin *Fratercula corniculata L 15" (38 cm)*
A stocky North Pacific species with thick neck, large head, massive bill; underparts are white in all plumages. **Breeding adult**'s
face is white, bill brightly colored. Dark, fleshy "horn" extending
up from eye is visible only at close range. **Winter adult**'s bill is
smaller, duller; face is dusky. Bill of **juvenile** and first-winter
birds smaller and duskier than adult; full adult bill takes several
years to develop. In flight, bright orange legs are conspicuous;
wings are rounded; wing linings grayish; wings lack white trailing edge. **Range:** Locally common; winters well out to sea. Rare
and irregular. Irregular straggler off the West Coast to southern
California, mainly in late spring.

Tufted Puffin *Fratercula cirrhata L 16" (41 cm)*
Stocky, with thick neck, large head, massive bill. Underparts are
dark in adults. **Breeding adult**'s face is white, bill brightly colored; pale yellow head tufts droop over back of neck. **Winter adult**
has smaller, duller bill; face is gray, tufts shorter or absent. **Juvenile** has smaller, dusky bill; dark eye; white or dark underparts.
First-winter bird looks like juvenile until spring molt. As in other
puffins, full adult bill and plumage take several years to develop.
Red-orange feet are conspicuous in flight; wings are rounded;
wing linings grayish; wings lack white trailing edge. **Range:** Common to abundant in northern breeding range; uncommon to rare
off California. Winters far out at sea.

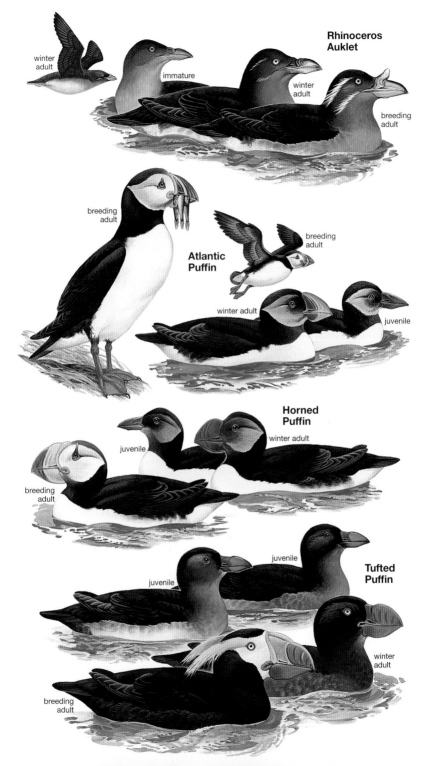

Rhinoceros Auklet

winter adult

immature

winter adult

breeding adult

Atlantic Puffin

breeding adult

breeding adult

winter adult

juvenile

Horned Puffin

juvenile

winter adult

breeding adult

Tufted Puffin

juvenile

juvenile

winter adult

breeding adult

Pigeons, Doves (Family Columbidae)

The larger species of these birds usually are called pigeons, the smaller ones doves. All are strong, fast fliers. Juveniles have pale-tipped feathers and lack the neck markings of adults. Pigeons and doves feed chiefly on grain, other seeds, and fruit. *Species: 308 World, 18 N.A.*

Band-tailed Pigeon *Patagioenas fasciata* L 14½" (37 cm)
Purplish head and breast; dark-tipped yellow bill, yellow legs; broad gray tail band; narrow white band on nape, absent on juvenile. Flocks in flight resemble Rock Doves but are uniform, not varied, in plumage and lack contrasting white rump and black band at end of tail. **Call** is a low *whoo-whoo.* **Range:** Locally common in low-altitude coniferous forests in the Northwest, and oak or oak-conifer woodlands in the Southwest; also increasingly common in suburban gardens, and parks. Uncommon in southeast Alaska; casual in eastern North America.

Red-billed Pigeon *Patagioenas flavirostris* L 14½" (37 cm)
Dark overall, with a mainly red bill. Distinctive **call** heard in early spring and summer, a long, high-pitched *cooooo* followed by three loud *up-cup-a-coo* notes. Perches in tall trees above a brushy understory; forages for seeds, nuts, and figs. Seldom comes to the ground except to drink. **Range:** Uncommon, local, and declining in Texas; rare in winter.

White-crowned Pigeon *Patagioenas leucocephala*
L 13½" (34 cm) **Range:** Flocks commute from nest colonies in coastal mangroves to feed inland on fruit. Most winter on Caribbean islands. A large, square-tailed pigeon of the Florida Everglades and Keys. Crown patch varies from shining white in **adult males** to grayish white in most **females** and grayish brown in juveniles. Otherwise this species looks all-black; the iridescent collar is visible only in good light. **Calls** include a loud, deep *coo-cura-cooo* or *coo-croo.*

Rock Pigeon *Columba livia* L 12½" (32 cm)
The highly variable city pigeon; multicolored birds were developed over centuries of near domestication. The birds most closely resembling their wild ancestors have head and neck darker than back, black bars on inner wing, white rump, and black band at end of tail. Flocks in flight show a variety of plumage patterns, unlike Band-tailed Pigeon. **Call** is a soft *coo-cuk-cuk-cuk-coooo.* **Range:** Rock Pigeon was introduced from Europe by early settlers, now widespread and common, particularly in urban settings. Nests and roosts chiefly on high window ledges, bridges, and barns. Feeds during the day in parks and fields.

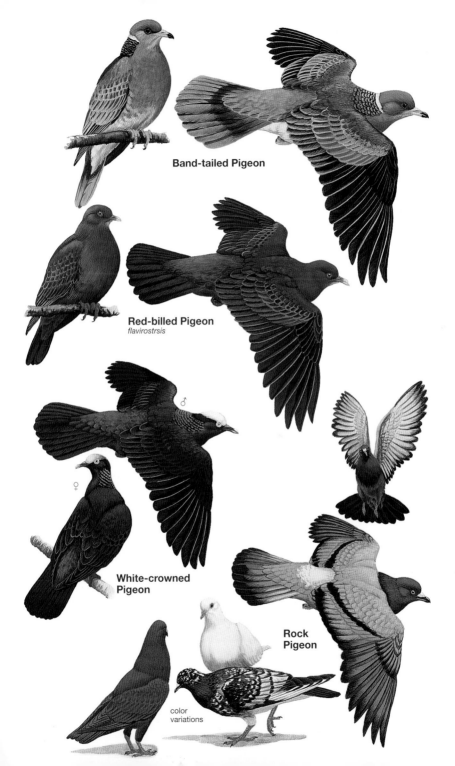

Band-tailed Pigeon

Red-billed Pigeon
flavirostrsis

White-crowned Pigeon

♂

♀

Rock Pigeon

color variations

Zenaida Dove *Zenaida aurita* *L 10" (25 cm)*

Range: Primarily West Indian species; now accidental on the Florida Keys (where it was reported as breeding by Audubon in 1832), and on southernmost Florida mainland. Distinguished from Mourning Dove by white on trailing edge of secondaries that shows as a square white spot on inner secondaries of folded wing; and by shorter, rounded, gray-tipped tail. Lacks white wing bars and tail tips of White-winged Dove. Feeds close to water. **Call,** similar to Mourning Dove's but faster. Generally shy.

Mourning Dove *Zenaida macroura* *L 12" (31 cm)*

Trim body; long tail tapers to a point. Black spots on upperwing; pinkish wash below. In flight, shows white tips on outer tail feathers. **Juvenile** has heavy spotting; scaled effect on wings. **Call** is a mournful *oowoo-woo-woo-woo.* Wings produce a fluttering whistle as the bird takes flight. **Range:** Our most abundant and widespread dove, found in a wide variety of habitats.

Spotted Dove *Streptopelia chinensis* *L 12" (31 cm)*

Range: An Asian species introduced in Los Angeles in the early 1900s; formerly well established in southwestern California but sharp declines in last decade. Named for spotted collar, distinct in **adults,** obscured in **juveniles.** Wings and long, white-tipped tail are more rounded than in Mourning Dove; wings unmarked. **Calls** include a rather harsh *coo-coo-croooo* and *coo-crrooo-coo,* with emphasis respectively on the last and middle notes.

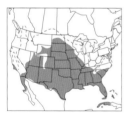

Eurasian Collared-Dove *Streptopelia decaocto*

L 12½" (32 cm) Very pale gray-buff; black collar. Escapes of domesticated **Ringed Turtle-Dove,** formerly named *S. risoria,* an Old World species, may form small populations, but do not do well in the wild. Ringed Turtle-Dove is smaller, paler; has whitish undertail coverts, gray primaries; tail shorter, less black from below. Believed to derive from African Collared-Dove, *S. roseogrisea.* **Range:** Eurasian species; introduced to Bahamas, spread to Florida. Common; now nearly throughout U.S.

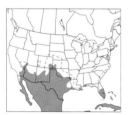

White-winged Dove *Zenaida asiatica* *L 11½" (29 cm)*

Large white wing patches and shorter, rounded tail distinguish this species from Mourning Dove. On sitting bird, wing patch shows only as a thin white line. Drawn-out, cooing **call,** *who-cooks-for-you,* has many variations. **Range:** Nests singly or in large colonies in dense mesquite, mature citrus groves, riparian woodlands, and saguaro-paloverde deserts; also found in desert towns. Casual mainly on East Coast to the Maritime Provinces.

Oriental Turtle-Dove *Streptopelia orientalis*

L 13½" (34 cm) **Range:** Asian species; casual to Aleutians and Bering Sea in spring and summer; accidental on Vancouver Island and California. Large and stocky; scaly pattern above with buffy, gray, and reddish fringes on black feathers; black-and-white streaked patch on neck. North American records are nominate *orientalis,* which is dark with gray rump and tail tip.

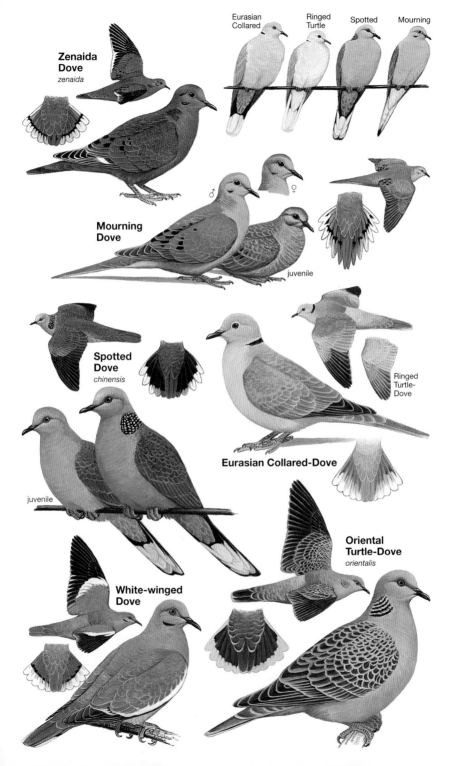

Zenaida Dove
zenaida

Eurasian Collared

Ringed Turtle

Spotted

Mourning

Mourning Dove

♂

♀

juvenile

Spotted Dove
chinensis

Ringed Turtle-Dove

Eurasian Collared-Dove

juvenile

White-winged Dove

Oriental Turtle-Dove
orientalis

Common Ground-Dove *Columbina passerina*
L 6½" (17 cm) Very small, with pink at base of bill; scaled effect on head and breast; short tail, often raised. Plain scapulars; bright chestnut primaries and wing linings visible in flight. **Male** has a slate gray crown, pinkish gray underparts. **Female** is grayer, more uniformly colored. **Call** is a repeated soft, ascending *wah-up.* **Range:** Forages on open ground in the East and brushy rangeland in the West. Declining in Gulf Coast region; casual as far north as New York and Oregon in fall and winter.

Ruddy Ground-Dove *Columbina talpacoti* L 6¾" (17 cm)
Range: Widespread in Latin America; rare to casual from southern Texas to southern California. Dark bill; lacks scaling of Common Ground-Dove. **Male** of the subspecies *eluta* has a gray crown, rufous color on upperparts. **Female** is mainly gray-brown overall. Both sexes show black on underwing coverts, black linear markings on scapulars. Most records in the U.S. are of west Mexican race *eluta;* some Texas records, however, are of east Mexican *rufipennis,* which is a richer cinnamon color overall.

Inca Dove *Columbina inca* L 8¼" (21 cm)
Plumage conspicuously scalloped. In flight, shows chestnut on wings like Common Ground-Dove, but note the Inca Dove's longer, white-edged tail. **Call,** a double *cooo-coo.* **Range:** Found usually near human habitations, often in parks and gardens. Casual wanderer north to North Dakota and Ontario, Canada.

White-tipped Dove *Leptotila verreauxi* L 11½" (29 cm)
This large, plump dove has a whitish forehead and throat and dark back. In flight, white tips show plainly on fanned tail. Low-pitched **call** is like the sound produced by blowing across the top of a bottle. Feeds on or near the ground, keeping close to woodlands with dense understory. Accidental to Dry Tortugas.

Key West Quail-Dove *Geotrygon chrysia* L 12" (31 cm)
Range: West Indian species. Reported as breeding on Key West by Audubon in 1832. Population eliminated by about mid-19th century. Casual on the Florida Keys and south Florida. Larger and with longer tail than Ruddy Quail-Dove, with a white line under the eye. Upperparts, primaries, and tail are chestnut, glossed with purple and green. **Male** is highly iridescent above; female is duller. Both sexes are whitish below.

Ruddy Quail-Dove *Geotrygon montana* L 9¾" (25 cm)
Range: A chunky tropical dove; five records for Florida and one for southern Texas. **Male**'s primarily rich rufous upperparts and prominent buffy line under the eye are distinctive. **Females** are brown above; have a plainer facial pattern. In both sexes, underparts are cinnamon-buff. Quail-doves are so named because they resemble quail and have a similar terrestrial lifestyle.

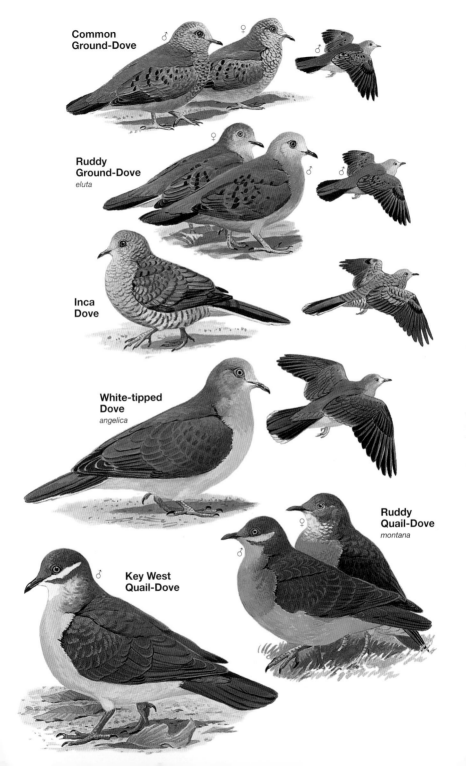

**Common
Ground-Dove**

♂ ♀

♂

**Ruddy
Ground-Dove**
eluta

♀

♂

♂

**Inca
Dove**

**White-tipped
Dove**
angelica

**Ruddy
Quail-Dove**
montana

♂

♀

**Key West
Quail-Dove**

♂

Lories, Parakeets, Macaws, Parrots
(Family Psittacidae)

Most parrots in the wild in North America are descendants of escaped cage birds. Shown are those with established populations, mostly from southern parts of California, Texas, and Florida. ABA accepts White-winged, Yellow-chevroned, Monk, and Green Parakeets; Red-crowned Parrot; and Budgerigar. *Species: 364 World, 8 N.A.*

White-winged Parakeet *Brotogeris versicolurus*
L 8¾" (22 cm) **Range:** From northern Amazon area. Small numbers established in south of Florida and California by 1960s, but have declined in recent years. Note white outer secondaries and inner primaries; yellow greater coverts; unfeathered lores.

Yellow-chevroned Parakeet *Brotogeris chiriri*
L 8¾" (22 cm) **Range:** Southern Amazon to northern Argentina. Now outnumbers White-winged in south of California and Florida. Lacks white on flight feathers; body yellow-green.

Monk Parakeet *Myiopsitta monachus L 11½" (29 cm)*
Range: Species of temperate South America. The most widespread parrot in south Florida. Some also found in cities of Northeast, Midwest, Texas. Note extensive gray on face and underparts.

Dusky-headed Parakeet *Aratinga weddellii L 11" (28 cm)*
Range: From western Amazon basin. Some established in Miami area. Gray head with white around eye and black bill.

Black-hooded Parakeet *Nandayus nenday*
L 13¾" (35 cm) **Range:** Southwest Brazil to north Argentina. Found Los Angeles area; widely established Pinellas County, Florida. Black on head, black bill, blue wash on breast, red thighs.

Green Parakeet *Aratinga holochlora L 13" (33 cm)*
Range: Mexican species; populations in towns in extreme southern Texas may include Mexican strays. Large, nearly all-green.

Blue-crowned Parakeet *Aratinga acuticaudata*
L 14" (36 cm) **Range:** South American species. Small numbers established on Key Biscayne and Key Largo, Florida, and in Los Angeles area. Blue face; bicolored bill; base of tail reddish below.

Mitred Parakeet *Aratinga mitrata L 15" (38 cm)*
Range: South American species. Numerous in Los Angeles area, a few in south Florida. Large, green, with white eye ring; red face, forehead, variable elsewhere on head; underwings yellow-olive.

Red-masked Parakeet *Aratinga erythrogenys*
L 13" (33 cm) **Range:** From southwest Ecuador and northwest Peru. In Los Angeles area, often associates with Mitred. Some also in Dade County, Florida. Similar to Mitred, but note red on leading edge of wing and underwing coverts, more red on head.

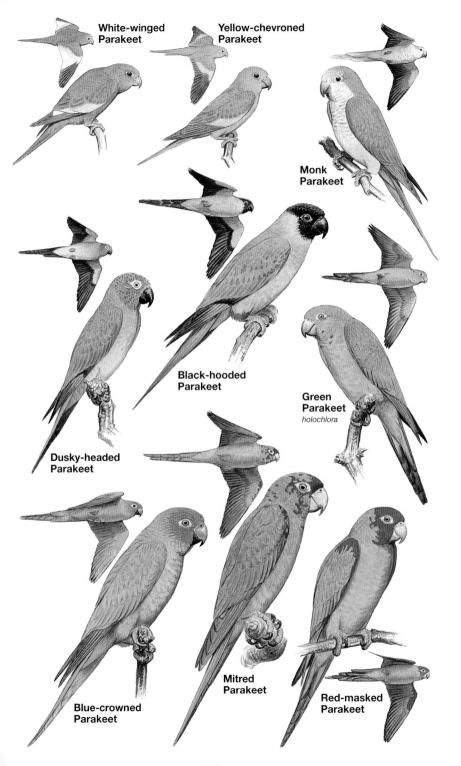

White-winged Parakeet

Yellow-chevroned Parakeet

Monk Parakeet

Black-hooded Parakeet

Dusky-headed Parakeet

Green Parakeet
holochlora

Blue-crowned Parakeet

Mitred Parakeet

Red-masked Parakeet

Thick-billed Parrot *Rhynchopsitta pachyrhyncha*
L 16¼" (41 cm) **Range:** Declining species in northwest Mexico. Former sporadic visitor primarily to Chiricahua Mountains, Arizona. Last valid record in 1938; recent New Mexico record (2003) not accepted (origin). Releases into Chiricahuas in 1980s were unsuccessful. **Adult** green overall with red forehead, eyebrow, thighs, marginal coverts; tail long and pointed. Yellow underwing bar; slow, shallow wingbeats. Immature's bill paler, no red on eyebrow and wing. Loud, laughing **calls** carry far.

Rose-ringed Parakeet *Psittacula krameri*
L 15¾" (40 cm) **Range:** Small numbers of this Asian and African species are established in Miami and Los Angeles areas. Appear to be of Indian race, *manillensis.* Slender tail with very long central feathers; bright red upper mandible. **Adult males** show black, rose-edged collar. **Call** is a loud, flickerlike *kew.*

Red-crowned Parrot *Amazona viridigenalis*
L 13" (33 cm) **Range:** Native of northeast Mexico. Established in towns of southernmost Texas; some may be visitors from Mexico, but most or all are probably descendants of escaped cage birds. Also found in Los Angeles and Fort Lauderdale areas. Pale blue on sides of head, yellow eyes, yellowish band across tip of tail. **Adult male** has red crown; **female** and juvenile show less red. **Calls** generally raucous but include a mellow, rolling *rreeoo.*

Orange-winged Parrot *Amazona amazonica*
L 12¼" (31 cm) **Range:** South American species. Small numbers established in Miami area. Note blue stripe and nape on yellow head; orange at base of outer tail feathers.

Lilac-crowned Parrot *Amazona finschi L 13" (33 cm)*
Range: West Mexican species. Small numbers established in Los Angeles area; a few seen in south Texas and Florida. Like Red-crowned, but has lilac wash on crown and nape; maroon band across forehead; orange eye; longer tail has entirely green central tail feathers. **Calls** include a distinctive upslurred whistle.

Yellow-headed Parrot *Amazona oratrix L 14½" (37 cm)*
Range: Drastically declining species from Mexico and Belize. Small but declining numbers established in Los Angeles area; a few also in south Texas and Florida. Large, with yellow head; immature shows less yellow. Some escapes are of closely related Yellow-naped (*A. auropalliata*) and Yellow-crowned (*A. ochrocephala*) Parrots, formerly treated as subspecies of Yellow-headed.

Budgerigar *Melopsittacus undulatus L 7" (18 cm)*
Range: Australian species. Native birds green, as were populations established in southwest Florida in early 1960s; reached tens of thousands before 1980s. Only a few now present in Hernando and Pasco Counties, maybe due to competition for nest cavities with European Starling. Note barred upperparts and white wing stripe visible in flight. Escapes may be blue, white, or yellow.

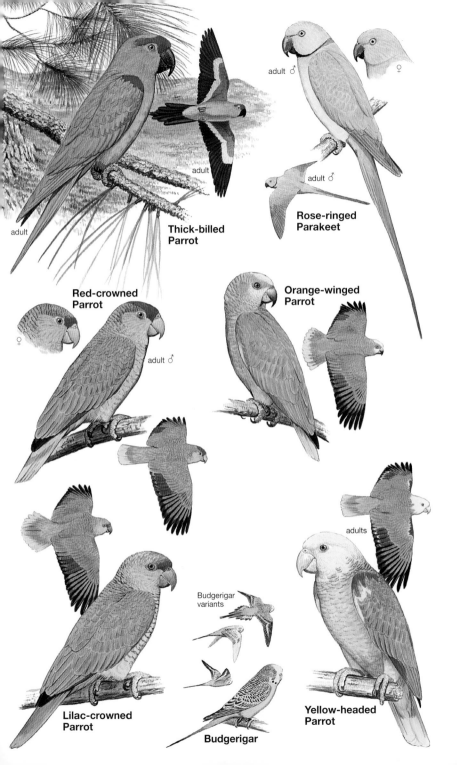

Thick-billed Parrot

adult

adult

Rose-ringed Parakeet

adult ♂

adult ♀

adult ♂

Red-crowned Parrot

♀

adult ♂

Orange-winged Parrot

Lilac-crowned Parrot

Budgerigar variants

Budgerigar

adults

Yellow-headed Parrot

Cuckoos, Roadrunners, Anis
(Family Cuculidae)

Of this large family, widespread in the Old World, only a few species are seen in North America. Most are slender with long tails; two toes point forward, two back. *Species: 140 World, 8 N.A.*

Mangrove Cuckoo *Coccyzus minor L 12" (31 cm)*
Black mask and buffy underparts distinguish this species from other cuckoos. Upperparts grayish brown; lacks rufous primaries of Yellow-billed Cuckoo. Black tail feathers are broadly tipped with white. Species is usually considered monotypic, but Mexican birds average brighter below; two variations shown. An accidental vagrant along our Gulf Coast from Mexico to northwest Florida. In all juveniles, mask is paler, tail pattern muted. Found chiefly in mangrove swamps. Like other cuckoos, perches quietly near center of tree. **Call** is a slow, guttural *gaw gaw gaw.*

Yellow-billed Cuckoo *Coccyzus americanus*
L 12" (31 cm) Grayish brown above, white below; rufous primaries; lower mandible yellow. Undertail patterned in bold black and white. In **juvenal** plumage, held well into fall, tail has a much paler pattern and bill may show little or no yellow; may be confused with Black-billed Cuckoo. One **song** sounds hollow and wooden, a rapid staccato *kuk-kuk-kuk* that usually slows and descends to a *kakakowlp-kowlp* ending. **Range:** Common in open woods, orchards, and streamside willow and alder groves. Once numerous but now a rare breeder in California. Rare vagrant to Atlantic Canada during fall migration.

Black-billed Cuckoo *Coccyzus erythropthalmus*
L 12" (31 cm) Grayish brown above, pale grayish below. Bill is usually all-dark. Lacks the rufous primaries of Yellow-billed Cuckoo. Note also reddish orbital ring. Undertail patterned in gray with white tipping; compare juvenile Yellow-billed. **Juvenile** Black-billed has a buffy orbital ring; undertail is paler; underparts may have buffy tinge, especially on undertail coverts; primaries may show a little rusty brown. **Song** usually consists of monotonous *cu-cu-cu* or *cu-cu-cu-cu* phrases. **Range:** Uncommon to fairly common; found in woodlands and along streams. Very rare breeder in northern Texas, western Tennessee, and western Idaho; casual in Pacific states.

Greater Roadrunner *Geococcyx californianus*
L 23" (58 cm) A large, ground-dwelling cuckoo streaked with brown and white. Note the long, heavy bill, conspicuous bushy crest, and long, white-edged tail. Short, rounded wings show a white crescent on the primaries. Eats insects, lizards, snakes, rodents, and small birds. **Song** is a dovelike cooing, descending in pitch. **Range:** Common in scrub desert and mesquite groves; less common in chaparral and open woodland.

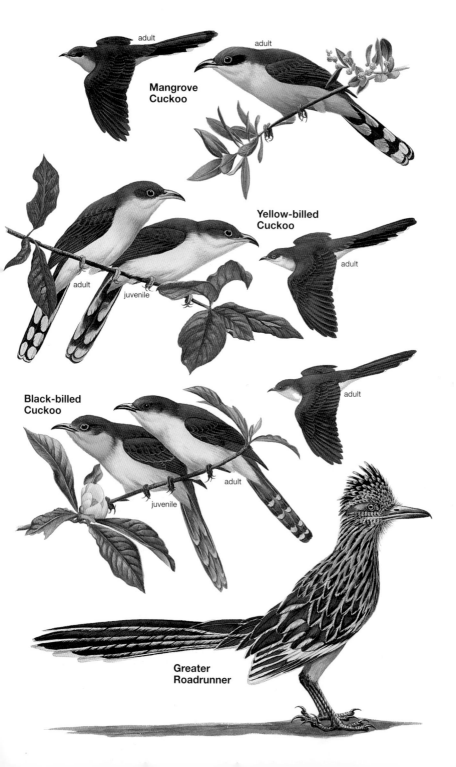

Mangrove
Cuckoo

adult

adult

Yellow-billed
Cuckoo

adult

adult

juvenile

Black-billed
Cuckoo

adult

adult

juvenile

Greater
Roadrunner

Common Cuckoo *Cuculus canorus* L 13" (33 cm)

Range: Old World species, rare spring and summer visitor to central and western Aleutians and Pribilofs. One late-June Anchorage record; accidental to Martha's Vineyard, Massachusetts. Closely resembles Oriental Cuckoo. **Adult male** and adult gray-morph female are gray above, paler below, with whitish belly narrowly barred with gray. Though variable, birds seen in Alaska are often paler below with narrower barring than Oriental. **Hepatic morph** (restricted to females in Common and Oriental Cuckoos) is pale rusty brown above, heavily barred with black on back and tail; rump is paler than hepatic-morph Oriental and either unmarked or only lightly spotted. In flight, both species resemble small falcons. Male's **song** is the familiar *cuc-coo* for which the family is named but **call** is rarely heard in North America.

Oriental Cuckoo *Cuculus optatus* L 12½" (32 cm)

Range: Eurasian species, casual from late spring through fall in western Aleutians, Pribilofs, and St. Lawrence Island (once on mainland). **Adult male** and adult gray-morph female are darker gray above than Common Cuckoo, paler below, with pale belly barred in dark gray. Barring is often slightly broader, and lower belly and undertail covert region buffier than in Common Cuckoo. In the hand, underwing shows largely unmarked white feathering below the primary coverts that is barred in Common Cuckoo; in flight, white on underwing coverts form more-contrasting bar than on Common. **Hepatic-morph female** is rusty brown above, heavily barred on back, rump, and tail. Oriental's **song**, a variable, hollow note often delivered four times, has not been heard here. The Oriental Cuckoo (*C. saturatus*) was formerly considered polytypic, but because of vocal differences it was split into three species: Himalayan Cuckoo (*C. saturatus*), Sunda Cuckoo (*C. lepidus*), and Oriental Cuckoo (*C. opatatus*); the latter is described here.

Smooth-billed Ani *Crotophaga ani* L 14½" (37 cm)

Bill size variable, but shape distinguishes both ani species from grackles (page 446). Black overall with iridescent bronze overtones. Long tail is often dipped and wagged. Found in brushy fields, scrublands; often feeds on insects stirred up by cattle. Both ani species are gregarious; several pairs usually share a nest and take turns incubating the eggs. **Call** is a whining, rising *quee-lick*. **Range:** Accidental north along Atlantic coast to New Jersey; also to Ohio. Has declined greatly in Florida and is on verge of being extirpated.

Groove-billed Ani *Crotophaga sulcirostris* L 13½" (34 cm)

Overall size and bill are smaller than in Smooth-billed Ani. Bill does not extend above crown; lower mandible straighter. Plumage is black overall with iridescent purple and green overtones; long tail is often dipped and wagged. Grooves in bill are visible only at close range; these and call are distinctive. **Call** is a liquid *tee-ho*, accented on the first syllable. **Range:** Common in summer in woodlands. Rare primarily in winter on Gulf Coast to Florida. Casual north to Minnesota, west to California, and east to Virginia.

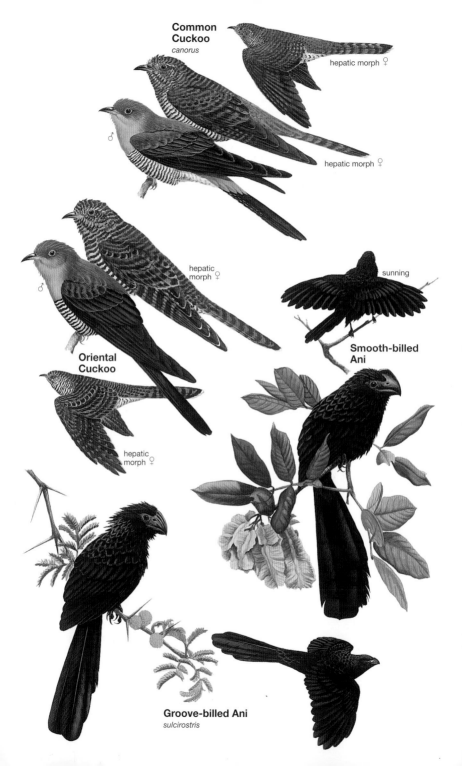

Common Cuckoo
canorus

hepatic morph ♀

hepatic morph ♀

♂

hepatic morph ♀

Oriental Cuckoo

♂

hepatic morph ♀

sunning

Smooth-billed Ani

Groove-billed Ani
sulcirostris

Owls (Families Tytonidae and Strigidae)

Distinctive birds of prey, divided by structural differences into two families, Barn Owls and Typical Owls. All have immobile eyes in large heads. Fluffy plumage makes their flight nearly soundless. Many species hunt at night and roost during the day. To find owls, search the ground for regurgitated pellets of fur and bone below a nest or roost. Listen for flocks of small songbirds noisily mobbing a roosting owl. *Species:* Tytonidae *15 World, 1 N.A.;* Strigidae *180 World, 21 N.A.*

Barn Owl *Tyto alba* L 16" (41 cm)
A pale owl with dark eyes in a heart-shaped face. Rusty brown above; underparts vary from white to cinnamon. Darkest birds are always **females,** palest birds **males.** Compare with Snowy Owl (next page). The Barn Owl roosts and nests in dark cavities in city and farm buildings, cliffs, and trees. Typical **call** is a raspy, hissing screech. **Range:** Rare to uncommon in parts of western range, uncommon and declining in the East.

Short-eared Owl *Asio flammeus* L 15" (38 cm)
Tawny; boldly streaked on breast; belly paler, more lightly streaked. Ear tufts are barely visible. In flight, long wings show buffy patch above, black "wrist" mark below; these markings are usually more prominent than in Long-eared Owl, which also has less distinct but more individual bars on primaries. A bird of open country, marshes, tundra, and weedy fields; nests on the ground. Flight is wavering, wingbeats erratic. During the day it roosts on the ground or on open, low perches: short poles, muskrat houses, and duck blinds. Typical **call,** heard in breeding season and sometimes in winter, is a raspy, high barking. **Range:** Fairly common. Somewhat gregarious in winter; groups may gather where prey is abundant. Short-eared Owls sighted on Florida Keys and Dry Tortugas are thought to have originated from West Indian populations, likely *domingensis* from Cuba.

Long-eared Owl *Asio otus* L 15" (38 cm)
A slender owl with long, close-set ear tufts. Boldly streaked and barred on breast and belly. Wings generally have a less prominent buffy patch with more dark barring and a smaller black "wrist" mark than Short-eared Owl; facial disk is rusty. Lives in thick woods; hunts at night over open fields, marshes. By day it roosts in a tree, close to the trunk. Generally silent except in breeding season. Common **call** is one or more long *hooo* notes. **Range:** Uncommon. More gregarious in winter; flocks may roost together.

Great Horned Owl *Bubo virginianus* L 22" (56 cm)
Size, bulky shape, and white throat separate this owl from the Long-eared Owl; ear tufts distinguish it from other large species. Nests in trees, caves, or on the ground. Chiefly nocturnal. Takes prey as large as skunks and grouse. **Call** is a series of three to eight loud, deep hoots; the second and third hoots are often short and rapid. **Range:** Common; habitats vary from forest to city to open desert. Widespread interior race, *subarcticus,* is paler.

Barn Owl
pratincola

Long-eared Owl

Short-eared Owl
flammeus

Great Horned Owl

subarcticus

Barred Owl *Strix varia L 21" (53 cm)*
A chunky owl with dark eyes, dark barring on upper breast, dark streaking below. Chiefly nocturnal; daytime roost well hidden. Easily flushed; does not generally tolerate close approach. Distinctive **call** is a rhythmic series of loud hoots: *who-cooks-for-you, who-cooks-for-you-all;* also a drawn-out *hoo-ah,* sometimes preceded by an ascending agitated barking. Much more likely than other owls to be heard in daytime. **Range:** Common in dense coniferous or mixed woods of river bottoms and swamps; also in upland woods. Northwestern portion of range is expanding rapidly; now overlaps and has hybridized with similar Spotted Owl. Probably a rare breeder in southeastern Alaska.

Great Gray Owl *Strix nebulosa L 27" (69 cm)*
Our largest owl. Heavily ringed facial disks make the yellow eyes look small. Lacks ear tufts. Hunts over forest clearings and nearby open country, chiefly by night but also at dawn and dusk; hunts by day during summer in northern part of range. **Call** is a series of deep, resonant *whoo* notes. **Range:** Inhabits boreal forests and wooded bogs in the far north, dense coniferous forests with meadows in the mountains farther south. Generally uncommon; rare and irregular winter visitor to limit of dashed line on map.

Spotted Owl *Strix occidentalis L 18" (46 cm)*
Large and dark-eyed, with white spotting on head, back, and underparts, rather than the barring and streaking of the similar Barred Owl. Tamer than Barred, with which it hybridizes. Strictly nocturnal. Main **call** is four doglike barks and cries; contact call, given mainly by females, is a hollow, upslurred whistle, *coooo-weep*. **Range:** Inhabits thickly wooded canyons, humid forests. Uncommon; decreasing in number and range due to habitat destruction, especially in the Northwest. The threatened northern race, *caurina* (**T**), is the largest and darkest race, with smaller white spots.

Snowy Owl *Bubo scandiacus L 23" (58 cm)*
Large white owl, with rounded head and yellow eyes. Dark bars and spots are heavier on females, heaviest on **immatures;** old males may be pure white. An owl of open tundra; nests on the ground; preys chiefly on lemmings, hunting by day as well as at night. **Range:** Retreats from northernmost part of range in winter; at least a few are seen annually to limit indicated by dashed line on map. In years when the lemming population plummets, Snowy Owls may wander in winter as far south as northern Alabama, Oklahoma, and central California, exceptionally to northern Florida and Texas. These irruptives, usually heavily barred younger birds, often perch conspicuously on the ground or on low stumps, fence posts, and buildings.

Barred
Owl

Great Gray
Owl
nebulosa

Spotted
Owl

Snowy
Owl

immature

Eastern Screech-Owl *Megascops asio L 8½" (22 cm)*
All three owl species shown on this page are small, with yellow eyes and pale bill tip; bill base is yellow-green on Eastern and Whiskered Screech-Owls and blackish or dark gray on Western. Ear tufts prominent if raised; when flattened, bird has a round-headed look. Underparts on all three are marked by vertical streaks crossed by dark bars: On Eastern, cross bars are spaced well apart and are nearly as wide as vertical streaks; on Western cross bars are closer together and much narrower; Whiskered is like Eastern, but markings have a bolder look. These markings are less distinct on the Eastern **rufous morph;** the latter pre-dominates in the South, the **gray morph** on the Great Plains and in southernmost Texas. Lightest and whitest, the *maxwelliae* race is found in the northwestern part of the range. Eastern Screech-Owls are common in a wide variety of habitats: woodlots, forests, swamps, orchards, parks, and suburban gardens. Nocturnal; best located and identified by voice. Two typical **calls:** a series of qua-vering whistles, descending in pitch; and a long single trill, all on one pitch. **Range:** Formerly classified with Western Screech-Owl as one species; range separation is not yet fully known. Both species are found at Big Bend National Park in Texas: Western is uncommon, Eastern rare and may not have been recorded recently. Accidental to southeastern New Mexico.

Western Screech-Owl *Megascops kennicottii*
L 8½" (22 cm) Generally gray overall; some birds in the humid coastal Northwest are brownish. Nocturnal; best located and identified by voice. Two common **calls:** a series of short whis-tles accelerating in tempo; and a short trill followed immediately by a longer trill, both on the same pitch. **Range:** Common in open woodlands, streamside groves, deserts, suburban areas, and parks. Where range overlaps that of Whiskered Screech-Owl, the Western Screech-Owl is generally found at lower elevations. Casual to southwestern Kansas.

Whiskered Screech-Owl *Megascops trichopsis*
L 7¼" (18 cm) Closely resembles gray Western Screech-Owl but slightly smaller with smaller feet and usually bolder cross barring, similar to Eastern. Identification best done by voice. Two common **calls:** a series of short whistles on one pitch and at a fairly even tempo; and a series of very irregular hoots, like Morse code. Nocturnal. **Range:** Inhabits dense oak and oak-conifer woodlands, at elevations from 4,000 to 6,000 feet, but mostly found around 5,000 feet. Generally at higher elevations than Western.

**Eastern
Screech-Owl**

rufous
morph

gray
morph

gray-morph
juvenile

maxwelliae

northwest
coast
kennicottii

**Western
Screech-Owl**

**Whiskered
Screech-Owl**
aspersus

Flammulated Owl *Otus flammeolus L 6¾" (17 cm)*

Dark eyes; small ear tufts, often indistinct; variegated red and gray plumage. Birds in the northwestern part of the range are the most finely marked; those in the Great Basin mountains are **grayish** and have the coarsest markings; and those breeding in the Southeast are **reddish**. Strictly nocturnal; nests and roosts in tree cavities, usually old woodpecker holes. Best located at night by its **call,** a series of single or paired low, hoarse, hollow hoots. **Range:** Common in oak and pine woodlands, especially ponderosa. Sometimes nests in loose colonies. Highly migratory. Accidental east to Louisiana and Florida. Rare in interior lowlands during migration, but likely overlooked.

Ferruginous Pygmy-Owl *Glaucidium brasilianum*

L 6¾" (17 cm) Long tail, reddish with dark or dusky bars. Upperparts gray-brown; crown faintly streaked. Eyes yellow; black nape spots look like eyes on the back of the head. White underparts streaked with reddish brown. Unlike other North American owls, pygmy-owls fly with quick, unmuffled wingbeats. Chiefly diurnal; active any time of day. Roosts in crevices and cavities. Most common **call** is a rapid, repeated *took.* **Range:** Found at lower elevations than Northern Pygmy-Owl. Inhabits saguaro deserts, and woodlands north to near Kingsville, Texas. Rare in Arizona and the slightly grayer subspecies there (*cactorum*) is considered endangered (**E**). The browner *ridgwayi* is resident in south Texas.

Elf Owl *Micrathene whitneyi L 5¾" (15 cm)*

Our smallest owl. Yellow eyes; very short tail. Lacks ear tufts. Strictly nocturnal; roosts and nests in cavities in saguaros and trees. **Call** is an irregular series of high *churp* notes and chattering notes. **Range:** Common in desert lowlands and in canyons, especially among oaks and sycamores; fairly common in foothills. Now almost eliminated in California. Casual in winter in southernmost Texas. Accidental to Los Angeles County.

Northern Pygmy-Owl *Glaucidium gnoma L 6¾" (17 cm)*

Long tail, dark brown with pale bars. Upperparts are either rusty brown or gray-brown; crown spotted; underparts white with dark streaks. Eyes yellow; black nape spots look like eyes on the back of the head. The grayest birds are to be found in the Rockies; those on the Pacific coast as far north as British Columbia are browner. Inhabits dense woodlands in foothills and mountains. Chiefly diurnal; most active at dawn and dusk. Nests in cavities. **Call** is a mellow, whistled, *hoo* or *hoo hoo,* repeated in a well-spaced series; also gives a rapid series of *hoo* or *took* notes followed by a single *took.* An aggressive predator, sometimes catching birds larger than itself, this owl is a favorite target for songbirds. Birders may locate the owl by watching for mobbing songbirds. Nominate race, *gnoma,* seen from southeastern Arizona south through the mountains of Mexico, gives a series of double *took-took* notes with occasional single notes interspersed. Considered by some to be a separate species "Mountain Pygmy-Owl," though no marked genetic differences.

reddish type

Flammulated Owl

grayish type

Ferruginous Pygmy-Owl
cactorum

Elf Owl
whitneyi

Northern Pygmy-Owl

Rockies type

Pacific coast type

Northern Saw-whet Owl *Aegolius acadicus L 8" (20 cm)*
Reddish brown above; white below with reddish streaks; bill
dark; facial disks reddish, without dark border. **Juvenile** strongly
reddish above, tawny rust below. **Call,** heard primarily in breeding season from late winter to late spring, is a monotonously
repeated single-note whistle; another, raspy call sounds like a saw
being sharpened. Strictly nocturnal; roosts during day in or near
nest hole in breeding season. In winter, preferred roost is in dense
evergreens, usually close to end of branch. Large concentrations
of regurgitated pellets and white "wash" build up below favored
winter roosts. Once found, this species can be closely approached.
Range: Northern Saw-whet Owls inhabit dense coniferous or
mixed forests, wooded swamps, and tamarack bogs. Very rare
over most of winter range. A distinctive subspecies, *brooksi,*
endemic to Queen Charlotte Islands, Canada, is much darker and
buffier on facial disks and belly.

Northern Hawk Owl *Surnia ulula L 16" (41 cm)*
Long tail, falconlike profile, and black-bordered facial disks identify this owl of the northern forests. Underparts are barred with
brown. Flight is low and swift; sometimes hunts during daylight
as well as at night. Is most often seen, however, perched high in
a spruce tree. Usually can be closely approached. **Range:** Basically nonmigratory, but retreats slightly in winter from northernmost part of range. Casual south of mapped range.

Boreal Owl *Aegolius funereus L 10" (25 cm)*
White underparts streaked with chocolate brown. Whitish facial
disk has a distinct black border; bill is pale. Darker above than
Northern Saw-whet Owl. **Juvenile** is chocolate brown below.
Boreal Owls are strictly nocturnal; roost during daylight in dense
cover, usually close to tree trunk. **Call,** heard primarily in breeding season from late winter to midspring, is a short, rapid series
of hollow *hoo* notes. **Range:** Inhabit dense northern forests and
muskeg. Irruptive, usually in small numbers; otherwise seldom
seen south of mapped range, but this may be due to difficulty of
locating them. Breed at isolated locations high in the Rockies.

Burrowing Owl *Athene cunicularia L 9½" (24 cm)*
Long legs distinguish this ground dweller from all other small
owls. Adult is boldly spotted and barred. **Juvenile** is buffy below.
An owl of open country, golf courses, and airports. Nests in single pairs or small colonies. Nocturnal; flight low and undulating;
often hovers like a kestrel. Perches conspicuously during daylight
at entrance to burrow nest or on low post. **Calls** include a soft
coo-coooo and a chattering series of *chack* notes. Disturbed in its
nest, the Burrowing Owl often gives an alarm call that imitates
the sound of a rattlesnake. **Range:** Casual vagrant (both North
American subspecies) in spring and fall to East Coast, north to
Maine. Declining in much of northern Great Plains; may be partly
due to destruction of prairie dog towns, which it frequents, by
agricultural growth. Declining Florida birds (*floridana*) are darker
above with more whitish spotting; less buffy below.

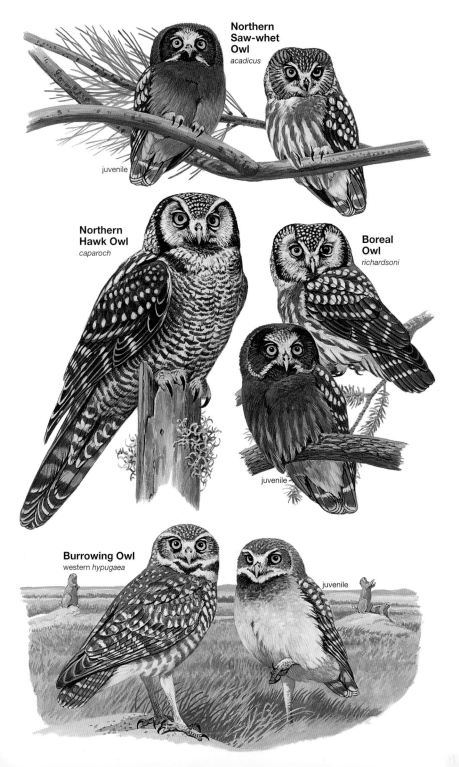

Northern Saw-whet Owl
acadicus

juvenile

Northern Hawk Owl
caparoch

Boreal Owl
richardsoni

juvenile

Burrowing Owl
western *hypugaea*

juvenile

Goatsuckers (Family Caprimulgidae)

Wide mouths help these night hunters snare flying insects. Most located and identified by distinctive calls. *Species: 89 World, 9 N.A.*

Lesser Nighthawk *Chordeiles acutipennis* L 8½" (22 cm)
Resembles Common Nighthawk but wings shorter and usually more rounded; whitish bar across primaries slightly closer to tip. Upperparts paler and more uniformly mottled; in Common paler wing coverts contrast more with back. Throat is white in **males,** usually buffy in **females** and juveniles. Underparts buffy, with faint barring. Male has white tail band. Female lacks tail band; note buffy wing bar and markings at base of primaries, often indistinct in juvenile female. Juvenile male's wing bar much smaller. Distinctive **call,** a rapid, tremulous trill, heard only on breeding grounds. Seen chiefly around dusk. Flies with a fluttery wingbeat. **Range:** Fairly common; found in dry, open country, scrubland, desert. Very rare spring and fall migrant on Gulf Coast. Rare to casual in winter in southern California, Texas, Florida.

Common Nighthawk *Chordeiles minor* L 9½" (24 cm)
Wings long and pointed; tail slightly forked. Bold white bar across primaries slightly farther from wing tip than in Lesser Nighthawk. Subspecies range from dark brown in eastern birds to more grayish in the northern Great Plains race, *sennetti;* color variations are subtle in adults, distinct in juveniles. Throat white in **male,** buffy in **female;** underparts whitish, with bold dusky bars. Female lacks white tail band. **Juvenile** shows less white on throat. In courtship display, male's wings make a hollow booming sound. Nasal *peent* **call** distinguishes Common from Lesser and Antillean Nighthawks. **Range:** Seen in woodlands, suburbs, and towns; more active in daylight than other goatsuckers. Roosts on the ground, on branches, posts, and roofs. Fairly common over parts of range, but declining in East where generally uncommon and local.

Antillean Nighthawk *Chordeiles gundlachii*
L 8" (20 cm) **Range:** Rare but regular in summer on Florida Keys; also seen on Dry Tortugas and southeastern Florida mainland. Accidental to Louisiana and Outer Banks, North Carolina. Wings are long and pointed; tail slightly forked. Females and juveniles lack white tail band. Very difficult to distinguish from variable but longer-winged and larger Common Nighthawk. **Call,** a varying *pity-pit-pit,* best identifies Antillean.

Common Pauraque *Nyctidromus albicollis* L 11" (28 cm)
In flight, long, rounded tail separates it from nighthawks; also shorter, rounder wings. Broad white bands on wings distinguish it from other nightjars (next page). White tail patches conspicuous on **male,** smaller and often buffy on **female.** In close view, note chestnut ear patch. Common in woodland clearings and scrub. Seen just before dawn and after dusk. Flies close to the ground; often lands on roads or roadsides. Distinctive **song,** one or more low *pur* notes followed by a higher, descending *wheeer.*

Lesser Nighthawk
texensis

Common Nighthawk
minor

juvenile
sennetti

Antillean Nighthawk

Common Pauraque
merrilli

Chuck-will's-widow *Caprimulgus carolinensis*

L 12" (31 cm) Our largest nightjar. Mottled buff-brown overall; wings rounded; tail long, rounded. Loud, whistling **song** sounds like *chuck-will's-widow,* the first note often inaudible. Much larger and redder than smaller-headed Whip-poor-will; buff-brown throat and whitish necklace contrast with dark breast. **Male**'s tail has less white than in male Whip-poor-will; tips of outer feathers are buff. **Female**'s tail lacks white. Rather shy; not usually approachable even when roosting during the day. Unlike eastern Whip-poor-will, birds will flush when disturbed. **Range:** Fairly common but local in oak-pine woodlands, live oak groves. Accidental west to New Mexico, Nevada, coastal northern California.

Whip-poor-will *Caprimulgus vociferus L 9¾" (25 cm)*

Mottled gray-brown overall; wings rounded; tail long, rounded. **Song** is a loud *whip-poor-will,* clear and mellow in eastern birds, with accent on first and last syllables; rough and burry in southwestern race *arizonae* (probably a separate species), with strongest accent on last syllable. Whip-poor-will is much smaller and grayer than Chuck-will's-widow; dark throat contrasts with white or buffy necklace and pale underparts. **Male**'s tail shows much more white than in male Chuck-will's-widow, especially with eastern nominate race. **Female**'s tail has contrasting pale tip on dark outer feathers. Unlike Chuck-will's-widow and southwestern Whip-poor-wills, members of the eastern race are tame; sitting birds will regularly stay put on a tree branch during daylight hours; southwestern birds usually roost on ground and don't allow close approach. **Range:** Fairly common but local in open coniferous and mixed woodlands in the East, wooded canyons in the Southwest. Breeds very locally in mountains of southern California (*arizonae*). Accidental to southeast Alaska (*vociferus*).

Buff-collared Nightjar *Caprimulgus ridgwayi*

L 8¾" (22 cm) **Range:** Rare, irregular, and local in desert canyons of extreme southwestern New Mexico (Guadalupe Canyon) and southeastern Arizona. Accidental in southern California (Ventura County). Usually roosts on the ground by day. Gray-brown plumage resembles Whip-poor-will, but is lighter and more finely marked; shows distinct buff collar across nape. **Song** is an accelerating series of *cuk* notes ending with *cukacheea.*

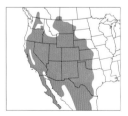

Common Poorwill *Phalaenoptilus nuttallii L 7¾" (20 cm)*

Our smallest nightjar, distinguished by short, rounded tail and short, rounded wings. Outer tail feathers are tipped with white, more boldly in **males** than in females. **Song** is a whistled *poorwill,* with a final *ip* note audible at close range. Plumage is variable; upperparts range from brownish gray to pale gray. Broad white band crosses dark throat and breast. **Range:** Fairly common in sagebrush and on chaparral slopes; often seen on roads or roadsides after dusk or before dawn. Roosts on the ground; flies up a short distance to catch an insect, then returns to the same or a nearby location. Known to hibernate in cold weather; may winter north into normal breeding range.

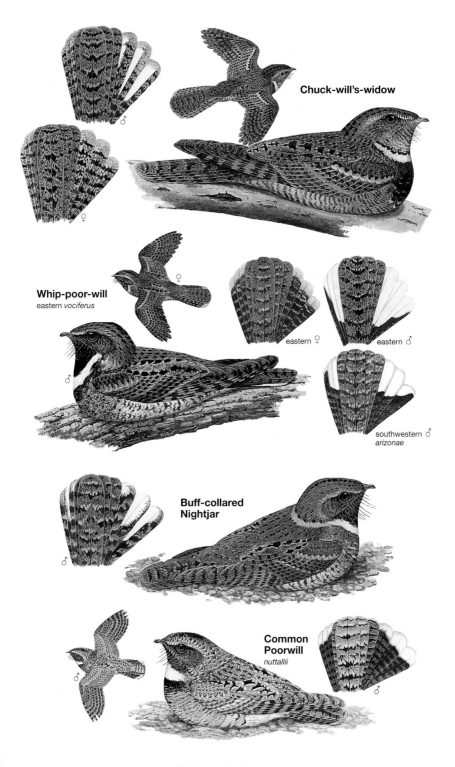

Chuck-will's-widow

♂

♀

Whip-poor-will
eastern *vociferus*

♀

♂

eastern ♀

eastern ♂

southwestern ♂
arizonae

**Buff-collared
Nightjar**

♂

**Common
Poorwill**
nuttallii

♂

♂

Swifts (Family Apodidae)

These fast-flying birds spend the day aloft. Long wings bend closer to the body than on similar swallows. *Species: 94 World, 9 N.A.*

Black Swift *Cypseloides niger* L 7¼" (18 cm)
Blackish overall; long, slightly forked tail, often fanned in flight. Nests in colonies on cliffs, beneath waterfalls; also on wet sea cliffs. Wingbeats rather more leisurely than in other swifts; often soars. **Range:** Uncommon. Thought to winter in South America.

Vaux's Swift *Chaetura vauxi* L 4¾" (12 cm)
Smaller than Chimney Swift; usually paler below and on rump; soars less. **Call** softer, higher and more insectlike. Nests in hollow trees. **Range:** Fairly common in woodlands near water. Rare in winter in southern California; casual on Gulf Coast.

Chimney Swift *Chaetura pelagica* L 5¼" (13 cm)
Cigar-shaped body; short, stubby tail. Chimney Swift is larger and usually darker below than similar Vaux's Swift; has longer wings, a louder, chattering **call,** and greater tendency to soar. Both species give a rocking display: Wings upraised, bird rocks from side to side. Nests in chimneys, barns, and hollow trees. **Range:** Rare in southern California. No winter records in the U.S.

Common Swift *Apus apus* L 6½" (17 cm)
Range: Breeds in Palearctic; winters in Africa. Accidental in summer on Pribilofs (twice) and Miquelon Island off Newfoundland; records from Bermuda and probably the Northeast. Long, thin winged, dark, with paler throat, long forked tail. Pribilofs specimen of eastern race *pekinensis* is paler than nominate.

White-collared Swift *Streptoprocne zonaris*
L 8½" (22 cm) **Range:** Tropical species, accidental at scattered coastal and Great Lakes locations in the U.S. and southern Canada. A very large, black swift; note white collar, more indistinct in **immatures,** and slightly forked tail. Soars with wings bent down.

White-throated Swift *Aeronautes saxatalis*
L 6½" (17 cm) Black above, black-and-white below, with long, forked tail. Distinguished from Violet-green Swallow (page 330) by longer, narrower wings, bicolored underparts. In poor light, may be mistaken for Black Swift but is smaller, with faster wingbeats. Common in mountains, canyons, cliffs. Nests in crevices.

White-throated Needletail *Hirundapus caudacutus*
L 8" (21 cm) **Range:** Large Asian swift, casual in spring on outer Aleutians. Dark overall, with pale patch on back; white throat and undertail coverts. Tail short and stubby.

Fork-tailed Swift *Apus pacificus* L 7¾" (20 cm)
Range: Asian species, casual to western Alaska's islands (and Middleton Island). White rump; long tail's fork not always apparent.

Black Swift
borealis

juvenile

adult

soaring

Vaux's Swift
vauxi

Chimney Swift

White-collared Swift

White-throated Swift
saxatalis

soaring

Common Swift
pekinensis

immature

soaring

Fork-tailed Swift
pacificus

White-throated Needletail
caudacutus

Hummingbirds (Family Trochilidae)

These birds hover at flowers to sip nectar with needlelike bills. Often identified by twittery calls. Males' throat feathers (gorget) look black in poor light. *Species: 331 World, 23 N.A.*

Green Violet-ear *Colibri thalassinus* L 4¾" (12 cm)
Range: Tropical species. Most records in summer in the Hill Country in Texas, where nearly annual; casual in eastern North America, accidental elsewhere. Green overall with dark subterminal tail band; bill slightly downcurved. **Adult male** has blue-violet patches on face and breast. Female and **immature** slightly duller, immature grayer on belly. **Song** is a repeated *tsip-tsup*.

Green-breasted Mango *Anthracothorax prevostii*
L 4¾" (12 cm) **Range:** Found from eastern Mexico to northern South America. Casual in fall and winter to southern Texas. Has curved bill and purplish color in outer tail feathers. **Adult male** is deep green overall. **Female** shows broad blackish green stripe on underparts bordered in white. **Immature** is similar to female but shows cinnamon border to sides of underparts.

Buff-bellied Hummingbird *Amazilia yucatanensis*
L 4¼" (11 cm) Green overall with buff belly and chestnut tail; bill pinkish red with black tip. **Calls** are shrill and squeaky. **Range:** Mexican species, fairly common in lower Rio Grande Valley. Rare in winter along Gulf Coast; casual to Florida.

Berylline Hummingbird *Amazilia beryllina* L 4¼" (11 cm)
Range: Very rare summer visitor from Mexico to mountains of southeastern Arizona; has bred there. Casual to southwestern New Mexico and west Texas. Green above and below, with chestnut wings, rump, and tail. Base of lower mandible red. **Male**'s lower belly is chestnut, **female**'s grayish.

Bahama Woodstar *Calliphlox evelynae* L 3¾" (10 cm)
Range: Bahamian endemic. Four records of five birds from southeast Florida. **Adult male** has broad white collar, light purple throat, long, forked tail; mixed olive and rich buff below. In **female** note tail projection past primary tips, cinnamon tips to outer tail feathers, slightly curved bill. **Calls** suggestive of Anna's Hummingbird.

Violet-crowned Hummingbird *Amazilia violiceps*
L 4½" (11 cm) Crown violet; underparts entirely white; upperparts bronze green; tail greenish. Long bill is mostly red. **Call** is a loud chattering; male's **song** is a series of sibilant *ts* notes. **Range:** Uncommon. Casual in California and west Texas.

Lucifer Hummingbird *Calothorax lucifer* L 3½" (9 cm)
Bill downcurved. **Adult male** has green crown, purple throat, long tail. **Female** is rich buff below; broadening pale stripe behind eye; outer tail feathers reddish at base. **Range:** Uncommon; rare in southeastern Arizona and southwestern New Mexico.

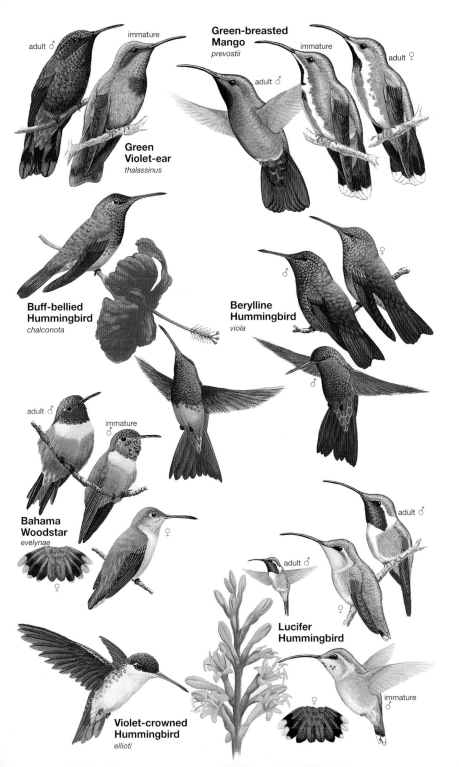

adult ♂

immature

Green-breasted Mango
prevostii

immature

adult ♀

adult ♂

Green Violet-ear
thalassinus

Buff-bellied Hummingbird
chalconota

Berylline Hummingbird
viola

♂

♀

♂

adult ♂

immature
♂

Bahama Woodstar
evelynae

♀

♀

adult ♂

adult ♂

♀

Lucifer Hummingbird

Violet-crowned Hummingbird
ellioti

♀

immature
♂

Broad-billed Hummingbird　*Cynanthus latirostris*

L 4" (10 cm) **Adult male** is dark green above and below, with white undertail coverts, blue gorget, and mostly red bill. Broad, forked tail is blackish blue. **Adult female** is duller above, gray below; often shows a narrow white eye stripe; has a square-tipped tail. Juveniles resemble female; by late summer, male begins to show blue and green flecks on throat, green on sides; dark, forked tail helps distinguish it from White-eared Hummingbird. Chattering *je-dit* **call** is similar to Ruby-crowned Kinglet. Male's display call is a whining *zing*. **Range:** Common in desert canyons and low mountain woodlands. Very rare in southern California and Texas during fall and winter; casual in East.

White-eared Hummingbird　*Hylocharis leucotis*

L 3¾" (10 cm) **Range:** Summer visitor to mountains of Southwest: rare in southeastern Arizona; very rare in southwest New Mexico and west Texas. Bill shorter than in Broad-billed Hummingbird; broad white stripe extends back from eye; has black ear patch, square tail. **Adult male** has dark purple crown and chin, emerald green gorget; display **call** is a repeated, silvery *tink tink tink*. Chattering calls are loud and metallic.

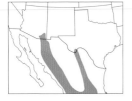

Blue-throated Hummingbird　*Lampornis clemenciae*

L 5" (13 cm) **Adult male**'s throat is blue, **female**'s gray. Broad white eye stripe and faint white malar stripe border dark ear patch. Tail has broad white tips on outer feathers; compare female Magnificent Hummingbird. Male's **call** is a loud, high, repeated *seep*. **Range:** Fairly common; found in mountain canyons, especially near streams. Casual north of mapped range.

Xantus's Hummingbird　*Hylocharis xantusii*

L 3½" (9 cm) **Range:** Endemic to southern Baja California, Mexico. Accidental vagrant to southern California and southwestern British Columbia. Plumages and **calls** similar to White-eared Hummingbird, but note buff on underparts and rufous in tail; **male** has black forehead and ear patches.

Magnificent Hummingbird　*Eugenes fulgens*

L 5¼" (13 cm) **Adult male** is green above, with purple crown; metallic green throat; breast and upper belly black and green; lower belly dull brown. Tail is dark green and deeply notched. **Female** is duller, lacks purple crown; squarish tail has small, grayish white tips on outer feathers; compare with female Blue-throated Hummingbird, which has stronger eyebrow. Main **call** is a sharp *chip*. **Range:** Fairly common in high mountain meadows and canyons. Casual away from mapped range.

Plain-capped Starthroat　*Heliomaster constantii*

L 5" (13 cm) **Range:** Casual stray in summer and fall from Mexico to arid foothills and deserts of southeastern Arizona. Broad white malar stripe, white eye stripe, and white patches on sides of rump are conspicuous. Throat shows variable amount of red; note also very long bill. **Call** is a sharp *chip*.

Broad-billed Hummingbird
magicus

♀

immature ♂

adult ♂

White-eared Hummingbird
borealis

adult ♀

adult ♂

♂

Blue-throated Hummingbird
bessophilus

♀

♂

♂

♀

Xantus's Hummingbird

♀

Magnificent Hummingbird
fulgens

adult ♂

Plain-capped Starthroat
pinicola

Ruby-throated Hummingbird *Archilochus colubris*

L 3¾" (10 cm) The only hummingbird regularly seen throughout most of the East. Metallic green above. **Adult male** has a brilliant red throat and black chin; underparts are whitish; sides and flanks dusky green; tail forked. **Female**'s throat is whitish; underparts grayish white, with buffy wash on sides; tail is similar to female Black-chinned Hummingbird. Immatures resemble adult female. Some **immature males** begin to show red spotting on throat by early fall. As with all hummingbirds, adult males migrate earlier than females and immatures. Ruby-throated Hummingbirds are fairly common in parts of range; found in gardens and woodland edges. *Archilochus* hummingbirds seen in the Southeast in winter are more likely to be Black-chinned, but females and immatures of these two species are almost indistinguishable. Ruby-throated generally has a greener crown, shorter bill; note darker face and more pointed shape of darker primaries, especially outermost. **Calls** very similar. **Range:** Casual west to California.

Black-chinned Hummingbird *Archilochus alexandri*

L 3¾" (10 cm) Metallic green above. In good light, **adult male** shows violet band at lower border of black throat. Underparts whitish; sides and flanks dusky green. **Female**'s throat can be all-white or show faint dusky or greenish streaks. Immatures resemble adult female; **immature male** may begin to show violet on lower throat in the fall. **Call** is a soft *tchew;* chase note combines high squeals and *tchew* notes. Twitches tail more than Ruby-throated while feeding. **Range:** Common in lowlands and low mountains. A few Black-chinned Hummingbirds winter in Southeast.

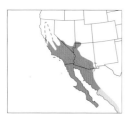

Costa's Hummingbird *Calypte costae* *L 3½" (9 cm)*

Adult male has deep violet crown and gorget extending far down sides of neck. **Female** is generally grayer above, whiter below, than female Black-chinned Hummingbird; note also tail differences. Best distinguished by voice. **Call** is a high, metallic *tink,* often given in a series. Male's call is a loud *zing.* **Range:** Fairly common in desert washes, dry chaparral. Casual north to south coastal Alaska and west to Texas.

Anna's Hummingbird *Calypte anna* *L 4" (10 cm)*

Adult male's head and throat are deep rose red, the color extending a short distance onto sides of neck. **Female**'s throat usually shows red flecks, often forming a patch of color. In both sexes, underparts are grayish, washed with a varying amount of green. Bill is disproportionately short. Immatures resemble female; **immature male** usually shows some red on crown. **Juveniles** lack red on throat; compare with smaller female Black-chinned and Costa's Hummingbirds. Common **call** note, a sharp *chick;* chase call is a rapid dry rattling. Male's **song** is a jumble of high squeaks and raspy notes. **Range:** Abundant in coastal lowlands and mountains; also in deserts, especially in winter. Casual north to south coastal Alaska and in eastern North America.

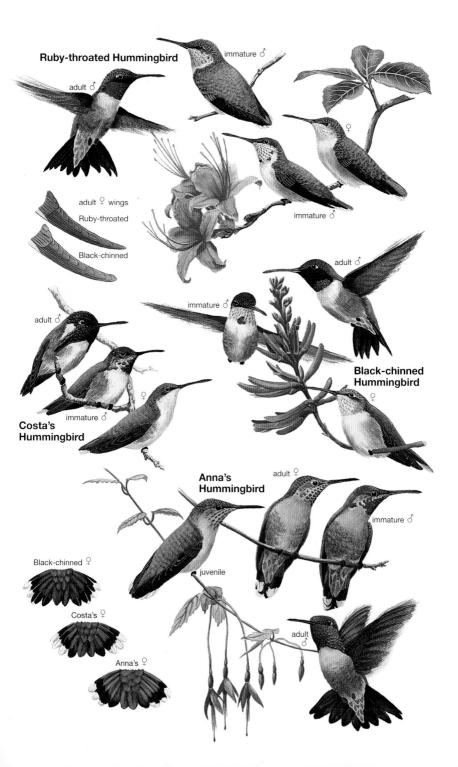

Ruby-throated Hummingbird

adult ♂

immature ♂

♀

adult ♀ wings
Ruby-throated

Black-chinned

immature ♂

adult ♂

immature ♂

adult ♂

Black-chinned Hummingbird

immature ♂

♀

Costa's Hummingbird

adult ♂

immature ♂

♀

Anna's Hummingbird

adult ♀

immature ♂

Black-chinned ♀

Costa's ♀

Anna's ♀

juvenile

adult ♂

Broad-tailed Hummingbird *Selasphorus platycercus*
L 4" (10 cm) Except during winter molt, all *Selasphorus* **adult males'** wingbeats produce a loud whistle, harsh and trilling in Broad-tailed. Male has rose red throat. **Female** has blended buff on underparts; similar to female Calliope, but note tail tip extends well past primaries. **Calls** include a metallic *chip*, often given in a short series. Summers in mountains. **Range:** Casual fall and winter to Gulf Coast.

Calliope Hummingbird *Stellula calliope L 3¼" (8 cm)*
Smallest North American bird; very short bill and tail; primary tips extend well past end of tail. Carmine streaks on **adult male**'s throat form a V-shaped gorget. **Female**'s underparts female Broad-tailed. **Immature** male like female but some show some red on throat by late summer. Relatively silent. **Range:** Common; summers in mountains. Very rare in Southeast in fall and winter.

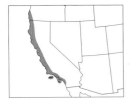

Rufous Hummingbird *Selasphorus rufus L 3¾" (10 cm)*
Tail mainly rufous. **Adult male** has rufous back, sometimes marked with green, very rarely entirely green; orange-red gorget. **Immatures** resemble **adult female**; immature male may show reddish brown back by winter before acquiring full gorget. Buzzy wing whistle and all **calls** identical to Allen's: Calls include a sibilant *chip*, often given in a series; chase note, *zeee-chuppity-chup*. **Range:** Rare in fall over much of the East.

Allen's Hummingbird *Selasphorus sasin L 3¾" (10 cm)*
Wing whistle and **calls** are identical to Rufous. **Adult male** has full, orange-red gorget; usually distinguishable from Rufous by solid green back. Adult female and immatures inseparable in the field from female Rufous, though tail feathers are comparatively narrower for each sex and age class. **Range:** Allen's migrates earlier in fall and spring than Rufous. Casual vagrant to eastern U.S.

Trogons (Family Trogonidae)

Colorful tropical birds with short, broad bills. *Species: 39 World; 2 N.A.*

Elegant Trogon *Trogon elegans L 12½" (32 cm)*
Yellow bill, white breast band; undertail delicately barred. **Male** is bright green above and has bright red belly. **Female** and juvenile are browner and duller. **Song** is a series of croaking *co-ah* notes. **Range:** Found in streamside woodlands, mostly at altitudes from 4,000 to 6,000 feet. Casual in southernmost Texas.

Eared Quetzal *Euptilotis neoxenus L 14" (36 cm)*
Range: Casual in mountain streamside woodlands of southeastern Arizona. Wary. Larger and with thicker body than Elegant Trogon; bill is black or gray; lacks white breast band and barring on undertail. **Calls** include a loud upslurred squeal ending in a *chuck* note; also a loud, hard cackling. Male's **song** is a long, quavering series of whistled notes that increase in volume.

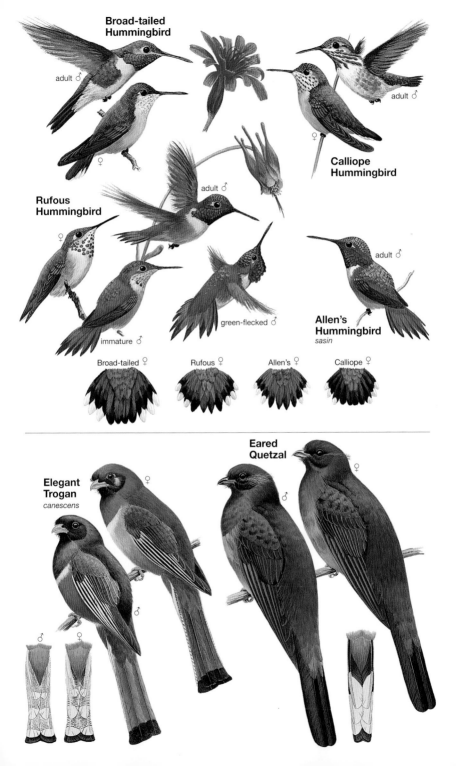

Broad-tailed Hummingbird

adult ♂

♀

Calliope Hummingbird

adult ♂

♀

Rufous Hummingbird

adult ♂

♀

immature ♂

green-flecked ♂

Allen's Hummingbird
sasin

adult ♂

Broad-tailed ♀   Rufous ♀   Allen's ♀   Calliope ♀

Eared Quetzal

Elegant Trogan
canescens

♀

♂

♂

♂

♀

♂   ♀

Kingfishers (Family Alcedinidae)

Stocky and short-legged, with a large head, a large bill, and, in two North American species, a ragged crest. Look for kingfishers near woodland streams and ponds and in coastal areas. They hover over water or watch from low perches, then plunge headfirst to catch a fish. With strong bill and feet, they dig nest burrows in stream banks. *Species: 91 World; 3 N.A.*

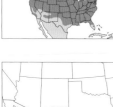

Belted Kingfisher *Ceryle alcyon L 13" (33 cm)*
The only kingfisher in most of North America. Both **male** and **female** have slate blue breast band; white belly and undertail coverts. Female has rust belly band and flanks; may be confused with female Ringed Kingfisher, note white belly and smaller size. Juvenile resembles adult but has rust spotting in breast band. **Call** is a loud, dry rattle. **Range:** Common and conspicuous along rivers and brooks, ponds and lakes, and estuaries. Generally solitary. Rare in winter north into summer range.

Ringed Kingfisher *Ceryle torquatus L 16" (41 cm)*
Larger than Belted Kingfisher; generally frequents larger rivers and ponds, perches on higher branches than Belted. Rufous underwing coverts of **female** distinctive in flight; white in **male.** Male is rust below with white undertail coverts. Female has slate blue breast, narrow white band, rust belly and undertail coverts. Juveniles resemble adult female, but juvenile male's breast is largely rust. **Calls** include a harsh rattle, lower and slower than in Belted Kingfisher, and single *chack* notes, given chiefly in flight. **Range:** Resident in lower Rio Grande Valley; casual elsewhere in southern Texas.

Green Kingfisher *Chloroceryle americana L 8¾" (22 cm)*
Smallest of our kingfishers; crest inconspicuous. **Male** is green above, with white collar; white below, with dark green spotting. **Female** has a band of green spots. Juvenile resembles adult female. One **call**, a faint but sharp *tick tick*, often ends in a short rattle; another, a squeaky *cheep*, is given in flight. Often perches on low, sheltered branches. Flight is direct and very fast; white outer tail feathers conspicuous in flight. **Range:** Uncommon and often hard to see. Resident of lower Rio Grande Valley; rarer on Edwards Plateau. Casual wanderer along the Texas coast; also to Big Bend region. In southeastern Arizona, a few pairs are resident along San Pedro River; also occasionally seen on Santa Cruz River near Nogales.

Belted Kingfisher

Ringed Kingfisher
torquatus

Green Kingfisher

Woodpeckers, Allies (Family Picidae)

Strong claws, short legs, and stiff tail feathers enable woodpeckers to climb tree trunks. Sharp bill is used to chisel out insect food and nest holes and to drum a territorial signal. *Species: 210 World; 25 N.A.*

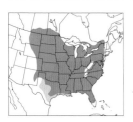

Red-headed Woodpecker *Melanerpes erythrocephalus*
L 9¼" *(24 cm)* Entire head, neck, and throat are bright red in **adults,** contrasting with blue-black back and snowy white underparts. **Juvenile** is brownish; acquires red head during gradual winter molt. Distinctive white inner wing patches and white rump are visible in all ages in perched and flying birds. In breeding season utters a loud *queark,* similar to Red-bellied Woodpecker (next page) but harsher and sharper; uncommon to fairly common **call** is a guttural rattle. Inhabits a variety of open and densely wooded habitats; often seen catching flies. **Range:** Now vagrant in the Northeast, chiefly in fall; no longer breeds there, due in part to habitat loss and competition with European Starlings for nest holes. Rare to Maritimes; casual to California and Arizona.

Acorn Woodpecker *Melanerpes formicivorus*
L 9" *(23 cm)* Black chin, yellowish throat, white cheeks and forehead, red cap. **Female** has smaller bill than **male,** less red on crown. In flight, white rump and small white patches on outer wings are conspicuous. Most frequent **call,** *waka,* usually repeated several times. Common in oak woods or pine forests where oak trees are abundant. Sociable; generally found in small, noisy colonies. Eats chiefly acorns and other nuts in winter, insects in summer. In the fall, is sometimes seen drilling small holes in a tree trunk and pounding a nut into each hole for a winter food supply. Colonies use the same "granary tree" year after year.

White-headed Woodpecker *Picoides albolarvatus*
L 9¼" *(24 cm)* Head and throat white. **Male** has a red patch on back of head. Body is black except for white wing patches. Juveniles have a variable patch of pale red on crown. **Calls** include a sharp *pee-dink* or *pee-dee-dink*. **Range:** Nests in coniferous mountain forests, especially ponderosa and sugar pine; feeds primarily on seeds from their cones; also pries away loose bark in search of insects and larvae. Casual at lower altitudes in winter. Fairly common over most of range; rare and local in the North.

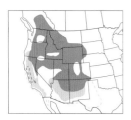

Lewis's Woodpecker *Melanerpes lewis* L 10¾" *(27 cm)*
Greenish black head and back; gray collar and breast; dark red face, pinkish belly. In flight, darkness, large size, and slow, steady wingbeats give it a crowlike appearance. **Juvenile** lacks collar and red face; belly may be only faintly pink; acquires more adultlike plumage from late fall through winter. Main food, insects, mostly caught in the air; also eats fruit and nuts. Stores acorns, which it first shells, in tree bark crevices. Generally silent. **Range:** Uncommon to fairly common in open woodlands of interior; rare on coast. Often gregarious; fall and winter movements unpredictable. Largely eliminated in coastal Northwest; accidental in East.

Red-headed
Woodpecker

juvenile

adults

Acorn
Woodpecker

♂

♀

♂

White-headed
Woodpecker

♂

♂

♀

juvenile

Lewis's
Woodpecker

adults

Golden-fronted Woodpecker *Melanerpes aurifrons*
L 9¾" (25 cm) Black-and-white barred back, white rump, usually an all-black tail; golden orange nape, paler in **females;** yellow feathering above bill. **Male** has a small red cap. Yellow tinge on belly not easily seen. Juvenile has streaked breast, brownish crown. In flight, all plumages show white wing patches, white rump as in Red-bellied and Gila Woodpeckers; unlike them, Golden-fronted shows black, not barred, tail. **Calls,** a rolling *churr-churr* and cackling *kek-kek,* are slightly louder and raspier than in Red-bellied. **Range:** Fairly common in dry woodlands, pecan groves, and mesquite brushlands.

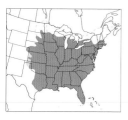

Red-bellied Woodpecker *Melanerpes carolinus*
L 9¼" (24 cm) Black-and-white barred back; white uppertail coverts; barred central tail feathers. Crown and nape are red in **males. Females** have red nape only; small reddish patch or tinge on belly. **Call,** a rolling *churr* or *chiv-chiv,* is slightly softer than that of Golden-fronted. **Range:** Red-bellied Woodpeckers are common in open woodlands, suburbs, parks. Breeding range extending northward. Rare to Maine and Maritimes; casual to New Mexico.

Gila Woodpecker *Melanerpes uropygialis* L 9¼" (24 cm)
Black-and-white barred back and rump; central tail feathers barred. **Male** has a small red cap. **Calls,** a rolling *churr* and a loud, sharp, high-pitched *yip,* often given in a series. **Range:** Inhabits towns, scrub desert, cactus country, and streamside woods.

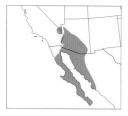

Northern Flicker *Colaptes auratus* L 12½" (32 cm)
Two distinct groups occur: **"Yellow-shafted Flicker"** in the East and far north, and **"Red-shafted Flicker"** in the West. These flickers have brown, barred back; spotted underparts, with black crescent bib. White rump is conspicuous in flight; no white wing patches. Intergrades are regularly seen in the Great Plains. Yellow-shafted Flicker" has yellow wing lining and undertail color, gray crown, and tan face with red crescent on nape. "Red-shafted Flicker" has brown crown and gray face, with no red crescent. "Yellow-shafted" male has a black moustachial stripe (red stripe in "Red-shafted" male); **females** lack these stripes. **Call** heard on the breeding ground is a long, loud series of *wick-er* notes; a single, loud *klee-yer* is given year-round. **Range:** Common in open woodlands and suburban areas. "Yellow-shafted" is rare in the West in fall and winter.

Gilded Flicker *Colaptes chrysoides* L 11½" (29 cm)
Restored to full species status from Northern Flicker. Gilded Flicker's head pattern more like "Red-shafted" Northern, but underwings and base of tail yellow; crown more cinnamon. Note also smaller size; larger black chest patch; paler back with narrower black bars; more crescent-shaped markings below. **Female** lacks red moustachial stripe. **Calls** are like Northern's. **Range:** Inhabits low desert woodlands; favors saguaro. Hybrids with "Red-shafted" are noted in cottonwoods at middle elevations in southern Arizona and along the lower Colorado River.

Golden-fronted Woodpecker
aurifrons

♂

♀

Red-bellied Woodpecker

♀

♂

♂

Gila Woodpecker
uropygialis

♂

♀

"Yellow-shafted" ♂

Northern Flicker

"Red-shafted" ♂

"Yellow-shafted" ♀

♂

Gilded Flicker

Gilded Flicker ♀

"Red-shafted" ♀

Sapsuckers

These woodpeckers drill evenly spaced rows of holes in trees and then visit these "wells" for sap and the insects it attracts. Red-breasted and Red-naped Sapsuckers were formerly considered subspecies of Yellow-bellied.

Williamson's Sapsucker *Sphyrapicus thyroideus*
L 9" (23 cm) **Male** has black back, white rump, and large white wing patch; black head with narrow white stripes, bright red chin and throat. Breast is black, belly yellow; flanks are barred with black and white. **Female**'s head is brown; back, wings, and sides barred with dark brown and white; rump white; lacks white wing patch and red chin; breast has large dark patch; belly variably yellow. Juveniles resemble adults but are duller; attain adult-like plumage by Nov. Juvenile male has white throat; juvenile female lacks black breast patch. Gives a harsh, shrill raptorlike **call. Range:** Fairly common in dry, piney forests of the western mountains; moves south or to lower elevations in winter. Accidental in eastern North America.

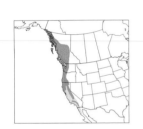

Red-breasted Sapsucker *Sphyrapicus ruber*
L 8½" (22 cm) This and next two species formerly considered one species. All show white wing patches and give a querulous descending mewing **call.** Red head, nape, and breast; large white wing patch; white rump. Back is black, lightly spotted with yellow in northern subspecies, *ruber;* more heavily marked with white in southern *daggetti.* Belly is yellow in *ruber; daggetti* has paler belly and duller head with longer white moustachial stripe. In both races, briefly held juvenal plumage is brownish, showing little or no red. **Range:** Common in coniferous or mixed forests in coastal ranges, usually at lower elevations and in moister forests than Williamson's Sapsucker. Most migrate south or move to lower elevations in winter. Red-breasted frequently hybridizes with Red-naped Sapsucker.

Yellow-bellied Sapsucker *Sphyrapicus varius*
L 8½" (22 cm) Red forecrown on black-and-white head; chin and throat red in **male,** white in **female.** Back is blackish, with white rump and large white wing patch. Underparts yellowish, paler in female. **Juvenile** retains largely brownish plumage until late in the winter. **Range:** Common in deciduous forests. Highly migratory; rare to very rare in the West during fall and winter. Hybridizes with Red-naped Sapsucker.

Red-naped Sapsucker *Sphyrapicus nuchalis*
L 8½" (22 cm) Very similar to Yellow-bellied, but has variable red patch on back of head; spotting on back more clearly organized into two rows. On **male,** extensive red on throat penetrates the surrounding black "frame"; on **female,** throat is partly red to almost entirely red on some birds. Juvenile is brownish overall; resembles adult by first fall except for lack of black chest. **Range:** Common in deciduous forests.

Williamson's Sapsucker

♂

♀

Red-breasted Sapsucker

ruber

daggetti

Yellow-bellied Sapsucker

adult ♀

adult ♂

Red-naped Sapsucker

adult ♂

adult ♀

Yellow-bellied juvenile

Williamson's ♂

Red-breasted *ruber*

Yellow-bellied adult ♂

Red-breasted *daggetti*

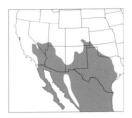

Ladder-backed Woodpecker *Picoides scalaris*
L 7¼" (18 cm) Black-and-white barred back, spotted sides; face and underparts slightly buffy or grayish; face marked with black lines. **Male** has red crown. In California, Ladder-backed may be confused with Nuttall's Woodpecker. Ladder-backed shows less black on face and is buffy-tinged rather than white below; white barring on back is more pronounced and extends to nape; white outer tail feathers are evenly barred rather than spotted; nasal tufts buffy. **Call** is a crisp *pik*, very similar to Downy Woodpecker's call and different from Nuttall's rattled *prrrt;* also gives a descending whinny. **Range:** Common in dry brushlands, mesquite and cactus country; also towns and rural areas. Feeds on beetle larvae from small trees; also eats cactus fruits and forages on the ground for insects. May hybridize with Nuttall's where ranges overlap.

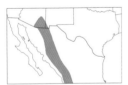

Red-cockaded Woodpecker *Picoides borealis* **E**
L 8½" (22 cm) Black-and-white barred back, black cap, and large white cheek patch identify this woodpecker; red tufts, seldom visible, on the **male**'s head. Similar Hairy and Downy Woodpeckers (next page) have solid white down backs. Distinctive **calls,** a raspy *sripp* and high-pitched *tsick,* are much more buzzy; recall a loud Brown-headed Nuthatch. Red-cockaded inhabits open, mature pine or pine-oak woodlands. Bores nest hole only in a large living pine afflicted with heartwood disease, then drills small holes around the nest opening. Pine pitch oozing down the trunk from these holes may repel predators; also makes the tree a distinctive signpost. Endangered: Populations continue to decline. Almost eliminated from Virginia, and has disappeared from Kentucky and Tennessee in the last decade. Accidental to Illinois and Ohio.

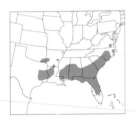

Arizona Woodpecker *Picoides arizonae*
L 7½" (19 cm) Solid brown back distinguishes this species from all other woodpeckers. **Female** lacks red patch on back of head. **Call** is a sharp *peek,* similar to call of Hairy Woodpecker but hoarser. **Range:** Uncommon resident in foothills and mountains; generally found in oak or pine-oak forests or canyons.

Nuttall's Woodpecker *Picoides nuttallii L 7½" (19 cm)*
Closely resembles Ladder-backed Woodpecker. Nuttall's shows more black on face; white bars on back are narrower, with more extensive solid black just below the nape. White outer tail feathers are sparsely spotted rather than barred; nasal tufts white. **Call** is a low, rattled *prrrt*, much lower than Ladder-backed's *pik;* also gives a series of loud, spaced, descending notes. Nuttall's prefers less arid habitat than Ladder-backed; usually seen in chaparral mixed with scrub oak and in wooded canyons and streamside trees. **Range:** Casual to western Nevada.

Great Spotted Woodpecker *Dendrocopos major*
L 9" (25 cm) **Range:** Widespread in Eurasia. Casual to western Aleutians and Pribilofs; accidental in winter north of Anchorage. Large size with large white cheek and scapular patch and red undertail coverts. Female lacks red nape patch. **Call,** a sharp *kick.*

Ladder-backed Woodpecker

♂

♀

Red-cockaded Woodpecker

♂

Arizona Woodpecker

♂

♀

Nuttall's Woodpecker

♂

♀

Great Spotted Woodpecker

♂

Ladder-backed ♂   Nuttall's ♂   Arizona ♂   Red-cockaded ♂

Downy Woodpecker *Picoides pubescens L 6¾" (17 cm)*
White back generally identifies both Downy and similar Hairy
Woodpecker. Downy is much smaller, with a smaller bill; outer
tail feathers generally have faint dark bars or spots. Birds in the
Pacific Northwest have pale gray-brown back and underparts.
Rocky Mountain birds have less white spotting on wings. Downy's
call, *pik,* and whinny are softer and higher-pitched than Hairy
Woodpecker's. **Range:** Common; active, and somewhat unwary;
often seen in suburbs, parklands, and orchards, as well as in
forests. A familiar visitor to feeders.

Hairy Woodpecker *Picoides villosus L 9¼" (24 cm)*
White back generally identifies both Hairy and similar Downy
Woodpecker. Hairy is much larger, with a larger bill; outer tail
feathers are entirely white. Birds in the Pacific Northwest have
pale gray-brown back and underparts. Rocky Mountain birds
have less white spotting on wings. **Juveniles,** particularly in the
Maritime Provinces, have some barring on back and flanks; sides
may be streaked. Juveniles on the Queen Charlotte Islands have
heavily barred outer tail feathers. In young males, the forehead
is spotted with white; crown streaked with red or orange. Hairy's
calls include a loud, sharp *peek* and a slurred whinny. **Range:**
Fairly common; inhabits both open and dense forests. Uncommon to rare in the South and in Florida.

American Three-toed Woodpecker *Picoides dorsalis*
L 8¾" (22 cm) Black-and-white barring down center of back
distinguishes most races of American Three-toed Woodpecker
from similar Black-backed. Both have heavily barred sides. **Male**'s
yellow cap is usually more extensive in Three-toed but less solid.
Density of barring on back is intermediate in northwestern race,
fasciatus. In Rocky Mountain race, nominate *dorsalis,* back is
almost entirely white. Back is much darker in eastern race, *bacatus;* thinner, white submoustachial stripe helps distinguish it
from Black-backed. **Range:** American Three-toed is found in
coniferous forests, especially in burned-over areas. Scarcer than
Black-backed in the East. Accidental south to Rhode Island in
winter; east to southwest Kansas (in summer!). New English and
scientific names reflect a recent split: The eight Old World subspecies are now considered their own species, *P. tridactylus.*

Black-backed Woodpecker *Picoides arcticus*
L 9½" (24 cm) Solid black back, heavily barred sides. **Male** has
a solid yellow cap. Compare especially with eastern race of Three-
toed Woodpecker, *bacatus,* which has a darker back than other
Three-toeds. Black-backed Woodpecker is larger; has longer,
stouter bill; and lacks white streak behind the eye. **Call** note is a
single, sharp *pik,* lower-pitched than call of Three-toed. **Range:**
Black-backed inhabits coniferous forests; often found in burned-
over areas. Forages on dead conifers, flaking away large patches
of loose bark rather than drilling into it, in search of larvae and
insects. Casual south of mapped range in the East, fewer records
in recent decades.

Downy Woodpecker

♀

♀

♀

Pacific Northwest
♂ *sitkensis*

juvenile

Hairy Woodpecker

American Three-toed Woodpecker

fasciatus

♀

♂

Black-backed Woodpecker

♂

♀

Hairy Rockies
♂ *orius*

Hairy Maritimes juvenile
♂ *terranovae*

Downy Rockies
♂ *leucurus*

Black-backed ♂

American Three-toed
♂ *fasciatus*

American Three-toed
♂ *dorsalis*

American Three-toed
♂ *bacatus*

Ivory-billed Woodpecker *Campephilus principalis* **E**
L 19½" (50 cm) **Range:** Formerly found north to the Ohio River,
near its confluence with the Mississippi. Perhaps extinct; last definite records from U.S. were in 1944 in the Singer Tract, near Tal-
lulah in northeastern Louisiana. Possibly valid sightings recorded
into the 1950s in Florida; from 1948, perhaps into the 1980s, in
Cuba (subspecies *bairdii*), but now probably extinct there. Unconfirmed sightings over the last 50 years come from eastern Texas,
Louisiana, Georgia, and Florida. In Apr. 2005 came the much
publicized announcement that the species had been rediscovered
more than a year earlier in the Big Woods of the White River-
Cache River system of eastern Arkansas. Documentation was provided in the form of sound recordings and videotape. However,
intense searching subsequently has yet to produce more documentation, and some authorities now question the conclusions
reached from the original evidence. The search continues. For
identification note Ivory-billed Woodpecker's black chin, striking ivory bill, and the extensive white wing patches and scapular
lines, visible in perched birds; tail longer than Pileated, especially
visible in flight. **Females** have black rather than red crests. Compare also the black-and-white wing patterns of Ivory-billed and
Pileated Woodpeckers in flight; in Ivory-billed from below, the
white leading edge and the white secondaries are divided by a black
bar; viewed from above, the white secondaries are diagnostic;
flight of Ivory-billed is more direct and swift. Distinctive **call** note
sounds like a toy trumpet, a high-pitched, nasal *yank,* given singly
or in short series, like a loud version of the call of eastern White-
breasted Nuthatch, but beware of Blue Jays giving similar calls;
double-rap drum is characteristic of genus *Campephilus.* Our
largest woodpecker, Ivory-billed required large tracts of old-
growth river forest; dead and dying trees supplied nesting sites
and food: the larvae of wood-boring beetles. Destruction of habitat at the end of the 19th century and early in the 20th century
led to the disappearance of this never-common species.

Pileated Woodpecker *Dryocopus pileatus*
L 16½" (42 cm) Perched bird is almost entirely black on back
and wings, lacking Ivory-billed Woodpecker's large white wing
patches. White chin and dark bill also distinguish Pileated Woodpecker, along with smaller size. Compare also the wing patterns
of the two species in flight; also note Pileated's deep, slow, crowlike wingbeats. This is the largest woodpecker now generally seen
in North America. **Female**'s red cap is less extensive than in
male. Juvenile plumage, held briefly, resembles adult but is duller
and browner overall. Generally shy. **Call** is a loud *wuck* note or
series of notes, given all year, often in flight; similar call of Northern Flicker is given only in the breeding season. **Range:** Prefers
dense, mature forest. In woodlots and parklands as well as deep
woods, listen for its loud, resonant, territorial drumming, given
by both sexes but less frequently by females; look for the long
rectangular or oval holes it excavates. Carpenter ants in fallen
trees and stumps are its major food. Common in Southeast;
uncommon and local elsewhere, but increasing in East.

Ivory-billed Woodpecker

Pileated Woodpecker

Tyrant Flycatchers (Family Tyrannidae)

A typical flycatcher darts out from a fixed perch to catch insects. Most have a large head, bristly "whiskers," and a broad-based, flat bill. *Species: 400 World; 44 N.A.*

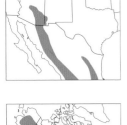

Greater Pewee *Contopus pertinax L 8" (20 cm)*
Note longer tail, more slender crest (usually visible), and more uniformly colored underparts than Olive-sided. Worn summer birds are overall grayer than freshly molted winter ones. Unlike *Empidonax* flycatchers (next page), most *Contopus* (pewees) do not wag their tails. **Song,** a whistled *ho-say ma-re-ah;* **call** is a repeated *pip.* **Range:** Fairly common in mountain pine-oak woodlands. Very rare in winter in southern Arizona, southern and central California; casual in south and west Texas.

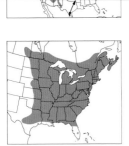

Olive-sided Flycatcher *Contopus cooperi L 7½" (19 cm)*
Large, with rather short tail. Brownish olive above; white tufts on sides of rump distinctive but often not visible. Throat, center of breast, and belly dull white. Sides and flanks brownish olive and streaked. Bill is mostly black; center and sometimes base of lower mandible dull orange. Distinctive **song,** a clear *quick-three-beers,* the second note higher; typical **call,** a repeated *pip.* **Range:** Fairly common in coniferous forests and bogs. Casual in winter on coastal slope of southern California.

Eastern Wood-Pewee *Contopus virens L 6¼" (16 cm)*
Plumage generally dark grayish olive above, with dull white throat, darker breast; underparts whitish or pale yellow. Bill of **adult** has black upper mandible, dull orange lower mandible. **Juvenile** and immature may have all-dark bill. Distinctive **song** is a clear, slow, plaintive *pee-a-wee,* the second note lower; this phrase often alternates with a downslurred *pee-yer.* **Calls** include a loud *chip* and clear, whistled, rising *pweee* notes; often given together, *chip pweee.* **Range:** Common in a variety of woodland habitats. Casual in the West. No winter records in U.S.

Western Wood-Pewee *Contopus sordidulus*
L 6¼" (16 cm) Plumage variable; slightly darker and less greenish than Eastern Wood-Pewee; base of lower mandible usually shows some yellow-orange. Identification very difficult; best done by range and voice. **Calls** include a harsh, slightly descending *peeer* and clear whistles suggestive of Eastern's *pee-yer.* **Song,** heard chiefly on breeding grounds, has three-note *tswee-tee-teet* phrases mixed with the *peeer* note. **Range:** Common in open woodlands. Casual in East. No winter records in U.S.

Cuban Pewee *Contopus caribaeus L 6" (15 cm)*
Range: West Indian species; accidental in south Florida. Short primary projection makes species look like *Empidonax,* but Cuban does minimal tail flicking. Note expansion of prominent white partial eye ring behind eye; dull wing bars; faint "vest." **Call,** a clear, steady *dee-dee-dee,* also a soft *dep* note.

spring adult

juvenile

Greater Pewee

adults

Olive-sided Flycatcher

variations

Eastern Wood-Pewee

fresh spring adult

worn late-summer adult

juvenile

variations

Western Wood-Pewee

paler adult

darker adult

Cuban Pewee

Empidonax Flycatchers

All empids are drab, with pale eye rings and wing bars. From spring to summer, plumages grow duller from wear. Some species molt before fall migration, acquiring fresh plumage in late summer. Identification depends on voice, habitat, behavior, and subtle differences in size, bill shape, primary projection, and tail length. Most flip their tails up.

Acadian Flycatcher *Empidonax virescens L 5¾" (15 cm)*
Olive above, with yellow eye ring, two buffy or whitish wing bars; very long primary projection. Long, broad-based bill, with mostly yellowish lower mandible. Most birds show pale grayish throat, pale olive wash across upper breast, white lower breast, and yellow belly and undertail coverts. Molts before migration; **fall** birds have buffy wing bars. Juvenile is brownish olive above, edged with buff. **Call** is a soft *peace,* extended in **song** to an emphatic *pee-tsup,* accented on first syllable. On breeding grounds, also gives a flickerlike *ti ti ti ti ti.* **Range:** Found in woodlands and swamps. Range is expanding in the Northeast.

Yellow-bellied Flycatcher *Empidonax flaviventris*
L 5½" (14 cm) Has rather short tail and big head. Olive above, yellow below. Broad yellow eye ring. Lower mandible entirely pale orange. Shows a more extensive olive wash across breast than Acadian Flycatcher; lacks pale area between olive and yellow belly. Also, throat is yellow, rather than whitish; bill smaller. Molts after migration; **worn fall** migrants slightly grayer above, duller below. **Song** is a liquid *je-bunk;* also a plaintive, rising *per-wee.* **Call,** a sharp, whistled *chiu* that sounds somewhat like Acadian. **Range:** Found in bogs, swamps, and damp coniferous woods.

Alder Flycatcher *Empidonax alnorum L 5¾" (15 cm)*
Very similar to Willow Flycatcher, but bill is slightly shorter, eye ring usually more prominent, back greener. Distinguished from eastern race of Willow by darker head; from western races by well defined tertial edges, bolder wing bars, long primary projection. Best identified by voice. **Call,** a loud *pip,* similar to Hammond's but louder. Distinctive **song,** a falling, wheezy *weeb-ew.* On breeding grounds, also gives a descending *wheer.* **Range:** Common in brushy habitats near bogs, birch and alder thickets.

Willow Flycatcher *Empidonax traillii L 5¾" (15 cm)*
Lacks prominent eye ring. Color ranges from pale gray head and greenish back of nominate eastern race to darker-headed, browner *brewsteri* in the Northwest. Great Basin race, *adastus* (not illustrated), is paler than *brewsteri;* endangered southwestern *extimus* (**E**) even paler. Western races have duller wing bars, blended tertial edges, and shorter primary projection. Distinguished from pewees (preceding page) by shorter wings and upward flicks of tail. **Call** is a liquid *wit.* **Songs,** a sneezy *fitz-bew;* on breeding grounds, also a rising *brreet;* often sings in spring migration. **Range:** Found in brushy habitats in wet areas; also in pastures, mountain meadows. Very rare migrant in Southeast.

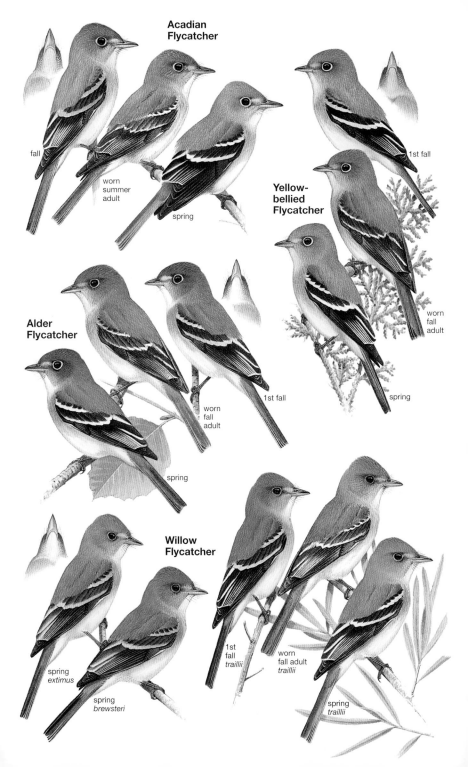

Acadian Flycatcher

fall

worn summer adult

spring

Yellow-bellied Flycatcher

1st fall

worn fall adult

spring

Alder Flycatcher

worn fall adult

1st fall

spring

Willow Flycatcher

spring *extimus*

spring *brewsteri*

1st fall *traillii*

worn fall adult *traillii*

spring *traillii*

Least Flycatcher *Empidonax minimus* L 5¼" (13 cm)
Smallest eastern empid. Large-headed; bold white eye ring; rather short primary projection. Throat whitish; breast washed with gray; belly and undertail coverts pale yellow. Underparts are usually paler than similar Hammond's Flycatcher. Bill short, triangular; lower mandible mostly pale. Molt occurs after fall migration. **First-fall** has buffier wing bars. **Song,** a dry *che-bek* accented on the second syllable, is usually delivered in a rapid series; **call,** a sharp *whit,* is sometimes also given in a series. **Range:** Inhabits deciduous woods, orchards, and parks. Common in East, rare migrant through most of West.

Hammond's Flycatcher *Empidonax hammondii*
L 5½" (14 cm) A small empid, with a fairly large head and short tail. White eye ring, usually expanded in a "teardrop" at rear. Grayish head and throat; grayish olive back; gray or olive wash on breast and sides; belly tinged with pale yellow. Molt occurs before migration; **fall** birds are much brighter olive above and on sides of breast, yellower below. Medium-length, slightly notched tail is edged with gray. Bill is slightly shorter, thinner, and usually somewhat darker than in similar Dusky Flycatcher; primary projection is longer. **Call** note is a sharp *peek.* **Song** resembles Dusky's but is hoarser and lower-pitched, especially on the second note. **Range:** Nests chiefly in coniferous forests. Most Hammond's Flycatchers migrate earlier in spring and later in fall than Dusky. Casual in the East.

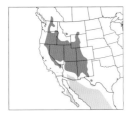

Gray Flycatcher *Empidonax wrightii* L 6" (15 cm)
Gray above, with a slight olive tinge in fresh fall plumage; whitish below, belly washed with pale yellow by late fall. Head is disproportionately small and rounded; white eye ring inconspicuous on pale gray face. Long bill; on most birds, lower mandible mostly pinkish orange at base, sharply divided from dark tip; on a few, entire lower mandible is pinkish orange. Short primary projection. Long tail, with thin whitish outer edge. Perched bird dips its tail down slowly, like a phoebe. Juvenile is brownish gray above, with pale, buffy wing bars; underparts are tinged brownish buff. **Song** is a vigorous *chi-wip* or *chi-bit,* followed by a liquid *whilp,* trailing off in a gurgle. **Call,** a loud *wit.* **Range:** Fairly common in dry habitat of Great Basin, in pine or piñon-juniper. Regular migrant on California coast. Accidental in the East.

Dusky Flycatcher *Empidonax oberholseri* L 5¾" (15 cm)
Grayish olive above; yellowish below, with whitish throat, pale olive wash on upper breast. White eye ring. Bill partly dark, orange at base of lower mandible blending into dark tip. Bill and tail slightly longer than Hammond's Flycatcher. Short primary projection. Molt occurs after fall migration; fresh late-fall birds are quite yellow below. **Calls** include a *wit* note, softer than Gray Flycatcher; a mournful *deehic,* heard on breeding grounds. **Song** has several phrases: A clear *sillit;* an upslurred *ggrrreep;* another high *sillit,* often omitted; and a clear, high *pweet.* **Range:** Breeds in open woodlands and brush of mountainsides.

Least Flycatcher

1st fall

worn fall adult

spring

Hammond's Flycatcher

fall

spring

Gray Flycatcher

winter

spring

Dusky Flycatcher

1st fall

worn fall adult

winter

spring

Pacific-slope Flycatcher   *Empidonax difficilis*

L 5½" (14 cm) Formerly considered same species as Cordilleran; known together as Western Flycatcher. Brownish green above; yellowish below with brownish tinge on breast. Broad pale eye ring, broken above, expanded behind eye; lower mandible entirely orange. Tail longer, wing tip slightly shorter than Yellow-bellied; wings and back slightly browner; less contrast in wing bars and tertial edges. Pacific-slope molts after arrival on winter grounds, so migrating **fall adults** appear more worn than spring birds. **First-fall** birds duller; wing bars buffy; variably whitish below, compare with Least Flycatcher (preceding page). Channel Islands race *insulicola* is slightly duller. **Call** is a sharp *seet;* male gives upslurred *psee-yeet* note. **Song,** a complex series of notes, including call notes. **Range:** Common in moist woodlands, coniferous forests, and shady canyons. Winters in lowlands of western Mexico. Common migrant through Southwest lowlands east to southeastern Arizona. Accidental in eastern North America.

Cordilleran Flycatcher   *Empidonax occidentalis*

L 5¾" (15 cm) Formerly considered same species as Pacific-slope Flycatcher. Nearly identical but slightly larger, darker, and greener above; more olive and yellow below. Separable in field only by male's **call,** a two-note *pit peet;* some populations in western portion of breeding range give more intermediate notes. *Seet* note seems sharper in Cordilleran than in Pacific-coast Flycatcher. **Range:** Breeds in coniferous forests and canyons in mountains of the West. Rare in lowlands in migration, even within breeding range. Casual on the Great Plains. Winters in mountains of Mexico.

Buff-breasted Flycatcher   *Empidonax fulvifrons*

L 5" (13 cm) Smallest *Empidonax* flycatcher. Brownish above; breast cinnamon-buff, paler on worn summer birds. Whitish eye ring; pale wing bars; small bill, with lower mandible entirely pale orange. Molts before migration. **Call** note is a soft *pwit.* Typical **song,** a quick *chicky-whew* or *chee-lick.* **Range:** Small colonies nest in dry woodlands of canyon floors. Very local in Huachuca and Chiricahua Mountains, Arizona; recently in Davis Mountains, Texas; now casual in New Mexico, but recorded recently in Peloncillo Mountains. Formerly more widespread as a breeder.

Northern Beardless-Tyrannulet   *Camptostoma imberbe*

L 4½" (11 cm) Grayish olive above and on breast; dull white or pale yellow below. Indistinct whitish eyebrow; small, slightly curved bill. Crown is darker than nape in many birds and often raised in a bushy crest. Distinguished from similar Ruby-crowned Kinglet (page 346) by buffy wing bars and lack of bold eye ring. Difficult to spot; most easily located by voice. **Song** on breeding grounds is a descending series of loud, clear *peer* notes; **call,** an innocuous, whistled *pee-yerp.* **Range:** Rather uncommon in U.S. Often found near streams in sycamore, mesquite, and cottonwood groves.

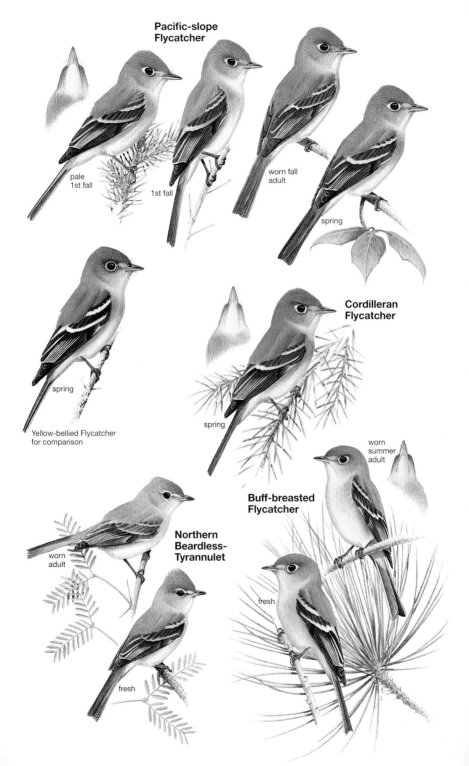

Pacific-slope Flycatcher

pale 1st fall

1st fall

worn fall adult

spring

spring

Yellow-bellied Flycatcher for comparison

Cordilleran Flycatcher

spring

worn summer adult

Buff-breasted Flycatcher

fresh

Northern Beardless-Tyrannulet

worn adult

fresh

Tufted Flycatcher   *Mitrephanes phaeocercus*

L 5" (13 cm) **Range:** Widespread tropical species; partially migratory at northern end of range (northern Mexico). Accidental in winter and early spring to west Texas and western Arizona. Distinctive small, crested flycatcher with cinnamon underparts and face; brownish olive above with faint cinnamon wing bars. Behavior suggests pewees. **Call,** a whistled *tchurree-tchurree.* Sometimes given singly; also a soft *peek* like Hammond's Flycatcher.

Eastern Phoebe   *Sayornis phoebe*   *L 7" (18 cm)*

Brownish gray above, darkest on head, wings, and tail. Underparts mostly white with pale olive wash on sides and breast; **fresh fall** birds are washed with yellow below. Molts before migration. All phoebes are distinguished from pewees (page 294) by their habit of pumping down and spreading their tails; Eastern Phoebe also by all-dark bill and lack of distinct wing bars. Also compare lack of eye rings and wing bars with *Empidonax* flycatchers (preceding pages). Distinctive **song,** a harsh, emphatic *fee-be,* accented on first syllable. Typical **call** note is a sharp *chip.* **Range:** Common in woodlands, farmlands, and suburbs; often nests under bridges, in eaves and rafters. Rare late fall migrant and winter visitor in the Southwest and on the West Coast.

Black Phoebe   *Sayornis nigricans*   *L 6¾" (17 cm)*

Black head, upperparts, and breast; white belly and undertail coverts. **Juvenal** plumage, held briefly, is browner, with two cinnamon wing bars, cinnamon rump. Four-syllable **song,** a rising *pee-wee* followed by a descending *pee-wee.* **Calls** include a loud *tseee* and a sharper *tsip,* slightly more plaintive than Eastern Phoebe's call. **Range:** Common near water; casual to Oklahoma.

Say's Phoebe   *Sayornis saya*   *L 7½" (19 cm)*

Grayish brown above, darkest on head, wings, and tail; breast and throat pale grayish brown; belly and undertail coverts tawny. **Song** is a fast *pit-tse-ar,* often given in fluttering flight. Typical **call,** a plaintive, whistled *pee-ee,* slightly downslurred. **Range:** Fairly common in dry, open areas, canyons, cliffs; perches on bushes, boulders, fences. Highly migratory; casual in eastern North America.

Vermilion Flycatcher   *Pyrocephalus rubinus*   *L 6" (15 cm)*

Adult male strikingly red and brown. **Adult female** grayish brown above, with blackish tail; throat and breast white, with dusky streaking; belly and undertail coverts are peach; note also whitish eyebrow and forehead. **Juvenile** resembles adult female but is spotted rather than streaked below; belly white, often with yellowish tinge. **Immature male** begins to resemble adult by midwinter. Male in breeding season sings during fluttery display flight. **Song,** a soft, tinkling *pit-a-see pit-a-see;* also sings while perched. Typical **call** note is a sharp, thin *pseep.* Frequently pumps and spreads its tail down. **Range:** Fairly common and approachable; found along streamsides, and near small wooded ponds. Rare winter visitor to coastal southern California and the Gulf Coast. Casual elsewhere in eastern North America, primarily in fall.

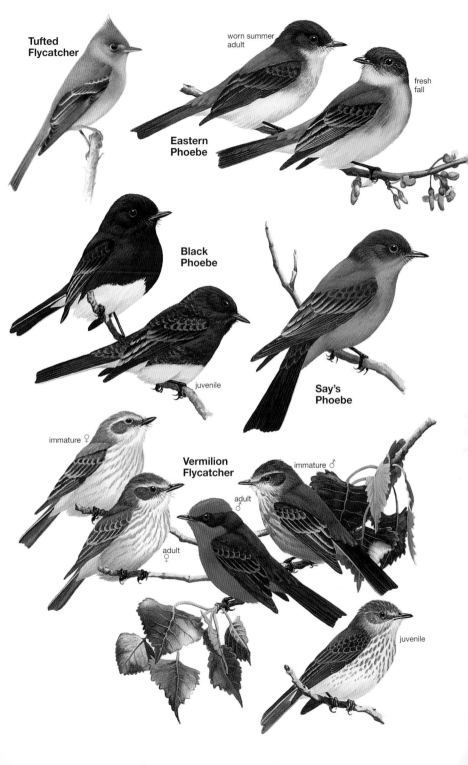

Tufted Flycatcher

Eastern Phoebe

worn summer adult

fresh fall

Black Phoebe

juvenile

Say's Phoebe

immature ♀

Vermilion Flycatcher

immature ♂

adult ♂

adult ♀

juvenile

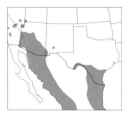

Brown-crested Flycatcher *Myiarchus tyrannulus*

L 8¾" (22 cm) Brownish olive above; as in all *Myiarchus* fly-catchers, shows a bushy crest, rufous in primaries; bill longer, thicker, broader than Ash-throated Flycatcher. Throat and breast are pale gray; belly slightly paler yellow than in Great Crested Fly-catcher. Tail feathers show reddish on outer two-thirds of inner webs. Texas race, *cooperi,* is smaller than southwestern *magister.* **Song** is a clear musical whistle, a rolling *whit-will-do.* **Call** is a sharp *whit.* **Range:** Fairly common in saguaro desert, river groves, lower mountain woodlands. Casual in Louisiana and Florida.

Great Crested Flycatcher *Myiarchus crinitus*

L 8½" (21 cm) Dark olive above. Gray throat and breast; bright lemon yellow belly and undertail coverts. Note broad, sharply contrasting edge to inner tertial. Outer tail feathers show entirely reddish inner webs. Distinctive **call,** a loud whistled *wheep.* **Range:** Common in a wide variety of open woods; feeds high in the canopy. Very rare on California coast during fall migration.

Nutting's Flycatcher *Myiarchus nuttingi*

L 7¼" (18 cm) **Range:** Tropical species; found from northwest Mexico to Costa Rica; three certain winter records from south-eastern Arizona and coastal southern California. Similar to Ash-throated Flycatcher but belly yellower; slightly more olive above; rufous primary edges blend to yellow-cinnamon secondary edges. Dark on outer webs of outer tail feathers does not extend across tip as in Ash-throated; orange, not flesh-colored, mouth lining. **Call,** a rather sharp *wheep,* different from Ash-throated.

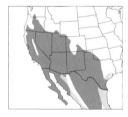

Ash-throated Flycatcher *Myiarchus cinerascens*

L 7¾" (19 cm) Grayish brown above; throat and breast pale gray; underparts paler than in Brown-crested. Tail shows rufous on inner webs with dark tips. As in all *Myiarchus* flycatchers, brief **juvenal** plumage shows mostly reddish tail. Distinctive **call,** heard year-round, is a rough *prrrt.* **Song,** heard on breeding grounds, is a series of burry *ka-brick* notes. **Range:** Common in a wide variety of habitats. Very rare fall and winter visitor to East.

La Sagra's Flycatcher *Myiarchus sagrae L 7½" (19 cm)*
Range: West Indian species from Bahamas, Cuba, and Caymans. Casual visitor, mainly in winter and spring, to south Florida; acci-dental to Alabama. Grayish brown upperparts, mainly white underparts suggestive of Ash-throated Flycatcher, but bill longer; inner tertial edge stronger; rufous on outer tail less extensive. Dis-tinctive **call,** a rather high-pitched *wink,* is often doubled.

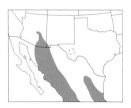

Dusky-capped Flycatcher *Myiarchus tuberculifer*

L 6¾" (17 cm) Smaller, bill larger, belly and undertail coverts usu-ally brighter yellow than in Ash-throated Flycatcher; tail shows less rufous. Secondaries have rufous edges, unlike other *Myiarchus.* **Call** is a mournful, descending *peeur.* **Range:** Fairly common in wooded mountain ranges. Casual in west Texas. Very rare in late fall and winter in southern and central California.

Brown-crested Flycatcher

southwest *magister*

Texas *cooperi*

Great Crested Flycatcher

juvenile

Nutting's Flycatcher

all tails from below

Ash-throated Flycatcher

adult   juvenile

La Sagra's Flycatcher
lucaysiensis

Dusky-capped Flycatcher
olivascens

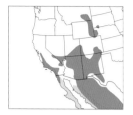

Cassin's Kingbird *Tyrannus vociferans* L 9" (23 cm)
Dark brown tail; narrow buffy tips and lack of white edges on outer tail feathers help distinguish this species from Western Kingbird. Bill is much shorter than in Tropical and Couch's Kingbirds. Upperparts darker gray than in Western, washed with olive on back; paler wings contrast with darker back. White chin contrasts with dark gray head and breast. Belly dull yellow. **Juvenile** is duller, slightly browner above, with bold buffy edges on wing coverts; paler below. Most common **call,** given year-round, is a short, loud *chi-bew,* accented on second syllable. **Range:** Fairly common in varied habitats; usually prefers denser foliage and hillier country than does Western Kingbird.

Western Kingbird *Tyrannus verticalis* L 8¾" (22 cm)
Black tail, with white edges on outer feathers. Bill much shorter than in Tropical and Couch's Kingbirds. Upperparts ashy gray, paler than in Cassin's Kingbird, tinged with olive on back; dark wings contrast with paler back. Throat and breast pale gray; belly bright lemon yellow. **Juvenile** has slightly more olive on back and buffy edges on wing coverts, brownish tinge on breast, paler yellow belly. Common **call** is a sharp *whit.* **Range:** Common in dry, open country; perches on fences, telephone lines. Regular straggler in fall and early winter along the East Coast from the Maritime Provinces south; winters in small numbers in central and southern Florida.

Couch's Kingbird *Tyrannus couchii* L 9¼" (24 cm)
Almost identical to Tropical Kingbird, with thicker, broader-based bill; back slightly greener and less gray; at close range, tips of individual primaries are evenly spaced on adults. Distinctive **calls,** a shrill, rolling *breeeer;* and a more common *kip,* similar to call of Western Kingbird, given singly or in a series. Distinguished from Western and Cassin's Kingbirds by larger bill, darker ear patch, and slightly notched brown tail. Juvenile is duller overall, with buffy edges on wing coverts. **Range:** Common in the lower Rio Grande Valley in summer; uncommon in winter. Found in groves and shrubs. Casual on Gulf Coast in fall and winter. Accidental to New Mexico and southern California.

Tropical Kingbird *Tyrannus melancholicus* L 9¼" (24 cm)
Almost identical to Couch's Kingbird. Bill is thinner and longer; back slightly grayer, less green; at close range, tips of individual primaries are unevenly staggered on adults. Distinctive **call** is a rapid, twittering *pip-pip-pip-pip.* Distinguished from Western and Cassin's Kingbirds by larger bill, darker ear patch, and slightly notched brown tail. **Range:** Uncommon and local in southeastern Arizona and Rio Grande Valley, Texas; found in lowlands near water; often nests in cottonwoods. Rare but regular during fall and winter along the West Coast to British Columbia, casually to southeast Alaska.

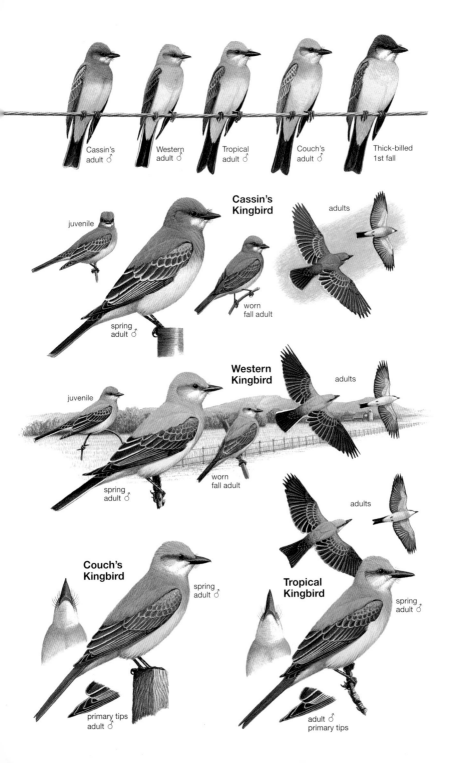

Cassin's adult ♂

Western adult ♂

Tropical adult ♂

Couch's adult ♂

Thick-billed 1st fall

Cassin's Kingbird

juvenile

adults

spring adult ♂

worn fall adult

Western Kingbird

juvenile

adults

spring adult ♂

worn fall adult

Couch's Kingbird

spring adult ♂

primary tips adult ♂

adults

Tropical Kingbird

spring adult ♂

adult ♂ primary tips

Fork-tailed Flycatcher *Tyrannus savana L 14½" (37 cm)*

Range: Widespread tropical species; casual vagrant on Atlantic coast and in Texas; accidental elsewhere: recorded north to north shore of Lake Superior (Ontario) and west to north coastal California. Recorded in fall (most records) and spring in East; the few western records are in fall. There are also several winter records from the Southwest. Extremely long black tail flutters in flight. Black cap, white underparts, white wing linings distinguish it from Scissor-tailed Flycatcher (next page). Many sightings are of immatures, which resemble **adult** but have a much shorter tail.

Eastern Kingbird *Tyrannus tyrannus L 8½" (22 cm)*

Black head, slate gray back; tail has a broad white terminal band. Underparts are white, with a pale gray wash across the breast. Orange-red crown patch is seldom visible. **Juvenile** brownish gray above, darker on breast. **Call** is a harsh *dzeet* note, also given in a series. **Range:** Common and conspicuous in woodland clearings, farms, and orchards; often seen near water. Rare migrant to Southwest and to Alaska, where recorded north and west to Nome and Point Barrow.

Gray Kingbird *Tyrannus dominicensis L 9" (23 cm)*

Pale gray above, with blackish mask. Red crown patch seldom visible. Bill long and thick. Underparts mostly white, with pale yellowish wash on belly and undertail coverts. Forked tail with no white terminal band. Juvenal plumage, held well into fall, is browner above. **Song** is a buzzy *pecheer-ry,* accented on second syllable. **Range:** Common on the Florida Keys, local in mangroves on the mainland. Casual wanderer north along the Atlantic coast to the Maritimes, inland to Michigan and Ontario, and along the Gulf Coast to coastal Texas. The Loggerhead Kingbird (*T. caudifasciatus*) of the West Indies had been on the Florida list on the basis of several records from the southern end of the state. These records are all now questioned, and the species was removed.

Thick-billed Kingbird *Tyrannus crassirostris*

L 9½" (24 cm) Large, with very large bill. **Adult** is dusky brown above, with a slightly darker head and seldom-seen yellow crown patch; whitish underparts washed with pale gray on breast, pale yellow on belly and undertail coverts. Yellow is brighter and more extensive in fresh fall adult and in **first-fall** birds, which have buffy edgings on wing coverts. Fall birds resemble Tropical Kingbird (preceding page), but have heavier bill and darker head. Common **call** is a loud, high, whistled *pureet.* **Range:** Perches high in sycamores of lowland streamsides. Breeds in Guadalupe Canyon and around Patagonia; rare elsewhere in southeastern Arizona. Casual during fall and winter west to southern California and in summer to western Texas (Big Bend). Accidental to British Columbia and Colorado.

Fork-tailed Flycatcher

adult

juvenile

Eastern Kingbird

juvenile

Gray Kingbird

1st fall

worn summer adult

Thick-billed Kingbird

pompalis

Scissor-tailed Flycatcher   *Tyrannus forficatus*

L 13" (33 cm) Pearl gray above; whitish and salmon pink below. Has very long outer tail feathers, white with black tips; also salmon pink wing linings with reddish axillaries. **Male**'s tail is longer than female's; **juvenile** is paler overall, with shorter tail. **Calls** similar to Western Kingbird. **Range:** Common; found in semi-open country. Very rare to casual wanderer in much of North America.

Piratic Flycatcher   *Legatus leucophaius*   L 6" (15 cm)

Range: Widespread tropical species. Accidental in U.S. on Dry Tortugas, Florida; on an oil rig in the Gulf of Mexico (Texas); Big Bend, Texas; and eastern New Mexico. Dark olive-brown above; blurry olive streaking below. Distinct head pattern; dark malar streak; pale throat; stubby black bill. Black tail can show rufous edges. Often perches out in the open.

Variegated Flycatcher   *Empidonomus varius*

L 7¼" (18 cm) **Range:** South American species; accidental in North America; three records in East. Similar to Piratic, but larger, longer bill has pale base; less distinct malar streak; more distinct streaking on upperparts, edging on wing coverts, and rufous edge on uppertail coverts and tail. Tends to perch lower than Piratic. Compare both to larger Sulphur-bellied Flycatcher. **Call** is a high, thin *pseee.*

Great Kiskadee   *Pitangus sulphuratus*   L 9¾" (25 cm)

Yellow crown patch on black-and-white head often concealed. Brown above, with reddish brown wings and tail. Found chiefly in wet woodlands or near watercourses; as well as fly-catching, dives for fish. **Calls** include a slow, deliberate *kis-ka-dee* and a loud *kreah*, given all year. **Range:** Common. Casual vagrant in southeastern Arizona and southern New Mexico and on Gulf Coast to Louisiana.

Sulphur-bellied Flycatcher   *Myiodynastes luteiventris*

L 8½" (22 cm) Boldly streaked above and below. Upperparts often show an olive tinge; rump and tail rusty red; underparts pale yellow. Loud **call** is an excited chatter, like the squeaking of a rubber duck. **Song** is a soft *tre-le-re-re.* **Range:** Fairly common in woodlands of mountain canyons, usually at elevations between 5,000 and 6,000 feet. Inconspicuous; often perches high in the canopy. Casual along the Gulf Coast and coastal California.

Rose-throated Becard   *Pachyramphus aglaiae*

L 7¼" (18 cm) Rosy throat distinctive in male; Arizona **adult male,** *albiventris*, has blackish cap, pale gray underparts. **Female** has slate gray crown, browner back. **First-fall male** shows partially pink throat; acquires full adult plumage after second summer. Larger *gravis* (eastern Mexico) found in Texas. Male darker; female more rufous than *albiventris*. Foot-long nest is suspended from a tree limb. **Call,** thin, mournful *seeoo,* sometimes preceded by chatter. **Range:** Rare and local in southeastern Arizona; casual (mostly in winter, but has bred) along lower Rio Grande, Texas.

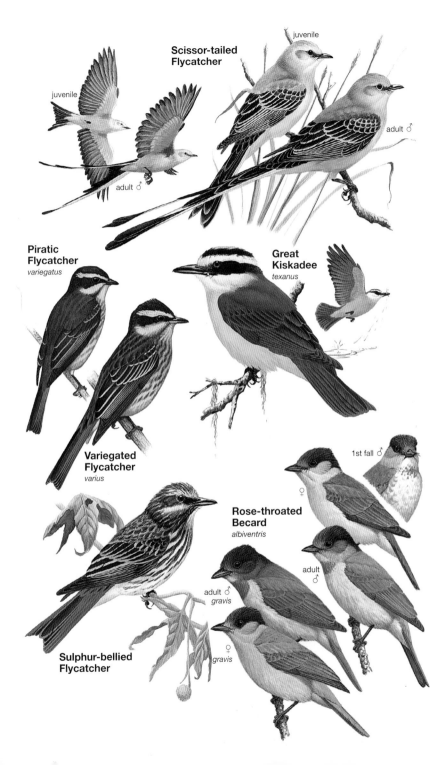

Scissor-tailed Flycatcher

juvenile

juvenile

adult ♂

adult ♂

Piratic Flycatcher
variegatus

Great Kiskadee
texanus

Variegated Flycatcher
varius

Rose-throated Becard
albiventris

1st fall ♂

♀

adult ♂

Sulphur-bellied Flycatcher

adult ♂
gravis

♀
gravis

Shrikes (Family Laniidae)

These masked hunters scan the countryside from lookout perches, then swoop down on insects, rodents, snakes, and small birds. Known as "butcher-birds," they mostly impale their prey on thorns. Recent research indicates that this is to mark territory and attract mates. *Species: 30 World; 3 N.A.*

Brown Shrike *Lanius cristatus* L 7½" (19 cm)
Range: Asian species; casual in Alaska where there are spring and fall records from western Aleutians, St. Lawrence Island, and Anchorage. Fall and winter records from California; late fall record from Nova Scotia. **Adult male** has distinct white border above black mask extending across forehead; warm brown upperparts, often brighter on rump and uppertail coverts; warm buff wash along sides and flanks. Lacks white wing patches. **Adult female** similar, but mask less solid; has some barring below. **Juveniles** are barred on sides and flanks; show distinct dark subterminal edges above; dark brown mask has short whitish border above and behind eye. Much juvenal plumage is retained into fall, some even into winter. Compare all ages and plumages to much larger, longer billed Northern Shrike. Old World Redbacked Shrike (*L. collurio*) and Isabelline Shrike (*L. isabellinus*) considered close relatives of Brown Shrike.

Loggerhead Shrike *Lanius ludovicianus* L 9" (23 cm)
Slightly smaller and darker than Northern Shrike. Head and back bluish gray; underparts white, very faintly barred. Broad black mask extends above eye and thinly across top of bill. All-dark bill, shorter than in Northern Shrike, with smaller hook. Rump varies from gray to whitish. **Juvenile** is paler and barred overall, with brownish gray upperparts; acquires **adult** plumage by first fall. Loggerheads hunt in open or brushy areas, diving from a low perch, then rising swiftly to the next lookout. Seen in flight, wings and tail are darker and white wing patches smaller than in Northern Mockingbird (page 362). **Song** is a medley of low warbles and harsh, squeaky notes; **calls** include a harsh *shack-shack*. **Range:** Fairly common over parts of range; rare to very rare and declining in the eastern Midwest and Northeast. The endangered race *mearnsi* (**E**) is endemic to San Clemente Island off southern California.

Northern Shrike *Lanius excubitor* L 10" (25 cm)
Larger than Loggerhead Shrike, with paler head and back, lightly barred underparts; rump whitish. Mask is narrower than in Loggerhead, does not extend above eye; feathering above bill is white. Bill longer, with a more distinct hook. Often bobs its tail. **Juvenile** is brownish above and more heavily barred below than adult. **Immature** is grayer; retains barring on underparts until first spring. Northern Shrike's **song** and **calls** are similar to those of Loggerhead. **Range:** Uncommon; often perches high in tall trees. Southern range limit and numbers on wintering grounds vary unpredictably from year to year.

Brown Shrike
cristatus

adult ♀

juvenile

adult ♂

juvenile

Loggerhead Shrike

Northern Mockingbird for comparison

adults

Northern Shrike

adult

immature

juvenile

Vireos (Family Vireonidae)

Short, sturdy bills slightly hooked at the tip characterize these small songbirds. Vireos are closely related to shrikes. Some have "spectacles" and wing bars. Others have eyebrow stripes and no wing bars. They are generally chunkier and less active than warblers. *Species: 52 World; 16 N.A.*

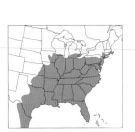

Black-capped Vireo Vireo atricapilla E

L 4½" (11 cm) Olive above, white below, with yellow flanks and yellowish wing bars. Hard to see, stays hidden in oak scrub, thickets. **Male**'s glossy black cap contrasts with broken white spectacles. Spectacles, smaller size, and secretive behavior distinguish **female;** immature males similar; **immature females** are more buffy. Best located by **song,** a persistent string of varied, twittering, two- or three-note phrases. Common **call** note, *tsidik,* almost identical to Ruby-crowned Kinglet. **Range:** Endangered. Extirpated from Kansas by 1930s and only a few left in Oklahoma. Major factors are habitat destruction and brood parasitism by Brown-headed Cowbird. Accidental to New Mexico and Ontario.

White-eyed Vireo Vireo griseus L 5" (13 cm)

Grayish olive above; white below, with pale yellow sides and flanks; two whitish wing bars; yellow spectacles. Distinctive white iris visible at close range. Juvenile is duller, with gray or brown iris. Subspecies on the Florida Keys, *maynardi,* is grayer above, with less yellow below; bill larger. Southern Texas race, *micrus,* is colored like *maynardi,* but smaller. Typical **song** is a loud, variable five- to seven-note phrase usually beginning and ending with a sharp *chick;* also gives a chatter **call** suggestive of House Wren. **Range:** Casual vagrant to the West.

Thick-billed Vireo Vireo crassirostris L 5½" (14 cm)

Range: Caribbean species, accidental or casual visitor to southeast Florida from Bahamas. Many reports from south Florida are misidentified White-eyed Vireos. Larger than White-eyed, with larger, slightly stouter and grayer bill. Note overall browner color, lack of gray on nape, and broken spectacles. Iris is darker than iris of adult White-eyed; **song** is similar but harsher; **call** notes slower and harsher.

Yellow-throated Vireo Vireo flavifrons L 5½" (14 cm)

Bright yellow spectacles, throat, and breast; white belly; two white wing bars. Upperparts olive, with contrasting gray rump. Compare with Pine Warbler, which has greenish yellow rump, streaked sides, thinner bill, and less complete and distinct spectacles. **Song,** a slow repetition of buzzy, low-pitched two- or three-note phrases separated by long pauses, often contains a rising *three-eight.* **Calls** include a rapid, harsh series of *cheh* notes. **Range:** Fairly common in most of breeding range. Rare or casual in southernmost Florida in winter. Most reports are misidentified Pine Warblers or Yellow-breasted Chats (page 396). Very rare vagrant in the West.

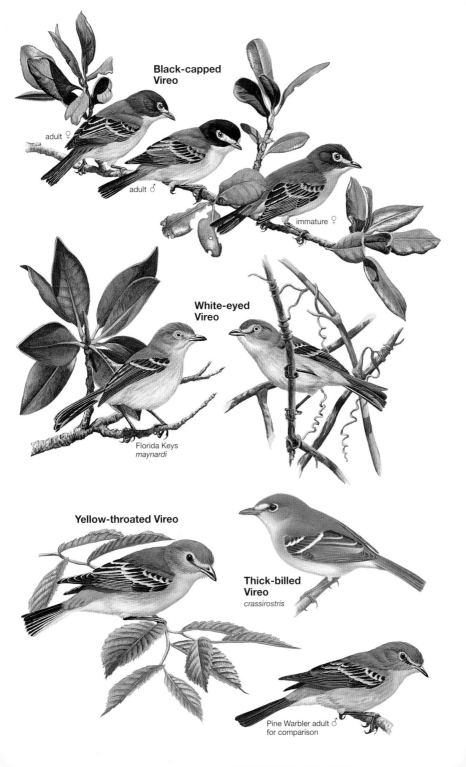

Black-capped Vireo

adult ♀

adult ♂

immature ♀

White-eyed Vireo

Florida Keys
maynardi

Yellow-throated Vireo

Thick-billed Vireo
crassirostris

Pine Warbler adult ♂
for comparison

Bell's Vireo *Vireo bellii* L 4¾" (12 cm)
Plumage variable. Endangered West Coast race, *pusillus* (**E**), is gray above, whitish below, with indistinct white spectacles; two whitish wing bars. More easterly nominate race is greenish above, yellowish below; often bobs tail. Southwestern *medius* and *arizonae* are intermediate. Active, rather secretive. **Song,** a series of harsh, scolding notes. **Range:** Uncommon in moist woodlands, bottomlands, mesquite, and in eastern part of range in shrubby areas on prairies.

Hutton's Vireo *Vireo huttoni* L 5" (13 cm)
Grayish olive above, with pale area in lores; white eye ring broken above eye. Subspecies vary from paler, grayer southwestern *stephensi* to greener coastal races such as *huttoni*. Separated from Ruby-crowned Kinglet by larger size, thicker bill, lack of dark area below lower wing bar. **Song** is a repeated or mixed rising *zu-wee* and descending *zoe zoo;* also a flat *chew*. **Calls** include a low *chit* and whining chatter; birds from interior Southwest give a harsher *tchurr-ree*. **Range:** Fairly common in woodlands.

Gray Vireo *Vireo vicinior* L 5½" (14 cm)
White eye ring; wings brownish, with faint wing bars, the lower more prominent; short primary projection; long tail. Compare with smaller West Coast race, *pusillus*, of Bell's Vireo. **Song** is a series of musical *chu-wee chu-weet* notes, faster and sweeter than Plumbeous. **Calls** include shrill, descending musical notes. **Range:** Found in semiarid habitat. Sticks to undergrowth; flicks tail as it forages.

Blue-headed Vireo *Vireo solitarius* L 5" (13 cm)
Adult male's solid blue-gray hood contrasts with white spectacles and throat; hood of female and immatures partly gray. All ages have bright olive back; yellow-tinged wing bars and tertials; greenish yellow edges to dark secondaries. Distinct white on outer tail; bright yellow sides and flanks, sometimes mixed with green. Larger Appalachian *alticola* has more slaty back; only flanks are yellow. **Song** is similar to Red-eyed Vireo, but slower. **Range:** Common in mixed woodlands.

Plumbeous Vireo *Vireo plumbeus* L 5¼" (13 cm)
Larger, with bigger bill than Cassin's Vireo; also has sharper head and throat contrast; gray upperparts. Pattern of tail feathers similar to Blue-headed Vireo. White wing bars and flight feather edges; pale yellow, if present, only on flanks. Sides of breast gray, sometimes tinged olive. Compare worn summer birds to shorter-winged Gray Vireo. **Song** is hoarser than Blue-headed. **Range:** Fairly common in varied woodland habitats.

Cassin's Vireo *Vireo cassinii* L 5" (13 cm)
Similar to Blue-headed, but slightly smaller and duller. Less contrast between head and throat; duller, whitish wing bars and tertial edges; less white in tail. Immature female can have entirely green head; compare to Hutton's Vireo. **Song** is hoarser than Blue-headed Vireo, like Plumbeous.

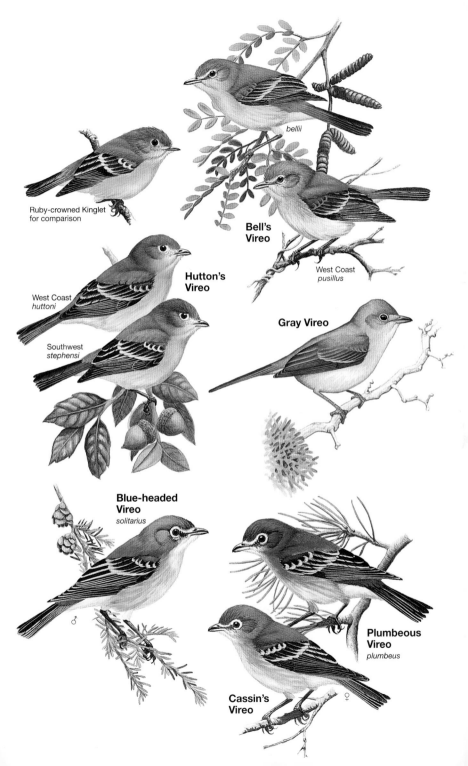

Ruby-crowned Kinglet
for comparison

bellii

**Bell's
Vireo**

West Coast
pusillus

West Coast
huttoni

**Hutton's
Vireo**

Southwest
stephensi

Gray Vireo

**Blue-headed
Vireo**
solitarius

♂

**Plumbeous
Vireo**
plumbeus

**Cassin's
Vireo**

♀

Yellow-green Vireo *Vireo flavoviridis L 6" (15 cm)*
Similar to Red-eyed Vireo, but bill longer; head pattern more
blended. Strong yellow-green wash above extends onto sides of
face; extensive yellow on sides, flanks, and undertail; brightest in
fall. **Song** is a rapid but hesitant series of notes, suggesting House
Sparrow. **Range:** Very rare in fall in coastal California and in summer in southern Texas. Casual in spring on the upper Gulf Coast.
Restored to full species from Red-eyed Vireo.

Red-eyed Vireo *Vireo olivaceus L 6" (15 cm)*
Blue-gray crown; white eyebrow bordered above and below with
black. Olive back, darker wings and tail; white underparts. Lacks
wing bars. Ruby red iris visible at close range. **First-fall** bird has
brown iris. Immatures and some fall adults have pale yellow on
flanks and undertail coverts. Persistent **song,** sung all day, a variable series of deliberate, short phrases. **Calls** include a nasal,
whining *quee.* **Range:** Common in eastern woodlands; rare
migrant west of dashed line on map.

Black-whiskered Vireo *Vireo altiloquus L 6¼" (16 cm)*
Variable dark malar stripe, often hard to see. Bill larger and
longer than in Red-eyed Vireo. Grayish brown crown; pattern
more diffuse than Red-eyed. Dull green above; whitish below,
with variable pale yellowish wash on sides and flanks. **Song,**
deliberate one- to four-note phrases, less varied and more
emphatic than Red-eyed. **Range:** Common in summer in the
mangrove swamps of Florida Keys and along Florida coasts.
Casual along rest of Gulf Coast.

Philadelphia Vireo *Vireo philadelphicus L 5¼" (13 cm)*
Adult variably yellow below, palest on belly. Greenish above, with
contrasting grayish cap, dull grayish olive wing bar, dull white
eyebrow, and dark eye line. First-fall birds and most **fall** adults
are often brighter yellow below. Distinguished from Warbling
Vireo by dark eye line extending through lores, darker cap, dark
primary coverts, and yellow at center of throat and breast. **Song**
resembles Red-eyed Vireo but is generally slower, thinner, and
higher-pitched. Similar Tennessee Warbler (page 376) has a thinner bill, white undertail coverts. **Range:** Uncommon; found in
open woodlands, streamside willows and alders. Casual to mostly
rare in West; chiefly occurs in fall.

Warbling Vireo *Vireo gilvus L 5½" (14 cm)*
Gray or olive-gray above; western birds, especially Pacific race
swainsoni, are smaller than nominate, with slighter bill. Underparts white. Dusky postocular stripe; white eyebrow, without
dark upper border; brown eye. Lacks wing bars. Smaller and
paler than Red-eyed Vireo; crown does not contrast strongly
with back. Birds in fresh **fall** plumage tend to be greener above,
pale yellow on sides of flanks. **Song** of *gilvus* is delivered in long,
melodious, warbling phrases; song of *swainsoni* less musical, with
higher tones and break near beginning. **Range:** Common across
most of North America in summer; found in deciduous woods.

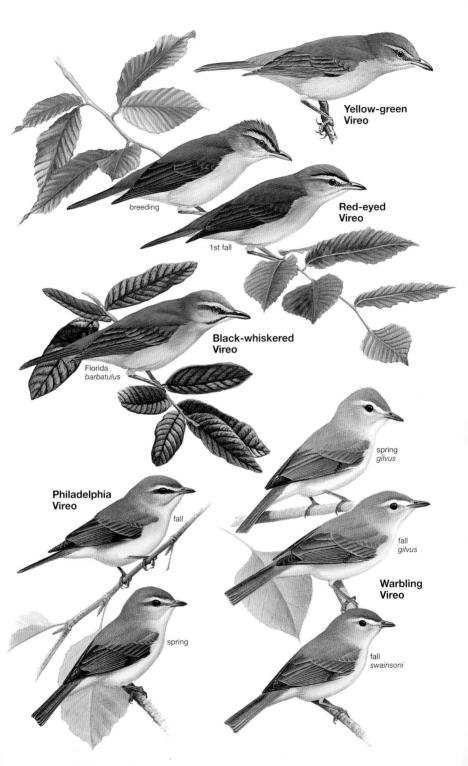

Yellow-green Vireo

Red-eyed Vireo

breeding

1st fall

Black-whiskered Vireo

Florida
barbatulus

Philadelphia Vireo

fall

spring

spring
gilvus

fall
gilvus

Warbling Vireo

fall
swainsoni

Crows, Jays (Family Corvidae)

Harsh voice and aggressive manner draw attention to these large, often gregarious birds. In most species, bristles cover nostrils. Powerful, all-purpose bill efficiently handles a varied diet. *Species: 117 World; 20 N.A.*

Blue Jay *Cyanocitta cristata L 11" (28 cm)*
Crested jay with black barring and white patches on blue wings and tail, black necklace on whitish underparts. Most common of varied **calls** is a piercing *jay jay jay;* also gives a musical *weedle-eedle* and mimics the call of Red-shouldered Hawk. Generally very noisy and bold. **Range:** Common in suburbs, parks, and woodlands. Often migrates in large flocks. Casual fall and winter visitor to the West, especially the Northwest.

Steller's Jay *Cyanocitta stelleri L 11½" (29 cm)*
Crested; dark blue and black overall. Some races, including nominate from coast to northern Rockies, have darker backs and bluish streaks on forehead. Central and southern Rockies race, *macrolopha,* has long crest, paler back, white streaks on forehead, white mark over eye; largest race, *carlottae* (not shown), resident on the Queen Charlotte Islands off British Columbia, is almost entirely black above. Where ranges overlap in the eastern Rockies, Steller's Jay occasionally hybridizes with Blue Jay. **Calls** include a series of *shack* or *shooka* notes and other calls suggestive of Red-shouldered and Red-tailed Hawks. **Range:** Common in pine-oak woodlands and coniferous forests. Bold and aggressive; often scavenges at campgrounds and picnic areas. Rare and irregular winter visitor to lower elevations of the Great Basin, southern California, and southwestern deserts.

Gray Jay *Perisoreus canadensis L 11½" (29 cm)*
A fluffy, long-tailed jay with small bill and no crest. The three subspecies groups are shown here: Nominate *canadensis,* one of several races common in northern boreal forests, has a white collar and forehead, with dark gray crown and nape; *capitalis,* in the southern Rockies, has a paler crown, head appears mostly white; *obscurus,* coastal resident in the Northwest from Washington to northernmost California, has a larger, darker cap extending to the crown, with underparts paler than in other races. **Juveniles** of all races are sooty gray overall, with a faint white moustachial streak. Gray Jays are familiar camp and cabin visitors. **Call** notes include a whistled *wheeoo* and a low *chuck.*

Clark's Nutcracker *Nucifraga columbiana L 12" (31 cm)*
Chunky gray bird with black wings and black central tail feathers. White wing patches and white outer tail feathers are conspicuous in flight. Wingbeats are deep, slow, crowlike. Locally common in high coniferous forests at timberline. **Calls** include a very nasal, grating, drawn-out *kra-a-a.* **Range:** Every 10 to 20 years, Nutcrackers irrupt out of core range into desert and lowland areas of the West. Accidental to eastern North America.

Blue Jay

Steller's Jay

stelleri

southern
Rockies
macrolopha

Gray Jay

juvenile

boreal
adult
canadensis

southern
Rockies
adult
capitalis

Northwest
adult
obscurus

adults

Clark's Nutcracker

Western Scrub-Jay   *Aphelocoma californica*
L 11" (28 cm) Long tail; blue above; variable bluish band on chest. Coastal races, including nominate *californica,* deeper blue above; contrasting brown patch; distinct white eyebrow and blue breast band; undertail coverts geographically variable; may or may not be bluish. Tame and widespread; found in urban areas. Interior races (possibly a separate species) range from duller, slender-billed *nevadae* of Great Basin to bluer, stouter-billed *texana* (neither shown); slender-billed *woodhouseii* is intermediate in color. Interior races rather shy; inhabit lower mountain woodland. All U.S. subspecies hold individual territories. **Calls** include raspy *shreep,* often in a short series. Western, Island, and Florida were formerly considered one species, Scrub Jay.

Island Scrub-Jay   *Aphelocoma insularis L 12" (30 cm)*
Range: Restricted to Santa Cruz Island, California, where it is the only scrub-jay. Larger and with much larger bill than Western; darker blue above; always shows rich blue undertail coverts. Birds hold individual territory; takes several years for young birds to acquire territory and breed.

Florida Scrub-Jay   *Aphelocoma coerulescens* **T**
L 11" (28 cm) Restricted to Florida scrub region where population has declined some 90 percent in 20th century due to habitat destruction. Optimum habitat is transitional, produced by fire: consists of scrub, mainly oak, about ten feet high with small openings. Distinguished from other scrub-jays by whitish forehead and eyebrow; shorter, broader bill; paler back; distinct collar; indistinct streaking below; disproportionately longer tail. Varied **calls** include raspy, hoarse notes. Has cooperative breeding system: Fledged young remain on territory and help rear nestlings.

Mexican Jay   *Aphelocoma ultramarina L 11½" (29 cm)*
Blue above, with slight grayish cast on back, brownish patch on center of back. Lacks crest. Distinguished from scrub-jays by absence of white throat and white eyebrow and by chunkier shape; flight is more direct. Texas race, *couchii,* has richer blue head. Arizona **juvenile** *arizonae* retains pale bill past post-juvenal molt. **Calls** include a loud, ringing *week,* given singly or in a series. **Range:** Common in montane pine-oak canyons of the Southwest, where it greatly outnumbers scrub-jays. Has cooperative breeding system similar to Florida Scrub-Jay.

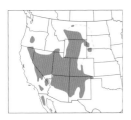

Pinyon Jay   *Gymnorhinus cyanocephalus L 10½" (27 cm)*
Blue overall; blue throat streaked with white; bill long and spiky; tail short. Immature is duller. Flight is direct, with rapid wingbeats, unlike scrub-jays' undulating flight. Typical flight **call** is a high-pitched, piercing *mew,* audible over long distances. Also gives a rolling series of *queh* notes. **Range:** Generally seen in large flocks, often numbering in the hundreds; nests in loose colonies. Common in piñon-juniper woodlands of interior mountains and high plateaus; also yellow pine woodlands. Casual to Plains states and coastal California.

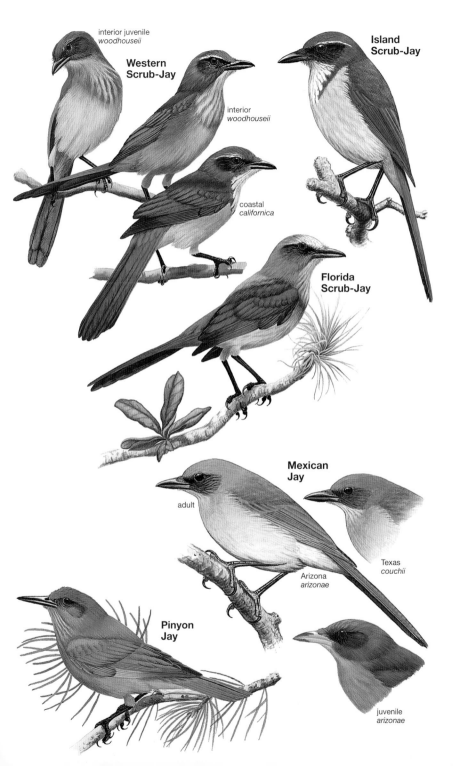

interior juvenile
woodhouseii

**Western
Scrub-Jay**

interior
woodhouseii

coastal
californica

**Island
Scrub-Jay**

**Florida
Scrub-Jay**

**Mexican
Jay**

adult

Texas
couchii

Arizona
arizonae

**Pinyon
Jay**

juvenile
arizonae

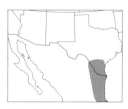

Brown Jay *Cyanocorax morio* *L 16½" (42 cm)*

Range: Tropical species; range barely extends to Texas, where it is resident but rare in woodlands and mesquite along the Rio Grande in vicinity of Falcon Dam. Very large jay with long, broad tail. Dark, sooty brown overall except for pale belly. **Adult** has black bill. **Juvenile** has yellow bill and eye ring, turning black by second winter; in transition, many have blotchy yellow-and-black bills. A noisy species; its harsh scream is similar to the **call** of a Red-shouldered Hawk. Another call sounds like a hiccup.

Green Jay *Cyanocorax yncas* *L 10½" (27 cm)*

Range: Tropical species; range extends to southern Texas. Resident and locally common in brushy areas and streamside growth of the lower Rio Grande Valley. Green and blue plumage blends with dappled sun and shade in woodland habitat. Somewhat inquisitive. Gregarious and noisy; most common **call** is a series of raspy *cheh-cheh-cheh* notes.

Black-billed Magpie 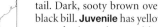 *Pica hudsonia* *L 19" (48 cm)*

Readily identified as a magpie by black and white markings and unusually long tail with iridescent green highlights. White wing patches flash in flight. Black bill and range distinguish this species from look-alike Yellow-billed Magpie. Ranges almost overlap, and Black-billed Magpies casually stray south and east of normal range in winter. Gregarious and noisy; typical **calls** include a whining *mag* and a series of loud, harsh *chuck* notes. Calls and many behavioral traits resulted in North American Black-billed Magpie being split from Old World populations of magpie, whose calls are faster and lower-pitched. **Range:** Common inhabitant of open woodlands and thickets in rangelands and foothills, especially along watercourses. Birds seen casually throughout the East may be escaped cage birds.

Yellow-billed Magpie *Pica nuttalli* *L 16½" (42 cm)*

Similar to Black-billed Magpie, but never occurs in Black-billed's normal range. Distinguished by its yellow bill and by a yellow patch of bare skin around the eye; extent of yellow variable, sometimes fully encircles eye; may be related to state of molt rather than individual variation, or may be a combination of both. **Calls** are similar to Black-billed; both species roost and feed in flocks, usually nest in loose colonies, but Yellow-billed Magpie's behavior is more colonial than Black-billed's. **Range:** Prefers oaks, especially more open oak grassland, also orchards and parks. Common resident of rangelands and foothills of central and northern Central Valley, California, and coastal valleys south to Santa Barbara County. Not prone to wandering, but casual north almost to Oregon. Some authorities believe that Yellow-billed Magpie is more closely related to the North American Black-billed than either is to the Old World races of magpies.

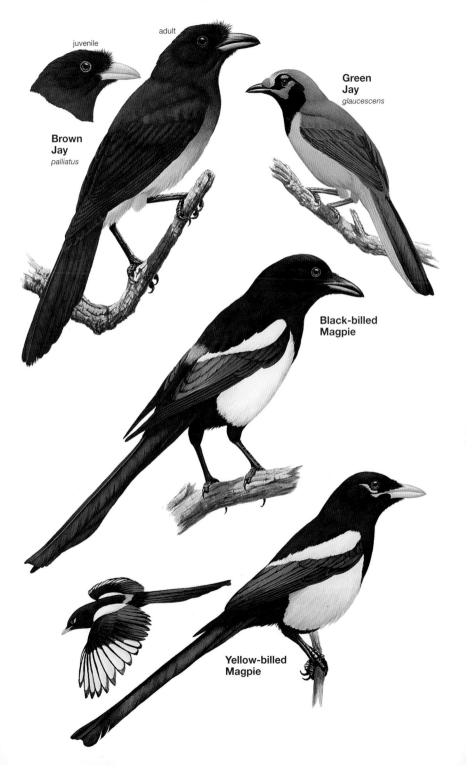

juvenile

adult

Brown Jay
palliatus

Green Jay
glaucescens

Black-billed Magpie

Yellow-billed Magpie

Eurasian Jackdaw *Corvus monedula L 13" (33 cm)*

Arrived in Northeast in early 1980s, most perhaps ship assisted. Found from Atlantic Canada to Pennsylvania. Few reports by 1990s, the last one in Apr. 1999 from Newfoundland. Small, black overall, with gray nape and face, pale grayish eyes. Lively and inquisitive. **Calls** include a metallic *kow* and a softer *jack* note.

Tamaulipas Crow *Corvus imparatus L 14½" (37 cm)*

Range: First appeared in U.S. in late 1960s at municipal dump near Brownsville, Texas, where it has nested. Present each winter since in varying numbers, sharply declining over last decade. Smaller, glossier than American Crow. **Call,** a low, froglike croak.

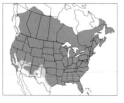

American Crow *Corvus brachyrhynchos L 17½" (45 cm)*

Our largest crow. Long, heavy bill is noticeably smaller than in ravens. Fan-shaped tail distinguishes all crows from ravens in flight. Adult American Crow is readily identified by familiar *caw* **call,** but juvenile's higher-pitched, nasal *cah* begging call resembles the call of the similar Fish Crow. **Range:** Generally common throughout most of its range in a wide variety of habitats.

Northwestern Crow *Corvus caurinus L 16" (41 cm)*

Not shown. **Range:** Inhabits northwestern coastal areas and islands, where a common scavenger along the shore. Nearly identical to American Crow but slightly smaller. **Call** is somewhat hoarser and lower than that of American. Best clue is range. Considered by some to be a subspecies of American Crow.

Fish Crow *Corvus ossifragus L 15½" (39 cm)*

Smaller than American Crow with smaller bill and feet; wings more pointed; wingbeats faster. Best distinguished by voice: **Call,** a high, nasal *uh uh,* the second note lower; also low, short *car* notes. **Range:** Favors tidewater marshes and low valleys along eastern river systems; less frequent inland, except along rivers. Often seen in winter in flocks with American Crows.

Chihuahuan Raven *Corvus cryptoleucus L 19½" (50 cm)*

Heavier bill and wedge-shaped tail distinguish both raven species from crows. Distinguished from Common Raven by shorter wings and shorter, less wedge-shaped tail; bristles extend farther out on shorter, thicker-appearing bill. Neck feathers white rather than grayish at base, but usually obscured. Frequent **call,** a drawn-out croak, usually slightly higher-pitched than call of Common Raven. **Range:** Common in desert areas and scrubby grasslands.

Common Raven *Corvus corax L 24" (61 cm)*

Large, with long, heavy bill and long, wedge-shaped tail. Most common **call** is a low, drawn-out croak. Larger than Chihuahuan Raven; note thicker, shaggier throat feathers and nasal bristles that do not extend as far out on larger bill. **Range:** Found in a variety of habitats, including mountains, deserts, and coastal areas. Numerous in western and northern part of range; uncommon and local, but slowly spreading, in Appalachians.

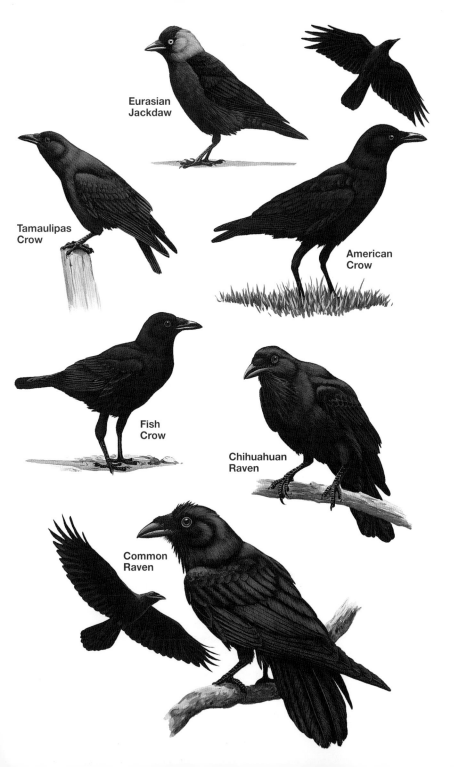

Eurasian
Jackdaw

Tamaulipas
Crow

American
Crow

Fish
Crow

Chihuahuan
Raven

Common
Raven

Larks (Family Alaudidae)

Ground dwellers of open fields, larks are slender-billed seed- and insect-eaters. They seldom alight on trees or bushes. On the ground, they walk rather than hop. *Species: 92 World; 2 N.A.*

Sky Lark *Alauda arvensis L 7¼" (18 cm)*
Range: Nominate *arvensis,* a widespread European race introduced to Vancouver Island in the early 1900s, is resident there on open slopes and fields. The population on San Juan Islands is now extirpated. Plain brown bird with slender bill; slight crest is raised when bird is agitated. Upperparts heavily streaked; buffy white underparts streaked on breast and throat. Dark eye prominent. Highly migratory Asian subspecies *pekinensis,* rare on western Aleutians and Pribilofs and casual on St. Lawrence Island, is darker and more heavily streaked above; accidental in winter in Washington and northern California. All juveniles have a scaly brown mantle. In flight, Sky Larks show a conspicuous white trailing edge on the inner wing and white edges on tail. **Song** is a continuous outpouring of trills and warblings, delivered in high hovering or circling song flight. **Call** is a liquid *chirrup* with buzzy overtones.

Horned Lark *Eremophila alpestris L 6¾-7¾" (17-20 cm)*
Head pattern distinctive in all subspecies: black "horns"; white or yellowish face and throat with broad black stripe under eye; black bib. **Female** duller overall than **male,** horns less prominent. Conspicuous in flight is the mostly black tail with white outer feathers, brown central feathers. Brief **juvenal** plumage has whitish markings above, streaks below; can be confused with Sprague's Pipit (page 370). Three widespread races are found in the East: **"Prairie Horned Lark,"** *praticola,* which breeds in southern Canada and the eastern U.S., is pale, with white eyebrows and throat. **"Northern Horned Lark,"** *alpestris,* is much darker, with a yellow throat. The central Arctic coast race, *hoyti,* is pale like *praticola,* but larger; *giraudi* from western Gulf Coast is quite yellow below. Western subspecies vary widely in overall color; selected extremes are shown here: *enthymia* (Plains, not illustrated), the Southwest deserts' *ammophila,* and large *arcticola* (northwest Canada, Alaska) are very pale; *sierrae* (northeast California) and *strigata* (coastal Northwest) are yellower on head and chest, *strigata* is also more streaked underneath; *rubea* (Central Valley, California) is redder dorsally; *insularis* (Channel Islands, California) is streaked below; *flava* from Palearctic (casual fall vagrant to Alaska) has a yellow throat and supercilium. Some subspecies are highly migratory, others are largely resident. Horned Lark's **calls** include a high *tsee-ee* or *tsee-titi.* **Song** is a weak twittering, delivered from the ground or in flight. **Range:** Widespread and common, Horned Lark prefers dirt fields, gravel ridges, and shores. The flocks in winter in the eastern U.S. are mainly *alpestris.*

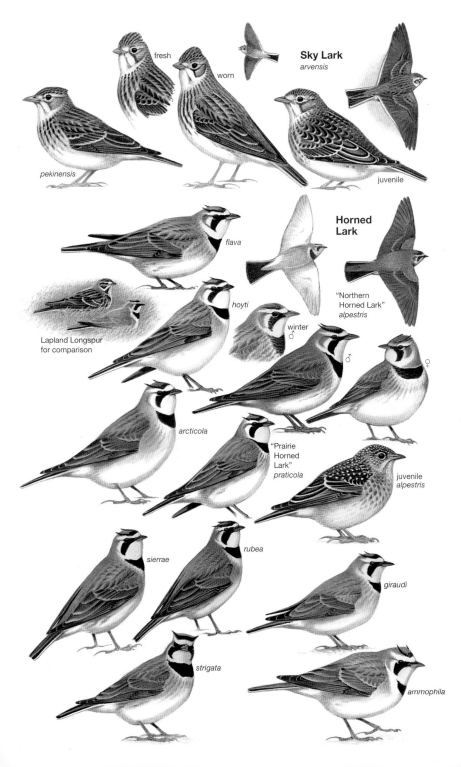

Sky Lark
arvensis

fresh

worn

pekinensis

juvenile

Horned Lark

flava

"Northern Horned Lark"
alpestris

hoyti

Lapland Longspur
for comparison

winter
♂

♂

♀

arcticola

"Prairie Horned Lark"
praticola

juvenile
alpestris

sierrae

rubea

giraudi

strigata

ammophila

330

Swallows (Family Hirundinidae)

Slender bodies with long, pointed wings resemble swifts, but "wrist" angle is sharper and farther from the body; flight is more fluid. Adept aerialists, swallows dart to catch flying insects. Flocks perch in long rows on branches and wires. *Species: 84 World; 15 N.A.*

Tree Swallow *Tachycineta bicolor L 5¾" (15 cm)*
Dark, glossy greenish blue above, greener in fall plumage; white below. White cheek patch does not extend above eye as in Violet-green Swallow. **Juvenile** is gray-brown above; usually has more diffuse breast band than Bank Swallow (next page). **First-spring female** shows varying amount of adult color on crown and back. **Range:** Common in wooded habitat near water, and where dead trees provide nest holes. Also nests in fence posts, barn eaves, nest boxes. Migrates in huge flocks; goes north earlier in spring and lingers farther north in fall than other swallows.

Bahama Swallow *Tachycineta cyaneoviridis*
L 5¾" (15 cm) **Range:** Endemic Bahamian species. Breeds in northern Bahamas and vicinity; casual visitor to the Florida Keys, especially Big Pine Key, and nearby mainland but unrecorded for over a decade. Greenish above. Deeply forked tail and white underwing coverts separate this species from similar Tree Swallow. Immatures have shorter tail fork, dusky wash on breast and wing linings.

Violet-green Swallow *Tachycineta thalassina*
L 5¼" (13 cm) White on cheek extends above eye; white flank patches extend onto sides of rump; compare with larger Tree Swallow. May also be confused with White-throated Swift (page 270). Female is duller above than **male. Juvenile** is gray-brown above; white except on rump may be mottled or grayish. **Range:** Common in a variety of woodland habitats. Nests in hollow trees or rock crevices, often forming loose colonies. Casual in the East.

Purple Martin *Progne subis L 8" (20 cm)*
Male is dark, glossy purplish blue. **Female** and juvenile are gray below. **First-spring males** have some purple below. In flight, male especially resembles European Starling (page 366); but note forked tail, longer wings, and typical swallow flight, short glides alternating with rapid flapping. **Range:** Locally common where suitable nest sites are available. Declining over much of North America, especially in Pacific states. Very early spring migrant in south; winters in South America.

Common House-Martin *Delichon urbicum L 5" (13 cm)*
Range: Old World species. Casual mainly in spring in western Alaska; one record for Saint-Pierre, off Newfoundland. Deep, glossy blue above; mostly white below with white rump; underwing coverts pale smoky gray. Female slightly grayer below; juvenile duller. Soars for long periods. **Call,** a rough scratchy *prrit,* somewhat similar to Rough-winged Swallow. One Alaska specimen of eastern race *lagopoda* has more extensive white on rump.

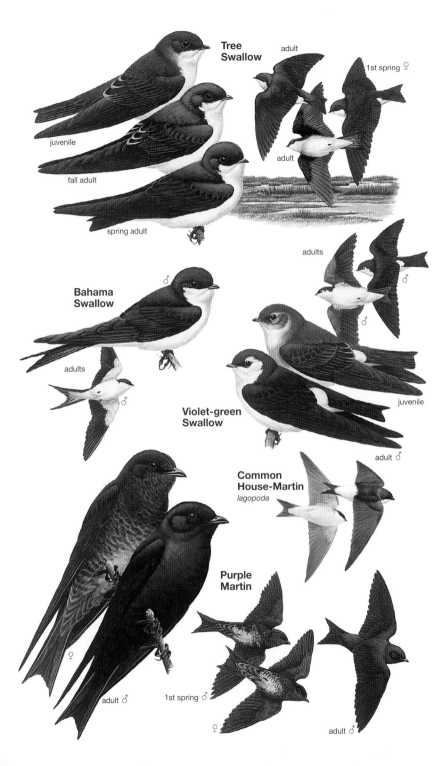

Tree Swallow
adult
1st spring ♀
juvenile
adult
fall adult
spring adult

Bahama Swallow
♂
adults
♂

adults
♂
♂

Violet-green Swallow
juvenile
adult ♂

Common House-Martin
lagopoda

Purple Martin

♀
adult ♂
1st spring ♂
♀
adult ♂

Bank Swallow *Riparia riparia L 4¾" (12 cm)*
Our smallest swallow. Distinct brownish gray breast band, often extending in a line down center of breast. Throat is white; white curves around rear border of ear patch. **Juvenile** has thin buffy wing bars; compare with juvenile Northern Rough-winged Swallow and juvenile Tree Swallow (preceding page). Locally common throughout most of range. Unlike Northern Rough-winged, wingbeats are shallow and rapid; also paler rump contrasts with wings. **Range:** Nests in large colonies, excavating nest burrows in steep riverbank cliffs, gravel pits, and highway cuts. Winters chiefly in South America; often migrates in large flocks.

Cliff Swallow *Petrochelidon pyrrhonota L 5½" (14 cm)*
Squarish tail and buffy rump distinguish this swallow from all others except Cave Swallow. Most Cliff Swallows have dark chestnut and blackish throat, pale forehead. A primarily southwestern race, *melanogaster,* has cinnamon forehead like Cave Swallow, but throat is dark chestnut. All **juveniles** are much duller and grayer than adults; throat is paler, forehead darker. **Range:** Locally common around bridges, rural settlements, and in open country on cliffs. Range has expanded greatly in last two decades. Nests in colonies, building gourd-shaped mud nests.

Northern Rough-winged Swallow
Stelgidopteryx serripennis L 5" (13 cm) Brown above, whitish below, with gray-brown wash on chin, throat, and upper breast. Lacks Bank Swallow's distinct breast band; wings are longer, wingbeats deeper and slower. **Juvenile** has cinnamon wing bars. **Range:** Nests in single pairs in riverbanks, cliffs, culverts, and under bridges. Migrates singly or in small flocks.

Barn Swallow *Hirundo rustica L 6¾" (17 cm)*
Long, deeply forked tail. Throat is reddish brown; underparts usually cinnamon or buffy. Two Eurasian, white-bellied races have occurred in western and northern Alaska: *rustica,* which has a solid dark breast band, and *gutturalis,* with incomplete breast band, which also has been found on Queen Charlotte Islands. In all **juveniles,** tail is shorter but still noticeably forked; underparts pale. **Range:** Common; generally nests on or inside farm buildings, under bridges, and inside culverts, in pairs or small colonies.

Cave Swallow *Petrochelidon fulva L 5½" (14 cm)*
Squarish tail; distinguished from Cliff by buffy throat color extending through auriculars and around nape setting off dark cap; rump averages a richer color; cinnamon forehead; juvenile much paler; compare with southwestern subspecies of Cliff also with cinnamon forehead. **Range:** Mexican and West Indian species: West Indies race, *fulva,* a local breeder in south Florida, is smaller than Mexican *pelodoma,* which is widespread in the Southwest; *fulva* also has more buff below and with darker rump. Nests in colonies in limestone caves, sinkholes, culverts, and under bridges, sometimes with Barn and Cliff Swallows. Very rare on East Coast, mainly in fall; casual to southern Arizona, southeastern California.

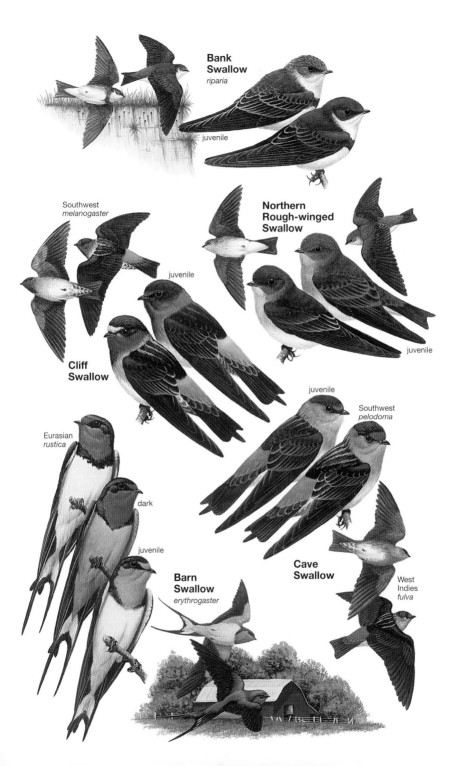

Bank Swallow *riparia*

juvenile

Southwest *melanogaster*

Northern Rough-winged Swallow

juvenile

Cliff Swallow

juvenile

juvenile

Southwest *pelodoma*

Eurasian *rustica*

dark

juvenile

Barn Swallow *erythrogaster*

Cave Swallow

West Indies *fulva*

334

Babblers (Family Timaliidae)

Species: 273 World; 1 N.A.

Wrentit *Chamaea fasciata* L 6½" (17 cm)
Color varies from reddish brown in northern populations to grayer in southern birds. Note distinct cream-colored eye and lightly streaked buffy breast; long, rounded tail usually cocked. Common in chaparral and coniferous brushland, Wrentits are usually heard before they are seen. Male's loud **song,** sung year-round, begins with a series of accelerating notes and runs into a descending trill: *pit-pit-pit-tr-r-r-r.* Female's song lacks trill.

Chickadees, Titmice (Family Paridae)

Species: 54 World; 12 N.A.

Bridled Titmouse *Baeolophus wollweberi* L 5¼" (13 cm)
Note distinct crest, black-and-white facial pattern, black throat. Most common **call** is a rapid, high-pitched variation of *chick-a-dee-dee,* similar to Juniper Titmouse. **Range:** Stands of oak, juniper, and sycamore in southern Arizona, New Mexico mountains.

Oak Titmouse *Baeolophus inornatus* L 5" (13 cm)
Grayish brown with a short crest. Northern race *inornatus* is slightly smaller, paler, and smaller billed than *affabilis* (shown here) from southwestern California and northern Baja; birds from Little San Bernadino Mountains are paler, grayer than *affabilis.* **Song** is variable, a repeated series of syllables made up of whistled, alternating, high and low notes. **Call** is a hoarse *tschick-a-dee.* **Range:** Common in warm, dry oak woodland.

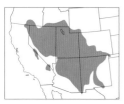

Juniper Titmouse *Baeolophus ridgwayi* L 5¼" (13 cm)
Like Oak Titmouse; range overlaps on northern California Modoc plateau. Larger, paler, grayer than Oak. **Song,** a rolling series of syllables, rapid, with uniform pitch. **Call,** a hoarse *tschick-a-dee* similar to Bridled. Overall, chattering call notes are more clipped and delivered much more rapidly than Oak's call. **Range:** Uncommon to fairly common in juniper or piñon-juniper woodland.

Tufted Titmouse *Baeolophus bicolor* L 6¼" (16 cm)
Note gray crest and distinct blackish forehead. **Juvenile** has brownish forehead and pale crest. In overlap zone in Texas, hybrids show variable brown foreheads, dark gray crests. Active, noisy; typical **song** is loud, whistled *peter peter peter;* but less vocal than Black-crested; calls softer and less nasal. **Range:** Deciduous woodlands, parks, and suburbs.

Black-crested Titmouse *Baeolophus atricristatus*
L 5¾" (15 cm) Resplit from Tufted. **Adult** has black crest, pale forehead. **Juvenile** crown darker than upperparts; forehead dirty white. **Calls** louder, sharper than Tufted. **Range:** Wooded areas.

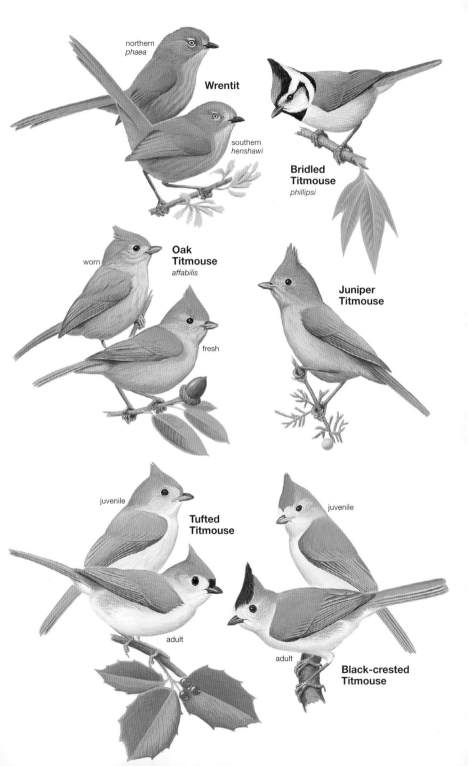

northern
phaea

Wrentit

southern
henshawi

Bridled Titmouse
phillipsi

worn

Oak Titmouse
affabilis

fresh

Juniper Titmouse

juvenile

Tufted Titmouse

adult

juvenile

adult

Black-crested Titmouse

Black-capped Chickadee *Poecile atricapillus*
L 5¼" (13 cm) Black cap and bib; cheeks more extensively and purer white than similar Carolina Chickadee. Note that Black-capped Chickadee's greater wing coverts and secondaries are broadly edged in white; tertials more boldly edged, with darker centers than Carolina's; flanks more olive, lower edge of black bib a bit more ragged. These differences are obscured in **worn summer** birds. Plumage is geographically variable: *occidentalis* from Pacific Northwest is darker; *nevadensis* from Great Basin is palest subspecies. Best distinction is voice. Black-capped's **call** is a lower, slower *chick-a-dee-dee-dee* than Carolina's; typical **song,** a clear, whistled *fee-bee* or *fee-bee-ee*, the first note higher in pitch; vocalizations show some geographic variation. **Range:** Common in open woodlands, clearings, and suburbs. Usually forages in thickets and low branches of trees. The usual ranges of Black-capped and Carolina barely overlap, but periodic fall irruptions push Black-capped's range south of mapped range. Where breeding ranges overlap, the two species hybridize. In the Appalachians, Black-capped inhabits higher elevations.

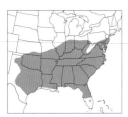

Carolina Chickadee *Poecile carolinensis* L 4¾" (12 cm)
Very similar to Black-capped Chickadee: black cap and bib, white cheeks. Note that Carolina lacks broad white edgings on greater wing coverts; lower edge of black bib is usually neater, has less olive on flanks than Black-capped. Westernmost race, *atricapilloides,* is grayer than nominate. Best distinction for separating species is voice. Carolina's **call** is a higher, faster version of *chick-a-dee-dee-dee* than Black-capped; typical **song** is a four-note whistle, *fee-bee fee-bay.* **Range:** Common in open deciduous forests, woodland clearings and edges, suburban areas. Feeds in trees and thickets; seldom descends to ground. At northern edge, its range in some winters is invaded by Black-capped. In the Appalachians, Carolina prefers valleys and foothills.

Mexican Chickadee *Poecile sclateri* L 5" (13 cm)
The only breeding chickadee in its range. Extensive black bib is distinctive, along with dark gray flanks. Lacks white eyebrow of Mountain Chickadee. **Song** is a warbled whistle; **call** note, a husky buzz. **Range:** A Mexican species, fairly common resident in coniferous and pine-oak forests; found in U.S. only in Chiricahua Mountains of southeastern Arizona and Animas and Peloncillo Mountains of southwestern New Mexico.

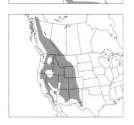

Mountain Chickadee *Poecile gambeli* L 5¼" (13 cm)
White eyebrow and pale gray sides distinguish this species from other chickadees; lack of crest separates it from the Bridled Titmouse (preceding page). Birds of Rocky Mountain nominate race *gambeli* are tinged with buff on back, sides, flanks, and have broader white eyebrow than *baileyae.* **Call** is a hoarse *chick-adee-adee-adee;* typical **song,** a three- or four-note descending whistle, *fee-bee-bay* or *fee-bee fee-bee.* **Range:** Common resident in coniferous and mixed woodlands. Some descend to lower elevations in winter.

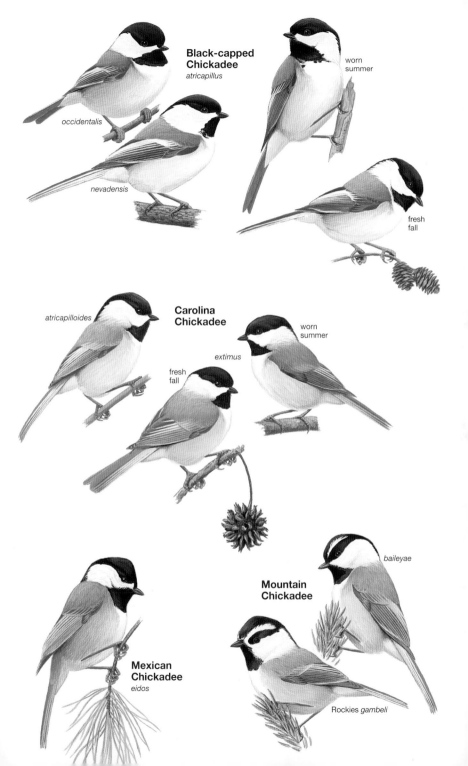

Black-capped Chickadee
atricapillus

occidentalis

nevadensis

worn summer

fresh fall

Carolina Chickadee

atricapilloides

extimus

fresh fall

worn summer

Mexican Chickadee
eidos

Mountain Chickadee

baileyae

Rockies *gambeli*

Chestnut-backed Chickadee *Poecile rufescens*
L 4¾" (12 cm) Sooty brown cap, white cheeks, black bib; back and rump chestnut. Over most of its range, this species has bright chestnut sides and flanks; *barlowi,* on central California coast south of Golden Gate Bridge, shows almost no chestnut below. **Call** is a hoarse, rapid *tseek-a-dee-dee.* **Range:** Found in coniferous forests, deciduous woodlands. Usually feeds high in trees.

Boreal Chickadee *Poecile hudsonicus L 5½" (14 cm)*
Grayish brown on crown and back, with pinkish brown flanks. Note that rear portion of cheeks is heavily washed with gray. **Call** is a nasal *tseek-a-day-day.* **Range:** Fairly common in coniferous forests. In some winters, small numbers wander hundreds of miles south of normal eastern range.

Gray-headed Chickadee *Poecile cinctus L 5½" (14 cm)*
Gray-brown above, whitish below, with white cheek patch, black bib, buffy sides and flanks. Distinguished from Boreal Chickadee by more extensively white cheeks, longer tail, paler flanks, and pale edges on wing coverts; also by **call,** a series of peevish *dee deer* notes. **Range:** Rare; found in willows and spruces edging tundra. Still known as the Siberian Tit in the Old World.

Penduline Tits, Verdins (Family Remizidae)

Small, spritely birds with finely pointed bills. They inhabit arid scrub country, feed in brush chickadee-style, and build spherical nests. *Species: 10 World; 1 N.A.*

Verdin *Auriparus flaviceps L 4½" (11 cm)*
Adult has dull gray plumage, chestnut shoulder patches, yellow head and throat. **Juvenile** is brown-gray overall; shorter tail helps separate it from Bushtit. Compare also with Lucy's Warbler (page 378). **Song** is a plaintive three-note whistle, the second note higher. **Calls** include rapid *chip* notes. **Range:** Common in mesquite and other dense thorny shrubs of the southwestern desert.

Long-tailed Tits, Bushtits
(Family Aegithalidae)

A longer tail distinguishes these tiny birds from other chickadee-like species. Except during nesting, usually feeds in large, busy, twittering flocks. Nest is an elaborate hanging structure. *Species: 11 World; 1 N.A.*

Bushtit *Psaltriparus minimus L 4½" (11 cm)*
Gray above, paler below; females have pale eyes, males' eyes are dark. Coastal birds have brown crown; interior birds show brown ear patch and gray cap, and have sharper, slower, twittering **calls.** **Juvenile male** and some adult males in the Southwest have a black mask, formerly considered a separate species, the **"Black-eared Bushtit." Range:** Common in a wide variety of woodlands.

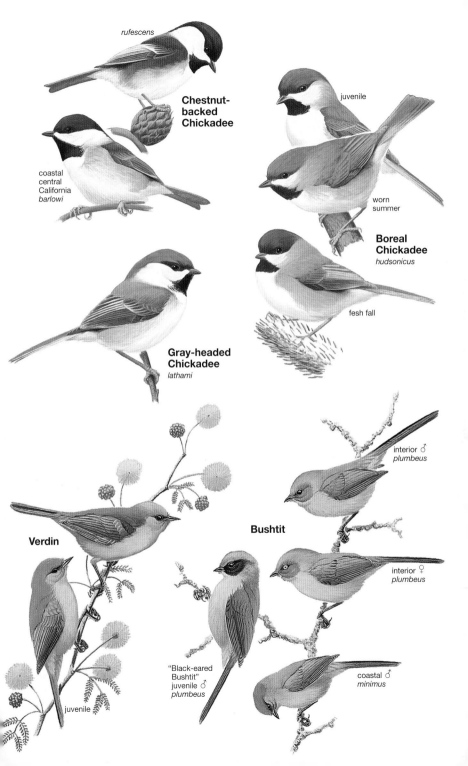

Chestnut-backed Chickadee

rufescens

coastal central California *barlowi*

juvenile

worn summer

Boreal Chickadee
hudsonicus

fesh fall

Gray-headed Chickadee
lathami

Verdin

juvenile

Bushtit

interior ♂ *plumbeus*

interior ♀ *plumbeus*

"Black-eared Bushtit" juvenile ♂ *plumbeus*

coastal ♂ *minimus*

Creepers (Family Certhiidae)

With curved bills, these little tree-climbers dig insects and larvae from bark. Stiff tail feathers serve as props. *Species: 8 World; 1 N.A.*

Brown Creeper *Certhia americana* L 5¼" (13 cm)
Camouflaged by streaked brown plumage, Creepers spiral upward from base of a tree, then fly to a lower place on another tree. **Call** is a soft, sibilant *see;* **song,** a high-pitched, variable *see see see titi see.* Fairly common but hard to spot. **Range:** Nests in coniferous, mixed, or swampy forests. Generally solitary, but sometimes seen in winter flocks of titmice and nuthatches.

Nuthatches (Family Sittidae)

These short-tailed acrobats climb up, down, and around tree trunks and branches. *Species: 25 World; 4 N.A.*

White-breasted Nuthatch *Sitta carolinensis*
L 5¾" (15 cm) Black cap tops all-white face and breast; extent of rust below is variable. **Females** in the Northeast have gray crowns more consistently than in the South. Western birds have longer, thinner bills. Typical **song** is a rapid series of nasal whistles on one pitch. **Call** is usually a low-pitched, repeated, nasal *yank* in eastern nominate race; high-pitched in West Coast *aculeata;* and higher-pitched and given in a rapid series by Great Basin *tenuissima* and Rockies *nelsoni.* **Range:** Common; found in leafy trees in the East, oaks and conifers in the West.

Red-breasted Nuthatch *Sitta canadensis* L 4½" (11 cm)
Black cap and eye line, white eyebrow, rust underparts; **female** and juveniles have duller head, paler underparts. High-pitched, nasal **call** sounds like a toy tin horn. **Range:** Resident in northern and subalpine conifers; gleans small branches and outer twigs. Irruptive migrant; numbers and winter range vary yearly. In the East, resident range is expanding southward.

Pygmy Nuthatch *Sitta pygmaea* L 4¼" (11 cm)
Gray-brown cap; creamy buff underparts. Pale nape spot visible at close range. Dark eye line bordering cap, most distinct in interior populations. Typical **calls,** a high, rapid *peep peep* and a piping *wee-bee;* grouped in three or more notes in coastal nominate race, *pygmaea.* **Range:** Favors yellow-pine forest, except for birds in coastal California pines. Roams in loose flocks.

Brown-headed Nuthatch *Sitta pusilla* L 4½" (11 cm)
Brown cap; dull buff underparts. Pale nape spot visible at close range. Narrow dark eye line borders cap. **Call** is a repeated double note like the squeak of a rubber duck. Feeding flocks also give twittering, chirping, and talky *bit bit bit* calls. **Range:** Fairly common; found in pine woodlands. Accidental north to Wisconsin, Ohio, and New Jersey.

Brown
Creeper

eastern
carolinensis

White-breasted
Nuthatch

Great Basin
♂ *tenuissima*

Red-
breasted
Nuthatch

Pygmy
Nuthatch

Brown-headed
Nuthatch

Wrens (Family Troglodytidae)

Found throughout most of North America, wrens are chunky birds with slender, slightly curved bills. Tails are often uptilted. Loud song and vigorous territorial defense belie the small size of most species. *Species: 76 World; 9 N.A.*

House Wren *Troglodytes aedon* L 4¾" (12 cm)
Brown above with faint eyebrow. Separated from Winter Wren by longer tail, less prominent barring on belly, and larger overall size. Western *parkmanii* breeds east to Ontario; grayer above, paler below. **Juvenile** shows a bright rufous rump and darker buff below. Birds from mountains of southeastern Arizona, formerly known as **"Brown-throated Wren,"** have a slightly buffier throat and breast and a bolder eyebrow. Exuberant **song** is a cascade of bubbling whistled notes. **Range:** Common in shrubs, farms, gardens, parks. Winters rarely north into summer range.

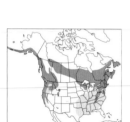

Winter Wren *Troglodytes troglodytes* L 4" (10 cm)
Stubby tail; dark barring on belly. Widespread eastern subspecies *hiemalis* from the north breeds west to northeastern British Columbia; similar *pullus* (not shown) breeds in the Appalachians. Western subspecies *pacificus* is richer buff on throat and breast, darker on back. Races from Bering Sea islands and Aleutians are larger, paler, and longer billed. Eastern subspecies give a *kelp-kelp* **call** like Song Sparrow; all western races a *timp-timp* call like Wilson's Warbler. **Song,** a rapid series of melodious trills, is much faster in western birds. **Range:** Rather secretive, nests in dense brush, especially along stream banks, in moist coniferous woods; in winter may be found in any type of woodland.

Carolina Wren *Thryothorus ludovicianus* L 5½" (14 cm)
Deep rusty brown above, warm buff below; white throat and prominent white eye stripe. Vivacious, melodious **song,** a loud, clear *teakettle tea-kettle teakettle* or *cheery cheery cheery.* Sings any time of day or year. **Range:** Common in the concealing underbrush of moist woodlands and swamps, wooded suburbs. Nonmigratory, but after mild winters resident populations expand north of mapped range. After harsh winters, range limits retract. Casual to Colorado, New Mexico, and Arizona.

Bewick's Wren *Thryomanes bewickii* L 5¼" (13 cm)
Long, sideways-flitting tail, edged with white spots; long white eyebrow. Subspecies differ mainly in dorsal color: Eastern *bewickii*, is reddish brown above; south Texas *cryptus* (not shown) duller, but still tinged red. Widespread *eremophilus* of the western interior is the grayest; western coastal races grow browner and darker as one travels north. Northwest *calaphonus* (not shown) is dark, richly colored, with a rufous cast. **Song** variable, a high, thin buzz and warble, similar to Song Sparrow. Calls include a flat, hollow *jip.* **Range:** Found in brushland, hedgerows, stream edges, open woods, and clear-cuts in the East. Sharply declining east of the Rockies, especially east of the Mississippi.

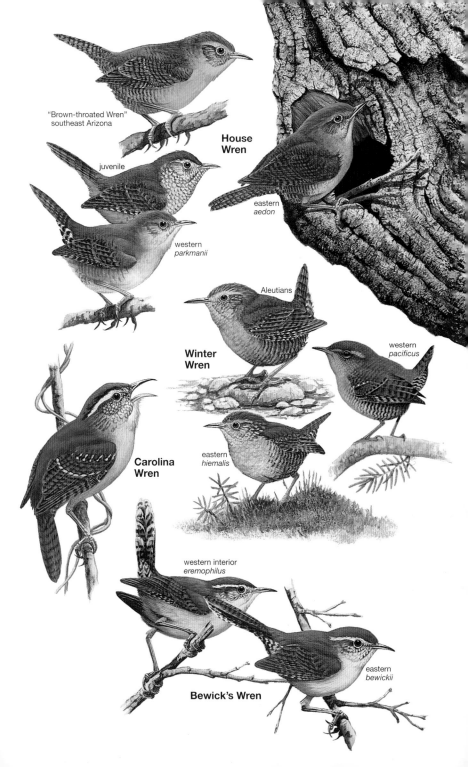

"Brown-throated Wren"
southeast Arizona

House Wren

juvenile

western
parkmanii

eastern
aedon

Aleutians

Winter Wren

western
pacificus

Carolina Wren

eastern
hiemalis

western interior
eremophilus

eastern
bewickii

Bewick's Wren

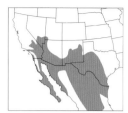

Cactus Wren *Campylorhynchus brunneicapillus*
L 8½" (22 cm) Large; dark crown, streaked back, heavily barred wings and tail, broad white eyebrow. Breast is densely spotted with black; threatened Californian subspecies, *sandiegense,* is less densely spotted. **Song,** heard all year, is a low-pitched, harsh, rapid *cha cha cha cha cha.* **Range:** Common in cactus country and arid hillsides and valleys. Bulky nests are tucked into the protective spines of cholla cactus or thorny bushes.

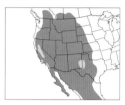

Rock Wren *Salpinctes obsoletus L 6" (15 cm)*
Dull gray-brown above with contrasting cinnamon rump, buffy tail tips, broad blackish tail band. Breast finely streaked. Frequently bobs its body, especially when alarmed. **Song** is a variable mix of buzzes and trills; **call,** a buzzy *tick-ear.* **Range:** Fairly common in arid and semiarid habitats, sunny talus slopes, scrublands, and dry washes. Casual in fall and winter to the East.

Canyon Wren *Catherpes mexicanus L 5¾" (15 cm)*
White throat and breast, chestnut belly. Long bill aids in extracting insects from deep crevices. Loud, silvery **song,** a decelerating, descending series of liquid *tee* and *tew* notes. Typical **call** is a sharp *jeet.* **Range:** Common in canyons and cliffs, often near water; may also build its cup nest in stone buildings and chimneys.

Marsh Wren *Cistothorus palustris L 5" (13 cm)*
Much plumage variation in eastern and western races. Where ranges overlap on Great Plains, eastern birds darker, more richly colored, with black-and-white speckled neck; western birds duller, with brownish smudges on neck. Football-shaped nest attached to reeds above water. **Songs,** more liquid in the East; harsher and much more variable in the West. Alarm **call,** a sharp *tsuk,* often doubled. **Range:** Common in reedy marshes and cattail swamps.

Sedge Wren *Cistothorus platensis L 4½" (11 cm)*
Crown and back streaked; eyebrow whitish and indistinct; underparts largely buff. **Song** begins with a few single notes followed by a weak staccato trill or chatter; **call** note, a rich *chip,* often doubled. Globular nest similar to that of Marsh Wren. **Range:** Found in wet meadows or sedge marshes. Generally common but local; uncommon to rare in the East. Rare and local in winter to New Mexico. Casual to California in late fall.

Dippers (Family Cinclidae)

Aquatic birds that wade and even swim underwater in clear, rushing mountain streams to feed. *Species: 5 World; 1 N.A.*

American Dipper *Cinclus mexicanus L 7½" (19 cm)*
Adult sooty gray; dark bill; tail and wings short. **Juvenile** has paler, mottled underparts and pale bill. **Song,** loud, musical, wrenlike. **Range:** Found along mountain streams. Descends to lower elevations in winter; casual vagrant well outside mapped range.

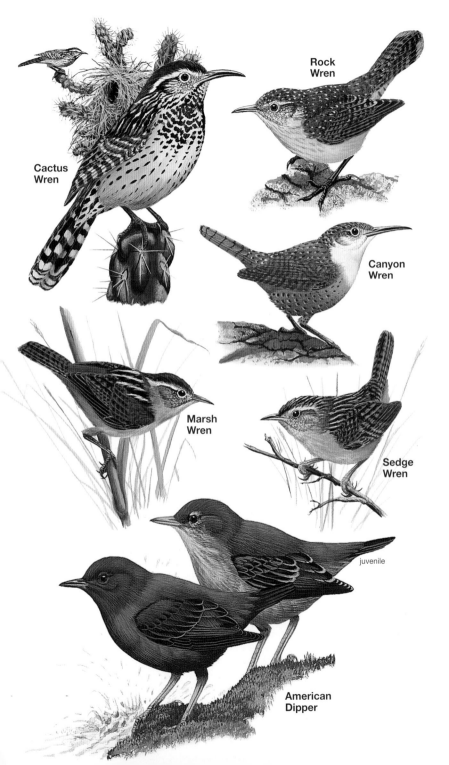

Rock
Wren

Cactus
Wren

Canyon
Wren

Marsh
Wren

Sedge
Wren

juvenile

American
Dipper

Kinglets (Family Regulidae)

Small, active birds that often hover to feed. *Species: 5 World; 2 N.A.*

Golden-crowned Kinglet *Regulus satrapa* L 4" (10 cm)
Orange crown patch of **male** is bordered in yellow and black; **female**'s crown is yellow. Head pattern and paler underparts are unlike Ruby-crowned Kinglet. **Call** is a series of high, thin *tsee* notes. **Song,** almost inaudibly high, is a series of *tsee* notes accelerating into a trill. **Range:** Common in coniferous woodlands.

Ruby-crowned Kinglet *Regulus calendula* L 4¼" (11 cm)
Male's red crown patch seldom visible; dusky underparts. Compare carefully with Golden-crowned Kinglet. Active; flicks wings rapidly. **Calls** include a scolding *je-ditt*. **Song,** several high, thin *tsee* notes followed by descending *tew* notes, ends with warbled three-note phrases. **Range:** Common in woodlands and thickets.

Old World Warblers, Gnatcatchers
(Family Sylviidae)

Old World Warblers are a large, diverse group. Sexes differ little, except in genus *Sylvia*. Gnatcatchers are found only in the New World. *Species: 279 World; 12 N.A.*

Blue-gray Gnatcatcher *Polioptila caerulea*
L 4¼" (11 cm) Long tail with white outer tail feathers is not graduated. **Male** is bluish above, in **breeding** plumage has black line on sides of crown. **Female** is grayer. **Call** is a querulous *pwee*. Active; favors woodlands, thickets, and chaparral.

Black-capped Gnatcatcher *Polioptila nigriceps*
L 4¼" (11 cm) **Range:** West Mexican species, very rare, in southeastern Arizona. Separated from Blue-gray and Black-tailed Gnatcatchers by more graduated white outer tail feathers and longer bill; **breeding male**'s black cap extends below eye. **Female** and winter male best identified by tail shape and pattern and by voice. **Calls** like California Gnatcatcher or Bewick's Wren.

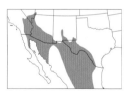

Black-tailed Gnatcatcher *Polioptila melanura*
L 4" (10 cm) White terminal spots on graduated tail feathers; short bill. **Breeding male** has glossy black cap, contrasting with eye ring. **Female** washed with brown. **Calls** include rasping *cheeh* and hissing *ssheh;* **song** is a rapid series of *jee* notes. Desert resident; partial to washes.

California Gnatcatcher *Polioptila californica* **т**
L 4¼" (11 cm) Similar to Black-tailed, but is darker with less white in outer tail feathers, less distinct eye ring. **Call,** a rising and falling, kitten-like *zeeer;* **song,** a series of *jzer* or *zew* notes. **Range:** Local resident in sage scrub of southwest California. Dark northern nominate race now threatened, due to habitat destruction.

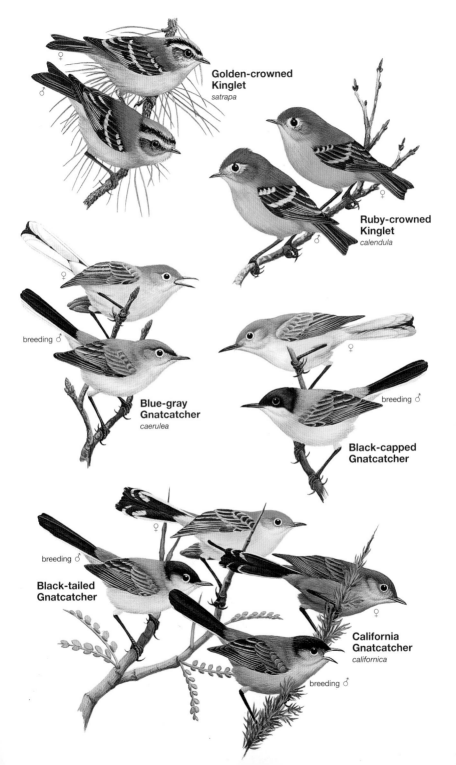

Golden-crowned Kinglet
satrapa

Ruby-crowned Kinglet
calendula

breeding ♂

Blue-gray Gnatcatcher
caerulea

breeding ♂

Black-capped Gnatcatcher

breeding ♂

Black-tailed Gnatcatcher

California Gnatcatcher
californica

breeding ♂

Lanceolated Warbler   *Locustella lanceolata*

L 4½" (11 cm) **Range:** Mainly Asian species. Many occurred in spring and summer of 1984 on Aleutian island of Attu. Accidental in fall in California. Resembles Middendorff's Grasshopper-Warbler but smaller; less broadly streaked above, including crown and rump, but streaks extend to feather tips; clear brown fringe on tertials. Breast, undertail coverts, and flanks are streaked. Highly secretive. Walks and runs; flicks its wings. Distinctive **call,** a metallic *rink-tink-tink,* delivered infrequently; also an explosive *pwit* and excited *chack* when disturbed. **Song,** a thin, insect-like reeling sound, like a fishing line makes.

Middendorff's Grasshopper-Warbler

Locustella ochotensis L 6" (15 cm) **Range:** East Asian species, casual migrant on westernmost Aleutians in fall; three spring to summer records. Recorded on St. Lawrence and Nunivak Islands and Pribilofs. Big, chunky warbler with whitish-tipped, wedge-shaped tail; hefty bill. Indistinct dark markings above; yellowish buff below with a faintly streaked breast, rustier above. By late spring, underparts are mostly whitish and lack streaking. Like all *Locustella* warblers, Middendorff's is very secretive.

Dusky Warbler   *Phylloscopus fuscatus L 5½" (14 cm)*

Range: Asian species, casual on islands off western Alaska, and in fall off south coastal Alaska and in California. Dusky brown, not greenish, upperparts and lack of wing bar distinguish this species from Arctic Warbler; tail slightly rounded; bill shorter and thinner. Usually has dark, slender legs; distinct eyebrow; dull white in front of eye; broad, dark brown eye line; whitish eye ring. Underparts creamy white, with buffy brown wash on flanks and undertail coverts. **Calls** include a hard, sharp *tschick,* not unlike *chip* note of Lincoln's Sparrow. Constantly flicks wings.

Arctic Warbler   *Phylloscopus borealis L 5" (13 cm)*

Long, yellowish white eyebrow, often curving upward behind eye; straw-colored legs and feet. Broad, dark eye line, mottled ear patches. Has square tail, olive upperparts, and pale wing bar on tips of greater coverts; faint second wing bar. Olive wash on sides and flanks; long primary projection. Stout bill is thicker, straighter than Orange-crowned Warbler (page 376); lacks streaking below. Compare also to accidental Willow Warbler (page 476) and Wood and Yellow-browed Warblers (page 477). Larger specimens taken in the western Aleutians with larger bills are either of nominate race *borealis,* with paler underparts, or yellower *xanthrodyas* (not shown). Alaskan race, *kennicotti,* is smaller, with smaller bill than either of the Asian races. Arctic Warbler's **song** is a long, loud series of toneless buzzy notes. **Calls** include a buzzy *dzik.* **Range:** Fairly common in western and central Alaska; four fall records for coastal California; nests on grassy tundra or in willow thickets.

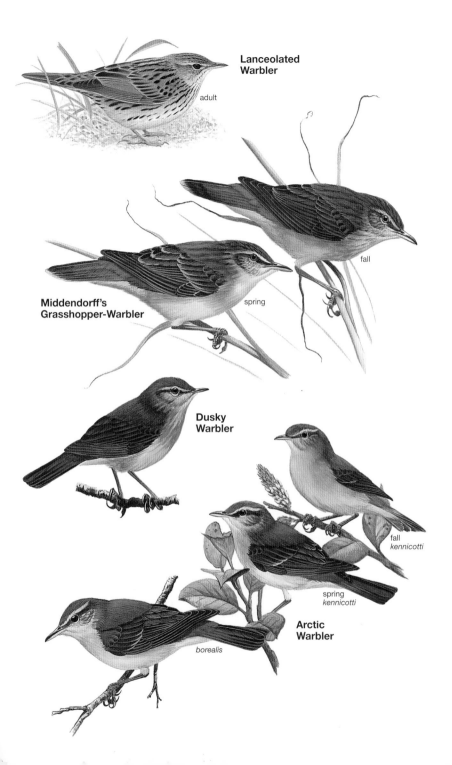

Lanceolated Warbler

adult

Middendorff's Grasshopper-Warbler

spring

fall

Dusky Warbler

fall
kennicotti

spring
kennicotti

Arctic Warbler

borealis

Old World Flycatchers (Family Muscicapidae)

Short-legged birds that perch upright and obtain insects primarily through fly-catching. May flick wings or tail. Species of genus *Ficedula* nest in cavities; genus *Muscicapa* build exposed nests. Not related to New World flycatchers. *Species: 275 World; 7 N.A.*

Narcissus Flycatcher *Ficedula narcissina* L 5¼" (13 cm)
Range: East Asian species; two spring records of males on Attu in the western Aleutians. **Adult male** overall black and yellow-orange; most orange on eyebrow and throat. Has yellow rump; white patch on inner secondary coverts. **First-spring male** similar, but duller. **Female** drab; brownish olive above, with green on rump; contrasting reddish-tinged uppertail coverts and tail; whitish throat; brownish mottling on breast. First-fall male similar to female.

Dark-sided Flycatcher *Muscicapa sibirica* L 5¼" (13 cm)
Range: Asian species; casual to western Aleutians; four spring records for Pribilofs; one fall record for Bermuda. Dark grayish brown upperparts and wash on sides and flanks; center of breast diffusely streaked. Whitish half collar; brownish supraloral spot; short bill; long primary projection; dark centers on undertail coverts may be concealed. Northern nominate race, *sibirica,* is darker and more diffusely streaked than southern races.

Taiga Flycatcher *Ficedula albicilla* L 5¼" (13 cm)
Range: Asian species; casual in late spring to western Aleutians; one spring record on St. Lawrence Island. Distinct white oval patches at base of outer tail feathers visible in flight, barely visible on folded tail from below; prominent eye ring. **Breeding male** with reddish throat. **Females** and winter males have whitish throats; grayish wash on breast. All show extensive patch of black on uppertail coverts. Formerly considered a subspecies of Red-breasted Flycatcher (*F. parva*). Perches low; often drops to ground to catch prey, then returns to perch. Frequently flicks tail up while giving rattled *trrt* **call;** also a metallic *tic* and harsh *ze-it.*

Gray-streaked Flycatcher *Muscicapa griseisticta*
L 6" (15 cm) **Range:** East Asian species; casual to western Aleutians in late spring; also several Pribilof records. Larger and with smaller head than Dark-sided; primary projection longer. Note distinctive, but variable, streaking below; paler supraloral spot; more distinct submoustachial stripe usually shows some markings; undertail coverts white.

Asian Brown Flycatcher *Muscicapa dauurica*
L 5¼" (13 cm) **Range:** Asian species; two spring records for Attu Island, Aleutians, and St. Lawrence Island. Grayish brown above; largely whitish below; grayish wash across chest or, rarely, some diffuse streaks. Bill larger than Dark-sided or Gray-streaked, extensively flesh-colored at base of lower mandible; primary projection shorter; supraloral area paler.

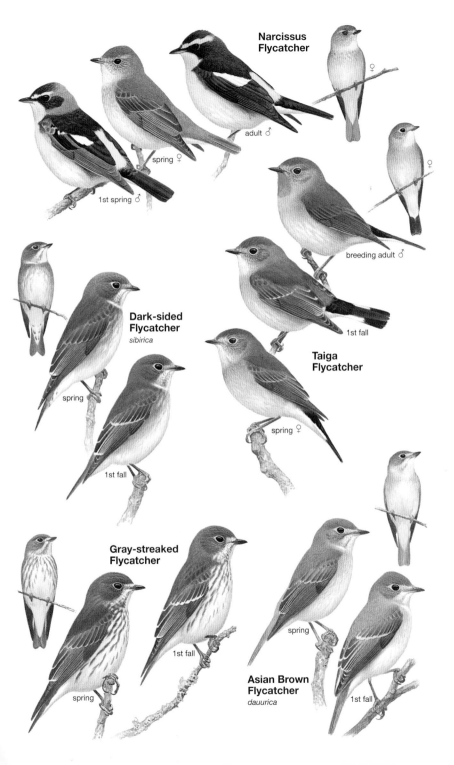

Narcissus Flycatcher

♀

adult ♂

spring ♀

1st spring ♂

♀

breeding adult ♂

1st fall

Dark-sided Flycatcher
sibirica

spring

1st fall

Taiga Flycatcher

spring ♀

Gray-streaked Flycatcher

spring

1st fall

Asian Brown Flycatcher
dauurica

spring

1st fall

Thrushes (Family Turdidae)

Eloquent songsters of many habitats. With narrow, notched bills, they feed on insects and fruit. *Species: 165 World; 29 N.A.*

Siberian Rubythroat *Luscinia calliope* L 6" (15 cm)

Range: Asian species; rare spring and fall migrant on western Aleutians, very rare on Pribilofs, casual on St. Lawrence Island. **Male** has a ruby red throat and broad, white submoustachial stripe. **Females** have white throats, often with some pink on adults and buffy on immatures; compare with smaller Bluethroat, which has rufous tail patches, dark breast band, paler underparts.

Bluethroat *Luscinia svecica* L 5½" (14 cm)

Colorful throat pattern distinguishes **breeding male** from all other birds. In all plumages, rufous patches at base of tail are conspicuous in flight, which is low off the ground. In **female** and immature, note dark breast band. Bluethroat runs on ground, usually with tail cocked. Generally furtive, but in courtship males sing from high perches and in elaborate display flight. Varied, melodious **song** often begins with a crisp, metallic *ting ting ting;* **call,** *tchak,* often given in a series. **Range:** Uncommon; nests in tundra thickets near water. Regular migrant on St. Lawrence Island; casual on Pribilofs and western Aleutians.

Red-flanked Bluetail *Tarsiger cyanurus* L 5½" (14 cm)

Range: Primarily Asian species; casual to western Aleutians and Pribilofs, mainly in spring; one late fall record for Farallones, off California. Note bluish tail, often flicked down; orangish flanks. **Adult male** has bright blue upperparts, but much individual variation; brightest birds may be several years old. Immature males closely resemble **females** until second fall. Rather secretive. **Calls** include a *hueet* and dry *keck-keck.*

Northern Wheatear *Oenanthe oenanthe* L 5¾" (15 cm)

Tail pattern distinctive: white rump, tail with dark central and terminal band. Greenland race, *leucorhea,* averages a little larger, is richer buff below; western birds are whitish, with a buff tinge. **Males** in fall and winter resemble females. Active; bob their tails. **Calls** include *chak* and whistled *wheet,* often combined. **Song,** a scratchy warbling mixed with call notes, often given in flight with tail spread. **Range:** Prefers open, stony habitats. Uncommon; very rare along Atlantic coast during fall; casual elsewhere.

Stonechat *Saxicola torquatus* L 5¼" (13 cm)

Range: Eurasian species; casual from scattered locations in Alaska; accidental in fall from New Brunswick and California. All records from the eastern *maurus* group of races, known as "Siberian Stonechat." Compact body; pale spot on inner coverts; paler rump. Note pattern of black on head of **adult male** obscured by fresh pale feather tips in **fall**; orange-buff wash on breast; extensive white on sides of neck, belly, and rump. **Female** and **first-fall male** have pale throat; pale buffy rump. Favors open country.

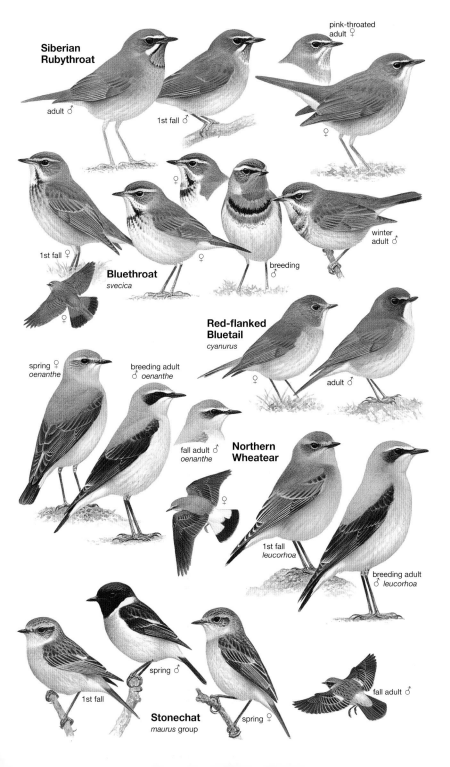

Siberian Rubythroat

adult ♂

1st fall ♂

pink-throated adult ♀

♀

Bluethroat
svecica

1st fall ♀

♀

♀

breeding ♂

winter adult ♂

♀

Red-flanked Bluetail
cyanurus

♀

adult ♂

spring ♀ *oenanthe*

breeding adult ♂ *oenanthe*

fall adult ♂ *oenanthe*

Northern Wheatear

♀

1st fall *leucorhoa*

breeding adult ♂ *leucorhoa*

1st fall

spring ♂

spring ♀

fall adult ♂

Stonechat
maurus group

Eastern Bluebird *Sialia sialis L 7" (18 cm)*

Chestnut throat, sides of neck, breast, sides and flanks; contrasting white belly, white undertail coverts. **Male** is uniformly deep blue above; **female** grayer. The subspecies resident in the mountains of southeastern Arizona, *fulva,* is paler overall. All subspecies distinguished from Western Bluebird by chestnut on throat and sides of neck and by white, not grayish, belly and undertail. **Call** note is a musical, rising *chur-lee,* extended in **song** to *chur chur-lee chur-lee.* **Range:** Found in open woodlands, farmlands, and orchards. Nests in holes in trees and posts; also in nest boxes. Serious decline in recent decades was due largely to competition with starling and House Sparrow for nesting sites. The provision of specially designed boxes by concerned conservationists has resulted in a promising comeback.

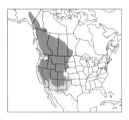

Western Bluebird *Sialia mexicana L 7" (18 cm)*

Male's upperparts and throat are deep purple-blue; breast, sides, and flanks chestnut; belly and undertail coverts grayish. Most birds show some chestnut on shoulders and upper back. **Female** duller, brownish gray above; breast and flanks tinged with chestnut, throat pale gray. **Call** note is a mellow *few,* extended in brief **song** to *few few fawee.* **Range:** Nests in holes in trees and posts; also in nest boxes. Common in woodlands, farmlands, orchards; in desert areas during winter, found in mesquite-mistletoe groves.

Mountain Bluebird *Sialia currucoides L 7¼" (18 cm)*

Male is sky blue above, paler below, with whitish belly and undertail coverts. **Female** is brownish gray overall, with white belly and undertail coverts; white edges on coverts give folded wing a scalloped look. In fresh fall plumage, female's throat and breast are tinged with red-orange; brownish rear flank contrasting with white undertail coverts distinguishes her from female Eastern Bluebird, which has reddish flank. Note also longer, thinner bill and longer primary tip projection of Mountain Bluebird. **Call** is a thin *few;* **song,** a low, warbled *tru-lee.* More often than other bluebirds, hovers above prey, chiefly insects, before dropping to catch them; also catches insects in flight. **Range:** Nests in tree cavities and buildings. Inhabits open rangelands, meadows, generally at elevations above 5,000 feet; in winter, found primarily in open lowlands and desert. Highly migratory; casual in the East during migration and winter.

Townsend's Solitaire *Myadestes townsendi*

L 8½" (22 cm) Large and slender; gray overall, with bold white eye ring. Buff wing patches and white outer tail feathers are most conspicuous in flight. **Call** note is a high-pitched *eek;* **song,** heard all year, a loud, complex, melodious warbling. Often seen on a high perch, from which it sometimes fly-catches. **Range:** Nests on the ground. Fairly common in coniferous forests on high mountain slopes; in winter, also in wooded valleys, canyons, wherever juniper berries are available. Highly migratory; casual in fall and winter in Midwest and Northeast.

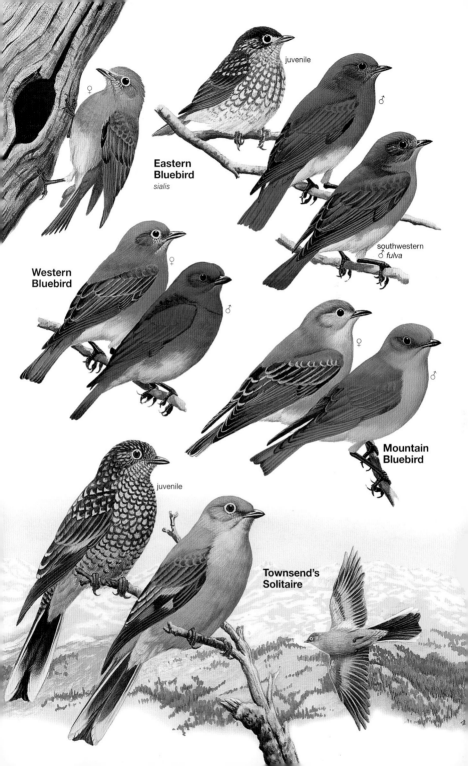

juvenile

Eastern Bluebird
sialis

southwestern
♂ *fulva*

Western Bluebird
♀
♂

Mountain Bluebird
♀
♂

juvenile

Townsend's Solitaire

Wood Thrush *Hylocichla mustelina* L 7¾" (20 cm)
Reddish brown above, brightest on crown and nape; rump and tail brownish olive. White eye ring conspicuous on streaked face. Large dark spots on whitish throat, breast, and sides. Loud, liquid **song** of three- to five-note phrases, each phrase usually ending with a complex trill. **Calls** include a rapid *pit pit pit.* **Range:** Common in moist deciduous or mixed woods. Casual in the West.

Veery *Catharus fuscescens* L 7" (18 cm)
Reddish brown above, white below, with gray flanks, grayish face, incomplete and indistinct gray eye ring. Upperparts duller, breast more spotted in more westerly *salicicola* than in eastern *fuscescens.* **Song** is a descending series of *veer* notes; **call,** a sharp, descending, whistled *veer.* **Range:** Fairly common; found in dense, moist woodlands and streamside thickets. Casual in Southwest.

Gray-cheeked Thrush *Catharus minimus* L 7¼" (18 cm)
Gray-brown above, with faint, incomplete eye ring. Dark spots on breast, which is usually less buffy than Swainson's; flanks brownish gray. Breeding *minimus* on Newfoundland can be warmer colored above, more like Bicknell's. Thin, nasal **song** is somewhat like Veery's, but first and last phrases drop, middle one rises; **call,** a sharp *pheu* similar to Veery's, but higher-pitched, not descending. **Range:** Favors coniferous or mixed woodlands.

Bicknell's Thrush *Catharus bicknelli* L 6¼" (16 cm)
Identification of Bicknell's Thrush when not singing is very difficult due to variation within Gray-cheeked, of which it formerly was considered a subspecies. Bicknell's is smaller, warmer brown above, especially on tail; lower mandible has more yellow. **Song** usually comes in three parts, the first and last rising.

Swainson's Thrush *Catharus ustulatus* L 7" (18 cm)
Brownish above, with buffy lores and bold buffy eye ring; bright buffy breast with dark spots; brownish gray sides and flanks. Pacific coast races such as *ustulatus* are reddish brown above, less distinctly spotted below; distinguished from *salicicola* race of Veery by face pattern, buffy brown sides and flanks, and voice. **Song** is an ascending spiral of varied whistles; common **call,** a liquid *whit* in Pacific coast races, a sharper *quirk* in others; at night a peeping *queep* is heard. **Range:** Fairly common; found in moist woods and swamps.

Hermit Thrush *Catharus guttatus* L 6¾" (17 cm)
Complete, often whitish eye ring; reddish tail. Upperparts vary from rich brown to gray-brown. Eastern races such as widespread *faxoni* have buff-brown flanks. Larger, paler western mountain races, such as *auduboni,* and smaller, darker north Pacific coast races, such as *guttatus,* have grayish flanks. **Song** is a serene series of clear, flutelike notes, the similar phrases repeated at different pitches. **Calls** include a deeper *chuck,* often doubled, and a whiny, upslurred *wee.* **Range:** Fairly common; found in coniferous or mixed woodlands, and thickets.

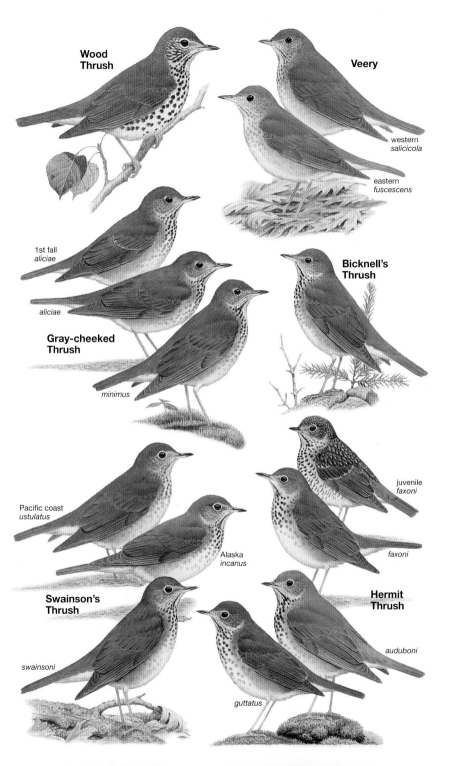

Wood Thrush

Veery

western
salicicola

eastern
fuscescens

1st fall
aliciae

aliciae

Bicknell's Thrush

Gray-cheeked Thrush

minimus

Pacific coast
ustulatus

juvenile
faxoni

faxoni

Alaska
incanus

Swainson's Thrush

Hermit Thrush

auduboni

swainsoni

guttatus

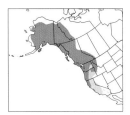

Varied Thrush *Ixoreus naevius L 9½" (24 cm)*
Male has grayish blue nape and back, orange eyebrow; underparts orange with black breast band; buffy orange bar on underwing prominent in flight. **Female** distinguished from American Robin (next page) by orange eyebrow and wing bar, dusky breast band, and unmarked throat. **Juvenile** resembles female but has white belly, scalier-looking throat and breast. In a very rare variant morph, all orange color is replaced by white. **Call** is a soft, low *tschook;* **song,** a slow series of variously pitched notes, rapidly trilled. **Range:** Common in dense, moist woodlands, especially coniferous forests. Generally feeds in trees. Very rare in winter as far east as New England and south to Virginia. Numbers vary from year to year in southern part of mapped winter range.

Eyebrowed Thrush *Turdus obscurus L 8½" (22 cm)*
Range: Asian species. Regular spring migrant on the Aleutians, casual in fall; casual on St. Lawrence Island and in northern Alaska; accidental California (late spring). Brownish olive above, with distinct white eyebrow. Belly is white, sides pale buffy orange. **Male** has dark gray throat and breast; **female**'s throat is white and streaked; browner head shows little contrast with rest of upperparts. Wing linings pale gray. Flight **call** is a high, piercing, drawn-out *dzee.*

Dusky Thrush *Turdus naumanni L 9½" (24 cm)*
Range: Asian species. Casual spring migrant on westernmost Aleutians; accidental on St. Lawrence Island, Point Barrow, and in winter south to coastal Washington. White eyebrow conspicuous on blackish head. Upperparts strongly patterned, with rust-colored rump; wings extensively rust, underwing almost entirely rufous. Below, white edgings give a scaly look to dark breast and sides. Note also distinctive white crescent across breast. Female and immatures average duller overall. Several sight records of redder nominate race for western Alaska's islands. **Call** is a series of *shack* notes; also a shrill, wheezy *shrree* similar to European Starling.

Fieldfare *Turdus pilaris L 10" (25 cm)*
Range: Eurasian species. Breeds from Greenland to Russian Far East. Casual vagrant to Alaska and northeastern North America. Accidental to Ontario and Minnesota. Large thrush with gray head and rump contrast with purplish brown upper back, blackish tail. Below, dark arrowhead-shaped spots pattern the buffy breast and extend along sides. White wing linings flash in flight. **Song** is a noisy twittering; **call** note is a series of *shack* notes, like Dusky Thrush; also gives a thin *seeh.*

Redwing *Turdus iliacus L 8¼" (21 cm)*
Range: Eurasian species; casual visitor to Newfoundland, mainly in winter; accidental south to Long Island, New York; once coastal Washington. Distinctive whitish to buffy eyebrow; boldly streaked below, with rusty red flanks; rusty red wing linings visible in flight. **Call** is a thin, penetrating *seeeh,* usually heard in flight; also a hard *kuk* note.

juvenile

Varied Thrush
meruloides

♀

♂

Eyebrowed Thrush

♀

♂

Dusky Thrush
eunomus

♂

♀

♂ *naumanni*

Fieldfare

immature

Redwing

immature

American Robin   *Turdus migratorius*   *L 10" (25 cm)*

Gray-brown above, with darker head and tail; bill yellow; underparts brick red; lower belly white. Most western birds paler and duller overall than eastern nominate *migratorius* (shown here), which breeds to western Alaska; in most, tail has white corners, visible in flight. Northwestern race, *caurinus,* is equally dark but lacks white tail spots; breeds north to southeast Alaska. **Juvenile**'s underparts are tinged with cinnamon, heavily spotted with brown. Loud, liquid **song,** is a variable *cheerily cheer-up cheerio.* **Calls** include a rapid *tut tut tut;* a high, thin *ssip* in flight. **Range:** Common, widespread. Often seen on lawns, head cocked as it searches for earthworms; also eats insects and berries. Nests in shrubs, trees, on sheltered windowsills, and eaves. In winter, found in moist woodlands, swamps, suburbs, and parks. Numbers vary greatly from winter to winter.

White-throated Robin   *Turdus assimilis*   *L 9½" (24 cm)*

Range: Tropical species; casual to southernmost Texas in winter. Distinct white collar in front; white throat with dark brown streaking; head and upperparts brownish; often shows yellow orbital ring; underparts mostly gray. Compare to Clay-colored Robin's less marked throat; lack of collar; overall tawnier color; more extensively yellow bill. **Call** is a nasal *rreeuh,* often doubled.

Rufous-backed Robin   *Turdus rufopalliatus*   *L 9¼" (24 cm)*

Range: West Mexican species, very rare winter visitor to southern Arizona, casual from southern and southwestern Texas to southern California. Distinguished from American Robin by reddish brown back and wing coverts, uniformly gray head with no white around eye, and more extensively streaked throat. **Calls** include a plaintive, drawn-out, whistled *teeeuu,* a clucking series of *chuk* notes, and in flight, a high, thin *ssi.* Somewhat secretive; found in treetops and dense shrubbery.

Clay-colored Robin   *Turdus grayi*   *L 9" (23 cm)*

Range: Species from east Mexico to north Colombia; rare visitor and very rare breeder in southernmost Texas. Brownish olive above; tawny buff below; pale buffy throat is lightly streaked with olive. Lacks white around eye conspicuous in American Robin. **Calls** include a slurred *reeeur-ee,* a clucking note, and, in flight, a high, thin *ssi;* **song** resembles American Robin's but is slower, clearer, much less varied. Rather secretive; forages in dense thickets, streamside brush, and woodlands. Will come to feeders.

Aztec Thrush   *Ridgwayia pinicola*   *L 9¼" (24 cm)*

Range: Mexican species, rare and irregular to southeast Arizona, mainly late summer; casual to southwestern Texas and the central Texas coast. **Male** is blackish brown above, with white patches on wings, white uppertail coverts; tail broadly tipped with white; contrasty underparts. **Female** is browner, more streaked on throat and breast. **Juvenile** is heavily streaked above with creamy white; underparts whitish and heavily scaled with brown. **Calls,** a quavering *wheeerr,* a metallic *wheer,* and a clear *sweee-uh.*

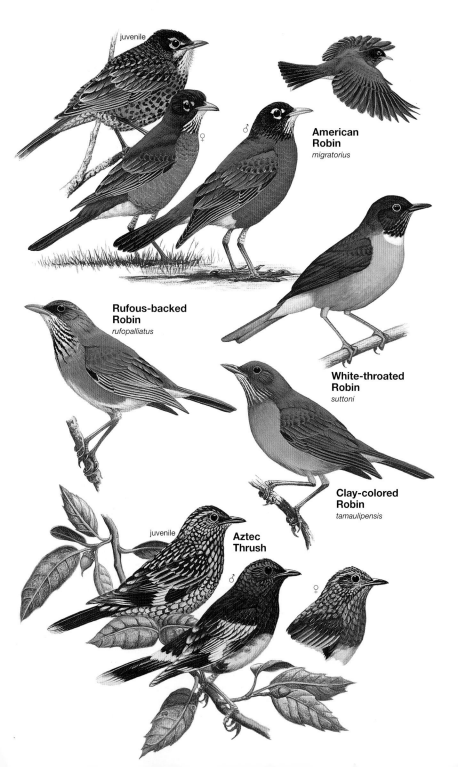

juvenile

**American
Robin**
migratorius

**Rufous-backed
Robin**
rufopalliatus

**White-throated
Robin**
suttoni

♀

♂

**Clay-colored
Robin**
tamaulipensis

juvenile **Aztec
Thrush**

♂

♀

Mockingbirds, Thrashers (Family Mimidae)

Notable singers, unequaled in North America for the rich variety and volume of their song. Some mimic the songs of other species. *Species: 34 World; 12 N.A.*

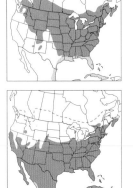

Gray Catbird *Dumetella carolinensis* L 8½" (22 cm)
Plain dark gray with a black cap and a long, black tail, often cocked; undertail coverts chestnut. **Song** is a mixture of melodious, nasal, and squeaky notes interspersed with catlike *mew* notes; some are good mimics. Most readily identified by harsh, downslurred *mew* **call**; also gives a low *quirt* and a clucking noise. **Range:** Generally common but rather secretive in thickets.

Northern Mockingbird *Mimus polyglottos* L 10" (25 cm)
White outer tail feathers and white wing patches flash in flight and in territorial and displays. **Song** is a mixture of original and imitative phrases, each repeated several times.Often sings at night. Imitates other species' songs and calls. Both sexes sing in fall, claiming feeding territories. **Call** is a loud, sharp *check*. **Range:** Found in a variety of habitats, including towns. Casual well north of mapped range, as far as Alaska.

Bahama Mockingbird *Mimus gundlachii* L 11" (28 cm)
Range: Caribbean species; casual south Florida. Larger and browner than Northern Mockingbird, with streaking on neck and flanks; white only on tail tip. Lacks white patches on wings; flight more direct. **Song** is varied but not known to include imitations; **call** slightly harsher, more downslurred than Northern.

Blue Mockingbird *Melanotis caerulescens* L 10" (25 cm)
Range: Mexican species which moves altitudinally. Casual in winter to southeast Arizona. Records from coastal southern California, New Mexico, and southern Texas of more questionable origin (though accepted). **Adult** deep slaty blue with black mask and red eye. Immature slightly duller, brownish tinge to wings, darker eye.

Brown Thrasher *Toxostoma rufum* L 11½" (29 cm)
Reddish brown above, heavily streaked below. Immature's eyes darker. Compare to Wood Thrush (page 356). **Sings** a series of varied melodious phrases, each phrase usually given only two or three times. Seldom imitates other birds. **Calls** include a sharp *spuck* and a low *churr*. **Range:** Common in hedgerows and woodland edges. Rare to West and Maritimes; casual to Newfoundland.

Long-billed Thrasher *Toxostoma longirostre*
L 11½" (29 cm) Closely resembles Brown Thrasher but much grayer above, with longer, more strongly curved bill; also has darker malar stripe, blacker streaking below, shorter primary projection. **Song** similar to Brown Thrasher. Gives *tsuck* **call** like Brown; other calls, a mellow *kleak*, and a loud, whistled *cheeooep*. **Range:** Inhabits dense bottomland thickets. Very rare in west Texas; casual in New Mexico and Colorado.

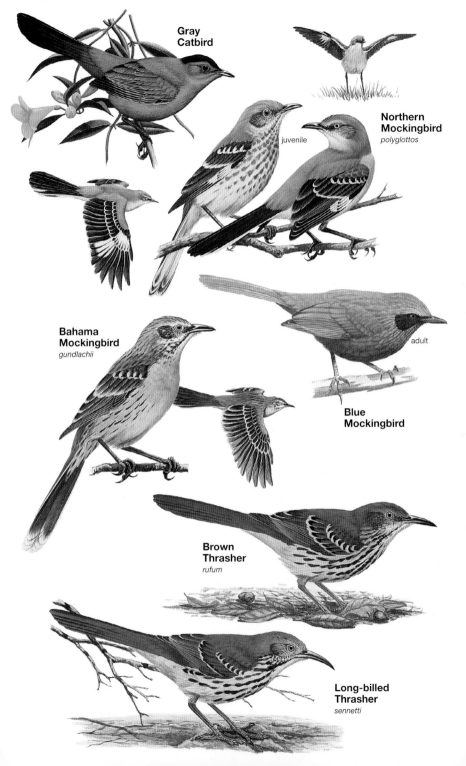

Gray Catbird

Northern Mockingbird
polyglottos

juvenile

Bahama Mockingbird
gundlachii

Blue Mockingbird

adult

Brown Thrasher
rufum

Long-billed Thrasher
sennetti

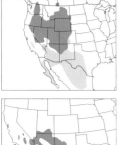

Sage Thrasher *Oreoscoptes montanus* L 8½" (22 cm)
Yellow eye, white wing bars, white-cornered tail. Grayish above,
boldly streaked below. **Worn** late-summer birds show much less
streaking, can resemble Bendire's Thrasher. Juvenile has streaked
head and back. **Song** is a long series of warbled phrases. **Calls**
include a *chuck* and a high *churr.* **Range:** Found in sagebrush
plains. Casual vagrant to eastern North America.

Bendire's Thrasher *Toxostoma bendirei* L 9¾" (25 cm)
Breast mottled; bill shorter and usually less curved than in
Curve-billed Thrasher; base of lower mandible pale. White tail
tips are similar to *oberholseri* race of Curve-billed. Distinctive
arrowhead-shaped spots on breast are not present in **worn** summer plumage. **Song** is a sustained, melodic warbling, each phrase
repeated one to three times. **Range:** Uncommon; found in open
farmlands, grasslands, and brushy desert. Casual to southern
California coast in late summer, fall, and winter.

Curve-billed Thrasher *Toxostoma curvirostre*
L 11" (28 cm) Breast mottled; bill all-dark, longer, heavier, and usually more strongly curved than in Bendire's Thrasher. Breast spots
indistinct in the westernmost race, *palmeri*. Race from extreme
southeastern Arizona to south Texas, *oberholseri*, shows clearer
spotting below; has pale wing bars; conspicuous white tips on
tail. **Juveniles** have shorter bills. Distinctive **call,** a sharp upslurred
whit-wheet, sometimes three-noted (*palmeri*) or even-pitched
whit-whit (*oberholseri*) **Song** is elaborate and melodic, and
includes low trills and warbles. **Range:** Common in canyons,
semiarid brushlands. Casual (*palmeri*) in southeastern California, the Great Plains, and upper Midwest.

California Thrasher *Toxostoma redivivum* L 12" (31 cm)
Dark above, with pale eyebrow, dark eye, dark cheeks. Pale throat
contrasts with dark breast; belly and undertail coverts tawny
buff. Darker overall than Crissal Thrasher. **Calls** are a low, flat
chuck and *chur-erp.* **Song** is loud and sustained, with mostly guttural phrases, often repeated once or twice. Imitates other species
and sounds. **Range:** Common in chaparral-covered foothills.

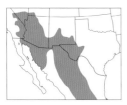

Crissal Thrasher *Toxostoma crissale* L 11½" (29 cm)
Large and slender, with a distinctive chestnut undertail patch and
a dark malar streak. **Song** is varied and musical, its cadence more
leisurely than in Curve-billed Thrasher. **Calls** include a repeated
chideery and a whistled *toit-toit-toit.* **Range:** Very secretive, hid-
ing in underbrush. Found mainly in dense mesquite and willows
along streams and washes; sometimes on lower mountain slopes.

Le Conte's Thrasher *Toxostoma lecontei* L 11" (28 cm)
Palest of the thrashers, with pale grayish brown upperparts,
darker tail; tawny undertail coverts. Bill and eye are dark. **Song,**
heard chiefly at dawn and dusk, is loud, melodious. **Calls** include
an ascending, whistled *tweeep.* **Range:** Prefers arid, sparsely vegetated habitats. Uncommon over most of range.

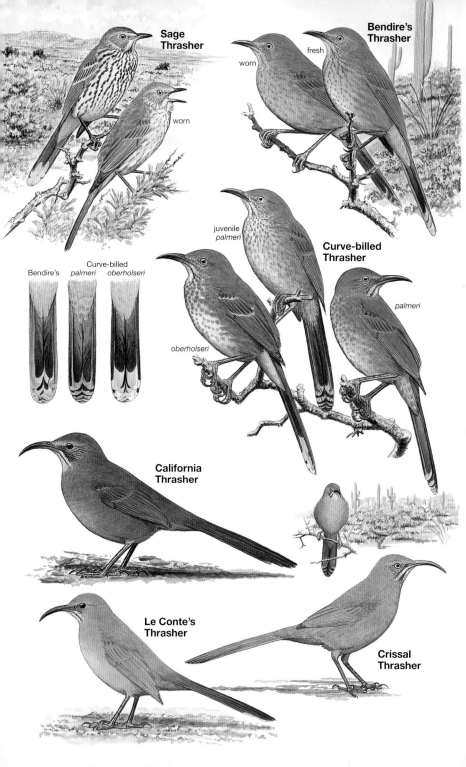

Sage Thrasher

worn

Bendire's Thrasher

worn

fresh

juvenile
palmeri

Curve-billed Thrasher

Bendire's

Curve-billed
palmeri   *oberholseri*

oberholseri

palmeri

California Thrasher

Le Conte's Thrasher

Crissal Thrasher

Bulbuls (Family Pycnonotidae)

Noisy, active Old World family of the tropics and subtropics. *Species: 118 World; 1 N.A.*

Red-whiskered Bulbul *Pycnonotus jocosus* L 7" (18 cm)
Range: Asian and African species. Escaped cage birds first noted in early 1960s in Miami, Florida; now established as a small population in suburbs and parklands south of Miami. Some also in Los Angeles area. Red ear spot and undertail coverts distinctive. **Juvenile** lacks ear patch; undertail coverts are paler.

Starlings (Family Sturnidae)

Widespread Old World family. Chunky and glossy birds; most species are gregarious and bold. *Species: 115 World; 4 N.A.*

Crested Myna *Acridotheres cristatellus* L 9¾" (25 cm)
Range: Asian species, introduced in Vancouver, British Columbia, in the 1890s; population numbered in the thousands in the 1920s, but declined to fewer than 100 by early 1990s and only two by 2002; they perished in Feb. 2003. A likely factor for their extirpation was competition from European Starlings. Identified by bushy crest on forehead, yellow bill and legs, white wing patch.

Common Myna *Acridotheres tristis* L 10" (25 cm)
Range: Southern Asian species; introduced elsewhere, including Hawaii, where it is common. Established in south Florida, where it is spreading. Dark brown, with black head and white undertail coverts; yellow bill and skin around eye; white tail tip, patch at base of primaries, and wing linings distinctive in flight. Juveniles have more brownish heads. **Calls** include gurglings, whistles, and screeches. Found in urban areas; also open country in native range.

Hill Myna *Gracula religiosa* L 10½" (27 cm)
Range: Asian species, fine mimic, popular as a cage bird. A small number of escaped birds, first noted in 1960s, persists but is very local in Miami. Glossy black; orange-red bill; yellow wattles and legs; white wing patch.

European Starling *Sturnus vulgaris* L 8½" (22 cm)
Adult in **breeding** plumage is iridescent black, with a yellow bill with blue base in male, pink in female. In fresh **fall** plumage, feathers are tipped with white and buff, giving a speckled appearance; bill brownish. In flight, note short, square tail, stocky body, and short, broad-based, pointed wings that appear pale gray from below. **Juvenile** is gray-brown, with brown bill. **Call** notes include squeaks, warbles, chirps, and twittering; also imitates songs of other species. **Range:** A Eurasian species introduced in New York in 1890-91, it soon spread across the continent. Abundant, bold, aggressive, it often competes successfully with native species for nest holes. Outside nesting season, usually seen in large flocks.

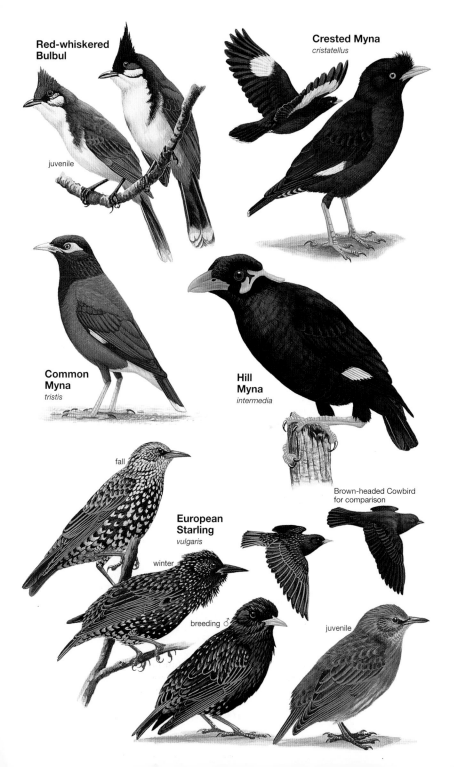

Red-whiskered Bulbul

juvenile

Crested Myna
cristatellus

Common Myna
tristis

Hill Myna
intermedia

Brown-headed Cowbird
for comparison

fall

European Starling
vulgaris

winter

breeding ♂

juvenile

Accentors (Family Prunellidae)

Small Eurasian family, most species found in mountainous country. One species strays to North America. *Species: 13 World; 1 N.A.*

Siberian Accentor *Prunella montanella L 5½" (14 cm)*
Range: Casual mainly fall and winter to Alaska and the Northwest. Bright tawny buff below; back and flanks are streaked. Dark crown, with broad gray median stripe. Note buffy eyebrow that broadens behind head; dark cheek patch with buff spots below; gray patch on side of neck. **Call** is a high, thin series of *see* notes.

Wagtails, Pipits (Family Motacillidae)

Slender-billed birds. Most species pump their tails as they walk. Wagtail flight is strongly undulating. *Species: 64 World; 10 N.A.*

Eastern Yellow Wagtail *Motacilla tschutschensis*
L 6½" (17 cm) Olive above, yellow below; tail shorter than other wagtails. In **breeding** plumage, Alaskan nesting *tschutschensis* has a speckled breast band. Asian *simillima*, recognized by some, seen on Aleutians and Pribilofs, averages greener above, yellower below. **Females** duller, **immatures** whitish below. **Call,** a loud *tsweep,* similar to Eastern Kingbird's. **Range:** Generally common on Alaska breeding grounds; casual fall migrant on California coast.

Gray Wagtail *Motacilla cinerea L 7¾" (20 cm)*
Range: Eurasian species. Very rare spring migrant on western Aleutians; casual on Pribilofs and St. Lawrence Island; accidental south to California. Gray above, with greenish yellow rump, yellow below; whitish tertial edges, but lacks wing bars. **Breeding male** has black throat. **Female** and winter birds have whitish throat, paler below. Distinctly longer tail and flesh-colored legs separate Gray from Yellow Wagtail. **Call,** a metallic *chink-chink*.

White Wagtail *Motacilla alba L 7¼" (18 cm)*
Breeding adult *ocularis* has black nape, gray back; eye line, throat, bib, and usually chin, black. In flight, shows mostly dark wings. In breeding adult male *lugens* upperparts are black, wings mostly white; chin usually white. **Breeding adult female** *lugens* similar, but duller above; **winter adults** retain distinct wing pattern. In nominate *alba* face is white in all plumages. Juveniles of all races are brownish above with two faint wing bars. **Immature** closer to adult but retains most of juvenile wing; immature *ocularis* has darker bases to median coverts than *lugens,* but separation problematic. **Calls** include a two-note *chizzik* given in flight and a whistled *chee-wee* given from perch. **Range:** Northeast Asian *ocularis* breeds sparingly in western Alaska; *lugens* breeds coastal East Asia (south of *ocularis*), has nested and hybridized with *ocularis* in western Alaska, was formerly treated as a separate species, the Black-backed Wagtail. Nominate *alba,* breeding as close as Iceland and Greenland, is accidental on Atlantic coast.

Siberian Accentor
badia

Eastern Yellow Wagtail
tschutschensis

breeding ♂

juvenile

immature

breeding ♂

breeding ♀

breeding ♂
simillima

Gray Wagtail

breeding ♂

♀

breeding ♂

White Wagtail

breeding
ocularis

breeding
adult ♂
lugens

breeding
adult ♂
lugens

breeding adult
♀ *lugens*

winter adult
♂ *lugens*

breeding ♂
alba

immature
lugens

American Pipit *Anthus rubescens* L 6½" (17 cm)

Breeding birds are grayish above and faintly streaked below, except for the *alticola* race, from the Rockies and California's high mountains, which has richly colored underparts with fewer or no streaks. In **winter** American Pipit becomes browner above and more streaked below. Bill mostly dark; legs dark or tinged with pink. Tail has white outer feathers. An Asian subspecies, *japonicus,* rare in western Alaska, is more boldly streaked below, with pink legs, white wing bars; casual in fall in coastal California. **Call,** given in flight, is a sharp *pip-pit;* **song,** a rapid series of *chee* or *cheedle* notes. **Range:** Common and widespread; nests on tundra in the far north, mountaintops farther south. Winter flocks are found in fields and on beaches.

Sprague's Pipit *Anthus spragueii* L 6½" (17 cm)

Dark eye prominent in pale buff face. Pale edges on rounded back feathers give a scaly look; rump is streaked. Underparts whitish, with a buffy wash and short, dark streaks on the breast. Legs pinkish. Outer tail feathers are more extensively white than in American Pipit. **Call** is a loud, squeaky *squeet,* usually given two or more times. **Song,** given continuously in high flight, is a descending series of musical *tzee* and *tzee-a* notes. Uncommon, secretive, and somewhat solitary. Does not pump tail. **Range:** Nests in grassy fields. Very rare in fall and winter to California; accidental in eastern North America.

Olive-backed Pipit *Anthus hodgsoni* L 6" (15 cm)

Range: Asian species. Rare migrant on western Aleutians; casual to Pribilofs and St. Lawrence Island; accidental to California and Nevada. Grayish olive back, faintly streaked. Eyebrow orange-buff in front of eye, white behind. Broken white stripe borders dark ear spot. Throat and breast rich buff, with rather large black spots on breast. Belly pure white; legs pink. **Call** is a buzzy *tsee.*

Pechora Pipit *Anthus gustavi* L 5½" (14 cm)

Range: Asian species. Casual in spring on the western Aleutians and St. Lawrence Island (mostly fall). Shows distinct primary projection. Resembles immature Red-throated Pipit, but compare Pechora Pipit's richly patterned back plumage, extending onto the nape; black centers with dull rufous edges contrast with white lines, or "braces," on the sides. Also a yellowish wash across the breast contrasts with the whitish belly. Quite secretive. **Call** is a hard *pwit* or *pit,* but Pechora is often silent when flushed.

Red-throated Pipit *Anthus cervinus* L 6" (15 cm)

Note unpatterned nape. Pinkish red head and breast are distinctive in **breeding male,** less extensive in **breeding female** and fall adults. Fall **immatures** and some breeding females show no red. **Call,** given in flight, is a high, piercing *tseee,* dropping in pitch at the end. Loud, varied **song** is delivered from the ground or in song flight. **Range:** Regular migrant on islands in Bering Sea; rare fall migrant along California coast; casual inland and in Northwest.

American Pipit
rubescens

breeding

winter

breeding
alticola

winter
japonicus

Sprague's Pipit

Olive-backed Pipit
yunnanensis

Pechora Pipit
gustavi

breeding ♀

Red-throated Pipit

breeding ♂

immature

Waxwings (Family Bombycillidae)

Red, waxy tips on secondary wing feathers are often indistinct, and sometimes they are absent altogether. All waxwings have sleek crests, silky plumage, and yellow-tipped tails. Where berries are ripening, waxwings come to feast in amiable, noisy flocks. *Species: 4 World; 2 N.A.*

Bohemian Waxwing *Bombycilla garrulus* L 8¼" (21 cm)

Larger and grayer than Cedar Waxwing; underparts gray; undertail coverts cinnamon. White and yellow spots on wings. In flight, white wing patch at base of primaries is conspicuous. **Juvenile** browner above, streaked below, with pale throat. Distinctive **call,** a buzzy twittering, lower and harsher than call of Cedar Waxwing. **Range:** Nests in open coniferous or mixed woodlands; often seen perched on top of a black spruce. Winter range varies widely and unpredictably; large flocks visit scattered locations, feeding on berries and small fruits. Also eat insects, flower petals, and sap. Irregular winter wanderer to the Northeast, usually in small numbers; annual in Maine, Maritimes, and Newfoundland. Individuals are sometimes seen in flocks of Cedar Waxwings.

Cedar Waxwing *Bombycilla cedrorum* L 7¼" (18 cm)

Smaller and browner than Bohemian Waxwing; belly pale yellow; undertail coverts white. Lacks yellow spots on wings. **Juvenile** is streaked; lacks white wing patches of juvenile Bohemian. Since this species usually nests late in summer, juvenal plumage is seen well into fall. **Call** is a soft, high-pitched, trilled whistle. **Range:** Found in open habitats where berries are available; also eats insects, flower petals, and sap. Highly gregarious in migration and winter.

Silky-flycatchers (Family Ptilogonatidae)

This New World tropical family of slender, crested birds is closely related to the waxwings. The family's common name describes their soft, sleek plumage and agility in catching insects on the wing. *Species: 4 World; 2 N.A.*

Phainopepla *Phainopepla nitens* L 7¾" (20 cm)

Male is shiny black; white wing patch conspicuous in flight. In both sexes, note distinct crest, long tail, red eyes. Juvenile resembles **adult female;** but has browner eyes; both have gray wing patches. Young males acquire patchy black in fall. Distinctive **call** note is a low-pitched, whistled, querulous *wurp?* **Song** is a brief warble, seldom heard. Flight is fluttery but direct, and often very high. **Range:** Phainopeplas nest in early spring in mesquite brushlands, feeding chiefly on insects and mistletoe berries. In late spring they move into cooler, wetter habitat and raise a second brood. Rare post-breeding wanderers north and east of mapped range. Accidental in eastern North America.

juvenile

Bohemian Waxwing
pallidiceps

juvenile

Cedar Waxwing

Phainopepla

Wood-Warblers (Family Parulidae)

A New World family. About half of its numerous species occur in North America. *Species: 112 World; 57 N.A.*

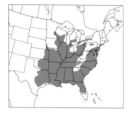

Prothonotary Warbler *Protonotaria citrea*
L 5½" (14 cm) Large, plump, short tailed, and very long billed. Eyes are large, dark, and prominent. **Male**'s head and underparts golden yellow, fading to white undertail coverts; wings blue-gray, without wing bars; blue-gray tail has large white patches. **Female** duller, head less golden. **Song** is a series of loud, ringing *zweet* notes; gives a dry *chip* note and buzzy flight **call. Range:** Fairly common. The only eastern warbler that nests in tree or other cavities and crannies; usually selects a low site along streams or surrounded by sluggish or stagnant water. Casual to rare vagrant across most of the continent during migration, especially in fall.

Blue-winged Warbler *Vermivora pinus* L 4¾" (12 cm)
Male has bright yellow crown and underparts, white or yellowish white undertail coverts, black eye line, blue-gray wings with two white wing bars. **Female** duller overall. In both sexes, bill is long and slender; extensive white on tail is visible from below. Main **song** is a wheezy *beee-bzzz*, the second note lower; alternate song is longer and more complex. **Range:** Locally common; inhabits brushy meadows, second-growth woodlands; nests on the ground. Rare to Atlantic Canada in fall; very rare vagrant to western U.S., but increasing. Blue-winged prefers a greater diversity of habitat than Golden-winged Warbler. Range is expanding at northern edge; gradually replacing Golden-winged. Hybridizes with Golden-winged where ranges overlap. Hybrids may vary considerably from parent species in amount of black on head and throat, amount of yellow below, and size and color of wing bars. Some variations are shown here of the two main types, the more frequent **"Brewster's Warbler"** and the rare **"Lawrence's Warbler"** backcross (most often produced by crossing a first-generation hybrid with one of the parent species).

Golden-winged Warbler *Vermivora chrysoptera*
L 4¾" (12 cm) **Male** has black throat; black ear patch bordered in white; yellow crown and wing patch. **Female** similar but duller. In both sexes, extensive white on tail is conspicuous from below; underparts are grayish white; bill long and slender. Main **song** is a soft *bee-bz-bz-bz;* also gives an alternate song similar to Blue-winged Warbler. **Range:** Prefers overgrown pastures, briery woodland borders; nests on the ground. Uncommon to rare and declining. Rare in fall to Maritimes; very rare vagrant to western U.S. Found farther north and at higher elevations in the Appalachians than Blue-winged. Songs of hybrids of these two species (see above) usually sound like one of the parent species.

Prothonotary
Warbler

♀

adult ♂

Blue-winged
Warbler

♀

♂

Blue-winged x
Golden-winged
hybrids

"Brewster's
Warbler"

♂

Golden-winged
Warbler

♀

♂

"Lawrence's
Warbler"

♀

♂

♂

Tennessee Warbler *Vermivora peregrina L 4¾" (12 cm)*
Plump, with short tail and long, straight bill. **Male** in spring is green above with gray crown, bold white eyebrow; white below. **Female** is tinged with yellow or olive overall, especially in fresh fall plumage. Adult male in fall resembles spring adult female but shows more yellow below. Immature also yellowish below; resembles young Orange-crowned, but is greener above and has a shorter tail and usually white undertail coverts. Spring male may be confused with Warbling and Red-eyed Vireos (page 318); note especially Tennessee Warbler's slimmer bill, greener back. Distinctive two- or three-part **song;** in three-part version, several rapid two-syllable notes are followed by a few higher single notes, ending with a staccato trill. **Range:** Fairly common. Found in coniferous and mixed woodlands in summer, mixed open woodlands and brushy areas during fall migration. Nests on the ground; generally feeds high in trees. Very rare in winter in coastal California.

Orange-crowned Warbler *Vermivora celata*
L 5" (13 cm) Olive above, paler below. Yellow undertail coverts and faint, blurred streaks on sides of breast distinguish this species from the similar Tennessee Warbler. Note also that Orange-crowned's bill is thinner and slightly downcurved; tail is longer. Plumage varies from the smaller, brighter, yellower birds of western U.S., such as Pacific *lutescens,* to the duller *orestera* (not shown) of the Great Basin and Rockies; to the dullest, *celata,* which breeds across Alaska and Canada and winters primarily in southeastern U.S.; *celata* is the latest fall migrant of the warblers. Tawny orange crown, absent in some **females** and **immatures,** is seldom discernible in the field. Immature *celata* can be particularly drab. Young birds are similar to immature Tennessees but show yellow undertail coverts and grayer upperparts. **Song** is a high-pitched staccato trill, faster in *lutescens;* **call** note, a sharp *chip.* **Range:** Inhabits open, brushy woodlands, forest edges, and thickets. Nests on the ground; generally feeds in low branches, often in dead leaf clumps. Common in the West; rarer in the East.

Bachman's Warbler *Vermivora bachmanii* **E**
L 4¾" (12 cm) Probably extinct; the last definite record was in 1962 near Charleston, South Carolina. **Range:** Bachman's once bred in canebrakes and wet woodlands; was known very locally in the southeastern U.S., from southeastern Missouri and Logan County in southern Kentucky east to South Carolina, but was probably never numerous. Wintered in Cuba and on Isle of Pines. Bill is very thin, long, somewhat downcurved; undertail coverts white in both sexes. **Male** has yellow forehead, chin, and shoulders; black crown and bib. Immature male has less black on crown and throat, less yellow on shoulders, and more white on lower belly. **Female** drabber, crown gray, throat and breast gray or yellow. Distinctive **song,** typically a rapid series of buzzes on one pitch; similar to Blue-winged Warbler's alternate song.

fall

fall

breeding ♀

Tennessee Warbler

breeding ♂

immature ♀

celata

♂

Orange-crowned Warbler

lutescens ♂

adult ♀

1st spring ♂

adult ♂

Bachman's Warbler

Nashville Warbler   *Vermivora ruficapilla*   L 4¾" (12 cm)

Bold white eye ring, gray head, olive upperparts, and white area below legs. Rump brighter on longer-tailed western race *ridgwayi* (not shown), which more often wags its tail. **Female** is duller than **male. Song** of eastern *ruficapilla* is a series of high *see-weet* notes and a lower short trill; **call,** a dull *chink.* In *ridgwayi,* song is sweeter, call is sharper. **Range:** Common; found in second-growth woodlands and spruce bogs.

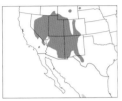

Virginia's Warbler   *Vermivora virginiae*   L 4¾" (12 cm)

Bold white eye ring on gray head; upperparts gray. Yellow patch on breast, yellow undertail coverts. Female is duller overall. Fall **immature** is browner; little or no yellow on breast. **Song** is a rapid series of thin notes, often ending with lower notes; **call** is a sharp *chink.* Often wags its long tail. **Range:** Common in mountain brushlands. Rare to coastal California. Casual in the East.

Colima Warbler   *Vermivora crissalis*   L 5¾" (15 cm)

Range: Mexican species; range extends to oak woodlands of Chisos Mountains, Big Bend National Park, Texas. Larger and browner than Virginia's Warbler; rufous crown patch usually visible. **Song** is a trill similar to Orange-crowned Warbler.

Lucy's Warbler   *Vermivora luciae*   L 4¼" (11 cm)

Pale gray above, whitish below, with a short tail. **Male**'s reddish crown, patch, and rump distinctive. Female and **immatures** duller. Lively **song** is a short trill followed by lower, whistled notes. **Call** is a sharp *chink.* Fairly common in mesquite and cottonwoods along watercourses; nests in tree cavities.

Crescent-chested Warbler   *Parula superciliosa*

L 4¼" (11 cm)   **Range:** Resident from northern Nicaragua to northern Mexico; casual to southeast Arizona; one sight record for Chisos Mountains, Texas. Bluish gray head with broad white eyebrow; green back; no wing bars or white in tail. Chestnut crescent distinct on **adult male;** reduced on female and immature male; absent or an orange wash on **immature female.**

Northern Parula   *Parula americana*   L 4½" (11 cm)

Short-tailed warbler, gray-blue above with yellowish green upper back, two bold white wing bars. Throat and breast bright yellow, belly white. In **adult male,** reddish and black bands cross breast. In female and immature male, bands are fainter or absent. One **song** is a rising buzzy trill, ending with an abrupt *zip* in eastern birds; no clear final note in more westerly birds. **Range:** Common in coniferous or mixed woods, especially near water. Rare vagrant throughout the West in migration.

Tropical Parula   *Parula pitiayumi*   L 4½" (11 cm)

Range: Uncommon in south Texas. Dark mask and lack of distinct white eye ring distinguish Tropical from Northern Parula. Also yellow of throat extends farther onto sides of face; **male** has more blended orange breast band. **Song** like Northern Parula.

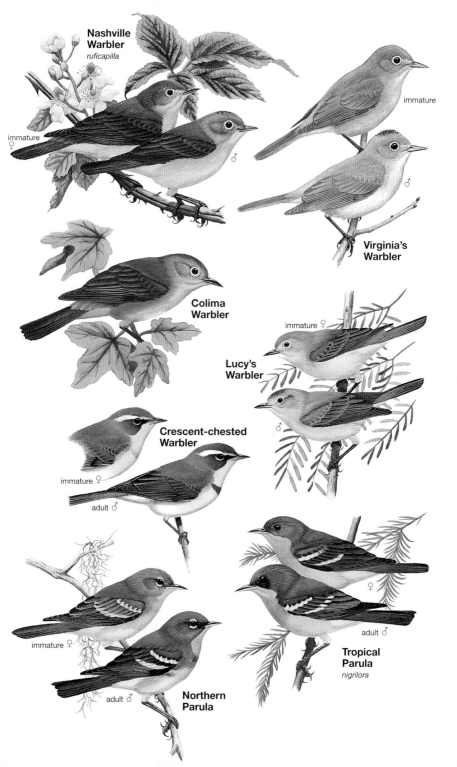

Nashville Warbler
ruficapilla

immature ♀

♂

immature

Virginia's Warbler

♂

Colima Warbler

immature ♀

Lucy's Warbler

♂

Crescent-chested Warbler

immature ♀

adult ♂

immature ♀

adult ♂

Northern Parula

adult ♂

♀

Tropical Parula
nigrilora

Chestnut-sided Warbler *Dendroica pensylvanica*

L 5" (13 cm) **Breeding male** has yellow crown, black eye line, black whisker stripe; extensive chestnut on sides; **female** has greenish crown, less chestnut. Fall adults and **immatures** are lime green above, with white eye ring, whitish underparts, yellowish wing bars. **Song** is a whistled *please please pleased to meetcha;* **call,** a *chip* note like Yellow Warbler. Chestnut-sided often cocks its tail. **Range:** Fairly common in second-growth deciduous woodlands. Rare migrant in West; casual in winter.

Cape May Warbler *Dendroica tigrina L 5" (13 cm)*

Most plumages have yellow on face, the color usually extending to sides of neck. Note also short tail; yellow or greenish rump; thin bill, slightly downcurved. **Breeding male**'s chestnut ear patch and striped underparts distinctive; wing patch white. **Female** drabber, grayer, with two narrow white wing bars. **Immature male**'s ear patch is less distinct. **Immature female** can be extremely drab, with gray face and only a tinge of yellow below and on rump; always has greenish edges on flight feathers. One **song** is a high, thin *seet seet seet seet;* **call,** a very high, thin *sip.* **Range:** Cape May Warbler shows aggressive behavior. Breeds in black spruce forests, where often uncommon except during spruce budworm outbreaks. Rare west to Texas in migration; very rare to casual throughout the West. Winters chiefly in the West Indies; a few birds winter in southernmost Florida.

Magnolia Warbler *Dendroica magnolia L 5" (13 cm)*

Male is blackish above, with white eyebrow, white wing patch, yellow rump; broad white tail patches. Underparts yellow, streaked on breast and sides; undertail coverts white; undertail white except for black band at tip. Female has two wing bars; some **first-spring females** have dull white eye ring; often confused with rare Kirtland's Warbler (page 386). **Fall adults** and **immatures** are drabber, with grayish olive upperparts; white eye ring; faint gray band across breast. Compare immature Prairie Warbler (page 386). Magnolia Warbler does not bob tail. **Song** is a short, whistled *weety-weety-weeteo.* **Range:** Fairly common to common in moist coniferous forests. Casual in winter in southern Florida. Rare throughout the West in migration.

Yellow-rumped Warbler *Dendroica coronata*

L 5½" (14 cm) Yellow rump, yellow patch on side, yellow crown patch, white tail patches. In northern and eastern birds, **"Myrtle Warbler,"** note white eyebrow, white throat and sides of neck, contrasting cheek patch. Western birds, **"Audubon's Warbler,"** have yellow throat, except for a few immature females. Some males in the mountains of the Southwest show more black. All **females** and fall males are duller than **breeding males** but show same basic pattern. **Song,** a slow warble, usually rising or falling at the end in "Audubon's," a musical trill in one song of "Myrtle." **Call** note of "Myrtle" is lower, flatter. **Range:** Abundant in coniferous or mixed woodlands. "Myrtle" is fairly common in winter on West Coast; "Audubon's" is casual in the East.

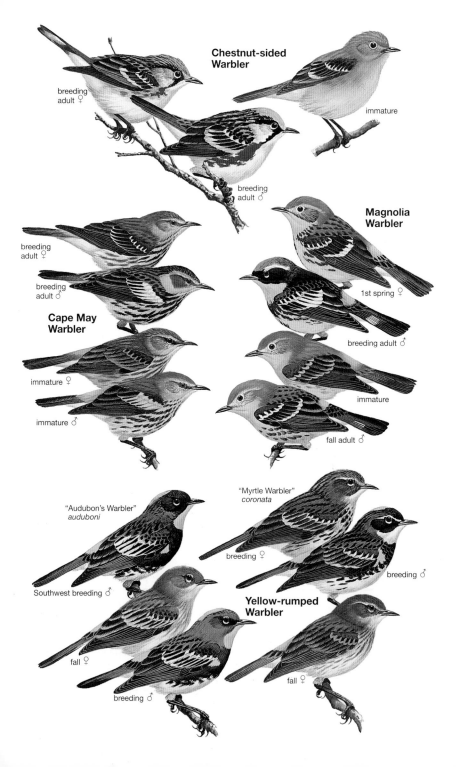

Chestnut-sided Warbler

breeding adult ♀

breeding adult ♂

immature

Magnolia Warbler

breeding adult ♀

breeding adult ♂

1st spring ♀

breeding adult ♂

immature

fall adult ♂

Cape May Warbler

immature ♀

immature ♂

"Audubon's Warbler" *auduboni*

Southwest breeding ♂

"Myrtle Warbler" *coronata*

breeding ♀

breeding ♂

fall ♀

breeding ♂

Yellow-rumped Warbler

fall ♀

Black-and-white Warbler *Mniotilta varia L 5¼" (13 cm)*

The only warbler that regularly creeps along branches and up and down tree trunks like a nuthatch. Boldly striped on head, most of body, and undertail coverts. **Male**'s throat and cheeks are black in breeding plumage; in winter, chin is white. **Female** and **immatures** have pale cheeks; female diffusely streaked on buffy flanks; buffy wash particularly bright on immatures. **Song** is a long series of high, thin *wee-see* notes. **Calls** include a sharp *chip* and high *seep-seep.* **Range:** Common in mixed woodlands.

Black-throated Blue Warbler *Dendroica caerulescens L 5¼" (13 cm)* **Male**'s black throat, cheeks, and sides separate blue upperparts, white underparts. Bold white patch at base of primaries. Appalachian males south of Susquehanna drainage average darker above; back largely black in the case of *cairnsi* in southern Appalachians. **Female**'s pale eyebrow is distinct on dark face; upperparts brownish olive; underparts buffy; wing patch smaller, occasionally absent on immature females. Typical **song** is a slow series of four or five wheezy notes, the last note higher: *zwee zwee zwee zweeee* or a slower *zur zurr zree.* **Call** is a single sharp *dit,* like the call of a Dark-eyed Junco. **Range:** Inhabits deciduous forests; usually seen in lower or mid-level branches. Rare fall vagrant in the West. A few birds winter in south Florida; most migrate to the West Indies.

Cerulean Warbler *Dendroica cerulea L 4¾" (12 cm)*

Small, with short tail and two wide white wing bars. **Adult male** is bluish above with dark streaks; white below, with dark breast band and dark blue-gray streaking on sides. **Female** has greenish mantle, blue-green or bluish crown; pale eyebrow broadens behind the eye; breast and throat are pale yellowish. Immature male is like female, but shows some bluish and dark streaks above. **Song** is a short, fast, accelerating series of buzzy notes on one pitch, ending with a long, single buzz note. **Range:** Sharply declining in the heart of its range. Found in tall trees in swamps, bottomlands, mixed woodlands near water. Fall migration begins from the second week of July. Range is expanding in Northeast.

Blackburnian Warbler *Dendroica fusca L 5" (13 cm)*

Fiery orange throat, broad white wing patch, triangular ear patch, conspicuous in **adult male. Female** and immature male have paler throat, **immature female** paler still; note also the two white wing bars, streaked back, and bold yellow or buffy eyebrow, broader behind the eye, that curls around onto side of neck. Orange or yellow forehead stripe and white in outer tail feathers are distinct in all males, less so in females. One **song,** a short series of high notes followed by a squeaky, ascending trill, ends on a very high note. **Range:** Fairly common in coniferous or mixed forests of northern breeding range; pine-oak woodlands in the Appalachians. Generally stays in the upper branches. Vagrants are seen rarely in coastal California in fall migration; casual elsewhere west of dashed line on map in spring and fall.

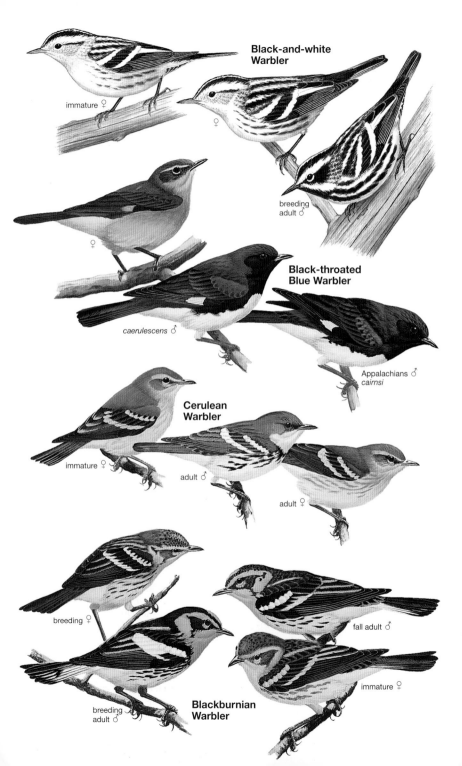

**Black-and-white
Warbler**

immature ♀

♀

breeding
adult ♂

♀

**Black-throated
Blue Warbler**

caerulescens ♂

Appalachians ♂
cairnsi

**Cerulean
Warbler**

immature ♀

adult ♂

adult ♀

breeding ♀

fall adult ♂

immature ♀

breeding
adult ♂

**Blackburnian
Warbler**

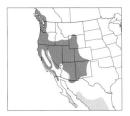

Black-throated Gray Warbler *Dendroica nigrescens*

L 5" (13 cm) **Adult** plumage is basically the same year-round: black-and-white head; gray back streaked with black; white underparts, sides streaked with black; small yellow spot between eye and bill. Lacks central crown stripe of the Black-and-white Warbler (preceding page); undertail coverts are white. Immature male resembles adult male; immature female is brownish gray above, throat white. Varied **songs** include a buzzy *weezy weezy weezy weezy-weet*. **Range:** Inhabits woodlands, brushlands, chaparral. Rare in winter in lower Rio Grande Valley, Texas; casual otherwise in eastern North America. Very rare during migration and in winter along the Gulf Coast.

Townsend's Warbler *Dendroica townsendi* L 5" (13 cm)

Dark crown, dark ear patch bordered in yellow. Olive above, streaked with black; yellow breast, white belly, yellowish black-streaked sides. **Adult male**'s throat and upper breast are black; **female** and immature male have streaked lower throat. **Immature female** is duller, lacks streaking on back; streaking on underparts is diffuse. Variable **song,** a series of hoarse *zee* notes. Frequently hybridizes with Hermit Warbler; **hybrids** usually have yellowish, streaked underparts of Townsend's, yellow head of Hermit. **Range:** Found in coniferous forests. Casual in the East.

Hermit Warbler *Dendroica occidentalis* L 5½" (14 cm)

Yellow head, with dark markings extending from nape onto crown. **Male** has black chin and throat; in **female** and **immatures,** chin is yellowish, throat shows less or no dark color. Immature female is more olive above. **Song** is a high *seezle seezle seezle seezle zeet-zeet*. **Range:** Fairly common in mountain forests; nests in tall conifers. During migration, also seen in lowlands. Casual in the East.

Black-throated Green Warbler *Dendroica virens*

L 5" (13 cm) Bright olive green upperparts; yellow face with greenish ear patch. Underparts are white, tinged with yellow on sides of vent and often on breast. **Male** has black throat and upper breast and black-streaked sides. **Female** and **immatures** show much less black below; immature female generally has dark streaking only on sides. One **song** is a hoarse *zeee zeee zee-zo-zee;* the other, often written as *trees, trees, whispering trees*. **Range:** Fairly common in coniferous or mixed forests in summer.

Golden-cheeked Warbler *Dendroica chrysoparia* **E**

L 5½" (14 cm) Dark eye line, unmarked yellow ear patches, and lack of any yellow on underparts distinguish this species from similar Black-throated Green Warbler. **Male** black above, with black crown, black bib, black-streaked sides. **Female** and immature male duller, upperparts olive with dark streaks; chin yellowish or white; sides of throat streaked. **Immature female** shows less black on underparts. **Song,** *bzzzz layzee dayzee,* ends on a high note. **Range:** Endangered; local in mixed cedar-oak woodland of the Edwards Plateau in central Texas.

Black-throated Gray Warbler

♀

adult ♂

adult ♀

Townsend's Warbler

adult ♂

Townsend's x Hermit hybrid

adult ♂

adult ♀

adult ♂

Hermit Warbler

adult ♀

Black-throated Green Warbler

adult ♂

Golden-cheeked Warbler

adult ♀

adult ♂

immature females

Golden-cheeked   Black-throated Green   Townsend's   Hermit

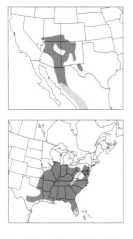

Grace's Warbler *Dendroica graciae L 5" (13 cm)*

Black-streaked gray back; throat and upper breast bright yellow; rest of underparts white, with black streaks on sides; short bill; yellow eyebrow becomes white behind eye. **Female** slightly duller and browner above. Grace's Warbler's **song** is a rapid, accelerating trill. **Range:** Inhabits coniferous or mixed forests of southwestern mountains, especially yellow pines. Usually forages high in the trees. Very rare to southern California.

Yellow-throated Warbler *Dendroica dominica*

L 5½" (14 cm) Plain gray back; large, white patch on each side of head. **Male** has black crown and face; in female, black is less extensive. Throat and upper breast bright yellow; rest of underparts white, with black streaks on sides; bold white eyebrow sometimes tinged with yellow. Eastern races *dominica* and *stoddardi* (of eastern Gulf Coast, not shown) have yellow supraloral area, unlike more westerly *albilora; stoddardi* and birds from Delmarva Peninsula have very long bills. **Song** is a series of clear, downslurred whistles ending with a rising note. **Range:** Fairly common in live oak and pine woodlands, cypress, and sycamores. Usually forages high in the trees, creeping methodically along the branches. Very rare northward to southern Ontario in spring and Newfoundland in fall. Casual in West during migration.

Kirtland's Warbler *Dendroica kirtlandii* **E**

L 5¾" (15 cm) Blue-gray above, strongly black-streaked on back; yellow below, streaked on sides; white eye ring, broken at front and rear; two whitish wing bars, thin and indistinct. Often confused with first-spring female Magnolia Warbler (page 380). **Adult female** is slightly duller; **immature female** brownish above. Kirtland's Warbler constantly wags its tail. **Song** is loud and lively, a variable series of low, sharp notes followed by slurred whistles. **Range:** An endangered species: The annual breeding census counted 1,420 singing males in 2005, up from the historic low of 167 singing males in 1987. Nests in northern Michigan, where controlled plantings and fires help produce the required habitat: thickets of young jack pines. Very rare in summer outside Michigan, with records from southern Ontario and especially Wisconsin. Very rarely seen in migration. Winters in the Bahamas.

Prairie Warbler *Dendroica discolor L 4¾" (12 cm)*

Olive above, with faint chestnut streaks on back; bright yellow eyebrow, yellow patch below eye; bright yellow below, streaked with black on sides of neck and body. Two indistinct wing bars. **Female** and immature male are slightly duller. **Immature female** is duller still, grayish olive above; lack of complete eye ring or gray breast band distinguish her from fall Magnolia Warbler (page 380). Distinctive **song**, a rising series of buzzy *zee* notes. **Range:** Generally common in open woodlands, scrublands, overgrown fields, and mangrove swamps. Usually forages in lower branches and brush, twitching its tail. Casual in the West, except in coastal California, where it is rare in fall. Also rare in fall to Maritimes and Newfoundland. Declining in upper Midwest.

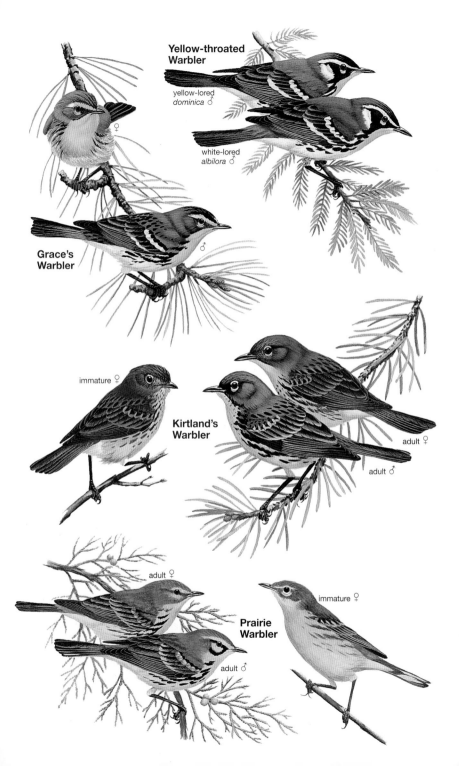

Yellow-throated Warbler

yellow-lored
dominica ♂

white-lored
albilora ♂

♀

Grace's Warbler

♂

immature ♀

Kirtland's Warbler

adult ♀

adult ♂

adult ♀

Prairie Warbler

adult ♂

immature ♀

Bay-breasted Warbler *Dendroica castanea*

L 5½" (14 cm) **Breeding male** has chestnut crown, throat, and sides; black face; creamy patch at each side of neck; two white wing bars. **Female** is duller. **Fall adults** and **immatures** resemble Blackpoll Warbler and Pine Warbler. Bay-breasted is brighter green above, wing bars are thicker; underparts show little or no streaking and little yellow; flanks usually show some buff or bay color; legs usually entirely dark; undertail coverts are buffy or whitish. Short tail projection past undertail coverts for both Bay-breasted and Blackpoll. **Song** consists of high-pitched double notes. **Range:** Fairly common; nests in coniferous forests. Migrates earlier in fall than Blackpoll. Very rare in the West.

Blackpoll Warbler *Dendroica striata* *L 5½" (14 cm)*

Solid black cap, white cheeks, and white underparts identify **breeding male;** back and sides boldly streaked with black. Compare with Black-and-white Warbler (page 382). **Female** is duller overall, variably greenish above and pale yellow below; some are gray; note streaking. **Fall adults** and immatures resemble Bay-breasted and Pine Warblers. Blackpoll is mostly pale greenish yellow below, with dusky streaking on sides; legs pale on front and back, dark on sides; undertail coverts long and usually white. **Song** is a series of high *tseet* notes. **Range:** Common; nests in coniferous forests. Migrates later in fall than Bay-breasted Warbler. Rare migrant over much of West. Very rare in fall in most of South because much migration is off East Coast.

Pine Warbler *Dendroica pinus* *L 5½" (14 cm)*

Relatively large bill; long tail projection past undertail coverts; throat color extends onto sides of neck, setting off dark cheek patch. **Male** is greenish olive above, without streaking; throat and breast yellow, with dark streaks on sides of breast; belly and undertail coverts white. **Female** is duller. **Immatures** are brownish or brownish olive above, with whitish wing bars and brownish tertial edges; male is dull yellow below, female largely white; both have brown wash on flanks. **Song** is a twittering musical trill, varying in speed. **Range:** Common in pines in summer; also in mixed woodlands in winter. Casual to very rare in the West; rare to Newfoundland in fall.

Palm Warbler *Dendroica palmarum* *L 5½" (14 cm)*

Upperparts olive. **Breeding adult** of eastern race, *hypochrysea,* has chestnut cap, yellow eyebrow, and entirely yellow underparts, with chestnut streaking on sides of breast. Fall adults and immatures lack chestnut cap and streaking; yellow is duller. Western nominate race, *palmarum,* has whitish belly and darker streaks on sides of breast; less chestnut. **Fall adults** and immatures are drab. **Song** is a rapid, buzzy trill. **Range:** Fairly common; nests in brush at edge of spruce bogs. During migration and winter, found in woodland borders, open brushy areas, and marshes. Habitually wags its tail as it forages. Regular on West Coast in fall and winter (*palmarum*); *hypochrysea* casual to California.

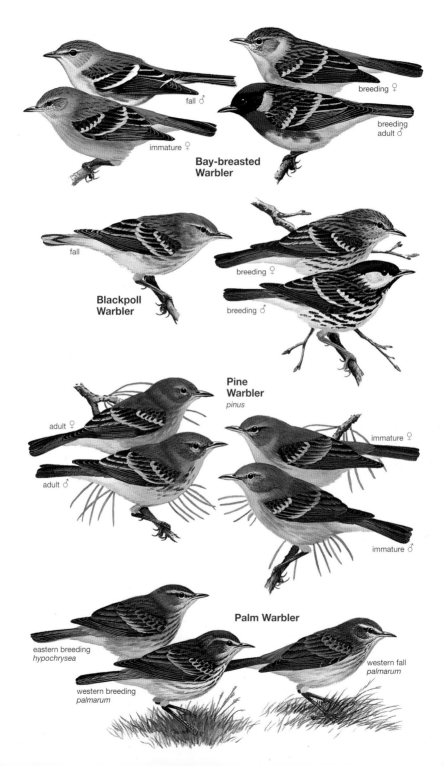

fall ♂

immature ♀

breeding ♀

breeding
adult ♂

**Bay-breasted
Warbler**

fall

**Blackpoll
Warbler**

breeding ♀

breeding ♂

**Pine
Warbler**
pinus

adult ♀

adult ♂

immature ♀

immature ♂

Palm Warbler

eastern breeding
hypochrysea

western breeding
palmarum

western fall
palmarum

Yellow Warbler *Dendroica petechia L 5" (13 cm)*
Plump, yellow overall, with short tail; dark eye prominent in uniformly yellow face; reddish streaks below are distinct in **male**, faint or absent in **female; immatures** are duller. Much geographic variation: Northern races are greener above; southwest *sonorana* is pale with faint red streaks below; resident *gundlachi* of southernmost Florida is of the "Golden" group of the West Indian races. Note green crown and short primary projection. Resident subspecies in mangroves from Mexico south are known as **"Mangrove Warbler"**; adult males of most subspecies have chestnut heads; immatures of this and **"Golden"** are dull. **Song,** rapid, variable, is sometimes written *sweet sweet sweet I'm so sweet.* **Range:** Favors wet habitats, especially willows and alders; open woodlands, orchards. A few "Mangroves" resident in mangroves in south coastal Texas.

Mourning Warbler *Oporornis philadelphia L 5¼" (13 cm)*
Lack of bold white eye ring distinguishes **adult male** from Connecticut Warbler. **Adult female** and especially **immatures** may show a thin, nearly complete eye ring, but compare with Connecticut. Immatures generally have more yellow on throat than MacGillivray's; compare also with female Common Yellowthroat (page 396). Immature males often show a little black on breast. Mourning Warblers hop rather than walk. **Call** is a flat, hollow *chip.* **Song** is a series of slurred two-note phrases followed by two or more lower phrases. **Range:** Fairly common in dense undergrowth, thickets, moist woods; nests on the ground. Most spring migration is west of the Appalachians. Very rare in the West.

MacGillivray's Warbler *Oporornis tolmiei L 5¼" (13 cm)*
Bold white crescents above and below eye distinguish all plumages from male Mourning and all Connecticut Warblers. Crescents may be very hard to distinguish from the thin, nearly complete eye ring found on female and immature Mourning Warblers. **Immature** MacGillivray's Warblers generally have grayer throat than immature Mournings and a fairly distinct breast band above yellow belly. Field identification is often difficult. MacGillivray's hops rather than walks. **Call** is a sharp, harsh *tsik.* **Song** has two parts: a buzzy trill ending in a downslur. **Range:** Fairly common; found in dense undergrowth; nests on the ground. Casual to East.

Connecticut Warbler *Oporornis agilis L 5¾" (15 cm)*
Large eye with bold white eye ring conspicuous on **male**'s gray hood and **female**'s brown or gray-brown hood. Eye ring is sometimes slightly broken on one side only. **Immature** has a brownish hood and brownish breast band. A large, stocky warbler, noticeably larger than Mourning and MacGillivray's Warblers. Like Mourning, long undertail coverts give Connecticut a short-tailed, plump appearance. Walks rather than hops. Loud, accelerating **song** repeats a brief series of explosive *beech-er* or *whip-ity* notes. **Range:** Uncommon; found in spruce bogs, moist woodlands; nests on the ground; generally feeds on the ground or on low limbs. Spring migration is almost entirely west of the Appalachians. Fall migrants uncommon in the East; very rare in the West.

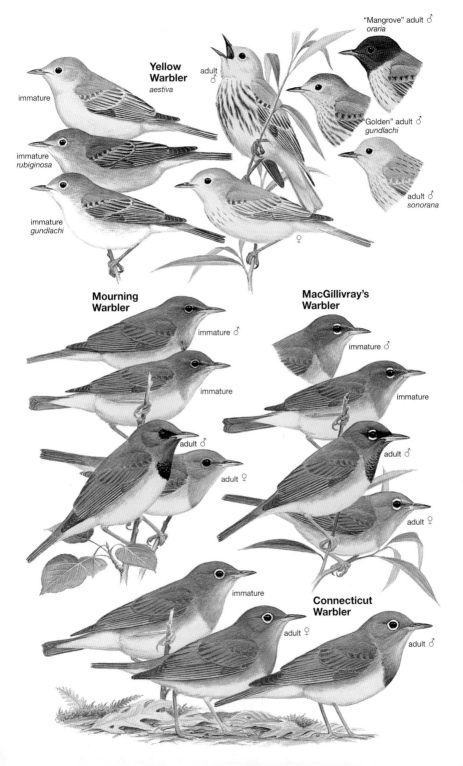

Yellow Warbler
aestiva

immature

adult ♂

"Mangrove" adult ♂
oraria

immature
rubiginosa

"Golden" adult ♂
gundlachi

immature
gundlachi

adult ♂
sonorana

♀

Mourning Warbler

immature ♂

immature

adult ♂

adult ♀

MacGillivray's Warbler

immature ♂

immature

adult ♂

adult ♀

immature

Connecticut Warbler

adult ♀

adult ♂

Kentucky Warbler *Oporornis formosus* L 5¼" (13 cm)

A short-tailed, long-legged warbler. Bold yellow spectacles separate black crown from black on face and sides of neck; underparts are entirely yellow, upperparts bright olive. Black areas are duller on **female,** olive on immature female. **Song** is a series of rolling musical notes, *churry churry churry,* much like the song of the Carolina Wren. **Call** is a low, sharp *chuck.* **Range:** Common in rich, moist woodlands; nests and feeds on the ground in dense undergrowth. Rare to Maritimes; casual to Newfoundland. Very rare vagrant to California and the Southwest.

Canada Warbler *Wilsonia canadensis* L 5¼" (13 cm)

Black necklace on bright yellow breast identifies **male;** note also bold yellow spectacles. In **females,** necklace is dusky and indistinct. Male is blue-gray above, females duller. All birds have white undertail coverts. **Song** begins with one or more short, sharp *chip* notes and continues as a rich and highly variable warble. **Range:** Common in dense woodlands and brush. Usually forages in undergrowth or low branches, but also seen flycatching. Winters in South America. Casual vagrant in the West; very rare in fall along California coast and in Newfoundland.

Wilson's Warbler *Wilsonia pusilla* L 4¾" (12 cm)

Olive above; yellow below, with yellow lores. Long tail is all-dark above and below, and often cocked. **Male** has black cap; in **females,** cap is blackish or absent, forehead yellowish. Yellow lores and lack of white in tail help distinguish female from female Hooded Warbler. Coloration varies geographically from bright *chryseola* of Pacific states to duller and olive-faced nominate *pusilla* of East; *pileolata* (shown) from Alaska and Rockies intermediate. Females average more black in western races. **Song** is a rapid, variable series of *chee* notes; common **call,** a sharp *chimp.* **Range:** Fairly common, much more numerous in the West than in the East; nests in dense, moist woodlands, bogs, willow thickets, and streamside tangles.

Hooded Warbler *Wilsonia citrina* L 5¼" (13 cm)

All ages have dark lores, unlike Wilson's Warbler; also bigger bill and larger eye. Extensive black hood identifies **male. Adult female** shows blackish or olive crown and sides of neck; sometimes has black throat or black spots on breast; **immature female** lacks black. Note that in both sexes tail is white below; seen from above, white outer tail feathers are conspicuous as the bird flicks its tail open. **Song** is loud, musical, whistled variations of *ta-wit ta-wit ta-wit tee-yo.* **Call** is a flat, metallic chink. **Range:** Fairly common in swamps, moist woodlands; generally stays hidden in dense undergrowth and low branches. Rare migrant in the Southwest and California, where it has nested; also has nested in Colorado; casual in other western states. Rare in fall to the Maritimes; casual to Newfoundland.

Kentucky Warbler

♂

♀

Canada Warbler

immature ♀

adult ♂

Wilson's Warbler
pileolata

♀

♂

Hooded Warbler

adult ♀

adult ♂

immature ♀

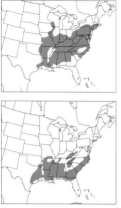

Worm-eating Warbler *Helmitheros vermivorum*
L 5¼" (13 cm) Bold, dark stripes on buffy head; upperparts brownish olive; underparts buffy; long, spikelike bill. **Song** is a series of sharp, dry *chip* notes, like Chipping Sparrow's song but faster. Common **call**, *zeep-zeep.* **Range:** Found chiefly in dense undergrowth on wooded slopes. Often feeds in clusters of dead leaves. Casual vagrant to California, the Southwest, and Atlantic Canada.

Swainson's Warbler *Limnothlypis swainsonii*
L 5½" (14 cm) Pale eyebrow, conspicuous between brown crown and dark eye line. Brown-olive above, grayish below. Bill very long and spiky. Uncommon and secretive. **Song** is a series of thin, slurred whistles like beginning of song of Louisiana Waterthrush; often ends with a rising *tee-oh.* **Calls** include a loud, dry *chip.* **Range:** Found in undergrowth in swamps and canebrakes; rare and local in mountain laurel and rhododendron. Walks or shuffles on the ground and shivers while picking up dead leaves. Casual north to Ontario and Nova Scotia and west to Colorado, New Mexico, and Arizona.

Ovenbird *Seiurus aurocapilla L 6" (15 cm)*
Russet crown bordered by dark stripes; bold white eye ring. Olive above; white below, with bold streaks of dark spots; pinkish legs. Generally seen on the ground; walks, with tail cocked, rather than hops. Typical **song** is a loud *teacher teacher teacher,* rising in volume. **Range:** A plump warbler, common in mature forests. Rare in the West. Rare in winter along Gulf and Atlantic coasts to North Carolina.

Louisiana Waterthrush *Seiurus motacilla L 6" (15 cm)*
Distinguished from Northern Waterthrush by contrast between white underparts and salmon-buff flanks; bicolored eyebrow, pale buff in front of eye, white and much broader behind eye; larger bill; bubblegum pink legs. A ground dweller; walks, rather than hops, bobbing its tail constantly but usually slowly. **Call** note, a sharp *chink,* is slightly flatter than that of Northern Waterthrush. **Song** begins with three or four shrill, slurred notes followed by a brief, rapid jumble. **Range:** Uncommon; found along mountain streams in dense woodlands, also near ponds and in swamps. Rare to Southwest; casual to California and Nova Scotia.

Northern Waterthrush *Seiurus noveboracensis*
L 5¾" (15 cm) Distinguished from Louisiana Waterthrush by lack of contrast in color between flanks and rest of underparts; buffy eyebrow, of even width throughout or slightly narrowing behind eye; smaller bill; drabber leg color. Some birds are whiter below, with whiter eyebrow. A ground dweller; walks, rather than hops, bobbing its tail constantly and usually rapidly. **Call** note, a metallic *chink,* is slightly sharper than that of Louisiana Waterthrush. **Song** begins with loud, emphatic notes and ends in lower notes, delivered more rapidly. **Range:** Found chiefly in woodland bogs, swamps, and thickets. Rare to uncommon migrant in California and the Southwest.

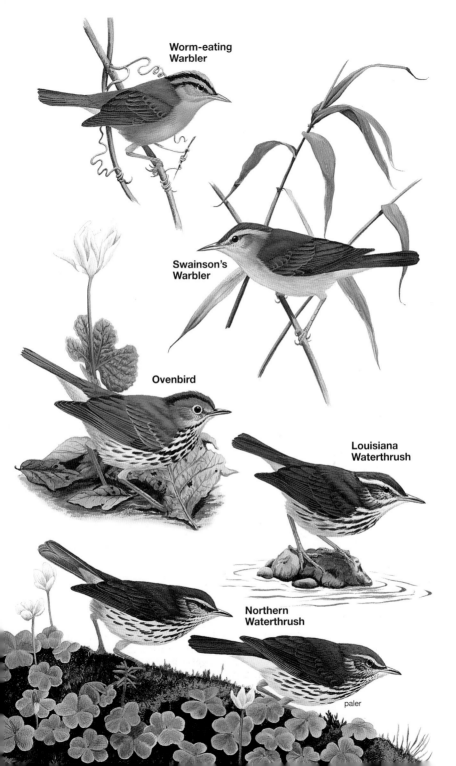

Worm-eating
Warbler

Swainson's
Warbler

Ovenbird

Louisiana
Waterthrush

Northern
Waterthrush

paler

Common Yellowthroat *Geothlypis trichas* L 5" (13 cm)
Adult male's broad black mask is bordered above by gray or white, below by bright yellow throat and breast; undertail coverts yellow. **Female** lacks black mask; has whitish eye ring. Races vary geographically in color of mask border and extent of yellow below. Southwestern race, *chryseola*, is brightest below and shows the most yellow. **Immatures** are duller and browner overall. Often cocks tail. Variable **song;** one version is a loud, rolling *wichity wichity wichity wich.* **Calls** include a raspy *chuck.* **Range:** Common; stays low in grassy fields, shrubs, and marshes.

Gray-crowned Yellowthroat *Geothlypis poliocephala*
L 5½" (13 cm) **Range:** Tropical species; former resident of the Brownsville area in southern Texas; population eliminated in early 20th century. Recently, several certain records in the lower Rio Grande Valley; other reports uncertain. Large, with a long, graduated tail; thick, bicolored bill with curved culmen; split white eye ring; lores blackish in **males,** slaty gray in **females.** **Song,** a rich, varied warble; **call,** a rising *chee dee.* Favors grassland with scattered bushes.

Fan-tailed Warbler *Euthlypis lachrymosa*
L 5¾" (15 cm) **Range:** Tropical species; casual, mainly late spring, to southeast Arizona. Large, with long, graduated, white-tipped tail held partly open and pumped sideways or up and down. Head pattern distinct with broken white eye ring; white lore spot; yellow crown patch. Note tawny wash on breast. **Song** of rich, loud slurred notes; **call,** a penetrating *schree.* Found low in canyons or ravines; often walks or shuffles on ground; secretive.

Golden-crowned Warbler *Basileuterus culicivorus*
L 5" (13 cm) **Range:** Tropical species, casual in southern Texas, chiefly in winter; accidental in eastern New Mexico (spring). Resembles Orange-crowned Warbler (page 376) but crown shows a distinct yellow or buffy orange central stripe, bordered in black; note also yellowish green eyebrow. **Call,** a rapidly repeated *tuck.*

Rufous-capped Warbler *Basileuterus rufifrons*
L 5¼" (13 cm) **Range:** Mexican species, casual to Edward's Plateau and Big Bend, Texas; also southeastern Arizona. Rufous crown, bold white eyebrow, throat extensively bright yellow. Long tail, often cocked. **Song** begins with musical *chip* notes and accelerates into a series of dry, whistled warbles; **call,** a *tik,* often doubled or in a rapid series. Inhabits brush and woodlands of foothills or low mountains, generally staying low in the undergrowth.

Yellow-breasted Chat *Icteria virens* L 7½" (19 cm)
Our largest warbler, with long tail, thick bill, and white spectacles. Lores black in **males,** gray in **females.** Unmusical **song,** a jumble of harsh, chattering clucks, rattles, clear whistles, and squawks, sometimes given in hovering display flight. **Range:** Inhabits dense thickets and brush. Rather shy. Regular straggler in fall to Maritimes and Newfoundland; rare in winter on the East Coast.

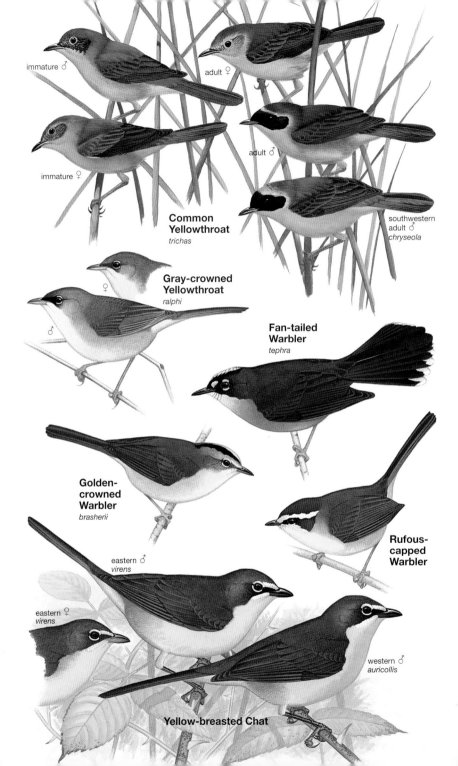

Common Yellowthroat
trichas

immature ♂

adult ♀

immature ♀

adult ♂

southwestern
adult ♂
chryseola

Gray-crowned Yellowthroat
ralphi

♀

♂

Fan-tailed Warbler
tephra

Golden-crowned Warbler
brasherii

Rufous-capped Warbler

eastern ♂
virens

eastern ♀
virens

western ♂
auricollis

Yellow-breasted Chat

American Redstart *Setophaga ruticilla* *L 5¼" (13 cm)*
Male glossy black, with bright orange patches on sides, wings, and tail; belly and undertail coverts white. **Female** is gray-olive above, white below with yellow patches. Immature male resembles female; by **first spring,** lores are usually black, breast has some black spotting; adult male plumage is acquired by second fall. Like redstarts of the genus *Myioborus,* often fans its tail and spreads its wings when perched. Variable **song,** a series of high, thin notes usually followed by a wheezy, downslurred note. **Range:** Common in second-growth woodlands. Rare to uncommon migrant in California and the Southwest.

Slate-throated Redstart *Myioborus miniatus* *L 6" (15 cm)*
Range: Middle and South American species, casual in southeast Arizona, southeast New Mexico, and west and south Texas. Head, throat, and back are slate black, breast dark red. Chestnut crown patch visible only at close range. Lacks white wing patch of similar Painted Redstart; white on outer tail feathers less extensive; tail strongly graduated. **Call,** a *chip* note, very different from Painted Redstart. Found in pine-oak canyons, forests.

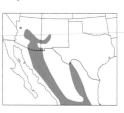

Painted Redstart *Myioborus pictus* *L 5¾" (15 cm)*
Bright red lower breast and belly; black head and upperparts; bold white wing patch. White outer tail feathers conspicuous as the bird fans its tail. **Juvenile** acquires full adult plumage by end of summer. **Song** is a series of rich, liquid warbles; **call,** a clear, whistled *chee.* **Range:** Found in pine-oak canyons. Very rare visitor to southern California; a scattering of records elsewhere.

Red-faced Warbler *Cardellina rubrifrons* *L 5½" (14 cm)*
Adult's red-and-black face pattern distinctive; back and tail gray, rump and underparts white. Immature is duller, face pinkish. **Song** is a series of varied, ringing *zweet* notes. **Range:** A warbler of high mountains, generally found above 6,000 feet. Fairly common, especially in fir and spruce mixed with oaks. Nests on the ground. Rare to west Texas; casual to southern California.

Olive Warbler (Family Peucedramidae)

Recently placed in its own family because relationships are uncertain.

Olive Warbler *Peucedramus taeniatus* *L 5¼" (13 cm)*
Dark face patch broadens behind eye. Long, thin bill; two broad white wing bars; outer tail feathers extensively white. **Adult male**'s head, throat, and nape tawny brown. **Female** has olive crown, yellow face; pale yellow throat and breast. Juveniles and **first-fall** birds resemble female but are paler or whitish below; crown is gray. Young male acquires adult plumage by second fall. Typical **song** is a loud *peeta peeta peeta,* similar to call of Tufted Titmouse; **call,** a soft, whistled *phew.* **Range:** Favors open coniferous forests at elevations above 7,000 feet. Nests and forages high in trees. A few remain on breeding grounds in winter.

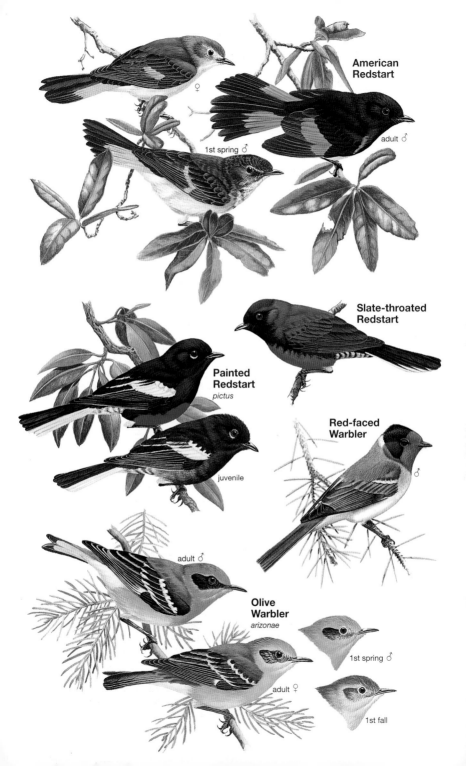

American Redstart

♀

1st spring ♂

adult ♂

Slate-throated Redstart

Painted Redstart
pictus

juvenile

Red-faced Warbler
♂

adult ♂

Olive Warbler
arizonae

1st spring ♂

adult ♀

1st fall

Tanagers (Family Thraupidae)

Brightly colored, mostly fruit-eating, tropical birds, related to warblers. *Species: 271 World; 6 N.A.*

Summer Tanager *Piranga rubra* L 7¾" (20 cm)

Adult male is rosy red year-round. **First-spring male** usually has red head. Some **females** show overall reddish wash; most have a mustard tone, lack olive of female Scarlet Tanager; bill larger. Western birds are larger and paler; females generally grayer above. **Song** is robinlike; **call,** a staccato *ki-ti-tuck.* **Range:** Common in pine-oak woods in the East, cottonwood groves in the West.

Hepatic Tanager *Piranga flava* L 8" (20 cm)

Large grayish cheek patch and gray wash on flanks set off brighter throat, breast, and cap in both sexes; dark bill with gray base. **Adult male** plumage is acquired by second fall; dull red plumage retained year-round. Juvenile resembles yellow-and-gray **female** but is heavily streaked overall. **Song** is robinlike. **Call** is a single low *chuck.* Inhabits mixed mountain forests.

Scarlet Tanager *Piranga olivacea* L 7" (18 cm)

Breeding male bright red and black. In late summer, becomes splotchy green-and-red as he molts to yellow-green winter plumage. **Female** has uniformly olive head, back, and rump; whitish wing linings; bill smaller than in Summer Tanager. Immature **male** resembles adult male, but note brownish primaries and secondaries. Some immatures show faint wing bars. Robinlike **song** (hoarser than Summer Tanager) of raspy notes, *querit queer query querit queer,* is heard in deciduous forests. **Call** is a hoarse *chip-burr.* **Range:** Very rare vagrant in the West, most in late fall.

Western Tanager *Piranga ludoviciana* L 7¼" (18 cm)

Conspicuous wing bars, often paler and thinner in **female,** upper bar yellow in **male.** Male's red head becomes yellowish and finely streaked in **winter.** Female's grayish back contrasts with greenish yellow nape and rump. Some females are duller below, grayer above. **Song** is like Scarlet Tanager's; **call,** *pit-er-ick.* **Range:** Breeds in coniferous forests. Rare in winter north along coastal slope to central California. Rare on Gulf Coast, casual in the East.

Flame-colored Tanager *Piranga bidentata*

L 7¼" (18 cm) **Range:** Resident from western Panama to northern Mexico; casual to mountains of southeast Arizona in spring and summer; casual to West and south Texas. Has gray bill with visible "teeth"; blackish rear border to ear patch; streaked back; white wing bars and tertial tips; whitish tail corners. Hybrids with Western Tanager are regularly noted in southeast Arizona. **Male** of nominate west Mexican race, *bidentata,* is flaming orange, eastern *sanguinolenta* male redder. **Female** and immatures are colored like female Western Tanager. **First-spring males** have brighter yellow head; some spotting. **Song** similar to Western and Scarlet Tanagers; **call** also, but huskier, low-pitched *prreck.*

Hepatic Tanager
hepatica

1st spring ♂

red morph ♀

Summer Tanager
rubra

♀

adult ♂

♀

adult ♂

1st spring ♂

♀

breeding adult ♂

1st fall ♂

fall adult ♂

Scarlet Tanager

1st fall ♂

gray morph ♀

♀

winter adult ♂

1st spring ♂

Flame-colored Tanager
bidentata

♀

Western Tanager

breeding adult ♂

adult ♂

Western Spindalis *Spindalis zena L 6¾" (17 cm)*
Formerly known as Stripe-headed Tanager. **Range:** West Indian species; very rare visitor, except in summer, from Bahamas to southeast Florida and Florida Keys. **Males** are strikingly patterned: Most are black-backed (*zena*); a few unconfirmed sightings of *townsendi*, restricted to Grand Bahama and Abaco, show greenish orange back; occasionally black with dull orange edgings. Recent winter record in Key West of male *pretrei* from Cuba. **Females** of both races are grayish olive, with pale eyebrow, pale greater covert patch, and distinct white spot at base of primaries. **Call** is a thin, high *tsee*, given singly or in a series.

Bananaquit (Incertae sedis)

Family affiliation of this species is uncertain. Prefers nectar.

Bananaquit *Coereba flaveola L 4½" (11 cm)*
Range: Tropical species; casual visitor from the Bahamas to southern Florida. Note thin, downcurved bill. **Adult** has conspicuous white eyebrow, yellow rump; underparts white, with yellow breast; small white wing patch. **Juvenile** is duller.

Emberizids (Family Emberizidae)

All have conical bills. This large family includes the towhees, sparrows, longspurs, and *Emberiza* buntings. *Species: 308 World; 60 N.A.*

White-collared Seedeater *Sporophila torqueola*
L 4½" (11 cm) Tiny, with thick, short, strongly curved bill; rounded tail. **Adult male** has black cap; white crescent below eye; incomplete buffy collar; white wing bars; white patch at base of primaries. **Females** are paler, lack cap and collar; wing bars duller. **Song** is pitched high, then low, a variable *sweet sweet sweet sweet cheer cheer cheer*. **Calls** include a distinct, high *wink*. In U.S., favors canes and river bottoms.

Black-faced Grassquit *Tiaris bicolor L 4½" (11 cm)*
Range: West Indian species; casual stray to south Florida. **Adult male** mostly black below, dark olive above; head is black. **Female** and immatures pale gray below, gray-olive above. **Song** is a buzzing *tik-zeee;* **call,** a lisping *tst*.

Yellow-faced Grassquit *Tiaris olivaceus L 4¼" (11 cm)*
Range: Tropical species. Accidental in southern Florida and southernmost Texas. **Adult male** of mainland race, *pusillus,* shows extensive black on head, breast, and upper belly; golden yellow supraloral, throat, and crescent below eye; olive above. Adult **female** and immature male have traces of same head pattern; olive above. Adult male of West Indian race, *olivaceus,* shows less black. Female lacks black below. **Song** is thin, insectlike trills; **call,** a high-pitched *sik* or *tsi*.

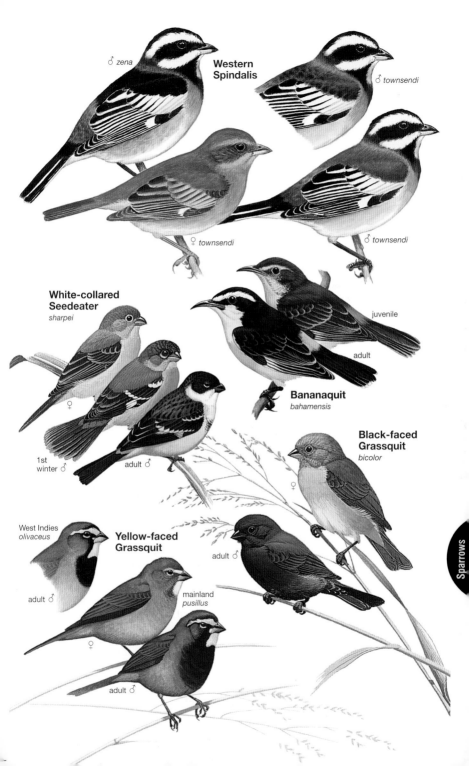

♂ *zena*

Western Spindalis

♂ *townsendi*

♀ *townsendi*

♂ *townsendi*

White-collared Seedeater
sharpei

juvenile

adult

Bananaquit
bahamensis

♀

1st winter ♂

adult ♂

Black-faced Grassquit
bicolor

♀

West Indies
olivaceus

Yellow-faced Grassquit

adult ♂

adult ♂

mainland
pusillus

♀

adult ♂

Sparrows

Olive Sparrow *Arremonops rufivirgatus L 6¼" (16 cm)*

Range: Tropical species, common in southernmost Texas in dense undergrowth, brushy areas, live oak. Dull olive above, with brown stripe on each side of crown. Lacks reddish cap of similar Green-tailed Towhee. **Juveniles** are buffier, with pale wing bars; faintly streaked on neck and breast. **Calls** include a dry *chip* and a buzzy *speeee*. **Song** is an accelerating series of *chip* notes.

Green-tailed Towhee *Pipilo chlorurus L 7¼" (18 cm)*

Olive above with reddish crown, distinct white throat bordered by dark stripe and white stripe. **Juvenile** has two faint olive wing bars; plumage is streaked overall; upperparts tinged with olive; lacks reddish crown. Clear, whistled **song** begins with *weet-chur*, ends in raspy trill. **Calls** include a catlike *mew*. **Range:** Fairly common in dense brush, chaparral, on mountainsides and high plateaus. Casual in winter throughout the East.

California Towhee *Pipilo crissalis L 9" (23 cm)*

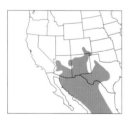

Brownish overall; crown slightly warmer brown than rest of upperparts. Buff throat is bordered by a distinct broken ring of dark brown spots; no dark spot on breast as in Canyon Towhee. Lores are same color as throat and contrast with cheek; undertail coverts warm cinnamon. **Juvenile** shows faint wing bars. **Call** is a sharp, metallic *chink* note; also gives some thin, lispy notes and an excited, squealing series of notes, often delivered as a duet by a pair. **Song,** accelerating *chink* notes with stutters in the middle, is heard mostly in late afternoon. **Range:** Resident in chaparral, parks, and gardens. The race *eremophilus* (**T**) of Inyo County, California, is threatened. With Canyon Towhee, California was formerly considered one species, Brown Towhee.

Canyon Towhee *Pipilo fuscus L 8" (20 cm)*

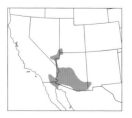

Similar to California Towhee. Canyon is paler, grayish rather than brown, with shorter tail; more contrast in reddish crown gives a capped appearance; crown is sometimes raised as short crest. Larger whitish belly patch with diffuse dark spot at junction with breast; paler throat bordered by finer streaks; lores the same color as cheek; distinct buffy eye ring. Juveniles are streaked below. **Call** is a shrill *chee-yep* or *chedep*. **Song,** more musical, less metallic, than California; opens with a call note, followed by sweet slurred notes. Also gives a duet of lisping and squealing notes, like California. **Range:** Favors arid, hilly country; desert canyons. Largely resident within range; casual southwestern Kansas (Morton County); no range overlap with California.

Abert's Towhee *Pipilo aberti L 9½" (24 cm)*

Black face; upperparts cinnamon-brown, underparts paler, with cinnamon undertail coverts. **Call** is a sharp *peek;* **song,** a series of *peek* notes. **Range:** Common within its range, but somewhat secretive. Inhabits desert woodlands and streamside thickets, at lower altitudes than similar Canyon Towhee. Also found in suburban yards and orchards.

juvenile

Olive Sparrow
rufivirgatus

spring

Green-tailed Towhee

fall

juvenile

juvenile

California Towhee

Canyon Towhee

Abert's Towhee

Eastern Towhee *Pipilo erythrophthalmus L 7½" (19 cm)*

Male's black upperparts and hood contrast with rufous sides and white underparts. Distinct white patch at base of primaries and distinct white tertial edges. White in outer tail feathers is conspicuous in flight, or seen from below when bird is perched. Most have red eyes. **Females** are similarly patterned, but black areas are replaced by brown. **Juveniles** are brownish and show distinct streaks below. The nominate race is largest and shows most extensive white in tail. Wing length, and the extent of white in wings and tail, declines from the northern part of the range to the Gulf Coast, while the size of bill, legs, and feet increases. The subspecies from the Florida peninsula, *alleni,* is smaller in all measurements, paler, and duller; has less white in wings and tail; has straw-colored eyes. The *rileyi* race (not shown), from northernmost Florida to east-central North Carolina, shows intermediate characteristics, eyes being either red or straw colored; eye color particularly variable in birds from southern Georgia and coastal South Carolina. Like other towhees, Eastern scratches with its feet together. Full **song** has three parts, often rendered as *drink your tea,* or shortened to two parts: *drink tea.* Northeastern birds' **call** is a slightly upslurred *chwee;* in *alleni,* a clearer, even-pitch or upslurred *swee.* **Range:** Partial to second growth with dense shrubs and extensive leaf litter; southern races, especially *alleni,* favor coastal scrub or sand dune ridges and pinelands. Nominate race is partly migratory; casual west to Colorado and Arizona. Has declined from the northeastern part of its range by as much as 90 percent in recent decades. Other races are largely resident. Eastern and Spotted Towhee have each been restored to full species status; formerly considered one species, Rufous-sided Towhee. The two interbreed along rivers in the Great Plains, particularly the Platte and its tributaries. Accidental in winter to Southwest.

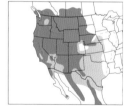

Spotted Towhee *Pipilo maculatus L 7½" (19 cm)*

Distinguished from similar Eastern Towhee by white spotting on back and scapulars; also on tips of median and greater coverts, which forms white wing bars. In general, **females** differ less from **males** than in Eastern, with *arcticus* from Great Plains showing the greatest difference. In both sexes the amount of white spotting above and white in tail shows marked geographical variation, with *arcticus* displaying most white. Races, principally *montanus,* from the Great Basin and Rockies show less white. The Northwest coast's *oregonus* is darkest and shows least white of all the races. White increases southward to *megalonyx* of southern California and *falcinellus* (not shown) of the Central Valley region. **Song** and calls also show great geographical variation. Interior races give introductory notes, then a trill. Pacific coast birds sing a simple trill of variable speed. **Call** of *montanus* is a descending and raspy mewing. Great Plains *arcticus* and all coastal races give an upslurred, questioning *queee.* **Range:** Some populations are largely resident while others are migratory; *arcticus* is the most migratory and is casual in eastern North America.

Eastern Towhee
erythrophthalmus

juvenile

Florida
♂ *alleni*

♀

♂

Spotted Towhee

♀ *arcticus*

♂ *arcticus*

♂ *montanus*

♀ *oregonus*

♂ *oregonus*

♀ *montanus*

juvenile
oregonus

♀ *megalonyx*

♂ *megalonyx*

Eastern

erythrophthalmus   *alleni*

Spotted

arcticus   *montanus*   *megalonyx*   *oregonus*

Bachman's Sparrow *Aimophila aestivalis* *L 6" (15 cm)*

A large sparrow with large bill, fairly flat forehead, and long, rounded, dark tail. **Adults** gray above, heavily streaked with chestnut or dark brown; sides of head buffy gray; a thin dark line extends back from eye. Breast and sides buff or gray; belly whitish. Subspecies range in overall brightness from the reddish *illinoensis* of the western part of range to the grayer and darker *aestivalis* of Florida. Birds from northeastern part of range are intermediate. **Juvenile** has a distinct eye ring; throat, breast, and sides are streaked. First-winter plumage usually retains some streaking. Quite secretive outside breeding season; best located and identified by **song:** one clear, whistled introductory note, followed by a variable trill or warble on a different pitch. Male sings from open perch; often heard in late summer. **Range:** Inhabits dry, open woods, especially pines; scrub palmetto. Northern range has markedly declined over last several decades.

Botteri's Sparrow *Aimophila botterii* *L 6" (15 cm)*

A large, plain sparrow with large bill, fairly flat forehead; tail long, rounded, dusky brown, lacking white tips and central barring of the very similar Cassin's Sparrow. Upperparts streaked with dull black, rust or brown, and gray; underparts unstreaked; throat and belly whitish, breast and sides grayish buff. Subspecies *arizonae* of southeastern Arizona is redder above; *texana* of extreme southern Texas is slightly grayer. **Juvenile**'s belly is buffy; breast broadly streaked, sides narrowly streaked. Best located and identified by **song:** several high sharp *tsip* or *che-lik* notes, often followed by a short, accelerating, rattly trill. **Range:** Generally secretive; inhabits grasslands dotted with mesquite, cactus, and brush. The *texana* race is declining because of habitat loss; now uncommon and local.

Cassin's Sparrow *Aimophila cassinii* *L 6" (15 cm)*

A large, drab sparrow, with large bill, fairly flat forehead. Long, rounded tail is dark gray-brown; distinctive white tips on outer feathers are most conspicuous in flight. Gray upperparts are streaked with dull black, brown, and variable amount of rust; blackish marks form anchor marks; underparts are grayish white, usually with a few short streaks on the flanks. **Juvenile** is streaked below; paler overall than juvenile Botteri's. In fresh fall plumage, shows bolder white wing bars than similar Botteri's Sparrow, and black-centered, white-fringed tertials. Best located and identified by **song,** often given in brief, fluttery song flight: typically a soft double whistle, a loud, sweet trill, a low whistle, and a final, slightly higher note; or a series of *chip* notes ending in a trill or warbles. Also gives a trill of *pit* notes. **Range:** Secretive; inhabits arid grasslands with scattered shrubs, cactus, and mesquite. Casual vagrant to the East and Far West.

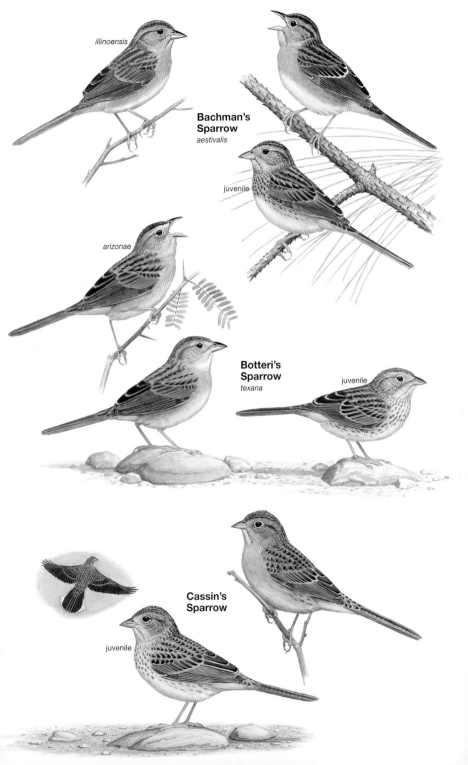

illinoensis

Bachman's Sparrow
aestivalis

juvenile

arizonae

Botteri's Sparrow
texana

juvenile

Cassin's Sparrow

juvenile

Rufous-winged Sparrow *Aimophila carpalis*

L 5¾" (15 cm) Pale gray head marked with reddish eye line and black moustachial and malar stripe on side of face; two-toned bill, with pale lower mandible; sides of crown streaked with reddish brown. Back is gray-brown, streaked with black; two whitish wing bars. Reddish lesser wing coverts distinctive but difficult to see. Underparts grayish white, without streaking. Tail long, rounded. **Juvenile**'s facial stripes are less distinct; wing bars buffier; bill dark; breast and sides lightly streaked; plumage can be seen as late as Nov. Distinctive **call** note, a sharp, high *seep*. Variable **song**, several chip notes followed by an accelerating trill of *chip* or *sweet* notes. **Range:** Fairly common but local; found in flat areas of tall desert grass mixed with brush and cactus.

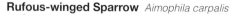

Rufous-crowned Sparrow *Aimophila ruficeps*

L 6" (15 cm) Gray head with dark reddish crown, distinct whitish eye ring, rufous line extending back from eye, single black malar stripe on each side of face. Gray-brown above, with reddish streaks; gray below; tail long, rounded. Subspecies range in overall color from paler, grayer *eremoeca*, found over most of eastern interior range, to widespread southwestern race, *scottii*, which is paler and reddish. Pacific coastal races are slightly smaller and darker and show variable amounts of reddish above. **Juvenile** is buffier above; breast and crown streaked; may show two pale wing bars. Distinctive **call**, a sharp *dear*, usually given in a series; **song**, a rapid, bubbling series of *chip* notes. Locally common on rocky hillsides and steep brushy or grassy slopes.

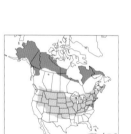

American Tree Sparrow *Spizella arborea* *L 6¼" (16 cm)*

Gray head and nape crowned with rufous; rufous stripe behind eye. Gray throat and breast, with dark central spot, rufous patches at sides of breast. Back and scapulars streaked with black and rufous. Tail notched; outer feathers thinly edged in white on outer webs. Underparts grayish white with buffy sides. **Winter** birds are buffier; rufous color on crown sometimes forms a central stripe. **Juvenile** is streaked on head and underparts. Western *ochracea* is paler overall. American Tree Sparrow gives a musical *teedle-eet* **call** and also gives a thin *seet*. **Song** usually begins with several clear notes followed by a variable, rapid warble. **Range:** Fairly common. Uncommon to rare west of Rockies. Breeds along edge of tundra, in open areas with scattered trees and brush. Winters in weedy fields, marshes, and groves of small trees.

Field Sparrow *Spizella pusilla* *L 5¾" (15 cm)*

Gray face with reddish crown, distinct whitish eye ring, bright pink bill. Back is streaked except on gray-brown rump. Breast and sides are buffy red; belly grayish white; legs pink. **Juvenile** streaked below; wing bars buffy. Birds in westernmost part of range, *arenacea*, are paler and grayer; extremes are shown here. **Song** is a series of clear, plaintive whistles accelerating into a trill; *chip* note similar to Orange-crowned Warbler. **Range:** Fairly common in open, brushy woodlands, fields. Uncommon to rare in Maritimes; casual west of mapped range.

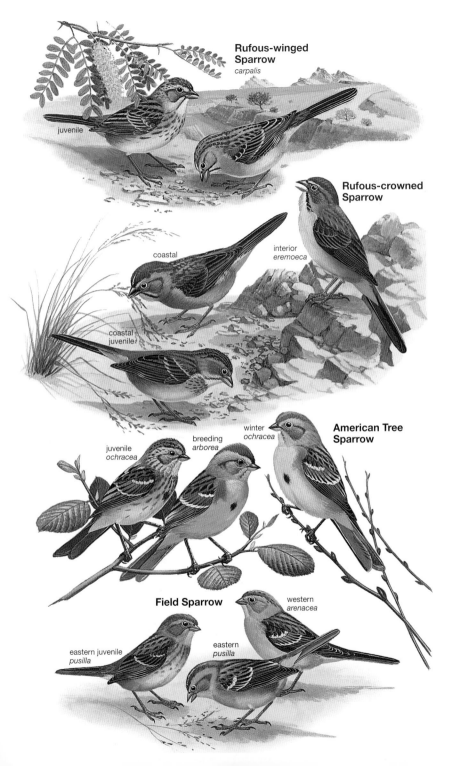

Rufous-winged Sparrow *carpalis*

juvenile

Rufous-crowned Sparrow

coastal

interior *eremoeca*

coastal juvenile

winter *ochracea*

American Tree Sparrow

juvenile *ochracea*

breeding *arborea*

Field Sparrow

western *arenacea*

eastern juvenile *pusilla*

eastern *pusilla*

Chipping Sparrow   *Spizella passerina*   L 5½" (14 cm)

Breeding adult identified by bright chestnut crown, distinct white eyebrow, and black line extending from bill through eye to ear; note also the gray nape and cheek with no dark moustachial stripe; gray unstreaked rump; and two white wing bars. As in all sparrows of the genus *Spizella*, the tail is fairly long and notched. **Winter adult** has browner cheek, dark lores, and streaked crown showing some rufous color. **First-winter** bird is similar but averages less rufous on the crown; breast and sides are tinged with buff. In **juvenile** plumage, often held into Oct, especially in the West, underparts are prominently streaked; crown usually lacks rufous; rump may show slight streaking. **Song,** rapid trill of dry *chip* notes, all on one pitch. Flight **call,** also given perched, is a high, hard *seep* or *tsik*. **Range:** Widespread and common, Chipping Sparrows are found on lawns and in fields, woodland edges, and pine-oak forests.

Clay-colored Sparrow   *Spizella pallida*   L 5½" (14 cm)

Brown crown with black streaks and a distinct buffy white or whitish median crown stripe. Broad, whitish eyebrow; pale lores; brown cheek outlined by dark postocular and moustachial stripes; conspicuous pale submoustachial stripe. Nape gray; back and scapulars are buffy brown, with dark streaks; rump is not streaked but color does not contrast with back as in Chipping Sparrow. Adult in fall and winter is buffier overall. **Juvenile** and **immature** birds are much buffier; gray nape and pale stripe on sides of throat stand out more; in juvenile, breast and sides are streaked. **Song** is a brief series of insectlike buzzes. Flight **call** is a thin *sip*. **Range:** Fairly common in brushy fields, groves, and streamside thickets. Winters primarily from Mexico south, uncommonly in southern Texas. Rare in fall, casual in winter and spring on both coasts and in Arizona. Rare in winter in south Florida.

Brewer's Sparrow   *Spizella breweri*   L 5½" (14 cm)

Brown crown with fine black streaks, without clearly defined, pale median crown stripe of Clay-colored; head pattern lacks Clay-colored's strong contrast. Distinct whitish eye ring; grayish white eyebrow; ear patch pale brown with darker borders; pale lores; dark malar stripe. Upperparts buffy brown and streaked; rump buffy brown, may be lightly streaked. **Juvenile** is buffier overall, lightly streaked on breast and sides. Immature, and fall and winter adult, are somewhat buffy below. **Song** is a series of varied bubbling notes and buzzy trills at different pitches. **Call** is a thin *sip*, like call of Clay-colored Sparrow. Common; breeds in mountain meadows and sagebrush flats. A separate subspecies, *taverneri* (not shown) of the alpine zone of the Canadian Rockies to east-central Alaska, has a slightly different song and larger bill. Juveniles are heavily streaked with blackish below. Some believe that this "Timberline Sparrow" may be a separate species.

breeding

Chipping Sparrow
passerina

winter adult

juvenile

1st winter

immature

juvenile

breeding

Clay-colored Sparrow

juvenile

Brewer's Sparrow
breweri

Lark Sparrow *Chondestes grammacus* L 6½" (17 cm)
Head pattern distinctive in adults; note dark central breast spot.
Juvenile's colors are duller; breast, sides, and crown streaked. In
all ages, white-cornered tail is conspicuous in flight. **Song** begins
with two loud, clear notes, followed by a series of rich, melodious notes and trills and unmusical buzzes. **Call** is a sharp *tsip*,
often a rapid series. **Range:** Gregarious, found in various types
of open country, often along roads. Formerly bred as far east as
New York and Maryland; now rare in the East.

Black-chinned Sparrow *Spizella atrogularis*
L 5¾" (15 cm) Medium gray overall; back and scapulars rusty,
with black streaks; bill bright pink; long tail. **Male** has black lores
and chin; lower belly is whitish gray; long tail is all-dark. **Female**
has less or no black. **Juvenile** and winter birds lack any black on
face. Juveniles resemble female but show light streaks below.
Plaintive **song** begins with slow *sweet sweet sweet* and continues
in a rapid trill. **Call** is a high, thin *seep*. **Range:** Inhabits brushy
arid slopes in foothills and mountains. Rarely seen in migration.

Black-throated Sparrow *Amphispiza bilineata*
L 5½" (14 cm) Black lores and triangular black patch on throat
and breast contrast with white eyebrow, white submoustachial
stripe, white underparts. Upperparts plain brownish gray. **Juvenal** plumage, often held well into fall, lacks black on throat, but
note bold white eyebrow; breast and back finely streaked. In all
ages, extent of white on tail is greater than in Sage Sparrow. **Song**
is rapid, high-pitched: two clear notes followed by a trill; **calls**
are faint, tinkling notes. **Range:** Fairly common in desert, especially on rocky slopes; casual to eastern U.S. in fall and winter.

Five-striped Sparrow *Aimophila quinquestriata*
L 6" (15 cm) Dark brown above; breast and sides gray; white throat
bordered by black and white stripes. Dark central spot at base of
breast. Juvenile lacks the streaks found on juveniles of other sparrows. **Range:** West Mexican species; range barely reaches southeastern Arizona. Highly specialized habitat: tall, dense shrubs on
rocky, steep hillsides, and canyon slopes. Very local; most often seen
in breeding season; few winter records, but likely overlooked.

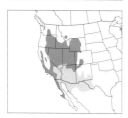

Sage Sparrow *Amphispiza belli* L 6¼" (16 cm)
White eye ring, white supraloral, broad white submoustachial
stripe bordered by dark malar stripe. Back buffy brown with dusky
streaks on interior (largest and palest) race *nevadensis*. Dark central breast spot, dusky streaking on sides. **Juvenile** is duller overall but more streaked. Smaller California coastal race, *belli*, is much
darker, lacks streaks on back, has stronger malar stripe. From a low
perch, male **sings** a geographically variable jumbled series of rising and falling phrases. Twittering **call** consists of thin, juncolike
notes. Runs on ground with tail cocked. **Range:** Interior *nevadensis* and slightly darker *canescens* favor alkaline flats in sagebrush,
saltbush. Coastal *belli* found in mountain chaparral. Ongoing studies may reveal that this complex represents two or three species.

Lark Sparrow
grammacus

juvenile

Black-chinned Sparrow

breeding ♀

breeding ♂

juvenile

Black-throated Sparrow
deserticola

juvenile

Five-striped Sparrow
septentrionalis

coastal
belli

Sage Sparrow

interior juvenile
nevadensis

interior
nevadensis

canescens

Grasshopper Sparrow *Ammodramus savannarum*

L 5" (13 cm) Buffy breast and sides, usually without obvious streaking. Small and chunky, with short tail and flat head. Dark crown has a pale central stripe; note also white eye ring and, on most birds, a yellow-orange spot in front of eye. Lacks broad buffy orange eyebrow and pale blue-gray ear patch of Le Conte's Sparrow (next page). Compare also with female Orange Bishop (page 464) and Savannah Sparrow (page 420). **Juvenile**'s breast and sides are streaked with brown. **Fall** birds are buffier below but never as bright as Le Conte's. Subspecies vary in overall color from dark Florida race, *floridanus* (**E**), to reddish *ammolegus* of southeastern Arizona. Eastern *pratensis* is slightly more richly colored than western *perpallidus,* which spreads east through the Great Plains. Typical **song** is one or two high chip notes followed by a brief, grasshopperlike *buzz;* also sings a series of varied squeaky and buzzy notes. **Range:** Found in pastures, grasslands, palmetto scrub, and old fields. Somewhat secretive; feeds and nests on the ground. Declining in East.

Baird's Sparrow *Ammodramus bairdii* L 5½" (14 cm)

Orange tinge to head (duller on worn summer birds), usually with less distinct median crown stripe than Savannah Sparrow (page 420); note especially the two isolated dark spots behind ear patch and lack of postocular line. Widely spaced, short dark streaks on breast form a distinct necklace; also shows chestnut on scapulars. **Juvenile**'s head is paler and creamier; central crown stripe is finely streaked; white fringes give a scaly appearance to upperparts; underparts are more extensively streaked. Very secretive, especially away from breeding grounds. **Song** consists of two or three high, thin notes, followed by a single warbled note and a low trill. **Range:** Uncommon, local, and declining. Found in grasslands and weedy fields. Casual east to Wisconsin and from coastal California. Accidental from East Coast and coastal Louisiana.

Henslow's Sparrow *Ammodramus henslowii*

L 5" (13 cm) Large flat head; large gray bill. Resembles Baird's Sparrow but head, nape, and most of central crown stripe are greenish; wings extensively dark chestnut. **Juvenile** is paler, yellower, with less streaking below; compare with adult Grasshopper Sparrow. Secretive, but after being flushed several times may perch in the open for a few minutes before dropping back into cover. Distinctive **song,** a short *se-lick,* accented on second syllable. **Range:** Uncommon, local, and declining; now occurs only casually in the Northeast; accidental to New Mexico (fall). Found in wet shrubby fields, weedy meadows, and reclaimed strip mines. In winter, found also in the understory of pine woods.

Grasshopper Sparrow

summer
perpallidus

floridanus

juvenile *pratensis*

fall *pratensis*

fall *ammolegus*

Orange Bishop ♀
for comparison

Baird's Sparrow

Henslow's Sparrow

juvenile

juvenile

Saltmarsh Sharp-tailed Sparrow

Ammodramus caudacutus L 5" (13 cm) Similar to Nelson's, but bill longer and head flatter; orange-buff face triangle contrasts strongly with paler, crisply streaked underparts. Also dark markings around eye and head are more sharply defined; eyebrow streaked with black behind eye. **Juvenile**'s crown is blacker than juvenile Nelson's; cheek darker; streaks below more widespread and distinct. **Song** softer, more complex than Nelson's, with which it hybridizes in Maine. With Nelson's Sharp-tailed Sparrow, formerly treated as one species, Sharp-tailed Sparrow.

Le Conte's Sparrow *Ammodramus leconteii L 5" (13 cm)*

White central crown stripe, becoming orange on forehead, chestnut streaks on nape, and straw-colored back streaks distinguish Le Conte's from sharp-tailed sparrows. Bright, broad, buffy orange eyebrow, grayish ear patch, thinner bill, and orange-buff breast and sides separate it from Grasshopper Sparrow (preceding page). Sides of breast and flanks have dark streaks. **Juvenal** plumage, seen on breeding grounds and in fall migration, is buffy; crown stripe tawny; breast heavily streaked. **Song** is a short, high, insect-like buzz. **Range:** A bird of wet grassy fields, marsh edges. Fairly common but secretive; scurries through matted grasses like a mouse. Casual migrant in the Northeast and in the West.

Nelson's Sharp-tailed Sparrow *Ammodramus nelsoni*

4¾" (12 cm) Distinguished from Le Conte's by gray median crown stripe; whitish or gray streaks on scapulars; gray, streakless nape. **Juvenile** has fainter median crown stripe; duller nape; variably thicker eye line; less contrast above; lacks streaking across breast. Plumage variable: *nelsoni*, of interior, has orange-buff triangle on face; streaked buffy breast contrasts with white belly; back strongly marked with black and white stripes; *subvirgatus*, of the Maritimes and coastal Maine, is duller overall; has diffuse streaking below; grayer upperparts. In *alterus* (not shown) from James and Hudson Bays, brightness is intermediate, streaks blurred. **Song,** a wheezy *p-tssssshh-uk*, ends on a lower note.

Seaside Sparrow *Ammodramus maritimus L 6" (15 cm)*

Long, spikelike bill with thick base, thin tip. Tail is short, pointed. Yellow supraloral patch. Dark malar stripe separates whitish throat and broad, pale stripe below cheek. Breast is white or buffy, with at least some streaking. **Juveniles** are duller, browner, than **adults.** Seaside Sparrows vary widely in overall color. Most races, like the widespread *maritimus,* are grayish olive above. The greener *mirabilis* (**E**), formerly called "Cape Sable Sparrow," inhabits a small area in southwestern Florida. Gulf Coast races such as *fisheri* have buffier breasts. The darkest race, *nigrescens,* formerly called "Dusky Seaside Sparrow," was found only near Titusville, Florida, and became extinct in June 1987. This subspecies was blackish above, heavily streaked below. Seaside Sparrow's **song** resembles that of Red-winged Blackbird but is buzzier. **Range:** Fairly common in grassy tidal marshes; accidental inland. Rare in Maine; very rare to the Maritimes.

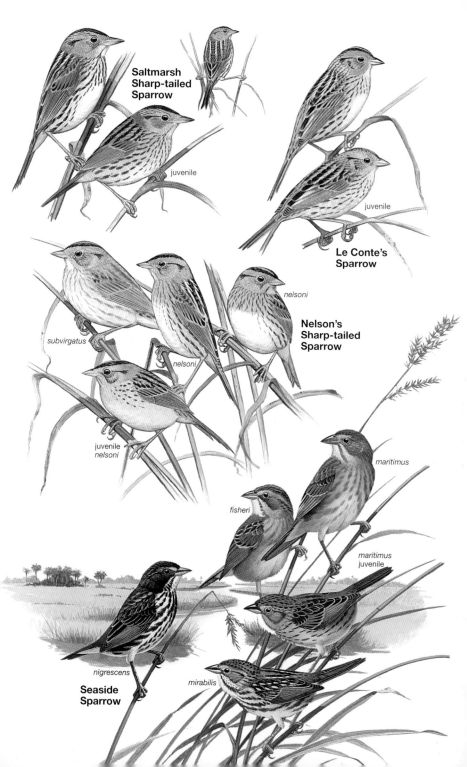

Saltmarsh Sharp-tailed Sparrow

juvenile

Le Conte's Sparrow

juvenile

subvirgatus

nelsoni

nelsoni

Nelson's Sharp-tailed Sparrow

juvenile nelsoni

maritimus

fisheri

maritimus juvenile

nigrescens

Seaside Sparrow

mirabilis

Fox Sparrow *Passerella iliaca L 7" (18 cm)*

Highly variable. Most subspecies have reddish rump and tail; reddish in wings; underparts heavily marked with triangular spots merging into a larger spot on central breast. The many named subspecies are divided into four subspecies groups; may represent distinct species. The brightest, *iliaca*, and slightly duller *zaboria* (**"Red"** group) breed in the far north, from Seward Peninsula, Alaska, to Newfoundland; winter in southeastern U.S. Western mountain races have gray head and back, grayish olive base to bill; range from small-billed Rockies *schistacea* (**"Slate-colored"** group) to large-billed California *stephensi* (**"Thick-billed"** group). Dark coastal races (**"Sooty"** group), with browner rumps and tails, vary from sooty *fuliginosa* of the Pacific Northwest to paler *unalaschcensis* of southwest Alaska. **Songs** are sweet, melodic in northern, "Red" group; include harsher trills in other races. Large-billed Pacific races give a sharp *chink* call, like California Towhee; others give a *tschup* note, like Lincoln's Sparrow but louder. **Range:** Uncommon to common; found in undergrowth in coniferous or deciduous woodlands and chaparral. Within "Sooty" group, paler northernmost races migrate the farthest south. The "Slate-colored" group migrates primarily southwest to California.

Lark Bunting *Calamospiza melanocorys L 7" (18 cm)*

Stocky, with short tail and whitish wing patches; bill bluish gray. **Breeding male** is mostly black. **Female** is streaked below, with buffy sides and brown primaries. **Winter male** is similar, but has black primaries; immature male darker, has some black around bill and chin. Distinctive **call** is a soft *hoo-ee*. **Song** is a varied series of rich whistles and trills. **Range:** Common; nests in dry plains and prairies, especially in sagebrush. Gregarious in migration and winter. In flight, looks short and round winged, with shallow wingbeats. Rare in fall and winter to West Coast; casual to Pacific Northwest and in the East.

Savannah Sparrow *Passerculus sandwichensis*

L 5½" (14 cm) Highly variable. Eyebrow yellow or whitish; pale median crown stripe; strong postocular stripe. **Song** begins with two or three chip notes, followed by two buzzy trills. Distinctive flight **call**, a thin *seep*. Common in a variety of open habitats, marshes, grasslands. The numerous subspecies vary geographically; extremes are shown here. West Coast races show increasingly darker color from north to south, with Alaskan and interior races paler, widespread *nevadensis* the palest; *beldingi* of southern California coastal marshes is darkest. The *rostratus* subspecies, **"Large-billed Sparrow,"** which winters on the edge of Salton Sea, rarely in coastal California, is very dull with a large bill. Its **song,** markedly different from other Savannah Sparrows, has short, high introductory notes, followed by about three rich, buzzy *dzeeee* notes; **call,** a soft, metallic *zink*. In the East, the degree of darkness is reversed: Arctic races are darker than more southerly Canadian and U.S. races. Large, pale *princeps*, **"Ipswich Sparrow,"** breeds on Sable Island, Nova Scotia; winters on East Coast beaches.

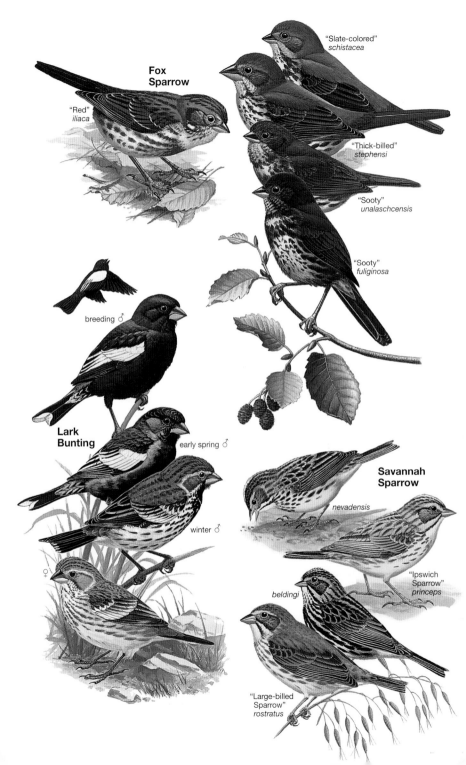

Fox Sparrow

"Red"
iliaca

"Slate-colored"
schistacea

"Thick-billed"
stephensi

"Sooty"
unalaschcensis

"Sooty"
fuliginosa

Lark Bunting

breeding ♂

early spring ♂

winter ♂

♀

Savannah Sparrow

nevadensis

"Ipswich Sparrow"
princeps

beldingi

"Large-billed Sparrow"
rostratus

Lincoln's Sparrow *Melospiza lincolnii L 5¾" (15 cm)*

Buffy wash and fine streaks on breast and sides, contrasting with whitish, unstreaked belly. Note broad gray eyebrow, whitish chin and eye ring. Briefly held **juvenal** plumage is paler overall than juvenile Swamp Sparrow. Distinguished from juvenile Song Sparrow by shorter tail, slimmer bill, and thinner malar stripe, often broken. Often raises slight crest when disturbed. Two **call** notes: a flat *tschup*, repeated in a series as an alarm call; and a sharp, buzzy *zeee*. Rich, loud **song,** a rapid, bubbling trill. Found in brushy bogs and mountain meadows; in winter prefers thickets.

Song Sparrow *Melospiza melodia L 4¾-6¾" (13-17 cm)*

All subspecies have long, rounded tail, pumped in flight. All show broad grayish eyebrow and broad, dark malar stripe bordering whitish throat. Highly variable. Upperparts are usually streaked. Underparts whitish, with streaking on sides and breast that often converges in a central spot. Legs and feet are pinkish. **Juvenile** is buffier overall, with finer streaking. Typical **song** has three or four short clear notes followed by a buzzy *tow-wee,* then a trill. Distinctive **call** note is a nasal, hollow *chimp.* The numerous subspecies vary geographically in size, bill shape, overall coloration, and streaking. Eastern races typified by *melodia;* large Alaskan races, the largest resident on the Aleutians, reach an extreme in the gray-brown *maxima;* paler races such as *saltonis* inhabit southwestern deserts; *morphna* represents the darker, redder races of the Pacific Northwest; *heermanni* is one of the blackish-streaked California races. **Range:** Generally common, Song Sparrows are found in brushy areas, especially dense streamside thickets.

Vesper Sparrow *Pooecetes gramineus L 6¼" (16 cm)*

White eye ring; dark ear patch bordered in white along lower and rear edges; white outer tail feathers. Lacks bold eyebrow of Savannah Sparrow (preceding page). Distinctive chestnut lesser coverts not easily seen. Eastern nominate race is slightly darker overall than the widespread subspecies, *confinis.* **Song** is rich and melodious: two long, slurred notes followed by two higher notes, then a series of short, descending trills. **Range:** Uncommon to fairly common in dry grasslands, farmlands, forest clearings, and sagebrush; declining in the East.

Swamp Sparrow *Melospiza georgiana L 5¾" (15 cm)*

Gray face; rich rufous upperparts and wings; variable black streaks on back; white throat. **Breeding adult** has reddish crown, gray breast, and whitish belly. **Winter adult** is buffier overall; crown is streaked, shows gray central stripe; sides are rich buff. Briefly held **juvenal** plumage is usually even buffier; darker overall than juvenile Lincoln's or Song Sparrow; wings and tail redder. **Immature** resembles winter adult. Typical **song** is a slow, musical trill, all on one pitch. Two **call** notes: a prolonged *zeee,* softer than Lincoln's Sparrow, and an Eastern Phoebe-like *chip.* **Range:** Nests in dense, tall vegetation in marshes and bogs. Winters in marshes and brushy fields. Generally rare in the West.

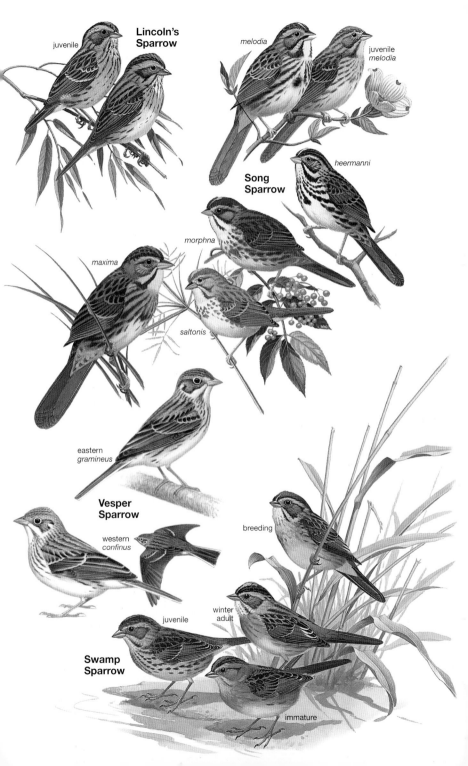

Lincoln's Sparrow

juvenile

melodia

juvenile *melodia*

Song Sparrow

heermanni

morphna

maxima

saltonis

eastern *gramineus*

Vesper Sparrow

western *confinus*

breeding

juvenile

winter adult

Swamp Sparrow

immature

Harris's Sparrow *Zonotrichia querula* L 7½" (19 cm)

A large sparrow with black crown, face, and bib; pink bill. **Winter adult**'s crown is blackish; cheeks buffy; throat may be all-black or show white flecks or partial white band. **Immature** resembles winter adult but shows less black; white throat is bordered by dark malar stripe. **Song** is a series of long, clear, quavering whistles, often beginning with two notes on one pitch followed by two notes on another pitch. **Calls** include a loud *wink* and a drawn-out *tseep.* **Range:** Fairly common; nests in stunted boreal forest; winters in open woodlands and brushlands. Rare to casual in winter in rest of North America outside mapped range.

White-throated Sparrow *Zonotrichia albicollis*

L 6¾" (17 cm) Conspicuous and strongly outlined white throat; mostly dark bill; dark crown stripes and eye line. Broad eyebrow is yellow in front of eye; remainder is either white or tan. Upperparts rusty brown; underparts grayish, sometimes with diffuse streaking. **Juvenile**'s eyebrow and throat are grayish, breast and sides heavily streaked. **Song** is a thin whistle, generally two single notes followed by three triple notes: *pure sweet Canada Canada Canada*, often heard in winter. **Calls** include a sharp *pink* and a drawn-out, lisping *tseep.* **Range:** Common in woodland undergrowth, brush, and gardens. Generally rare in the West.

White-crowned Sparrow *Zonotrichia leucophrys*

L 7" (18 cm) Black-and-white striped crown; pink, orange, or yellowish bill; whitish throat; underparts mostly gray. **Juvenile**'s head is brown and buff, underparts streaked. **Immature** has tan and brownish head stripes; compare with immature Golden-crowned Sparrow. Nominate race *leucophrys,* mainly found in the east Canadian tundra, and *oriantha* (not shown), of the High Sierra, southern Cascades, and Rockies, have a black supraloral area and large, dark pink bill; *gambelii,* found from Alaska to Hudson Bay, has whitish supraloral and a smaller, orange-yellow bill; in coastal *nuttalli* and *pugetensis* (not shown), breast and back are browner, bill dull yellow, supraloral pale. **Song,** often heard in winter, is usually one or more thin, whistled notes followed by a twittering trill; *leucophrys* and *gambelii* give a more mournful song with no trill at the end. **Calls** include a loud *pink* and sharp *tseep.* **Range:** Generally common in woodlands, grasslands, and roadside hedges.

Golden-crowned Sparrow *Zonotrichia atricapilla*

L 7" (18 cm) Yellow patch tops black crown; back brownish, streaked with dark brown; breast, sides and flanks grayish brown. Bill is dusky above, pale below. Yellow is less distinct on **immature**'s brown crown. Briefly held **juvenal** plumage has dark streaks on breast and sides. **Winter adults** are duller overall; amount of black on crown varies. **Song** is a series of three or more plaintive, whistled notes: *oh dear me.* **Calls** include a soft *tseep* and a flat *tsick.* **Range:** Fairly common in stunted boreal bogs and in open areas near tree line, especially in willows. Winters in dense woodlands, tangles, and brush; casual in East.

breeding

winter adults

Harris's Sparrow

immature

White-throated Sparrow

tan-striped morph

white-striped morph

juvenile

adult *gambelii*

juvenile *gambelii*

adult *leucophrys*

adult *nuttalli*

White-crowned Sparrow

immature *leucophrys*

Golden-crowned Sparrow

juvenile

immature

breeding

winter adult

Dark-eyed Junco *Junco hyemalis* L 6¼" (16 cm)
Variable; most races have a gray or brown head and breast sharply set off from white belly. White outer tail feathers are conspicuous in flight. **Male** of the widespread **"Slate-colored Junco"** group of subspecies has a dark gray hood; upperparts are entirely gray or have varying amount of brown at center of back. **Female** is brownish gray overall. **Juveniles** of all races are streaked. "Slate-colored" winters mostly in eastern North America; uncommon in the West. Male **"Oregon Junco"** of the West has slaty to blackish hood, rufous-brown to buffy brown back and sides; females have duller hood color. Of the eight subspecies in the "Oregon" group (two are resident in northern Baja California), the more southerly races are paler. "Oregon" types winter mainly in the West; very rare during winter in the East. **"Pink-sided Junco,"** *mearnsi* (considered within "Oregon" group)—breeding in the central Rockies and wintering from western Great Plains to the foothills of the Southwest and northern Mexico, rarely to southern California—has very broad, bright pinkish cinnamon sides that sometimes meet across the breast, blue-gray hood, and blackish lores. The **"White-winged Junco"** race, *aikeni*—breeding in the Black Hills area and wintering largely in the Front Range south to north-central New Mexico, rarely on Great Plains and casually to Southwest and California—is mostly pale gray above, usually with two thin, white wing bars; also larger, with a bigger bill and more white on tail. In the **"Gray-headed Junco"** of the southern Rockies, the pale gray hood is barely darker than the underparts; back is rufous. It winters on the western Great Plains and in the foothills of the Southwest and northern Mexico, rarely to California; accidental in Midwest. In much of Arizona and New Mexico, largely resident "Gray-headed," *dorsalis,* has an even paler throat and a large, bicolored bill, black above and bluish below. Intergrades between some races are frequent. Dark-eyed Junco's **song** is a musical trill on one pitch, often heard in winter. Varied **calls** include a sharp *dit* and, in flight, a rapid twittering. Some songs and calls of "Gray-headed" *dorsalis* are more suggestive of Yellow-eyed Junco. **Range:** Breeds in coniferous or mixed woodlands. In migration and winter, found in a wide variety of habitats.

Yellow-eyed Junco *Junco phaeonotus* L 6¼" (16 cm)
Bright yellow eyes, set off by black lores. Pale gray above, with a bright rufous back and rufous-edged greater wing coverts and tertials; underparts paler gray. **Juveniles** are similar to juveniles of gray-headed races of Dark-eyed Junco; eye is brown, becoming pale before changing to yellow of adult; look for rufous on wings. **Song** is a variable series of clear, thin whistles and trills. **Calls** include a high, thin *seep,* similar to call of Chipping Sparrow. **Range:** Yellow-eyed Junco is found on coniferous and pine-oak slopes, generally above 6,000 feet. Resident within its range. Some move to lower altitude in winter.

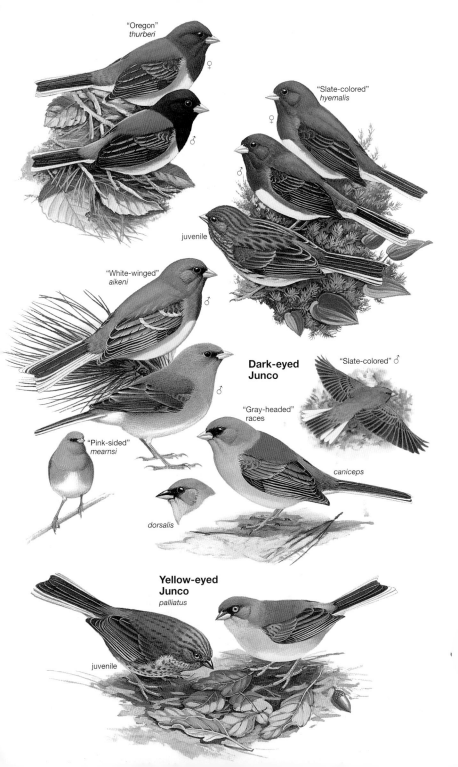

"Oregon"
thurberi
♀

♂

"Slate-colored"
hyemalis
♀

♂

juvenile

"White-winged"
aikeni
♂

**Dark-eyed
Junco**

"Slate-colored" ♂

♂

"Gray-headed"
races

"Pink-sided"
mearnsi

caniceps

dorsalis

**Yellow-eyed
Junco**
palliatus

juvenile

Chestnut-collared Longspur *Calcarius ornatus*

L 6" (15 cm) White tail marked with blackish triangle. Very short primary projection; primary tips barely extend to base of tail. **Breeding adult male**'s black-and-white head, buffy face, and black underparts are distinctive; a few have chestnut on underparts. Lower belly and undertail coverts whitish. Upperparts black, buff, and brown, with chestnut collar, whitish wing bars. **Winter males** are paler; feathers edged in buff and brown, obscuring black underparts. Male has small white patch on shoulder, often hidden; compare with Smith's Longspur (next page). Breeding adult female resembles **winter female** but is darker, usually shows some chestnut on nape. Juvenile's pale feather fringes give upperparts a scaled look; tail pattern and bill shape distinguish juvenile from juvenile McCown's Longspur. Fall and winter birds have grayer bills than McCown's. **Song,** heard only on breeding grounds, is a pleasant rapid warble, given in song flight or from a low perch. Distinctive **call,** a two-syllable *kittle,* repeated one or more times. Also gives a soft, high-pitched rattle and a short *buzz* call. **Range:** Fairly common; nests in moist upland prairies. Somewhat shy; generally found in dense grass; gregarious in fall and winter. Casual during migration to eastern North America and Pacific Northwest; more regularly to California.

McCown's Longspur *Calcarius mccownii L 6" (15 cm)*

White tail marked by dark inverted-T shape. Note also stouter, thicker-based bill than bills of other longspurs. Primary projection slightly longer than in Chestnut-collared Longspur; in perched bird, wings extend almost to tip of short tail. **Breeding adult male** has black crown, black malar stripe, black crescent on breast; gray sides. Upperparts streaked with buff and brown, with gray nape, gray rump; chestnut median coverts form contrasting crescent. **Breeding adult female** has streaked crown; may lack black on breast and show less chestnut on wing. In **winter adults,** bill is pinkish with dark tip; feathers are edged with buff and brown. Winter adult female is paler than female Chestnut-collared, with fewer streaks on underparts and a broader buffy eyebrow. Some winter males have gray on rump; variable blackish on breast; retain chestnut median coverts. **Juvenile** is streaked below; pale fringes on feathers give upperparts a scaled look; paler overall than juvenile Chestnut-collared. **Song,** heard only on breeding grounds, is a series of exuberant warbles and twitters, generally given in song flight. **Calls** include a dry rattle, a little softer and more abrupt than Lapland Longspur; also gives single finchlike notes. **Range:** Locally fairly common but range has shrunk significantly since the 19th century. Nests in dry shortgrass plains; in winter, also found in plowed fields and dry lake beds, often amid large flocks of Horned Larks. Look for McCown's chunkier, shorter-tailed shape, slightly darker plumage, mostly white tail, thicker bill, and undulating flight. Very rare visitor to interior California, Nevada. Casual in coastal California and southern Oregon; accidental to the East Coast.

breeding males

Chestnut-collared Longspur

winter ♂

winter ♀

McCown's Longspur

breeding ♂

breeding ♀

winter ♀

winter ♂

juvenile

Smith's Longspur   *Calcarius pictus   L 6¼" (16 cm)*

Outer two feathers on each side of tail are almost entirely white. Bill is thinner than in other longspurs. Note long primary projection, a bit shorter than Lapland, but much longer than Chesnut-collared or McCown's (preceding page); shows rusty edges to greater coverts and tertials. **Breeding adult male** has black-and-white head, rich buff nape and underparts; white patch on shoulder, often obscured. **Breeding adult female** and all **winter** plumages are duller, crown streaked, chin paler. Dusky ear patch bordered by pale buff eyebrow; pale area on side of neck often breaks through dark rear edge of ear patch. Underparts are pale buff with thin reddish brown streaks on breast and sides. Females have much less white on lesser coverts than males. Typical **call** is a dry, ticking rattle, harder and sharper than call of Lapland and McCown's Longspurs. **Song,** heard in spring migration and on the breeding grounds, is delivered only from the ground or a perch. It consists of rapid, melodious warbles, ending with a vigorous *wee-chew.* **Range:** Generally uncommon and secretive, especially in migration and winter. Nests on open tundra and damp, tussocky meadows. Winters in open, grassy areas; sometimes seen with Lapland Longspurs. Regular spring migrant in the Midwest, east to western Indiana. Casual vagrant to East Coast from Massachusetts to South Carolina, and to California.

Lapland Longspur   *Calcarius lapponicus   L 6¼" (16 cm)*

Outer two feathers on each side of tail are partly white, partly dark. Note also, especially in winter plumages, the reddish edges on the greater coverts and on the tertials. The reddish edges of the tertials form an indented, or notched, shape. **Breeding adult male**'s head and breast are black and well outlined: a broad white or buffy stripe extends back from eye and down to sides of breast; nape is reddish brown. **Breeding adult female** and all **winter** plumages are duller; note bold dark triangle outlining plain buffy ear patch; dark streaks (female) or patch (male) on upper breast; dark streaks on side. On all winter birds, note broad buffy eyebrow and buffier underparts; belly and undertail are white, unlike Smith's Longspur; also compare head and wing patterns. **Juvenile** is yellowish and heavily streaked above and on breast and sides. **Song,** heard only on the breeding grounds, is a rapid warbling, frequently given in short flights. **Calls** include a musical *tee-lee-oo* or *tee-dle* and, in flight, a dry rattle distinctively mixed with whistled *tew* notes. **Range:** Fairly common, Lapland Longspurs breed on Arctic tundra, winter in grassy fields, grain stubble, and on shores. Often found amid flocks of Horned Larks and Snow Buntings; look for Lapland's darker overall coloring and smaller size.

Smith's Longspur

breeding ♂

breeding ♀

winter ♂

breeding ♂

breeding ♀

Lapland Longspur

winter ♂

winter ♀

juvenile

buffy fall ♀

Snow Bunting   *Plectrophenax nivalis   L 6¾" (17 cm)*

Black-and-white breeding plumage acquired by end of spring by wear. Bill is black in summer, orange-yellow in winter. In all seasons, note long black-and-white wings. **Males** usually show more white overall than **females,** especially in the wings. **Juvenile** is grayish and streaked, with buffy eye ring; very similar to juvenile McKay's Bunting. First-winter plumage, acquired before migration, is darker overall than adult. **Calls** include a sharp, whistled *tew;* a short buzz; and a musical rattle or twitter. **Song,** heard only on the breeding grounds, is a loud, high-pitched musical warbling. **Range:** Fairly common; breeds on tundra, rocky shores, and talus slopes. During migration and winter, found on shores, especially sand dunes and beaches, in weedy fields and grain stubble, and along roadsides, often in large flocks that may include Lapland Longspurs and Horned Larks.

McKay's Bunting   *Plectrophenax hyperboreus*
L 6¾" (17 cm) **Adult breeding** plumage mostly white, with less black on wings and tail than Snow Bunting; **female** shows a white panel on greater coverts. **Winter** plumage is edged with rust or tawny brown, but male is whiter overall than Snow Bunting; female very similar to male Snow Bunting. Juvenile is buffy gray and streaked, with gray head, prominent buffy eye ring; very similar to juvenile Snow Bunting. **Calls** and **song** similar to Snow Bunting. **Range:** McKay's is known to breed only on Hall and St. Matthew Islands in the Bering Sea. A few sometimes present in late spring on St. Lawrence Island; summer rarely on Pribilofs. Rare to uncommon in winter along west coast of Alaska; casual in winter south on coast to Oregon, in interior of Alaska and on Aleutians. Some authorities think McKay's may be a subspecies of Snow Bunting.

Yellow-breasted Bunting   *Emberiza aureola*
L 6" (15 cm) **Range:** A declining, mostly Asian species; casual to Alaska, mostly on western Aleutians. Has the white outer tail feathers characteristic of most *Emberiza* buntings. **Breeding male** has rufous-brown upperparts, bright yellow underparts, white patch on lesser and median wing coverts. East Asian race, *ornata,* which has reached Alaska, has black on forehead and base of breast band. Winter adult male usually shows features of breeding plumage. **Female** and immatures have striking head pattern with median crown stripe; ear patches with dark border and pale spot in rear; yellowish underparts with sparse streaking; unmarked belly. **Call** is a *tzip,* similar to Little Bunting.

Gray Bunting   *Emberiza variabilis   L 6¾" (17 cm)*
Range: Asian species, casual spring vagrant on western Aleutians. A large, heavy-billed bunting; shows no white in tail. **Breeding male** is gray overall, prominently streaked with blackish above. Winter males are a bit browner above, paler below. **Adult female** is brown; chestnut rump is conspicuous in flight. **Immature male** resembles adult female above but is mostly gray below with some gray on the head; immature plumage is largely held through first spring. **Call** is a sharp *zhii.*

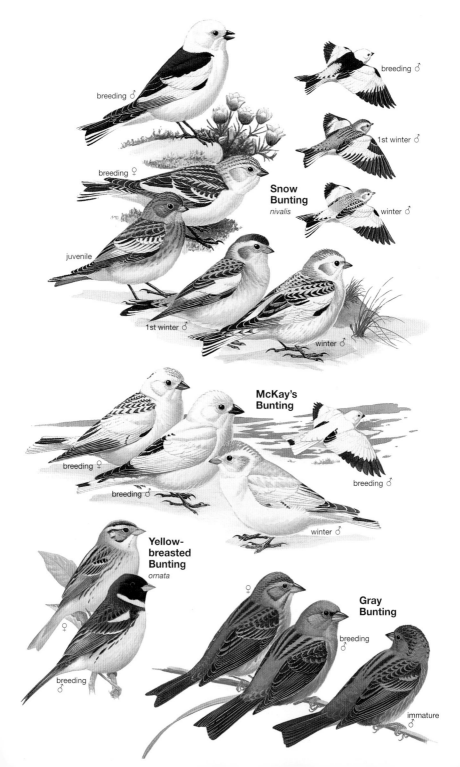

breeding ♂

breeding ♂

1st winter ♂

Snow Bunting
nivalis

breeding ♀

winter ♂

juvenile

1st winter ♂

winter ♂

McKay's Bunting

breeding ♀

breeding ♂

breeding ♂

winter ♂

Yellow-breasted Bunting
ornata

♀

breeding ♂

♀

breeding ♂

Gray Bunting

immature

Reed Bunting *Emberiza schoeniclus L 6" (15 cm)*
Range: Eurasian species, casual vagrant on westernmost Aleutians in late spring; one fall record on St. Lawrence Island. All records are of pale East Asian *pyrrhulina,* which resembles Pallas's Bunting in female and winter plumages. Reed Bunting has solid chestnut lesser wing coverts. Note also heavy, gray bill with curved culmen; cinnamon wing bars; dark lateral crown stripes, paler median crown stripe. **Breeding male** has black head and throat, a broad white submoustachial stripe, and white nape; upperparts streaked black and rust; rump gray. Underparts white with thin reddish streaks along sides and flanks. **Female** has pale brownish rump, broad buffy white eyebrow; compare with female Pallas's. **Fall male** resembles female Reed, but shows black on throat and a more distinct collar. Active and conspicuous, Reed Bunting often flicks its tail, showing white outer tail feathers. **Calls,** a *seeoo,* falling in pitch; flight note, a hoarse *brzee.*

Pallas's Bunting *Emberiza pallasi L 5" (13 cm)*
Range: Asian species, accidental spring vagrant at Point Barrow, Alaska; St. Lawrence Island; western Aleutians. Compare with Reed Bunting. Note Pallas's smaller size, smaller two-toned bill with straighter culmen (except **breeding male,** which has black bill); grayish lesser wing coverts; less rufous wing bars; shorter tail. **Female** has more indistinct eyebrow and lateral crown stripes than female Reed; lacks median crown stripe. **Call,** a *cheeep,* recalling Eurasian Tree Sparrow, very unlike Reed's call.

Little Bunting *Emberiza pusilla L 5" (13 cm)*
Range: Eurasian species, very rare in fall to St. Lawrence Island. Casual on western Aleutians and in California. Small, with short legs, short tail, a small triangular bill, bold creamy white eye ring, chestnut ear patch, and two thin, pale wing bars. Underparts whitish and heavily streaked; outer tail feathers white. In **breeding** plumage, shows chestnut crown stripe bordered by black stripes. Many **males** have chestnut on chin. **Immatures** and winter adults have chestnut crown, tipped and streaked with buff and black; compare especially with female Rustic and Reed Buntings. **Call** note is a sharp *tsick.*

Rustic Bunting *Emberiza rustica L 5¾" (15 cm)*
Range: Eurasian species; uncommon spring migrant on western and central Aleutians, rare in fall; very rare on other islands in Bering Sea; casual elsewhere from West Coast. Has a slight crest, whitish nape spot, and prominent pale line extending back from eye. **Male** has black head; upperparts bright chestnut with buff and blackish streaks on back; outer tail feathers white. Underparts are white, with chestnut breast band and streaks on sides. **Female** and fall and winter males have brownish head pattern, with pale spot at rear of ear patch. Female may be confused with Little Bunting; note Rustic's larger size, heavier bill with pink lower mandible, diffuse rusty streaking below, and lack of eye ring. **Call** note is a hard, sharp *jit* or *tsip.* **Song,** a soft, bubbling warble.

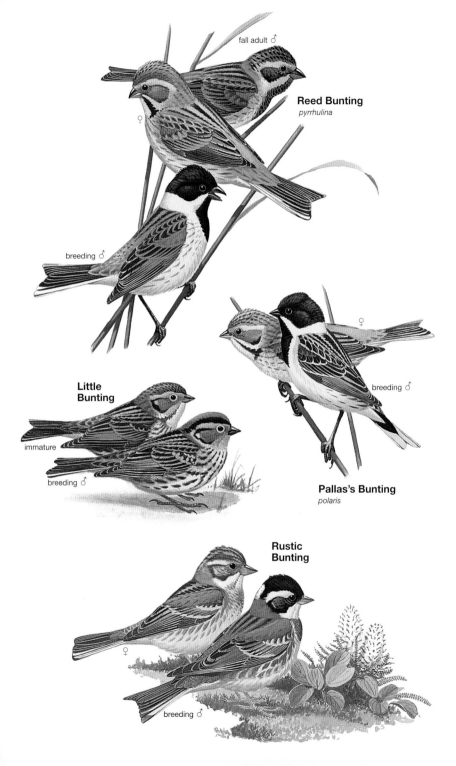

fall adult ♂

Reed Bunting
pyrrhulina

♀

breeding ♂

♀

breeding ♂

**Little
Bunting**

immature

breeding ♂

Pallas's Bunting
polaris

**Rustic
Bunting**

♀

breeding ♂

Cardinals, Saltators, Allies
(Family Cardinalidae)

In North America, these seedeaters include Northern Cardinal, certain grosbeaks, the *Passerina* and other buntings, and Dickcissel. *Species: 42 World; 13 N.A.*

Rose-breasted Grosbeak *Pheucticus ludovicianus*
L 8" (20 cm) Large size; very large, triangular bill; upper mandible paler than Black-headed Grosbeak. **Breeding male** has rose red breast, white underparts, white wing bars, white rump. Rose red wing linings show in flight. Brown-tipped **winter** plumage is acquired before migration. **Female**'s streaked plumage and yellow wing linings resemble female Black-headed, but underparts are more heavily and extensively streaked. Similar **first-fall male** is buffier above, with buffy wash across breast; often has a few red feathers on breast; red wing linings distinctive. Rich, warbled **songs** of both species are nearly identical. Rose-breasted's **call,** a sharp *eek,* is squeakier than Black-headed's. **Range:** Common in wooded habitat along watercourses. Rare throughout West in migration.

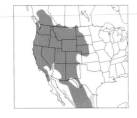

Black-headed Grosbeak *Pheucticus melanocephalus*
L 8¼" (21 cm) Large, with a very large, triangular bill, upper mandible darker than in Rose-breasted Grosbeak. **Male** has cinnamon underparts, all-black head. In flight, both sexes show yellow wing linings. **Female** plumage is generally buffier above and below than female Rose-breasted, with less streaking below. **First-fall male** Black-headed is rich buff below, with little or no streaking. **Songs** and **calls** of the two species are nearly identical, but Black-headed's call is lower-pitched. **Range:** Common in open woodlands and forest edges. Casual during migration and winter to the Midwest and East. Black-headed hybridizes occasionally with Rose-breasted in range of overlap on the Great Plains.

Crimson-collared Grosbeak *Rhodothraupis celaeno*
L 8½" (22 cm) **Range:** Endemic to northeast Mexico; casual to south Texas, mainly in winter. Stubby, mostly black bill; long tail; black on head variable. **Adult male** collar and much of underparts an intense shade of red; upperparts darker. **Adult female** is olive above; has thin yellowish wing bars; yellow-green rear collar; yellowish olive underparts. Immatures show less black than female; male shows some red and black patches by first spring. Often skulks on or near ground; often raises rear crown feathers. **Song,** a variable warble; **call,** a penetrating, rising and falling *seeiyu.*

Yellow Grosbeak *Pheucticus chrysopeplus* *L 9¼" (24 cm)*
Range: Mexican species, casual vagrant to southeastern Arizona in late spring to early summer, chiefly in open woodlands and river courses of low mountains. **Male** distinguished by large size, massive bill, yellow plumage. **Females** similar to male but duller; crown streaked; immature male has yellower head than female; like adult male by second fall. Compare with Evening Grosbeak (page 462). **Call** and **song** are like Black-headed's.

Rose-breasted Grosbeak

breeding adult ♂

winter adult ♂

breeding adult ♂

1st fall ♂

1st spring ♂

♀

Black-headed Grosbeak

♀

breeding adult ♂

1st fall ♂

adult ♀

adult ♂

Crimson-collared Grosbeak

adult ♂

adult ♀

Yellow Grosbeak

Northern Cardinal *Cardinalis cardinalis* L 8¾" (22 cm)

Conspicuous crest; cone-shaped reddish bill. **Male** is red overall, with black face. **Female** is buffy brown or buffy olive, tinged with red on wings, crest, and tail. **Juvenile** browner overall, dusky bill; juvenile female lacks red tones. Bill shape helps distinguish female and juveniles from similar Pyrrhuloxia. **Song** is a loud, liquid whistling with many variations, including *cue cue cue* and *cheer cheer cheer* and *purty purty purty*. Both sexes sing almost year-round. Common **call** is a sharp *chip*. **Range:** Abundant throughout the East, inhabits woodland edges, swamps, streamside thickets, and suburban gardens. Nonmigratory, but this species has expanded its range northward during the 20th century.

Pyrrhuloxia *Cardinalis sinuatus* L 8¾" (22 cm)

Thick, strongly curved, pale bill helps distinguish this species from female and juvenile Northern Cardinal. **Male** is gray over-all, with red on face, crest, wings, tail, and underparts. **Female** shows little or no red. **Song** is a liquid whistle, thinner and shorter than Northern Cardinal's; **call** is a sharper *chink*. **Range:** Fairly common in thorny brush, mesquite thickets, desert, woodland edges, and ranchlands. Casual to southern California.

Dickcissel *Spiza americana* L 6¼" (16 cm)

Yellowish eyebrow, thick bill, and chestnut wing coverts are distinctive. **Breeding male** has black bib under white chin, bright yellow breast. **Female** lacks black bib, but has some yellow on breast; chestnut wing patch muted. **Winter adult male**'s bib is less distinct. **Immatures** are duller overall than adults, breast and flanks lightly streaked; female may show almost no yellow or chestnut. The Dickcissel's common **call,** often given in flight, is a distinctive electric-buzzer *bzrrrrt*. **Song,** a variable *dick dick dickcissel*. **Range:** Breeds in open weedy meadows, grainfields, and prairies. Abundant and gregarious, especially in migration, but numbers and distribution vary locally from year to year outside core breeding range. Irregular east of the Appalachians; occasional breeding is reported outside mapped range. Rare migrant to both coasts; more common in the East, where a few winter.

Blue Grosbeak *Passerina caerulea* L 6¾" (17 cm)

Wide chestnut wing bars, large heavy bill, and larger overall size distinguish **male** from male Indigo Bunting (next page). **Females** of these two species also similar; compare bill shape, wing bars, and overall size. Juvenile resembles female; in first fall, some **immatures** are richer brown than female. **First-spring male** shows some blue above and below; resembles adult male by second winter. In poor light, Blue Grosbeak resembles Brown-headed Cowbird (page 448); note Blue Grosbeak's bill shape and wing bars; also the habit of twitching and spreading its tail. Listen for distinctive **call,** a loud, explosive *chink*. **Song** is a series of rich, rising and falling warbles. **Range:** Fairly common; found in low, overgrown fields, streamsides, woodland edges, and brushy roadsides. Uncommon to rare in fall north to New England and the Maritime Provinces.

Northern Cardinal
cardinalis

♂

♀

juvenile ♂

Pyrrhuloxia
fulvescens

♀

♂

Dickcissel

breeding ♂

breeding ♀

winter adult ♂

immature ♀

immature ♂

Blue Grosbeak
caerulea

breeding adult ♂

♀

immature

1st spring ♂

Indigo Bunting *Passerina cyanea L 5½" (14 cm)*

Breeding male deep blue. Smaller than Blue Grosbeak (preceding page); bill much smaller; lacks wing bars. In **winter** plumage, blue is obscured by brown and buff edges. Female is brownish, with diffuse streaking on breast and flanks. Young birds resemble female. **Song,** a series of varied phrases, usually paired. **Range:** Common in woodland clearings and borders. Uncommon to rare to Maritimes and Newfoundland; rare to Pacific states.

Lazuli Bunting *Passerina amoena L 5½" (14 cm)*

Adult male bright turquoise above and on throat; cinnamon across breast; thick white upper wing bars. **Female** is grayish brown above, rump grayish blue; whitish underparts with buffy wash across breast. Juveniles resemble female but have distinct fine streaks across breast; immature male is mostly blue by **first spring.** Winter adult male's blue color is obscured by brown and buff edges. **Song** is a series of varied phrases, sometimes paired; faster and less strident than Indigo Bunting's song. **Range:** Found in open deciduous or mixed woodlands and chaparral, especially in brushy areas near water. Occasionally hybridizes with Indigo.

Painted Bunting *Passerina ciris L 5½" (14 cm)*

Adult male's gaudy colors are retained year-round. **Female** is bright green above, paler yellow-green below. **Juvenile** is much drabber; look for telltale hints of green above, yellow below. Fall molt in eastern nominate race takes place on breeding grounds; western *pallidior* molts on winter grounds. First-winter male resembles adult female; by spring, may show tinge of blue on head, red on breast. **Song** is a rapid series of varied phrases, thinner and sweeter than song of Indigo Bunting. **Call** is a loud, rich *chip.* **Range:** Locally common in low thickets, streamside brush, and woodland borders. Casual vagrant north on Atlantic coast to New York; west to Midwest, California. Declining in Southeast.

Varied Bunting *Passerina versicolor L 5½" (14 cm)*

Breeding male's plumage is colorful in good light; otherwise appears black. In **winter,** colors are edged with brown. **Female** is plain gray-brown or buffy brown above, slightly paler below; resembles female Indigo Bunting but lacks streaks and all wing markings; note also that Varied Bunting's culmen is slightly more curved. First-spring male resembles female. **Song** is similar to song of Painted Bunting. **Range:** Locally common in thorny thickets in washes and canyons, often near water.

Blue Bunting *Cyanocompsa parellina L 5½" (14 cm)*

Range: Tropical species, very rare and irregular winter visitor to southern Texas. Smaller than Blue Grosbeak; lacks wing bars. Found in brushy fields and woodland edges. **Adult male** is blackish blue overall, paler blue on crown, cheeks, shoulder, and rump. Immature male similar, but with brownish cast to wings. Contrasting colors and thick, strongly curved bill distinguish male from male Indigo Bunting. separated by female Blue Bunting's richer, uniform color, and lack of streaking below.

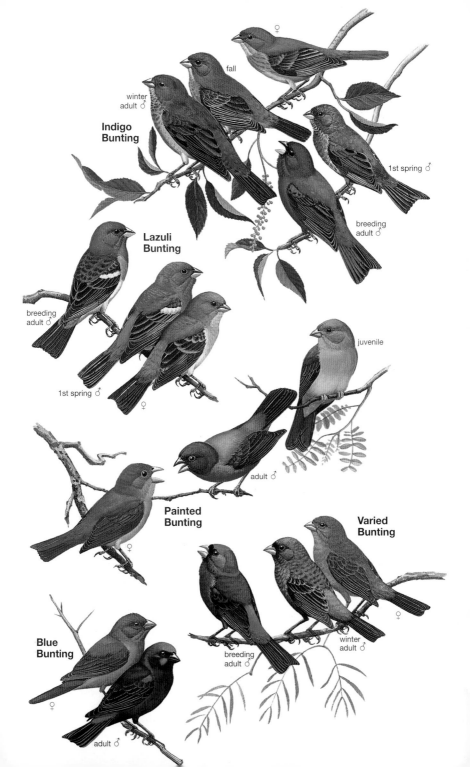

Indigo Bunting

winter adult ♂

fall

♀

1st spring ♂

breeding adult ♂

Lazuli Bunting

breeding adult ♂

1st spring ♂

♀

juvenile

adult ♂

Painted Bunting

Varied Bunting

♀

Blue Bunting

♀

breeding adult ♂

winter adult ♂

adult ♂

Blackbirds (Family Icteridae)

Strong, direct flight and pointed bills mark this diverse group.
Species: 98 World; 25 N.A.

Bobolink *Dolichonyx oryzivorus L 7" (18 cm)*
Breeding male entirely black below; hindneck is buff, fading to whitish by midsummer; scapulars and rump white. Male in **spring** migration shows pale edgings. **Breeding female** is buffy overall, with dark streaks on back, rump, and sides; head is striped with dark brown. Juvenile resembles female, but lacks streaking below; has indistinct spotting on throat and upper breast. All **fall** birds resemble female, but are rich yellow-buff below—especially, on average, the immatures. In all plumages, note sharply pointed tail feathers. Bobolinks nest primarily in hayfields, weedy meadows, where male's loud, bubbling *bob-o-link* **song**, often given in flight, is heard in spring and summer. Flight **call** heard year-round is a repeated, whistled *ink*. **Range:** Most birds migrate east of the Great Plains. Rare in fall on West Coast.

Eastern Meadowlark *Sturnella magna L 9½" (24 cm)*
Black V-shaped breast band on yellow underparts is characteristic of both meadowlark species after post-juvenal molt. In fresh **fall** plumage, birds are more richly colored overall, with partly veiled breast band and rich buffy flanks. On Eastern females, yellow does not reach submoustachial area, and barely does so on males. In widespread northern nominate race, dark centers are visible on central tail feathers, uppertail coverts, secondary coverts, and tertials. Southeastern *argutula* is smaller and darker, especially those from Florida. Southwestern *lilianae* is pale, like Western Meadowlark, but note more extensively white tail. South Texas birds, *hoopesi,* are intermediate in color. **Song** is a clear, whistled *see-you see-yeeer;* distinctive **call** a high, buzzy *drzzt,* given in a rapid series in flight. **Range:** Generally common in fields and meadows; has declined in the East in recent decades.

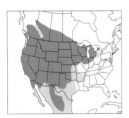

Western Meadowlark *Sturnella neglecta L 9½" (24 cm)*
Plumages similar to those of Eastern Meadowlark, but in **spring** and summer yellow extends well into the submoustachial area, especially in males; yellow often veiled in **fall.** Lack of dark centers to feathers of upperparts helps to separate from the more easterly races of Eastern, in areas where ranges overlap. Also, in fresh fall and winter plumage, upperparts, flanks, and undertail region are much paler. Distinguished from pale Eastern *lilianae* by mottled cheeks, more mottled postocular and lateral crown stripes, and less white in tail. Northwestern *S. n. confluenta* is darker above and can show dark feather centers like Eastern. **Song** is a series of bubbling, flutelike notes of variable length, usually accelerating toward the end. Sharp *chuck* note; rattled flight **call** similar to Eastern, but lower-pitched; also gives a whistled *wheet.* **Range:** Westerns are gregarious in winter; large flocks often gather along roadsides, while Easterns usually prefer taller cover. Eastern and Western Meadowlarks hybridize in Midwest.

Bobolink

early spring ♂

breeding ♂

breeding ♀

fall

spring *magna*

fall *magna*

juvenile *magna*

Eastern Meadowlark

spring *argutula*

spring *hoopesi*

spring *lilianae*

spring *neglecta*

Western Meadowlark

spring *confluenta*

fall *neglecta*

juvenile *neglecta*

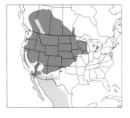

Yellow-headed Blackbird

Xanthocephalus xanthocephalus L 9½" (24 cm) **Adult male**'s yellow head and breast and white wing patch contrast sharply with black body. **Adult female** is dusky brown, lacks wing patch; eyebrow, lower cheek, and throat are yellow or buffy yellow; belly streaked with white. **Juvenile** is dark brown with buffy edgings on back and wing; head mostly tawny. **Immature male** resembles female but darker; wing coverts tipped with white; acquires adult plumage by following fall. **Song** begins with a harsh, rasping note, ends with a long, descending buzz. **Call** note is a rich *croak*. **Range:** Locally common throughout most of range; uncommon and very local in the Midwest. Prefers freshwater marshes or reedy lakes; often seen foraging in nearby farmlands. Rare fall and winter visitor to the East Coast. Casual in spring and fall as far north as southern Alaska.

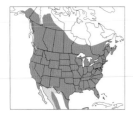

Red-winged Blackbird *Agelaius phoeniceus*

L 8¾" (22 cm) More rounded wings and usually stouter bill than Tricolored Blackbird. Glossy black **male** has red shoulder patches broadly tipped with buffy yellow. In perched birds, red patch may not be visible; only the buffy or whitish border shows. **Females** are dark brown above, heavily streaked below; sometimes show a red tinge on wing coverts or pinkish wash on chin and throat. **First-year male** plumage is distinguished from female Tricolored by reddish shoulder patch. Males in races of California's Central Valley and central coast region nearly or totally lack the buffy band behind red shoulder patch; known collectively as **"Bicolored Blackbird."** Females have darker bellies, more like female Tricolored; but note chestnut-buff edging on feathers of upperparts, except when worn away; more rounded wings; stouter bill, except for *aciculatus* of Kern Basin in south-central California, which has a bill like Tricolored. Red-winged Blackbird's **song** is a liquid, gurgling *konk-la-reee*, ending in a trill. Most common **call** is a *chack* note. **Range:** This abundant, aggressive species is often found in immense flocks in winter. Generally nests in thick vegetation of freshwater marshes, sloughs, and dry fields; forages in surrounding fields, orchards, and woodlands.

Tricolored Blackbird *Agelaius tricolor* L 8¾" (22 cm)

More pointed wings and bill than Red-winged Blackbird. Glossy (slightly grayish sheen) black **male** has dark red shoulder patches, often hidden, broadly tipped with white; tips are buffy white in fresh fall plumage. **Females** usually lack any red on shoulder and never show pinkish on throat; plumage is sooty brown and streaked overall; darker than female Red-winged Blackbird, particularly on belly; note more pointed wings and bill. In fresh fall plumage, all Tricolored Blackbirds have grayish buff edging on feathers of upperparts, unlike chestnut-buff of Red-winged. Distinction between females is more difficult when feathers are worn. Tricolor's variety of **calls** are much like Red-winged's, but its harsh, braying *on-ke-kaaangh* **song** lacks Red-winged's liquid tones. **Range:** Gregarious; found year-round in large flocks in open country and dairy farms; nests in large colonies in marshes.

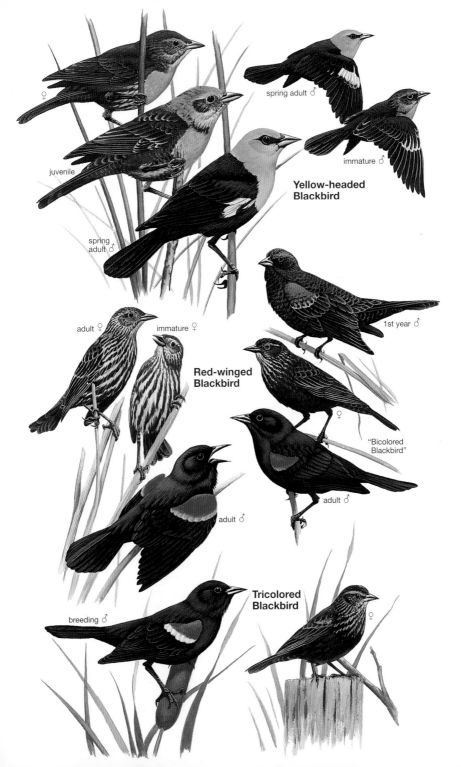

spring adult ♂

immature ♂

juvenile

Yellow-headed Blackbird

spring adult ♂

1st year ♂

adult ♀   immature ♀

Red-winged Blackbird

♀

"Bicolored Blackbird"

adult ♂

adult ♂

Tricolored Blackbird

breeding ♂   ♀

Common Grackle *Quiscalus quiscula* L 12½" (32 cm)

Long, keel-shaped tail; pale yellow eyes. Plumage appears all-black at a distance. In good light, **males** show glossy purplish blue head, neck, and breast. Widespread race *versicolor,* called "Bronzed Grackle," occurs in most of New England and west of the Appalachians; it has a bronze back, blue head, and purple tail. Smaller "Purple Grackle," *quiscula* of the Southeast, has a narrow bill, purple head, bottle green back, and blue tail. An intergrade population from the mid-Atlantic (*stonei*) shows variable head color and purplish back with iridescent bands of variable color. Females are smaller and duller than males. **Juveniles** are sooty brown, with brown eyes. Common Grackle's **song** is a short, creaky *koguba-leek;* **call** note, a loud *chuck.* **Range:** Abundant and gregarious, roaming in mixed flocks in open fields, marshes, parks, and suburban areas. Casual in Pacific states and Alaska, primarily in late spring.

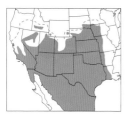

Boat-tailed Grackle *Quiscalus major*

♂ L 16½" (42 cm) ♀ L 14½" (37 cm) Large grackle with a very long, keel-shaped tail; smaller overall size, duller eye color, and more rounded crown than Great-tailed Grackle. **Adult male** is iridescent blue-black. **Adult female** is tawny brown with darker wings and tail. Male and female eye color is mostly brown in nominate race of coastal Texas and Louisiana and *westoni* of Florida; *alabamensis* of coastal Mississippi to northwest Florida and the largest race, *torreyi,* on the Atlantic coast, have a yellow iris. **First-fall male** is black but lacks iridescence; **juvenile** shows a hint of spotting or streaking on breast. Immatures resemble respective adults by mid-fall. **Calls** include a quiet chuck and a variety of rough squeaks, rattles, and other chatter. Most common **song** is a series of harsh *jeeb* notes. **Range:** This common, noisy grackle seldom strays beyond coastal saltwater marshes except in Florida, where it also inhabits inland lakes and streams. Nests in small colonies. Range is slowly expanding northward on the Atlantic coast.

Great-tailed Grackle *Quiscalus mexicanus*

♂ L 18" (46 cm) ♀ L 15" (38 cm) A large grackle with very long, keel-shaped tail and golden yellow eyes. **Adult male** is iridescent black with purple sheen on head, back, and underparts. **Adult female**'s upperparts are brown; underparts cinnamon-buff on breast to grayish brown on belly; shows less iridescence than male. **Juveniles** resemble adult female but are even less glossy and show some streaking on underparts. Immature males are duller, with shorter tails and darker eyes than adults by mid-fall. Females west of central Arizona are smaller and paler below than races to the east. In narrow zone of range overlap, Great-tailed Grackle is distinguished from Boat-tailed by bright yellow eyes, larger size, and flatter crown. Varied **calls** include clear whistles and loud *clack* notes. **Range:** Common, especially in open flatlands with scattered groves of trees and in marshes and wetlands. Casual far north of breeding range; rapidly expanding north and west in western U.S.

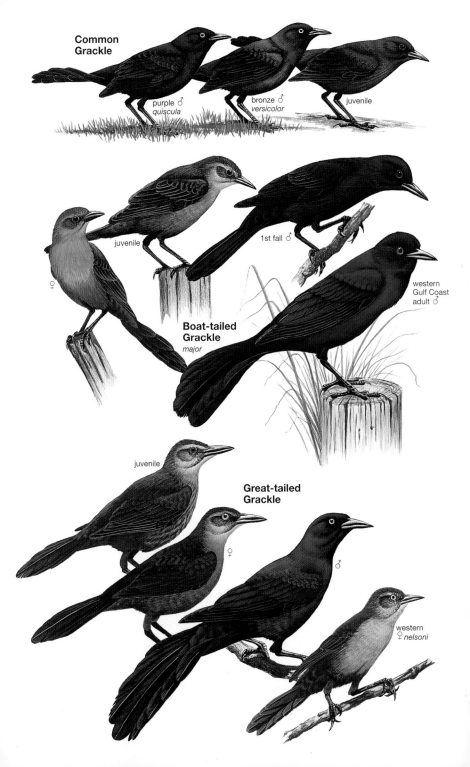

Common Grackle

purple ♂
quiscula

bronze ♂
versicolor

juvenile

juvenile

1st fall ♂

♀

Boat-tailed Grackle
major

western Gulf Coast adult ♂

juvenile

Great-tailed Grackle

♀

♂

western ♀ *nelsoni*

Rusty Blackbird *Euphagus carolinus* L 9" (23 cm)

Adults and fall immatures have yellow eyes. Fall adults and immatures are broadly tipped with rust; tertials and wing coverts edged with rust. **Fall female** has broad, buffy eyebrow, buffy underparts, gray rump. **Fall male** is darker; eyebrow fainter. The rusty feather tips wear off by spring, producing the dark **breeding** plumage. Juveniles have dark eyes. **Call** is a harsh *tschak;* **song,** a high, squeaky *koo-a-lee.* **Range:** Overall uncommon and declining in wet woodlands and swamps; nests in shrubs or conifers near water. Gregarious in fall and winter. Very rare in West.

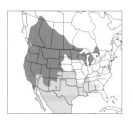

Brewer's Blackbird *Euphagus cyanocephalus*

L 9" (23 cm) **Male** has yellow eyes; **female**'s are usually brown. Male is black year-round, with purplish gloss on head and neck, greenish gloss on body and wings. **Immature males** show variable buffy feather edgings, but never on tertials or wing coverts, as in Rusty Blackbird; note also the shorter, thicker bill. Female and juveniles are gray-brown. Typical **call** is a harsh *check;* **song,** a wheezy *que-ee* or *k-seee.* **Range:** Common in open habitats; gregarious. Casual in winter to East Coast.

Shiny Cowbird *Molothrus bonariensis* 7½" (19 cm)

Range: Mainly South American species, which spread through the West Indies, arriving in south Florida in 1985. Uncommon in coastal south Florida; rare to eastern Gulf coast; casual to Texas and North Carolina; accidental to Oklahoma, Maine, and Maritimes. Sleeker, with longer tail, flatter head, and longer, more pointed bill than Brown-headed. **Male** blackish with purple gloss on head, breast, and back. **Female** and juveniles resemble female Brown-headed except for shape, darker color, and more prominent eyebrow. **Song,** whistled notes followed by trills.

Brown-headed Cowbird *Molothrus ater* L 7½" (19 cm)

Male's brown head contrasts with metallic green-black body. **Female** is gray-brown above, paler below. **Juvenile** is paler above, more heavily streaked below; pale edgings give its back a scaled look. Young males molting to adult plumage in late summer are a patchwork of buff, brown, and black. Southwestern *obscurus* is distinctly smaller than eastern nominate *ater;* Rockies and Great Basin *artemisiae* is largest. Male's **song** is a squeaky gurgling. **Calls** include a harsh rattle and squeaky whistles. Common; found in woodlands, farmlands, and suburbs. Feeds with tail cocked up. All cowbirds lay their eggs in nests of other species.

Bronzed Cowbird *Molothrus aeneus* L 8¾" (22 cm)

Red eyes distinctive at close range. Bill larger than Brown-headed Cowbird. **Adult male** is black with bronze gloss; wings and tail blue-black; thick ruff on nape and back gives a hunchbacked look. **Adult female** of the Texas race, *aeneus,* is duller than the male; **juveniles** are dark brown. In southwestern *loyei,* females and juveniles are gray. **Call** is a harsh, guttural *chuck.* **Song** is wheezy and buzzy. **Range:** Locally common in open country, brushy areas, and wooded mountain canyons; forages in flocks.

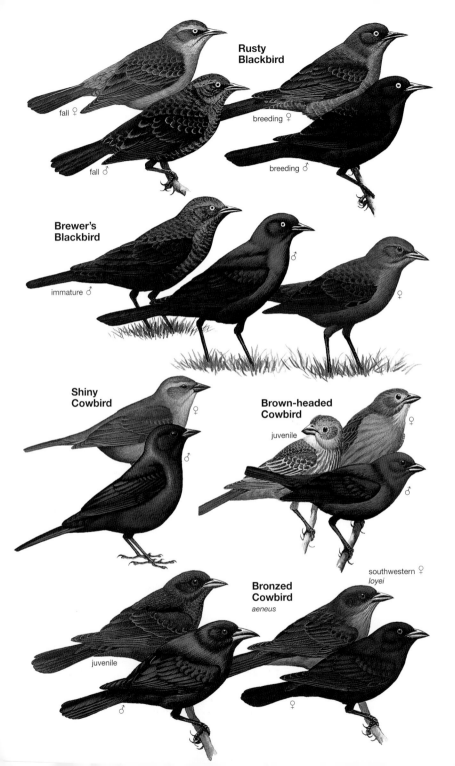

Rusty Blackbird

fall ♀

breeding ♀

fall ♂

breeding ♂

Brewer's Blackbird

immature ♂

♂

♀

Shiny Cowbird

♀

♂

Brown-headed Cowbird

juvenile

♀

♂

Bronzed Cowbird
aeneus

southwestern ♀
loyei

juvenile

♂

♀

Orchard Oriole *Icterus spurius* L 7¼" (18 cm)

Adult male is chestnut overall, with black hood. During winter, **female** is olive above, yellowish below. Immature male resembles female; acquires black bib and, sometimes, traces of chestnut by first spring. Smaller size, lack of orange tones or whitish belly, and thinner, more curved bill distinguish female and immature male from Baltimore and Bullock's Orioles. Compare especially with *nelsoni* race of Hooded Oriole. Locally common in suburban shade trees and orchards. **Calls** include a sharp *chuck*. **Song** is a loud, rapid burst of whistled notes, downslurred at the end. **Range:** Rare vagrant to Arizona, California, the Maritimes.

Hooded Oriole *Icterus cucullatus* L 8" (20 cm)

Bill long and slightly curved. **Breeding male** is orange or orange-yellow; note black patch on throat. Western birds (*nelsoni*) are yellower; the two Texas races—*sennetti* (shown) and *cucullatus*—are orange. All **winter adult males** have buffy brown tips on back, forming a barred pattern; compare with Streak-backed Oriole (next page). Hooded **female** and immature male lack pale belly of Bullock's Oriole; bill is more curved. Compare *nelsoni* also with female and immature male Orchard Orioles, which are smaller and purer lemon yellow below, with smaller bill. Immature male acquires black patch on throat by winter. **Calls** include a whistled, rising *wheet;* **song** is a series of whistles, trills, and rattles. Common in varied habitats, especially near palms. **Range:** Breeding has expanded northward on West Coast.

Baltimore Oriole *Icterus galbula* L 8¼" (21 cm)

Adult male has black hood and back, bright orange rump and underparts; large orange patches on tail. **Adult females** are brownish olive above and orange below, with varying amounts of black on head and throat; those with maximum black (shown) resemble first-spring males. Extent and intensity of color on underparts of **fall immatures** is highly variable; has distinctly contrasting wing bars and palish lores; no eye line or yellowish eyebrow. Common **call** is a rich *hew-li;* also gives a series of rattles. **Song** is a musical, irregular sequence of *hew-li* and other notes. **Range:** Common breeder in deciduous woodland over much of the East. Some winter in the South. Rare vagrant to West.

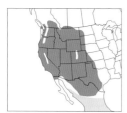

Bullock's Oriole *Icterus bullockii* L 8¼" (21 cm)

Formerly considered same species as Baltimore Oriole; some interbreeding on Great Plains. **Adult male** has less black on head: crown, eye line, throat patch; note bold white patch on wing, entirely orange outer tail feathers. **Females** and **immatures** have yellow throat and breast, unlike Baltimore's extensive orange; note Bullock's dark eye line, less contrasting wing bars. Most birds show dark "teeth" intruding into white of median covert bar. By **first spring,** males have black lores, throat. **Song,** mix of whistles and harsher notes; **call,** a harsh *cheh* or series of same. **Range:** Breeds where shade trees grow. Small numbers winter in coastal California. Casual vagrant to the East; most reports are of dull, immature Baltimores.

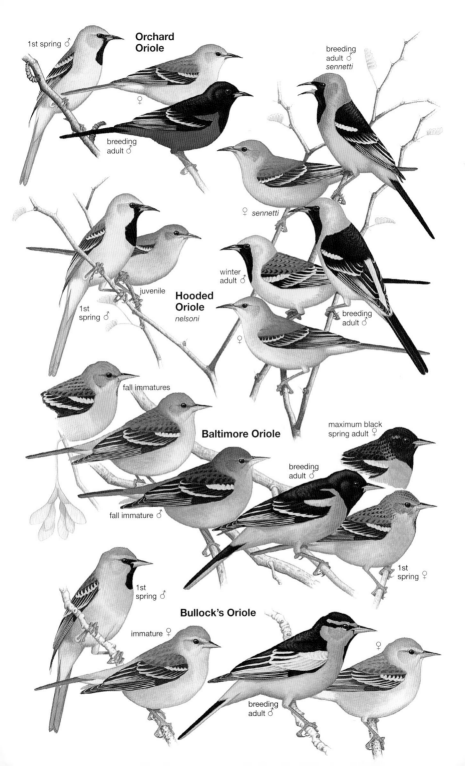

1st spring ♂

Orchard Oriole

♀

breeding
adult ♂

breeding
adult ♂
sennetti

♀ *sennetti*

juvenile

1st
spring ♂

Hooded Oriole
nelsoni

winter
adult ♂

breeding
adult ♂

♀

fall immatures

Baltimore Oriole

fall immature ♂

breeding
adult ♂

maximum black
spring adult ♀

1st
spring ♀

1st
spring ♂

Bullock's Oriole

immature ♀

♀

breeding
adult ♂

Black-vented Oriole *Icterus wagleri L 8½" (22 cm)*

Range: Resident from central Nicaragua to northern Mexico; accidental to south and west Texas, southeast Arizona. Long, narrow bill and long, graduated tail. **Adult** has solid black head, back, undertail coverts, tail, and wings, except for yellow shoulders; the border between breast and belly is chestnut. **First-spring** has black lores and chin; streaked back. Juvenile lacks black bib. Black-vented Oriole's **call** is a nasal *nyeh*, often repeated.

Streak-backed Oriole *Icterus pustulatus L 8¼" (21 cm)*

Range: Mexican species, casual in fall and winter in southeastern Arizona, southern California; accidental to New Mexico, east Texas, and Wisconsin. Distinguished from winter Hooded Oriole (preceding page) by broken streaks on upper back; deeper orange head; and much thicker-based, straighter bill. **Female** is duller than **male.** Immatures resemble adult female. *Wheet* **call** is softer than Hooded Oriole's call and does not rise in pitch. Chatter calls resemble those of Baltimore Oriole.

Altamira Oriole *Icterus gularis L 10" (25 cm)*

Distinguished from Hooded Oriole (preceding page) by larger size, much thicker-based bill, and, in **adult,** by orange shoulder patch. Lower wing bar whitish. **Immatures** are duller than adults, shoulder patch yellow; like adults by second fall. **Calls** include a low, raspy *ike ike ike;* **song** is a series of clear, varied whistles. **Range:** Found in southernmost Texas in tall trees and willows.

Audubon's Oriole *Icterus graduacauda L 9½" (24 cm)*

Range: Tropical species, resident but uncommon in south Texas. **Male** has greenish yellow back. Female is slightly duller. Rather secretive; often seen foraging on ground. **Song** is a series of soft, tentative, three-note warbles.

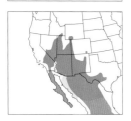

Spot-breasted Oriole *Icterus pectoralis L 9½" (24 cm)*

Adults have an orange or yellow-orange patch on shoulders; black lores and throat; dark spots on upper breast; extensive white on wings. **Juveniles** are yellower overall; **immatures** may lack breast spots. **Song** is a long, loud series of melodic whistles. **Range:** Middle American species, introduced and now established in southern Florida. Prefers suburban gardens. Florida population has declined over past three decades.

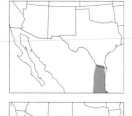

Scott's Oriole *Icterus parisorum L 9" (23 cm)*

Adult male's black hood extends to back and breast; rump, wing patch, and underparts bright lemon yellow. Adult female is olive and streaked above, dull greenish yellow below; throat shows variable amount of black. **Immature male**'s head is mostly black by first spring. **Females** and immatures larger, grayer, more streaked above; have straighter bill than female Hooded Oriole (preceding page). Common **call** note is a harsh *shack;* **song** is a mixture of rich, whistled phrases. **Range:** Found in arid and semiarid habitats. Casual east to Minnesota, Wisconsin, Louisiana. A few winter in southern California.

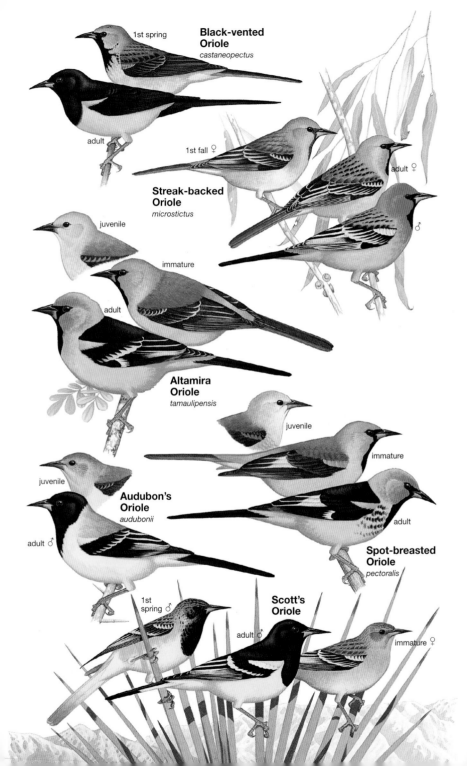

Black-vented Oriole
castaneopectus

1st spring

adult

Streak-backed Oriole
microstictus

1st fall ♀

adult ♀

♂

juvenile

immature

adult

Altamira Oriole
tamaulipensis

juvenile

immature

adult

Audubon's Oriole
audubonii

juvenile

adult ♂

Spot-breasted Oriole
pectoralis

1st spring ♂

Scott's Oriole

adult ♂

immature ♀

Fringilline and Cardueline Finches,
Allies (Family Fringillidae)

Seedeaters with undulating flight. Many nest in the North; in fall, flocks of "winter finches" may roam south. *Species: 168 World; 23 N.A.*

Oriental Greenfinch *Carduelis sinica L 6" (15 cm)*
Range: Asian species. Casual migrant, mainly in spring, on outer Aleutians; one Pribilofs record. **Adult male** has greenish face and rump, dark gray nape and crown, bright yellow wing patch and undertail coverts. **Adult female** is paler, with a brownish head. **Juvenile** has same yellow areas as adults but is streaked overall.

Brambling *Fringilla montifringilla L 6¼" (16 cm)*
Range: Eurasian species; fairly common but irregular migrant on Aleutians; rare on Pribilofs and St. Lawrence Island; casual in fall and winter in Canada and northern U.S. **Adult male** has tawny orange shoulders, spotted flanks; head and back fringed with buff in fresh fall plumage that wears down to black by spring. **Female** and juvenile have mottled crown, gray face, striped nape. Flight **call,** a nasal *check-check-check;* also gives a nasal *zwee.*

Common Chaffinch *Fringilla coelebs L 6" (15 cm)*
Range: Palearctic species; casual to northeastern North America; reports elsewhere possibly escaped cage birds. Has white patches on lesser coverts, base of primaries, wing bar; outer tail feathers white. **Male**'s crown and nape are blue-gray; shows pinkish below, pinkish brown above. **Female**'s head is mostly gray with brown lateral stripes. **Call** a metallic *pink-pink;* also a *hweet.*

Gray-crowned Rosy-Finch *Leucosticte tephrocotis*
5½-8¼" (14-21 cm) Dark brown, with gray on head; pink on wings and underparts; underwings silvery. Female less pink, **juveniles** grayish. All have yellow bill in **winter,** black by spring. Western *littoralis,* **"Hepburn's Rosy-Finch,"** and much larger, darker Pribilofs *umbrina* and Aleutians *griseonucha* show more gray on face than widespread nominate race and closely allied *dawsoni* from Sierra Nevada and White Mountains. **Call,** a high, chirping *chew,* often given in courtship flight. **Range:** Descends from higher elevations in winter. Some races are migratory.

Brown-capped Rosy-Finch *Leucosticte australis*
L 6" (15 cm) Plumages, behavior, and voice like Gray-crowned. Lacks gray head band of other North American Rosy-Finches. **Male** rich brown; darker crown; extensive pink on underparts. **Female** much drabber; some young female Gray-crowneds can be very similar.

Black Rosy-Finch *Leucosticte atrata L 6" (15 cm)*
Plumages, behavior, and voice like Gray-crowned. Darkest Rosy-Finch. **Male** is blackish; in fresh plumage, scaled with silver-gray; has gray head band; shows extensive pink. **Female** is blackish gray with little pink. **Range:** Casual to California, Arizona.

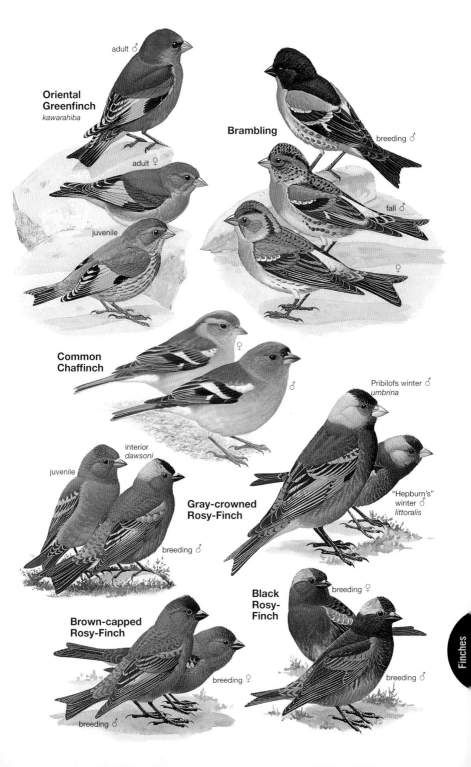

Oriental Greenfinch
kawarahiba

adult ♂

adult ♀

juvenile

Brambling

breeding ♂

fall ♂

♀

Common Chaffinch

♀

♂

Gray-crowned Rosy-Finch

Pribilofs winter ♂
umbrina

"Hepburn's" winter ♂
littoralis

interior
dawsoni

juvenile

breeding ♂

Brown-capped Rosy-Finch

breeding ♂

breeding ♀

Black Rosy-Finch

breeding ♀

breeding ♂

Purple Finch *Carpodacus purpureus L 6" (15 cm)*

Not purple, but rose red over most of **adult male**'s body, brightest on head and rump. Rose color is acquired in second fall. Back is streaked; tail notched. Pacific coast race, *californicus,* is buffier below and more diffusely streaked than the widespread *purpureus,* especially in females. **Adult female** and immatures are heavily streaked below; closely resemble Cassin's Finch. Ear patch and whitish eyebrow and submoustachial stripe are slightly more distinct in Purple Finch; bill slightly stubbier and more curved; undertail coverts are often not streaked. Compare also with female House Finch. **Calls** include a musical *chur-lee* and, in flight, a sharp *pit,* a bit sharper in *californicus.* **Song** is a rich warbling, longer and more variable in *purpureus;* shorter than Cassin's song, lower and less strident than House Finch song. **Range:** Fairly common; found in coniferous or mixed woodland borders, suburbs, parks, and orchards; in the Pacific states, inhabits coniferous forests, oak canyons, and lower mountain slopes.

Cassin's Finch *Carpodacus cassinii L 6¼" (16 cm)*

Crimson of **adult male**'s cap ends sharply at brown-streaked nape. Throat and breast paler than Purple Finch; streaks on sides and malar stripe more distinct. Red hues begin to appear late in second summer. Tail strongly notched. Undertail coverts always distinctly streaked, unlike many Purples. **Adult female** and immatures otherwise closely resemble Purple Finch. Cassin's facial pattern is slightly less distinct; culmen is straighter and longer; has longer primary projection. Cassin's gives a dry *kee-up* or *tee-dee-yip* **call.** Lively **song,** a variable warbling, longer and more complex than song of Purple Finch, especially *californicus.* **Range:** Fairly common in upper mountain forests, evergreen woodlands. Casual in winter east of range and to West Coast.

House Finch *Carpodacus mexicanus L 6" (15 cm)*

Male has brown cap; front of head, bib, and rump are typically red but can vary to orange or occasionally yellow. Bib is clearly set off from streaked underparts. Tail is squarish. **Adult female** and juveniles are streaked with brown overall; lack distinct ear patch and eyebrow of Purple and Cassin's Finches. Young males acquire adult coloring by first fall. Lively, high-pitched **song** consists chiefly of varied three-note phrases; includes strident notes, unlike Purple Finch's song; usually ends with a nasal *wheer.* **Calls** include a whistled *wheat.* **Range:** Abundant; found in semiarid lowlands and slopes up to about 6,000 feet. Introduced in the East in the 1940s, where its range is fast expanding; range has expanded rapidly also in the West; especially numerous in towns.

Common Rosefinch *Carpodacus erythrinus*

L 5¾" (15 cm) **Range:** Eurasian species; very rare migrant, chiefly in spring, on the western Aleutians and other western Alaska islands. Strongly curved culmen. Lacks distinct eyebrow. **Adult male** has red head, breast, and rump. **Female** and immatures diffusely streaked above and below except on pale throat. **Call** is a soft, nasal *djuee.*

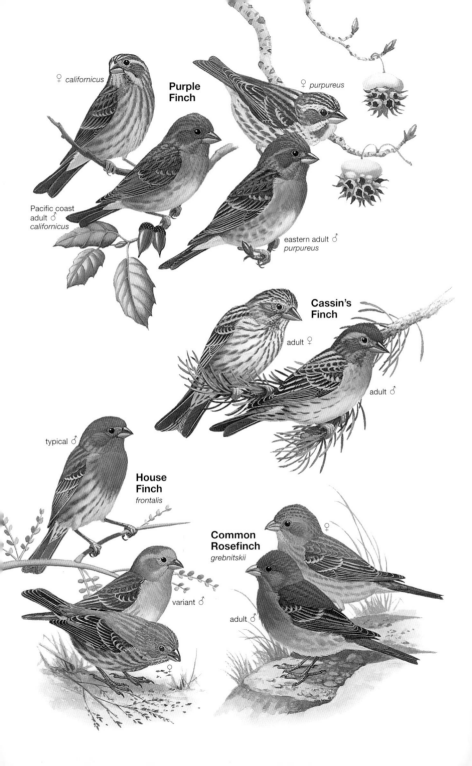

♀ *californicus*

Purple Finch

♀ *purpureus*

Pacific coast
adult ♂
californicus

eastern adult ♂
purpureus

Cassin's Finch

adult ♀

adult ♂

typical ♂

House Finch
frontalis

Common Rosefinch
grebnitskii

♀

variant ♂

adult ♂

♀

Red Crossbill *Loxia curvirostra* L 5½-7¾" (14-20 cm)

Bill with crossed tips identifies both crossbill species. Red Crossbill's dark brown wings lack the bold white bars of White-winged Crossbill. Plumage highly variable. Most **males** are reddish overall, brightest on crown and rump, but may be pale rose or scarlet or largely yellow; always have red or yellow on throat. Most **females** are yellowish olive; may show patches of red; throat is always gray, except in a small northern subspecies where yellow extends to center, but not sides, of throat. **Juveniles** are boldly streaked; a few juveniles and a very few adult males show white wing bars, the upper bar thinner than the lower. Immatures are like the respective adult but juvenile wing is retained. All birds except adult males have olive edges on wings. Subspecies vary widely in size, including bill size; extremes are shown here. All have their "home range." Distinct differences in vocalizations have led some authorities to believe that there may be a half dozen or more cryptic separate species in the Red Crossbill complex. All have large heads and short, notched tails. **Calls,** given chiefly in flight, vary from one subspecies to another. **Song** begins with several two-note phrases followed by a warbled trill. **Range:** Fairly common, Red Crossbills inhabit coniferous woods. May nest at any time of year, especially in southern range. Highly irregular in their wanderings, dependent upon cone crops. Any race may turn up almost anywhere. Irruptive migrant. Has bred as far south as Georgia.

White-winged Crossbill *Loxia leucoptera* L 6½" (17 cm)

All ages have black wings with white tips on the tertials; two bold, broad white wing bars. Upper wing bar is often hidden by scapulars. **Adult male** is bright pink overall, paler in winter. **Immature male** is largely yellow, with patches of red or pink. **Adult female** is mottled with yellowish olive or grayish; rump pale yellow; underparts grayish olive, with yellow wash on breast and sides. **Juvenile** is heavily streaked; wing bars thinner than in adults. White-winged Crossbill's distinctive flight **call** is a rapid series of harsh *chet* notes. Variable **song,** often delivered in display flight, combines harsh rattles and musical warbles. **Range:** Inhabits coniferous woods. Highly irregular in its wanderings, dependent upon spruce cone crops. Irruptive migrant.

Pine Grosbeak *Pinicola enucleator* L 9" (23 cm)

Large and plump, with long tail. Bill is dark, stubby, strongly curved. Two white wing bars, sometimes tinged with pink in adult male. **Male**'s gray plumage is tipped with red on head, back, and underparts; pinker in fresh fall plumage. **Female** and immatures are grayer overall; head, rump, and underparts variably yellow or reddish; some females and immature males are **russet.** Typical flight **call** is a whistled *pui pui pui;* alarm call, a musical *chee-vli.* Location call shows considerable geographic variation. **Song** is a rather short, musical warble. **Range:** Fairly common; inhabits open coniferous woods. In winter, found also in deciduous woods, orchards, and suburban shade trees. Usually unwary and approachable. Irruptive winter migrant in the East.

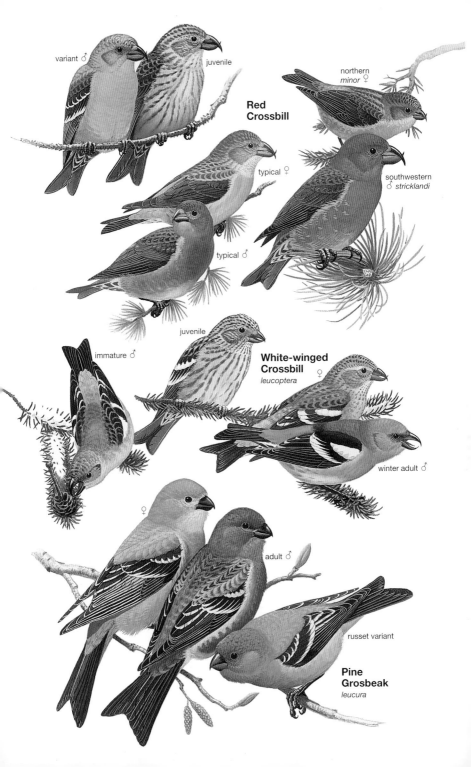

variant ♂

juvenile

Red Crossbill

northern
minor ♀

typical ♀

typical ♂

southwestern
♂ *stricklandi*

immature ♂

juvenile

White-winged Crossbill
leucoptera ♀

winter adult ♂

♀

adult ♂

russet variant

Pine Grosbeak
leucura

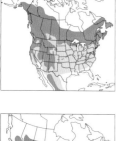

Pine Siskin *Carduelis pinus* L 5" (13 cm)

Prominent streaking; yellow at base of tail and in flight feathers conspicuous in flight; bill thinner than in other finches. **Juvenile**'s overall yellow tint is lost by late summer. **Calls** include a rising *tee-ee* and, in flight, a harsh, descending *chee*. **Song** is similar to that of American Goldfinch but much huskier. **Range:** Gregarious; may flock with goldfinches in winter. Found in coniferous and mixed woods in summer; forests, shrubs, and fields in winter. Winter range is erratic. Casual to Bering Sea islands.

American Goldfinch *Carduelis tristis* L 5" (13 cm)

Breeding adult male is bright yellow with black cap; black wings have white bars, yellow shoulder patch; uppertail and undertail coverts white, with black-and-white tail. **Female** is duller overall, olive above; lacks black cap and yellow shoulder patch. White undertail coverts distinguish female from most Lesser Goldfinches. **Winter adults** and immatures are either brownish or grayish above; male may show some black on forehead. **Juvenal** plumage, held into Nov., has cinnamon-buff wing markings and rump. **Song** is a lively series of trills, twitters, and *swee* notes. Distinctive flight **call,** *per-chik-o-ree*. **Range:** Common and gregarious; found in weedy fields, open second-growth woodlands, and roadsides, especially in thistles and sunflowers. Casual north to southeast and south-coastal Alaska.

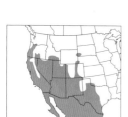

Lesser Goldfinch *Carduelis psaltria* L 4½" (11 cm)

All birds have a white wing patch at base of primaries. Entire crown black on **adult male;** back varies from black in eastern part of range to greenish in western birds. Most **adult females** are dull yellow below; except for a few extremely pale birds, they lack the white undertail coverts typical of American Goldfinch. **Immature male** lacks full black cap. Juveniles resemble adult female. **Call,** a plaintive, kittenlike *tee-yee*. **Song** is somewhat similar to that of American Goldfinch. **Range:** Common in dry, brushy fields, woodland borders, and gardens. Range expanding northward. Casual in Great Plains; accidental in the East.

Lawrence's Goldfinch *Carduelis lawrencei*

L 4¾" (12 cm) Wings extensively yellow; upperparts grayish in breeding plumage; large yellow patch on breast. **Male** has black face and yellowish tinge on back. **Winter** birds are browner above, duller below. **Juvenile** is faintly streaked, unlike other goldfinches. **Call** is a bell-like *tink-ul*. Mixes *tink* notes into jumbled, melodious **song.** Lawrence's and Lesser Goldfinches often mimic other species' songs. **Range:** Fairly common in spring and early summer; may sometimes flock with other goldfinches, but generally prefers drier interior foothills and mountain valleys; also western fringe of desert near watercourses. Erratic but usually uncommon at other seasons. Irregular fall movements to southwestern U.S. Casual as far east as western Texas.

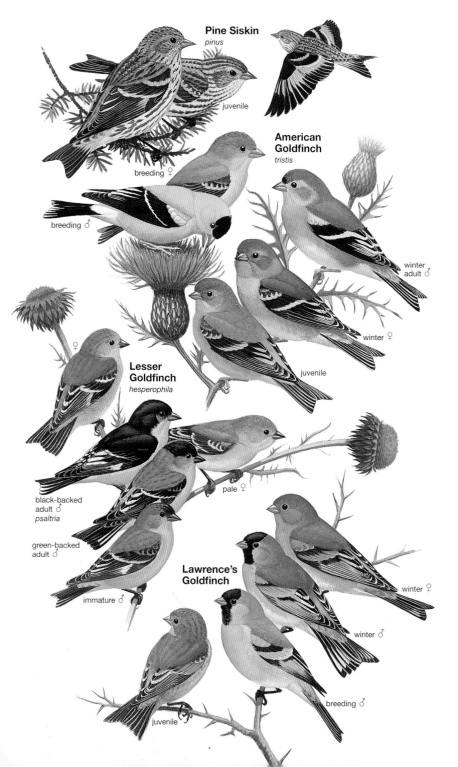

Pine Siskin
pinus

juvenile

American Goldfinch
tristis

breeding ♀

breeding ♂

winter adult ♂

winter ♀

juvenile

Lesser Goldfinch
hesperophila

♀

black-backed adult ♂
psaltria

green-backed adult ♂

pale ♀

immature ♂

Lawrence's Goldfinch

winter ♀

winter ♂

breeding ♂

juvenile

Common Redpoll *Carduelis flammea L 5¼" (13 cm)*

Red or orange-red cap or "poll," black chin. Closely resembles Hoary Redpoll, but usually has distinct streaks on flanks, rump, undertail coverts; bill is slightly larger. **Male** usually has bright rosy breast and sides. Both sexes paler, buffier in winter. **Juveniles** lack red cap until late-summer molt; males acquire pinkish breast by end of second summer. Extent of interbreeding between Common and Hoary Redpolls is unknown. When perched, Common gives a *swee-ee-eet* **call;** flight call, a dry rattling. **Song** combines trills and twittering. **Range:** Fairly common; breeds in subarctic forests and tundra scrub. Unwary. Forms large winter flocks; frequents brushy, weedy areas, also catkin-bearing trees like alder and birch.

Hoary Redpoll *Carduelis hornemanni L 5½" (14 cm)*

Closely resembles Common Redpoll but is usually frostier and paler overall, with a slightly smaller bill. Streaking below and on rump minimal or absent. **Male**'s breast is usually paler and pinker than on Common; color does not extend to cheeks or sides. **Calls** and **song** similar to Common. **Range:** Fairly common; nests on or near the ground above Arctic tree line. The race *hornemanni*, of Canadian Arctic islands and Greenland, is larger and paler than more widespread *exilipes*. Rare sightings, especially of *exilipes,* occur south of Canada in winter, almost always with Commons.

Evening Grosbeak *Coccothraustes vespertinus*

L 8" (20 cm) Stocky, noisy finch. Big bill pale yellow or greenish by spring, whitish by fall; prominent white patch on inner wing. Yellow forehead and eyebrow on **adult male;** dark brown and yellow body. Grayish tan **female** has thin, dark malar stripe, white-tipped tail; second wing patch, on primaries, is conspicuous in flight. **Juveniles** have brown bills; female resembles adult female; male yellower overall, wing and tail like adult male. Loud, strident **call:** *clee-ip* or *peeer.* **Range:** Breeds in mixed woods; in the West, mainly in mountains. In winter frequents woodlots, shade trees, and feeders; numbers and range limits vary greatly.

Hawfinch *Coccothraustes coccothraustes L 7" (18 cm)*

Range: Eurasian species. Rare spring stray on western Aleutians; casual off other islands of western Alaska. Stocky; yellowish brown above; pinkish brown below; has black throat and lores; shows conspicuous white band on extended wing. Big bill is blue-black in spring, yellowish in fall. Female resembles **male,** but is duller; has grayish secondaries and inner primaries. Walks with parrotlike waddle. **Call** is a loud, explosive *ptik.*

Eurasian Bullfinch *Pyrrhula pyrrhula L 6½" (17 cm)*

Range: Eurasian species. Casual migrant on Aleutians; casual in winter on Alaskan mainland. Cheeks, breast, and belly intense reddish pink in **male,** brown in **female.** Black cap and face, gray back, prominent whitish bar on wing, distinct white rump. In profile, top of head and bill form unbroken curve. Juvenile resembles female, but with brown cap. **Call** is a soft, piping *pheew.*

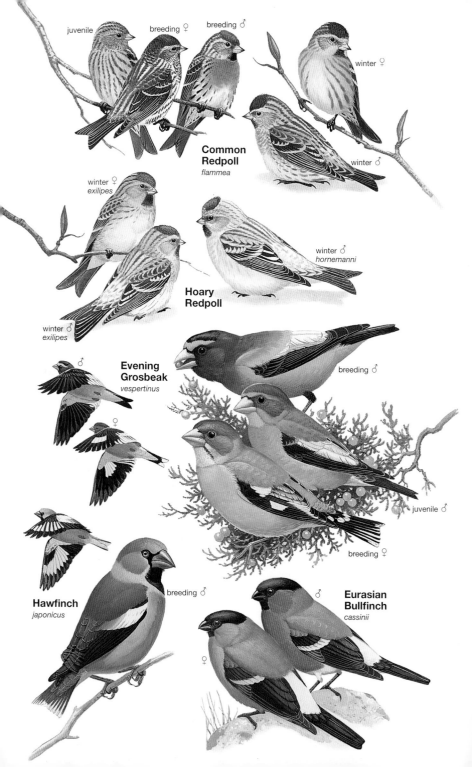

Common Redpoll
flammea

juvenile
breeding ♀
breeding ♂
winter ♀
winter ♂

Hoary Redpoll

winter ♀
exilipes
winter ♂
hornemanni
winter ♂
exilipes

Evening Grosbeak
vespertinus

♂
♀

breeding ♂
juvenile ♂
breeding ♀

Hawfinch
japonicus

breeding ♂

Eurasian Bullfinch
cassinii

♂
♀

464

Old World Sparrows (Family Passeridae)

Old World family. Gregarious; two species have become established in North America. *Species: 40 World; 2 N.A.*

House Sparrow *Passer domesticus* L 6¼" (16 cm)
Breeding male has gray crown, chestnut nape, black bib, black bill. Fresh **fall** plumage is edged with gray, obscuring these markings; bill becomes brownish. **Female** is best identified by the combination of streaked back, buffy eye stripe, and unstreaked breast. Juveniles resemble adult female. **Range:** Common and aggressive, House Sparrows are omnipresent in populated areas. Gregarious in winter. Also known as English Sparrow.

Eurasian Tree Sparrow *Passer montanus* L 6" (15 cm)
Range: Old World species, introduced and now locally common in parks, suburbs, and farmlands around St. Louis, Missouri, and in nearby Illinois. Accidental in Indiana, Wisconsin, Manitoba, Kentucky, Ontario. Gregarious all year. Brown crown, black ear patch, black throat distinguish **adult.** Compare with House Sparrow's gray crown and more extensively black throat. **Juvenile** has dark mottling on crown, dark gray throat and ear patch.

Weavers (Family Ploceidae)

Large, primarily African family. Breeding males are often highly colored. Known for elaborate woven nests. *Species: 108 World; 1 N.A.*

Orange Bishop *Euplectes franciscanus*
L 4" (10 cm) **Range:** Native to sub-Saharan Africa; widely introduced. Established in Los Angeles (1980s) and Phoenix (1998) areas, where it favors weedy areas, especially river bottoms. **Breeding male** is bright orange-red with black cap, breast, and belly; long tail coverts obscure tail. **Females,** immatures, and winter birds are streaked above. Compare especially with Grasshopper Sparrow (page 416); note Orange Bishop's thicker, pinkish bill; short, blunt tail, often flicked open. Complex **song,** high and buzzy. **Calls** include a sharp *tsip* and a mechanical *tsik tsik tsk.*

Estrildid Finches (Family Estrildidae)

Large, Old World family found from Africa to Australia and South Pacific islands. Most are small, with pointed tails. Related to weavers. *Species: 108 World; 1 N.A.*

Nutmeg Mannikin *Lonchura punctulata*
L 4½" (11 cm) **Range:** Widespread in Southeast Asia, found in greater Los Angeles area. Small, with heavy bill, pointed tail. **Adults** rich reddish brown above; scaled below; bill black. **Juveniles** are tan; bill slate gray. **Song,** *tiks* and whistles, is nearly inaudible; **call,** a loud *kibee.* Favors grassy, weedy areas.

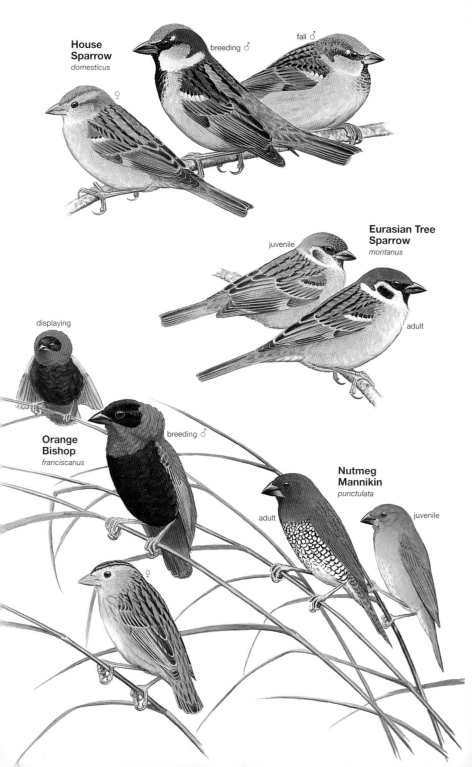

House Sparrow
domesticus

breeding ♂

fall ♂

♀

Eurasian Tree Sparrow
montanus

juvenile

adult

displaying

Orange Bishop
franciscanus

breeding ♂

♀

Nutmeg Mannikin
punctulata

adult

juvenile

Accidentals, Extinct Species

These 71 species have been recorded for North America, but for nearly all there are fewer than three records in the past two decades or five records in the last hundred years. Four species that have gone extinct in the past two centuries are also included.

Graylag Goose *Anser anser*

L 29-33" (74-84 cm) WS 59-66" (150-168 cm) Palearctic species that has become widely domesticated (page 50). The nominate European race is a common summer resident on Iceland; recently recorded from Greenland. From 24 Apr. to 2 May 2005, one landed and remained on a ship some 120 miles southeast of St. John's, Newfoundland. Largest and bulkiest of gray geese with heavy head, neck, and bill. Pink legs and orange (in nominate *anser*) bill. Head and neck gray, uniform with rest of body, unlike other gray geese, which have a darker head and neck. In flight, striking pale gray forewing and contrasting pale gray underwing coverts.

adult
anser

Lesser White-fronted Goose *Anser erythropus*

L 22-26" (55-66 cm) Palearctic species. Closely resembles Greater White-fronted Goose (page 20) and plumages similar, but smaller and more stocky, with shorter neck and stubbier bill. The yellow orbital ring is conspicuous. It has a darker neck than Greater White-fronted (except for the *elgasi* and *flavirostris* subspecies of Greater). The wings extend beyond the tail when folded. Specimen record from Attu Island, Alaska, on 5 June 1994. Population is declining, especially from the western Palearctic.

adult

Labrador Duck *Camptorhynchus labradorius* **EX**

L 22½" (57 cm) Extinct. An endemic North American species. Note the unique bill shape that broadens towards tip. Much of **adult male**'s head, neck, and chest white; remainder of body plumage blackish. Adult females, immatures, and eclipse males more grayish-brown overall, the throat being whiter than the head. Never common, it was best known from the winter grounds on the mid-Atlantic coast, especially the southern shore of Long Island where the last definite record (specimen) was obtained in 1875. Breeding grounds unknown, perhaps Labrador, perhaps farther north. Accidental inland in spring from Montreal, Quebec (1862).

adult ♂

Light-mantled Albatross *Phoebetria palpebrata*

L 31-35" (79-89 cm) WS 72-86" (183-218 cm) A circumpolar species of the southern oceans that breeds on subantarctic islands. A very graceful flyer. **Adult** has dark head with prominent white eye crescents and strikingly pale mantle and body. The long, dark, wedge-shaped tail is distinctive. At close range, note bluish line of skin on the lower mandible (sulcus). Juvenile is similar to adult but browner overall, with less prominent eye crescents and gray sulcus. One individual was well documented at Cordell Bank, off northern California, on 17 July 1994. The origin of this record has been questioned by the ABA Checklist Committee.

adult

Wandering Albatross *Diomedea exulans*

L 42-53" (107-135 cm) WS 100-138" (254-351 cm) Circumpolar in southern oceans, breeding on subantarctic islands. A polytypic species (5 to 7 subspecies), some authorities recognize up to five species. Huge size and immense wingspan (reaches over 11 feet). Massive pinkish bill and white underwings with narrow dark trailing edge and primary tips. **Adult** has extensively white back and wings. Juvenile is dark chocolate brown with conspicuous white face. Maturation takes up to 15 years. Becomes white first on the mantle, body, and head, eventually spreading to upperwing coverts. One onshore record at Sea Ranch, Sonoma County, California, 11 to 12 July 1967. Five European records.

adult ♀

Black-bellied Storm-Petrel *Fregetta tropica*

L 8" (20 cm) WS 18" (46 cm) A widespread southern ocean species, one was well photographed off Manteo, North Carolina, on 31 May 2004. Black-and-white coloration distinctive on all individuals, but diagnostic black line up through white belly (separating it from another southern oceans species, White-bellied Storm-Petrel, *F. grallaria*) can be hard to see. Note long legs and feet project past tail. Foraging behavior distinctive: splashes breast into water, then springs forward pushing off with long legs.

Ringed Storm-Petrel *Oceanodroma hornbyi*

L 8¼-9" (21-23 cm) South American species of the Humboldt Current from Chile to southern Ecuador; casual to Colombia. Nesting grounds unknown, but possibly in the central Andes. Recent well-documented record off San Miguel Island, California, on 2 Aug. 2005. Note large size and striking plumage pattern, including blackish cap and breast band; tail is deeply forked.

Nazca Booby *Sula granti* *L 32" (81 cm) WS 62" (158 cm)*

Recently split from the Masked Booby, this eastern tropical Pacific endemic ranges north to Mexico. One immature landed on a ship off northern Baja California and rode to San Diego (29 May 2001). Other records of immatures off southern and central California remain problematic. Similar to Masked Booby (page 100) in all plumages; subtle shape differences include shorter and thinner bill, shorter legs, and longer wings and tail. Note **adult**'s orange-pink bill and more orange (not yellow) iris. Juvenile averages paler than Masked, and pale collar is less marked or absent.

adult

Great Frigatebird *Fregata minor*

L 37" (95 cm) WS 85" (216 cm) Extensive breeding range in Indian and Pacific Oceans. Closely resembles Magnificent Frigatebird (page 98). Adult male distinguished from Magnificent by russet bar on upper wing coverts, pink feet and often by whitish scallops on axillars. Note **adult female**'s dark head with pale gray throat, rounder (less tapered) black belly patch, and red orbital ring. When fresh, juvenile has rusty wash to head and chest, and pink feet. Specimen from Perry, Oklahoma (3 Nov. 1975). Two photographed records of adults off California (male in Monterey Bay on 13 Oct. 1979, and female Southeast Farallon Island on 14 Mar. 1992).

adult ♀

adult ♂

adult

adult

breeding
adult

dark-
morph
adult

Lesser Frigatebird *Fregata ariel*
L 30" (76 cm) WS 73" (185 cm) Widespread in southwest and central Pacific and Indian Ocean; a few colonies in south Atlantic. Our smallest frigatebird, in all plumages a white spur extends from the flanks into the axillars. Juvenile has pale, rusty head. Recorded at least once from North America, an **adult male** photographed at Deer Island, Maine, on 3 July 1960; a photographed bird from Michigan in fall of 2005 is under review.

Yellow Bittern *Ixobrychus sinensis*
L 15" (38 cm) WS 21" (53 cm) Widespread Asian species. One specimen record from Attu Island, Alaska (17 to 22 May 1989). In **adults** (sexes similar), head and neck are buffy, cap and tail are black, and neck is streaked. Juvenile is more streaked overall. In flight, note black primary coverts and flight feathers. An Asian congener, Schrenck's Bittern (*Ixobrychus eurhythmus*), though scarce, is highly migratory and could occur in North America. It is slightly larger than Yellow Bittern, more cinnamon dorsally, and has a slaty gray trailing edge to its wing.

Gray Heron *Ardea cinerea*
L 33-40" (84-102 cm) WS 61-69" (155-175 cm) Widespread Old World species; one found on Newfoundland coast in Oct. 1999, subsequently died in a rehabilitation center. There is a sight record from St. Paul Island, Alaska, 1 Aug. 1999. Similar to Great Blue Heron (page 114), but smaller, with shorter legs and neck. In all plumages lacks rufous thighs of Great Blue; in flight leading edge of wing shows prominent white area, rather than rufous.

Chinese Egret *Egretta eulophotes*
L 27" (65 cm) WS 41" (104 cm) Threatened Asian species, breeding on islands off Korea, China, and perhaps the Russian Far East; winters in the Philippines and Borneo, some on coastal mainland of Southeast Asia. One specimen record from Agattu Island, Alaska, 16 June 1974. Note shorter legs than Little Egret (page 112). In **breeding** plumage has shaggy crest, turquoise lores, entirely orange-yellow bill, and black legs with yellow feet. Nonbreeding birds lack crest; legs and feet are yellowish green and bill mostly dark.

Western Reef-Heron *Egretta gularis*
L 23½" (60 cm) WS 37½" (95 cm) Old World species; casual to the West Indies. A **dark morph** was present on Nantucket Island, Massachusetts, from 26 Apr. to 13 Sept. 1983; another dark morph summered (2005) at Stephenville Crossing, western Newfoundland. Structurally resembles closely related Little Egret (page 112), but has slightly thicker neck; thicker-based bill is longer and a little more curved. Two color morphs. Much more numerous dark morph is slaty gray overall with white chin and throat; lores and bill dusky yellow; legs black and feet yellow. White morph resembles Little Egret, but note slight structural differences; immatures often have scattered dark feathers.

Chinese Pond-Heron *Ardeola bacchus*

L 18" (46 cm) WS 34" (86 cm) Migratory East Asian species that occurs rarely, but with increasing frequency, to Japan and Korea. A breeding-plumaged adult was on St. Paul Island, Alaska, 4 to 9 Aug. 1996. Members of this genus are short and stocky and most have entirely white wings, rump, and tail (especially visible in flight); yellow legs and feet. **Breeding male** has bright chestnut head, neck, and upper breast, slaty lower breast, and blue-based bill. Breeding female lacks slaty lower breast. Immatures and non-breeding adult much duller with streaked neck and not separable from several other congeners from south and Southeast Asia.

breeding adult ♂

adult

light-morph adult

Crane Hawk *Geranospiza caerulescens*

L 18-21" (46-53 cm) WS 36-41" (91-104 cm) Neotropical species from northeastern and northwestern Mexico to South America. One wintered at Santa Ana National Wildlife Refuge, southern Texas, from 20 Dec. 1987 to 9 Apr. 1988. Distinctive, long profile with small head, long orange legs, and long banded tail; iris reddish. Northeastern subspecies (*nigra*) is darkest. In flight, note white crescent at base of primaries. Juvenile has some whitish in face and undertail, whitish barring below, and duller soft parts.

Collared Forest-Falcon *Micrastur semitorquatus*

L 20" (52 cm) WS 31" (79 cm) Neotropical species found from northeastern and northwestern Mexico to South America. Recorded once in south Texas at Bentsen-Rio Grande Valley State Park, from 22 Jan. to 24 Feb. 1994 (light-morph adult). Distinctive structure: very short, rounded wings (wing tips barely reach base of tail), long graduated tail, and long legs. Three color morphs: more numerous **light morph** is black above, white below; note black crescent on white cheek and thin white bars on tail; juvenile similar but browner above, also barred and more buffy below. In buff morph, white areas replaced with buff; dark morph is rare. Usually seen within forest canopy; often located by loud calls.

Red-footed Falcon *Falco verspertinus*

L 11" (27 cm) WS 29" (73 cm) A medium-sized falcon that breeds in eastern Europe and western Asia and winters in southern and southwestern Africa. Regular, especially in spring, to northwestern Europe; casual to Iceland. One **first-summer male** was present at Martha's Vineyard, Massachusetts, 8 to 24 Aug. 2004. Adult male is slaty gray overall with rufous thighs and undertail. Adult female has buffy crown and underparts, dark moustache, pale sides of neck; adults have red legs and feet. Juvenile similar but browner and more streaked, duller legs and feet. Often hovers.

1st summer ♂

Paint-billed Crake *Neocrex erythrops*

L 7¼-8" (18-20 cm) Found eastern Panama through South America and Galápagos Islands. Specimens from Brazos County, Texas, on 17 Feb. 1972 (*erythrops*) and near Richmond, Virginia, on 15 Dec. 1978 (*olivascens*). Olive-brown above with gray forecrown and face; throat whitish; sides, flanks, and undertail coverts barred; red legs and yellow-green bill with bright orange base.

adult

Spotted Rail *Pardirallus maculatus* L 10-11¼" (25-28 cm)

Resident on Cuba and Isle of Pines, Hispaniola, and from central Mexico to South America and the Galápagos Islands. Specimens (*insolitus*) from Beaver County, Pennsylvania, on 12 Nov. 1976 and from Brown County, Texas, on 9 Aug. 1977. Rather large, blackish rail. **Adult** is spotted with white on head and upperparts; remainder of underparts banded with white; long, slender greenish yellow bill has red spot at base; iris, legs, and feet red. Juveniles are polymorphic, have duller legs and bill, and brown iris. Dark morph is plain dark brown above, sooty gray below; pale morph has grayish brown throat and breast with fine white bars on breast; barred morph has gray throat with white spots, breast and belly barred with white.

Double-striped Thick-knee *Burhinus bistriatus*

L 16½" (42 cm) Resident from northeastern Mexico to Brazil; recent nesting record from Great Inagua, Bahamas. A specimen record on 5 Dec. 1961 from the King Ranch, Kleberg County, Texas. A bird at Yuma, Arizona, was transported. Crepuscular and terrestrial, with ploverlike gait of runs and abrupt stops. Adults with dark lateral crown stripe and bold white supercilium; dark-tipped yellow bill and yellow legs. Juvenile slightly duller. In flight, upper wing two-toned; prominent broken white bar on primaries.

Greater Sand-Plover *Charadrius leschenaultii*

L 8½" (32 cm) Old World species. Only North American record is one that wintered at Bolinas Lagoon, California, from 29 Jan. to 8 Apr. 2001. Overall closely resembles Lesser Sand-Plover (page 158), but bill distinctly longer; legs longer and not as dark, more greenish yellow. In flight, wing stripe broader and feet project beyond tail. In breeding plumage, colored breast band is not as dark or extensive.

Collared Plover *Charadrius collaris* L 5" (14 cm)

Resident from northern Mexico to South America. Only North America record, 9 to 11 May 1992 at Uvalde, Texas. Small with disproportionately long legs, small thin black bill, pinkish legs; lacks white collar around nape. Adult with dark forecrown, often with rusty border; auriculars, nape, and sides of breast often with rusty fringes, especially in males; narrow but complete black breast band, often with distinct rusty fringes at sides, especially in male. Juvenile has incomplete breast band and pale rusty edges above.

Eurasian Oystercatcher *Haematopus ostralegus*

L 16½" (42 cm) Palearctic species, breeding west to Iceland; rare migrant to Greenland (over 30 records). Two spring records from Newfoundland: Fox Island, Tors Cove, 22 to 25 May 1994; and Eastport, from 3 Apr. to 2 May 1999. Similar to American Oystercatcher (page 160), but has black back and red iris. In flight white wing bar is bolder and more extensive, and white extends up back. Nonbreeding birds have a white bar across throat.

winter

adult

breeding adult

adult

adult

Black-winged Stilt *Himantopus himantopus L 13" (33 cm)*
Widespread in Old World. Two spring records for Alaska from
western Aleutians: Nizki Island from 24 May to 3 June 1983; and
Shemya Island, 1 to 9 June 2003. One specimen record from St.
George Island, Alaska, 15 May 2003. Similar to Black-necked Stilt
(page 160), but paler on rear neck and lacks white spot above eye.
Adults vary from having entirely white head and neck to being
darker; adult males have glossy black backs, females browner.

Slender-billed Curlew *Numenius tenuirostris* **E**
L 15" (39 cm) Critically endangered, possibly extinct. Only known
nests found near Tara, north of Omsk, southwestern Siberia, Russia, early in 20th century. Wintered in western Mediterranean
region and coastal northwest Africa, where several recorded from
one Moroccan location until 1995; last record from Northum-
berland, United Kingdom, 4 to 7 May 1998, ironically the United
Kingdom's first record. In North America a specimen from Crescent Beach, Ontario, from "about 1925." Size of Whimbrel but patterned like Eurasian Curlew (page 173), but with slender bill and
black heart-shaped spots, not chevrons, on sides and flanks.

Eurasian Woodcock *Scolopax rusticola L 13" (33 cm)*
Widespread Old World species. Casual to North America, where
most records are old and from the Northeast; older records are
from Newfoundland (1862), Quebec (twice in 1862), Pennsylvania (1886, 1890), New Jersey (1859), and Alabama (1889). The last
record, and the only one accepted from the 20th century, was one
at Goshen, New Jersey, 2 to 9 Jan. 1956, although one from Ohio
(specimen lost) in 1935 may have been this species. All dated
records fall between early Nov. and early Mar. Distinctly larger than
similar American Woodcock (page 190); also duller and heavily
barred below.

Oriental Pratincole *Glareola maldivarum*
L 9" (23 cm) WS 23½-25½" (60-65 cm) Asian species. Winters
south to Australia. Recorded twice in Alaska: a specimen from
Attu Island, 19 to 20 May 1985; one at Gambell, St. Lawrence
Island, 5 June 1986. Short-tailed pratincole with no white trailing
edge to wing and chestnut underwings. Collared Pratincole (*G.
pratincola*), breeding in the western Palearctic, has occurred once
on Barbados and could occur in eastern North America. Collared
has longer tail than Oriental and has a white trailing edge to wing.

breeding
adult

Gray-hooded Gull *Larus cirrocephalus*
L 16" (41 cm) WS 43" (109 cm) A native to Africa and South
America. One adult was photographed on 26 Dec. 1998 at
Apalachicola, Florida. **Breeding adult** has pale gray hood with
darker border, long dark red bill, and long red legs; wing pattern
distinctive. In winter loses hood and has dark ear spot and
smudge around eye and dark tip to bill. First-year has similar
outer wing pattern to adult, but a diagonal brown bar across the
inner wing and a dark secondary bar, and a dark tail band. The
pinkish yellow bill has a dark tip.

breeding
adult

breeding
adult

Whiskered Tern *Chlidonias hybridus*

L 9½-10" (24-25 cm) WS 26½-28½" (67-72 cm) Widespread Old World species. Two North American records, both adults. In 1993 one at Cape May, New Jersey, 12 to 15 July, later moved to Delaware shore from 19 July to 24 Aug. Another at Cape May, 8 to 12 Aug. 1998. Like congeners, secures food by picking it off surface. **Adults** have short stout dark red bill and medium length red legs; dark gray underparts set off contrasting white cheeks and undertail. In winter, head and underparts white with thin black postocular patch, blackish bill and legs; compare head pattern to "ear muff" effect of White-winged Tern (page 224).

Great Auk *Pinguinus impennis* **EX** *L 30" (81 cm)*

Extinct. North Atlantic species known in North America from three nesting colonies on islands off Quebec and Newfoundland, the largest on Funk Island off Newfoundland. Wintered within breeding range and south to Massachusetts, casually to South Carolina. Extirpated from Funk Island about 1800; last definite record was two clubbed on Eldey Stack, Iceland, on 3 June 1844. Flightless. Resembled a large Razorbill with similarly shaped bill. Distinct, white circular patch in lores. Winter plumage imperfectly known.

adult

Scaly-naped Pigeon *Patagioenas squamosa*

L 14" (36 cm) Resident throughout most of the West Indies. Two old specimen records from Key West: 24 Aug. 1898 and 6 May 1929. A large dark pigeon; in good light, head and upper breast are dark maroon; feathers on sides of neck more reddish, tipped black, forming diagonal lines giving scaled appearance; dark red bill with yellow tip; orange-red iris; orange orbital ring.

adult ♂

Passenger Pigeon *Ectopistes migratorius* **EX**

L 15¾" (40 cm) Extinct. Believed to have been the most abundant bird species in North America—in migration, flocks said to have numbered in the millions. Formerly found in eastern North America, casually in the West. By 1870s relegated to scattered breeding locations. Last records were a specimen from Ohio in 1900 and a reliable sight record in Missouri in 1902. Last individual died in captivity in a Cincinnati zoo on 1 Sept. 1914. Destruction of old-growth deciduous forests and overhunting, especially in breeding colonies, led to its demise. Resembled a large Mourning Dove. **Adult male** bluish gray above and pinkish below; female browner above and paler below; juvenile similar to female.

adult ♂

Carolina Parakeet *Conuropsis carolinensis* **EX**

L 13½" (34 cm) Extinct. Only native breeding North American psittacid. Formerly resident in Southeast, especially along rivers. Last certain records were from Florida and Kansas in 1904; a reliable sight record from Missouri in 1905 and perhaps another in 1912. Last captive died on 21 Feb. 1918. **Adult** had green body with yellow patches on shoulder, thighs, and vent, a yellow head, and reddish orange face. Immature entirely green, except for orange patch on forehead.

adult

Oriental Scops-Owl *Otus sunia*

L 7½" (19 cm) WS 21" (53 cm) A small, nocturnal, insectivorous owl of eastern Asia. Multiple subspecies, northern ones are migratory. Two records (*japonicus*) of rufous morphs from Aleutian Islands, Alaska: a dried wing found on Buldir Island on 5 June 1977 and one found alive on Amchitka Island on 20 June 1979, subsequently died (specimen). Three color morphs: gray-brown, reddish gray, and **rufous.** Fine dark streaks on head; breast streaked vertically and horizontally with thin crossbars. Short ear tufts. Northern subspecies may be specifically distinct, calls differ.

rufous morph
japonicus

Mottled Owl *Cicabba virgata*

L 14" (36 cm) WS 33" (84 cm) A medium-size and very vocal nocturnal owl found in a variety of woodland habitats from northwest and northeast Mexico to South America. A road-killed specimen was salvaged in front of Bentsen-Rio Grande Valley State Park, southern Texas, on 23 Feb. 1983. Note round head with no ear tufts and streaked underparts; brown facial disk with bold white eyebrows and whiskers is distinctive. Larger Barred Owl (page 258) has prominent barring across upper breast and paler facial disk.

Stygian Owl *Asio stygius* L 17" (43 cm) WS 42" (107 cm)

A medium-size, forest-dwelling nocturnal owl occurring from northern Mexico to South America; also Hispaniola and Gonâve Island, West Indies. Two winter records of birds found roosting and photographed at Bentsen-Rio Grande Valley State Park: 9 Dec. 1994 and 26 Dec. 1996. Deep chocolate brown overall with close-set ear tufts and blackish facial disk with contrasting white forehead; underparts show distinct dark streaks and crossbars. Compare to Long-eared Owl (page 256), which is browner and has a rufous facial disk.

Gray Nightjar *Caprimulgus indicus* L 11-12¾" (28-32 cm)

Asian species, formerly known as Jungle Nightjar. One desiccated specimen (*jotaka*) salvaged on Buldir Island, Alaska, on 31 May 1977. Overall color is grayish brown, patterned with black, buff, and grayish white. Note long wing-tip projection. Adult male has large white subterminal patch on inner primaries and white tips to all but central pair of tail feathers; on female, wing patch and tail tips more buffy. The two more northerly and migratory subspecies (*jotaka* and *hazarae*) have different vocalizations and are treated as a distinct species by some authors, *C. jotaka*.

♂ *jotaka*

Antillean Palm-Swift *Tachornis phoenicobia*

L 4¼" (11 cm) A tiny Caribbean swift that is resident in the Greater Antilles (except Puerto Rico). Two were present and photographed at Key West, Florida, from 7 July to 13 Aug. 1972. Distinctive are dark cap, dark sides, and thin line across breast contrasting with white throat, belly, and rump; tail has shallow fork. Batlike flight with rapid wingbeats and short glides and twists; generally flies low, among trees and palms.

Cinnamon Hummingbird *Amazilla rutila*
L 4-4½" (10-12 cm) Resident in lowlands from Sinaloa and Yucatán Peninsula, south to Costa Rica. Two records from Southwest: 21 to 23 July 1992 at Patagonia, Arizona; 18 to 21 Sept. 1993 at Santa Teresa, New Mexico. Adults have a cinnamon tail and underparts and a black-tipped red bill. Immature is similar but upperparts edged cinnamon when fresh, and upper mandible is mostly dark.

Bumblebee Hummingbird
Atthis heliosa L 2¾-3" (7-8 cm) Endemic to montane forests of Mexico north of the Isthmus of Tehuantepec. Two specimens taken on 2 July 1896 in Ramsey Canyon, Arizona. That two would be taken on the same date from one locality with no records since seems unlikely, but the specimens are extant and the records have not yet been refuted. The question is whether the collector was actually in the present-day Ramsey Canyon or was farther south in Mexico. A tiny hummingbird with a short bill and a short, rounded or double-rounded, rufous-based tail with white tips. **Adult males** have an elongated magenta-rose gorget. Females and immatures closely resemble female-type Calliope Hummingbirds, which have darker tails that fall shorter than or equal to wing tips; on Bumblebee, tail extends beyond wing tips.

adult ♂

Eurasian Hoopoe *Upupa epops L 10½" (27 cm)*
Widespread Old World species. One North American record, a specimen (*saturata*) from Old Chevak, Yukon-Kuskokwim Delta, Alaska, 2 to 3 Sept. 1975. Unmistakable: pinkish brown coloration; long crest (sometimes raised); long, thin, slightly decurved bill. Striking black-and-white wing pattern in flight; wingbeats slow and floppy. The two races from equatorial Africa and farther south and from Madagascar are each treated as separate species by some authors.

adult
saturata

Eurasian Wryneck *Jynx torquilla L 6" (17 cm)*
Widespread in Old World. Two fall records from Alaska: a specimen (*chinensis*) taken at Cape Prince of Wales, 8 Sept. 1945, and one photographed at Gambell, St. Lawrence Island, 2 to 5 Sept. 2003. A dead bird found in southern Indiana was believed to have been artificially transported. Patterned in browns and grays, the Wryneck is quite unlike a woodpecker, except for the sharply pointed bill. Note dark mask, dark vertical band on sides of back, and the long and sparsely barred tail. Often forages on ground, but also perches on branches in a somewhat horizontal posture.

adult

Greenish Elaenia *Myiopagis viridicata L 5½" (14 cm)*
Resident in Mexico from southern Durango and southern Tamaulipas, south to northern Argentina. Recorded once in North America on upper Texas coast at High Island, 20 to 23 May 1984. Overall greenish above with a contrasting grayish head and dark eye stripe with distinct, pale supercilium. Primaries edged with olive; bright yellowish on secondaries; short primary projection. Grayish throat and olive breast contrast with yellow belly. Distinctive call note, a high, thin, and descending *seei-seeur*.

Caribbean Elaenia *Elaenia martinica* L 5½" *(14 cm)*
Resident on many Caribbean Islands, including throughout Lesser
Antilles, but absent from Greater Antilles, except for Puerto Rico.
Recorded once (photographs) from Santa Rosa Island, Escambia
County, Florida, on 28 Apr. 1984. The AOU, while accepting the
record as an elaenia, does not consider the record definitive to
species. Overall plumage plain. Short crest rarely raised to show
white-based crown feathers. Indistinct pale gray supercilium; dusky
lores; pale yellowish wing bars and edges to secondaries; lower
mandible flesh-colored at base. **Call,** a clear whistled *wheee-u.*

Social Flycatcher *Myiozetetes similis* L 6¾"-7¼" *(17-18 cm)*
Common from northeastern and northwestern Mexico to northeastern Argentina. Only one fully documented record at Bentsen-
Rio Grande Valley State Park, Texas, 7 to 14 Jan. 2005. A
medium-sized, colorful flycatcher vaguely suggestive of the much
larger Greater Kiskadee, but black bill is much smaller. **Adult** also
lacks rufous in the wings and tail, which eliminates Middle American races of Great Kiskadee, although juvenile Social Flycatcher
does show rufous edges. The reddish orange central crown patch
is concealed by dark gray. Distinctive **call** is a loud *che cheechee
cheechee cheechee;* also a harsh *cree-yooo.*

Masked Tityra *Tityra semifasciata* L 9" *(23 cm)*
Common from northwestern and northeastern Mexico to Brazil.
One record from south Texas at Bentsen-Rio Grande Valley State
Park, from 17 Feb. to 10 Mar. 1990. Large and chunky; **males** are
pale gray above and whitish below with contrasting black on face,
most of wings, and thick subterminal tail band. Bare skin on face
and base of thick bill is pinkish red. Female is similar, but is darker
and duller. Distinctive **call** is a double, nasal grunt, *zzzr-zzzrt.*

Yucatan Vireo *Vireo magister* L 6" *(15 cm)*
Resident on Yucatán Peninsula and its offshore islands; also on
Grand Cayman and islands off Honduras. Overall brownish above
with dark eye line, but no dark lateral crown stripe as in Red-eyed
Vireo (page 318). Dull whitish below with grayish brown flanks,
short primary projection, and very large, heavy bill. **Call** a nasal
benk, often strung together in a series.

Cuban Martin *Progne crytoleuca* L 7½" *(19 cm)*
Breeds Cuba and Isle of Pines; wintering grounds unknown, but
presumably South America. Only acceptable record is specimen
taken on 9 May 1895 at Key West, Florida. Adult male closely
resembles Purple Martin (page 330), but has relatively longer and
more deeply forked tail; in hand, note concealed white feathers on
belly. **Female** resembles female Purple, but with unmarked white
belly and undertail coverts; lacks grayish collar. Separation from
Caribbean (*P. dominicensis*) and Sinaloa Martins (*P. sinaloae*), with
which it sometimes is treated as conspecific, is difficult; Cuban is
darker overall with dark shaft smudges on the undertail coverts
and usually with some shaft streaking on the breast and sides.

adult

adult ♂

adult ♀

adult ♀

adult ♀

adult
fusca

adult

adult
yakutensis

Gray-breasted Martin *Progne chalybea L 6¾" (17 cm)*
Breeds in Mexico from southern Sinaloa and southern Tamauli-pas, south to Argentina. Withdraws from northeastern portion of range in winter. Two old specimen records for south Texas: 25 Apr. 1880 at Rio Grande City; 18 May 1889 from Hidalgo County; all other reports unsubstantiated. Similar to female Purple Martin (page 330), but smaller with a less deeply forked tail; also browner on forehead, a less well-defined collar, and paler underparts.

Southern Martin *Progne elegans L 7" (18 cm)*
An austral migrant from South America. One specimen record from Key West, Florida, on 14 Aug. 1890. Adult male resembles Purple Martin (page 330), but smaller with slightly longer and more forked tail, and in hand, lacks concealed white patch on sides and flanks. **Female** is darker below than female Purple Martin.

Brown-chested Martin *Progne tapera L 6½" (16 cm)*
South American species. Southern subspecies, *fusca*, is an austral migrant to northern South America. Two North American records: a specimen (*fusca*) from Monomoy Island, Massachusetts, 12 June 1983, and one seen at Cape May, New Jersey, 6 to 15 Nov. 1997. Smaller than Purple Martin with brownish upper parts, white below with brown sides, and brown band across breast.

Mangrove Swallow *Tachycineta albilinea L 5¼" (13 cm)*
A small swallow found from coastal slopes of central Sonora and southern Tamaulipas, Mexico, south through Panama; isolated population in Peru. An adult was at the Viera Wetlands in Bre-vard County, Florida, 18 to 25 Nov. 2000. **Adults** have an irides-cent greenish crown and back; auriculars and lores black; narrow white line, usually meets across forehead; partial white collar; and distinct white rump. Juvenile is like adult, but brownish above. Compare also to Tree and Violet-green Swallows and Common House-Martin (page 330). Within normal range, seldom found far from water.

Willow Warbler *Phylloscopus trochilus L 4½" (11 cm)*
A highly migratory Old World species. Only record for North America at Gambell, St. Lawrence Island, Alaska, 25 to 30 Aug. 2002, was thought to pertain to *yakutensis* (illustrated), but was greener above and more yellowish below. There is an additional specimen record from northeast Greenland. Like the similar Arc-tic Warbler (page 348) in overall coloration and long primary pro-jection, but smaller, with smaller bill and a plainer wing. Whistled *hoo-eet* **call** note is very unlike Arctic's buzzy note. Another *Phyl-loscopus*, the widespread Chiffchaff (*P. collybita*), could occur in North America. It is very similar to Willow Warbler, but has a shorter primary projection and a different wing formula (primary spacing). Eastern breeding populations of Chiffchaff average grayer or browner than European populations. Typically leg color is a good indicator (pale on Willow, dark on Chiffchaff), but the Gam-bell bird had dark legs as it can in the easterly breeding subspecies of Willow Warbler.

Wood Warbler *Phlloscopus sibilatrix L 5" (13 cm)*
Breeds in the western Palearctic; winters in tropical Africa. Two
fall records for western Alaska: one collected on Shemya Island,
western Aleutians, 9 Oct. 1978; one photographed on St. Paul
Island, 7 Oct. 2004. A colorful *Phylloscopus* with yellow throat and
upper breast contrasting sharply with white lower breast and belly;
the yellow supercilium is well defined by a complete dark eye line;
yellow-green edges to flight feathers and greater coverts; and dark
centered tertials with sharply defined pale edges. Note very long
primary projection, which contributes to short-tailed appearance.

fall
adult

Yellow-browed Warbler *Phylloscopus inornatus*
L 4½" (11 cm) Primarily breeds in the northeastern Palearctic
region. Two photographed fall records from Gambell, St.
Lawrence Island, Alaska: 12 to 14 Sept. 1999 and 30 Aug. 1992.
Distinctly patterned with bold supercilium and two pale wing
bars and dark band at base of secondaries; tertials with sharply
defined, pale edges. Note small and mostly dark bill. **Call** a distinctive upslurred *swee-eet,* not too unlike call of male Pacific-
slope Flycatcher. Most authorities have now split the less
migratory and more southerly breeding subspecies (*humei* and
mandellii) as a separate species, Hume's Leaf -Warbler (*P. humei*).

1st fall
inornatus

Lesser Whitethroat *Sylvia curruca L 5½" (14 cm)*
Old World species. Only record was one photographed at Gambell, St. Lawrence Island, Alaska, 8 to 9 Sept. 2002. Distinctive,
with a rather long tail, outer rectrices tipped with white; gray
crown with a dark mask, a warm brown back and wings, and
whitish underparts with a tan wash on the sides and flanks. **Call**
is a hard *tik,* often repeated. Multiple subspecies groups are
treated by Old World authorities as up to four species.

1st fall
blythi

Mugimaki Flycatcher *Ficedula mugimaki L 5¼" (13 cm)*
Highly migratory species of eastern Asia. Only record is from Shemya Island, Alaska, on 24 May 1985, supported by marginal photos. Note long wings. Adult male is striking, with blackish head
and upper parts, white wing patch, short but broad downcurving
white supercilium, and extensively orange underparts. Female is
brownish above, burnt orange on throat and breast; has two thin
pale wing bars. **First-year male** closer to female, but with partial,
broad and downcurving supercilium. In Asian range feeds from
mid- to upper canopy.

1st year ♂

Spotted Flycatcher *Muscicapa striata L 6" (15 cm)*
Widespread breeder in the Palearctic, east to about Lake Baikal;
winters in Africa, south of the Sahara. One photographed from
Gambell, St. Lawrence Island, Alaska, on 14 Sept. 2002. Overall
grayish brown above, with fine streaking on crown and forecrown,
and indistinct whitish eye ring; lacks distinct malar and submoustachial markings; below indistinctly streaked, not spotted,
across throat and breast. Juvenile is spotted with buff above and
has dark mottling below.

adult

adult ♀

Siberian Blue Robin *Luscinia cyane* L 5½" (14 cm)
Highly migratory Asian species. One certain North American specimen record from Attu Island, Alaska, 21 May 1985; an additional spring sighting of an adult male from the Yukon is disputed. Adult male is deep blue above, clear white below. **Adult female** brownish above with faint buffy eye ring; buffy wash across breast with faint stippling, and most have some bluish on tail (lacking on immature females). Immature male has some blue on scapulars, wings, and tail. Frequently vibrates tail.

Orange-billed Nightingale-Thrush
Catharus amantiirostris L 6½" (17 cm)
Widespread in Neotropics. Two records from south Texas: one photographed in hand on 8 Apr. 1996 at Laguna Atascosa National Wildlife Refuge, and a specimen from Edinburg on 28 May 2004. Orange-brown above, pale gray and whitish below with distinctive bright orange bill, legs, and orbital ring. In flight, lacks pale underwing bar of northern breeding *Catharus* thrushes.

Black-headed Nightingale-Thrush *Catharus mexicanus*
L 6½" (17 cm) Found from northeastern Mexico to western Panama. Only record was one at Pharr, in south Texas, from 28 May to 29 Oct. 2004. Distinctive, with blackish crown and face, whitish throat and belly; otherwise gray below. Bright orange orbital ring, bill, and legs.

♂

Eurasian Blackbird *Turdus merula* L 10½" (27 cm)
Palearctic species. Only accepted record was a **male** found dead on 16 Nov. 1994 at Bonavista, Newfoundland. Other records, mainly from northeastern Canada, are of uncertain origin. There are a dozen Greenland records. Male is all-black; orange-yellow orbital eye ring and bill (duller on immatures). Female is browner with pale throat and dark-streaked chest; soft parts duller.

winter
adult ♂

Citrine Wagtail *Motacilla citreola* L 6½" (17 cm)
Palearctic species that winters farther north than either Western or Eastern Yellow Wagtail. Only North American record was from Starkville, Mississippi, from 31 Jan. to 1 Feb. 1992. All plumages have gray back and bold, well-defined white wing bars. Breeding adult male has bright yellow head and underparts and a dark nape. Adult female and **winter adult male** have yellow-centered, grayish brown auriculars completely surrounded by yellow. Immatures lack all yellow, but have similar, winter-adult face pattern. **Call** is loud buzzy *tsweep*, like Eastern Yellow Wagtail.

Tree Pipit *Anthus trivialis* L 6" (15 cm)
Palearctic breeding species, wintering mainly in Africa south of the Sahara and in India. Three records for western Alaska: a specimen from Cape Prince of Wales on 23 June 1978, and two photographed at Gambell, St. Lawrence Island, Alaska (6 June 1995; 21, 27 Sept. 2002). Resembles Olive-backed Pipit (page 370), but browner above and with distinct back streaks; face pattern more blended and no dark spot in rear of cheek; **call** similar.

Gray Silky-flycatcher *Ptilogonys cinereus* L 7½" (20 cm)
Resident (some seasonal movement) from northern Mexico to
Guatemala; largely montane. Two accepted Texas records: from 31
Oct. to 11 Nov. 1985 at Laguna Atascosa National Wildlife Refuge
and from 12 Jan. to 5 Mar. 1995 in El Paso. Four well-documented
southern California records have been questioned on origin. Struc-
tured like Phainopepla. **Adult males** are gray with orange-yellow
flanks and bright yellow undertail coverts; note white eye ring and
white base of tail. Females and juveniles are similar, but duller.

Worthen's Sparrow *Spizella worthenii* L 5½" (14 cm)
Critically endangered. Only extant populations are in northeastern Mexico in Coahuila and Nuevo Léon. Only U.S. record at Sil-
ver City, New Mexico, on 16 June 1884, the type specimen of the
species; probably part of a small resident population, subsequently
extirpated. Resembles *aranacea* Field Sparrow (page 410), but
crown solidly rufous and rump grayish; vocalizations differ.

Pine Bunting *Emberiza leucocephalus* L 6½" (17cm)
Primarily an eastern Palearctic species. Two fall records from Attu
Island, Alaska, both males: one photographed 18 to 19 Nov. 1995
and a specimen (nominate *leucocephalus*) on 6 Oct. 1993. Breeding male is rusty overall, with chestnut head, and bold white eyebrow and cheek patch; in winter, duller head lacks white crown
patch. Female is duller still with a weak malar, but has a rusty eyebrow and at least a small white spot at rear of cheek.

Yellow-throated Bunting *Emberiza elegans* L 6" (15 cm)
East Asian species. One record of a male photographed on Attu
Island, Alaska, 25 May 1988. Note prominent crest. Yellow-and-
black head pattern of **adult male** is striking. Female and immature male are similar, but duller, with brownish auriculars.

Tawny-shouldered Blackbird *Agelaius humeralis*
L 8" (20 cm) Resident on Cuba and in Haiti. Only U.S. record was
two secured (specimens) at the Key West Lighthouse on 27 Feb.
1936. Smaller and slimmer than Red-winged Blackbird and with
a slim, pointed bill; lesser coverts tawny, not red, and rear border
has a narrow blended edge. More arboreal than Red-winged and
buzzy, muffled song is more drawn out.

Eurasian Siskin *Carduelis spinus* L 4¾" (12 cm)
Palearctic species. Two records of males from Attu Island: a specimen, 21 to 22 May 1993 and a sight record on 4 June 1978. About
six records from northeast North America, but the origin of these
has been questioned; a male photographed at Saint-Pierre and
Miquelon on 23 June 1983 is perhaps the most compelling.
Unrecorded from Greenland. **Male** is distinctive with black forecrown and chin, olive above, and extensively yellow below. Female
is much duller, the yellow restricted to sides of breast, and a wash
of yellow on face, eyebrow, and rump; juvenile duller still. Some
Pine Siskins (page 460) are very similar, but wing coverts of
Eurasian average darker.

adult ♂

fall
adult ♂

adult ♂

adult ♂

fall
adult ♂

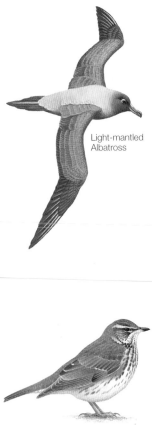

Light-mantled
Albatross

AOU and ABA Checklist Differences

As noted in the introduction of this book, the AOU and ABA checklist committees serve different purposes. The differences can be summarized as follows:

Light-mantled Albatross *Phobetria palpebrata*. Origin questioned by ABA (page 466). **Azure Gallinule** *Porphyrula flavirostris*. A specimen from Suffolk County, New York, on 14 Dec. 1986 was initially accepted by both committees, but subsequent information revealed that it may have escaped from a local aviculturalist. Still accepted by AOU. **Caribbean Elaenia** *Elaenia martinica*. Not accepted by AOU (page 475). **European Turtle-Dove** *Streptopelia turtur*. One at Lower Matecumbe Key, South Florida, 9-11 Apr. 1990 (photos), was accepted by AOU; its origin was questioned by ABA.

Greenland

Greenland is the largest island in the World, most of it lying north of the Arctic Circle, and forms the most northeastern part of North America. Over 230 species have been recorded there, and nearly all are substantiated by specimens. The definitive ornithological reference is *An Annotated Checklist to the Birds of Greenland* (1994) by David Boertmann (*Bioscience* 38). Boertmann divides Greenland into four regions (north, west, northeast, and southeast) and details the bird distribution for each. Greenland's avifauna is a mix of both Palearctic and Nearctic species, many of which are strays respectively from Europe (including Iceland) and mainland North America. The breeding avifauna includes Pink-footed, White-fronted (the endemic breeding subspecies *flavirostris*), and Barnacle Geese, White-tailed Eagle, Fieldfare, Redwing, White Wagtail (nominate *alba*), and Meadow Pipit. Three subspecies of Rock Ptarmigan are found in Greenland, two of which (*saturata* and *capta*) are endemic. Two subspecies of Dunlins breed in Greenland, one of which (*arctica*) is an endemic breeder in the northeast; the other (*schinzii*) breeds in southern Greenland as well as northwestern Europe. The Black Scoters recorded are of the nominate *nigra* subspecies from northwest Europe. The Merlin specimens from Greenland are of *subaesalon*, an endemic breeder on Iceland; also recorded is the more widespread *aesolon*, breeding mainly in northern Europe. The Red Crossbills collected are of nominate *curvirostra* from the Palearctic. These, along with the following list of species *not* recorded in our area of coverage, should alert observers to the potential visitors to northeast North America. For polytypic species, the trinomial subspecies name is given, if known:

Eurasian Spoonbill *Platalea leucorodia leucorodia*. One Oct. record (1909) for the West. **Ruddy Shelduck** *Tadorna ferruginea*. Four collected in the summer of 1892, an invasion year for the species in northwest Europe. (See also page 96.) **Water Rail** *Rallus aquaticus hibernans*. Four records. The subspecies *hibernans* is endemic to Iceland. **Spotted Crake** *Porzana porzana*. Eleven

Redwing

White Wagtail
alba

records, nearly all in fall, from the West! **Oriental Plover** *Charadrius veredus.* One May record (1948) from the West. A remarkable record, as it breeds on the steppes of eastern Asia and winters in Australia. **Rook** *Corvus frugilegus frugilegus.* One Mar. record (1901) for the Southeast. **Carrion Crow** *Corvus corone cornix.* Two spring records (1897, 1907) were of the "Hooded Crow." **Meadow Pipit** *Anthus pratensis pratensis.* Scarce breeder in eastern Greenland. **White's Thrush** *Zoothera aurea aurea.* One Oct. record (1954) for the Northeast. It is here treated as a separate species from the Scaly Thrush, *Z. dauma,* following other authorities. **Song Thrush** *Turdus philomelos philomelos.* One June record (1982) for the Northeast. **Blackcap** *Sylvia atricapilla atricapilla.* One Nov. record (1916) for the Southeast. **Lesser Redpoll** *Carduelis cabaret.* One Sept. record (1933) for the Southeast.

Dunlin
schinzii

Bermuda

Bermuda is a series of some 300 small islands, most of which are uninhabited. It is best known as the only breeding site of the Bermuda Petrel (also called the Cahow), which was discovered early in the 17th century and then thought to be extinct until it was rediscovered in 1951. The White-tailed Tropicbird reaches its northernmost breeding range here. The only endemic breeding land bird is a nonmigratory subspecies of the White-eyed Vireo (*bermudianus*). Established exotics not found in North America include European Goldfinch, Common Waxbill, and Orange-cheeked Waxbill. Bermuda is well known for its migrants and vagrants, which make up most of Bermuda's extensive species list—in excess of 360 species. Surprising northern species that have occurred include Northern Hawk Owl, Snowy Owl, Bohemian Waxwing, White-winged Crossbill, and Pine Grosbeak. The single Snowy Owl (1987) took to predating the endangered Bermuda Petrels and had to be collected—sometimes conservationists have to make hard choices! Most of the vagrants come from North America (including the West) or Europe, but a few (Large-billed Tern and Fork-tailed Flycatcher) are from South America. The Red-necked Stint and, even more surprisingly, the Dark-sided Flycatcher (a late Sept. specimen of nominate *sibirica*) are from Asia. The most recent birding references for Bermuda are *A Guide to the Birds of Bermuda* (1991) by Eric Amos and *A Birdwatching Guide to Bermuda* (2002) by Andrew Dobson.

Bermuda Petrel

The following are the species recorded from Bermuda but not from mainland North America:

West Indian Whistling-Duck *Dendrocygna arborea.* One record (1907). This species is resident on some of the Bahamian islands. (A recent record from Virginia is of uncertain origin.) **Ferruginous Duck** *Aythya nyroca.* A winter sight record (1987). **Striated Heron** *Butorides striatus.* One record (1985) of a long-staying bird. **Booted Eagle** *Hieraaetus pennatus.* A Sept. sight record (1989). **White Tern** *Gygis alba.* A remarkable Dec. record (1972). Photographic evidence indicates that it was not the expected nominate race from the south Atlantic but, rather, one of the Pacific races!

White-tailed Tropicbird

Index

The main entry for each species is listed in **boldface** type and refers to the text page opposite the illustration.

Art Credits

Jonathan Alderfer: Inside front cover; 2-3; 6-Buller's Shearwater; 11-Pacific Golden-Plover and Short-tailed Albatross; 12-Black-bellied Plover; 14-American Golden-Plover; 16-Short-billed Dowitcher; 19-Carolina Parakeet; 31-Spot-billed Duck; 45-White-winged Scoter *stejnegeri;* 47-Goldeneye hybrid; 49-Goosander; 75; 77-heads; 79; 81; 83-Parkinson's Petrel and Murphy's Petrel; 85; 89-Cory's Shearwater, Cape Verde Shearwater, and small comparison figures; 91-Wedge-tailed Shearwater, Bulwer's Petrel, left Short-tailed Shearwater, and heads; 93; 101; 107; 155; 175; 177-flying Black Turnstone; 189; 191; 233-flying winter Dovekie; 235-Long-billed Murrelet; 239; 241-flying Rhinoceros Auklet; 245-with N. John Schmitt; 307; 311-Rose-throated Becard; 347-female Blue-gray Gnatcatcher tail; 363-Blue Mockingbird; 367-Common Myna; 466-except Lesser White-fronted Goose; 467-except Great Frigatebird; 468-Gray Heron; 472-except Whiskered Tern and Scaly-naped Pigeon; 475-Social Flycatcher and Masked Tityra; 476-Mangrove Swallow; 479-Gray Silky-flycatcher; 480-except Redwing. **David Beadle:** 11-Least Flycatcher; 13-Acadian Flycatcher; 14; 83-Great-winged Petrel; 295; 297; 299; 301; 303-Tufted Flycatcher; 309-Gray Kingbird and Thick-billed Kingbird; 315-Thick-billed Vireo; 319-Philadelphia Vireo and Warbling Vireo; 329; 343-western Winter Wren; 379-Crescent-chested Warbler; 389-fall Bay-breasted Warbler; 399-Red-faced Warbler; 415-Sage Sparrow *canescens;* 423-Vesper Sparrow; 427-Pink-sided Dark-eyed Junco; 469-Paint-billed Crake; 470-Spotted Rail and Double-striped Thick-knee; 472-Scaly-naped Pigeon; 473-Gray Nightjar and Antillean Palm-Swift; 474-Bumblebee Hummingbird and Greenish Elaenia; 475-except Social Flycatcher and Masked Tityra; 476-except Mangrove Swallow and Willow Warbler; 478-Orange-billed Nightingale-Thrush and Black-headed Nightingale Thrush; 479-Worthen's Sparrow and Tawny-shouldered Blackbird. **Peter Burke:** 6-male White-collared Seedeater; 12-Flycatcher tails; 13-Scarlet Tanager; 17-Shiny Cowbird; 109; 117-Glossy Ibis (except flying) and White-faced Ibis; 305; 311-Piratic Flycatcher and Variegated Flycatcher; 317-Gray Vireo; 361-White-throated Robin; 397-except Common Yellowthroat; 401; 403-adult male White-collared Seedeater and Yellow-faced Grassquit; 405; 407; 437-Crimson-collared Grosbeak; 449-Shiny Cowbird; 451; 453. **Marc R. Hanson:** 83-Northern Fulmar; 89-

Greater Shearwater, Manx Shearwater, Audubon's Shearwater, and Little Shearwater; 91-Flesh-footed Shearwater, Sooty Shearwater, and right Short-tailed Shearwater; 95-except European Storm-Petrel; 97; 147; 149; 151-except Purple Swamphen. **Cynthia J. House:** 9-Lesser and Greater Scaups; 12-American Black Duck; 21; 23; 25-except flying and Taverner's Cackling Goose and Lesser Canada Goose; 27-except juvenile Whooper Swan; 29-except flying Muscovy Duck; 31-except head of female American Black Duck and Spot-billed Duck; 33; 35; 37; 39; 41; 43; 45-except White-winged Scoter *stejnegeri;* 47-except Goldeneye hybrid; 49-except Goosander; 51-except Egyptian Goose; 52-53; 54-55. **H. Jon Janosik:** 77-except heads; 99; 103; 105; 161; 481-White-tailed Tropicbird. **Donald L. Malick:** 8; 9-American Three-toed Woodpecker; 18; 19-Red-cockaded Woodpecker; 119; 121; 125-except Stellar's Sea-Eagle and 3rd year Bald Eagle; 127-except flying figures; 129-perched figures of juvenile Common Black-Hawk, Zone-tailed Hawk, and Short-tailed Hawk; 133; 135-except dark-morph Ferruginous Hawk and flying adult and dark juvenile White-tailed Hawks; 137-perched Aplomado Falcons and Crested Caracara; 139-all perched figures except Merlin *suckleyi* and upper flying American Kestrel; 141-except flying figures of adult male Prairie Falcon, Peregrine Falcon, and Gyrfalcon; 247; 257; 259; 261; 263; 265; 281; 283; 285; 287; 289-except Great Spotted Woodpecker; 291; 293. **Killian Mullarney:** 17-Ruff; 159; 187; 193; 196-Little Ringed Plover. **Michael O'Brien:** 87, 163-Willet; 335; 337; 339-except Verdin and Bushtit; 481-Bermuda Petrel. **John P. O'Neill:** 279-Elegant Trogan and Eared Quetzal; 339-Verdin and Bushtit. **Kent Pendleton:** 57-Gray Partridge and Chukars on ground; 59; 61; 63; 65; 67; 69; 123-except Northern Harrier; 141-flying figures of adult male Prairie Falcon, Peregrine Falcon, and Gyrfalcon; 142-except Hook-billed Kite; 143; 144; 145. **Diane Pierce:** 10-Chipping Sparrow; 16-Indigo Bunting; 19-Dusky Seaside Sparrow; 111; 113-except Little Egret; 115; 117-flying Glossy Ibis, White Ibis, Scarlet Ibis, and Roseate Spoonbill; 153; 409-except Bachman's Sparrow; 411; 413; 415-except Sage Sparrow *canescens:* 417-except Orange Bishop; 419-Seaside Sparrow; 421; 423-except Vesper Sparrow; 425; 427-except Pink-sided Dark-eyed Junco and Slate-colored Dark-eyed Junco; 429; 431; 433-except Yellow-breasted Bunting; 435; 437-except

Crimson-collared Grosbeak; 439; 441; 455-except Common Chaffinch; 457; 459; 461; 463; 468-Yellow Bittern. **John C. Pitcher:** 157; 163-except Willet and flying Yellowlegs; 165-standing Common Grenshank and standing Spotted Redshank; 167; 169; 177-except flying Black Turnstone; 181; 183; 185. **H. Douglas Pratt:** 6-female and 1st winter male White-collared Seedeater; 7-Crested Myna; 9-Cerulean Warbler; 10-Northern Parula; 14-Painted Redstart; 16-European Starling; 243; 253; 255; 273-except immature Green Violet-ear, Green-breasted Mango, and Lucifer Hummingbird; 275-except Xantus's Hummingbird; 277-except wing figures; 279-except Elegant Trogan and Eared Quetzal; 303-except Tufted Flycatcher; 309-adult Fork-tailed Flycatcher and Eastern Kingbird; 311-except Piratic Flycatcher, Variegated Flycatcher, and Rose-throated Becard; 313-except Brown Shrike; 315-except Thick-billed Vireo; 317-except Gray Vireo; 319-except Philadelphia Vireo and Warbling Vireo; 321; 323-except Island Scrub-Jay and adult Mexican Jays; 325; 327; 331-except Common House-Martin; 333; 341; 343-except western Winter Wren; 345; 347-except female Blue-gray Gnatcatcher tail; 349-except Lanceolated Warbler; 355; 359-Varied Thrush; 361-except White-throated Robin; 363-except Blue Mockingbird; 367-except Common Myna; 369-except Siberian Accentor; 373; 375; 377; 379-except Virginia's Warbler and Crescent-chested Warbler; 381; 383-except Black-and-white Warbler; 385; 387; 389-except fall Bay-breasted Warbler; 393; 395; 397-Common Yellowthroat; 399-except Red-faced Warbler; 403-female and 1st winter male White-collared Seedeater, Bananaquit, and Black-faced Grassquit; 445; 447; 449-except Shiny Cowbird. **David Quinn:** 6-Mugimaki Flycatcher; 7-Asian Brown Flycatcher; 17-Redwing and Eurasian Hoopoe; 71; 73; 95-European Storm-Petrel; 113-Little Egret; 151-Purple Swamphen; 165-Marsh Sandpiper and Common Redshank; 195-Common Redshank; 289-Great Spotted Woodpecker; 313-Brown Shrike; 331-Common House-Martin; 349-Lanceolated Warbler; 351; 353; 359-except Varied Thrush; 369-Siberian Accentor; 371; 433-Yellow-breasted Bunting; 455-Common Chaffinch; 466-Lesser White-fronted Goose; 468-Chinese Egret and Western Reef-Heron; 469-Chinese Pond-Heron; 470-except Spotted Rail and Double-striped Thick-knee; 471; 472-Whiskered Tern; 474-except Bumblebee Hummingbird and Greenish Elaenia; 476-Willow Warbler; 477; 478-except Nightingale-Thrushes; 479-Pine Bunting, Yellow-throated Bunting and Eurasian Siskin; 480-Redwing. **Chuck Ripper:** 233-except flying winter Dovekie; 235-except Long-billed Murrelet; 237; 241-except flying Rhinoceros Auklet; 267; 269-except southwestern Whip-poor-will tail. **N. John Schmitt:** 7-Orange Bishop; 10-Common Black-Hawk; 13-House Sparrow; 25-flying and Taverner's Cackling Goose and Lesser Canada Goose; 27-juvenile Whooper Swan; 29-flying Muscovy Duck; 51-Egyptian Goose; 57-Plain Chachalaca and flying Chukar; 123-Northern Harrier; 125-Stellar's Sea-Eagle and 3rd year Bald Eagle; 127-flying figures; 129-except perched figures of juvenile Common Black-Hawk, Zone-tailed Hawk, and Short-tailed Hawk; 131; 135-dark-morph Ferruginous Hawk and flying adult and dark juvenile White-tailed Hawks; 137-Eurasian Hobby and flying Aplomado Falcons; 139-Merlin *suckleyi* and all flying figures except upper American Kestrel; 142-Hook-billed Kite; 171-Little Curlew; 173-standing figures of Bristle-thighed Curlew and Eurasian Curlew; 194-Little Curlew; 245-with Jonathan Alderfer; 249; 251; 271; 309-juvenile Fork-tailed Flycatcher; 323-Island Scrub-Jay and adult Mexican Jays; 365; 417-Orange Bishop; 419-except Seaside Sparrow; 427-Slate-colored Dark-eyed Junco; 465. **Thomas R. Schultz:** 11-Great Black-backed Gull wing, and Western and California Gulls; 12-Common Tern; 179; 199; 201; 203; 205; 207; 209; 211; 213; 215; 216-217; 219; 221; 223; 225; 227; 229; 231, 357; 379-Virginia's Warbler; 383-Black-and-white Warbler; 391; 403-Western Spindalis; 409; 443; 467-Great Frigatebird; 468-Lesser Frigatebird; 469-except Chinese Pond-Heron and Paint-billed Crake; 473-except Gray Nightjar and Antillean Palm-Swift; 481-Dunlin. **Daniel S. Smith:** 163-flying Yellowlegs; 165-flying Common Grenshank and flying Spotted Redshank; 171-except Little Curlew; 173-except standing figures of Bristle-thighed Curlew and Eurasian Curlew; 194-except Little Curlew; 195-except Common Redshank; 196-except Little Ringed Plover; 197. **Patricia A. Topper:** Cover. **Sophie Webb:** 269-southwestern Whip-poor-will tail; 273-immature Green Violet-ear, Green-breasted Mango, and Lucifer Hummingbird; 275-Xantus's Hummingbird; 277-wing figures.

502

Acknowledgments

The editors wish to thank the following individuals and institutions for their valuable assistance in the preparation of the fifth edition:
M. Adams, Natural History Museum, Tring, UK; Jim Arterburn, Tulsa, Oklahoma; Ken Behrens, Pittsburg, Pennsylvania; Gavin Bieber, Tucson, Arizona; Chuck Carlson, Fort Peck, Montana; John Carlson, Helena, Montana; Robin Carter, Columbia, South Carolina; Allen Chartier, Inkster, Michigan; Ricky Davis, Rocky Mount, North Carolina; James Dinsmore, Iowa City, Iowa; Richard Erickson, Irvine, California; Doug Faulkner, Denver, Colorado; Dr. C. T. Fisher, World Museum Liverpool, UK; Robert Fisher, Independence, Missouri; Rick Fridell, Hurricane, Utah; Kimball L. Garrett, Los Angeles County Museum of Natural History, Los Angeles, California; Daniel D. Gibson, University of Alaska, Fairbanks, Alaska; Britt Griswold, Annapolis, Maryland; Robert Hamilton, Long Beach, California; Tom and Jo Heindel, Big Pine, California; Rich Hoyer, Tucson, Arizona; Dan Kassebaum, Belleville, Illinois; Tom Kent, Iowa City, Iowa; Rudolf Koes, Winnipeg, Manitoba; Dr M. Largen, World Museum Liverpool, UK; Tony Leukering, Brighton, Colorado; Mark Lockwood, Alpine, Texas; Derek Lovitch, Portland, Maine; Rich MacIntosh, Kodiak, Alaska; Ron Martin, Sawyer, North Dakota; Terry McEneaney, Yellowstone NP, Wyoming; Mick McHugh, Shawnee Mission, Kansas; Ian McLaren, Halifax, Nova Scotia; Steve Mlodinow, Everett, Washington; Glenn Murphy, Royal Ontario Museum, Ontario, Canada; Kenny Nichols, Pangburn, Arkansas; Jerry Oldenettel, Socorro, New Mexico; Mike Overton, Boone, Iowa; A. Parker, World Museum Liverpool, UK; John Parmeter, Albuquerque, New Mexico; Michael Patten, Bartlesville, Oklahoma; Mark Peck, Royal Ontario Museum, Ontario, Canada; Bill Pranty, Bayonet Point, Florida; David Quady, Berkeley, California; Mark Robbins, Lawrence, Kansas; Don Roberson, Pacific Grove, California; Bill Rowe, St Louis, Missouri; Larry Sansone, Hollywood, California; Larry Semo, Westminster, Colorado; John Sterling, Woodland, California; Mark Stevenson, Tucson, Arizona; Sherman Suter, Alexandria, Virginia; Peder Svingen, Duluth, Minnesota; Charles Trost, Pocatello, Idaho; David Willard, Field Museum of Natural History, Chicago, Illinois; Chris Wood, Ithaca, New York.

The editors also wish to thank the following for their contributions to previous editions of this guide:
Thomas A. Allen; David Agro; J. Phillip Angle; Stephen Bailey; Lawrence G. Balch; Dr. Richard C. Banks; John Barber; Jon Barlow; Jen and Des Bartlett; Giff Beaton; Louis Bevier; Eirik A.T. Blom; Daniel Boone; Jack Bowling; Edward S. Brinkley; the Department of Ornithology at the British Museum, Tring; Dawn Burke; Danny Bystrak; Richard Cannings; Steven W. Cardiff; Charles Carlson; Graham Chisholm; Carla Cicero; Charles T. Clark; William S. Clark; Rene Corado; Marian Cressman; Denver Museum of Natural History, Colorado; Bruce Deuel; Donna L. Dittman; Robert Dixon; Peter J. Dunn; Peter Dunne; Cameron Eckert; Victor Emanuel; Richard Erickson; Field Museum of Natural History, Chicago; Dr. Clemency Fisher; John W. Fitzpatrick; David Fix; Kimball L. Garrett; Freida Gentry; Daniel D. Gibson; Peter Grant; John A. Gregoire; Dr. James L. Gulledge; Jon S. Greenlaw; Dr. George A. Hall; J.B. Hallett, Jr.; Robert Hamilton; Jo and Tom Heindel; Matt Heindel; Steve Heinl; Paul M. Hill; Chris Hobbs; Phill Holder; Steve N.G. Howell; Rebecca Hyman; Frank Iwen; Greg Jackson; Alvaro Jaramillo; Joseph R. Jehl, Jr.; Ned K. Johnson; Roy Jones; Colin Jones; Lars Jonsson; Kenn Kaufman; Wayne Klockner; Marianne G. Koszorus; Lasse J. Laine; Los Angeles County Museum of Natural History; Daniel Lane; Dr. Malcolm Largen; Greg Lasley; Paul E. Lehman; Nick Lethaby; Tony Leukering; Rich Levad; Liverpool Museum, England; Mark Lockwood; Los Angeles County Museum of Natural History; Tim Loseby; Aileen Lotz; Rich MacIntosh; Bruce Mactavish; Laura Martin; Guy McCaskie; Terry McEneaney; Doug McRae; Dominic Mitchell; Steve Mlodinow; Joseph Morlan; Killian Mullarney; Museum of Natural History, Santa Barbara, California; Museum of Natural Science, Louisiana State University, Baton Rouge; Museum of Vertebrate Zoology, University of California, Berkeley; Glen Murphy; National Museum of Natural History, Smithsonian Institution, Washington, D.C.; Natural History Museum, San Diego, California; Harry Nehls; Michael O'Brien; Jerry Oldenettel; Gerald Oreel; Tony Parker; John Parmeter; Michael Patten; Brian Patteson; Dennis Paulson; Mark Peck; Paul Prior; Peter Pyle; Betsy Reeder; Dr. J.V. Remsen; Robert F. Ringler; Don Roberson; Mark Robins; Gary Rosenberg; Philip D. Round; John Rowlett; Rose Ann Rowlett; Royal Ontario Museum; Will Russell; San Diego Natural History Museum; Larry Sansone; Rick Saval; Robert T. Scholes; Brad Schram; Thomas Schulenberg; Scott Seltman; David Sibley; Ross Silcock; Mark Stackhouse; James Stasz; Rick Steenberg; Andrew Stepniewski; Doug Stotz; Sherman Suter; Thede Tobish; Dr. John Trochet; Charles Trost; Laurel Tucker; Nigel Tucker; Bill Tweit; Philip Unitt; U.S. Fish and Wildlife Service's Patuxent Wildlife Research Center in Laurel, Maryland; Arnoud van den Berg; T.R. Wahl; George Wallace; Western Foundation of Vertebrate Zoology; Mel White; Tony White; Hal Wierenga; Claudia P. Wilds; David W. Willard; Jeff Wilson; Alan Wormington; Louise Zemaitis; Barry Zimmer; Kevin Zimmer.

National Geographic Field Guide to the Birds of North America

Edited by Jon L. Dunn and Jonathan Alderfer

Published by the National Geographic Society

John M. Fahey, Jr., *President and Chief Executive Officer*

Gilbert M. Grosvenor, *Chairman of the Board*

Nina D. Hoffman, *Executive Vice President; President, Books Publishing Group*

Prepared by the Book Division

Kevin Mulroy, *Senior Vice President and Publisher*

Leah Bendavid-Val, *Director of Photography Publishing and Illustrations*

Marianne R. Koszorus, *Director of Design*

Barbara Brownell Grogan, *Executive Editor*

Elizabeth Newhouse, *Director of Travel Publishing*

Carl Mehler, *Director of Maps*

Staff for this Book

Barbara Levitt, *Editor*

Jennifer Conrad Seidel, *Text Editor*

Lyle Rosbotham, *Art Director*

Paul E. Lehman, *Chief Map Researcher/Editor*

Matt Chwastyk, *Map Production Manager*

Sven M. Dolling, Steven D. Gardner, Thomas L. Gray, *Map Research and Production*

Rick Wain, *Production Project Manager*

Meredith Wilcox, *Illustrations Coordinator*

Teresa Tate, Abby Leopold, *Illustrations Specialists*

Michael Greninger, *Editorial Assistant*

Cameron Zotter, *Design Assistant*

Rebecca Hinds, *Managing Editor*

Gary Colbert, *Production Director*

Manufacturing and Quality Management

Christopher A. Liedel, *Chief Financial Officer*

Phillip L. Schlosser, *Vice President*

John T. Dunn, *Technical Director*

Vincent P. Ryan, *Director*

Chris Brown, *Director*

Maryclare Tracy, *Manager*

Founded in 1888, the National Geographic Society is one of the largest nonprofit scientific and educational organizations in the world. It reaches more than 285 million people worldwide each month through its official journal, NATIONAL GEOGRAPHIC, and its four other magazines; the National Geographic Channel; television documentaries; radio programs; films; books; videos and DVDs; maps; and interactive media. National Geographic has funded more than 8,000 scientific research projects and supports an education program combating geographic illiteracy.

For more information, please call 1-800-NGS LINE (647-5463) or write to the following address:
National Geographic Society
1145 17th Street N.W.
Washington, D.C. 20036, U.S.A.

Visit us online at
www.nationalgeographic.com/books

For information about special discounts for bulk purchases, please contact National Geographic Books Special Sales: ngspecsales@ngs.org

Library of Congress Cataloging-in-Publication Data available upon request.

Hard cover
ISBN-10: 1-4262-0072-2
ISBN-13: 978-1-4262-0072-4

Soft cover
ISBN-10: 1-4262-0071-4
ISBN-13: 978-1-4262-0071-7

Printed in China

NATIONAL GEOGRAPHIC

GUIDE TO

Birding Hot Spots

OF THE UNITED STATES

Using the Guide

In the following pages, you'll find nearly 500 of the best places to go bird-watching in the 48 contiguous United States. (Hawaii and Alaska are not covered because of the disparate bird life of the former and the complications of travel in the latter.)

States are grouped by region, with sites throughout each state arranged in a logical flow. Site numbers are keyed to a regional map at the beginning of each section to aid you in finding your way from one site to the next. (A map key can be found on page 551.) For each state, you will find web addresses and telephone numbers for the sites or their administrative offices.

Be advised that facilities may be seasonal and limited. Call or write ahead for specific information, including directions to sites, tour and fee information, proximity to restrooms and concessions, and wheelchair accessibility.

If you're new to this business of traveling to see birds, remember that birds travel, too. Some sites are rewarding year-round; others are at their best only in nesting season or winter, or in spring and fall migration.

A Few Other Ideas

New birders should first join their local National Audubon Society chapter or birding club. The leading national organization for bird-watchers is the American Birding Association, or ABA (www.americanbirding.org). One of the benefits of ABA is its membership guide, published annually, which lists birders all over the country who will give advice to travelers or guide visitors to good birding sites in their home regions.

Check the web sites of bird clubs and ornithological societies across the nation, which offer guides to birding locations, information about local contacts, and schedules of field trips. Start your search with the National Audubon Society (www.audubon.org); check here for local chapters in the area you'll be visiting. Another important step in planning your trip is checking regional rare bird alerts—recorded messages, updated frequently, that list unusual species seen in a state or locality, often with directions to sites or numbers to call for more information. These can be found at www.birder.com/birding.

Also attend one of the birding festivals held annually across the nation, with programs and field trips led by experts, often concentrating on regional species. Find a list of festivals at the ABA web site.

Beyond Your List

Birding is rewarding even if you approach it only as a sport or hobby. After they've been at it awhile, though, most birders become conservationists. Understanding a bit about ecosystems and birds' habitat requirements leads to some inescapable conclusions. For instance, Sprague's Pipits need naturally managed prairie; if all our grasslands are plowed or overgrazed, there won't be any more Sprague's Pipits. Increasingly, birders are realizing that they are not exempt from responsibility. Playing a tape of a bird's song or call is often an effective way to bring it in close, but for some vulnerable species, it is bad practice. Really wanting to see a Yellow Rail doesn't mean you can enter a marsh to flush one up, especially when it's nesting. Parks and refuges may close areas where a sensitive species is nesting; ethical birders obey such regulations, realizing that a bird's welfare comes before the desire to check it off a list.

Get Started

Birding ranks among the fastest growing outdoor pursuits. Equipment is minimal, and the pleasures derived are legion. The rewards include observing some of the earth's most colorful and interesting creatures and traveling to scenic wild places that you might otherwise never have discovered. The challenges will last a lifetime, for no one will ever see all the different kinds of birds there are.   —Mel White

New England

All the New England states save Vermont have a seacoast, and it's along this meeting of land and water—which can be rocky, sandy, or marshy, as well as bluff-lined or flat—that many of the region's top birding sites are located.

One reason these sites are so valuable is that they host myriad seabirds. Given the relative uniformity of their ocean habitat, and including in their number some of the world's most accomplished fliers, these birds are notorious wanderers. Birders who brave the chilly winter wind of Rhode Island's Sachuest Point or Halibut Point in Massachusetts, or who take to the sea on a whale-watching boat, always hope for a true rarity to put an exclamation point on the day. Even species a bit more frequently seen make the coast an excit-ing place. Few birders become so jaded that their hearts don't speed up at the powerful flight of a jaeger or the beauty of a Harlequin Duck.

Atlantic Puffin

The coast is a great place to look for land birds, as well. In fall, north winds blow south-bound migrants down against the coast, concentrating flocks into higher than normal num-bers. The ocean acts as a barrier to their movement, so vagrants from the West often end their roaming on the coastline or on an island such as Block, off Rhode Island, or South Monomoy, in Massachusetts.

Other New England highlights include northern specialties in Maine's Baxter State Park, Bicknell's Thrush on New Hampshire's Mount Washington, and geese and wetland species at Vermont's Dead Creek Wildlife Management Area.

SPECIAL BIRDS OF NEW ENGLAND

Cory's Shearwater	White-winged Scoter	Black-legged Kittiwake	Gray Jay
Greater Shearwater	Black Scoter	Roseate Tern	Boreal Chickadee
Sooty Shearwater	Long-tailed Duck	Arctic Tern	Bicknell's Thrush
Wilson's Storm-Petrel	Spruce Grouse	Razorbill	Magnolia Warbler
Leach's Storm-Petrel	Piping Plover	Black Guillemot	Blackburnian Warbler
Northern Gannet	Purple Sandpiper	Atlantic Puffin	Saltmarsh Sharp-tailed Sparrow
Great Cormorant	Hudsonian Godwit	Snowy Owl	Nelson's Sharp-tailed Sparrow
Glossy Ibis	Red-necked Phalarope	Northern Saw-whet Owl	Snow Bunting
Mute Swan	Red Phalarope	Black-backed Woodpecker	Rusty Blackbird
Brant	Pomarine Jaeger	Pileated Woodpecker	Red Crossbill
King Eider	Parasitic Jaeger	Yellow-bellied Flycatcher	White-winged Crossbill
Common Eider	Black-headed Gull		
Harlequin Duck	Iceland Gull		
Surf Scoter	Glaucous Gull		

Maine

1 **Kennebunk Plains**
www.state.me.us/spo/lmf/projects
207-287-8000

2 **East Point Sanctuary**
www.maineaudubon.org
207-781-2330

3 **Scarborough Marsh Nature Center**
www.maineaudubon.org
207-883-5100

4 **Acadia National Park**
www.nps.gov/acad
207-288-3338

5 **Bar Harbor Yarmouth Ferry Service**
www.catferry.com
207-288-3395 or 888-249-7245

6 **Norton's Tours**
www.machiassealisland.com
207-497-5933

6 Bold Coast Charter Company
www.boldcoast.com
207-259-4484

7 Quoddy Head State Park
www.state.me.us/doc/prkslnds/prkslnds.htm
207-733-0911(park season)
or 207-941-4014 (off season)

8 Baxter State Park
www.baxterstateparkauthority.com
207-723-5140

New Hampshire

9 Hampton Beach State Park
www.nhstateparks.com/hampton.html
603-926-3784

10 Odiorne Point State Park
www.nhstateparks.com/odiorne.html
603-436-8043

11 Great Bay National Wildlife Refuge
www.fws.gov/northeast/nh/gtb.htm
603-431-7511

12 Sandy Point Discovery Center
www.greatbay.org/sandy_point/index.html
603-778-0015

13 White Mountain National Forest
www.fs.fed.us/r9/white
603-528-8721

14 Connecticut Lakes Region
www.nhconnlakes.com
603-538-7118

Vermont

15 Wenlock Wildlife Management Area
www.vtfishandwildlife.com/wmaguide.cfm
802-751-0100

16 Victory Basin Wildlife
Management Area
www.vtfishandwildlife.com/wmaguide.cfm
802-751-0100

17 Mount Mansfield Natural Area
www.nature.nps.gov/nnl
802-241-3670

18 Dead Creek Wildlife Management Area
www.vtfishandwildlife.com/wmaguide.cfm
802-759-2398

18 Chimney Point State Historic Site
www.vtfishistoricvermont.org/chimneypoint
802-759-2412

19 West Rutland Marsh
www.wrutland.org/bc/marsh/marsh.html
802-438-2381

20 Herrick's Cove
vt.audubon.org/iba.html
802-434-4686

Massachusetts

21 Joppa Flats Education Center
and Wildlife Refuge
www.massaudubon.org
978-462-9998

22 Parker River National
Wildlife Refuge
parkerriver.fws.gov
978-465-5753

23 Halibut Point State Park
www.mass.gov/dcr/forparks.htm
978-546-2997

24 Mount Auburn Cemetery
www.mountauburn.org
617-547-7105

25 Monomoy National Wildlife Refuge
monomoy.fws.gov
508-945-0594

26 Wellfleet Bay Wildlife Sanctuary
www.wellfleet.org
508-349-2615

27 Cape Cod National Seashore
www.nps.gov/caco
508-255-3785

Rhode Island

28 Block Island National Wildlife Refuge
www.fws.gov/blockisland
401-364-9124

29 Trustom Pond National Wildlife Refuge
www.fws.gov/northeast
401-364-9124

30 Point Judith Lighthouse
www.cr.nps.gov/maritime/light/ptjudith.htm
401-789-0444

31 Sachuest Point National
Wildlife Refuge
www.fws.gov/northeast/sachuestpoint
401-847-5511

32 Swan Point Cemetery
swanpointcemetery.com
401-272-1314

Connecticut

33 Audubon Center in Greenwich
greenwich.center.audubon.org
203-869-5272

34 Connecticut Audubon Coastal Center
www.ctaudubon.org/visit/milford.htm
203-878-7440

34 Stewart B. McKinney National
Wildlife Refuge
www.fws.gov/refuges
860-399-2513

35 Hammonasset Beach State Park
dep.state.ct.us/stateparks
203-245-2785

36 Devil's Hopyard State Park
dep.state.ct.us/stateparks
860-873-8566

37 White Memorial Foundation
and Conservation Center
www.whitememorialcc.org
860-567-0857

ADDITIONAL SITES

1 Lighthouse Point Park
www.cityofnewhaven.com/parks
203-946-8005

2 East Rock Park
cityofnewhaven.com/parks
203-787-6086

3 Bluff Point State Park
and Coastal Reserve
dep.state.ct.us/stateparks
860-445-1729

White-Winged and Red Crossbills

The White-winged Crossbill and its relative the Red Crossbill are famous—perhaps *notorious* is a better word—for the irregularity and unpredictability of their movements. Some years they're seen all over the North Woods, using their specially adapted crossed bills to feed on seeds of pine, fir, spruce, and hemlock. Other years there are none to be found, and a visiting birder looking for one of these finches leaves frustrated, having searched in vain.

Mid-Atlantic

Here sprawls the southern part of one of the world's great urban corridors, the Washington-to-Boston supermetropolis. Here highways entwine with rail lines and more highways, and city and suburb alternate seemingly without end along Atlantic shore and harbors, until from an airplane the landscape seems one glowing band of light. Here in large part we have reconfigured the natural landscape to serve our own purposes, for better or worse.

Here, too, is Cape May, New Jersey, unquestionably one of America's top birding spots, where hawks and land birds pass by each fall, sometimes by the hundreds of thousands. Northern New Jersey holds Great Swamp National Wildlife Refuge, where conservationists fought off a proposed airport in the days before ecology was a buzzword. In the expansive tidal marshes along Delaware Bay, rails carry on their furtive affairs as they did in the days before the first European explorers appeared. To the north, herons, egrets, and shorebirds enthrall watchers next door to John F. Kennedy and Philadelphia international airports, at Jamaica Bay Wildlife Refuge and John Heinz National Wildlife Refuge, respectively.

Nature yet endures in our largest metropolitan agglomeration, and there are plentiful opportunities for great birding. For beginners, the wonderful thing about the mass of people in the crowded Northeast is that there are just that many more birders and a valuable body of collective expertise to take advantage of. Gulls in their multifarious plumages can seem impossible to sort out, for example, but visit Niagara Falls in December or January and you will find people peering through telescopes who will point out the darker underside of the primary feathers of the one Black-headed Gull amid all those Bonapartes. Settle in for a weekend at any one of the region's many excellent hawk-watching locations, and it is possible to learn quite a bit about the shapes and sizes and wing-flapping patterns of raptors. While you may encounter the inevitable can't-be-bothered birder who is single-mindedly pursuing just one particular species, you'll discover many more friendly folks who are willing and even eager to share their birding knowledge and experience with other enthusiasts.

SPECIAL BIRDS OF THE MID-ATLANTIC

Cory's Shearwater	Black Scoter	Purple Sandpiper	Black Skimmer
Greater Shearwater	Common Eider	Ruff	Pileated Woodpecker
Sooty Shearwater	Surf Scoter	Pomarine Jaeger	Yellow-bellied Flycatcher
Wilson's Storm-Petrel	White-winged Scoter	Parasitic Jaeger	Bicknell's Thrush
Northern Gannet	Black Scoter	Little Gull	Golden-winged Warbler
Great Cormorant	Long-tailed Duck	Lesser Black-backed Gull	
Glossy Ibis	Ruffed Grouse	Black-legged Kittiwake	Cerulean Warbler
Brant	Black Rail	Least Tern	Prothonotary Warbler
Mute Swan	Piping Plover	Gull-billed Tern	Saltmarsh Sharp-tailed Sparrow
Tundra Swan	American Oystercatcher	Roseate Tern	Seaside Sparrow
Eurasian Wigeon			

New York

1 Fort Niagara State Park
nysparks.state.ny.us/parks
716-745-7273

2 Braddock Bay Fish and Wildlife Management Area
www.dec.state.ny.us/website/reg8/wma/braddock.html
716-948-5182

3 Derby Hill Bird Observatory
www.dec.state.ny.us/website/education/drbyhill.html
315-963-8291

4 Montezuma National Wildlife Refuge
www.fws.gov/r5mnwr
315-568-5987

5 Ferd's Bog
www.nybirds.org/Articles/ferds_bog.htm

6 Central Park
www.centralparknyc.org
212-310-6600

7 Jamaica Bay Wildlife Refuge
www.nature.nps.gov/jbi
718-318-4340

8 Jones Beach State Park
nysparks.state.ny.us/parks
516-785-1600

8 Robert Moses State Park
nysparks.state.ny.us/parks
631-669-0470

9 Montauk Point
nysparks.state.ny.us/parks
631-668-3781

New Jersey

10 Cape May Bird Observatory
www.njaudubon.org/Centers/CMBO
609-884-2736

10 Cape May Point State Park
www.state.nj.us/dep/parksandforests/parks
609-884-2159

10 Higbee Beach Wildlife
Management Area
www.state.nj.us/dep/fgw
609-628-2103

11 Brigantine Division, Edwin B. Forsythe
National Wildlife Refuge
www.fws.gov/northeast/forsythe
609-652-1665

11 Barnegat Lighthouse State Park
www.state.nj.us/dep/parksandforests/parks
609-494-2016

12 Sandy Hook, Gateway National
Recreation Area
www.njaudubon.org/Centers/SHBO
732-872-2500

13 Great Swamp National Wildlife Refuge
www.fws.gov/northeast/greatswamp
973-425-1222

14 Delaware Water Gap National
Recreation Area
www.nps.gov/dewa
570-588-2452

Pennsylvania

15 John Heinz National Wildlife Refuge
www.fws.gov/northeast/heinz
215-365-3118

16 Ridley Creek State Park
www.dcnr.state.pa.us/stateparks
610-892-3900

16 Tyler Arboretum
www.tylerarboretum.org
610-566-9134

17 Middle Creek Wildlife
Management Area
*www.dep.state.pa.us/dep/deputate/enved
/mcreek.htm*
717-733-1512

18 Lake Ontelaunee
www.hamburgpa.org
610-562-3106

19 Hawk Mountain Sanctuary
www.hawkmountain.org
610-756-6000

20 Delaware Water Gap National
Recreation Area
www.nps.gov/dewa
570-588-2452

20 Pocono Environmental
Education Center
www.peec.org
570-828-2319

21 Wyoming State Forest
www.dcnr.state.pa.us/forestry
570-387-4255

22 Presque Isle State Park
www.presqueisle.org
814-833-7424

Delaware

23 Bombay Hook National
Wildlife Refuge
www.fws.gov/northeast/bombayhook
302-653-6872

24 Little Creek Wildlife Management Area
www.dnrec.state.de.us/fw/wildlifemaps.htm
302-739-5297

25 Ted Harvey Conservation Area
www.dnrec.state.de.us/fw/wildlifemaps.htm
302-284-4795

26 Cape Henlopen State Park
www.destateparks.com/chsp/chsp.htm
302-645-8983

27 White Clay Creek State Park
www.destateparks.com/wccsp/index.asp
302-368-6900

27 Brandywine Creek State Park
www.destateparks.com/bcsp/bcsp.asp
302-577-3534

Maryland

28 Ocean City
www.ococean.com
410-250-0125

29 Assateague Island
National Seashore
www.nps.gov/asis
410-641-1441

29 Assateague State Park
www.dnr.state.md.us
410-641-2120

30 Great Cypress Swamp
302-378-2736

31 Blackwater National
Wildlife Refuge
www.fws.gov/blackwater
410-228-2677

32 Rock Creek Park
www.nps.gov/rocr
202-426-6070

33 Herrington Manor State Park
www.dnr.state.md.us
301-334-9180

33 Swallow Falls State Park
www.dnr.state.md.us
301-387-6938

Purple Sandpiper

The Purple Sandpiper, which breeds in the Arctic, might better be
called a "rockpiper," since in winter it's almost always found on wave-
splashed rocks along the North Atlantic coast. It especially favors rock jetties, and with the
building of these structures where once there was only sand and marsh, it now winters much
farther south than before. Look for this sandpiper at Barnegat Lighthouse State Park in New
Jersey and the Ocean City jetty in Maryland.

Band-rumped
Storm-Petrel

South Atlantic

The natural world seems especially near on the Atlantic coastal islands.
The fecund smell of a salt marsh, the raucous cries of gulls, the stirring sight of a flock
of Dunlins whirling in unison as they come to rest on a beach—we experience these and realize instinctively that we are witness to earth's grand and endless cycle of renewal.

If we look closely we may see a pale little Piping Plover running along the sand, a secretive
Virginia Rail in the marsh grass, or a fierce Merlin skimming over the dunes. Popular places
like Assateague Island and Cape Hatteras still offer opportunities for solitary observation.

This region offers some spectacular sights, including the fall hawk migration at Kiptopeke
State Park and the gathering of thousands of Tundra Swans at Mattamuskeet National Wildlife
Refuge. Imagine more subtle encounters: a Black-throated Blue Warbler singing in a dark
Appalachian hemlock forest or a Least Bittern picking its way through the cattails.

Every season in the South Atlantic area has its own birding highlights. Spring sees waves of beautiful warblers heading up the mountains. From coastal lookouts, seabird migration can provide exciting viewing. In early summer, heronries are full of noisy life, mountain breeders are singing, and regional specialties are nesting. Shorebirds throng beaches in late summer and fall, hawks move south, and songbird migration can be excellent along the coast. In winter, waterfowl are in every watery environment, and birders check hot spots for rarities.

SPECIAL BIRDS OF THE SOUTH ATLANTIC

Black-capped Petrel	Wood Stork	Sandwich Tern	Swainson's Warbler
Cory's Shearwater	Swallow-tailed Kite	Bridled Tern	Bachman's Sparrow
Audubon's Shearwater	Mississippi Kite	Black Skimmer	Nelson's Sharp-tailed Sparrow
Band-rumped Storm-Petrel	Black Rail	Common Ground-Dove	Saltmarsh Sharp-tailed Sparrow
White-tailed Tropicbird	Purple Gallinule	Red-cockaded Woodpecker	Seaside Sparrow
White Ibis	Wilson's Plover	Brown-headed Nuthatch	Painted Bunting
	Purple Sandpiper		
	Royal Tern		

Virginia

1 Chincoteague National Wildlife Refuge
www.fws.gov/northeast/chinco
757-336-6122

2 Kiptopeke State Park
www.dcr.state.va.us/parks/kiptopek.htm
757-331-2267

2 Eastern Shore of Virginia NWR
www.fws.gov/northeast/easternshore
757-331-2760

3 Chesapeake Bay Bridge-Tunnel
www.cbbt.com
757-331-2960

4 Back Bay National Wildlife Refuge
www.fws.gov/backbay
757-721-2412

5 Great Dismal Swamp National Wildlife Refuge
www.fws.gov/northeast/greatdismalswamp
757-986-3705

6 Huntley Meadows Park
www.fairfaxcounty.gov/parks/huntley
703-768-2525

7 Shenandoah National Park
www.nps.gov/shen
540-999-3500

7 Blue Ridge Parkway
www.nps.gov/blri
828-271-4779

North Carolina

8 Pea Island National Wildlife Refuge
www.fws.gov/peaisland
252-473-1131

8 Cape Hatteras National Seashore
www.nps.gov/caha
Bodie 252-441-5711; Hatteras 252-995-4474;
Ocracoke 252-928-4531

9 Mattamuskeet National Wildlife Refuge
www.fws.gov/mattamuskeet
252-926-4021

10 Croatan National Forest
www.cs.unca.edu/nfsnc
252-638-5628

11 Fort Fisher State Recreation Area
www.ils.unc.edu/parkproject/ncparks.html
910-458-5798

12 Weymouth Woods–
Sandhills Nature Preserve
www.ils.unc.edu/parkproject/ncparks.html
910-692-2167

13 Blue Ridge Parkway
www.nps.gov/blri
828-271-4779

14 Grandfather Mountain
www.grandfather.com
828-733-2013

14 Mount Mitchell State Park
www.ils.unc.edu/parkproject/ncparks.html
828-675-4611

South Carolina

15 Huntington Beach State Park
www.discoversouthcarolina.com/stateparks
843-237-4440

16 Francis Marion National Forest
and Cape Romain NWR
www.fws.gov/seweecenter
843-928-3368

17 Francis Beidler Forest Sanctuary
and Center
www.beidlerforest.com
843-462-2150

18 Bear Island Wildlife Management Area
www.dnr.sc.gov/managed
843-844-8957

19 Savannah National Wildlife Refuge
www.fws.gov/savannah
912-652-4415

20 Santee National Wildlife Refuge
www.fws.gov/santee
803-478-2217

21 Congaree Swamp National Monument
www.nps.gov/cosw
803-776-4396

22 Carolina Sandhills NWR
www.fws.gov/carolinasandhills
843-335-8401

23 Caesars Head State Park
www.discoversouthcarolina.com/stateparks
864-836-6115

Georgia

24 Brasstown Bald
www.fs.fed.us/conf/rec/btb_overview.htm
706-745-6928

25 Kennesaw Mountain National
Battlefield Park
www.nps.gov/kemo
770-427-4686

26 CCWA Wetlands Center and
E. L. Huie Land Application Facility
www.ccwa1.com/facilities
770-603-5606

27 Sweetwater Creek State
Conservation Park
gastateparks.org/info/sweetwater
770-732-5871

28 Piedmont National Wildlife Refuge
www.fws.gov/piedmont; 478-986-5441

29 Okefenokee National Wildlife Refuge
www.fws.gov/okefenokee; 912-496-7836

29 Stephen C. Foster State Park
gastateparks.org/info/scfoster
912-637-5274

30 Jekyll Island
www.jekyllisland.com; 912-635-3636

31 Harris Neck National Wildlife Refuge
www.fws.gov/harrisneck; 912-652-4415

32 Fort Pulaski National Monument
www.nps.gov/fopu
912-786-5787

Florida

"The flocks of birds that covered the shelly beaches, and those that hovered overhead, so astonished us that at first we could scarcely believe our eyes." This was John James Audubon's reaction on visiting the Florida Keys in the early 1830s, and it's still the vision that appears to many travelers when they think of Florida: masses of herons, egrets, ibises, spoonbills, and storks feeding in shallow wetlands or flying to roost at dusk, in a setting of lush, subtropical vegetation. In places this scene is just what you'll find, an avian spectacle that still has the power to astonish.

Unfortunately, persecution in the late 19th and early 20th centuries and, of late, the burgeoning human population and exploding econmy of South Florida and the attendant loss and degradation of habitat mean that never again will we see the huge numbers of wading birds that once flourished here.

It's sobering to imagine, as you look out over a teeming, colorful flock of waders in Big Cypress National Preserve or the famed J. N. "Ding" Darling National Wildlife Refuge, that once there were many more of these birds—in some cases ten times as many—and many more places where they could nest and feed.

Florida has more to entice birders than flashy herons and egrets, beautiful as they are. As a continental extremity, the peninsula is home to species seldom or never found elsewhere in the United States. Apart from regularly occurring specialties, Florida also sees rare strays that wander from the Bahamas and the Caribbean islands. Among the sought-after regular species are Swallow-tailed and Snail Kites, Short-tailed Hawk, Limpkin, Roseate Tern, White-crowned Pigeon, Mangrove Cuckoo, Smooth-billed Ani, Antillean Nighthawk, Gray Kingbird, Black-whiskered Vireo, the endemic (and threatened) Florida Scrub-Jay, and Shiny Cowbird. The pinelands, scrub, and prairies of central and northern Florida harbor Crested Caracara, Sandhill Crane, Red-cockaded Woodpecker (endangered), and Bachman's Sparrow, among other species. With a huge pet trade, abundant fruit trees, and a subtropical climate that allows escaped birds to survive, southern Florida is home to a broad and colorful variety of free-flying exotic birds. And beaches (less than two hours away no matter where you are in the state) host an array of shorebirds that changes with the seasons.

Mangrove Cuckoo

SPECIAL BIRDS OF FLORIDA

Fulvous Whistling-Duck	Short-tailed Hawk	Mangrove Cuckoo	
Masked Booby	Crested Caracara	Smooth-billed Ani	
Brown Booby	Limpkin	Burrowing Owl	
Magnificent Frigatebird	Sandhill Crane	Antillean Nighthawk	Yellow Warbler (golden race)
Roseate Spoonbill	Roseate Tern	Red-cockaded Woodpecker	Bachman's Sparrow
Wood Stork	Bridled Tern		
Greater Flamingo	Sooty Tern	Gray Kingbird	Shiny Cowbird
Swallow-tailed Kite	Brown Noddy	Black-whiskered Vireo	
Snail Kite	Black Noddy	Florida Scrub-Jay	
	White-crowned Pigeon	Cave Swallow	

Southern Everglades and the Keys

1 Everglades National Park
www.nps.gov/ever
305-242-7700

2 Florida Keys
www.fla-keys.com

3 Dry Tortugas National Park
www.nps.gov/drto
305-242-7700

Southeastern and Southwestern Florida

4 Jonathan Dickinson State Park
www.floridastateparks.org/jonathandickinson
772-546-2771

5 Arthur R. Marshall Loxahatchee NWR
oxahatchee.fws.gov
407-732-3684

6 Big Cypress National Preserve
www.nps.gov/bicy
239-695-2000

6 Fakahatchee Strand State Preserve
www.floridastateparks.org/fakahatcheestrand
239-695-4593

7 Corkscrew Swamp Sanctuary
www.audubon.org
239-348-1522

8 J. N. "Ding" Darling National
Wildlife Refuge
www.fws.gov/dingdarling
239-472-1100

9 Myakka River State Park
www.myakkariver.org
941-361-6511

9 Avon Park Air Force Range
www.avonparkafr.com
863-452-4254

ADDITIONAL SITES

1 John U. Lloyd Beach SRA
www.floridastateparks.org/lloydbeach
954-923-2833

2 Hugh Taylor Birch SRA
www.floridastateparks.org/hughtaylorbirch
954-564-4521

3 Shark Valley
www.nps.gov/ever/visit
305-221-8776

4 Conservancy Nature Center
www.conservancy.org
239-262-0304

5 Oscar Scherer State Park
www.floridastateparks.org/oscarscherer
941-483-5956

Northern Peninsular Florida

10 Merritt Island National Wildlife Refuge
www.fws.gov/merittisland
321-861-0667

11 Paynes Prairie State Preserve
www.floridastateparks.org
352-466-3397

Florida Panhandle

12 St. Marks National Wildlife Refuge
www.fws.gov/saintmarks
850-925-6121

13 Gulf Islands National Seashore
www.nps.gov/guis
Florida 850-934-2600
Mississippi 228-875-9057

ADDITIONAL SITES

6 Edward Ball Wakulla Springs
State Park
www.floridastateparks.org/wakullasprings
850-224-5950

7 Apalachicola National Forest
www.fs.fed.us/r8/florida
850-643-2282

Snail Kite

The Snail Kite's distinctive bill is adapted for feeding on apple snails, large gastropods common in South Florida marshes. The curved, pointed bill easily reaches inside the snail's shell. The kite's ability to find snails is greatly affected by water levels, so the birds wander widely. Once reduced to just a few pairs in Florida, the Snail Kite has made something of a comeback, though it remains vulnerable to drought and human-caused disruptions in water flow through the "river of grass."

South-Central

Roseate Spoonbill and Canada Warbler are seldom mentioned in the same paragraph. Here, though, they illustrate the avian extremes of this chapter, which encompasses the salt marshes of Louisiana and the 6,000-foot peaks of eastern Tennessee, with a correspondingly broad range of birding possibilities. In one corner of the region, Fulvous Whistling-Duck and Purple Gallinule nest; in the other, Northern Saw-whet Owl, Common Raven, Black-capped Chickadee, and other northern birds extend their ranges south along the Appalachian Mountains.

Between these extremes lie temperate lands favored by southern birds such as Anhinga, Little Blue Heron, Swallow-tailed Kite, Prothonotary and Swainson's Warblers, and Painted Bunting. Other habitats reward birders, too. Pinewoods are home to Red-cockaded Woodpecker, Brown-headed Nuthatch, and Bachman's Sparrow, all southern specialties. Sandy beaches provide nesting sites for Snowy and Wilson's Plovers, Least Tern, and Black Skimmer. Some of America's most famous spring migration "fallout" sites lie along the Gulf Coast, and great inland reservoirs such as Alabama's Guntersville Lake attract wintering loons, grebes, waterfowl, Bald Eagles, and gulls.

Due in part to human-caused habitat loss, the Carolina Parakeet and Bachman's Warbler are gone. And in 2005 Hurricanes Katrina and Rita ravaged the Gulf Coast. Comeback may be slow.

On the other side of the scale, Ospreys and Bald Eagles are beginning to breed in places where they were long absent. Brown Pelicans have made a strong comeback after declines in population caused by pesticides. Colonies of wading birds, once vulnerable to hunting and harassment, enjoy strong protection. And a growing corps of conservationists works to safeguard the remaining natural areas, many of which are among America's finest places to see birds.

SPECIAL BIRDS OF THE SOUTH-CENTRAL STATES

Brown Pelican	Fulvous Whistling-Duck	Snowy Plover	Red-cockaded Woodpecker
Neotropic Cormorant	Ross's Goose	Wilson's Plover	Scissor-tailed Flycatcher
Anhinga	Mottled Duck	American Oystercatcher	Brown-headed Nuthatch
Reddish Egret	King Rail	Royal Tern	
Roseate Spoonbill	Swallow-tailed Kite	Sandwich Tern	Swainson's Warbler
Yellow Night-Heron	Mississippi Kite	Common Ground-Dove	Bachman's Sparrow
White Ibis	Purple Gallinule		Painted Bunting
Glossy Ibis			

Tennessee

1 Great Smoky Mountains National Park
www.nps.gov/grsm; 865-436-1200

2 Roan Mountain State Park
www.state.tn.us/environment/parks
423-772-0190 or 800-250-8620

3 Sharp's Ridge Memorial Park
www.ci.knoxville.tn.us/parks/sharpsridge.asp
865-215-2000

4 TVA Kingston Steam Plant Wildlife Observation Area
www.tva.gov
865-632-2101

5 Brainerd Levee
www.chattanooga.gov/PRAC/30_1086.htm
423-757-5167

6 Radnor Lake State Natural Area
www.tennessee.gov; 615-373-3467

7 Tennessee National Wildlife Refuge
www.fws.gov/tennesseerefuge; 731-642-2091

8 Reelfoot National Wildlife Refuge
www.fws.gov/reelfoot; 731-538-2481

8 Reelfoot Lake State Park
www.state.tn.us/environment; 731-253-7756

9 Maxson Wastewater Treatment Plant
901-789-0510

ADDITIONAL SITE
1 Blythe Ferry Unit of Hiwassee Refuge
www.state.tn.us/twra
931-484-9571

Alabama

10 Dauphin Island Bird Sanctuaries
www.dauphinisland.org/bird.htm
251-861-3607

10 Fort Morgan
www.alabamacoastalbirdingtrail.com
334-540-7125

10 Bon Secour National Wildlife Refuge
www.fws.gov/bonsecour
251-540-7720

10 Gulf State Park
www.alapark.com; 251-948-7275

11 Eufaula National Wildlife Refuge
www.fws.gov/eufaula; 334-687-4065

12 Lake Guntersville State Park
www.alapark.com; 256-571-5444

13 Wheeler National Wildlife Refuge
www.fws.gov/wheeler; 256-353-7243

14 Bankhead National Forest and Brushy Lake Recreation Area
www.fs.fed.us/r8/alabama; 205-489-5111

ADDITIONAL SITE
2 Leighton
www.colbertcountytourism.org
256-383-0783

Mississippi

15 Lower Pascagoula River WMA
www.mdwfp.com; 228-588-3878

16 Mississippi Sandhill Crane NWR
www.fws.gov/mississippisandhillcrane
228-497-6322

17 Gulf Islands National Seashore
www.nps.gov/guis; 228-875-9057

17 Buccaneer State Park
www.mdwfp.com; 228-467-3822

18 St. Catherine Creek NWR
www.fws.gov/saintcatherinecreek
601-442-6696

19 Yazoo National Wildlife Refuge
www.fws.gov/yazoo; 662-839-2638

20 Noxubee National Wildlife Refuge
www.fws.gov/noxubee; 662-323-5548

21 Sardis Lake
www.sardislake.com

Arkansas

22 Lake Chicot State Park
www.arkansasstateparks.com; 870-265-5480

23 Felsenthal National Wildlife Refuge
www.fws.gov/felsenthal; 870-364-3167

24 Millwood State Park
www.arkansasstateparks.com; 870-898-2800

25 Devil's Den State Park
www.arkansasstateparks.com; 479-761-3325

26 Buffalo National River
www.nps.gov/buff; 870-741-5443

27 Holla Bend National Wildlife Refuge
www.fws.gov/southeast; 479-229-4300

28 Wapanocca National Wildlife Refuge
www.fws.gov/southeast; 870-343-2595

ADDITIONAL SITES

❸ Charlie Craig State Fish Hatchery
www.agfc.com; 877-795-2470

❹ St. Francis National Forest
www.fs.fed.us/oonf/ozark; 479-968-2354

Louisiana

29 Peveto Woods Sanctuaries
www.braudubon.org; 225-768-9874

30 Sabine National Wildlife Refuge
www.fws.gov; 337-762-3816

30 Cameron Prairie NWR
www.fws.gov; 337-598-2216

31 Lacassine National Wildlife Refuge
www.fws.gov; 337-774-5923

32 Sherburne Wildlife Management Area
www.wlf.state.la.us; 318-566-2251

32 Cypress Island Preserve
nature.org/wherewework; 225-338-1040

33 Grand Isle State Park
www.lastateparks.com
985-787-2559 or 888-787-2559

34 Jean Lafitte National Historical Park
and Preserve
www.nps.gov/jela; 504-589-3882

35 Alexander State Forest
www.ldaf.state.la.us/divisions/forestry
318-487-5172

35 Catahoula National Wildlife Refuge
www.fws.gov/catahoula; 318-992-5261

ADDITIONAL SITES

❺ Bayou Sauvage National
Wildlife Refuge
bayousauvage.fws.gov; 985-882-2000

❻ Pearl River Wildlife Management Area
225-765-2360

Eastern Texas

In an election to choose the birding capital of the United States, the Texas coast would be a serious contender. The geographic range of this 370-mile sweep of Gulf of Mexico shoreline, combined with the subtropical environment of the lower Rio Grande Valley, attracts birders on regular pilgrimages.

Sandy beaches, salt marshes, and prairie make up much of the Texas Gulf Coast. Some of the region's scattered woodlands are famed for spring songbird migration. Bolivar Flats is the best known of several excellent shorebird-watching sites, while rice fields and other agricultural areas west of Houston can attract impressive flocks of waterfowl from fall through spring, as well as migrant shorebirds. Farther south, an array of Mexican species are in the brushlands along the lower Rio Grande.

Every season has something to offer in this diverse, extensive region. Even midsummer, perhaps the least appealing time of year, affords birders interesting breeding species and such post-nesting wanderers as Magnificent Frigatebird and Wood Stork. Fall shorebird migration begins as early as July. In fall, Hazel Bazemore County Park has one of the great hawk-watching spectacles. Winter brings flocks of waterfowl and the annual return of Whooping Cranes to Aransas National Wildlife Refuge. Spring means the excitement of migration, from warblers on the upper coast to hawks moving north in flocks.

Making planning easier for the traveling birder, the Great Texas Coastal Birding Trail (see sidebar page 525) directs visitors to excellent birding sites with maps and special road signs.

More and more, communities along the Gulf Coast and in the lower Rio Grande Valley are waking up to their birding possibilities and working to spread the word about them. One of the ways they're doing this is by holding birding festivals, most of which feature field trips aimed at finding local specialties, guest speakers, and workshops on improving identification skills. Attending these is a great way for birders to get an introduction to the wonders of this marvelous area.

Plain Chachalaca

SPECIAL BIRDS OF EASTERN TEXAS

Least Grebe	Gray Hawk	Groove-billed Ani	
Northern Gannet	Harris's Hawk	Ferruginous Pygmy-Owl	Brown Jay
Brown Pelican	Yellow Rail	Elf Owl	Tamaulipas Crow
Neotropic Cormorant	King Rail	Lesser Nighthawk	Chihuahuan Raven
Magnificent Frigatebird	Purple Gallinule	Common Pauraque	Cave Swallow
Reddish Egret	Sandhill Crane	Buff-bellied Hummingbird	Clay-colored Robin
Roseate Spoonbill	Whooping Crane		Long-billed Thrasher
Black-bellied Whistling-Duck	Snowy Plover	Ringed Kingfisher	Tropical Parula
Fulvous Whistling-Duck	Plain Chachalaca	Green Kingfisher	White-collared Seedeater
Muscovy Duck	Wilson's Plover	Golden-fronted Woodpecker	Olive Sparrow
Ross's Goose	Piping Plover	Northern Beardless-Tyrannulet	Botteri's Sparrow
Mottled Duck	American Oystercatcher	Brown-crested Flycatcher	Nelson's Sharp-tailed Sparrow
Masked Duck	Hudsonian Godwit	Great Kiskadee	Seaside Sparrow
White-tailed Hawk	Gull-billed Tern	Couch's Kingbird	Pyrrhuloxia
Crested Caracara	Sandwich Tern	Scissor-tailed Flycatcher	Bronzed Cowbird
Hook-billed Kite	Red-billed Pigeon		Altamira Oriole
White-tailed Kite	White-tipped Dove	Green Jay	Audubon's Oriole
	Green Parakeet		
	Red-crowned Parrot		

Upper Texas Coast

1 Sabine Woods
www.texasbirds.org

2 Sea Rim State Park
www.tpwd.state.tx.us
409-971-2559

2 Anahuac National Wildlife Refuge
www.fws.gov/refuges
409-267-3337

3 High Island Sanctuaries
www.houstonaudubon.org
713-932-1639

4 Bolivar Flats
www.houstonaudubon.org
713-932-1639

5 San Bernard National Wildlife Refuge
www.fws.gov/refuges
979-849-7771

6 Brazos Bend State Park
www.tpwd.state.tx.us
409-553-5101

7 Attwater Prairie Chicken NWR
www.fws.gov/refuges; 949-234-3278

Central Texas Coast

8 Aransas National Wildlife Refuge
www.fws.gov/refuges
361-286-3559

9 Port Aransas Birding Center
www.cityofportraransas.org
361-749-4158

10 Padre Island National Seashore
www.nps.gov/pais
361-949-8068

11 Hazel Bazemore County Park
512-387-4231

Lower Texas Coast and Rio Grande

12 King Ranch
www.king-ranch.com
361-592-8055

13 Laguna Atascosa NWR
www.fws.gov/refuges
956-748-3607

14 Brownsville
www.brownsville.org
800-626-2639

15 Sabal Palm Audubon Center
and Sanctuary
www.audubon.org/local
956-541-8034

16 Santa Ana National Wildlife Refuge
www.fws.gov/refuges
956-787-3079

17 Bentsen–Rio Grande Valley State Park
www.tpwd.state.tx.us
956-519-6448

19 Falcon State Park
www.tpwd.state.tx.us
956-848-5327

20 Zapata
www.zapatausa.com
956-765-4871

ADDITIONAL SITE

1 Galveston Island
www.tpwd.state.tx.us
409-737-1222

Great Texas Coastal Birding Trail

Recognizing the Gulf Coast's fame among birders, government agencies and private enterprise cooperated to establish the Great Texas Coastal Birding Trail (GTCBT), an auto tour route of over 400 miles that links more than 300 sites from the Sabine River to the Rio Grande. Travelers can obtain special maps showing birding locations, and road signs depicting a Black Skimmer point the way to sites ranging from such well-known areas as Anahuac National Wildlife Refuge to small-town parks.

Heartland

When birders think of the upper Midwest, one image often predominates in their collective imagination: A car winds slowly along a back road through a snowy forest, its occupants fighting off the cold with coffee and hopeful, half-hearted jokes. All eyes are on the roadside trees, constantly scanning. Someone calls, "Stop! There it is!" and all look up to see another set of eyes staring back at them in the piercing yellow gaze of a Great Gray Owl, that huge, elusive predator of the North Woods.

But perhaps this scenario is too specific. The subject might be an elusive Boreal Owl, a band of Common Redpolls, or a flock of sleek Bohemian Waxwings. The glamour birds of this region are mostly the species of the far north, which barely reach the lower 48 states in their breeding ranges or appear only as irregular winter visitors. A trip to northern Minnesota or Wisconsin in winter is as much a part of a birder's agenda as fall at Pennsylvania's Hawk Mountain or spring at the Texas coast.

Other seasons and places have their own attractions. Spruce Grouse, Black-backed Woodpecker, and Gray Jay reward birders year-round, and the sought-after Connecticut Warbler nests here. Wisconsin's Crex Meadows is a premier birding area. Missouri's prairies are home to Greater Prairie-Chicken and Henslow's Sparrow. Refuges in Iowa and Illinois host migrant waterfowl and shorebirds. The Great Lakes attract many waterbirds, and their shorelines concentrate migrant raptors and songbirds. All these are just highlights in a region of surprising diversity, of prairies and lakes, of spruce-fir forests and Mississippi River bottomlands.

SPECIAL BIRDS OF THE HEARTLAND

Northern Goshawk	Great Gray Owl	Boreal Chickadee	
Spruce Grouse	Boreal Owl	Bohemian Waxwing	
Sharp-tailed Grouse	Northern Saw-whet Owl	Connecticut Warbler	
Greater Prairie-Chicken		Henslow's Sparrow	
Yellow Rail	Black-backed Woodpecker	Chestnut-collared Longspur	Common Redpoll
Sandhill Crane	Yellow-bellied Flycatcher	Pine Grosbeak	Hoary Redpoll
Snowy Owl		Red Crossbill	Evening Grosbeak
Northern Hawk Owl	Gray Jay	White-winged Crossbill	Eurasian Tree Sparrow

Yellow-bellied Flycatcher

Missouri

1 Table Rock State Park
www.mostateparks.com; 417-334-4704

2 Prairie State Park
www.mostateparks.com; 417-843-6711

3 Squaw Creek National Wildlife Refuge
www.fws.gov/midwest; 660-442-3187

4 Eagle Bluffs Conservation Area
www.mdc.mo.gov; 573-445-3882

5 Shaw Arboretum of the Missouri Botanical Garden
www.mobot.org; 314-577-9400

6 Riverlands Environmental Demonstration Area
www.mvs.usace.army.mil/Rivers/eda.htm
636-899-2600

7 Mingo National Wildlife Refuge
www.fws.gov/midwest; 573-222-3589

ADDITIONAL SITES

① Taberville Prairie Conservation Area
mdc.mo.gov/areas/natareas; 417-876-5226

② Schell-Osage Conservation Area
mdc.mo.gov/areas/natareas; 417-876-5226

③ Swan Lake National Wildlife Refuge
www.fws.gov/midwest
660-856-3323

Illinois

8 Chicago Park District,
Lakefront Region
www.chicagoparkdistrict.com
312-742-7529

9 Illinois Beach State Park
dnr.state.il.us/lands/landmgt/parks
708-662-4811

10 Goose Lake Prairie State Natural Area
dnr.state.il.us/lands/landmgt/parks
815-942-2899

11 Chautauqua National Wildlife Refuge
www.fws.gov/midwest/Chautauqua
309-535-2290

12 Lincoln Memorial Garden
www.lmgnc.org; 217-529-1111

12 Eldon Hazlet and South Shore
State Parks
dnr.state.il.us/lands/landmgt/parks
618-594-3015

13 Carlyle Lake Wildlife
Management Area
dnr.state.il.us/lands/landmgt/parks
618-425-3533

14 Shawnee National Forest
www.fs.fed.us/r9/forests/shawnee
618-253-7114

ADDITIONAL SITES

④ Union County Conservation Area
dnr.state.il.us/lands/landmgt/parks
618-833-5175

⑤ Cache River State Natural Area
dnr.state.il.us/lands/landmgt/parks
618-634-9678

Iowa

15 Waubonsie State Park
www.iowadnr.com/parks/index.html
712-382-2786

16 Riverton Wildlife Area
www.iowadnr.com/parks/index.html
712-374-2510

17 Lake Red Rock
www.lakeredrock.org; 641-828-7522

18 Lacey-Keosauqua State Park
www.iowadnr.com/parks/index.html
319-293-3502

19 Yellow River State Forest
www.iowadnr.com/forestry/yellowriver.html
319-586-2254

19 Effigy Mounds National Monument
www.nps.gov/efmo; 563-873-3491

20 Lost Island Nature Center
www.paccb.org/WildlifeAreas.html
712-837-4866

ADDITIONAL SITES

⑥ Saylorville Lake
www.saylorvillelake.org
515-276-4656

⑦ Shimek State Forest
www.iowadnr.com/forestry/shimek.html
319-878-3811

⑧ Cone Marsh Wildlife Area
www.iowadnr.com/wildlife
319-335-1575

Minnesota

21 Gunflint Trail
www.gunflint-trail.com; 800-338-6932

22 Sax-Zim Bog
www.irontrail.org/Attractions; 218-749-8161

23 Rice Lake National Wildlife Refuge
midwest.fws.gov/ricelake; 218-768-2402

23 McGregor Marsh State Natural Area
www.dnr.state.mn.us; 651-296-6157

24 Agassiz National Wildlife Refuge
www.fws.gov/midwest/agassiz; 218-449-4115

25 Felton Prairie
www.dnr.state.mn.us; 651-296-6157

26 Rothsay Wildlife Management Area
www.dnr.state.mn.us; 218-739-7576

27 Big Stone National Wildlife Refuge
www.fws.gov/midwest/bigstone
320-273-2191

ADDITIONAL SITES

9 Beaver Creek Valley State Park
www.dnr.state.mn.us; 507-724-2107

10 Minnesota Valley National
Wildlife Refuge
www.fws.gov/Midwest/MinnesotaValley
952-854-5900

Wisconsin

28 Wyalusing State Park
www.dnr.state.wi.us/org/land/parks
608-996-2261

29 Horicon National Wildlife Refuge
midwest.fws.gov/horicon; 920-387-2658

30 North Point Park
ci.sheboygan.wi.us; 920-459-3444

31 Crex Meadows Wildlife Area
www.dnr.state.wi.us/org/land/wildlife
715-463-2739

32 Nicolet National Forest
www.exploringthenorth.com/nicolet
/nicmain.html
715-362-1359

ADDITIONAL SITES

11 Devil's Lake State Park
www.dnr.state.wi.us/org/land/parks
608-356-8301

12 Kettle Moraine State Forest,
Northern Unit
www.dnr.state.wi.us/org/land/parks
262-626-2116

Duluth's Raptor Road

Duluth, Minnesota, sits at the extreme western end of Lake Superior, a location that becomes a virtual raptor superhighway in fall. Thousands of hawks migrating south, reluctant to cross the broad expanse of water before them, turn southwest and follow the shore. Duluth's renowned Hawk Ridge Nature Reserve provides a chance to see literally thousands of hawks on good days. Here beginners will often find experienced birders and naturalists who can provide tips on identifying the more than two dozen species that regularly pass by.

North-Central

The Great Lakes wrap around the top of this part-northern, part-eastern, part-midwestern section of the country, acting as both a passageway and a barrier for birds. They're a path mostly for waterbirds, of course—even those usually thought of as seabirds, which find familiar territory on the broad expanses of these "inland seas." As a result, diligent birders can at times turn up such anomalies as King Eider in Ohio or Parasitic Jaeger in Indiana.

The lakes are a barrier, too—a fact that birders put to good use in spring migration. Northbound land birds arrive at the lakes, look out over seemingly endless stretches of water offering no food or place to rest, and often take a break before going on. As a result, impressive numbers of birds can pile up along shorelines, especially at isolated patches of trees. On any day from mid-April through May, or during September and October, one is likely to find birders scanning such patches in anticipation of a "fallout" day when 20 or more species of warblers may be found in just a few hours. Beginning birders do well to visit such popular sites, since there's always a veteran around willing to share his or her knowledge, and more birds may be seen in one place in a single morning than in days of solitary wandering.

This region's birds are as varied as its geography, from Ohio River bottomland in Kentucky to Indiana beaches to the boreal forests of Michigan's Upper Peninsula. For city birding, Columbus has its Green Lawn Cemetery and Arboretum, Indianapolis its Eagle Creek Park, Louisville its Falls of the Ohio. For solitude, travel to Kentucky's expansive Land Between the Lakes, walk the trails at Michigan's Warren Woods State Natural Area, or explore the highlands of West Virginia, where great birding is set in one of the most beautiful landscapes of the eastern United States.

Spruce
Grouse

SPECIAL BIRDS OF THE NORTH-CENTRAL STATES

Spruce Grouse	Snowy Owl	Kirtland's Warbler	
Sharp-tailed Grouse	Great Gray Owl	Henslow's Sparrow	
Yellow Rail	Black-backed Woodpecker	Le Conte's Sparrow	
Sandhill Crane		Pine Grosbeak	
Upland Sandpiper	Gray Jay	Red Crossbill	Common Redpoll
Common Tern	Bohemian Waxwing	White-winged Crossbill	Hoary Redpoll

Michigan

1 Warren Dunes State Park
www.michigan.gov/dnr
269-426-4013

2 Lake Erie Metropark
www.metroparks.com
734-379-5020

2 Pointe Mouillee State Game Area
www.michigan.gov/dnr
734-379-9692

3 U.S. Fish and Wildlife Service, East Lansing
www.fws.gov/midwest
517-351-2555

4 Seney National Wildlife Refuge
midwest.fws.gov/seney
906-586-9851

5 Whitefish Point Bird Observatory
www.wpbo.org
906-492-3596

ADDITIONAL SITES

1 Maple River State Game Area
www.michigan.gov/dnr
517-373-9358

2 Nayanquing Point State Wildlife Area
www.michigan.gov/dnr
989-697-5101

3 Tawas Point State Park
www.michigan.gov/dnr
989-362-5041

4 Sault Ste. Marie
www.saultstemarie.com
906-632-3366 or 800-647-2858

Indiana

6 Lakefront Park and Sanctuary
hmdin.com/parks
219-853-6378

7 Indiana Dunes National Lakeshore
www.nps.gov/indu
219-926-7561

7 Indiana Dunes State Park
www.IN.gov/dnr/parklake
219-926-1952

8 Michigan City Parks and Recreation
www.emichigancity.com
219-873-1506

9 Kingsbury Fish and Wildlife Area
www.in.gov/dnr/fishwild/publications/kings.htm
219-393-3612

10 Willow Slough Fish and Wildlife Area
www.in.gov/dnr/fishwild/publications/willow.htm
219-285-2704

11 Eagle Creek Park
www.indygov.org/eGov/City/DPR/Parks
317-327-7110

12 Muscatatuck National Wildlife Refuge
www.fws.gov/midwest/muscatatuck
812-522-4352

ADDITIONAL SITE
6 Minnehaha Fish and Wildlife Area
www.in.gov/dnr/fishwild/publications/hillen.htm
812-268-5640

Ohio

13 Headlands Beach State Park
www.dnr.state.oh.us/parks
216-881-8141

13 Mentor Marsh State Nature Preserve
www.dnr.state.oh.us/dnap
800-317-9155

14 Resthaven Wildlife Area
419-684-5049

15 Magee Marsh Wildlife Area
www.dnr.state.oh.us/parks
419-836-7758

15 Ottawa National Wildlife
Refuge Complex
www.fws.gov/midwest/Ottawa
419-898-0014

16 Oak Openings Preserve Metropark
www.metroparkstoledo.com
419-826-6463

17 Killdeer Plains Wildlife Area
www.dnr.ohio.gov/wanderings
740-496-2254

18 Mohican State Park
www.dnr.state.oh.us/parks
419-994-5125

18 Mohican-Memorial State Forest
www.dnr.state.oh.us/forestry
330-339-2205

19 Clear Creek Nature Preserve
www.metroparks.net
614-891-0700

20 Adams Lake State Park
www.dnr.state.oh.us/parks
740-858-6652

ADDITIONAL SITE
6 Green Lawn Cemetery

West Virginia

21 Green Bottom Wildlife
Management Area
wvweb.com/www/hunting/area.html
304-675-0871

22 Robert C. Byrd Locks and Dam
www.lrh.usace.army.mil/projects/locks/rcb
304-399-5211

23 Cranesville Swamp Nature Preserve
nature.org
304-637-0160

24 Monongahela National Forest
www.fs.fed.us/r9/mnf
304-636-1800

ADDITIONAL SITES
7 Highland Scenic Highway
www.fs.fed.us/r9/mnf/sp/highland_hwy.html
304-846-2695

8 Gaudineer Knob
and **Gaudineer Scenic Area**
www.fs.fed.us/r9/mnf/sp/gaudineer.html
304-456-3335

9 Dolly Sods Wilderness
www.fs.fed.us/r9/mnf/sp/dolly_sods
_wilderness.htm
304-636-1800

Kentucky

25 Black Mountain
www.kingdomcome.org
606-589-5812

26 Minor E. Clark Fish Hatchery
www.kdfwr.state.ky.us
606-784-6872

27 Falls of the Ohio State Park
www.fallsoftheohio.org
812-280-9970

28 Sauerheber Unit of Sloughs Wildlife
Management Area
www.kdfwr.state.ky.us
270-827-2673 or 800-858-1549

29 Kentucky Lake Visitor Center
www.tva.gov/sites/kentucky.htm
502-362-4128 or 800-467-7145

29 Lake Barkley
www.orn.usace.army.mil/pao/lakeinfo/BAR.htm
270-362-4236

30 Land Between the Lakes National
Recreation Area
www.lbl.org
270-924-2000 or 800-525-7077

ADDITIONAL SITE
10 Red River Gorge Geologic Area
www.fs.fed.us/r8/boone
859-745-3100

Short-Eared Owl

Though owls are often thought of as forest birds, Short-eared Owl prefers
open grassland for nesting and wintering. At dusk it flies low over the ground
like a huge moth, searching for mice and other rodents, or an occasional small bird.
While mostly nocturnal, it is sometimes seen in daylight sitting on the ground. Look for it in
prairies and fields such as those at Killdeer Plains Wildlife Area in Ohio. Short-eared Owl is
irregular in occurrence from year to year.

The Plains

Looking at this strip of states in America's midsection, a birder is bound to think: prairie. Yet while many adaptable grassland species are still common, prairie in its various forms is one of our most imperiled habitats.

The grassland of Lostwood National Wildlife Refuge, in North Dakota, is one of the best places in the country to find the scarce Sprague's Pipit and Baird's Sparrow. Lesser Prairie-Chicken, another dwindling species, still dances at leks in Cimarron National Grassland in Kansas. Its relative, the Greater Prairie-Chicken, is more widespread and can be seen at numerous sites throughout the region, including Fort Pierre National Grassland in South Dakota and Burchard Lake Wildlife Management Area in Nebraska.

These states are also appealing because of the "East meets West" aspect of their bird life. Areas in the west, like South Dakota's Black Hills, host birds with Rocky Mountain affinities. Eastern species find deciduous-forest habitat at places such as Little River National Wildlife Refuge in Oklahoma. There are superb wetlands here, too. Quivira National Wildlife Refuge and Cheyenne Bottoms in Kansas and Nebraska's Rainwater Basin are among the best.

And any list of America's most thrilling birding phenomena has to include the gathering of Sandhill Crane on Nebraska's Platte River in spring migration. The sights and sounds of countless thousands of these impressive birds has become one of the "must see" spectacles of North American natural history. Each of these states offers more diversity than residents of other parts of the country might realize, and each will reward exploration with a surprising variety of birds.

Sprague's Pipit

SPECIAL BIRDS OF THE PLAINS

Trumpeter Swan	Snowy Plover	Chihuahuan Raven	Harris's Sparrow
Sharp-tailed Grouse	Piping Plover	Sprague's Pipit	
Greater Prairie-Chicken	Burrowing Owl	Cassin's Sparrow	McCown's Longspur
Lesser Prairie-Chicken	Scissor-tailed Flycatcher	Baird's Sparrow	Smith's Longspur
Black Rail		Le Conte's Sparrow	Chestnut-collared Longspur
Sandhill Crane	Bell's Vireo	Nelson's Sharp-tailed Sparrow	
Whooping Crane	Black-capped Vireo		Painted Bunting

Oklahoma

1 Little River National Wildlife Refuge
www.fws.gov/refuges
580-584-6211

2 Beavers Bend Resort Park
www.beaversbend.com
580-494-6300

3 Sequoyah National Wildlife Refuge
www.fws.gov/refuges
918-773-5252

4 Oxley Nature Center
www.oxleynaturecenter.org
918-669-6644

5 Lake Overholser
www.okc.gov
405-297-3882

6 Wichita Mountains NWR
wichitamountains.fws.gov
580-429-3221

7 Hackberry Flat Wildlife
Management Area
580-335-5262

8 Salt Plains National Wildlife Refuge
saltplains.fws.gov
580-626-4794

9 Black Mesa State Park
touroklahoma.com
580-426-2222

9 Black Mesa Preserve
nature.org
918-585-1117

Kansas

10 Weston Bend Bottoms
www.mostateparks.com
816-640-5443

11 Perry Lake
*www.nwk.usace.army.mil/perry
/perry_home.htm*
785-597-5144

12 Marais des Cygnes Wildlife Area
and La Cygne Lake and Wildlife Area
maraisdescygnes.fws.gov
913-352-8941

13 Quivira National Wildlife Refuge
www.fws.gov/quivira
316-486-2393

14 Wilson State Park
www.kdwp.state.ks.us/news/state_parks
785-658-2465

15 Cimarron National Grassland
www.fs.fed.us/r2/psicc
620-697-4621

ADDITIONAL SITE

1 Cheyenne Bottoms
www.cheyennebottoms.net
877-427-9299

Nebraska

13 Indian Cave State Park
www.ngpc.state.ne.us
402-883-2575

17 Fontenelle Forest Nature Center
www.fontenelleforest.org
402-731-3140

18 Burchard Lake State Wildlife
Management Area
www.ngpc.state.ne.us
402-335-2534

19 Lillian Annette Rowe Sanctuary
www.rowesanctuary.org
308-468-5282

19 Crane Meadows Nature Center
www.cranemeadows.org
308-382-1820

19 Fort Kearny State Historical Park
www.ngpc.state.ne.us
308-865-5305

20 Rainwater Basin
www.rwbjv.org; 308-865-5310

21 Lakes McConaughy and Ogallala
State Recreation Areas
www.ngpc.state.ne.us
308-284-3542

22 Oliver State Recreation Area
www.ngpc.state.ne.us
308-436-2383

23 Gilbert Baker WMA
www.ngpc.state.ne.us
308-665-2924

23 Chadron State Park
www.ngpc.state.ne.us
308-432-6167

ADDITIONAL SITE

2 Branched Oak Lake State
Recreation Area
www.ngpc.state.ne.us; 402-783-3400

South Dakota

24 Sica Hollow State Park
www.sdgfp.info/Parks
605-448-5701

25 Waubay National Wildlife Refuge
waubay.fws.gov
605-947-4521

26 Sand Lake National Wildlife Refuge
sandlake.fws.gov
605-885-6320

27 Oahe Dam
www.nwo.usace.army.mil
605-224-5862

28 Black Hills National Forest
www.fs.fed.us/r2/blackhills
605-673-2251

29 Badlands National Park
www.nps.gov/badl
605-433-5361

30 Lacreek National Wildlife Refuge
lacreek.fws.gov
605-685-6508

ADDITIONAL SITES

3 Hartford Beach State Park
www.sdgfp.info/Parks
605-432-6374

4 Fort Pierre National Grassland
www.fs.fed.us/r2/nebraska
605-224-5517

5 Newton Hills State Park
www.sdgfp.info/Parks
605-987-2263

North Dakota

31 Sheyenne National Grassland
www.fs.fed.us/r1
701-683-4342

32 Long Lake National Wildlife Refuge
Complex
longlake.fws.gov
701-387-4397

33 Garrison Dam National
Fish Hatchery
www.r6.fws.gov
701-654-7451

34 Theodore Roosevelt National Park
www.nps.gov/thro
701-623-4466

35 Lostwood National Wildlife Refuge
lostwood.fws.gov
701-848-2722

36 J. Clark Salyer NWR
www.fws.gov/jclarksalyer
701-768-2548

37 Wakopa Wildlife Management Aare
www.state.nd.us/gnf
701-662-3617

38 Grahams Island State Park
www.ndparks.com
701-766-4015

38 Sullys Hill National Game Preserve
www.fws.gov/sullyshill
701-766-4272

39 Icelandic State Park
www.ndparks.com
701-265-4561

ADDITIONAL SITES

6 Oak Grove Park
www.fargoparks.com
701-241-1350

7 Big Gumbo
www.bowmannd.com
701-523-5880

Southwest

The typical traveler is likely to visualize the southwestern deserts through a wide-angle lens: broad panoramas of arid terrain covered in spined cactus and mesquite, with rugged hills on the horizon, all seen in harsh midday light. The birder's image is more tightly cropped: a dry wash in the soft light of a cool morning, with the calls of wrens, thrashers, and sparrows against the crunch of sand underfoot.

Birders know that the Southwest has far more than deserts. Cottonwood-lined streams create oases where Gray Hawk and Green Kingfisher nest. Mountains near the Mexican border host regional specialties such as Elegant Trogon and Red-faced Warbler, in lush canyons shaded by oaks and junipers. High country is home to Blue Grouse, American Three-toed Woodpecker, Clark's Nutcracker, and Gray Jay, resident in forests of Douglas-fir, spruce, and aspen. Refuges and reservoirs shelter waders, waterfowl, and shorebirds.

The Southwest has two of America's finest birding locales. Southeastern Arizona ranks with the nation's best birding destinations. Its "sky islands"—mountain ranges in a sea of desert—and riparian areas such as the San Pedro River shelter great diversity in a small area.

Another famed birding destination is Texas' Big Bend National Park. Its stark desert contrasts with green riparian areas and the striking Chisos Mountains. The tiny Colima Warbler

SPECIAL BIRDS OF THE SOUTHWEST

Neotropic Cormorant

Black-bellied Whistling-Duck

Gray Hawk

Common Black-Hawk

Harris's Hawk

Zone-tailed Hawk

Scaled Quail

Montezuma Quail

Mountain Plover

Whiskered Screech-Owl

Elf Owl

Spotted Owl

Broad-billed Hummingbird

Violet-crowned Hummingbird

Blue-throated Hummingbird

Magnificent Hummingbird

Lucifer Hummingbird

Elegant Trogon

Green Kingfisher

Gila Woodpecker

Arizona Woodpecker

Northern Beardless-Tyrannulet

Greater Pewee

Buff-breasted Flycatcher

Vermilion Flycatcher

Dusky-capped Flycatcher

Brown-crested Flycatcher

Sulphur-bellied Flycatcher

Tropical Kingbird

Thick-billed Kingbird

Rose-throated Becard

Black-capped Vireo

Gray Vireo

Mexican Jay

Cave Swallow

Bridled Titmouse

Verdin

Rose-throated Becard

Black-tailed Gnatcatcher

Bendire's Thrasher

Crissal Thrasher

Phainopepla

Olive Warbler

Lucy's Warbler

Grace's Warbler

Red-faced Warbler

Painted Redstart

Hepatic Tanager

Abert's Towhee

Rufous-winged Sparrow

Cassin's Sparrow

Botteri's Sparrow

Yellow-eyed Junco

McCown's Longspur

Pyrrhuloxia

Varied Bunting

Bronzed Cowbird

nests here and only here in the U.S., rewarding hikers who climb to the oak woods where it sings its trilling song in spring and early summer.

Also visit New Mexico's southwestern corner for many of the same specialties found in Arizona, and travel to Bosque del Apache National Wildlife Refuge for remarkable concentrations of Sandhill Crane. The Texas Hill Country offers many western birds for Eastern visitors, including the endangered Golden-cheeked Warbler, which nests only in its oak-juniper woods.

Arizona

1 Coronado National Forest
www.fs.fed.us/r3/coronado
520-364-3468

2 Sulphur Springs Valley
www.explorecochise.com
800-862-5273

3 San Pedro Riparian National Conservation Area
www.blm.gov/nlcs
520-458-3559

4 Ramsey Canyon Preserve
www.nature.org
520-378-2785

4 Fort Huachuca
www.army.mil
520-533-7083

5 Patagonia-Sonoita Creek Preserve
www.nature.org
520-622-3861

5 Patagonia Lake State Park
www.pr.state.az.us
520-287-6965

6 Madera Canyon Recreation Area
www.fs.fed.us/r3/coronado
520-281-2296

7 Arizona-Sonora Desert Museum
www.desertmuseum.org
520-883-2702

7 Saguaro National Park
www.nps.gov/sagu
520-733-5158

8 Coronado National Forest
www.fs.fed.us/r3/coronado
520-749-8700

9 Boyce Thompson
Southwestern Arboretum
arboretum.ag.arizona.edu
520-689-2811

10 Apache-Sitgreaves National Forest
www.fs.fed.us/r3/asnf
520-333-4301

11 Humphreys Peak
www.fs.fed.us/r3/coconino
928-527-3600

12 Lake Havasu
www.golakehavasu.com
928-453-3444

New Mexico

13 Maxwell National Wildlife Refuge
www.fws.gov/southwest
505-375-2331

14 Randall Davey Audubon Center
www.audubon.org
505-983-4609

14 Hyde Memorial State Park
www.emnrd.state.nm.us
505-983-7175

15 Cibola National Forest
www.fs.fed.us/r3/cibola
505-281-3304

15 Rio Grande Nature Center
State Park
www.emnrd.state.nm.us
505-344-7240

16 Hawk Watch International Fall
Migration Site
www.hawkwatch.org
505-255-7622

17 Bosque del Apache National
Wildlife Refuge
www.fws.gov/southwest
505-835-1828

18 Elephant Butte State Park
www.emnrd.state.nm.us
505-744-5421

18 Caballo Lake State Park
www.emnrd.state.nm.us
505-743-3942

19 Bitter Lake National Wildlife Refuge
www.fws.gov/southwest
505-622-6755

20 Carlsbad Caverns National Park
www.nps.gov/cave
505-785-2232

21 Gila National Forest
www.fs.fed.us/r3/gila
505-388-8201

21 Gila Riparian Preserve
www.nature.org
505-988-3867

Western Texas

22 Big Bend National Park
www.nps.gov/bibe
915-477-2251

23 Davis Mountains State Park
www.tpwd.state.tx.us/spdest
915-426-3337

24 Lake Balmorhea
www.tpwd.state.tx.us/spdest
432-375-2370

25 Guadalupe Mountains National Park
www.nps.gov/gumo
915-828-3251

26 Muleshoe National Wildlife Refuge
www.fws.gov/southwest
806-946-3341

27 Palo Duro Canyon State Park
www.tpwd.state.tx.us/spdest
806-488-2227

28 Balcones Canyonlands National Wildlife Refuge
www.fws.gov/southwest
512-339-9432

28 Emma Long Metropolitan Park
www.ci.austin.tx.us/parks
512-346-1831

28 Hornsby Bend Biosolids Management Facility
www.hornsbybend.org
512-929-1000

29 Pedernales Falls State Park
www.tpwd.state.tx.us/spdest
830-868-7304

30 Lost Maples State Natural Area
www.tpwd.state.tx.us/spdest
830-966-3413

Elegant Trogon

Trogons compose a colorful family of mostly tropical species, including Resplendent Quetzal of Central America, one of the world's most spectacular birds. The Elegant Trogon is one of the most sought-after specialties of southeastern Arizona. Its hoarse *co-ah* call is heard in spring and early summer in Cave Creek and Madera Canyons, among other wooded riparian sites. The species is much rarer in southwestern New Mexico. Its larger relative the Eared Quetzal is found only rarely in southeastern Arizona mountains.

Central Rockies

Some of the birding highlights of this region are very high, indeed. In Colorado's Rocky Mountain National Park, for example, Trail Ridge Road ascends to more than 12,000 feet. Lucky birders find White-tailed Ptarmigan or Brown-capped Rosy-Finch near the highway. Colorado's Mount Evans Scenic Byway, Wyoming's Snowy Range Scenic Byway, Utah's Mirror Lake Scenic Byway, and Nevada's Great Basin National Park are a few of the other highland areas where Clark's Nutcrackers and Mountain Bluebirds brighten stunning landscapes. Find noisy Steller's Jay and elusive Blue Grouse, too.

In Colorado, birders at Pawnee National Grassland may see McCown's Longspurs perform their song flights or see the declining species Ferruginous Hawk and Mountain Plover. Dinosaur National Monument hosts Gray Flycatcher, Pinyon Jay, and Juniper Titmouse. Corn Creek in Nevada's Desert National Wildlife Refuge is one of the country's best desert-oasis "migrant traps."

Fine wetlands in this region include the renowned Bear River Migratory Bird Refuge, on Utah's Great Salt Lake west of Brigham City; Wyoming's Seedskadee National Wildlife Refuge; and Nevada's Lahontan Valley. In the Arkansas River Valley of eastern Colorado, waders and shorebirds frequent a series of shallow lakes that dot the High Plains.

S. D A K.

90

N E B R.

N. Platte

TABLE MT. W.H.M.U. 5

Cheyenne

80

HUTTON LAKE N.W.R.

PAWNEE
NAT. GRASSLAND

76

6

ROOSEVELT
NAT. FOR.

CACHE LA POUDRE-
NORTH PARK SCENIC
BYWAY

BARR LAKE S.P.

15

BONNY LAKE
S.P.

10

70

Denver

Colorado Springs

40

O

Fountain

19

Pueblo

Great Plains
Reservoirs

Ordway

21

Arkansas

Lamar

50

25

La Junta

COMANCHE
NATIONAL
GRASSLAND

22

SPECIAL BIRDS OF THE CENTRAL ROCKIES

Clark's Grebe
Trumpeter Swan
Barrow's Goldeneye
Ferruginous Hawk
Chukar
Himalayan Snowcock
Greater Sage-Grouse
White-tailed Ptarmigan
Blue Grouse
Lesser Prairie-Chicken
Snowy Plover
Mountain Plover
Wilson's Phalarope
Flammulated Owl
Great Gray Owl
Boreal Owl

Black Swift
Lewis's Woodpecker
Williamson's Sapsucker
American Three-toed
   Woodpecker
Gray Flycatcher
Gray Vireo
Pinyon Jay
Chihuahuan Raven
Juniper Titmouse
Sage Thrasher
Curve-billed Thrasher
Le Conte's Thrasher
Phainopepla
Virginia's Warbler
Cassin's Sparrow
Black-chinned Sparrow

Sage
Thrasher

Sage Sparrow
McCown's Longspur
Chestnut-collared
   Longspur
Gray-crowned
   Rosy-Finch
Black Rosy-Finch
Brown-capped
   Rosy-Finch
Pine Grosbeak

Wyoming

1 National
Elk Refuge
nationalelkrefuge.fws.gov
307-739-9322

1 Grand Teton National Park
www.nps.gov/grte; 307-739-3300

2 Yellowstone National Park
www.nps.gov/yell; 307-344-7381

3 Story Fish Hatchery
gf.state.wy.us; 307-683-2234

4 Edness Kimball Wilkins State Park
www.wyoparks.state.wy.us; 307-577-5150

5 Table Mountain and Rawhide
Wildlife Habitat Management Areas
gf.state.wy.us; 307-777-4600

6 Hutton Lake National Wildlife Refuge
www.fws.gov/refuges; 970-723-8202

7 Medicine Bow-Routt National Forest
www.fs.fed.us/r2/mbr; 307-745-2300

8 Rock Springs
www.rockspringswyoming.net; 307-362-3771

9 Seedskadee National Wildlife Refuge
seekskadee.fws.gov; 307-875-2187

Colorado

10 Bonny Lake State Park
parks.state.co.us; 970-354-7306

11 Pawnee National Grassland
www.fs.fed.us/r2/arnf; 970-353-5004

11 Central Plains Experiment Range
www.ars.usda.gov; 970-897-2226

12 Rocky Mountain National Park
www.nps.gov/romo; 970-586-1206

13 Roosevelt National Forest
www.fs.fed.us/r2/arnf; 970-498-1100

14 Arapaho National Wildlife Refuge
arapaho.fws.gov; 970-723-8202

15 Barr Lake State Park
parks.state.co.us; 303-659-6005

16 Arapaho National Forest
www.fs.fed.us/r2/arnf; 303-567-2901

17 Colorado National Monument
www.nps.gov/colm; 970-858-3617

18 Box Canyon Falls Park
www.ouraycolorado.com; 970-325-4464

19 Fountain Creek Regional Park and Nature Center
adm.elpasoco.com/parks; 719-520-6745

20 Valco Ponds State Wildlife Area
gppbt.org; 719-561-4909

20 Lake Pueblo State Park
parks.state.co.us; 719-561-9320

21 Lake Henry
parks.state.co.us; 303-297-1192

22 Comanche National Grassland
www.fs.fed.us/r2/psicc; 719-523-6591

Utah

23 Bear River Migratory Bird Refuge
www.fws.gov/bearriver; 435-723-5887

24 Antelope Island State Park
www.utah.com/stateparks; 801-773-2941

24 Farmington Bay Waterfowl Management Area
www.wildlife.utah.gov; 801-451-7386

25 Wasatch-Cache National Forest
www.fs.fed.us/r4/wcnf; 801-524-3900

26 Mirror Lake Scenic Byway
www.utah.com/byways

27 Dinosaur National Monument
www.nps.gov/dino; 970-374-3000

28 Ouray National Wildlife Refuge
ouray.fws.gov; 435-789-0351

29 Fish Springs National Wildlife Refuge
fishsprings.fws.gov; 435-831-5353

30 Lytle Nature Preserve
mlbean.byu.edu/lytle; 801-378-5052

Nevada

31 Sunset Regional Park
www.co.clark.nv.us; 702-455-8293

31 Henderson Bird Viewing Preserve
www.cityofhenderson.com; 702-565-4264

32 Red Rock Canyon National Conservation Area
www.discovernlcs.org; 702-363-1921

32 Spring Mountain Ranch State Park
parks.nv.gov/smr; 702-875-4141

33 Humboldt-Toiyabe National Forest
www.fs.fed.us/r4/htnf; 702-873-8800

34 Desert National Wildlife Range
www.nvwf.org; 702-646-3401

35 Great Basin National Park
www.nps.gov/grba; 775-234-7331

36 Lamoille Canyon Scenic Byway

37 Ruby Lake National Wildlife Refuge
pacific.fws.gov/refuges; 775-779-2237

38 Stillwater National Wildlife Refuge
www.fws.gov/stillwater; 775-423-5128

38 Carson Lake
www.ndow.org; 775-423-3171

39 Lake Tahoe Nevada State Park
parks.nv.gov/lt; 702-831-0494

California

California has a greater variety of terrain than any other state. Within its 800-mile range are Mojave Desert scrub, redwood forests, Pacific Ocean cliffs, and Sierra Nevada peaks. Such diversity means a correspondingly long list of birds. More than 600 species have been found here—about 70 percent of the total seen in the lower 48 states.

Of its specialties (below) the California Quail and California Thrasher are common and easily seen. The threatened California Gnatcatcher and the endangered California Condor are harder to find. The Island Scrub-Jay and the Yellow-billed Magpie are special specialties: neither has been seen in another state or country.

Highlights include the Salton Sea, where odd waterbirds flock; pelagic trips from Monterey Bay, where seabirds wander in from around the globe; Yosemite National Park, where high-country birds nest; and Point Reyes, where land birds and waterbirds share the area.

SPECIAL BIRDS OF CALIFORNIA

Chukar	Clapper Rail	Great Gray Owl	*Yellow-billed Magpie*
Greater Sage-Grouse	Pacific Golden-Plover	Black Swift	
Blue Grouse	Mountain Plover	Anna's Hummingbird	
Mountain Quail	Wandering Tattler	Costa's Hummingbird	California Gnatcatcher
California Quail	Black Turnstone	Allen's Hummingbird	Varied Thrush
Ross's Goose	Surfbird	Red-breasted Sapsucker	Wrentit
Eurasian Wigeon	Rock Sandpiper		California Thrasher
Barrow's Goldeneye	Heermann's Gull	Nuttall's Woodpecker	Le Conte's Thrasher
Pacific Loon	Mew Gull	White-headed Woodpecker	Phainopepla
Black-footed Albatross	Thayer's Gull	Black-backed Woodpecker	Hermit Warbler
Buller's Shearwater	Yellow-footed Gull		California Towhee
Black-vented Shearwater	Elegant Tern	Pacific-slope Flycatcher	Black-chinned Sparrow
Ashy Storm-Petrel	Common Murre	Cassin's Vireo	Sage Sparrow
Black Storm-Petrel	Pigeon Guillemot	Hutton's Vireo	Golden-crowned Sparrow
Brandt's Cormorant	Marbled Murrelet	Island Scrub-Jay	Tricolored Blackbird
Pelagic Cormorant	Xantus's Murrelet	Yellow-billed Magpie	Hooded Oriole
California Condor	Cassin's Auklet	Chestnut-backed Chickadee	Scott's Oriole
White-tailed Kite	Rhinoceros Auklet	Oak Titmouse	Gray-crowned Rosy-Finch
Black Rail	Tufted Puffin	Verdin	Lawrence's Goldfinch
	Spotted Owl		

Northern California

1 Klamath Basin
klamathbasinrefuges.fws.gov; 530-667-2231

2 Patrick's Point
www.parks.ca.gov; 707-677-3570

3 Arcata Marsh
www.arcatacityhall.org; 707-826-2359

3 Samoa Dunes
www.redwoodvisitor.org; 707-825-2300

3 Humboldt Bay
www.fws.gov/pacific; 707-733-5406

4 Sacramento National Wildlife Refuge
www.fws.gov/pacific; 530-934-2801

5 Westside and Doran County Parks
www.sonoma-county.org/parks
707-875-3540

6 Point Reyes
www.nps.gov/pore; 415-663-1092

6 Tomales Bay
www.parks.ca.gov; 415-669-1140

6 Audubon Canyon Ranch
www.egret.org; 415-868-9244

7 Golden Gate National Recreation Area
www.nps.gov/goga; 415-556-0560

8 Golden Gate Park
www.parks.sfgov.org; 415-831-2745

9 Don Edwards SF Bay NWR
www.fws.gov/desfbay; 510-792-0222

9 Coyote Hills Regional Park
www.ebpakrs.org; 510-795-9385

9 Palo Alto Baylands Preserve
www.abag.ca.gov; 650-329-2506

10 Pillar Point
www.smharbor.com/pillarpoint
650-726-5727

11 Año Nuevo State Reserve
www.anonuevo.org; 650-879-0227

12 Moss Landing State Beach
www.parks.ca.gov; 831-384-7695

12 Elkhorn Slough National Estuarine
Research Reserve
www.elkhornslough.org; 831-728-2822

13 Shearwater Journeys
www.shearwaterjourneys.com; 831-637-8527

14 Little Panoche Reservoir
www.dfg.ca.gov/lands/wa; 209-826-0463

15 Merced NWR and San Luis NWR
www.fws.gov/pacific; 209-826-3508

16 Yosemite National Park
www.nps.gov/yose; 209-372-0200

17 Mono Basin National Forest
www.monolake.org; 760-647-3044

18 Bodie State Historic Park
www.parks.ca.gov; 760-647-6445

Southern California

19 Morro Bay
www.parks.ca.gov; 805-772-2694

19 Montaña de Oro State Park
www.parks.ca.gov; 805-528-0513

20 Santa Barbara Museum
www.sbnature.org; 805-682-4711

20 Santa Barbara Botanic Garden
www.sbbg.org; 805-682-4726

21 Los Padres National Forest
www.fs.fed.us/r5/lospadres; 805-245-3731

22 Angeles National Forest
www.fs.fed.us/r5/angeles; 626-574-5200

23 Channel Islands
www.nps.gov/chis; 805-658-5730

24 McGrath Beach
www.parks.ca.gov; 850-899-1400

24 Point Mugu
www.parks.ca.gov; 818-880-0350

25 Bolsa Chica
www.dfg.ca.gov; 714-846-1114

26 Huntington Beach
www.parks.ca.gov; 714-536-1454

26 Upper Newport Bay Reserve
www.dfg.ca.gov; 949-640-6746

26 Crystal Cove
www.parks.ca.gov; 949-494-3539

27 Big Morongo Canyon
www.bigmorongo.org; 760-363-7190

28 San Bernardino
www.fs.fed.us/r5; 909-383-5588

28 Mount San Jacinto State Park
www.sanjac.statepark.org; 909-659-2607

29 San Jacinto Wildlife Area
www.dfg.ca.gov; 909-654-0580

30 Anza-Borrego
www.anzaborrego.statepark.org; 760-767-5311

31 Sonny Bono Salton Sea Refuge
www.pacific.fws.gov; 760-348-5278

32 San Dieguito River Park,
Bernardo Bay Natural Area
www.sdrp.org; 858-674-2270

35 Cabrillo National Monument
www.nps.gov/cabr; 619-557-5450

35 Tijuana Slough
www.fws.gov/pacific; 619-575-3613

Northwest

Just as it does in many areas, water defines some of the best and most characteristic birding opportunities in the Northwest. The Pacific Ocean meets land in beautiful scenes of rock and sand along the Washington and Oregon coasts, and water in the form of abundant rainfall fuels the lush greenery of Washington's Olympic National Park. Varied Thrush sings here, and American Dipper haunts rocky mountain streams. Spotted Owl still calls in areas where dense old-growth forest remains.

Farther east, rainfall dwindles so much that semidesert conditions prevail in some areas. Arid-country species add appealing variety to regional birding, and where water does occur in the midst of desert terrain, it can attract substantial numbers of breeders and migrants.

Lakes and marshes host great flocks of waterfowl at Montana's Freezout Lake Wildlife Management Area, Idaho's Camas National Wildlife Refuge, Washington's Ridgefield National Wildlife Refuge, and many other sites throughout the region. Where waterfowl gather, birders assemble to look for eagles and large falcons. The Skagit and Samish Flats area in northwestern Washington is famed for sightings of the powerful Gyrfalcon, and the Klamath Basin, on the Oregon-California border, serves as winter home to hundreds of Bald Eagles.

This region stretches more than a thousand miles from corner to corner. Habitats include coniferous forest, riparian woodland, sagebrush shrub-steppe, oak chaparral, coastal salt marsh, and others providing good birding throughout the year. Whether your idea of fun is scanning for rare seabirds on a pelagic trip, hiking up rugged mountains to tundra in search of White-tailed Ptarmigan, or driving through a wildlife refuge to marvel at masses of geese, you'll find the Northwest full of possibilities.

SPECIAL BIRDS OF THE NORTHWEST

Trumpeter Swan
Eurasian Wigeon
Harlequin Duck
Barrow's Goldeneye
Spruce Grouse
Blue Grouse
White-tailed
  Ptarmigan
Pacific Loon
Black-footed Albatross
Pink-footed Shearwater
Buller's Shearwater
Fork-tailed
  Storm-Petrel
Brandt's Cormorant
Pelagic Cormorant
Gyrfalcon
Pacific Golden-Plover
Black Oystercatcher
Black Turnstone

Surfbird
Sharp-tailed Sandpiper
Rock Sandpiper
Mew Gull
Thayer's Gull
Common Murre
Pigeon Guillemot
Marbled Murrelet
Ancient Murrelet
Cassin's Auklet
Rhinoceros Auklet
Tufted Puffin
Spotted Owl
Boreal Owl
Black Swift
Vaux's Swift
Rufous Hummingbird
Calliope Hummingbird
Red-breasted
  Sapsucker

White-headed
  Woodpecker
American Three-toed
  Woodpecker
Black-backed
  Woodpecker
Pacific-slope
  Flycatcher
Cassin's Vireo
Northwestern Crow
Chestnut-backed
  Chickadee
Boreal Chickadee
Varied Thrush
Wrentit
Sage Thrasher
Sprague's Pipit
Townsend's Warbler
Hermit Warbler
Sage Sparrow
Baird's Sparrow

Washington

1 Bayview State Park
www.parks.wa.gov; 360-757-0227

2 Washington State Ferries
www.wsdot.wa.gov/ferries; 206-464-6400

3 Olympic National Park
www.nps.gov/olym; 360-565-3130

4 Dungeness National Wildlife Refuge
pacific.fws.gov/refuges; 360-457-8451

**5 Ocean Shores Environmental
Interpretive Center**
www.oceanshoresinterpretivecenter.com
360-289-4617

6 Grays Harbor National Wildlife Refuge
www.fws.gov/pacific; 360-268-5222

7 Willapa National Wildlife Refuge
www.fws.gov/pacific; 360-484-3482

7 Leadbetter Point State Park
www.parks.wa.gov; 360-642-3078

8 Ridgefield National Wildlife Refuge
www.fws.gov/pacific; 360-887-4106

9 Mount Rainier National Park
www.nps.gov/mora; 360-569-2211

10 Hazel Wolf Wenas Bird Sanctuary
www.nwlink.com/~cyrus/wenas.html

11 Walla Walla
www.wallawalla.org; 509-525-0850

12 Okanogan National Forest
www.fs.fed.us/r6/oka; 509-826-3275

Oregon

13 Sauvie Island Wildlife Area
www.dfw.state.or.us; 503-621-3488

14 Fort Stevens State Park
www.oregonstateparks.org; 503-861-1671

15 Oregon Coastal Refuges
www.fws.gov/oregoncoast; 541-867-4550

16 Boiler Bay State Scenic Viewpoint
www.oregonstateparks.org; 541-265-4560

17 Yaquina Head Outstanding
Natural Area
www.blm.gov/nlcs/ona; 541-574-3100

17 Hatfield Marine Science Center
hmsc.oregonstate.edu; 541-867-0100

18 Bandon Marsh NWR
www.fws.gov/oregoncoast; 541-347-1470

19 William L. Finley NWR
www.fws.gov/refuges; 541-757-7236

20 Fern Ridge Wildlife Area
www.dfw.state.or.us; 541-935-2591

21 Deschutes National Forest
www.fs.fed.us/r6; 541-383-5300

22 Crater Lake National Park
www.nps.gov/crla; 541-594-3100

23 Lower and Upper Table Rocks
www.nature.org; 503-230-1221

24 Summer Lake Wildlife Area
www.dfw.state.or.us; 541-943-3152

25 Malheur National Wildlife Refuge
www.fws.gov/pacific; 541-493-2612

Idaho

26 Sandpoint
www.cityofsandpoint.com/Parks_Rec
208-263-3613

27 Heyburn State Park
www.idahoparks.org/parks; 208-686-1308

28 Deer Flat National Wildlife Refuge
www.fws.gov/refuges; 208-467-9278

29 Hagerman Wildlife Management Area
fishandgame.idaho.gov/cms/wildlife/wma
208-324-4350

30 Caribou National Forest
www.fs.fed.us/r4; 208-524-7500

31 Camas National Wildlife Refuge
pacific.fws.gov/refuges; 208-662-5423

32 Market Lake WMA
fishandgame.idaho.gov/cms/wildlife/wma
208-228-3131

ADDITIONAL SITE

① American Falls
www.americanfallschamber.org
208-226-7214

Montana

33 Glacier National Park
www.nps.gov/glac; 406-888-7800

34 Ninepipe National Wildlife Refuge
www.fws.gov/bisonrange/Ninepipe
406-644-2211

35 Freezout Lake WMA
fwp.state.mt.us/habitat/wma/freezout.asp
406-467-2646

36 Benton Lake National Wildlife Refuge
bentonlake.fws.gov; 406-727-7400

37 Bowdoin National Wildlife Refuge
bowdoin.fws.gov; 406-654-2863

38 Fort Peck Dam and Lake
www.nwo.usace.army.mil/html/Lake_Proj
406-526-3411

39 Medicine Lake National
Wildlife Refuge
medicinelake.fws.gov; 406-789-2305

ADDITIONAL SITES

② Westby
geocities.com/westbymt; 406-385-2445

③ Billings
ci.billings.mt.us; 406-252-4016

MAP KEY AND ABBREVIATIONS

National Monument .... NAT. MON., N.M.
National Park .... N.P.
National Preserve .... NAT. PRES.
National Recreation Area .... N.R.A.
National Seashore .... N.S.
National Conservation Area .... N.C.A.
National River

National Forest .... NAT. FOR., N.F.
State Forest .... S.F.
National Grassland

National Wildlife Refuge .... N.W.R.
National Wildlife Range

State Park .... S.P.

ADDITIONAL ABBREVIATIONS

Conservation Area .... C.A.
County .... CO.
Environmental Demonstration Area .... ENV. DEM. AREA
Fish and Wildlife Area .... F.W.A.
International .... INTL.
Memorial .... MEM.
National .... NAT.
National Battlefield Park .... N.B.P.
National Historical Park .... N.H.P.
National Lakeshore .... N.L.
Natural Area .... N.A.
Preserve .... PRES.
Recreation Area .... R.A.
Refuge .... REF.
Scenic Area .... S.A.
State Beach .... S.B.
State Conservation Park .... S.C.P.
State Game Area .... S.G.A.
State Historic Park .... S.H.P.
State Natural Area .... S.N.A.
State Nature Preserve .... S.N.P.
State Recreation Area .... S.R.A.
State Scenic Viewpoint .... S.S.V.
State Wildlife Area .... S.W.A.
State Wildlife Management Area .... S.W.M.A.
Wilderness .... WILD.
Wildlife Area .... W.A.
Wildlife Habitat Management Unit .... W.H.M.U.
Wildlife Management Area .... W.M.A.

Interstate Highway

U.S. Federal Highway

State Road

County, Local, or Other Road

Trans-Canada Highway

Other Canadian Highway

Ferry

State Boundary

National Boundary

National Forest Boundary

1   Featured Area
1   Additional Site
•   Point of Interest
⊛   National Capital
⊛   State or Provincial Capital
I   Dam
+   Peak

Staff for National Geographic Guide to Birding Hot Spots of the United States Jennifer Conrad Seidel, *Project Editor;* Jennifer Frink, *Designer;* Rick Wain, *Production Project Manager;* Rebecca Hinds, *Managing Editor*

Text Based on the *National Geographic Guide to Birding Hot Spots of the United States,* by Mel White with Paul Lehman, Copyright © 2006 National Geographic Society.

Illustrations All the bird paintings are from the *National Geographic Field Guide to the Birds of North America,* Third Edition, Copyright © 1999, reproduced with permission of the National Geographic Society.